Innovation-Driven Business and Sustainability in the Tropics

Emiel L. Eijdenberg • Malobi Mukherjee
Jacob Wood
Editors

Innovation-Driven Business and Sustainability in the Tropics

Proceedings of the Sustainability, Economics, Innovation, Globalisation and Organisational Psychology Conference 2023 (SEIGOP 2023)

Springer

Editors
Emiel L. Eijdenberg
Centre for International Trade and Business in Asia
James Cook University
Singapore, Singapore

Malobi Mukherjee
Centre for International Trade and Business in Asia
James Cook University
Singapore, Singapore

Jacob Wood
Centre for International Trade and Business in Asia
James Cook University
Singapore, Singapore

ISBN 978-981-99-2908-5 ISBN 978-981-99-2909-2 (eBook)
https://doi.org/10.1007/978-981-99-2909-2

This Springer imprint is published by the registered company Springer Nature Singapore Pte Ltd.
The registered company address is: 152 Beach Road, #21-01/04 Gateway East, Singapore 189721, Singapore

Foreword

The SEIGOP conference kicked off in March 2023 as many observers around the world looked nervously at their screens for news of war in Europe, tensions in East Asia, natural disasters in the Middle East and the polarization of domestic politics in several "stable" economies. Whilst we all feel the ripples from these events in our daily lives through living costs and the impact on global supply chains, it is important to place these things in context, perhaps to remind ourselves that it is the peoples of the global south whose fragile circumstances are such that a crop failure which affects supermarket prices in the West represents an existential threat to rural communities in the tropics.

Sitting more or less on the Equator, Singapore provides a unique lens through which to study these challenges. Its mature public institutions, strong economic position, and international talent pool help to paint a picture of an aspirational society for many surrounding nations. But even Singapore, with its ageing population and scarcity of natural resources, remains dependent on more fragile economies to provide labour and essential commodities. While Singapore has made significant progress in developing its economy and achieving high levels of prosperity, its reliance on cheap labour and food imports has raised concerns about its sustainability and ethical implications. As we discuss issues related to food security, sustainability, and economic development, we must also consider the challenges and opportunities that arise from Singapore's dependence on its neighbours in Association of Southeast Asian Nations (ASEAN). It is, of course, impossible to look at these issues through a mono-disciplinary lens. Trade policy, immigration rules, human behaviour, and consumer choice all compound to create a complex, inter-dependent problem space even before we factor in the impacts of climate change and the need to transition to more sustainable models of consumption.

The COVID-19 pandemic has had a significant impact on Southeast Asian economies, with many countries facing unprecedented economic challenges. Lockdowns, travel restrictions, and supply chain disruptions have disrupted trade and investment flows, leading to job losses, business closures, and significant economic contraction. While some countries have managed to recover to some extent, the pandemic has highlighted the vulnerabilities and limitations of the region's economies. The long-term impacts of COVID-19 on Southeast Asian economies remain unclear, but it is evident that the pandemic has exposed structural weaknesses and highlighted the need for greater resilience and sustainability in the region's economic systems. As we discuss issues related to economic development and sustainability, we must also consider the lessons learned from the COVID-19 pandemic and work towards building more resilient and sustainable economies in the region.

Prior to the pandemic, tourism was a significant contributor to the gross domestic product (GDP) of many Southeast Asian economies. According to the World Travel & Tourism Council, the travel and tourism sector accounted for 12.6% of total GDP in Southeast Asia in 2019. Countries such as Thailand, Malaysia, and Indonesia were particularly reliant on tourism, with the sector accounting for 20% or more of their GDP. However, the pandemic has had a significant and highly apparent impact on the tourism sector, with international travel grinding to a halt and domestic travel severely curtailed. With weaker public institutions and limited capacity for government intervention, many families in the tourist hotspots will have faced 2+ years with little or no income. The long-term impact of this on the economies of the region remains to be seen, but it is evident that the pandemic has highlighted the need for diversification and greater resilience in the region's economies.

It follows then that Southeast Asian countries need to diversify their tourist markets to reduce their reliance on a few key source countries. One way to achieve this could be to make it easier for foreign investors to invest in the region and gain residency. Countries like Thailand and Indonesia have already introduced policies to encourage foreign investment and long-term residency, and this could be expanded to other countries in the region although recent conservative legislation announced in Indonesia concerning unmarried relationships is an example of misalignments in the policy space. Another opportunity could be to create retirement clusters in places like Chiang Mai and Bali, which have already become popular destinations for retirees from Western countries. These clusters could be designed to provide tailored services and facilities for retirees and could attract a new type of long-term tourist. As we discuss issues related to economic development and sustainability, we must also consider the opportunities presented by diversifying the region's tourism markets and work towards creating policies and infrastructure to support this goal.

At the same time, recent trade agreements like the Regional Comprehensive Economic Partnership (RCEP) have created new opportunities for Southeast Asian countries to diversify their trade and reduce their reliance on China. With China facing wage inflation and increasing competition from other manufacturing destinations, countries like Vietnam and Indonesia with significant manufacturing capabilities stand to gain. The RCEP, which includes 10 Southeast Asian countries as well as Australia, China, Japan, New Zealand, and South Korea, is expected to create a regional free trade area covering almost a third of the world's population and GDP. This presents significant opportunities for countries in the region to increase their trade and investment flows and reduce their reliance on any one market. As we discuss issues related to economic development and sustainability, we must also consider the opportunities presented by trade agreements like the RCEP and work towards building stronger economic ties with our regional partners.

Whilst the (generally) young countries of Southeast Asia continue to urbanise and the rapid transition from predominantly agricultural work to higher productivity sectors there are consequently a pressing need and opportunity for expansion of skills provision and higher education. Public and private universities across the region exhibit a huge appetite for the international links that will speak to their reputation as well as providing their students and staff with mobility and development opportunities. It is a privilege for us, as Western educators in the region, to play a small role in driving the generational changes that are taking place across Southeast Asia and to provide a platform for discussion of these fascinating issues.

James Cook University, Singapore, Singapore
March 2023
Professor Chris Rudd OBE
chris.rudd@jcu.edu.au

Contents

Chapter 1
Putting the Tropics on the Academic Map: The Raison d'Être of the SEIGOP Conference

Manisha Agarwal, Thomas Chong, Emiel L. Eijdenberg, Malobi Mukherjee, and Jacob Wood

Abstract The Tropics is the region located between the Tropic of Cancer and the Tropic of Capricorn. Apart from its distinctive climate, tropical regions share many other characteristics, including exotic but vulnerable bio-diversity and natural eco-systems such as rain forests and coral reefs. More than 20 years before publication of this edited volume, Sachs et al. (2001) defined three factors that contribute to the economic successes enjoyed across the Tropics. These include, coastal proximity, prevalence (or rather: absence) of infectious diseases, and agricultural productivity. Accordingly, northern Australia, Hong Kong, Singapore and the southern part of Taiwan could be considered as the only successful, high-income and socio-economically advanced places in the Tropics. Notwithstanding these three factors, the Tropics have witnessed tremendous transitions which, in turn, have triggered varied levels of socio-economic development in the region. These changes call for a renewed focus into the socio-economic potential of the Tropics. The proceedings of the SEIGOP Conference are an endeavor to provide a collection of research and practice papers that shed some nuanced insights into the contemporary socio-economic state of the Tropics.

Keywords Conference · Sustainability · Economics · Innovation · Globalisation · Organisational psychology · Tropics

---

M. Agarwal
James Cook University, Singapore, Singapore

T. Chong
Director Engagement, Newcastle Australia Institute of Higher Education, Singapore, Singapore

E. L. Eijdenberg (✉) · M. Mukherjee · J. Wood
Centre for International Trade and Business in Asia, James Cook University, Singapore, Singapore
e-mail: emiel.eijdenberg@jcu.edu.au

E. L. Eijdenberg et al. (eds.), *Innovation-Driven Business and Sustainability in the Tropics*, https://doi.org/10.1007/978-981-99-2909-2_1

The Tropics is a region located between the Tropic of Cancer at 23°26′11.5′ N and the Tropic of Capricorn at 23°26′11.5′ S (Feeley & Stroud, 2018). The Tropics is well known for its warm climate, lots of sunshine and tropical rainfall, with very little seasonal change in daily temperatures. Apart from its climate, tropical regions share many other characteristics, including exotic but vulnerable bio-diversity and natural ecosystems such as rain forests and coral reefs. More than 20 years before publication of this edited volume, Sachs et al. (2001) defined three factors that contribute to the economic successes enjoyed across the Tropics. These include, coastal proximity, prevalence (or rather: absence) of infectious diseases, and agricultural productivity. Accordingly, Australia, Hong Kong, Singapore and Taiwan could be considered as the only successful, high-income and socio-economically advanced places in the Tropics. Notwithstanding these three factors, the Tropics have witnessed numerous transitions which in turn have triggered varied levels of socio-economic development in the region. These changes call for a more nuanced focus into the socio-economic potential of the tropical region. The proceedings of the SEIGOP Conference are an endeavor to provide a collection of research papers which shed some refined insights into the contemporary state of the Tropics.

The Tropics is the most populous (i.e., with around 40% living there), most bio-diverse (i.e., 80% of the terrestrial species and more than 95% of the world's corals and mangroves) region on the planet (State of the Tropics, 2021a). Propelled by rapid population growth, the Tropics is a region full of economic development opportunities and exciting international trade and investment opportunities (Case et al., 2022). Densely populated emerging countries such as India, Indonesia and Nigeria will be among the world's largest economies by the end of the century, which is driven by massive entrepreneurial activity. Some notable emerging countries in the Tropics, such as Colombia and Panama, score remarkably high (30% of the adults between 18 and 64 years old) in total early-stage entrepreneurial activities (TEA) (Global Entrepreneurship Monitor, 2021).

These upward socioeconomic trends are compromised by the impact of climate change on the Tropics' biodiversity as well as humanity's ecological footprint (State of the Tropics, 2020). Deforestation, desertification, disease outbreaks (e.g., COVID-19 pandemic) and natural disasters (e.g., drought, floods, heat waves) may cause natural resources to be depleted. For instance, environmental pollution in the northern parts of tropical Zambia negatively affect entrepreneurs' life satisfaction, which results in less-profitable businesses (Choongo et al., 2021). This calls for individuals being forced to seek creative ways to live and work.

Moving forward, adaptive and creative responses by individuals and businesses will redefine societies in the Tropics (Thirumaran & Azzali, 2021). An increasing stream of research focuses on how businesses use and apply (technological) innovation as a means of achieving sustainability goals (George et al., 2021; Lüdeke-Freund, 2020; Schaltegger & Wagner, 2011). An important innovation in the Tropics has been the increased use of mobile phone technology as a connector of people in remote, urban, rural, developed and underdeveloped areas. According to the published State of the Tropics Report (2021b), access to mobile phones in the Tropics has increased dramatically since the turn of the century but still trails behind the rest of the world. In 2000, there were fewer than five mobile phones per 100 people in the Tropics. By 2019, this number had grown to more than 97 per 100 people.

Prior to the COVID-19 pandemic, the State of the Tropics (2019) report had also highlighted that mental health issues are an area of societal concern in the Tropics because they are a significant contributor to morbidity in the region. The COVID-19 pandemic pointed at stark differences between tropical and non-tropical regions. Access to education and healthcare were already challenging the pre-COVID-19 environment in many tropical countries. This was exacerbated by the pandemic and resulted in increased school dropouts and the absence of resources to provide quality remote education and healthcare (State of the Tropics, 2022). Perhaps a few of the main lessons learnt from the COVID-19 pandemic are that in the future innovative education and healthcare systems would need to more inclusive by design to be accessible to rural and urban populations while also being resilient to disruptive external forces. Another factor redefining the post-COVID-19 society will be the ability of workplaces to effectively deal with mental health issues which have risen dramatically due to prolonged periods of lockdown and separation from family and friends.

All in all, a complex interplay of well-being, social, economic, environmental factors pose significant challenges for the future of the Tropics and yet most of the research on business innovation for sustainable development are focused on the Western and industrialised world, which lies largely above the Tropic of Cancer. Little is known about how innovation-driven economic, environmental and social sustainability is exercised by or for businesses in the Tropics, i.e., the region of the world that is probably the most jeopardised in all aspects of sustainability (State of the Tropics, 2020). With that in mind, the *Sustainability, Economics, Innovation, Globalisation and Organisational Psychology* (SEIGOP) Conference—hosted by the Centre for International Trade and Business in Asia (CITBA) at James Cook University, Singapore (JCUS)—aimed to provide a platform where academics and industry professionals could converge and deliberate on theoretical and practical implications that could benefit the Tropics and it's inhabitants.

The SEIGOP Conference was led by Co-Chairs Dr. Emiel L. Eijdenberg, Associate Professor Jacob Wood and Dr. Malobi Mukherjee. The Conference Management Team comprised Ms. Erica Neo, Ms. Janice Lim, Ms. Manisha Agarwal, Dr. Michele Chew and Dr. Thomas Chong. Professor May Tan-Mullins (James Cook University, Singapore) played a key role as Advisor to the Co-Chairs and the Conference Management Team. The SEIGOP Conference took place on the 1st to 3rd of March 2023. After the pre-conference workshops (i.e., "Assessing Oral Communication Workshop & Advancement in Assessment Workshop" by Mr. Syed Mohamed, PBS, PK; and "Publishing in Top Journals" by Professor Eero Vaara), the conference kicked off with a Welcome Reception at the Australian High Commission in Singapore on Wednesday the 1st of March. This reception also marked the official launch of the *Journal of Tropical Future* by SAGE: a JCUS-born journal dedicated to the Tropics. On the second of March, Associate Professor Jonathan Reynolds (Saïd Business School, University of Oxford) provided a Key

Note, after which paper presentations in parallel sessions commenced at the JCUS campus. The presented papers were allocated in the following tracks led by Session Chairs & Discussants:

- Tourism 1, Thursday, 2nd March 2023, 11:15–12:45.
- Organisation Psychology, Thursday, 2nd March 2023, 11:15–12:45.
- Healthcare, Thursday, 2nd March 2023, 11:15–12:45.
- Sustainable Business 1, Thursday, 2nd March 2023, 13:45–15:45.
- Information Technology, Thursday, 2nd March 2023, 13:45–15:45.
- Sustainable Business 2, Thursday, 2nd March 2023, 16:15–18:15.
- Human Resource Management, Thursday, 2nd March 2023, 16:15–18:15.
- Sustainable Business 3, Friday, 3rd March 2023, 09:00–11:00.
- Finance and Economic Development 1, Friday, 3rd March 2023, 09:00–11:00.
- Tourism 2, Friday, 3rd March 2023, 11:15–12:45.
- Finance and Economic Development 2, Friday, 3rd March 2023, 11:15–12:45.

In the afternoon of Friday the 3rd of March, all participants took part in a corporate tour of Schneider Electric's Singapore office. Schneider Electric is a leading French multinational company in digital transformation of energy management and automation and that has an office in Singapore. The Scientific Council members (i.e., Professor Abhishek Bhati, James Cook University, Singapore; Professor Alexander Josiassen, Copenhagen Business School, Denmark; Professor Chris Rudd OBE, James Cook University, Singapore; Professor Eddy Ng, Queen's University, Canada; Professor Enno Masurel, Vrije Universiteit Amsterdam, the Netherlands; Associate Professor Jie Wu, Zhejiang University of Technology, China; Associate Professor Taha Chaiechi, James Cook University, Australia; Professor Wim Naudé, Cork University Business School, Ireland) provided guidance in different ways and on different occasions prior and during the conference. Additionally, the conference was sponsored by AECUS Asia, eKenjo Pte Ltd., Charis Manor Nursing Home, Dr. Gary Tsu, Chew Investment Advisor, Raymond Teo & Associates, Mr. Tan Yong Siang, Ms. Tina Tan of Tatgu, and GLOO Public Relations. In total, SEIGOP Conference had 55 participants; 31 paper presentations by academics and industry professionals from Kenya, India, South Korea, Japan, amongst others. This edited volume comprises a selection of 31 blind peer-reviewed papers which were presented at the conference.

References

Case, P., Wood, J., & Ng, E. (2022). Journal of tropical futures inaugural editorial. *Journal of Tropical Futures, 0*, 1–9. https://doi.org/10.1177/27538931221143352

Choongo, P., Eijdenberg, E. L., Lungu, J., Chabala, M., Taylor, T. K., & Masurel, E. (2021). The influence of environmental pollution and drought on the satisfaction with life of entrepreneurs in Zambia's mining sector. In *Economic effects of natural disasters* (pp. 147–160). Academic.

Feeley, K. J., & Stroud, J. T. (2018). Where on earth are the "tropics"? *Frontiers of Biogeography, 10*(1–2), e38649.

George, G., Merrill, R. K., & Schillebeeckx, S. J. (2021). Digital sustainability and entrepreneurship: How digital innovations are helping tackle climate change and sustainable development. *Entrepreneurship Theory and Practice, 45*(5), 999–1027.

Global Entrepreneurship Monitor. (2021). 2020/2021 Report https://www.gemconsortium.org/report/gem-20202021-global-report

Lüdeke-Freund, F. (2020). Sustainable entrepreneurship, innovation, and business models: Integrative framework and propositions for future research. *Business Strategy and the Environment, 29*(2), 665–681.

Sachs, J. D., Mellinger, A. D., & Gallup, J. L. (2001). The geography of poverty and wealth. *Scientific American, 284*(3), 70–75.

Schaltegger, S., & Wagner, M. (2011). Sustainable entrepreneurship and sustainability innovation: Categories and interactions. *Business Strategy and the Environment, 20*(4), 222–237.

State of the Tropics. (2019). *2019 State of the tropics report.* https://www.jcu.edu.au/__data/assets/pdf_file/0012/864993/SOTT-Health-Report-2019-Webv02.pdf

State of the Tropics. (2020). *2020 State of the tropics report.* https://www.jcu.edu.au/__data/assets/pdf_file/0004/1271956/State-of-the-Tropics-2020-Summary.pdf

State of the Tropics. (2021a). *Why do the Tropics matter?* https://www.jcu.edu.au/state-of-the-Tropics/why-do-the-Tropics-matter

State of the Tropics. (2021b). *2021 State of the tropics report.* https://www.jcu.edu.au/__data/assets/pdf_file/0011/1870391/SOTT-Report-2021-Web.pdf

State of the Tropics. (2022). *2022 State of the tropics report.* https://www.jcu.edu.au/__data/assets/pdf_file/0003/1973703/SOTT-Report-2022_web.pdf

Thirumaran, K., & Azzali, S. (2021). Adapting to constraints: Businesses and societies in the tropics. In *Tropical constrained environments and sustainable adaptations: Businesses and communities* (pp. 1–5).

Chapter 2
Seeking a Sustainable Technology of Governance to Support Small and Medium Enterprises: A Study from the ASEAN Countries

Harun Harun, David Carter, and Habib Khan

Abstract The study aims to provide a better understanding with respect to key institutional environment and challenges associated with the adoption of technology of governance by small and medium enterprises (SMEs) in ten countries of the Association of the Southeast Asia Nations (ASEAN). The empirical data of the study was collected from a survey of 200 professional accountants in 10 ASEAN countries, in-depth interviews with 65 participants including the owners of SMEs, regulators, and government officials in the region. We find that although all ASEAN countries recognize the significant economic role of SMEs, incoherent and contradictory definitions of SMEs across ASEAN countries persist. Beyond this, there is a naive assumption among policy makers and the accounting profession who believe that the success of SME companies is how to become a big company like a multinational firm. Unfortunately, such an assumption has an impact on policy making in support of SMEs. Consequently, training, skills uptakes and technological support provided by the accounting, professional, international, and governmental bodies in the ASEAN also fail to meet the real needs of SMEs from the economic and sustainability perspective of these entities. The study warns that micro-entrepreneurs have been excluded from all accounting service processes, standard-setting processes and government support according to the needs of SMEs. Finally, this study provides recommendations for government agencies, accounting professional bodies

---

In this paper the term "technology of governance" refers to the nature and application of accounting and financial information in supporting business planning, performance evaluation and value creation of business entities from multiple perspectives (Kaplan and McMillan, 2021).

H. Harun (✉)
James Cook University, Singapore, Singapore
e-mail: harun.harun@jcu.edu.au

D. Carter · H. Khan
Canberra Business School, The University of Canberra, Canberra, Australia
e-mail: david.carter@canberra.edu.au; habib.khan@canberra.edu.au

E. L. Eijdenberg et al. (eds.), *Innovation-Driven Business and Sustainability in the Tropics*, https://doi.org/10.1007/978-981-99-2909-2_2

and standard setters across the ASEAN to enhance the existing roles of SMEs in the future with the support of sustainable technology of governance.

Keywords SMEs · emerging economies · IFRS · the ASEAN · micro enterprises

2.1 Introduction

In recent years there has been increased attention of business researchers with various methodologies and theoretical lenses to investigate accounting and financial practices by small and medium enterprises (SMEs) across world including the ASEAN region (Zhang & Si, 2008; Sian & Roberts, 2009; Ahmad & Mohamed Zabri, 2015; Ritchi et al., 2019). Meanwhile, given the roles SMEs are crucial in the global economy, it is equally important to formulate a clear set of principles of policies to support these entities (Pratama, 2019). However, there is a lack of studies of SMEs which concentrated on understanding the key challenges faced by SMEs and how to strengthen the supporting roles of professional, government and transnational institutions to assist in the empowerment of this critical sector (Stone, 2011; Del Baldo, 2017; Warren et al., 2019). In addition, despite accounting profession is regarded as a trusted source of advisory services, limited progress has been made to develop uniform reporting standards such as the International Reporting Standard (IFRS) for SMEs in order to compare the financial performance of SMEs across nations (Ram & Newberry, 2012; Devi & Samujh, 2015; Ramirez et al., 2015). In fact, accounting professionals play a central role in empowering SMEs with the provision of professional assistance with respect to business services, accounting, reporting, taxes, auditing and organizational planning and development (Albu et al., 2013). Prior studies on accounting and auditing were concentrated on listed big companies and only large audit firms that significantly shape the whole processes of accounting harmonization and increasingly control the profession as well as the production of knowledge (Aburous, 2018). This trend reinforces the notion that in seeking and maintaining legitimacy powerful states and transnational associations such as the European Union and the ASEAN increasingly continues to seek legitimacy through the adoption of the IFRS within a context of increased institutional complexity and the interconnectedness of national and global forces (Aburous, 2018; Irvine, 2008).

Prior studies on SMEs have offered an increased understanding of a variety of perspectives in terms of methodologies, and other issues such as key business obstacles, government support and policies, internationalization of reporting rules, regional development and the empowerment potential of intelligent technologies in the context of SMEs (Stone, 2011; Ramirez et al., 2015; Devi & Samujh, 2015). However, despite this range of SME research, there remains a lack of empirical studies examining the nature of the roles of accountants in providing effective and meaningful support to SMEs. Additionally, the survey data informing prior studies tended to reflect participants representing established medium enterprises. As

Fearnley and Hines (2007) argue, despite SMEs being the dominant employer in many economies, their voices are often ignored in debates dominated by larger, global players. This contributes to low levels of responsiveness from SMEs. This is not surprising as the International Accounting Standards Board (IASB) traditionally focuses on advanced financial capital. In a critical sense, this engenders a 'cosy arrangement for a narrow band of stakeholders such as investment bankers, international institutional investors and Big Four accounting firms, but not for other member groups of the global community that IAS/IFRS claim to serve' (Brown, 2004, p. 385).

In recent years criticisms have been raised to question how the public interests are represented by the IASB (see for example, Gallhofer et al., 2012; Gaffikin, 2008; Dellaportas & Davenport, 2008; Botzem, 2012; Devi & Samujh, 2015). In addition, SMEs in developing nations have been largely excluded from the international radar simply because they were not significant players in international capital markets (Brown, 2004). Meanwhile, to understand critical issues, challenges and solutions needed by SMEs, including micro entities, and how the interests of SMEs be represented – further studies should be undertaken. And our study intends to fill these gaps. The rest of this paper progresses into the following sections: (a) Aim and contributions of the study, (b) a literature review on the roles of SMEs in the ASEAN, (d) the methodology used in the study, (e) main findings and the discussion of these findings, and (f) conclusions and recommendations for policy makers and future studies in this area.

2.2 Aims and Contributions

Drawing from the issues earlier discussed, the aim of the study is to provide a better understanding with respect to (a) the current approaches to regulations and definitions of SMEs in the ASEAN; (b) the nature of accounting and financial management practices adopted by SMEs, and (c) the demands of SMEs from accounting profession the ASEAN in the future. Our study contributes to the literature by providing empirical evidence on the extent to which SMEs in the region have engaged in business reporting policy-making and supporting initiatives for themselves. As Gaffikin (2008), Dellaportas and Davenport (2008), Botzem (2012) point out that the focus IASF for example, is on big and multinational companies. In this sense, this study contributes to the ongoing debate around the relationship between SMEs and the accounting profession, internationalization of SME reporting requirements and the role of governments in empowering SMEs.

2.3 SMEs in the ASEAN: A Literature Review

In today competitive global market, SMEs play a major role in most nations across the globe. In emerging economies, SMEs contribute to the creation of 4 out of every 5 new jobs in both developed and emerging economies, despite their access to finance is limited (Gaffikin, 2008). Without access to capital, many SMEs languish and stagnate (World Bank, 2019). In the ASEAN context, SMEs account 59% of Indonesia's GDP, 33% of Malaysia's GDP and 47% of Singapore's GDP. Equally, the employment contribution of this sector is in Indonesia is 97% for Indonesians, 58% for Malaysians, 63% for Filipinos, 70% for Singaporeans, and 81% for Thais. (ERIA, 2015). Nonetheless, there is a lack of consensus about what defines an SME, what conditions are critical to the success of these firms and what sort of government policies are most helpful to support SMEs. Additionally, evidence suggests that the lack of adequate financial management and accounting knowledge, growth and financial stability of SMEs have been jeopardized as owners of SMEs experience difficulties to prepare financial statements, budgeting, cash flows projections, leading to weak projections, estimations of costs and growth of SMEs (Birley & Niktari, 1995). Given accountants have been considered as valuable and trusted advisors for SMEs, their professional and technical skills are necessary to assist SMEs owners in terms of management of financial accounts, pricing, budgeting, effective mechanism of costs determinations, cost controlling and assist them to reporting and tax requirements (ACCA, 2016).

Internationally, a study by Leung et al. (2008) finds that SMEs in Australia regard accountants are rated particularly well on the potential for a long-term relationship with the business, technical understanding of the regulatory, ability to meet the needs of the business and understanding of the business of the SMEs and their operation. As Wilson (1995:93) asserts that the needs of users of financial statements should determine the objectives of financial reporting, leading ultimately to the form and content of financial statements. Hence, McAleese (2001) concluded that the needs of information users must be prioritized in making financial statement forms. In this case the consultants need to be involved with users of financial statements from small and medium sized companies. However, it has been too long, SMEs were ignored in the development of accounting standards. Whilst SMEs are too significant in the global economy, these sectors have been ignored to date, by the international accounting standard setters (Coetzee, 2007, p. 32).

This study is motivated by the observation that accounting scholars should undertake the hard theoretical and experiential task to uncover the political mechanisms and transformation of 'thought into action' as Tinker and Carter (2003) observed. For example, it took two decades before the IASB recognized that 'one size fits all' is not appropriate (UNCTAD, 2008). A preparatory committee was appointed but no work was undertaken. The issue of 'political visibility' of complying with the IAS was an issue. Many developed nations also regard the requirements of the IFRS are difficult to adopt by small entities and implemented a differential reporting regime, despite they have better technical expertise and supportive regulatory infrastructure. Therefore, in Australia and New Zealand, for example, only those entities defined as 'reporting entities' are required to comply with IFRS (Potter, 2013). In Europe, a high level of country-specific differentiation for non-listed companies is also practiced (Jermakowicz & Gornik-Tomaszewski, 2006). This is particularly important to note when considering the situation in many developing nations where the biggest enterprise is equivalent to, if not smaller than, a relatively small enterprise in a mature economy. Therefore, we argue that the initiatives for a global convergence of accounting standards were mainly motivated by the globalization of financial markets efforts and to meet securities regulators' expectations as suggested by UNCTAD (2008).

2.4 Research Methodology

This case study situates within the ten ASEAN nations. We treated the ASEAN states as the setting of this study. Our data collection methods involved multiple phases. Phase one of the project involved document collection and analysis. We collected and analyzed publicly available, official and research documents in relation to: (a) the nature as well as the economic, employment and other contributions of SMEs in all ASEAN members; (b) definitions, legal and institutional frameworks surrounding SMEs in all ASEAN members countries (and in other jurisdictions) of SMEs; (c) services needed by SMEs in ASEAN members nations from accounting professionals and professional accounting bodies and (d) key challenges faced by SMEs in all ASEAN members in today's economy.

Phase two involved a survey of professional accountants and a time-use survey. We developed a survey to help us to map the time allocations of accountants in regular practice with SMEs. This allowed us to understand the nature of the work of accountants in the ASEAN region. We delivered this survey electronically through Survey Monkey. We aimed for 400 responses from the region, but we received over 200 responses. This is considered an appropriate number for analytical purposes. Table 2.1 presents the number and percentage of participants of the survey for each ASEAN country. And Table 2.2 reveals the key profiles of these participants.

Phase three involved interviews with participants who have extensive experience, knowledge and professional engagement relating to accounting, management and regulatory aspects of SMEs in the ASEAN. This involved regulators, peak industry bodies, SME accountants, SME owners, academics, standard setters, and others related to the SME process. Our methodology for selecting participants reflects a form of stratified respondents reflecting the interests in SMEs. In total, we had 65 respondents from Indonesia, Thailand, Malaysia, Singapore and Brunei Darussalam. Interviews lasted on an average 50–60 min and interviews were conducted according to the time and places suitable for the participants. In most of the cases, interviews were taped but note was also taken when permission was not granted to record conversation. Interviews conducted other than English were back translated by the corresponding author who are fluent in Indonesian, Thai and others. Interviews were conducted in major cities in different countries such as Jakarta, Singapore city, Kuala Lumpur, Bangkok, and others. Less than one-fourth of interviews were taken over phone where face-to-face meeting was not possible. The detailed break-down and profiling of interview participants are given in the Table 2.3.

2.5 Findings and Discussion

2.5.1 *The ASEAN and Its Context*

The ASEAN was formed in 1967 by Indonesia, Malaysia, the Philippines, Singapore, and Thailand to promote political and economic cooperation and regional stability. Brunei Darussalam joined in 1984, shortly after its independence from the United Kingdom, and Vietnam joined the ASEAN as its seventh member in 1995. Laos and Burma were admitted into full membership in July 1997 as celebrated its 30th anniversary (Albert, 2017). Cambodia became ASEAN's tenth member in 1999. The ASEAN Declaration in 196 established its legal identity as an international organization and took a major step in its community-building process. Table 2.4 highlights key demographic and economic parameters of the ASEAN members. In the ASEAN, SMEs including micro enterprises are integral to the economic development and growth of the ASEAN Member States (Albert, 2017). They constitute the largest number of establishments and contribute significantly to the labor force of ASEAN Member States (henceforth AMS). As Albert (2017) states that SMEs account for between 88.8% and 99.9% total establishments in AMS and between 51.7% and 97.2% of total employment. The contribution of these enterprises to each AMS' GDP is between 30% and 53% and the contribution of SMEs to exports is between 10% and 29.9%. Albert's (2017) report also highlights the regional importance of SMEs and why their effective regulation, and the support of accountants, is important.

Table 2.1 Survey participants of study by nation

Nations	Total	Percentage
Thailand	63	32%
Philippines	48	24%
Indonesia	39	20%
Malaysia	10	5%
Singapore	5	3%
Other ASEAN members	35	18%
Grand total	200	100%

Table 2.2 Ky profiles of survey participants

Profession	Total	Percentage
Senior external auditors	46	23%
Senior internal accountants	43	22%
Academics	35	18%
Senior internal auditors	28	14%
Government officials	26	13%
Accounting & tax consultants	22	11%
Grand total	200	100%

Table 2.3 Key profiles of interview participants

Profession	Total	Percentage
Peak industry bodies	17	26%
SME accountants	15	23%
SME owners	12	18%
Academics	8	12%
Standard setters	7	11%
Government officials	6	9%
Grand total	65	100%

2.5.2 Definitions and Approaches for SMEs in the ASEAN

In terms of definition, we find that there is a significant variation within the ASEAN states. Table 2.5 details the exact specification for SMEs in each AMS and in the national, transnational and supranational entities that we refer to. In our estimation, this reflects the complexity of the region, and is especially reflective of the differences from the most developed of the AMS in comparison to those AMS who have more recently commenced the development journey. Currently, the ASEAN region recognizes local definitions of AMS. While there might be benefits in developing a shared definition in providing a foundation for regional solutions to take advantage of the opportunities for the SME sector across the region, including the potential for economic growth, there are risks associated with the imposition of a common definition, given the relativity across the region in terms of development, access to finance, infrastructure and support systems like business incubators. Negotiating a consensus around a common SME definition may prove inherently problematic, as a study of the existing AMS SME regulatory frameworks reveals significant inconsistencies.

Despite initial encouragement for AMS to adopt a common SME definition, in preparation for the formation of the ASEAN economic community, most AMS have instituted their own individual approaches. Some AMS have no legislative source for a SME definition. The challenges associated with the adoption of singular definition with clear legal basis become apparent when considering the regulatory framework approaches of more advanced economies, and indeed, development

Table 2.4 Key demographic and economic indicators of ASEAN members

No	Country	Population on	GDP (PPP)	Income per capita (PPP in US$)
1	Brunei Darussalam	0.417 million	33.376 billion	77,699
2	Cambodia	16 million	70.242 billion	1559
3	Indonesia[a]	261 million	3.492 trillion	13,162
4	Laos	6.758 million	53.752 billion	7932
5	Malaysia	32.049 million	1.002 trillion	30,858
6	Myanmar	53.582 million	334.856 billion	6139
7	Philippines	100.981 million	960.7 billion	9862
8	Singapore	5.638 million	554.855 billion	98,014
9	Thailand	68.863 million	1.311 trillion	18,944
10	Vietnam	94.569 million	705.774 billion	7463

International Monetary Fund (2018)
[a]The only ASEAN member which is also the member of G 20

agencies and other NGOs. The simple point is that definitions based on numbers of employees, assets, revenue, or some other parameters are ultimately arbitrary criteria that potentially impacts on growth, development and other consequences. There is no 'correct' SME definition, and all definitions have limits. We see evidence of this complexity in many ways: a) The Asian Development Bank has no definition of SMEs; b) the IASB in the standard, *IFRS for SMEs*, chooses to define not by criteria, but by their nature (not having public accountability, but might benefit from reporting to external users); and Federal states, such as the United States of America and Australia have multiple definitions of SMEs that vary in criteria and parameters across different regulators and agencies. Given the complexities associated with the adoption of a common definition within national borders, we believe that these are compounded when considering the adoption of a common SME definition across national borders. This was a common theme within our interviews. One of our interviewees, a senior Accounting Professor, comments:

> At this stage, I find it difficult to find and set up a common definition of SMEs for all ASEAN nations. And the key question is whether all governments in the ASEAN are willing to have a common definition and whether they can negotiate if there are differences.

While there are significant variations in definitions of SMEs, the majority of AMSs adopt criteria based upon quantitative parameters, such as number of employees and financial criteria. However, this is not necessarily the norm. Certain of the transnational bodies have moved away from quantitative parameters. For example, the Organization for Economic Co-operation and Development (OECD) recognizes that SMEs employ 'fewer' (comparative to larger entities) but abstains from the articulation of any parameters. The OECD definition for SMEs is that they are "non-subsidiary, independent firms which employ fewer than a given number of employees", which varies across countries (OECD, 2005). The International Accounting Standards Board, in recognition arguably of the complexity and arbitrariness of measurement-based criteria determined to define SMEs by their function: "*Small*

Table 2.5 SME definitions – Summary of features

Country	Legal basis/regulatory framework	Features					Notes
		No of Employees	Turnover	Other Financial	Sector	Distinguishes between micro, small and medium enterprises	
Brunei Darussalam	Ministry of industry and primary resources	100				✓	
Cambodia	Small and medium enterprise development framework, 2005 RGC Subcommittee on small and medium enterprises	100		✓		✓	Definition bases of full time employees used for statistical purposes. The financial definition may be used if more suitable for other purposes. Financial criteria in US$, not in the Cambodian Riel (៛).
Indonesia	Ministry for cooperatives and small medium enterprises (Law No, 20/2008 Regarding micro, small and medium enterprises, article 6)	×		✓		✓	
Laos	The Decree on SME division, number 25/LG, dated January 16, 2017	100	✓	✓		✓	
Malaysia	SME Corp Malaysia endorsed at the 14th NSDC Meeting in July 2013	200	✓		✓	✓	

(continued)

Table 2.5 (continued)

		Features					Notes
Country	Legal basis/regulatory framework	No of Employees	Turnover	Other Financial	Sector	Distinguishes between micro, small and medium enterprises	
Myanmar	Department of small and medium enterprises development. Law on the development of small and medium businesses – Pyidaungsu Hluttaw Law No. 23/2015	600	✓	✓	✓	✓	Financial criteria differ by sector.
Philippines	The Department Trade Industry (DTI) *Micro, Small and Medium Enterprise Development (MSMED) Council*. Republic Act No. 9501. Magna Carta for Micro, Small and Medium Enterprises (MSMEs)	×		✓		✓	
Singapore	SPRING Singapore	200		✓			Requirement for 30% local shareholding
Thailand	Office of SME Promotion (OSMEP), a government agency under the governance of the Ministry of Industry	200		✓	✓	✓	
Vietnam	Government Decree No. 56/2009/ND-CP The enterprise development department of the ministry of planning and investment	300		✓	✓	✓	

		Features					Notes
Country	Legal basis/regulatory framework	No of Employees	Turnover	Other Financial	Sector	Distinguishes between micro, small and medium enterprises	
Japan	SME Basic Act Different criteria in the Corporation Tax Act (financial)	✓		✓		✓	Different criteria based on sector (Manufacturing, Wholesale, Services, Retail). Distinguishes Micro from SMEs
Australia		200	✓	✓	✓		No universal definition. Classification criteria vary across government agencies.
USA		1500			✓	✓	No universal definition. Classification criteria vary according to industry, and across government agencies and programs.
IFRS	*IFRS for SMEs*						Definition not based on quantitative criteria
IFC		300	✓	✓		✓	
EU		250	✓	✓		✓	
Asian Development Bank	No definition						No Definition. Accepts legal/ regulators definition within each jurisdiction.

and medium-sized entities are entities that: (a) do not have public accountability, and (b) publish general purpose financial statements for external users.

Definitions based on size are inherently problematic, due a fundamental arbitrariness. What really is the incremental effect of a 51-employee business vis-à-vis a 49-employee business, if the criteria were based on 50 employees? The rigidity of size-oriented criteria fails to acknowledge or address contextual factors such as social and economic conditions and development needs. This is particularly relevant to the ASEAN community, as AMSs exhibit diversity across the quantitative parameters. As one of our interviewees (a senior practitioner) comments:

> The definitions of SMEs are so complicated and even the definitions between government rules within a country like Indonesia are different.

Such a comment is reflected by our one senior auditor in Thailand and a professional accountant in Brunei Darussalam. Table 2.6 provides a summary of economic and social development indicators across AMSs, as well as definitional parameters for SMEs.

While SMEs are best defined by their characteristics and attributes, these are difficult to 'measure', and subsequently definitions tend to be quantitative in nature. In developing such a definition within the ASEAN, participants need to be highly cognizant that quantitative criteria should be regarded only as a proxy for the qualitative, and not the defining features in themselves. As such, methods for neutralizing disparities in economic conditions, such as multipliers based on GNI per capita, GINI coefficient, or poverty rates will need to be considered.

Furthermore, there is considerable variation across the SME sector with respect to definition for Small and Medium and whether to differentiate micro-SMEs, as different. As an example, a Thai academic argued:

> The definition is required for medium, national and transnational companies, but is not really relevant to micro firms.

The inclusion of micro-entities is varied between AMS, as Cambodia, Indonesia, Malaysia and Vietnam do define micros through some combination of employees and other financial criteria, but employees seem to be the driving criteria (Brunei Darussalam only uses employee-number for example). The Philippines, uniquely, distinguishes only by Total Assets excluding land. However, Thailand, Singapore, Laos and Myanmar do not differentiate between Small and Micro. The literature tends to be split on this. Some literature suggests that micro should be excluded, as they are contributing small amounts to an economy and thus, their growth potential is largely irrelevant. The competing argument is that micros are increasingly being included in definitional schemes from the World Bank, the European Union and the OECD. This is not surprising given the number of micro enterprises are the majority particularly for employment in country like Indonesia or Vietnam. Most of our participants in this study share this argument as stated by the owner of a traditional cake seller in Indonesia.

Table 2.6 Reporting standards and audit requirements adopted by ASEAN members

	IFRS adoption	*IFRS for SMEs*	Audit requirement	Comments
Brunei Darussalam	✓			Brunei Darussalam is currently in the process of considering suitable accounting standards for SMEs. Brunei Darussalam does not have a stock exchange, therefore, while IFRS has been adopted, it applies only to publicly accountable entities such as financial institutions and insurance companies
Cambodia	✓	✓	✓	Statutory audit is required for companies meeting thresholds of revenue, assets, and employee numbers. SMEs that are not publicly accountable, but subject to statutory audit have a choice of *IFRS for SMEs* or full IFRS.
Indonesia			✓	The Indonesian Financial Accounting standards Board has developed Tier 2 – SAK ETAP for entities with no public accountability using *IFRS for SMEs* as a reference
Laos	✓	✓	✓	The LFRS for SMEs is based on *IFRS for SMEs* year 2009, and required to be adopted by Large-sized entities and SMEs (please see the LFRS for non-public interest enterprises);
Malaysia	✓	✓	✓	SMEs are permitted to use the Malaysian Private Entities Reporting Standard (MPERS). These are essentially the *IFRS for SMEs* verbatim, excepting income tax and property development requirements, and some terminology changes.
Myanmar	✓	✓	✓	Myanmar has already signed the Open License Agreement with IFRS Foundation and full IFRS will soon be adopted nation-wide by issue of the Notification by MAC.As such, SMEs shall be required to use IFRS for SMEs. SMEs not using the IFRS for SMEs must use full IFRSs.
Philippines	✓	✓	✓	Large or publicly accountable entities must use the Philippine equivalent of IFRS of full FPRS. Small and medium-sized entities that are not publicly accountable are eligible to use the Philippine equivalent of IFRS for SMEs, subject to specific criteria. Effective January 1, 2019, small entities that meet specific criteria are allowed to use the PFRS for small entities with early adoption permitted.

(continued)

Table 2.6 (continued)

	IFRS adoption	*IFRS for SMEs*	Audit requirement	Comments
Singapore	✓	✓	✓	Entities that are not publicly accountable are eligible to use the Singapore equivalent of *IFRS for SMEs*, the SFRS for Small entities, subject to specific criteria
Thailand	✓	In progress	✓	Thailand is in the process of adopting *IFRS for SMEs* in full. The criteria for determining which entities are permitted or required to use TFRS for SMEs is under consideration
Vietnam	✓		✓	The Ministry of Finance has developed a simplified version of the Vietnamese Accounting Standards for use by SMEs

Note: ✓ = adopted

> For us who do not have enough training and university degrees doing this kind of business is the only option for live. And I believe millions of people in this country rely on this business to run our household and cost of living of our children.

Such a statement indicates that there are potential risks associated with the development of a common regional definition. Each articulation of an SME definition involves choices, and a particular definition is ultimately arbitrary, whether this reflects the boundaries between micro, small and medium entities, whether to differentiate between the three types, employee numbers, sector variations or the specification of financial measures such as turnover, fixed assets, total capital or similar. This is rendered more complex by differentiations across institutional, governmental and taxation regimes. Consequently, without a whole of region approach, with government buy-in, any further layer of definition is likely to be counter-productive. In this sense, no current definitional approach is better than the other. The more general *IFRS for SMEs* approach, for example, avoids the arbitrariness around measurement, but perhaps, introduces another arbitrariness with respect to when and whether certain SMEs do have external users. This also does not deal with those entities that are within the informal economies in the region or with companies that do not meet reporting/taxation requirements.

We also hold that any approach needs to reflect the actual numbers of SMEs within the region, including micro, small and medium entities. We argue that there appears to be a lack of focus on micro-SMEs within the regulatory and institutional frameworks in the broader sense. While the immediate financial returns might be greater with respect to small and medium entities, the future development of the ASEAN region will be driven from development and growth in micro-entities. Tables 2.7 and 2.8 respectively highlight the type of client organization and proportion of firms' revenues from SME clients respectively.

2.5.3 Existing Accounting Practices and Roles of Accountants

The dominance of SMEs as a proportion of clients and revenues for public accounting firms facilitates an insight into the current accounting and financial management practices within this sector. Through data gathered from an online time-use survey and interviews, we have an overview of relevant accounting practices. However, it must be noted that evidence from our interviews, as well as a review of prior studies, indicates that significant challenges remain surrounding the regulatory status of micro and small enterprises within AMSs. Therefore, the data and analysis with respect to current practices can be said to pertain only to those enterprises that have taken steps towards formalization and compliance.

As expected, the traditional reporting and compliance functions of accountants are well represented in time use survey data of services provided to SME clients in the previous 2 years. Such activities, including financial reporting, preparation of taxes, and external audit and assurance services comprised and average of 31% of participants time. Interview subjects in Indonesia indicated the perceived role of professional accountants as being largely restricted to reporting and compliance functions within the local context. Survey data does indicate a limited demand for technical accounting services that are not related to reporting and compliance functions, such as budgeting, forecasting, and planning. Table 2.9 highlights the types of services required by SME clients.

However, within the ASEAN region more broadly, both survey respondents and interview participants indicated that significant time (28%), was devoted to the provision of support services. Such services as book-keeping and payroll activities, while often financially oriented, do not require the services of a professional accountant, and would typically be performed in- house given the availability of administrative resources, and the required financial literacy. Interview participants in Thailand in particular, described a significant role for professional accountants in providing assistances with such activities. Subjects in Brunei Darussalam, Singapore and Malaysia discussed the support role of accountants more in terms of providing training aimed at increasing administrative and financial capabilities within the SME sector. While Indonesian participants indicated a dearth of financial literacy and basic business skills, the assistance provided by professional accountants remains largely confined to technical compliance. A general theme in our interviews was recognizing the role of accounting information in a broader context of financial

Table 2.7 Type of organisations by size (N = 200 people)

No	Type of client organizations	Percentage
1.	Small	34%
2.	Micro	32%
3.	Medium	24%
4.	Large	10%
Total		100%

Table 2.8 Type of SMEs client by revenues (N = 200 people)

No	Type of client organizations	Revenue (%)
1.	Micro	40%
2.	Medium	32%
3.	Large	16%
4.	Small	12%
Total		100%

Table 2.9 Types of services to SMEs clients (N = 200 people)

No	Type of client organizations	Revenue (%)
1.	Governance and compliance services	31%
2.	Business support services	28%
3.	Technical accounting	21%
4.	Other services	20%
Total		100%

literacy. For example, one interview, discussing this matter commented that the major issue was

> The lack of understanding regarding the roles of financial reports

This was reflected by most of our interviewees. For example, this was succinctly stated by another interviewee, who commented:

> …I think most firms are micro firms and they provide most of the nation's employments. It is great to see all firms to be able to produce and make use of financial reports, but if we are honest about empowering SMEs, what they need the most is not about having international based financial information but how to survive for everyday live.

Despite the role of the professional accountant traditionally being associated with the conventional functions of compliance and technical accounting, evidence of time-use survey indicates that this accounts for only half of the picture. Evidence from the survey and through interview responses illustrates that demand from SME clients necessitated the evolution of the accountants' role, to include extensive business support and advisory functions. To better understand the relationship between the functions performed by professional accountants on behalf of SME clients, and the challenges confronting SMEs, survey responses were further categorized as either governance and compliance related, training and development related, or value added, growth and development oriented in nature.

Governance and compliance related activities are those that relate to internal control and reporting such as budget variance analysis, setting of performance targets and preparation of financial reports, as well as activities required to meet various legal obligations. These may include tax requirements, employer obligations, and social and sustainability reporting where required. Value added, growth and development-oriented activities include budgeting, forecasting, planning and analysis of financial information, as well as issues relating to finance and mergers and expansion, and those relating to human capital requirements. Training and skill development refer both to undertaking professional development activities and providing training services to clients. Predictably, most of the accountant's time in compliance services was spent on compliance type activities, such as audit processes and preparation of taxes. However, over a quarter of time spent on compliance services was devoted to training and skill development, and value-added type activities. These included analyses of financial information, and training on various regulatory requirements. Time usage data strongly corresponds with anecdotal evidence from interviews suggesting that accountants are being called upon to respond to skill shortfalls within the SME sector.

Overall, the role of accountants is varied between compliance and organisational development activities. Some of our interview subjects suggested that, comparatively, the regulatory compliance levels and cost of compliance is unfairly burdensome for SMEs. Certainly, interview participants typically described IFRS as too complex, too costly and beyond the needs of most SMEs. The complexity of reporting standards determines the extent to which SMEs can undertake financial management activities in-house given the requisite financial literacy. Where complexity demands a level of technical expertise, beyond the financial skills required for effective business management, SMEs not only are forced to expend precious resources on accountants, but understandably feel that they do so in return for financial information that is not relevant, useful or meaningful. This resonated strongly with the majority of our interviewees. Table 2.9 provides a summary of financial reporting requirements across the ASEAN region. The formal adoption of IFRS or the plan to adopt IFRS (at varying stages and to varying degrees) is almost universal across AMSs. However, there are also a significant number of non-reporting, non-formalized entities as well. In this context, it must be acknowledged, that increasing the complexity of reporting standards may act as a significant disincentive to further formalization, due to multiple definitions across regulatory agencies (accounting, tax, etc.) and issues with financial literacy and cost of compliance. For instance, many interviewees shared this sentiment, expressed by a practicing accountant:

> I know most of my firms have financial literacy problems, but the issue is who will pay for their access to information necessary for them to understand more formal accounting

While there are some advantages to universal reporting standards, particularly in terms of economic integration, certain considerations will determine their net impact on the SME sector and consequently the accounting industry. First, the requirement to comply with *IFRS for SMEs* must be weighed against the relevance and complexity. Most SMEs in the ASEAN region are not seeking international capital and are not engaged in international trade. Notably, the *IFRS for SMEs* approach also would likely exclude many SME firms across the region as they do not necessarily have to '*publish general purpose financial statements for external users.* Furthermore, SMEs must be developed as educated consumers of the financial information that they are required to collect and provide.

2.5.4 Future Accounting and Management Needs of SMEs

Given the highly level of interaction with the SME sector, the accounting industry can be considered a key stakeholder in its future. In many ways, the relationship between professional accountants facilitates a unique insight into the business environment of SME clients, and challenges confronting the sector. Often, the accountant represents the first point of professional contact for SMEs, and often the first step towards formalization. The services of an accountant are often initially sought out of necessity, perhaps resulting from a need for finance, or some form of regulatory compliance. With the relationship between accountant and client established in the infancy of an enterprise, and due to the management characteristics of small enterprises, a close working relationship typically develops. Table 2.10 reveals the future demands of SMEs from accounting profession.

Survey participants overwhelmingly (46%) anticipated that planning and advisory services, including tax and financial planning, and business planning, would represent the most significant area of future demand. This is supported by responses from interview subjects with Thai participants highlighting the financial leadership role for accountants in undertaking controllership and value-added activities. Two academics we interviewed in Indonesia, one academic in Malaysia and two accounting professionals in Thailand also stressed that issue. An accounting professional in Thailand says:

> I believe the future roles of this [accounting] profession should be focused on providing services relating to business planning about the nature of SMEs products, financial feasibility of their business and costs of business.

The high representation of planning and advisory services relative to other anticipated future need reflects the assumption that as SMEs mature and develop the necessary capacity, administrative, technical and compliance activities are increasingly internalized. At this stage of the business development cycle, the expertise of the professional accountant, combined with the accumulated trust upon which the relationship has developed completes the evolution of the accountants' role from technocrat to trusted business advisor.

Our surveys also reveal that following planning and advisory services, 19% of our online survey participants argue that compliance services are still regarded as the most important service they need in the future. Interviewees in Brunei Darussalam and Indonesia identified the significant role of accountants in improving financial literacy and capabilities of SME clients, including understanding of financial reports and reporting standards, as well as planning and financial management. These participants also identified the need for the challenges and business environments of SMEs to be addressed within accounting qualifications. Interestingly, despite their unique relationship with the SME sector, and capacity to advocate on behalf of SME clients, participants did not foresee a significant future role in legal services and lobbying provided by accounting profession.

Table 2.10 Future demands from accounting profession in ASEAN (N = 200 people)

No.	Services	Percentage
1.	Planning and advisory	46
2.	Compliance services	19
3.	Technical services	17
4.	Legal issues	10
5.	Lobbying, communications and marketing	7
6.	Other services	2
Total		100

2.6 Conclusions and Recommendations

Our study aims to provide a better understanding of the institutional environment of accounting regulations, accounting practices and future demands of SMEs from accounting profession in the ASEAN. According to our examination of documents sources, online surveys and interviews with our participants, several conclusions can be drawn. Firstly, significant issues were identified surrounding incoherent and contradictory definitions of SMEs. Within a country, for example, the definition of SMEs may vary across regulatory bodies, government departments, banking, tax authorities and professional institutions. We find that the existing government laws/rules and regulatory framework for SMEs reveals significant inconsistencies that will impede the negotiation and adoption of a common and coherent definition throughout the ASEAN. This contrasts with the need to establish a common business reporting and accounting parameters for SMEs in the region and beyond. Undoubtedly, a shared definition forms the foundation of any regional solution to the factors limiting the potential of SMEs as drivers of economic growth. Our finding support Singleton and Green's (2016) assessment which shows that, while accounting requirements for listed companies around the world are increasingly moving toward a common approach based on International Financial Reporting Standards, requirements for private companies — and particularly for SMEs — still vary widely internationally. This pattern is also evident in the US and the EU.

Secondly, in relation to accounting practices, the common challenges faced by SMEs in the ASEAN region include the lack of skills to understand, prepare and utilize financial information for business decision making and to add value to firms through strategic partnerships and business expansion. Beyond this, our data shows that persistent obstacles, particularly for micro enterprises include limited access to basic business skills (marketing, human capital and human resources, and production), financing, innovation and technology, and importantly is the lack of effective, cohesive, and integrated of government policies for SMEs. Clearly, the challenge ahead for the accounting profession in this region is to provide leadership and support for SMEs, beyond traditional services such as reporting, taxing, and auditing services.

Thirdly, participants overwhelmingly anticipated that that planning and advisory services, including tax, and business and financial planning will represent the most significant area of future demands. This is supported by responses from interview subjects highlighting the financial leadership role of accountants in providing controllership and value-added activities. Weaknesses were also identified in relation to the efficacy of current accounting qualifications, in preparing professional accountants for the demands and distinctiveness of the SME environment. Interestingly, despite their unique relationship with the SME sector, and capacity to advocate on behalf of SME clients, participants did not foresee a significant future role in lobbying and communication. Interviewees in Brunei Darussalam and Indonesia identified the significant role of accountants in improving financial literacy and capabilities of SME clients, including understanding of financial reports and reporting standards, as well as planning and financial engagement. At this stage of a business development cycle, the expertise of the professional accountant, combined with the accumulated trust upon which the relationship has developed completes the evolution of the accountants' role from technocrat to trusted business professional.

Finally, it is important to note given that most SMEs are micro enterprises, that ultimately, they have substantively different business problems requiring tailored solutions in comparison to medium and major firms with greater market opportunities. The contention that adoption of a reporting rules (IFRS for example), is a prioritized concern for all SMEs across nations in the ASEAN is a naïve assumption. Nonetheless, this does not suggest that having the ability to prepare and effectively utilize financial reports is not important for all types of enterprises, irrespective of location and size. The research implicitly suggests that despite accounting information being theoretically and practically useful in alleviating inconsistencies associated with reporting and measuring business assets, debt and productivity of all entities, it is beyond the prioritized concerns of micro entrepreneurs. Improved access to basic educational skills in business, genuine and consistent government support and greater ease of doing business are almost universally identified as priorities. Public policy makers and professional accounting bodies should be cognizant of these findings in their efforts to develop and implement solutions for the empowerment of SMEs throughout ASEAN economies.

Further studies should seek to expand both sample size and demographic aspects of participants. While the current survey provides significant insight from the perspective of the accounting profession, future studies would benefit from the participation of a larger and more comprehensive sample of stakeholders. Targeted participants of future studies should extend beyond those with direct professional affiliations with SMEs, including business owners, representatives of government and development agencies, educators, and other community representatives. Analysis and interpretation of data by country of origin would also provide greater dimension, and a more comprehensive understanding of the diverse social, economic, and environmental contexts, and factors constraining SME development. Comparison of interview data from Indonesia, Thailand, Malaysia and Singapore indicate significantly disparate views and experiences across AMSs.

Throughout this study, we observed clear instances of a need to develop easier ways of accessing small finance opportunities, but also for sourcing alternative methods of financing. This is a challenging question, and the associated complexities beyond the scope of this study. Further research with a focus on alternative financing models for micro entities would seem critical, and we would argue that this should be directed towards the exploration of resource sharing alternatives as a means of meeting the needs of micro enterprise minus the debt imperative.

Acknowledgement The authors thank the ASEAN Federation of Accountants and Chartered Accountants Australia & New Zealand for their finding support for the study.

References

Aburous, D. (2018). *IFRS and institutional work in the accounting domain. Critical Perspectives on Accounting*. Available at https://doi.org/10.1016/j.cpa.2018.10.001.

ACCA. (2016). *SME development in ASEAN*. Available at http://www.accaglobal.com/content/dam/ACCA_Global/Technical/smb/pi-sme-development-asean.pdf. Accessed Oct 2018.

Ahmad, K., & Mohamed Zabri, S. (2015). Factors explaining the use of management accounting practices in Malaysian medium-sized firms. *Journal of Small Business and Enterprise Development, 22*(4), 762–781. https://doi.org/10.1108/JSBED-04-2012-0057

Albert, E. (2017). ASEAN: The Association of Southeast Asian Nations. *Council on Foreign Relations*, Available at https://www.cfr.org/backgrounder/asean-association-southeast-asian-nations. Accessed June 2018.

Albu, C. N., et al. (2013). Implementation of IFRS for SMEs in emerging economies: Stakeholder perceptions in The Czech Republic, Hungary, Romania and Turkey. *Journal of International Financial Management & Accounting, 24*(2), 142–185.

Barcelo, Y. (2007). Standard overload blues. *CA Magazine, 140*(4), 25–30.

Birley, S., & Niktari, N. (1995). The failure of owner-managed businesses: The diagnosis of accountants and bankers. In P. Hemington (Ed.), *A survey of small businesses and the reasons for failure*. Research Board Institute of CA in England and Wales.

Botzem, S. (2012). *The politics of accounting regulations: Organizing transnational standard setting in financial reporting*. Edward Elgar Publishing Ltd.

Brown, A. M. (2004). The Milieu of the IASB. *Journal of American Academy of Business, 5*(1–2), 385–390.

Chin, Y. W., & Lim, E. S. (2018). Policies and performance of SMEs in Malaysia. *Journal of Southeast Asian Economies, 35*(3), 470–487.

Cleminson, J., & Rabin, E. (2002). *The reporting problems faced by small business entities in South Africa*. Southern African Accounting Association.

Coetzee, S. (2007, May). IFRS for SMEs: Is small, small enough? *Accountancy SA*, pp. 32.

Del Baldo, M. (2017). The implementation of integrating reporting IR in SMEs: Insights from a pioneering experience in Italy. *Meditari Accountancy Research, 25*(4), 505–532.

Dellaportas, S., & Davenport, L. (2008). Reflections on the public interest in accounting. *Critical Perspectives on Accounting, 19*(7), 1080–1098.

Devi, S. S., & Samujh, S. H. (2015). The political economy of convergence: The case of IFRS for SMEs. *Australian Accounting Review, 25*(2), 124–138.

ERIA. (2015). Accounting standards for small and medium sized enterprises in ASEAN in Mizunoura K. (Ed.), Economic Research Institute for ASEAN and East Asia. Available at http://www.eria.org/RPR_FY2015_22.pdfSingapore. Accessed Jan 2017.

Fearnley, S., & Hines, T. (2007). How IFRS has destabilised financial reporting for UK non-listed entities. *Journal of Financial Regulation and Compliance, 15*(4), 394–408.

Gaffikin, M. J. (2008). *Accounting theory: Research, regulation and accounting practice* (1st ed.). Pearson Education.

Gallhofer, S., Haslam, J., & Kamla, R. (2012). The accountancy profession and the ambiguities of Globalisation in a post-colonial, middle eastern and Islamic context: Perceptions of accountants in Syria. *Critical Perspectives on Accounting, 22*(4), 376–395.

Hora, J. A., Onkar, R. H., & Adhikari, A. (1997). International accounting standards in capital markets. *International Accounting, Auditing, and Taxation, 6*(2), 171–190.

Irvine, H. (2008). The global institutionalization of financial reporting: The case of the United Arab Emirates. *Accounting Forum, 32*(2), 125–142.

Jermakowicz, E., & Gornik-Tomaszewski, S. (2006). Implementing IFRS from the perspective of EU publicly traded companies. *Journal of International Accounting, Auditing and Taxation, 15*, 170–196.

Kaplan, R. S., & McMillan, D. (2021). Reimagining the balanced scorecard for the ESG Era. *Harvard Business Review Digital Articles*, (February 3).

Leung, P., Raar, J., & Tangei, G. (2008). *Accounting services and SMEs: An Australian Study*. Certified Accountants Educational Trust for the Association of Chartered Certified Accountants.

OECD. (2005). *OECD SME and entrepreneurship outlook*. OECD.

Potter, B. (2013). Forum introduction: Differential reporting. *Australian Accounting Review, 23*(1), 1.

Pratama, A. (2019). *SMEs as the Backbone of Southeast Asia's Growing Economy*, International federation of Accountants. Available at https://www.ifac.org/knowledge-gateway/contributing-global-economy/discussion/smes-backbone-southeast-asia-s-growing-economy

Ram, A., & Newberry, S. (2012). IFRS for SMEs: The IASB's due process. *Australian Accounting Review, 23*(3), 3–17.

Ramirez, C., Stringfellow, L., & Maclean, M. (2015). Beyond segments in movement: A "small" agenda for research in the professions. *Accounting, Auditing & Accountability Journal, 28*(8), 1341–1372.

Ritchi, H., Azis, Y., Adrianto, Z., Setiono, K., & Sanjaya, S. (2019). In-app controls for small business accounting information system: A study of domain understanding. *Journal of Small Business and Enterprise Development, 27*(1), 31–51. https://doi.org/10.1108/JSBED-12-2018-0372

Sharma, D., & Sharma, U. (2020). Analysis of balanced scorecard usage by private companies, *Pacific Accounting Review*, Vol. ahead-of-print No. ahead-of- print. https://doi.org/10.1108/PAR-06-2019-0076.

Sian, S., & Roberts, C. (2009). UK small owner-managed businesses: Accounting and financial reporting needs. *Journal of Small Business and Enterprise Development, 16*(2), 289–305. https://doi.org/10.1108/14626000910956065

Stone, G. (2011). Let's talk: Adapting accountants' communications to small business managers' objectives and preferences. *Accounting, Auditing & Accountability Journal, 24*(6), 781–809.

Tinker, T., & Carter, C. (2003). Spectres of accounting: Contradictions or conflicts of interest? *Organization, 10*(3), 577–582.

UNCTAD [United Nations Conference on Trade and Development]. (2008). *Accounting and financial reporting guidelines for small and medium-sized enterprises (SMEGA) – Level 3 Guidance*. UNCTAD.

Warren, R., Carter, D., & Napier, C. (2019). Opening up the politics of standard setting through discourse theory: The case of IFRS for SMEs. *Accounting, Auditing & Accountability Journal, 33*, 124–151.

Wilson, A. (1995). A GAAP in understanding. *Accountancy, 115*(9), 1218.

World Bank. (2019). *A small and medium enterprises (SMED) finance*. Available at https://www.worldbank.org/en/topic/smefinance. Accessed Jan 2018.

Zhang, Y., & Si, C. (2008). The impacts of external factors on the growth of Chinese entrepreneurial enterprises: An empirical study. *Journal of Small Business and Enterprise Development, 15*(4), 689–703. https://doi.org/10.1108/14626000810917807

Chapter 3
An Empirical Study on the Impact of Trade Facilitation on Chinese Exports to South American Countries: The Case of Commodities and Electronic Products

Xinru Luan, Jungsuk Kim, Sook Rei Tan, and Jacob Wood

Abstract After the significant reduction in tariffs, trade flows are more influenced by other factors, one of which is trade facilitation, and it has been increasingly researched and mentioned. This study attempts to assess the impact of South American countries' logistics performance on exports of Chinese products. We use the Logistics Performance Index, tariffs, and FTA signature as comprehensive indicators to reveal the level of trade facilitation. To investigate the impact, the gravity model with Feasible Generalized Least Square was conducted. We found that LPI has a positive correlation with China's exports in relation to all commodity trade and E-products at 2-digit HS code level. However, tariffs and signing agreements have mixed effects. For E-products at 4-digit HS code level, LPI has no significant impact on trade, while signing an FTA can lead to a significant decrease in the export of China.

Keywords Logistics performance index (LPI) · Trade facilitation · Gravity model · Electronic products · South America · China

X. Luan
Independent Scholar, Dalian, Liaoning, China
e-mail: luanxinru2018@126.com

J. Kim
Department of Economics, Sejong University, Seoul, South Korea
e-mail: js_kim@sejong.ac.kr

S. R. Tan · J. Wood (✉)
James Cook University, Singapore, Singapore
e-mail: sookrei.tan@jcu.edu.au; jacob.wood@jcu.edu.au

E. L. Eijdenberg et al. (eds.), *Innovation-Driven Business and Sustainability in the Tropics*, https://doi.org/10.1007/978-981-99-2909-2_3

3.1 Introduction

As a result of the General Agreement on Tariffs and Trade (GATT) and World Trade Organization (WTO) multilateral negotiations, tariffs have dramatically reduced over the past 50 years, to the extent that they are no longer a major restricting factor of trade between countries. Instead, trade facilitation has provided an alternative way to reduce trade barriers. WTO members concluded negotiations on the landmark Trade Facilitation Agreement (TFA) at the 2013 Bali Ministerial Conference. The TFA includes provisions for technical assistance and capacity building and covers provisions to expedite the movement, release and clearance of goods, including goods in transit, and provides effective cooperation measures between customs and other relevant authorities in trade facilitation and customs compliance. The advent of TFA provides a legal text that seeks to address the bureaucracy and red tape of cross-border trade. It simplifies and harmonizes trade procedures and speeds up the transnational movement of factors across borders which has become an important issue in the world trading system.

The term "trade facilitation" has no common definition. The Institute for International Cooperation and Development defines it as the "simplification, harmonization and automation of international trade procedures, particularly import and export procedures, transit requirements and the procedures applied by customs and other agencies." And WTO describes it as: "the simplification and harmonization of international trade procedures [...] in collecting, presenting, communications and processing data required for the movement of goods in international trade."

Developing economies are particularly vulnerable to high trade costs. Thus, reducing trade costs will encourage developing economies to engage in more international trade, facilitate the flow of goods and promote economic development. Some exporting and importing nations are severely constrained by institutional trade barriers. These barriers which are multidimensional, impede trade flows and performance in many developing countries (Sakyi & Afesorgbor, 2019). In many South American countries, importers pay relatively more in transport costs than in tariffs (World Bank, 2001). Consequently, any effort in infrastructure development will reduce costs and ease trade (Ramasamy & Yeung, 2019; Du et al., 2021). Broadly speaking, trade facilitation refers to all measures used to increase border and transport efficiency and lower transaction costs related to trade flows (Sakyi & Afesorgbor, 2019).

Due to the accelerated process of international trade integration, countries at different levels of development are connected through trade, and changes in a country's economic environment will affect the economies linked to its economy (Dornbusch, 1976; Obstfeld & Rogoff, 1996). Trade between China and South American countries has grown rapidly since China acceded to the WTO in 2001. Free trade agreements are being negotiated between China and many South

American nations based on changing political and economic ties. (Jenkins, 2009). In order to increase its sway in the region, China published its first policy document on ties with Latin America in 2008 and joined the Inter-American Development Bank (IDB) as a full member in the same year. At the same time, China started its membership with the Asia-Pacific Economic Cooperation (APEC) and initiated negotiations with the Southern Common Market (MERCOSUR) and the Andean Community of Nations. South America has entered a period of stagnant economic growth since the 1980s. Meanwhile, China's economy has entered a stage of rapid growth. After entering the twenty-first century, China's economy has grown significantly (Wu, Huh, & Wood, 2021a; Wu, Wood, et al., 2021b), with strong trade growth and exports that accounts for nearly 13% of the world's total exports in 2020 (World Trade Organization, 2021). Calculated in Chinese Yuan, the Association of Southeast Asian Nations (ASEAN), the European Union, the United States, Japan, and South Korea are China's top five trading partners. Although South American countries account for less than 5%[1] of China's export value, China is still the main trading partner of many South American countries, with bilateral import and export trade rising rapidly (Silva et al., 2019).

Since 2001, China's trade surplus with South American countries has gradually increased due to the prosperity of Chinese manufacturing products and the decline in global bulk commodity prices. This progress particularly relates to the exports of electronic products, accounting for more than 35%[2] of China's exports to South American countries. China began to aggressively grow its electronic product processing industry as the country's most vital strategic industry at the end of the past century. It has made China's electronic industry to be a crucial part of the country's industrial structure (Wu et al., 2007), with electronic product exports making up 43%[3] of China's total exports.

The purpose of this study is to analyze the impact of trade facilitation on South American imports of Chinese commodities, especially electronic products. We use the gravity model to study the relationship between international trade and several selected indicators. The remainder of this paper is organized as follows. Section 3.2 focuses on the trade overview between China and South American countries. Section 3.3 summarizes the literature review on Logistics Performance Index (LPI). Section 3.4 presents the methodology and the variables selected in this paper. Section 3.5 documents the regression results, while Sect. 3.6 draws a series of conclusions.

[1] Calculated from UN Comtrade data.

[2] Average data of 2007-2021 from UN Comtrade data (using HS84&85 as E-products classification).

[3] Calculated from UN Comtrade data (using HS84&85 as E-products classification).

3.2 Trade Overview Between China and South American Countries

China is the largest trading partner of South American countries, and through the Belt and Road Initiative, China is a significant source of loans and foreign direct investment for these nations' infrastructure and energy development (Wang et al., 2020). Over the past two decades, the advent of China as a major commercial power has had a significant impact on world trade, with South American nations emerging as big winners. China mainly imports bulk commodities from South America and exports manufacturing products (up to 95%) (Sanborn & Ching, 2017). In the early 2000s, China started mining trade with Peru and Chile and subsequently imported oil, and agricultural products, especially soybeans, from South American countries (Estay, 2018). China's dominant position in the global economy helped contain the regional spillover effects of the 2008 global financial crisis, and South America's GDP shrank by 6.0%[4] in 2020 with the outbreak of the COVID−19 pandemic, while resilient bilateral trade has provided important opportunities for economic recovery. Between 2002 and 2021, China's exports to South American countries showed an increasing trend year by year. In terms of the trade value of China's exports to the world, the proportion of South American countries has experienced the same growth trend (see Fig. 3.1). This indicates that South American countries' imports from China are on the rise as a whole. As shown in Fig. 3.1, over the past 20 years, the global financial crisis in 2008 and the downturn in global commodity prices in 2014 had a greater impact on South

Fig. 3.1 Overall Export Value from China to Main South American Countries. (Data source: UN Comtrade)

[4] Calculated from World Bank Data, using GDP (constant 2015 $US).

American countries' imports from China. At the second meeting of the China-CELAC[5] Forum held in Chile in 2018, representatives of China and Latin American countries reached an agreement on a joint action plan for 2019–2021. In the early stages of the epidemic, China and Latin American countries reached an agreement to cooperate. The impact of the epidemic has made South American countries need to cooperate more than ever to revive the region's hard-hit economies and forge a more sustainable and inclusive development path. In 2020, the outbreak of COVID-19 caused a large number of factories to shut down and suspend production, causing serious disruption to world trade which affected both the supply and demand sides of the global economy (Gruszczynski, 2020). While during the COVID-19 crisis, South American countries imported more from China than in previous years, with the import value exceeding USD $120 billion in 2021, up 56.61% year-on-year (see Fig. 3.1).

As mentioned above, electronic products are a key area of trade between China and South American countries. When compared with Figs. 3.1 and 3.2, from 2002 to 2021, the trade trends of electronic products were similar to the overall trade trends. The economic impact brought by the economic crisis in 2008 and the global commodity price slump in 2014 also led to a decline in the import value of electronic products. The share of South American countries in global exports of Chinese electronics is in line with overall trade. In the post-COVID-19 era in 2021, imports of electronic products from South American countries increased by 46.12% year over year. According to UN Comtrade data, Brazil, Chile, and Argentina have been China's top three South American export partners over the past 20 years, and the ranking of electronic product export is the same as that of all commodity exports. Electronics account for more than 40% of all

Fig. 3.2 Export Value of Electronic Products from China to Main South American Countries. (Data source: UN Comtrade)

[5] The Community of Latin American & Caribbean States.

Table 3.1 Value of all commodities and electronic products export from China to main South American countries from 2002 to 2021

Rank	Partner	E value ($US mil) *	Total value ($US mil) *	E value/ total value (%)**	GDP (constant 2015 $US mil) ***
1	Brazil	187,442	460,421	40.71%	1,829,902
2	Chile	50,697	195,059	25.99%	275,165
3	Argentina	47,682	113,999	41.83%	567,607
4	Colombia	36,587	105,553	34.66%	330,299
5	Peru	27,397	93,067	29.44%	217,030
6	Ecuador	12,413	42,195	29.42%	97,754
7	Uruguay	9772	28,724	34.02%	54,391
8	Paraguay	6851	19,251	35.58%	42,038
9	Bolivia	2971	7985	37.20%	36,984
10	Guyana	797	2777	28.68%	8726

Data source: *UN Comtrade; **calculated by author; ***World Bank open data

products imported from China by Brazil and Argentina. Overall, around 30% of the total value of imports comes from Chinese electronic goods by various nations in South America (see Table 3.1). In recent years, China and South American countries have successively signed trade agreements and introduced several trade facilitation policies to promote the development of China's foreign trade export industry.

In the following part, we will summarize the trade relations between China and 10 major South American countries, including bilateral policies, trade value, commodities, and trade facilitation levels. China has signed trade facilitation documents with 10 South American countries. Brazil stands out among them as China's biggest trading partner in the region, where the country mainly exports bulk commodities and imports electronic products.

3.2.1 *Argentina*

Argentina is a member of the WTO and a party to the Multilateral Agreement on Trade in Goods (MTA), the General Agreement on Trade in Services (GATS), and the Agreement on Trade-Related Aspects of Intellectual Property Rights (TRIPS). In March 1991, Argentina, along with Brazil, Uruguay, and Paraguay, initiated and established MERCOSUR. Argentina is also a member of the Latin American Integration Association (ALADI). According to Chinese Customs statistics, bilateral trade between China and Argentina totaled USD $13.89 billion in 2020, down 2.68% year-on-year. China's exports to Argentina were USD $7.09 billion, up 2.95% year-on-year.[6] China continues to maintain its position as Argentina's second largest trading partner, export market, and source of imports. Argentina mostly imports Chinese telephone sets and automated data processing equipment.

[6] Data Source: General Administration of Customs Peoples Republic of China.

Ministry of Commerce of China reports that in December 2019, after the Fernandez administration took office, Argentina chose protectionism as its first major trade priority and introduced a series of trade control measures to strengthen trade barriers in the face of the triple challenges of the debt crisis, economic crisis, and the COVID-19 pandemic.[7]

3.2.2 *Bolivia*

Bolivia is an associate member of MERCOSUR and a member of the Andean Community of Nations and the Latin American Integration Organization. Since 2006, Bolivia's new government has sought closer diplomatic ties with China, and China has become its second largest trading partner. According to Chinese Customs statistics, in 2020, the trade value between China and Bolivia was USD $982 million, of which China's export value was USD $688 million.[8] China mainly exports electromechanical products, high-tech products, metal products, and vehicles. According to the Ministry of Commerce of China, on May 1, 2016, the Bolivian Government adopted three decrees to adopt a pre-licensing system for some imported products. Strengthening ties with Bolivia offers China an opportunity to show that Chinese cooperation and financing may help Bolivia achieve sustainable national development (Estay, 2018).

3.2.3 *Brazil*

Brazil is a member of MERCOSUR, with which China has not yet signed a free trade agreement. Since 2009, China has been Brazil's biggest trading partner. As of 2020, China is both Brazil's largest import and export market and its biggest trading partner in Latin America. Bilateral trade soared in the 2000s due to the commodities boom (2003–2008) and China's manufacturing exports to Brazil, which were dominated by soybeans and iron ore. The Brazilian Government also supports the agricultural sector through an active national trade policy in the WTO. And Brazil, along with China, India, South Africa, and Russia, formed the BRICS.

Chinese Customs records show that bilateral trade reached USD $119.040 billion in 2020, up 3.06% year-on-year, with China's exports to Brazil amounting to USD $34.956 billion, down 1.64% year-on-year.[9] The primary items that China sells to Brazil are ships, machinery, electrical devices, integrated circuits, etc.

[7] Foreign Investment Cooperation Country (Argentina) Guide 2021 by Ministry of Commerce, PRC, 2022b.

[8] Data Source: General Administration of Customs People's Republic of China.

[9] Data Source: General Administration of Customs People's Republic of China.

Brazilian law is quite complex, and there are differences in legal provisions and implementation around the country. Moreover, Brazil's foreign trade management regulations are more frequently modified.[10]

3.2.4 Chile

Chile is an associate member of MERCOSUR, a member of the Pacific Alliance, and a member of APEC. In 2016, Chile joined the Treaty of Amity of Southeast Asian Nations (TAC), while expressing interest in joining The Regional Comprehensive Economic Partnership (RCEP). In March 2018, Chile signed the Comprehensive and Progressive Agreement for the Trans-Pacific Partnership (CPTPP) with 11 countries, including Canada and Japan, in Santiago. Chile has actively negotiated free trade agreements and is one of the most open economies in the world. To date, Chile has signed 31 regional trade agreements around the world.[11] In November 2016, China and Chile jointly issued the Joint Declaration on a Comprehensive Strategic Partnership of the People's Republic of China and the Republic of Chile. And the China-Chile Free Trade Agreement was implemented in 2006.

Copper is Chile's main mineral resource. Rising copper prices and growing Chinese demand for Chilean copper have led to a marked increase in bilateral trade (Estay, 2018). China-Chile trade has maintained a stable level of development, and China has become Chile's top trading partner, the biggest export market, and the biggest source of imports since 2012. In 2020, bilateral trade between China and Chile amounted to USD $40.9 billion, up 11% year-on-year, of which, China's exports were USD $15.2 billion, up 3.6% year-on-year.[12] According to Chinese Customs statistics, electric motors, electrical, audio-visual equipment, and their spare parts, and mechanical appliances have been China's leading exports to Chile in recent years.[13]

According to the China's Ministry of Commerce, Chile's trade strategy aims to improve the efficiency and competitiveness of domestic producers; reduce physical protection and remove obstacles to exports; promote regional economic cooperation; and promote exports and attract foreign investment. Since 1997, Chile has been implementing a liberalized trade management system, and in 2003 further unilaterally reduced tariffs, reformed trade remedies, and developed export

[10] Foreign Investment Cooperation Country (Brazil) Guide 2021 by Ministry of Commerce, PRC, 2022b.

[11] Data source: WTO Regional Trade Agreements Database.

[12] Data Source: General Administration of Customs People's Republic of China.

[13] Foreign Investment Cooperation Country (Chile) Guide 2021 by Ministry of Commerce, PRC, 2022b.

promotion measures.[14] Chile does not have any quantitative restrictions or licensing measures for imported products, but prohibits the import of used cars, motorcycles, used recycled tires, toxic and hazardous goods, and endangered plants and animals.

3.2.5 Colombia

Colombia is a member of the Organization for Economic Cooperation and Development (OECD) and an associate member of MERCOSUR. In 2020, China was Colombia's second largest trading partner. According to Chinese Customs statistics, total bilateral trade between China and Colombia was USD $13.62 billion, down 12.9% year-on-year. Of this amount, China's exports were USD $9.32 billion, up 0.9% year-on-year.[15]

Since 1984, Colombia has been reforming its foreign trade system and liberalizing trade. The main manifestation of the foreign trade system reform is the significant reduction of tariffs and the elimination of non-tariff barriers. According to China's Ministry of Commerce, The Colombian Ministry of Trade, Industry and Tourism, together with other relevant ministries such as the General Directorate of Taxation and Customs, have significantly improved government efficiency by establishing a single window mechanism for foreign trade, providing a unified one-stop management of import and export trade, and simplifying import and export procedures.[16]

3.2.6 Ecuador

Ecuador is also an associate member of MERCOSUR and a member of the Andean Community of Nations and the Latin American Integration Association. In 2020, China was the second largest trading partner of Ecuador, and the bilateral trade value reached USD $7.56 billion in 2020, up 4.0% year-on-year, of which China's exports amounted to USD $3.25 billion, down 10.3% year-on-year.[17] China's Ministry of Commerce reports that Ecuador customs requires importers to register their qualifications with the competent authorities and they can selectively contact local insurance companies in Ecuador for import insurance before the goods arrive at the port.[18]

---

[14] Free Trade Agreement between the Government of the People's Republic of China and the Government of the Republic of Chile.

[15] Data Source: General Administration of Customs People's Republic of China.

[16] Foreign Investment Cooperation Country (Colombia) Guide 2021 by Ministry of Commerce, PRC, 2022b.

[17] Data Source: General Administration of Customs People's Republic of China.

[18] Foreign Investment Cooperation Country (Ecuador) Guide 2021 by Ministry of Commerce, PRC, 2022b.

3.2.7 Guyana

Guyana is an associate member of MERCOSUR and is a member of the Caribbean Community and Common Market (CARICOM). Guyana can enjoy the free trade agreements that CARICOM has signed with other countries or regions. In 2001, China signed a trade agreement with Guyana. The agreement is a programmatic document that stipulates that both governments agree on the following matters: to take appropriate measures to promote the development of economic and trade relations between the two countries, to gradually reduce and eliminate obstacles in the process of trade in goods and services, and to strengthen technical cooperation by their respective existing laws, regulations and binding international agreements.[19] In 2020, trade in goods between China and Guyana amounted to USD $570 million, an increase of 78.7% year-on-year. Of this amount, China's exports were USD $265 million, down 2.9% year-on-year.[20]

3.2.8 Paraguay

Paraguay is also a member of MERCOSUR, and China has not signed any bilateral economic and trade agreements with Paraguay. Statistics from Paraguayan Central Bank show that commerce between China and Paraguay was USD $2.869 billion in 2020, with China's exports totaling USD $2.855 billion, down 28.61% year-on-year.[21] According to China's Ministry of Commerce, Paraguay has continued to take measures to modernize its trade system in recent years, including measures such as the ongoing simplification of customs procedures. After the establishment of a single export window, Paraguay also established a single import window, enabling electronic clearance of all imports and exports.[22]

3.2.9 Peru

Peru actively participates in global multi-bilateral trade mechanisms as a way to expand its foreign trade markets and create a favorable trade environment. According to China's Ministry of Commerce, trade between Peru and its partners in various regional trade agreements accounts for more than 80% of the country's total foreign

[19] Foreign Investment Cooperation Country (Guyana) Guide 2021 by Ministry of Commerce, PRC, 2022b.

[20] Data Source: General Administration of Customs People's Republic of China.

[21] Data Source: General Administration of Customs People's Republic of China.

[22] Foreign Investment Cooperation Country (Paraguay) Guide 2021 by Ministry of Commerce, PRC, 2022b.

trade. Overall, Peru is a global leader in the development of free trade agreements. Peru is an associate member of MERCOSUR, and China and Peru signed the China-Peru Free Trade Agreement (CPFTA) in April 2009, see Table 3.2 for more bilateral trade agreements.

Gaining preferential access to the Chinese market and pursuing a policy of deeper integration into Asian industrial "supply chains" and becoming the commercial hub of South America were objectives of Peru's FTA with China (OECD/CAF/ECLAC, 2015). China and Peru are now discussing to upgrade their existing free trade agreement (Ministry of Commerce, PRC, 2022a).

China has been Peru's top trading partner for seven consecutive years, with total trade between China and Peru amounting to USD $20.75 billion, down 11.2% year-on-year, and China's exports to Peru amounting to USD $9.64 billion, down 1.5% year-on-year.[23] Since 2006, the Peruvian government has decided to unilaterally and significantly reduce import tariffs and simplify customs management measures, while trying to promote the diversification of export markets and non-traditional export products. Currently, imports of capital goods, foodstuffs, raw materials, etc. are being liberalized to the maximum extent possible, except for products that undermine Peru's sovereignty, security, and social morals and disrupt the market order. The role of China as an important economic partner of Peru, coupled with the development of Peru's own economic diversification strategy, has reduced Peru's economic dependence on the United States (Sanborn & Ching, 2017).

3.2.10 *Uruguay*

Uruguay is a member of MERCOSUR, and the economies of China and Uruguay are highly complementary. According to Chinese Customs statistics, bilateral trade between China and Uruguay was USD $4.07 billion in 2020, down 17.0 percent year-on-year. Among them, China's exports to Uruguay were USD $1.70 billion, down 12.6% year-on-year.[24] Electromechanical equipment, automobiles and locomotive parts, high-tech products, cell phones and communication equipment, data processing equipment and components, and household appliances make up the majority of China's exports to Uruguay. Uruguay is one of the South American nations with the most open policies for foreign trade. The government places a strong emphasis on the development of foreign trade as means of promoting economic growth. This emphasizes the diversification of export commodities and export markets, and highlights the importance of diplomacy for economics and trade.[25]

[23] Data Source: General Administration of Customs People's Republic of China.

[24] Data Source: General Administration of Customs People's Republic of China.

[25] Foreign Investment Cooperation Country (Uruguay) Guide 2021 by Ministry of Commerce, PRC, 2022b.

Table 3.2 Trade policies between China and main South American countries

Country	Trade facilitation policy	Time
Argentina	Trade Agreement	1977.2
	Maritime Transport Agreement	1978.5
	Protocol amending the Agreement on maritime transport	1995.1
	Memorandum of Understanding (MoU) on Investment Promotion and Trade Diversification	2010.7
	Cooperation Agreement between the China Council for the Promotion of International Trade and the Argentine Investment and International Trade Agency (AAICI)	2017.5
	MoU on Trade and Investment Promotion between Department of International Trade and Economic Affairs of the Ministry of Commerce of the People's Republic of China and Argentine Investment and Trade Promotion Agency	2017.5
	MoU on the Belt and Road Initiative	2022.2
Bolivia	Joint Declaration on Strategic Partnership between the People's Republic of China and the Government of the Plurinational State of Bolivia	2018.6
	MoU on Jointly Promoting the Construction of the Silk Road Economic Belt and the twenty-first Century Maritime Silk Road	2018.6
Brazil	Trade Agreement	1978.1
	Maritime Transport Agreement	1979.5
	Supplementary Protocol to the Trade Agreement	1984.5
	MoU on Trade and Investment Cooperation Between the People's Republic of China and the Federative Republic of Brazil	2004.11
	MoU on Services Cooperation between Ministry of Commerce of China and the Ministry of Economy of Brazil	2019.11
	MoU on Investment Cooperation between Ministry of Commerce of China and the Ministry of Economy of Brazil	2019.11
Chile	Trade Agreement	1971.4
	Agreement on Encouragement and Reciprocal Protection of Investments	1994.3
	Maritime Transport Agreement	1995.11
	Market Access Agreement	1999.11
	China-Chile Free Trade Agreement	2005.11
	Supplementary Agreement on Trade in Services of the Free Trade Agreement	2008.4
	Supplementary Agreement on Investment of the Free Trade Agreement	2012.9
	Protocol to Amend the Free Trade Agreement and the Supplementary Agreement on Trade in Services of the Free Trade Agreement Between the Government of the People's Republic of China and the Government of the Republic of Chile	2017.11
	MoU on Jointly Promoting the Construction of the Silk Road Economic Belt and the twenty-first Century Maritime Silk Road	2018.11
	Joint Statement on Strengthening Free Trade Cooperation in Combating the New Coronary Pneumonia Epidemic	2020.7

(continued)

Table 3.2 (continued)

Country	Trade facilitation policy	Time
Colombia	Agreement on the Mutual Protection and Promotion of Investment	1981.7
	MoU on Strengthening of Production Capacity Cooperation between National Development and Reform Commission of China and The Ministry of Commerce, Industry and Tourism of Colombia	2015.5
	MoU to Deepen Cooperation on Infrastructure Development between Ministry of Commerce of China and Ministry of Transport of Government of the Republic of Colombia	2015.5
	MoU on Infrastructure Cooperation between China Development Bank and the Development Finance Corporation of Colombia	2015.5
Ecuador	Agreement For Avoidance of Double Taxation and Prevention of Fiscal Evasion	2013
	MoU on Cooperation on Industrial Parks and Special Economic Zones	2016
	Framework of Production Capacity and Investment Cooperation	2016
	MoU on the Belt and Road Initiative	2018
Guyana	Trade Agreement	2001
	MoU on the Belt and Road Initiative	2018.7
	Agreement on the Mutual Protection and Promotion of Investment	2003.3
Paraguay		
Peru	Trade Agreement	1972.8
	Agreement Between the Government of the People's Republic of China and the Government of the Republic of Peru Concerning the Encouragement and Reciprocal Protection of Investments	1994.6
	The China-Peru Free Trade Agreement	2009.4
	Joint Declaration on the Deepening of the Comprehensive Strategic Partnership between China and Peru	2016.9
	2016–2021 Joint Action Plan between the Government of the People's Republic of China and the Government of the Republic of Peru	2016.11
	MoU Between the Ministry of Foreign Trade and Tourism of the Republic of Peru and The Ministry of Commerce of The People's Republic of China for Optimization of the Peru-China Free Trade Agreement	2016.11
	MoU on Jointly Promoting the Construction of the Silk Road Economic Belt and the twenty-first Century Maritime Silk Road	2019.4
Uruguay	Trade Agreement	1988.2
	MoU on Trade and Investment Cooperation	2009.3
	MoU on the Belt and Road Initiative	2018.8

Source: Foreign Investment Cooperation Country (Region) Guide 2021 by Ministry of Commerce, PRC (2022b)

3.3 Literature Review

The World Bank introduced the Logistic Performance Index (LPI) levels for more than 150 countries in 2007. Customs clearance, infrastructure, logistics services, transportation services, tracking of goods, and timeliness are the six components of the LPI. Through giving assessment and scoring, the index comprehensively evaluates the logistics level of various countries.

The LPI is based on a worldwide survey of operators on the ground including global freight forwarders and express carriers, to elicit feedback on the logistics "friendliness" of the countries that they operate and trade with. The LPI combines in-depth knowledge of the countries in which they operate with informed qualitative assessments of other countries where they trade and experience of global logistics environment. Principal Component Analysis (PCA) is used to calculate the weights of the six indicators that make up the LPI. The LPI include following indicators[26]:

1. The efficiency of customs and border management clearance ("Customs").
2. The quality of trade and transport infrastructure ("Infrastructure").
3. The ease of arranging competitively priced shipments ("Ease of arranging shipments").
4. The competence and quality of logistics services—trucking, forwarding, and customs brokerage ("Quality of logistics services").
5. The ability to track and trace consignments ("Tracking and tracing").
6. The frequency with which shipments reach consignees within scheduled or expected delivery times ("Timeliness").

Previous research showed that the logistics index was positively correlated with trade level. Taking 26 OECD member countries as research objects, Guner and Coskun (2012) studied the relationship between logistics development and other economic and social factors by LPI. Martí et al. (2014) measured the impact of LPI on the level of trade facilitation of South America, Africa, Middle East, Far East, and Post-Soviet States. Recent study by Zaninović et al. (2021) discovered that differences in LPI have heterogeneous effects on bilateral trade, especially when different categories of goods and trade between different country pairs are taken into account.

More studies on LPI effects have been conducted by several academics. According to research by Arvis et al. (2016), the quality score of railway facilities was generally lower due to the popularity of automated border management network facilities, and the quality score of railways was also generally lower. In addition, service facilities had a great impact, and countries varied significantly between air and sea transportation. Dang and Yeo (2018) used LPI to prioritize and analyze the factors that affect the efficiency of Vietnam's logistics, and they found that logistics costs had the greatest impact, followed by logistics services. In 2010, a study by the World Bank on the impact of trade facilitation in Southeast Asia was conducted,

[26] World Bank, International LPI. URL: https://lpi.worldbank.org/international

in which infrastructure, information and communication technology, border and transport efficiency, and the environment of the trading system were all considered. In terms of the trade costs associated with South American countries, Wilmsmeier et al. (2006) argued that port efficiency, infrastructure, private sector participation, and connectivity between ports can profoundly affect transportation costs. Although Scholars have mixed opinions on the use of LPI, it has developed into a useful indicator of the country's logistics level and level of trade facilitation (Duzbaievna Sharapiyeva et al., 2019; Katrakylidis & Madas, 2019; La & Song, 2019; Takele, 2019; Takele & Buvik, 2019; Bugarčić et al., 2020).

3.4 Methodology

Tinbergen (1962) and Pöyhönen (1963) are generally considered to be the first scholars to use gravity models in international trade. Gravity models have been widely used to analyze and predict economic variables, especially bilateral trade flows (Frankel & Rose, 2002; Anderson & Van Wincoop, 2003; Head & Mayer, 2014; Baier et al., 2014; Wood et al. 2017a, b; Chaney, 2018; Wood et al., 2020; Wu et al., 2022). The initial version of the model assumes that bilateral GDP and distance affect bilateral trade volume, stating that trade volume is proportional to the GDP of the two countries and inversely proportionate to the distance between them (Frankel & Rose, 2002).

Although some scholars believe that the gravity model is more theoretical and lacks consideration of complex factors, it is widely used due to its success in predicting trade volume (Deardorff, 1984). Harris et al. (2012) presented that its high acceptance is largely due to its success in understanding the effects of trade liberalization and assessing the effects of geographical distribution and trade agreements on trade flows. Baier et al. (2014) also concurred that due to the widespread use of gravity models in practice, it has become the dominant econometric method in the international trade literature. In particular, gravity models have been widely used to assess the effects of regional economic integration, national borders, trade unions, languages, and other factors on trade flows (Bergstrand & Egger, 2013).

The basic notion behind a gravity equation is that bilateral trade can be explained by:

- Factors related to the potential of a country to export goods and services
- Factors that can explain the tendency of a country to import goods and services
- Other forces that attract bilateral trade

The empirical model used in this paper is based on the gravity model proposed by Linnemann (1967), who used the gravity model in an extensive empirical analysis. The basic model is expressed as Eq. (3.1), that is, the trade volume between countries is proportional to the national GDP and inversely proportional to the distance between the two countries.

$$\log\left(Trade_{ijt}\right)=\beta_0+\beta_1\log\left(GDP_{it}\right)+\beta_2\log\left(GDP_{jt}\right)+\beta_3\log\left(Dist_{ij}\right)+u_{ijt} \quad (3.1)$$

In addition to bilateral GDP, population and distance, we choose weighted average tariffs and whether to sign an FTA with China as variables to reflect the level of trade openness of each country in South America. At the same time, South America contains both coastal countries and inland countries, therefore we selected LPI to reflect the variations in transportation. This study adjusts the original gravity model following the characteristics of South America, adding FDI levels, tariffs, and LPI as variables, and whether to sign FTA as a dummy variable. Besides, since this paper is devoted to the study of electronic products, the number of mobile phone subscriptions of South American countries is also considered.

$$\begin{aligned}\log\left(Export_{ijt}\right)=&\ \beta_0+\beta_1\log\left(GDP_{it}\right)+\beta_2\log\left(GDP_{jt}\right)+\beta_3\log\left(Dist_{ij}\right)\\&+\beta_4\tau_{ijt}+\beta_5CFDIout_t+\beta_6SAFDIin_{jt}+\beta_7pop_{jt}\\&+\beta_8mobile_{jt}+\beta_9LPI_{jt}+\beta_{10}FTA_{jt}+u_{ijt}\end{aligned} \quad (3.2)$$

In the Eq. (3.2), $Export_{ijt}$ represents China's export trade value to South American country j at 2-digit HS code level in year t. GDP_i and GDP_j stand for the gross domestic product of country i (China) and country j in year t respectively, and this variable is expected to be positively correlated with trade value. $Dist_{ij}$ is the distance between the capital of country i and country j. We predict the further the distance between the two countries, the less the trade value, due to the fact that geographically closer countries have lower trade costs and higher levels of bilateral trade (see Anderson & van Wincoop, 2004). In addition, the population of South American countries is also considered as a measure of overall purchasing power. In the existing literature of trade gravity model, the population effect is indeterminate. For examples, Hutchinson (2005) and Dell'Ariccia (1999) uncovered negative relationship between population and trade flows, while Jafari et al. (2011) and Karagöz and Karagöz (2009) found such relationship to be positive.

$CFDIout_t$ represents China's FDI outflows in year t. We predicted the export value increases with greater level of China's outward FDI, especially for intermediate products, such as raw materials and components. If the increase in CFDI outflow is accompanied by an increase in trade value, it means that China's foreign direct investment and exports to South American countries are positively correlated. $SAFDIin_{jt}$ represents the inflow of FDI to South American countries in year t. We expect that an increase in inflow of FDI, will follow the overall trade value, especially in intra-MNC[27] trade (Hejazi & Safarian, 2001). With the continuous increase of FDI inflow in South American countries in recent years, we expect a strong correlation with trade value.

A more open political and economic environment means easier market access, which is positively related to trade value (Wu et al., 2007). Three variables will be

[27] Multi National Company.

used to reflect the degree of trade facilitation in the South American countries. In order to show the logistics level, this paper uses the LPI as a variable to reflect the customs clearance level of cargo transportation in South American countries. This variable and trade value are expected to have a positive correlation. Since there are multiple indicators in the LPI, this study uses the overall LPI as a research indicator. Nevertheless, imposing tariffs is also a significant tool for restricting trade, and the tariff levels between South American countries are quite different. Therefore, this paper uses the weighted average tariff at 2-digit HS code level, which corresponds to the trade value. Due to the lagged effect of tariffs, this study uses tariffs of the previous year as variables. It is expected that the tariff and trade value are negatively correlated. As a dummy variable, FTA_{jt} means whether the South American country has ratified a free trade agreement with China.

Finally, due to the particularity of electronic products trade, we choose mobile phone subscriptions in South American countries as a variable. According to our predictions, countries with high mobile phone subscriptions rate would import more electronic products from China, and vice versa.

3.5 Results

This study examines China's export to 10 South American countries from 2007 to 2021. The required data have been retrieved from international organizations databases such as United Nations Comtrade database, World Bank Open Data, *CEPII*, UNCTAD FDI online database, and WTO Tariff Analysis Online (TAO) database. Furthermore, we collected FTA agreements from China Free Trade Zone Network. To deal with the zero trade flows problem, we choose Feasible Generalized Least Square (FGLS) as the estimation method, which is also robust to heteroscedasticity (Tables 3.3 and 3.4).

Table 3.3 Descriptive statistics for the variables

	Unit	Count	Mean	SD	Min	Max
TradeValue	US $	14,400	7.10e+07	3.57e+08	0	1.41e+10
CGDP	US $	14,400	1.05e+13	3.13e+12	5.69e+12	1.58e+13
SAGDP	US $	14,400	3.20e+11	5.03e+11	3.32e+09	1.87e+12
SAFDIinflow	US $	14,400	10,397.77	17,777.75	-1821.10	97,421.79
CFDIoutward	US $	14,400	112,008.20	46,406.45	26,506.09	196,149.40
lpi	Index	14,400	2.77	0.29	2.05	3.32
Tariff	Ratio	14,400	11.05	8.44	0.00	100.00
mobilecellpop	number	14,400	4.17e+07	6.24e+07	447,769	2.81e+08
population	number	14,400	3.78e+07	5.70e+07	746,477	2.14e+08
Distance	kilometers (km.)	14,400	17,229.85	1669.73	14,808.48	19,297.47
fta	Dummy variable	14,400	0.19	0.39	0.00	1.00

Note: the nominal export value (*TradeValue*), China's GDP (*CGDP*), South American countries' GDP (*SAGDP*), FDI inflow of South American countries (*SAFDIinflow*), FDI outflow of China (*CFDIoutward*), Logistics Performance Index (*lpi*), Tariff rate (*tariff*), Mobile population (*mobilecellpop*), population (*population*), Distance (*Distance*), Dummy variable fta (*fta*)

Table 3.4 Variance covariance matrix

	distance	tariff	sagdp	cgdp	cfdiout	lpi	fta	safdiin	mobile	pop	_cons
distance	11.9398										
tariff	−0.0029	0.0036									
sagdp	−0.4994	0.0003	0.2393								
cgdp	0.1017	0.0002	−0.0439	0.1130							
cfdiout	0.0180	0.0000	0.0089	0.0582	0.0448						
lpi	−0.0771	0.0001	−0.0228	0.0040	−0.0086	0.1278					
fta	−0.0853	0.0028	−0.0012	0.0013	0.0004	0.0071	0.1442				
safdiin	0.0056	0.0000	−0.0019	0.0014	−0.0001	−0.0005	0.0000	0.0009			
mobile	0.0847	0.0000	−0.0828	0.0158	−0.0296	−0.0090	−0.0320	0.0001	0.1475		
pop	0.3599	−0.0003	−0.1534	0.0184	0.0234	0.0207	0.0297	0.0010	−0.0670	0.2687	
_cons	−114.1352	0.0116	3.9884	−3.1774	0.9524	0.7648	0.8060	−0.0701	−0.1614	−3.8327	1159.9888

As expected, the results of three regressions show the GDP of South American countries is positively related to bilateral trade, and distance is negatively related to trade, except when analyzing electronics at 2-digit HS code level without considering the mobile subscription. An increase in South American GDP will boost trade and the greater the distance between South American countries and China, the more trade will be hindered. The outcomes of all commodities exports are displayed in columns 1–4 of Table 3.5. Without considering FTA signing (column 3), there is a positive correlation between China's GDP and exports at the 5% significant level, which suggests that an increase in China's GDP will drive the export of all goods to South America. FDI inflows to South American countries also had an unexpectedly adverse impact on trade, probably because the aggregate rise in investment received by South American countries boosted their exports rather than purchasing power. But FDI outflows from China have no significant impact on exports. The open trade of South American countries has a major favorable impact on China's commodity exports, which is reflected both in the LPI and whether FTA signing at the 1% significant level. However, the increase in tariff levels in South American countries has brought about a significant increase in the export of Chinese goods to South American countries. This positive impact is also seen in Cheong and Tang's (2018) analysis of the impact of tariffs in two FTAs, which demonstrates that duties under the Prepared Foodstuffs category show a boosting effect on trade. Since the tariffs are that imposed by South American countries towards all WTO members in the prior year, there is a possibility of deviations for Chinese exports. The increase in tariffs in South American countries has largely denied high-cost goods to the South American market, which may also boost China's exports of many cheap manufactured goods. Additionally, exports and the number of mobile cellular customers are strongly statistically connected. Moreover, the South American country population shows a somewhat negative relationship, which is in line with the findings of Hutchinson (2005) and Dell'Ariccia (1999).

Columns 5 – 8 of Table 3.5 show the results of China's electronics exports to South American countries at 2-digit HS code level (HS84&85). Bilateral GDP is positively correlated with electronics exports, which is consistent with the findings for all merchandise exports. The export of electronic products is unquestionably impacted by FDI inflows to South American countries, which have a considerable positive link at 5% significant level. But China's outward FDI does not reveal a significant correlation. In terms of three trade facilitation indicators, tariff levels and LPI show negative and positive correlations with trade at less than 5% significant level. Signing FTA with China can promote trade only when LPI is ignored. Furthermore, there is a strong positive correlation between mobile cellular usage and electronics exports. Besides, the population of South American countries shows a somewhat unfavorable relationship with electronics imports.

Results of electronic product exports from China to South American countries at the 4-digit HS code level are shown in Columns 9–12 of Table 3.5. Bilateral distance and GDP of South American countries show a good correlation with trade. China's GDP, CFDI outflow, and SAFDI inflow do not show clear correlations with trade value. Regarding the trade facilitation indicators, only FTA signing shows a negative correlation with trade at 5% significant level, indicating that the export of

Table 3.5 Estimation result

	All commodity at 2-digit HS code level				E-products at 2-digit HS code level				E-products at 4-digit HS code level			
distance	−7.2012***	−6.9876***	−6.4774***	−6.6412***	−0.6896***	−0.5158**	−0.6628***	−0.3666	−1.8537***	−1.7237**	−2.0026***	−1.9700***
	(0.0000)	(0.0000)	(0.0000)	(0.0000)	(0.0051)	(0.0065)	(0.0065)	(0.1332)	(0.0084)	(0.0135)	(0.0043)	(0.0039)
sagdp	2.4151***	2.6390***	1.9206***	2.7514***	0.8838***	1.0691***	0.8872***	1.0965***	1.8098***	1.9679***	1.9414***	1.7358***
	(0.0000)	(0.0000)	(0.0000)	(0.0000)	(0.0000)	(0.0000)	(0.0000)	(0.0000)	(0.0000)	(0.0000)	(0.0000)	(0.0000)
cgdp	0.4967	0.4567	0.6533**	0.4145	0.6416***	0.6063***	0.6442***	0.6020***	0.5467	0.5193	0.5024	0.5692
	(0.1264)	(0.1596)	(0.0457)	(0.2015)	(0.0000)	(0.0001)	(0.0000)	(0.0001)	(0.1877)	(0.2106)	(0.2264)	(0.1690)
pop	−2.4939***	−2.6057***	−2.3316***	−1.5534***	−0.7842***	−0.9002***	−0.7687***	−0.2961***	−0.3942	−0.4730	−0.4193	−0.6006***
	(0.0000)	(0.0000)	(0.0000)	(0.0000)	(0.0000)	(0.0000)	(0.0000)	(0.0000)	(0.2372)	(0.1507)	(0.2091)	(0.0001)
cfdiout	−0.0117	0.0522	−0.1197	0.2820	−0.0543	−0.0006	−0.0534	0.0936	0.2935	0.3351	0.3231	0.2263
	(0.9549)	(0.8001)	(0.5664)	(0.1476)	(0.5568)	(0.9947)	(0.5638)	(0.2959)	(0.2700)	(0.2054)	(0.2249)	(0.3619)
safdiin	−0.0673**	−0.0646**	0.0025	−0.0736***	0.0282**	0.0298**	0.0302**	0.0286**	0.0525	0.0546	0.0367	0.0538
	(0.0131)	(0.0172)	(0.9256)	(0.0066)	(0.0202)	(0.0194)	(0.0107)	(0.0228)	(0.1266)	(0.1117)	(0.2781)	(0.1163)
tariff	1.0392***	1.0414***	0.7786***	1.0213***	−0.1483***	−0.1248**	−0.1682***	−0.2388***	---	---	---	---
	(0.0000)	(0.0000)	(0.0000)	(0.0000)	(0.0016)	(0.0108)	(0.0000)	(0.0000)	---	---	---	---
lpi	0.8024***		2.5712***	0.7421**	0.7260***		0.7643***	0.7218***	0.5585		0.1208	0.5734
	(0.0075)		(0.0000)	(0.0133)	(0.0000)		(0.0000)	(0.0000)	(0.1463)		(0.7252)	(0.1353)
fta	1.8748***	2.0301***		1.8925***	0.0503	0.2100***		−0.0195	−0.4108**	−0.3038**		−0.4177**
	(0.0000)	(0.0000)		(0.0000)	(0.4836)	(0.0022)		(0.7878)	(0.0117)	(0.0368)		(0.0103)
mobile	1.2305***	1.1905***	1.3634***		0.6759***	0.6704***	0.6540***		−0.2707	−0.3018	−0.3296	
	(0.0000)	(0.0001)	(0.0000)		(0.0000)	(0.0000)	(0.0000)		(0.4834)	(0.4342)	(0.3933)	
_cons	23.7769**	21.1433**	16.4637*	13.9509	−14.5816***	−16.6135***	−14.9891***	−14.5816***	−24.0158**	−25.6303**	−22.2742*	−22.0270*
	(0.0132)	(0.0267)	(0.0876)	(0.1330)	(0.0007)	(0.0002)	(0.0004)	(0.0000)	(0.0493)	(0.0352)	(0.0682)	(0.0638)
N	14,400	14,400	14,400	14,400	300	300	300	300	2047	2047	2047	2047
adj. R-sq	Not applicable in FGLS method.											

p-values in parentheses * $p < 0.1$ ** $p < 0.05$ *** $p < 0.01$. HS84&85 is used as the classification of electronic products in this paper. At 4-digit HS code level, this paper takes HS 8471, 8473, 8517, 8523, 8529, 8531, 8532, 8533, 8534, 8535, 8541, 8542, 8543, 9013 as the electronic product classification electronic goods will decline as a result of FTA signing. In terms of other variables, mobile cellular subscription and population likewise do not reveal significant correlations with exports.

3.6 Conclusion

Trade facilitation is seen as an important means to reduce trade costs due to the dramatic reduction in tariffs over the past five decades. Countries can enhance logistics and streamline trade processes in places where tariffs have been drastically cut to boost international trade. This paper supports this assertion in light of the expanding trade ties between China and South American nations. During the COVID-19 crisis, the level of trade between China and its South American trading partners reached all-time highs. Thus, we cite the Logistics Performance Index (LPI) as an indicator of the level of trade facilitation to study the overall logistics level of South American countries importing all commodities and electronic products from China, and to put forward the direction of further cooperation for bilateral trade.

The gravity model is conducted in the research with extra indicators such as GDP, population, distance, FDI, etc. The LPI, tariffs, and the signing of FTAs are also introduced as measures of trade facilitation. Additionally, we incorporate mobile cellular subscription as a variable to investigate the trade of electronic products. According to the regression analysis, there are negative and positive correlations between distance and South American countries' GDP for both all commodities and electronic goods. FDI inflows to South American countries show different effects on the export under three situations, and China's FDI outflow presents no significant relationship with trade in all situations. The population shows a negative relationship in all commodities and electronics at 2-digit HS code level analysis, and the same conclusion was also obtained when analyzing electronic products at 4-digit HS code level without considering mobile cellular subscriptions.

For the level of trade facilitation, tariffs show a positive correlation with the trade value of all commodities which is contrary to predictions but appear to be trade-restrictive when analyzing electronics. LPI exhibits a positive correlation with trade in both all commodities and electronic products at 2-digit HS code level. Signing an FTA has a positive effect on trade flows in all product trades, while a negative relationship was shown in electronics trade at the 4-digit HS code level. Regarding the mobile phone subscription variable, it shows a positive effect on trade value in the first two scenarios. To conclude, China can promote trade facilitation with South American countries by raising the level of LPI, and the signing of FTA can also have a greater positive impact on all merchandise export.

We use the gravity model to explain the strategic role of trade logistics enhancement of China's exports to South American countries. Although there is much space for development in the LPI in South American nations, the precise indicators of different LPI components have not been taken into account. In the short term, it is easier to improve the level of customs clearance and logistics services than infrastructure construction. However, through the Belt and Road Initiative, China's infrastructure expansion in South American countries will improve the flow of trade in and out of the region. Therefore, in future research, more possibilities can be dug deeper.

References

Anderson, J. E., & Van Wincoop, E. (2003). Gravity with gravitas: A solution to the border puzzle. *American economic review, 93*(1), 170–192.

Anderson, J. E., & van Wincoop, E. (2004). Trade Costs. *Journal of Economic Literature, 42*(3), 691–751.

Arvis, J. F., Saslavsky, D., Ojala, L., Shepherd, B., Busch, C., & Raj, A. (2016). *Trade logistics in the global economy: The logistics performance index and its indicators*. World Bank. https://openknowledge.worldbank.org/handle/10986/24598

Baier, S. L., Bergstrand, J. H., & Feng, M. (2014). Economic Integration Agreements and the Margins of International Trade. *Journal of International Economics, 93*(2), 339–350.

Bergstrand, J. H., & Egger, P. (2013). Gravity Equations and Economic Frictions in the World Economy. In D. Bernhofen, R. Falvey, D. Greenaway, & U. Kreickemeier (Eds.), *Palgrave handbook of international trade* (pp. 532–570). Palgrave Macmillan. https://doi.org/10.1007/978-0-230-30531-1_17

Bugarčić, F. Ž., Skvarciany, V., & Stanišić, N. (2020). Logistics Performance Index In International Trade: Case Of Central And Eastern European And Western Balkans Countries. *Business: Theory and Practice, 21*(2), 452–459. https://doi.org/10.3846/btp.2020.12802

Chaney, T. (2018). The gravity equation in international trade: An explanation. *J Polit Econ, 126*(1), 150–177.

Cheong, J., & Tang, K. K. (2018). The trade effects of tariffs and non-tariff changes of preferential trade agreements. *Economic Modelling, 70*, 370–382.

Dang, V. L., & Yeo, G. T. (2018). Weighing the key factors to improve Vietnam's logistics system. *The Asian Journal of Shipping and Logistics, 34*(4), 308–316.

Deardorff, A. V. (1984). Testing trade theories and predicting trade flows. *Handbook of International Economics, 1*, 467–517.

Dell'Ariccia, G. (1999). Exchange rate fluctuations and trade flows: Evidence from the European Union. *IMF Staff papers, 46*(3), 315–334.

Dornbusch, R. (1976). Expectations and exchange rate dynamics. *Journal of political Economy, 84*(6), 1161–1176.

Du, Q., Deng, D., & Wood, J. (2021). Differences in distance and spatial effects on cross-border e-commerce and international trade: An empirical analysis of China and One-Belt One-Road Countries. *Journal of Global Information Management, 30*(2), 1–24.

Duzbaievna Sharapiyeva, M., Antoni, A., & Yessenzhigitova, R. (2019). The impact of port transport-logistics infrastructure and LPI for economic growth: On the example of landlocked countries. *Pomorstvo, 33*(1), 63–75. https://doi.org/10.31217/p.33.1.7

Estay, J. (2018). Past and present of Latin American regionalisms, in the face of economic reprimarization. In E. Vivares (Ed.), *Regionalism, development and the post-commodities boom in South America* (pp. 76–105). Springer.

Frankel, J., & Rose, A. (2002). An estimate of the effect of common currencies on trade and income. *The quarterly journal of economics, 117*(2), 437–466.

Gruszczynski, L. (2020). The COVID-19 pandemic and international trade: Temporary turbulence or paradigm shift? *European Journal of Risk Regulation, 11*(2), 337–342.

Guner, S., & Coskun, E. (2012). Comparison of impacts of economic and social factors on countries' logistics performances: A study with 26 OECD countries. *Research in logistics & production, 2*, 330–343.

Harris, M. N., Kónya, L., & Mátyás, L. (2012). Some stylized facts about international trade flows. *Review of International Economics, 20*(4), 781–792.

Head, K., & Mayer, T. (2014). Gravity equations: Workhorse, toolkit, and cookbook. In *Handbook of international economics* (Vol. 4, pp. 131–195). Elsevier.

Hejazi, W., & Safarian, A. E. (2001). The complementarity between US foreign direct investment stock and trade. *Atlantic Economic Journal, 29*(4), 420–437.

Hutchinson, W. K. (2005). "Linguistic distance" as a determinant of bilateral trade. *Southern Economic Journal, 72*(1), 1–15.

Jafari, Y., Ismail, M. A., & Kouhestani, M. S. (2011). Determinants of trade flows among D8 countries: Evidence from the gravity model. *Journal of Economic Cooperation & Development, 32*(3), 21–38.

Jenkins, R. (2009). The Latin American case. In R. Jenkins & E. D. Peters (Eds.), *China and Latin America. Economic relations in the twenty-first century* (pp. 21–64). Deutsches Institut für Entwicklung (DIE) and Universidad Nacional Autónoma de México (UNAM)/CECHIMEX. https://doi.org/10.22201/cechimex.9783889854858p.2009

Karagöz, K., & Karagöz, M. (2009). Determining factors of trade flows blacksea economic cooperation (BSEC) region: A panel gravity model. *Akademik Araştırmalar ve Çalışmalar Dergisi (AKAD), 1*(1), 63–75.

Katrakylidis, I., & Madas, M. (2019). International trade and logistics: An empirical panel investigation of the dynamic linkages between the logistics and trade and their contribution to economic growth. *International Journal of Economics and Business Administration, VII*(Issue 4), 3–21. https://doi.org/10.35808/ijeba/328

La, K. W., & Song, J. G. (2019). An Empirical Study on the Effects of Export Promotion on Korea-China-Japan Using Logistics Performance Index (LPI). *Journal of Korea Trade, 23*(7), 96–112. https://doi.org/10.35611/jkt.2019.23.7.96

Linnemann, H. (1967). An Econometric Study of International Trade Flows. *The Economic Journal, 77*(306), 366–368.

Martí, L., Puertas, R., & García, L. (2014). The importance of the Logistics Performance Index in international trade. *Applied economics, 46*(24), 2982–2992.

Ministry of Commerce, PRC (2022a). China FTA Network. Chinese Government. http://fta.mofcom.gov.cn/english/index.shtml

Ministry of Commerce, PRC. (2022b). *Foreign Investment Cooperation Country (Region) Guide*. Chinese Government. http://fec.mofcom.gov.cn/article/gbdqzn/

Obstfeld, M., & Rogoff, K. (1996). Intertemporal trade and the current account balance. In M. Obstfeld & K. Rogoff (Eds.), *Foundations of international macroeconomics*. MIT press.

OECD/CAF/ECLAC the Economic Commission for Latin America and the Caribbean (UN ECLAC), and the Development Bank of Latin America (CAF). (2015). *Latin American Economic Outlook 2016*. OECD. https://read.oecd-ilibrary.org/development/latin-american-economic-outlook-2016_9789264246218-en#page3

Pöyhönen, P. (1963). Toward a General Theory of International Trade. *The Journal of the Economic Society of Finland, 16*(2), 69–77.

Ramasamy, B., & Yeung, M. C. (2019). China's one belt one road initiative: The impact of trade facilitation versus physical infrastructure on exports. *The World Economy, 42*(6), 1673–1694.

Sakyi, D., & Afesorgbor, S. K. (2019). The effects of trade facilitation on trade performance in Africa. *Journal of African Trade, 6*(1–2), 1–15.

Sanborn, C., & Ching, V. C. (2017). Chinese Investment in Peru's Mining Industry: Blessing or Curse? In R. Ray, K. Gallagher, A. López, & C. Sanborn (Eds.), *China and Sustainable Development in Latin America* (pp. 183–226). Anthem Press. https://www.cambridge.org/core/books/abs/china-and-sustainable-development-in-latin-america/chinese-investment-in-perus-mining-industry-blessing-or-curse/C14F2790980B0EC57B885992 14E4957A

Silva, G. D., Gomes, M. F. M., & Teixeira, E. C. (2019). The spillover effect of Chinese growth on South America: An analysis from international trade. *CEPAL Review, 2018*(126), 43–56.

Takele, T. B. (2019). The relevance of coordinated regional trade logistics for the implementation of regional free trade area of Africa. *Journal of Transport and Supply Chain Management, 13*, 1–11. https://doi.org/10.4102/jtscm.v13i0.417

Takele, T. B., & Buvik, A. S. (2019). The role of national trade logistics in the export trade of African countries. *Journal of Transport and Supply Chain Management, 13*, 1–11. https://doi.org/10.4102/jtscm.v13i0.464

Tinbergen, J. (1962). An Analysis of World Trade Flows. *Shaping the World Economy, 5*(1), 27–30.

Wang, C., Wood, J., Wang, Y., Geng, X., & Long, X. (2020). CO2 emission in transportation sector across 51 countries along the Belt and Road from 2000 to 2014. *Journal of Cleaner Production, 263*, 122000.

Wilmsmeier, G., Hoffmann, J., & Sanchez, R. J. (2006). The impact of port characteristics on international maritime transport costs. *Research in transportation economics, 16*, 117–140.

Wood, J., Wu, J., Li, Y., & Kim, J. (2017a). TBT and SPS Impacts on Korean exports to China: Empirical analysis using the PPML method. *Asian-Pacific Economic Literature, 31*(2), 96–114.

Wood, J., Wu, J., Li, Y., & Jang, H. (2017b). The economic impact of SPS measures on agricultural exports to China: An empirical analysis using the PPML method. *Social Sciences, 6*(51), 1–18.

Wood, J., Wu, J., & Oh, K. (2020). Do Technical Barriers to Trade Restrict Exports? Evidence from South Korea. *Korea and the World Economy, 21*(2), 1–26.

World Bank. (2001). *Global economic prospects and the developing countries 2002: Making trade work for the poor*. World Bank. https://documents.worldbank.org/en/publication/documents-reports/documentdetail/327261468136791217/global-economic-prospects-and-the-developing-countries-2002-making-trade-work-for-the-worlds-poor

World Trade Organization. (2021). *World trade statistical review 2021*. World Trade Organization. https://www.wto.org/english/res_e/statis_e/wts2021_e/wts2021_e.pdf

Wu, H. L., Chen, C. H., & Chen, L. T. (2007). Foreign trade in China's electronics industry. *Eurasian Geography and Economics, 48*(5), 626–642.

Wu, J., Huh, C.-G., & Wood, J. (2021a). Globally Chained Economies: Unwitting Victims of the US-China Trade War. *Asian-Pacific Economic Literature, 35*(2), 60–76. https://doi.org/10.1111/apel.12334

Wu, J., Wood, J., Oh, K., & Jang, H. (2021b). Evaluating the cumulative impact of the US–China trade war along global value chains. *World Economy, 44*(12), 3516–3533. https://doi.org/10.1111/twec.13125

Wu, J., Wood, J., Oh, K., Li, Y., & Bhuyan, M. I. (2022). The impact of TBT and SPS measures on Domestic value-added exports: Evidence from the United States. *Asia-Pacific Journal of Accounting & Economics*, 1–15. https://doi.org/10.1080/16081625.2022.2077779

Zaninović, P. A., Zaninović, V., & Skender, H. P. (2021). The effects of logistics performance on international trade: EU15 vs CEMS. *Economic Research-Ekonomska Istraživanja, 34*(1), 1566–1582.

Chapter 4
The Use of Blockchain in Vietnam's Global Fishery Supply Chain Management

Linh Hoang Tuan Nguyen, Jungsuk Kim, Benedict Atkinson, Jacob Wood, and Haejin Jang

Abstract The issue of traceability has emerged as a fundamental tenet of sound logistics and supply chain management. In order to assess this issue, our study investigates the use of blockchain-based traceability frameworks to manage fisheries supply chains in Vietnam. From a methodological perspective, we assessed the contemporary empirical literature to research to achieve four key objectives. First, to provide a comprehensive analysis of the advantages and potential applications of blockchain from a Vietnamese fisheries perspective. Second, to present an application framework that consists of four stages, with the aim of improving the transparency and security of transaction information by adopting Internet of Things (IoT) and blockchain in each of the connections throughout the fishery supply chain. Third, to illustrate the five transformational phases in which blockchain technology can be applied to small and medium enterprises (SMEs) operating in the fishery industry. Finally, to establish a set of policy implications based around the infrastructural, regulatory gaps and human capital that exist in the fishery industry in Vietnam and affect blockchain. From our analysis, we find substantial cause for optimism about the role of blockchain can play as an engine of growth in Vietnam's fishery export industry.

Keywords Blockchain · Traceability · Transparancy · Vietnam fishery · Logistics · Supply chain

---

L. H. T. Nguyen
Graduate School of International Studies (GSIS), Sogang University, Seoul, South Korea
e-mail: nht.linh2605@gmail.com

J. Kim
Department of Economics, Sejong University, Seoul, South Korea
e-mail: js_kim@sejong.ac.kr

B. Atkinson · J. Wood (✉) · H. Jang
James Cook University, Singapore, Singapore
e-mail: benedict.atkinson@jcu.edu.au; jacob.wood@jcu.edu.au; haejin.jang@jcu.edu.au

E. L. Eijdenberg et al. (eds.), *Innovation-Driven Business and Sustainability in the Tropics*, https://doi.org/10.1007/978-981-99-2909-2_4

4.1 Introduction

The logistics and supply chain management process play an important role in the international trade area as the logistics and supply chain is part of every aspect of the trading and production process (Wu et al., 2021a, b, c). Companies use these concepts to plan, control, and implement procedures that manage not only the flow of goods and services, but also the effective and efficient storage and transportation of products, as well as the tracking of the products from the point of origin to the point of consumption. In Vietnam, these two activities have formed essential components of all major logistics and supply chain related industries, including the fishery sector, which plays a key role in Vietnam's export and trade development. This study focuses on issues of logistics and supply chain management that relate to Vietnam's fishery sector.

One persistent problem of the fishery logistics and supply chain in Vietnam is lack of transparency, which leads to a decrease in product quality. As a result, the product's added value remains low with a lot of products returned from the importers because they do not meet the food hygiene and safety standards of the importers. In this context, traceability is widely recognized as essential to ensure that important food safety standards are met. Using transparency as a foundation, supply chain traceability allows organizations and the government to access critical information about the origins of raw materials or a finished product. Organizations and government can also obtain information about the production processes that raw materials and finished products have undergone (Francisco & Swanson, 2018).

At the moment, the existing traceability systems for fishery products in developing countries like Vietnam are inadequate and seemingly far outstripped by those in developed countries. This issue has resulted in discussion about whether the applications of advanced technologies such as blockchain could actually narrow the food quality gaps in developing countries (Tan & Ngan, 2020). As Woodside et al. (2017) have stated, blockchain is an emerging technology that is expected to transform businesses across different industries. One promising feature of blockchain is to provide transparency, which supports traceability in ways that older technologies cannot.

Given the potential of blockchain application in the traceability of Vietnam's fishery logistics and supply chain management, as well as the future application of blockchain to international trade, the authors have decided to research on the topic: "The use of Blockchain in Vietnam's global fishery supply chain management". The focus of this study is to explain whether the applications of blockchain could increase the quality of Vietnam's fish exports, and how the use of blockchain can improve traceability and transparency in Vietnam's fishery logistics.

This research provides an assessment of the relevant contemporary literature to better understand how blockchain technologies can be used to manage Vietnam's global fishery supply chains. From our examinations of the empirical literature, we found that while most studies use a variety of empirical approaches to analyze supply chain management practices, more can be done to address Vietnam's seafood industry development and the way in which technology can be used to manage relevant supply chains. Our analysis provides a series of relevant policy recommendations and areas of future research endeavor. In particular, a more detailed evaluation of the feasibility of the blockchain-based traceability system is needed as efforts to design a better mechanism for introducing new pilot applications.

4.2 Literature Review

Most countries have engaged in blockchain technology research and development. Research on blockchain technology began after 2008, when Satoshi Nakamoto proposed the use of bitcoin – the first peer-to-peer digital currency (Nakamoto, 2008). In later years, due to the huge influence of bitcoin, blockchain gained widespread attention from both academia and policymakers. A White Paper on Blockchain in Trade Facilitation by the United Nations Centre for Trade Facilitation and Electronic Business (UN/CEFACT, 2019) and a study on the Distributed Ledger Technology (DLT) and Blockchain (2017) by the World Bank do much to explain the concept, advantages, and operation methods of blockchain platforms. They also detail areas of possible applications, such as: currency, payment, securities, insurance, and other non-financial fields, including global logistics and supply chain.

The adoption of technology and the availability of innovative solutions in the logistics and supply chain sector industry have evolved over the past 15 years, mainly focusing on the traceability and transparency of data. According to Bateman (2015, p. 8), traceability "affects supply chain efficiency, product safety and security, managing deep tier risks, on-time delivery performance, troubleshooting customer issues, controlling costs, and regulatory compliance". The world has witnessed many lost, damaged, or delayed shipments, the consequence of which is decrease of product quality. A main reason for the decrease in product quality is lack of transparency and central control. Other reasons include miscommunication between vendors and suppliers, as well as confusion in the supply chain. In the food industry, according to WHO (2017), every year around 600 million people (almost 1 in 10 people) in the world fall ill and 420,000 die by diseases due to the consumption of contaminated food. One of the reasons is that foods are not manufactured, processed, transported, and stored safely.

Therefore, for years, many research papers have been conducted to find out the solution to the problem of traceability. Multiple approaches to supply chain traceability have been applied, ranging from traditional paper-based ones to sophisticated and advanced technologies. In 2015, Alexis H. Bateman drew attention to a new system called blockchain-based supply chain traceability system. Francisco and Swanson (2018) agree with Alexis H. Bateman's suggestion that the characteristics of blockchains indeed make them especially suited for traceability applications. Christidis and Devetsikiotis (2016) state that blockchain is considered to be a good solution for connecting and managing Internet of Things (IoT) objects. A large amount of such objects is found in a logistics environment (vehicles, shipments, etc.), The IoT is one of the most promising fields of application. By integrating the IoT with blockchain, Madakam et al. (2015) indicate that the efficiency of the food traceability system can be improved to build an open and comprehensive network of devices that can automatically organize and share resources and data. In recent years, blockchain applications have been developed, such as a project to track the origin of fish by a UK-based company named Provenance, or the development of traceability solutions for pork in China and for mangos in the US by Walmart and IBM (Kamath, 2018).

Hofmann and Rüsch (2017) suggest that the application of blockchain will help facilitate further supply chain integration. In order to facilitate progress, government policies are adopted around the world to support digital technology development. Focusing on the fishery logistics and supply chain management of Vietnam – where the standards are mainly based on the ISO standards – this paper also recognizes the occurrence of the blockchain concept in several ISO standards, such as ISO 22739:2020. These standards define basic terms relating to blockchain and distributed ledger technologies. ISO 22005:2007 provides general principles and basic requirements for the design and implementation for a feed and food traceability system.

Francisco and Swanson (2018) argue that industries and firms that are already well developed may not be willing to invest in blockchain if the innovation does not provide significant benefits over existing solutions. They continue to share that, according to the United Nations Global Compact on Traceability (2014), some companies with a profound understanding of their supply chains and supply chain partners prefer to have their own traceability protocols. In industries such as agriculture or manufacturing, which present a wide and diverse multi-stakeholder framework, several traceability protocols already exist to develop a stable and trustworthy chain of product custody standards and certification. Besides, according to Bello et al. (2005), less developed countries still have the tendency to trace product in supply chains by a paper-based approach or, as Wognum et al. (2011) state, by leveraging their integrated system to avoid overspending rather than exploiting cutting-edge techniques.

Nguyen et al. (2020) argue that although there have been quite a few system applications for the traceability of pork or agricultural products in Vietnam, most of these systems involve using QR code or bar code with lots of limitations. These limitations include: data that is impossible to be reused; data that is short in reading range and scope; data that is highly environmentally sensitive; data security is weak; and especially, traceability applications have not yet been applied to seafood traceability. Most Vietnamese fishermen and farmers are not familiar even with recording documents and exchanging them with wholesalers who buy their products, let alone participating in a complex computer-based system. The number of studies on seafood traceability in Vietnams is still relatively small, and most of them are about overall supply chain management. They do not focus on traceability, information security, or export financing, etc.

Much is still yet to be learned about blockchain, but as Zheng et al. (2017) argue, it is undeniable that blockchain has much potential to become a realistic technological option to address the challenge of transparency across the supply chain. With the help of blockchain, the systems can be made completely "end-to-end" with information tracked going far beyond origin of products, which can include data on storage temperatures, shipping details, batch number and so on.

4.3 Background Information

4.3.1 Fishery Logistics and Supply Chain of Vietnam

In the structure of Vietnam's export market, seafood is one of the key commodities that actively contribute to the growth of export turnover. Indeed, Vietnam is the third major exporting country of aquaculture products, with exports worth $8.89 billion in 2021 (Fig. 4.1) and a high export rate of major fishery products (shrimp, pangasius and tuna) to the world's top markets such as the US, EU, and Japan (Table 4.1).

Currently, the value-add to Vietnam's fishery products is low and Vietnam's fish export trade is affected by issues of quality. In 2017, Vietnam was issued a yellow card by the European Union (EU) related to Illegal, Unreported and Unregulated Fishing – IUU, which led to a decrease in efficiency, export value and market share. From being the then 2nd biggest import market of Vietnamese fishery products, the EU quickly dropped to the 5th position, entailing a great impact on Vietnam's seafood reputation and trading volume to other markets.

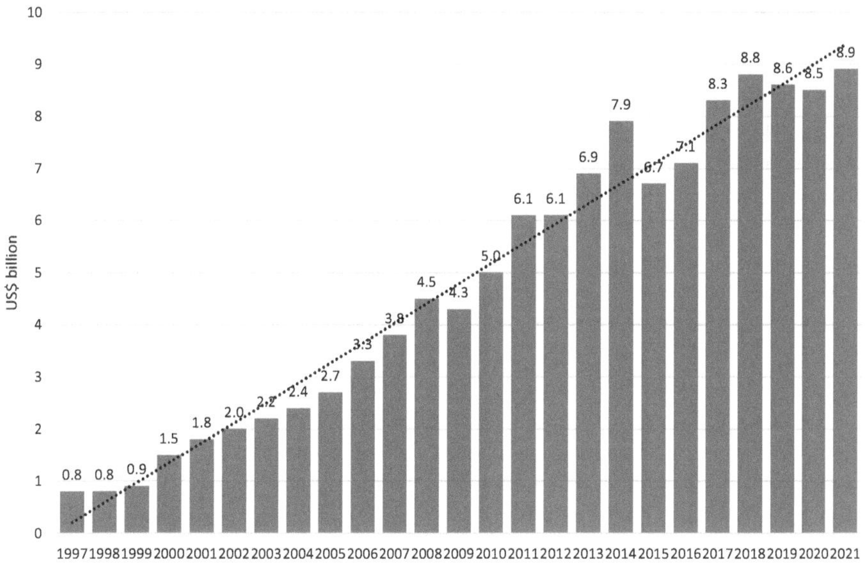

Fig. 4.1 Vietnam seafood exports, 1997–2020. Source: Fishery profile – Vietnam Association of Seafood Exporters and Producers (VASEP)

Table 4.1 Top 10 single markets importing Vietnamese seafood in 2020–2021 (US$ mil)

Markets	2020	2021	Change (%)	Proportion (%)
The US	1620.629	2049.359	26.5	23.0
Japan	1422.252	1325.597	−6.8	14.9
China	1,203,234	990.648	−17.7	11.1
South Korea	768.518	807.785	5.1	9.1
The UK	344.638	316.137	−8.3	3.6
Thailand	244.357	267.034	9.3	3.0
Canada	262.760	265.618	1.1	3.0
Australia	228.202	265.457	16.3	3.0
Netherland	219.382	228.085	4.0	2.6
Germany	180.010	200.052	11.1	2.2

Source: Report on Vietnam's seafood exports in 2021, Vietnam Association of Seafood Exporters and Producers

In addition, according to the United Nations Industrial Development Organization (2019), Vietnam is one of the top three countries that received the most cases of import rejection regarding fish and aquatic products from four major importers: the EU, the US, Japan, and Australia, from which Vietnam accrued annual financial losses (in the study period) up to 14 million USD. The main reason for such import rejection is Vietnam's weak management regarding Sanitary and Phytosanitary Measures (SPS) in all stages of the fishery value chain. Poor quality control during fish farming, fish processing and delivering leads to problems such as: veterinary drug residues (EU market), hygiene and labeling conditions (US market), industrial contaminants and foreign objects (Japan market). Hygiene problems can occur at any stage from the point of origin to the point of distribution. In order to reduce the rate of import rejection, logistics and supply chain companies need to adopt a comprehensive solution for better control and management of all stages in the value chain.

The Vietnamese seafood sector is under pressure. There is a continuous use of fishing equipment and methods that destroy original resources, such as explosives, electric pulses, trawling nets, small fish catching, fishing in coastal waters or marine protected areas, etc. In addition, spontaneous and sporadic aquaculture farming caused serious damage to the environment. At the same time, in order to maximize profit, many fish breeding establishments used hormones to stimulate reproduction, leading to the deterioration of fingerlings quality to an alarming level. Signs of deterioration included a lower survival rate, and the increased probability of a higher rate of infection, leading to disease.

Adopting blockchain technology to build a traceability system is essential to facilitate supply chain management and tracking. Such tracking extends from any given point in the supply chain backwards to the origin of seafood with blockchain allows for the strict control of off-shore fishing and effective monitoring of aquaculture. As a result of applying blockchain, Vietnam will be able to provide efficient decision-making that would improve the seafood value chain and enhance the reputation and brand name of the Vietnamese seafood industry in the world market.

4.3.2 What Is Blockchain Technology?

In the simplest terms, "blockchain" is a chain of blocks that are connected by cryptography, an information security technique (Hans & Rhea, 2021). The original idea of blockchain technology came from the development of cryptography in which encryption methods were invented to convert comprehensible messages into incomprehensible forms. Encrypted data could only be read by a small number of people who created and agreed to use a decryption key (Rouse, 2020). Over time, this technique was applied to digital and computing data and to secure information on the internet, especially in Blockchain technology.

Blockchain was assumed to be invented firstly in 2008 in a paper named "Bitcoin: A Peer-To-Peer Electronic Cash System" by an unknown person, or a group of people, using the name Satoshi Nakamoto, for the purpose of creating the cryptocurrency bitcoin. This was "the first digital currency that solved the double-spending problem without the need of a trusted authority or central server" (Nakamoto, 2008).

According to Nakamoto, a blockchain is a distributed ledger that is completely open to anyone. A block is a piece of digital information that can store up to 1 megabyte (MB) data, which once recorded inside the blockchain, becomes very difficult to change. Each block contains data, the hash of the block and the hash of the previous block (Doruk, 2022). These data stored in the block could be the transaction details (date, time, amount), transaction parties (each party is recorded under a unique identity, called digital signature or username), and special information to distinguish it from other blocks.

The hash of the block is just like a fingerprint that can be used to identify a block and all of its contents. Once a block is created, its hash will be calculated and when some data inside the blocks is changed, all of the hash changes will be updated as well. The hash of the previous block that is stored inside of each block connects blocks and makes a blockchain. As someone tampering with one block of the chain will cause the hash of that block to change as well, this action makes all the following blocks invalid because they are no longer storing a valid hash of the previous block (Haque & Rahman, 2020).

Another element of blockchain is the proof-of-work mechanism that slows down the creation of new blocks. This mechanism makes it very hard to tamper with the blocks, because if you tamper with a block, you will need to recalculate the proof-of-work for all the following blocks. Moreover, blockchain assures a high-level of security is achieved along the peer-to-peer network. All the nodes in this network create consensus, which agree about which blocks are valid and which are not, for example, blocks that are tampered with will be rejected by other nodes in the network. To successfully tamper with a blockchain, someone needs to tamper with all the blocks on the chain, redo the proof-of-work for each block, and take control of more than 50% of the peer-to-peer network (EdifyPath, 2022). Only then will that tampered block be accepted by everyone else. Given this context, blockchain technologies are therefore extremely secure methods of data storage.

In short, with the above-mentioned operating mechanism, blockchain is able to provide outstanding features and advantages such as: Data preservation, transparency, immutability, intermediaries' elimination, reducing transaction time and costs, and high verifiability. These features create a basis for determining ownership. Blockchain applications are also constantly evolving, with one of the more recent developments in blockchain applications is the creation of smart contracts. In a simple way, blockchain can be applied in almost every activity in our daily life and sectors in international trade.

4.4 Blockchain Application in Vietnam's Fishery Logistics and Supply Chain Management

4.4.1 Potential Application of Blockchain in Fishery Logistics and Supply Chain Management

As discussed, blockchain offering enormous potential, acting as a new means of improving the processes and business models of the fishery sector and in particular its logistics and supply chain management. There are three blockchain-based innovations that offer the most benefits when adopted. These are: (i) verifying goods; (ii) reducing paperwork and cost; and (iii) end-to-end tracking. Blockchain applications in logistics are expected to provide a relative advantage as they provide features such as immutability, transparency, and decentralization.

Firstly, blockchain technology can effectively be used to create a digital certificate for each piece of fish, tracking from the moment they are caught or processed, to when they end up in the hands of customers. If contamination is detected, products can be traced back to their roots, and the person who detects contamination can instantly notify other people who bought the same batch of bad food. Such a system can also battle counterfeit goods by allowing anyone to verify whether or not the product comes from the manufacturer they think it does. By being able to share information and to prove to consumers that their products originate from safe and sustainable producers, producers can develop more loyal customer bases and in doing so grow the profitability of their business (Luh et al., 2020).

Secondly, global fishery supply chains normally contain verifying documentation in the form of letters of credit or bills of lading. As these letters are actually moving across time and space and involving multiple actors, they face the risk of forgery, theft, and alteration (Lehmacher, 2017). Kim and Laskowski (2018) highlight that blockchain creates access to crucial data since the information is stored across several computers, providing a secure, duplicated, and synchronized ledger, such as digital bills of lading "which cannot be secretly altered [...] because the original is always visible" (Morley, 2017). Deploying blockchain solutions can significantly reduce the chance to manipulate an item as information in the blockchain cannot be changed. Besides, digital bills of lading also facilitate a speeding up of current processes and lead to a reduction in cost, as they allow for the elimination or reduction of paperwork associated with today's business practices (Hackius & Petersen, 2017). An adoption of blockchain technology would improve the management of the current cumbersome administrative paperwork, as consignment validation and control process are time-consuming and possibly affected by human error. More importantly, smart contracts can provide advantages as they might eliminate or substantially reduce transaction costs through the recording and auditing functions of the blockchain, as well as executing payments automatically.

Thirdly, the ability to trace the origins of goods or to gain more knowledge about them in the current logistics system is rather limited (Yang & Lirn, 2017). Although current practices have the ability to track the shipment of a package through the company's internal tracking system on their home page, the information is often limited to timestamps of when the package enters the logistics service provider's handling system (Shermin, 2017). With one of the more recent developments of blockchain, which is the creation of smart contracts, the technology provides a secure platform for actors to not only follow the movements throughout the supply chain, but also share and exchange information concerning their delivery, package, and shipments. Data can also be allowed to be automatically exchanged based on certain conditions (such as only sharing the data a partner wants to reveal). Similarly, the awareness of environmental impact stemming from fishing and freight has increased and logistics providers have introduced sustainable options. However, the various layers of subcontractors involved in typical processes make it difficult to verify environmentally friendly standards. By having such information on the blockchain, customers would be able to trace the goods back to the first node in the chain of fishing to transport, providing insight into the chosen fishing method, transport route and carrier choice (Dobrovnik et al., 2018).

However, there are still risks associated with adopting this technology, particularly in the field of logistics and supply chain management. Logistics and supply chain are not only huge but also complex. On the other hand, blockchain is still in the nascent stages of development, with relatively few designers familiar with the technology. This can make implementation complex and costly.

4.4.2 A Framework for Adopting Blockchain to the Vietnam's Fishery Logistics and Supply Chain Management

Based on recent studies, the authors would like to summarize a structure that emphasizes blockchain-based quality traceability to improve transparency and security of transaction information throughout the process of Vietnam's fishery logistics and supply chain management:

(i) *Business practice stage:*

This stage consists of a business cycle for the entire seafood supply chain. At present, there are two common types of seafood suppliers: fresh seafood and processed seafood. A fresh seafood supply chain includes multiple stages: Purchasing input materials (fish seeds), farming, catching, transporting, preserving, distributing, or exporting and finally reaching the consumer. A similar concept is applied to the processed seafood products supply chain, with the only additional processing stage occurring after seafood is purchased and before distribution or export. Each of such connections inside the supply chain can be exploited for the purpose of controlling and managing traceability information for seafood products.

Traceability can begin during the collection of raw fish. After being caught or processed, the seafood is then packaged and labelled with identifiable tags such as barcodes, QR codes, RFID tag readers,[1] NFC-connected devices,[2] etc., before being registered into the system as new products (Giang & Trang, 2020). From here, all the information of such product can be stored into the product's database. The data for the corresponding fish seeds, including breed, feeds and health will in turn then be updated on the blockchain, which makes it very difficult to tamper with the information. If any package is not able to meet the initial requirements it is rejected by fish collectors. At this point, the farmer is then able to identify the exact batch of fish that has been rejected by scanning the tag on the returned package. In order to have common and consistent data standards, producers should operate in a manner that is in accordance with the World Trade Organization's SPS and TBT regulations such as: GlobalGAP, Hazard Analysis Critical Control Point (HACCP) and ISO standards. In this way, related information on catching or processing procedures can be traced back and understood with the help of identifiable tags and blockchain, such as whether the fish breed is healthy, who was the person performing the fish catch for this batch of fish, which catching machine was used, if storage equipment was cleaned correctly, etc. Meanwhile, with a new identifiable security seal attached, fish collectors can use blockchain technology to upload all pertinent information onto the distributed ledger, such as the fish batch number, collecting time and location, original farms, total volume, initial test results and transportation vehicle details (Tan & Ngan, 2020).

(ii) *Internet of Things stage:*

Information for each of the supply chain linkages can be traced back to its direct origins, including quality information, logistics information, and transaction data. After receiving the seafood, the processing/consuming agent can then read and register the new data into the product's profile, once again through identification technologies (barcode, QR code, RFID, NFC, etc.) that can automatically and

[1] Radio frequency identification reader (RFID reader): a device used to gather information from an RFID tag, which is used to track individual objects.

[2] Near Field Communication (NFC) technology allows users to make secure transactions, exchange digital content, and connect electronic devices with a touch.

continuously collect and transmit ambient information about weather, humidity, oxygen, CO2, etc. (Giang & Trang, 2020). After processing, new tags/labels continue to be attached to the handled/processed products. These connected devices can then easily communicate with the ledger in the blockchain (Giang & Trang, 2020).

In the next stage, the fresh seafood/processed seafood are preserved at the storage facility. Through the installation of IoT devices inside the warehouse, the data of the registered seafood can be automatically extracted. For example, with wireless sensors and monitoring devices, seafood data including quantity, category, temperature, humindity and storage time can be stored in real-time, which then can be checked and updated in both of the digitized database and on the product's labels/tags (Giang & Trang, 2020).

Inventory information can also be queried directly inside the system or by means of an RFID reader which can also meet the requirements for dynamic storage management (Giang & Trang, 2020). In the next stage of distribution, factors around hygiene, safety and the quality of the seafood can be determined using the 3 T factors (Time, Temperature and Turbulence). Moreover, one of the options is to design and install a sensor system at different spots on the transporting vehicle to monitor the quality of seafood by collecting real-time data on humidity, temperature, and seafood preservation environment, and then sending this information to a digitized database where the goods can be tagged and labelled.

(iii) *Blockchain stage:*

Smart contracts are helpful in supporting real-time monitoring and providing quality control check for each block. With logistics data, smart contracts are even able to automate logistics planning (Kshetri, 2018), such as to automate transactions between farmers and manufacturers or between exporter and importer. When the blockchain layer combines with the IoT layer, smart contracts will get even "smarter", as the application of blockchain can be further exploited in the IoT environment – such as when the automated payments between systems (when two systems are interconnected, they can start negotiating and applying prices based on the logistics operational efficiency) (Giang & Trang, 2020).

The distributed ledger system will assist retailers and consumers in storing transaction information, and increase transparency of information throughout the product's flows, from producer to processor, to distributors, importers, and supermarkets/markets/retail shops, etc., and finally consumers (Giang & Trang, 2020).

(iv) *Application stage:*

This final stage allows for the smooth interaction between actors in the seafood traceability chain and the blockchain system. The actors participating in the chain can review the entire product flow, information flows and financial flows through the distributed ledger system. Data related to quality management, price management, financial management and sales management can all be continuously updated into the blockchain. Ultimately, the end consumers can use their smartphone to scan the product QR code at the Point of Sale (POS) and check its provenance as well as authenticity (Tan & Ngan, 2020). They will be redirected to a webpage containing information that could answer some of the questions about a particular fish item such as: the original farm or the processor of the fish product, the time of manufacturing, the processing stages, the food safety standards, the date and time of distribution and display, and the expiration date, etc.

4.5 Transformation Phases of Blockchain Application for Vietnam's Small and Medium Enterprises

Once a company recognizes the potential of blockchain technology to drive efficiency and value, the next step is to establish an application roadmap. This should start from a willingness to collaborate, involving building blockchain knowledge and capabilities with a focus on driving value for all stakeholders. There are three main success factors for every blockchain initiative: (i) Create a culture of collaboration; (ii) Build up blockchain knowledge and capabilities; and (iii) Focus on value and engage with stakeholders on blockchain opportunities (Heutger & Kueckelhaus, 2018).

According to Iansiti and Lakhani (2017), the use of blockchain applications will happen in different transformation stages and will require different levels of collaboration and consensus, as well as legislative and regulatory efforts. Moreover, organizational processes, capabilities, capital, and infrastructure have to be established in order to facilitate the implementation of these blockchain applications. The below framework created with reference from Iansiti and Lakhani (2017) can help managers of SMEs in different development stages to identify suitable business opportunities and corresponding starting points in the supply of seafood.

Phase #1 – The Planning This phase builds toward a prototype for the proof of concept. During the proof-of-concept phase, stakeholders should learn all the nuances of using blockchain technology in the proposed application.

Phase #2 – Approaching and Experiment For most small and medium logistics companies, the best way to start on blockchain is to adopt blockchain gradually case by case, which minimizes risk because stakeholders can test the application on a small scale based on existing systems. Gradual adoption involves little coordination with third parties while permitting a high-level assessment of roll out at scale. Another low-risk approach is to use the blockchain internally as a database that manages the physical and digital assets, recording internal transactions, and verifying identities (Heutger & Kueckelhaus, 2018).

Phase #3 – Localization This is the phase where logistics companies can tackle specific problems in the area of transactions across boundaries by using blockchain to digitize paper records so that the global network of shippers, carriers, ports, and customs authorities are connected (Dobrovnik et al., 2018). First result of the established platform is when every relevant document or approval is stored on the blockchain, with every partner having full visibility of the container (Allison, 2017).

Phase #4 – Substitution Developing substitute applications requires careful planning and a shift of perspective – from achieving success with an internal solution to now onboarding multiple parties and testing the solution across a network. One path to follow could be to focus on replacements that do not require end users to significantly change their behavior but presents alternatives to expensive or unattractive solutions in a way so that it is not difficult for the ecosystem to absorb and adopt.

Phase #5 – Transformation Transformative applications may require departure of value and business operation logics from existing approaches. These applications are, however, argued by Iansiti and Lakhani (2017) to be "many years away". They have, however, the potential to unlock future growth for companies. A transformative blockchain business model involves scaling the solution which, in turn, requires a transformation of business processes and depends heavily on their acceptance across internal parties and multiple stakeholders and even business partners (Dobrovnik et al., 2018). Stakeholder participation is arguably the most critical success factor in blockchain adoption, as the success of the project hinges on everyone adjusting their business practices and fully leveraging the blockchain implementation. In 2020, Walmart decided to improve the last mile deliveries through coordinating delivery drones using the blockchain. Whether this strategy has succeeded remains controversial. Moreover, it is argued that the current Internet architecture with its server infrastructure might not be able to handle such a number of devices and data, which also entails a large number of data security concerns.

4.6 Current Situation in Vietnam & Some Policy Recommendations

4.6.1 Current Situation of Blockchain Adoption and Management in Vietnam

While many countries around the world have been deploying multiple application models of IoT, artificial intelligence, and blockchain technology platforms in order to build a digital economy, in Vietnam, those technologies are still brand-new fields (Giang & Trang, 2020). Predicting the rapid development trend of digital technology, Vietnamese government has adopted several legal amendments to resolve existing problems. An orientation for technology development in the period 2021–2030 was introduced: "Application and development of new technologies, prioritizing digital technology, 5G and post 5G connectivity, artificial intelligence, blockchain, 3D printing, Internet of Things, cybersecurity, clean energy, environmental technology to transform and improve energy productivity and efficiency of the economy". Many laws and legal documents related to information technology have also been promulgated.

Nevertheless, the factors of technological innovation and education that are ready for Vietnam's 4.0 industrial revolution stays measured at a low level – total 4.9 point out of 10 (World Economic Forum, 2018). Not only those regulatory efforts are not comprehensive and up to date, the absence of a central authority as well as a censorship authority for the current blockchain system has the potential to, according to Reyna et al. (2018), create a lot of instability. Report No. 70/BC-BTP dated March 23, 2020 submitted by Vietnam's Ministry of Justice to the Prime Minister made representations about the legal framework related to the application and development of services and products based on blockchain platforms. The report found that in relation to seafood traceability using blockchain alone, many businesses stated that they basically do not have any problems with their existing system. According to these businesses, in order to build a traceability chain using blockchain, the most important factor is to develop an ecosystem friendly to the application of blockchain where publicity, transparency and anti-fraud practices are nurtured.

4.6.2 Some Policy Recommendations for the Vietnamese Government

First and foremost, governance and monitoring of the development of blockchain are the fundamental factors that should be identified as a long-term goal, requiring the government's considerable investment in a comprehensive legal framework regulating the automation and digitization of procedures related to business operations.

(i) In this blockchain application journey, the "standardization of production" will be the most difficult problem for Vietnamese businesses as now all input issues such as the use of seeds, feeds, medicines, or vaccines will be exposed. Therefore, it is necessary for the regulatory authority to be involved in the implementation of related plans as well as to assist businesses by providing multiple blockchain standard guidelines for farmers to follow.

(ii) The government needs to create a complete and consistent legal framework for the management of blockchain-related transactions to identify and support legitimate real-life applications of blockchain, such as cross-sector digital databases, the problem of data sharing, information security, personal data protection, privacy protection, e-authentication, etc. Regarding this issue, Vietnam should refer to the best practice of other countries that are ahead of the curve in digital technology regulatory adoption, such as those on protection of personal data and privacy of users of Singapore or Malaysia. Moreover, the use of Electronic Identification, Authentication and Trust Service (eIDAS) Regulation of the European Union (EU), or the Electronic Signatures in Global and Nation Commerce Act as are used in US may also be of benefit. Many governments have also introduced regulations on sharing banking data or a controlled trial management mechanism such as the Financial Conduct Authority (FCA) of the UK, or the Monetary Authority of Singapore (MAS), etc.

(iii) In addition, government authorities and state-owned enterprises should pioneer the application of scientific and technological systems, including blockchain technology. This workstream not only serves the purposes of improving the efficiency of administration, governance, and provision of public services, but also taking the lead in building a blockchain ecological environment. After a blockchain environment is built, the ability to connect relevant stakeholders into the ecosystem could be more easily achieved. Nevertheless, while an optimal environment for innovation is created, it is necessary to ensure the neutrality of technology development in the direction that the market decides on technology selection. The current legal framework should be flexible in managing and handling related issues. Exceptions should always be allowed, and the government should react in a quick manner if any arising issue (or issue groups) requires a regulatory amendment.

(iv) To create a competitive yet united blockchain ecosystem that attracts more participants from the private sector, it is also necessary to develop policies that support businesses – especially the SME groups – not only in terms of operations and processes, but also financially. Examples include policies that seek to cut taxes, and provide financial support by way of loans, etc. Vietnam can first develop these supportive policies for a group of pioneering enterprises, thereby creating a competitive environment for other businesses as well as other actors of the economy to take advantage of and go for the general growth acceleration.

(v) At the same time, it is necessary to maintain strong effective relationships between the business community and those working in technology service sector – both domestically and internationally. The ability to do so promotes not only the exchange of knowledge and technology, but also helps to handle any problems and difficulties that may arise during the process of implementation. Capacity and quick adaptation to the system can also be improved by the increase of understanding and awareness of people, businesses, and enterprises, which can be achieved through means of communication, dissemination, training, and retraining activities.

4.7 Conclusion

This study revealed valuable insights and potential benefits of blockchain adoption in Vietnam's fishery logistics and supply chain management system. The study also proposes a model framework for blockchain application in tracing the origins of seafood in the sector, as well as requirements for Vietnam's trade policy to build a suitable blockchain model. The immutable nature of blockchain will help tracing products from the point-of-producer to the point-of-customer, and allow anyone to check if the system has been compromised somewhere, or not. Transparency in the blockchain reduces delays and disputes while preventing fishery products from getting stuck at any stage of the supply chain. Since each product can be tracked in real time, errors are also kept to a minimum. In addition to the guarantee in product integrity, as well as the efforts to combat poor quality seafood products that do not meet the requirements of importers, blockchain technology can also help retailers and small businesses overcome the financial problems that they are facing in the global logistics and supply chain.

The development of application models for seafood traceability is not new in the world, but the application of blockchain technology in seafood traceability in Vietnam is still a challenging field due to short-comings in the production and distribution of fish in Vietnam. Therefore, future studies can aim to adjust and evaluate the feasibility of a blockchain-based traceability system, or even consider blockchain technology applications to enhance the sustainability of other products' logistics supply chains as well, such as those involved with agricultural and medical products, etc.

References

Allison, I. (2017). Maersk and IBM want 10 million shipping containers on the global supply blockchain by year-end. *International Business Times, 8.*

Bateman, A. H. (2015). Tracking the value of traceability. *Supply Chain Management Review, 9*, 8–10.

Bello, L. L., Mirabella, O., & Torrisi, N. (2005, September). A general approach to model traceability systems in food manufacturing chains. *2005 IEEE Conference on Emerging Technologies and Factory Automation, 2*, 8–214.

Blaha, F., & Katafono, K. (2020). Blockchain application in seafood value chains. *FAO Fisheries and Aquaculture Circular*. (C1207), I-43.

Christidis, K., & Devetsikiotis, M. (2016). Blockchains and smart contracts for the internet of things. *IEEE Access, 4*, 2292–2303.

Crosby, M., Pattanayak, P., Verma, S., & Kalyanaraman, V. (2016). Blockchain technology: Beyond bitcoin. *Applied Innovation Review, 2*, 6–10.

Dobrovnik, M., Herold, D. M., Fürst, E., & Kummer, S. (2018). Blockchain for and in logistics: What to adopt and where to start. *Logistics, 2*(3), 18.

Doruk, S. (2022). Market applications of Blockchain with a focus on government and public sector. *Readwrite*. https://readwrite.com/market-applications-of-blockchain-with-a-focus-on-government-and-public-sector/

Dutta, P., Choi, T. M., Somani, S., & Butala, R. (2020). Blockchain technology in supply chain operations: Applications, challenges, and research opportunities. *Transportation research part e: Logistics and transportation review, 142*, 102067.

EdifyPath. (2022). *Introduction to Cryptocurrency and Blockchain*. https://edifypath.com/blog/post/global-outlook-of-blockchain

Food and Agriculture Organization of the United Nations. (2021). *GLOBEFISH – Information and Analysis on World Fish Trade, World exports declined due to COVID-19 impacts,* https://www.fao.org/in-action/globefish/news-events/trade-and-market-news/april-2021/en/

Francisco, K., & Swanson, D. (2018). The supply chain has no clothes: Technology adoption of Blockchain for supply chain transparency. *Logistics, 2*(1), 2. MDPI AG.

Giang, P. T. H., & Trang, K. H. (2020, November). Applying blockchain technology to improve the efficiency of the agricultural products supply chain in Vietnam. *Review of Finance, 4*(1), 105–111.

Hackius, N., & Petersen, M. (2017). Blockchain in logistics and supply chain: Trick or treat? Digitalization in supply chain management and logistics: Smart and digital solutions for an industry 4.0 environment. *Proceedings of the Hamburg International Conference of Logistics (HICL), 23*, 3–18.

Hans, P. P., & Rhea N. (2021). Blockchain applications in the legal field. *Speedlegal.Io*. https://speedlegal.io/post/blockchain-applications-in-the-legal-field

Haque, A. K. M., & Rahman, M. (2020). Blockchain technology: Methodology, application, and security issues. *IJCSNS International Journal of Computer Science and Network Security, 20*(2).

Heutger, M., & Kueckelhaus, M. (2018). Blockchain in logistics. *DHL Trend Research.*

Hofmann, E., & Rüsch, M. (2017). Industry 4.0 and the current status as well as future prospects on logistics. *Computer in Industry, 89*, 23–34.

Iansiti, M., & Lakhani, K. R. (2017). The truth about Blockchain. *Harvard Business Review, 95*(1), 118–127. https://hbr.org/2017/01/the-truth-about-blockchain

Kamath, R. (2018). Food traceability on blockchain: Walmart's pork and mango pilots with IBM. *The Journal of the British Blockchain Association, 1*(1), 3712. 1-12.

Kim, H. M., & Laskowski, M. (2018). Toward an ontology-driven blockchain design for supply-chain provenance. *Intelligent Systems in Accounting, Finance and Management, 25*(1), 18–27.

Kshetri, N. (2018). Blockchain's roles in meeting key supply chain management objectives. *International Journal of Information Management, 39*, 80–89.

Lehmacher, W. (2017, May). Why blockchain should be global trade's next port of call. *World Economic Forum, 23.*

Levitt, T. (2016). Blockchain technology trialed to tackle slavery in the fishing industry. *The Guardian.*

Luh, P. M., et al. (2020). Mapping the potentials of blockchain in improving supply chain performance. *Cogent Business & Management, 7*(1).

Madakam, S., Ramaswamy, R., & Tripathi, S. (2015). Internet of things (IoT): A literature review. *Journal of Computer and Communications, 3*, 164–173.

Mathisen, M. (2018, June). *The application of blockchain technology in Norwegian fish supply chains-A case study*. Master's thesis, Norwegian University of Science and Technology Faculty of Engineering.

Morley, H. R. (2017). *Industry skeptical of pace of logistics tech adoption*. JOC.

MUTRAP European Trade Policy and Investment Support Project. (2014). *Report – Output 2: Study on Sanitary Phytosanitary measures (SPS) and Technical Barriers to Trade (TBT) faced by Vietnamese exporters in major export market* (pp. 65–66).

Nakamoto, S. (2008). Bitcoin: A peer-to-peer electronic cash system.

Nguyen, S., Chen, P. S. L., & Du, Y. (2020). Risk identification and modeling for blockchain-enabled container shipping. *International Journal of Physical Distribution & Logistics Management, 51*(2), 126–148.

Phu, N. A., Tu, L. T. C., & Tien, N. T. (2020). The combination of RFID and blockchain to develop the traceability system model for aquaculture activities in Mekong Delta, Vietnam. *Vietnam Industry and Trade Magazine, 4*, 138–143.

Pilkington, M. (2016). Blockchain technology: Principles and applications. *Research Handbook on Digital Transformations, 11*, 1–39.

Reyna, A., Martín, C., Chen, J., Soler, E., & Díaz, M. (2018). On blockchain and its integration with IoT: Challenges and opportunities. *Future Generation Computer Systems, 88*, 173–190.

Rouse, M. (2020). Cryptography definition. *TechTarget.* https://searchsecurity.techtarget.com/definition/cryptography

Shermin, V. (2017). Disrupting governance with blockchains and smart contracts. *Strategic Change, 26*(5), 499–509.

Tan, A., & Ngan, P. T. (2020). A proposed framework model for dairy supply chain traceability. *Sustainable Futures, 2*, 100034.

Tian, F. (2016, June). An Agri-food supply chain traceability system for China based on RFID & blockchain technology. *IEEE 13th international conference on service systems and service management (ICSSSM)*, 1–6.

United Nations Economic Commission for Europe. (2020). *White Paper on Blockchain in Trade Facilitation (ECE/TRADE/457).* https://unece.org/DAM/trade/Publications/ECE-TRADE-457E_WPBlockchainTF.pdf

United Nations Global Compact. (2014). *A Guide to Traceability—A Practical Approach to Advance Sustainability in Global Supply Chains.* https://www.unglobalcompact.org/docs/issues_doc/supply_chain/Traceability/Guide_to_Traceability.pdf

United Nations Industrial Development Organization. (2019). Vietnam industry white paper 2019: Manufacturing and subsector competitiveness.

Vietnam Association of Seafood Exporters and Producers. (2020). *Fishery Profile.* http://seafood.vasep.com.vn/why-buy-seafood/fishery-profile

Wang, X., & Li, D. (2006, June). Value added on food traceability: A supply chain management approach. *2006 IEEE international conference on service operations and logistics, and informatics*, 493–498.

Wognum, P. N., Bremmers, H., Trienekens, J. H., Van Der Vorst, J. G., & Bloemhof, J. M. (2011). Systems for sustainability and transparency of food supply chains–Current status and challenges. *Advanced Engineering Informatics, 25*(1), 65–76.

Woodside, J. M., Augustine, F. K., Jr., & Giberson, W. (2017). Blockchain technology adoption status and strategies. *Journal of International Technology and Information Management, 26*(2), 65–93.

World Bank. (2017). Distributed ledger technology (DLT) and blockchain. *Fintech Note, 1.* https://openknowledge.worldbank.org/bitstream/handle/10986/29053/WP-PUBLIC-Distributed-Ledger-Technology-and-Blockchain-Fintech-Notes.pdf?sequence=5

World Economic Forum. (2018). *Readiness for the future of production assessment 2018, 251.* https://www3.weforum.org/docs/FOP_Readiness_Report_2018.pdf

Wu, J., Huh, C.-G., & Wood, J. (2021a). Globally chained economies: Unwitting victims of the US-China trade war. *Asian-Pacific Economic Literature, 35*(2), 60–76. https://doi.org/10.1111/apel.12334

Wu, J., Wood, J., & Huang, X. (2021b). How does GVC reconstruction affect economic growth and employment? Analysis of USA–China decoupling. *Asia Pacific Economic Literature, 35*(1), 67–81. https://doi.org/10.1111/apel.12319. (SSCI, IF 0.952) (SDG 9, 7, 11).

Wu, J., Wood, J., Oh, K., & Jang, H. (2021c). Evaluating the cumulative impact of the US– China trade war along global value chains. *The World Economy, 44*(12), 3516–3533. https://doi.org/10.1111/twec.13125

Yang, C. S., & Lirn, T. C. (2017). Revisiting the resource-based view on logistics performance in the shipping industry. *International Journal of Physical Distribution & Logistics Management, 47*, 884–905.

Zheng, Z., Xie, S., Dai, H., Chen, X., & Wang, H. (2017, June). An overview of blockchain technology: Architecture, consensus, and future trends. *IEEE international congress on big data (BigData congress), 2017*, 557–564.

Chapter 5
Power Up Sustainability: A Lean-Agile Perspective for the Tropics

Christine Wing Kit Yip

Abstract Enabling innovation from the ground up is the way for businesses in the tropic. This paper presents insights from research, observation and management frameworks to implement such a strategy from a practitioner's perspective. It drastically differs from tropical organisations' top-down, hierarchical, and authoritarian leadership. The paper highlights some of the most urgent environmental, social and governance (ESG) priorities in the tropical region to elaborate on the severity and importance of successful ESG strategy implementation in the region. Moreover, businesses must be resilient in a challenging environment with ongoing uncertainty and disruptions in technologies and supply chains. Leaders must have emotional and mental health resilience to drive innovation and implement sustainable development. The paper is written from a management practitioner's perspective to examine the cultural, philosophical and managerial aspects of Lean-Agile innovation. An implementation practice framework has been proposed as a way forward.

Keywords Innovation · Implementation · Lean-agile · Well-being · Team

5.1 Introduction

Fresh thinking and pragmatic solutions are needed to solve the pressing problem of sustainability in the Tropics and worldwide. Sustainability encompasses many aspects of environmental, social and governance (ESG) initiatives (Abdi et al., 2021).

The paper is written from a management practitioner's perspective to examine some of the most urgent priorities in understanding the region's correlation and interdependencies of ESG management challenges. By inspecting the complexity in the geopolitical, cultural and organisational context of those priorities, it is

C. W. K. Yip (✉)
University of Otago, Dunedin, New Zealand

C WHY International Limited, Auckland, New Zealand
e-mail: christine@cwhy.co.nz

E. L. Eijdenberg et al. (eds.), *Innovation-Driven Business and Sustainability in the Tropics*, https://doi.org/10.1007/978-981-99-2909-2_5

identified that the probability of success in the ESG strategy management is heavily reliant on the organisational structure, belief systems and people's ability to be innovative in problem-solving and developing new solutions.

While an overwhelming amount of scientific research focuses on environmental and climate factors (Lu et al., 2018; Sadiq et al., 2021; Sharma et al., 2020), the social and governance expectations are largely up for interpretation by individual organisations. Some scholars and international institutions have interchangeably used Corporate Social Responsibility (CSR) with ESG due to their similar corporate governance and leadership characteristics (Gillan et al., 2020; Kuo et al., 2022; Saxena et al., 2022). The United Nations Industrial Development Organization states, 'CSR is a management concept whereby companies integrate social and environmental concerns in their business operations and interactions with their stakeholders'. CSR is generally understood as being the way through which a company achieves a balance of economic, environmental and social imperatives ("Triple-Bottom-Line- Approach"(Elkington, 2018)), while at the same time addressing the expectations of shareholders and stakeholders.'(United Nations Industrial Development Organization [UNIDO], n.d.)

Similar to the evolution of definition of CSR (Fordham & Robinson, 2018), even though ESG is a common term today, the definition and criteria are ever evolving. The ESG elements are summarised by the author of *Greensight: The Sustainability Guide for Company Directors*:

- Environment – pollution, waste and environmental impact
- Social – modern slavery, diversity and inclusion and payment conditions
- Governance – decision-making, anti-corruption and bribery, risk management and business codes of conduct.

The expectations in social and governance responsibility for businesses vary. Some definitions go beyond the law to incorporate social, ethical, and consumer concerns into business operations to create value for stakeholders and shareholders. Others expect the business to comply with the law (Newman et al., 2020).

Despite sharing a similar drive to mitigate environmental risks and the climate change crisis in management, social responsibility and governance needs in the Tropics are markedly different from the rest of the world due to the historical geopolitical structure and socioeconomic and demographic makeup (Balls, 2001). For example, when the business is expected to integrate social and governance sustainability initiatives to comply with a legal standard in a less developed country, the rule of law may not be enforced to the extent expected (Newman et al., 2020). The implementation, therefore, requires an approach that is meeting the cultural and geographic needs of the Tropics.

A combination of qualitative research methods has been used to provide insights and recommendations for the paper. Direct observation and participatory immersion at several organisations in the past decade and through innovation events throughout 2018 to 2022 provide in-depth insights into leadership and management perspectives. Additionally, relevant past research and case studies are used to draw interdisciplinary connections through the domains of philosophy, social science, health and environment, impacting the performance in team activities and how it may influence the success of ESG strategy implementation (Munduate & Gravenhorst, 2003; Vallance et al., 2011; Noji, 2019;Silva, 2022).

Global organisations are affected by government regulations and corporate compliance with sustainability. The European Union is enforcing the Corporate Sustainability Reporting Directive (CSRD) starting from January 2023 (European Union – European Commission, n.d.). This paper provides a practical framework for leaders tasked to develop sustainability solutions and transformational changes in businesses and communities.

Thus, the final part focuses on the practical aspects and explores philosophical, and cultural elements impacting individuals in the implementation of ESG strategy in business. The proposed implementation framework incorporates indigenous and Lean-Agile philosophies. The framework aims to balance the immediate needs of organisations in the region. By tapping into the collective wisdom of diverse cultures, innovations and pragmatic solutions can be found and implemented at speed.

5.2 Context

5.2.1 Operational Complexity

The tropical region is vibrant and highly diverse in languages, cultures and history, wealth distribution, politics and equality (James Cook University, 2022). The diversity and potential of the area are attractive, yet challenging to operate in business.

Climate and history significantly affect the economic status of the countries (Saxena et al., 2022). Research has found that the physical geographic location and regional climate contributed substantially to the lag of economic development at the start of the twenty-first century (Balls, 2001). In the past, the climate was too challenging for manual labour work, and most investors were more attracted to businesses in the temperate zone (Balls, 2001).

Political unrest from the mid-1970s to the 1990s and rapid urbanisation triggered informal settlements in cities across developing countries. Providing health, education and infrastructure services to these communities has proved challenging (Mbokazi, 2006). History informs the present. Past ideas and actions directly impact and influence our current mental, physical and emotional state at personal and global levels (Trim, 2020). The Tropics are culture-rich, with many indigenous communities whose collective history needs to be understood.

Indigenous worldviews have often met opposition and conflict from Western worldviews (Harmsworth & Awatere, 2013). Historically, this has led to the voices of indigenous communities being silenced or widely absent. A guardian advocating for a healthy ecosystem and well-being was silenced in favour of a mono-perspective of economic development as the only game worth playing (Meyer & Kamaka, 2019).

Being part of an international enterprise can be exceptionally challenging in the Tropics, given the historical background and geospatial location. Every city is unique, yet company headquarters need to standardise their working processes to maximise efficiency and achieve service consistency (Bates et al., 2007; Smith, 2017; United Nations – CEPAL, 1999). Drawing from first-hand experience managing projects across different Asia Pacific countries, the culture, working environment, and availability of standardised equipment vary from place to place (APQC, 2022a).

In contrast, despite the number of countries in Europe, most follow a unified set of standards as part of the economic and political partnership of the European Union. That shared understanding makes navigating and implementing a single set of regional standards and policies easier (Meyer & Kamaka, 2019).

Despite some conceptual ideas to form a region-wide economy, there is yet a single regional standard and policies across the tropics (United Nations – CEPAL, 1999). The political systems and ideologies vary significantly in the Tropics, ranging from restricted authoritarianism to transparent democracy (Jackson & Rosberg, 1985; United Nations – CEPAL, 1999). Differences between the philosophies underpinning societal systems impact how policies are shaped and presented for enforcement (Pieris & King, 2017). In the same way, thinking impacts organisation management processes, flowing through to how teams work together and the implementation of new initiatives (Hodgkinson & Healey, 2008; Bovey & Hede, 2001).

Moreover, the merger and acquisition history of international organisations adds to the complexity, with multiple ownership, people, systems and assets (Hwang, 2016). It would be easy if a change of name and a fresh coat of paint gave people a new sense of identity and the ability to work differently, but change is often far more complex (Bovey & Hede, 2001).

While the benefit of change may be justifiable for the highest decision-makers, it is not always cost-effective for local subsidiaries (Bovey & Hede, 2001). There is a need for international transparency with technologies and data at the headquarters, while local teams have always enjoyed the freedom to work without being closely monitored. The result is push-and-pull tension (Yip, 2022).

Different needs and perspectives can widen the gap between the local team and headquarters. Distance and multiple locations mean that managing a change of perspective is limited to short sting visits or virtual discussions. It takes conscious leadership to bring teams together with mutual understanding and demonstrate the shared benefits of the changes (Yip, 2022).

5.2.2 Paradigm Shift

Ways of working often come with particular mentalities and ideologies (Kniberg & Ivarsson, 2012): thinking impacts people's behaviour, the work environment and the organisational culture (Hodgkinson & Healey, 2008).

Organisation and management methodologies are used to focus solely on financials with little concern for the environment or people's well-being (Flinn, 2022). Those organisations and methods are like stale bread; fragile, crumbly, soulless and past their use-by date. Stale management is hierarchical, has a rigid power structure and disempowers people and nature (Munduate & Gravenhorst, 2003). It can offer basic survival in the short term but doesn't help the organisation go forward and stay afloat (Campbell, 2019).

Table 5.1 represents the three paradigms in observation: Stale, Fresh and Ultra-fresh. Due to past under-development and the pandemic's recent impact, tropical organisations are likely to be located between Stale and Fresh.

The paradigm comes with a different organisational structure. With the breakdown of the hierarchical, static organisational structure, strategic, tactical and operational management can be more interconnected with multi-directional communication and greater engagement across the levels of responsibility (Kniberg & Ivarsson, 2012; Vitalari & Shaughnessy, 2012).

Figure 5.1 describes the difference in communication structure in hierarchical and agile organisations. The traditional hierarchical structure follows a static one-way pathway with layers of upward approval. It creates disconnection from the strategic to the operational layers and delays in communication (Kniberg & Ivarsson, 2012;Vitalari & Shaughnessy, 2012). Organisations like Spotify have evolved to agile-at-scale and flatter organisation structures to remove such barriers (Kniberg & Ivarsson, 2012). Adapting to a more agile and de-centralised tribal structure in

Table 5.1 Three paradigms of organisational structure

Stale	Fresh	Ultra-fresh
Centralised hierarchical organisation structure (Rust, 1919)	Combination of hierarchical matrix (Stuckenbruck, 1979) and network structure (Antivachis & Angelis, 2015)	De-centralised network of tribes (Kniberg & Ivarsson, 2012;Vitalari & Shaughnessy, 2012)
Manufacturing standards to produce quality goods (APQC, 2022a)	Value-driven priorities to create quality services (APQC, 2022b)	Data-driven approach to creating innovative digital services (Process Excellence Network, 2022)
Static (Campbell, 2019)	Vary in agility (Kniberg & Ivarsson, 2012)	Elastic (Vitalari & Shaughnessy, 2012)
Technology-centric implementation (Process Excellence Network, 2022	Human-centric implementation (Process Excellence Network, 2022)	Blended human-robotic implementation (Sondh, 2021)
ESG Scope 1: Focus only on direct-controlled legal entities, their operations and their impact on the value chain. (Flinn, 2022) E.g., sustainable procurement policy and culture	ESG Scope 2: Extend to cover the critical inputs of resources used in the business and their impact on the value chain. (Flinn, 2022) E.g., using a sustainable supply of material for production to reduce emissions and impact	ESG Scope 3: Cover the entire upstream and downstream value chain of the business and its impact. (Flinn, 2022) E.g., sub-contractors, and outsourced service providers' actions are in the range

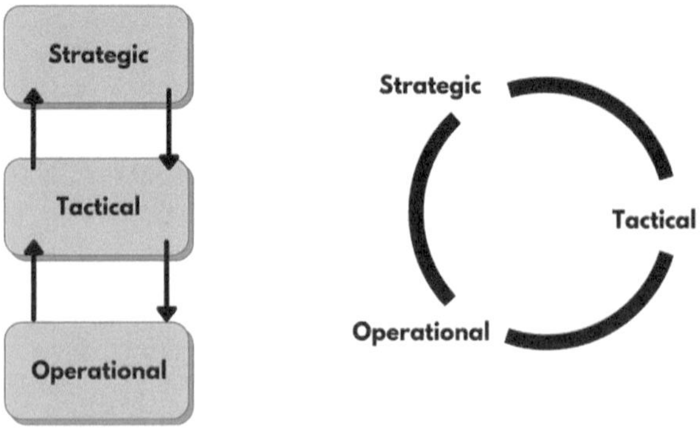

Fig. 5.1 Hierarchical to Agile organisation with circular communication. (Yip, 2022)

global organisations has reduced inefficiencies and increased strategy implementation speed (Kniberg & Ivarsson, 2012).

Each paradigm shift toward Ultra-fresh brings more transparency in communication with participation and autonomy (Kniberg & Ivarsson, 2012;Vitalari & Shaughnessy, 2012). The holistic view of the value chain impact on ESG aligns with the values of looking after people and the environment. With the shared value of collaboration and creativity, organisations and communities in the Tropics can adapt quickly to the fresh management paradigm as it is similar to original cultural settings (Meyer & Kamaka, 2019; Kniberg & Ivarsson, 2012). Along with the disruption of technologies, evolving demographics and better education (James Cook University, 2022;Sarfraz et al., 2021) in ESG will foster incredible innovation in this region.

5.2.3 *Environmental*

While it is acceptable to live with creative messiness, living with mountains of rubbish in the environment is unlikely to do anyone well. Unfortunately, this is the reality for many in undeveloped areas of the Tropics (United Nations Environment Programme, n.d.; Van Trotsenburg & Lim, 2022; Agency, 2023).

Pollution is a critical environmental issue due to the acceleration of urbanisation, lack of waste infrastructure and heavy reliance on the plastic economy (Niyommaneerat et al., 2023). Over recent decades, plastic products have become the world's most popular 'go-to' material in retail packaging because of rapid urbanisation and a rising middle class (World Bank Group, 2022). Single-use plastic and a lack of coordinated plastic recycling mean tropical countries throw usable materials (made from fossil fuels) into landfills or the ocean (Van Trotsenburg & Lim, 2022).

The World Bank estimated that 95% of the value of plastic packaging (US$80–120 billion per year) is lost to the economy when single-use plastic is discarded and not recycled (Van Trotsenburg & Lim, 2022). The severity of pollution and loss of value scaled rapidly through the COVID-19 pandemic with single-use personal protective equipment and increased consumption of online delivery packaging (Auto, 2021).

It leads to another urgent issue in the region- water resource management (Edwards et al., 1983). Water is a scarce resource, and fish provide livelihoods for many communities. However, these natural resources are contaminated by plastic due to improper disposal, manufacturing processes and commercial fishing practice (Fava, 2022).

Plastic pollution spreading across urbanised water streams and flowing to the ocean has been an issue across the Tropics and globally. Researchers estimate that between 1.15 and 2.41 million tonnes of plastic waste currently enters the ocean annually from rivers, with more than 74% of emissions occurring between May and October (Lebreton, 2017). The study found that the top 122 polluting rivers (4% of the total landmass surface area and 36% of the global population) contributed more than 90% of the plastic inputs. 103 rivers are located in Asia, eight in Africa, eight in South and Central America, and one in Europe (Lebreton, 2017).

Countries of the Association of Southeast Asian Nations (ASEAN) collaborated in the ASEAN Framework of Action on Marine Debris. The Regional Action Plan, developed at the 34th ASEAN Summit in June 2019, proposed an integrated approach to address marine plastic pollution over 5 years, from 2021 to 2025, in three key stages. These involve: Reducing inputs into the system, enhancing collection and minimising leakage, and creating value for waste reuse (ASEAN Secretariat, 2021). The World Bank approved a US$20 million grant to support the action plan, which includes strengthening and harmonising policies that govern the production and use of plastics across the region. Manuela V. Ferro, World Bank vice president for East Asia and the Pacific, commented that reducing plastic pollution in the world's rivers and oceans requires country-level action and collective, coordinated efforts (World Bank Group, 2022).

While tropical countries are putting policies in place to reduce pollution, connecting those policies with corporate governance and building action plans for effective frontline implementation will dictate the success of these initiatives. Government policy initiative is only a starting point in problem-solving. The water industry and organisations need to move away from the business-as-usual approach and collaborate with the public sector to generate synergy in the implementation (Silva, 2022).

With a concentration of global factories based in Tropical regions, a significant portion of the environmental issues originates from the actions of business communities as a collective. Manufacturing, Food and beverage, agriculture, power generation and mining industries are among the thirstiest sectors (Silva, 2022). The Imperative of Sustainability Responsiveness surveyed 100 executives in Asia in 2022 and found many businesses still need to build an effective action plan to address current elements comprising ESG. Thirty-five percent of business leaders still need to address environmental sustainability in plastic pollution and 50% in water resource management (Flinn, 2022). It is noted that low awareness levels among the stakeholders undermine the implementation collaboration focused on driving sustainability, stakeholders, leaders and management practitioners are unaware of their responsibilities in engaging in practices that can improve sustainability and reduce wastage, and the lack of financial resources hinders the long-term implementation of sustainable strategy initiatives. The combination results in the pilot projects being abandoned (Silva, 2022).

Sustainable water resource management depends on factors such as population, rainwater harvesting, land resource planning and the use of innovative technologies in the water industry (Silva, 2022). There is light at the end of the tunnel if all parties are on board in integrating sustainability initiatives in water management across sectors and resolving this existential threat to humanity due to water scarcity in the region. In that case, long-term sustainable solutions must lie in education, engagement and cooperation in responsive action as a collective to achieve a clean, healthy living environment that sparks joy.

5.2.4 *Mental Health*

Mental health is linked to almost every key issue in international development and the World Health Organization's sustainable development goals (World Health Organization, 2022). Development and achievements are not sustainable without joy.

Tropical countries have become a powerhouse of global manufacturing and economic growth with increasing prospects for future development (James Cook University Australia, 2020). This has led to increased job opportunities and a rural-to-urban movement for job seekers. Relocating rural communities to urban areas brings a change of pace that can pose a challenge for those seeking to make a living and prosper. Living conditions for workers who move into urban areas for job prospecting can be horrifying and depressing. In 2018, researchers estimated that 47% of the tropical population lived in an urban setting, and roughly 37% of that population inhabited slum conditions (James Cook University Australia, 2020). Workers are exposed to poor working conditions as well as the change to urban living. These lifestyle changes and the energy required to adapt to the new environment are significant.

Equal pay and supplier employee welfare are pressing areas that require attention on the social side of ESG. Over 60% of business leaders have not yet taken responsive action in those elements of sustainability in their supply chain (Flinn, 2022). Out of sight, out of mind. Over the decades, businesses have become used to passing the buck of CSR to their suppliers and contractors. This lack of awareness and action continues to put vulnerable workers under pressure.

Non-profit organisations have focused on support for basic survival needs such as food, medicine and education to combat the impact of disease and undernourishment (Barhate et al., 2021). Mental health has largely been neglected due to other pressing issues. Mental and emotional health is often lower priorities and treated as taboo in communities and workplaces, even in the health sector itself. It is because raising the issues on mental and emotional health issues often couple with discomfort in the self and impact the individual's notions of perfection. (Patel et al., 2021).

The World Health Organization has estimated that almost 15% of the world's working population experienced a mental disorder in 2019 (World Health Organization, 2022). The Gallup annual workplace survey into daily negative emotions has provided significant insight into how global and regional workers are faring in their mental and emotional health. The Gallup State of the Global Workplace 2022 report showed worldwide workplace stress levels have increased from 31% in 2009 to an average of 38% in the years leading up to 2019. These levels reached 43% in 2020 when COVID-19 arrived and were at 44% in 2021 (Gallup, 2022). South Asia (53%), Latin America and the Caribbean regions (49%) record the highest daily worry. In East Asia, Latin America and the Caribbean, over 50% of workers experience daily stress (Gallup, 2022).

We cannot underestimate the impact of the COVID-19 pandemic on workers' well-being. Pandemic fatigue is caused by the sudden pressure to respond and perform during a crisis, operating instantly in a different environment. The ongoing exhaustion and uncertainty of changes in lifestyle and the pandemic are having a long-lasting effect on the wellness of organisations and individuals. Unlike other diseases, there is no quick-fix immunisation vaccine for emotional well-being.

Acute stress is the compound result of ongoing stress, prolonged sleeping issues, using caffeine or other means to boost energy and continuing to act as if nothing has happened. This is not uncommon when someone starts a new lifestyle, such as a new job or moving to a new country. Adding to the mix is the pressure of being 'always on call' for sub-contractors and business leaders. Acute stress leads to trauma responses in the physiological reaction. The fight or flight responses, coined by American physiologist Walter Cannon in 1915, are well-known (Frothingham, 2021). When facing a stressful or dangerous situation, the ancient human survival instinct is to confront danger or flee from it. When the sympathetic nervous system perceives a threat, it prompts an unconscious physiological action and a range of stress responses.

Based on Cannon's model, psychologists have developed a deeper understanding of acute stress and trauma responses (Munier, 2021). It turns out that our stress reactions vary. Dr. Stephen Porges' 2009 Polyvagal theory indicated 'freeze' as an additional response that immobilises the body. In 2014, Peter Walkers expanded the fight, flight, and freeze responses, adding 'fawn' through the lens of trauma typology perspective. It is a passive, submissive reaction that attempts to reduce the perceived danger. Dr. Curtis Reisinger suggested the psychological reactions of 'flood' and 'flop' as further stress responses. Flood is where an individual is overwhelmed by emotions, while flop is the disassociation of threat with physical tiredness and sleep as trauma responses (Munier, 2021). A variety of human personalities and stress reactions can be hard to spot and difficult for colleagues, peers and family to identify.

Disproportionate stress responses to perceived danger led to a range of reactionary consequences. This is when we are not in real danger but still experience an acute stress reaction. It reduces the person's access to clear headspace, rational action and the ability to participate in proactive problem-solving.

Individuals are used to paying attention to physical health because it is easier to discuss symptoms that can be identified and seen. Cultural values and practices often mean that unconscious bias about physical health takes precedence over emotional and mental health. In cultures where trust is low and judgement is high, it is difficult to express emotional vulnerability with others who do not share the same sentiment or understanding (Patel et al., 2021). This results in the lack of diagnosis of emotional and mental disorders, even by medical professionals (De Silva et al., 2013).

Joint research in the United Kingdom (UK) and Pakistan identified that Southeast Asians in the UK have a history of lack of diagnosis in chronic fatigue syndrome or myalgic encephalitis. This was due to barriers of cultural perception, despite the patients experiencing severe, disabling, medically unexplained fatigue that was not alleviated by rest and lasted for at least 6 months (De Silva et al., 2013).

A World Health Organization multinational study that included South Asia found the prevalence of disabling fatigue to be 1.69%. A community study among women in India revealed chronic fatigue in one in ten women. These statistics show the lack of diagnosis of emotional and mental health issues is widespread. With medically unexplained symptoms, patients reported that the lack of serious illness meant even health professionals did not take fatigue symptoms seriously (De Silva et al., 2013).

Because emotional and mental health is so taboo in workplaces (Patel et al., 2021) and communities, organisations and leaders risk misunderstanding and mislabelling individuals and groups. This leads to inaccurate judgements, misdiagnosis of performance and further disempowerment of vulnerable workers.

When cultural factors are woven with the disruption of health and the economic impact of COVID-19, it puts the health systems, business leaders and workers at risk. Poor mental health and well-being thus become part of the ongoing barrier for individuals and organisations in the region to achieve sustainable development. Social well-being and governance in organisations are underdeveloped in the ESG arena globally.

5.3 An Implementation Framework for Sustainable Development

Implementing sustainable development is similar to bringing the parties together to treat the wounds on the planet earth and to reduce the existential threat to humanity. Upon examining the most urgent priorities in the Tropical regions, a solution is needed to help organisations and community leaders address and eliminate the barriers to people's well-being and management issues in implementation. A framework is proposed to address some challenges and progress toward effectively implementing regional action plans from a management practitioner's perspective.

5.3.1 Anchoring Philosophies

> Health, life and good living are a complex interdependent whole that is part of interconnected relational networks, of human communities, social relations and relations with Mother Earth. (Kain & Hinojosa, 2020)

The proposed framework is anchored in the richness of worldviews, cultures and values of indigenous communities across the Tropics. Deeply ingrained cultural values impact the day-to-day interactions and decisions of people in the region. Despite their differences, cultures have many shared experiences and values. The proposed framework is a starting point for further ground-up discussion, iteration and trial.

Connectivity between communities and mother earth is a universal value that must be honoured as a fundamental principle in sustainable development for the region. Lean Agile is a continuous improvement philosophy and an effective management methodology (Beck et al., 2001). It has proven helpful in mobilising teams and organisations, private and public, to tackle complex problems and identify solutions at speed.

5S is a well-known Lean management method for increasing efficiency and effectiveness worldwide in the supply chain, manufacturing and logistics sector. The method originated from five Japanese words: Sort (*seiri* 整理), Set in order (*seiton* 整頓), Shine (*seisō* 清掃), Standardise (*seiketsu* 清潔), and Sustain (*shitsuke* 躾). The heavy focus on cleanliness is much more than the organisation of the place. It helps 'eliminate the gloom in our hearts', according to Shoukei Matsumoto, a Buddhist monk from Koyoji Temple (Smith, 2018). A clean place equals clean headspace.

As an easily understood concept, 5S is applied wide and far. It is effective in personal and workspace organisation and in organising conflicting priorities at scale. 5S can be used to build organisational resilience in times of disruption.

Sorting the status quo provides clarity and calmness by reducing chaos and unnecessary distractions. Before starting anything new, it is essential to understand the baseline of the environment in the organisation as part of the voice of the employee. Is there clutter in the physical workplace, computer systems, legacy processes and mental demands impacting people's actions?

People rarely come on board with new initiatives and changes if they are experiencing distress. That includes understanding the physical and psychological health of the group. If people are already at capacity, deliberate action must be taken to identify the causes. The outcome is a baseline measurement of the organisational environment.

The ability to cater to new demands and address them differentiates an organisation. Employee needs with priorities from the voice of the business and the customer are turned into goals and outcomes. These are set in order by conceptually re-arranging the needs and workflow ready for further action.

The early stages help streamline the needs and priorities to make way for improvement. Traditionally, the shine process is about sweeping and cleaning the factory to enhance safety and efficiency. It is about resolving old issues and implementing changes to improve organisational resilience and health. Shoukei Matsumoto describes it as 'an ascetic practice to cultivate the mind' (Smith, 2018).

Like a spring clean, creating change from scratch requires more effort than if it is only done occasionally. Standardising generates consistent and regular occurrences. Creating processes across the organisation ensures the work stays in place with the day-to-day management. Traditionally, it is a daily inspection before and after the factory shift. In organisational resilience, the leadership observes and reviews the priority pipeline consistent with the vision and holds daily stand-up discussions and regular retrospective dialogue.

The ultimate goal of the 5S method is to sustain a new level of resilience. A new norm is cultivated through training and growing new leaders to champion the new processes. Maintaining a lean and supportive environment allows employees to problem-solve and offer solutions. New initiatives can be delegated to motivated individuals, trusting their ability to take ownership of the organisation's vision as an autonomous team.

5.3.2 The Four Quadrants

The Four Quadrants are the intrinsic value and motivation to mobilise the various parties to participate in problem-solving and innovation in sustainability implementation. The framework's core elements are Free, Fun, Focus and Fire. The sequence of the elements in the application depends on the organisational culture and the level of motivation in the status quo, allowing agility in the decision-making process. The elements are described and elaborated with case studies and observations (Fig. 5.2).

5.3.3 Free

> By the way we live our daily life, we contribute to peace or to war. It is mindfulness that can tell me that I am going in the direction of war and it is the energy of mindfulness that can help me to make a turn and to go in the direction of peace. – Thich Nhat Hanh (Hanh, n.d.)

Growing development comes with a highly stressful lifestyle for many in the Tropics. Constant stressors limit our ability to stay calm amid chaos.

Zen master Thich Nhat Hanh was a peace movement activist who promoted mindfulness in daily routine, embedding a gratitude meditation practice in an urban environment. Hanh recognised the widespread need for peace and calmness in individuals, yet traditional sitting meditation can be prohibitive given our lack of understanding, time and space. He revolutionised meditation practices by incorporating

Fig. 5.2 The four quadrants

them into daily routines such as face washing, preparing breakfast and walking (Hanh, 2011).

By expanding mindfulness practices outside of religion, these exercises support conscious engagement in daily activities, increasing the awareness of self and the surrounding environment. The exercises lead to better emotional health, where the mind focuses only on the present, not the past or the future. Headspace is free when the mind stops wandering with stressful thoughts.

Every human has a history, as does every organisation, country and region. Stressors from the past and present cause deep angst in the population, individuals and society (Jowf et al., 2022). Differences in worldview and distrust of authority are barriers to cooperation between communities (Kain & Hinojosa, 2020).

It is never pleasant to feel constantly hurt by life events. Acknowledging the past helps bring closure to trauma, freedom from stress and peace to the present.

Meyer and Kamaka are two educators who led an artistic project with the indigenous Hawaiian community as part of expression and connection with ancestral wisdom. Participants co-designed and created artwork while sharing and processing collective emotions from historical events. They processed traumatic emotions that resulted from colonisation and racism. The process allowed new expressions to emerge in an artistic form in response to current times. The participants completed two artworks and strengthened their social bonds connecting heritage and ancestral wisdom to face future endeavours (Meyer & Kamaka, 2019). It was a transformational and healing experience.

While facilitated activities can vary in form, the essence is for a group to develop a common goal, connect with trust and share the emotional experience. The goal is to bring harmony between past and present, the inner self and the external environment. This non-duality view is similar to the practice of Zen and connecting intuition in activities. (Japanese Zen Buddhist Philosophy (Stanford Encyclopedia of

Philosophy), 2019) Inner space and the external world are the two sides of the same coin. When we heal and integrate from past pain, it becomes a nutrient for present and future growth.

Creativity streams from an open mind with calmness and involves removing boundaries and red tape (De Bono, 1985; Meyer & Kamaka, 2019). This can be temporary in a designated setting, such as creating art as a group. It can be done through a company-wide, online innovation forum, a team-building exercise, or an innovation retreat. That means that while team members are specialists in their day jobs, they can contribute creativity as members of the wider organisation. If the platform is well-facilitated, groups with shared interests can learn from each other's insights, work to solve complex problems and develop ideas to test out potential solutions.

Group creativity can be unleashed through intentional facilitation using the Six Thinking Hats theory proposed by Edward de Bono, the father of lateral thinking (De Bono, 1985). The idea is that various functions and perspectives are hats you put on to consider the topic. The colour of the hat dictates a way of thinking; for example, yellow for optimism, black for risk, and red for feeling and intuition.

Facilitating the group through a process can avoid groupthink, which happens when members do not want to challenge or share a different opinion. This is often due to varying status, political power or language barriers. It is hard to talk about different perspectives if the participants and teams are from a culture with little psychological safety. No one likes being judged, criticised, or feeling out of place in workplaces.

A process such as Six Thinking Hats allows the team to be bolder in expressing themselves and helps break behavioural habits in communication (Kaya, 2013). Emerging creativity comes from rich and diverse discussions. Self-expression and different opinions are expected and become a regular part of the process.

Freedom to make honest decisions dictates the success of the implementation. Research from Cornell University estimated that the average person makes 226.7 decisions per day on food alone (Wansink & Sobal, 2007). As humans, we often go for the most familiar and safe options. It saves time and energy to work and avoids the risk of coming across unpleasant food choices.

That high volume of decisions is similar when implementing a new strategy, regardless if it is sustainability (Silva, 2022; Kniberg & Ivarsson, 2012). Alternative feasible options are unlikely to be supported without a blind review process and strong advocacy. This reiterates the importance of breaking behavioural habits in communications and allowing freedom of choice in decision-making.

The Toyota Production System is a classic lean management example of activating ground-up problem-solving. It is world-famous for productivity and quality improvement, but we know little about its intent to develop innovative leadership. Kiichiro Toyoda, the founder of Toyota, began as a textile manufacturer. He envisioned building a fully Japanese-made car and 'catching up with America' in car manufacturing. That vision drove the family business to find a way to design and manufacture vehicles in Japan from scratch in the 1930s (Noji, 2019). At the time, cars were manufactured in Europe or America and imported into Japan for assembly. Toyoda's vision led to the creation of a local supply chain. He knew that once the challenge of building the supply chain had started, the cost of parts and production must come down for the end products to be accepted by the consumers as affordable, privately owned transportation.

With limited resources, fulfilling the vision required a thinking team that shared the dream and could create new solutions independently. A team that would dare to identify areas of improvement from the status quo, come up with new ideas, and make sound judgments on the viability of potential solutions. Once a solution was identified, they were tasked with implementing and sustaining it as their own – until another improvement was identified and newer solutions implemented. The team had the freedom to improve the business they worked for. And so, the Toyota production system was born.

Innovation starts with observation (Berkhout et al., 2006). The team had time to watch others completing production tasks over days or weeks. Whether the job was big or small, the ultimate goal was to identify improvements and generate ideas.

In today's manufacturing operations, where the focus is on optimising every minute of the people's hours, the value of intentional observation of the status quo is often underestimated. It is a crucial step in independent fact-gathering and critical thinking processes.

Unlike today where pre-made parts and technologies are readily available, the start-up Toyota did not have the luxury of designing or purchasing machinery to drive improvement (Noji, 2019). The leaders even discouraged purchasing external machinery as an improvement solution because it was seen as 'outsourcing the thinking', thus taking away opportunities for the team to go through the ideas development process.

The production system educated the team on the quality of their thinking and output. The Andon traffic light system gave any team member authority to stop production if there was a defect on the line. Once stopped, the leader would go through the problem-solving process until the root cause was found. When the quality issue was resolved, production could resume with a green light for this line and the subsequent processes (Noji, 2019). While this effectively eliminated defects from the manufacturing process, it was also an educational opportunity for the team to take ownership of problem-solving and implement a solution to enable the product to continue.

These are a few examples of how the Toyota production system builds innovative leaders from a shared vision and creates norms for the team to be thinkers and idea creators. These activities promote a strong sense of ownership around solving problems and facilitate a culture that continually reinvents itself.

At Toyota, a continual invention from a community of innovative leaders enabled the company to grow from an impossible vision of building a locally-made car to a global corporation throughout challenging times.

5.3.4 Fun

Two opposing spectrums of creativity are accepted across different cultures — demonstrative and reserved (Hondzel & Gulliksen, 2015; Shao et al., 2019). While many cultures endorse creativity and expression in arts and music, in a number of tropical countries, any perception of standing out from the crowd is discouraged in organisations and workplaces. Fitting in with the group is a natural human instinct and is comforting.

From a collective cultural perspective, it is desirable to behave like others, in line with common norms and create a sense of belonging and a shared identity (Raudenbush, 2012). There is a strong preference for some cultures to seek approval from authority figures before expressing a different idea. Fun activities help release the team from these restrictions and form a new norm within the team. This work is conducted through the forming, storming and norming stages in team building as per Tuckman's model of group development (Tuckman, 1965). Through experiencing different stages in team development, the shared experiences and connections form a new group identity and norms. The people become familiar with each other and form a new dynamic.

Despite differences in backgrounds, personal connections develop through shared interests fostering inter-generational and inter-regional teamwork and trust. Meetup.com has had worldwide success in connecting people with different interests for this very reason.

Observing and understanding the expression, demographic and personalities through team activities help leaders determine tactics for team engagement. Using constructive methods to gather objective data can uncover ways to bring the team on board with the purpose of work. The team profile provides perspective and insight into shared values and motivation drivers (Maslow, 1943). Anonymous surveys, sports and recreational group activities provide informal qualitative and quantitative data to help understand individuals.

One such example is the female-led hackathon held at the Auckland University of Technology in 2022, where participants created AI technology-driven solutions to environmental issues. The team members had not met before the event, which was held over 36 hours period. The compressed time frame forced an intensive team-building process that started with informal introductions, getting to know each other and initial pitching of ideas. That informal social interaction in a creative space outside their usual workplaces helped individuals be open to working differently. They gathered information about possible teammates, shared stories about causes they cared about and then formed teams.

While the organisers facilitated the social activities, teams were free to build a culture that best suited their personalities and skill profiles. The upfront social interaction allowed teams to move swiftly through the storming and norming stages as they worked to develop solutions and a prototype over the 2 days.

Forming their communities and teams created space for creative solutions. The leadership structure was flat, with equal contributions from all team members.

Alongside the goal of completing a design and pitching a possible prototype, teams embedded fun in their solutions to environmental issues. They built solutions based on their passions for fashion, photography, food and technology. They had fun while toying with new possibilities to disrupt the status quo.

Harnessing the power to create, innovate and evolve the organisations and technology is the solution to a shift in behaviours in implementing sustainability changes. Scientists and artists have moments of insight that naturally transform their work. Their cumulative efforts lead to significant breakthroughs (Meyer & Kamaka, 2019). The enjoyment, and fun in iterations with integrity in the decision and planning processes safeguard the evolutionary journey in sustainable development, despite the technology disruption.

5.3.5 Focus

The immediate needs of the tropical region vary widely, even within the same country, making collaboration on sustainability and other social issues challenging.

Maslow's hierarchy of needs is a timeless description of human needs. At the most basic level, we must have our physiological needs of food, shelter, and warmth to survive (see Fig. 5.3). As those needs are met, we are more likely to explore love, belonging and self-fulfilment and contribute to a cause for a wider group through our actions (Maslow, 1943).

Understanding the dynamics of various stakeholder needs through analysis, assessment and dialogue is essential in strategy implementation. The level of need can be identified across multiple layers in complex problems.

An example is the transformation of road and transport modes described in the New Zealand Transport Agency (NZTA) National Action Plan 2019–2021. Given the need to reduce carbon emissions, the growing urban population must lessen car dependency to reduce traffic congestion and improve urban mobility. NZTA found

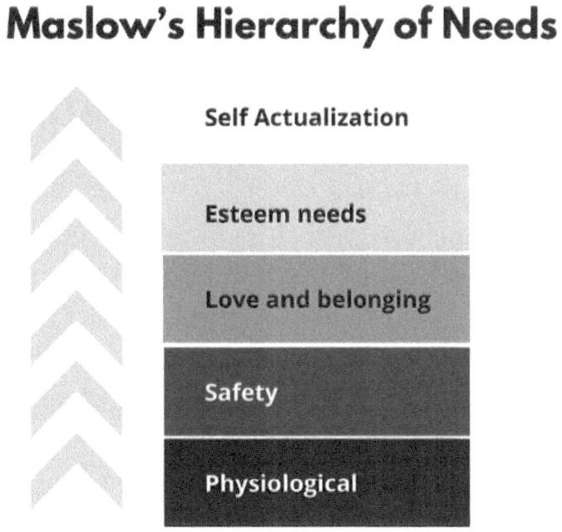

Fig. 5.3 Maslow's hierarchy of needs. (Maslow, 1943)

that 65.5% of all transport trips in New Zealand are less than five kilometres and these short trips in private vehicles contribute to the country's carbon emissions (Waka Kotahi NZ Transport Agency, n.d.-a).

Convenience is a need. When applying the hierarchy of needs on a larger scale, it is evident that keeping carbon emissions down is crucial for the government in urban planning and regulation, while the immediate convenience of driving a private vehicle takes precedence for the population. Other needs, such as safety in public transport systems, road infrastructure and accessibility, were considered as part of the initiative (Waka Kotahi NZ Transport Agency, n.d.-a, n.d.-b). The NZTA National Action Plan report did not consider the significant psychological factors of private vehicle ownership as identity and social status. Car ownership is a form of esteem and even self-actualisation. The simple act of driving a car meets many people's needs for individual freedom, flexibility and higher social status.

As part of its community engagement to support the national strategy, NZTA hosted an innovative hackathon weekend. One hundred and twenty community and technology sector volunteers worked on technology-enabled solutions to increase travel choices (NZ Transport Agency, 2019). Partnerships with communities explored user perspectives to assess the complexity of needs in transport mobility. The initiatives opened up government national transport databases, providing the public access to direct conversation with the countries' transport designers, planners and regulators to a greater level of exchange in opinion and co-designing potential solutions. Some ideas from the hackathon, including public transport occupancy data, were eventually used as part of the COVID-19 crisis response in social distancing on public transport (PricewaterhouseCoopers, 2021a).

This case study from the New Zealand Transport Agency demonstrates the complexity of needs related to a sustainable strategy and potential ways to progress the strategy through broader community engagement (NZ Transport Agency, 2019). Opening access to direct collaboration and focusing on user needs provided opportunities to reach common ground between the New Zealand Government agency, policy-makers and the general public for innovative, sustainable solutions and strategy implementation.

Thriving through innovation requires a coordinated effort. One of the most overlooked elements is the voice of the process. This includes strategic planning, operational activities, data measurements, and performance metrics. Embedding lean and agility in the framework enables the organisation to change fast in a coordinated manner. An adaptive enterprise process framework is a competitive advantage in challenging times.

The manufacturing and logistics industry worldwide has evolved with new technologies. From the introduction of electricity in the First Industrial Revolution, new materials and standardisation in the Second, and computerisation in the Third, we are in the Fourth with digital technologies, and the Fifth is now emerging.

Industry 4.0 started in 2011 and focused on smart technologies to perform automation and data to drive intelligent actions (Callaghan Innovation, 2022). Joint cyber-and-physical robotic systems, the IoT, AI, and cloud computing are key technologies being incorporated into the workflow of manufacturing and logistics businesses to improve the efficiency and accuracy of services (Sondh, 2021). These technologies are now widely used in intelligent transport system development around the globe to digitalise transport operation processes to achieve safety, environmental and efficiency outcomes (UNECE, 2021). New urban infrastructures are built with future smart city development in mind.

2020 Global Digital IQ found that the 5% of companies that invest in digital technologies enterprise-wide have 17% higher profit margin growth over 3 years (Oxford Economics, 2021). Mastering the integration of adaptive process management and the ongoing investment in industry 4.0 technologies will transform regions and organisations to thrive in the foreseeable future.

The Fifth Industrial Revolution, which arguably started in 2020, involves cognitive computing working with human intelligence (Sarfraz et al., 2021). It is a time when the human mind combines with machine intelligence for more radical innovation in personalising products and services for the masses (Sondh, 2021). Technologies and minds working together can lead us toward an exponential problem-solving ability and potentially achieving a state of 'neuroenlightment', as Dr. John Vervaeke of Toronto University calls it (Vervaeke, 2013). For example, the ability of the human mind to spontaneously resolve the Nine Dots problem was statistically zero, but with the support of neurotechnologies, the statistics rose to 40%.

Technology and human minds joining forces in the field of cognitive science can potentially significantly impact our ability to solve previously inaccessible problems, such as the climate and environmental issues that threaten society (Vervaeke, 2013). Projecting the population behaviours in Digital Twin Cities is still a major challenge because of the complexities of human nature, how we interact with the infrastructure and the nature of the changing environment, including the climate (Yang, 2022). Greater problem-solving power will potentially help us deal with some of the most critical issues in our supply chain, intelligent transport and logistics systems. These developments present disruption or opportunity to the sector and the global communities.

With a glimpse into technological advancement, it is crucial to start building a level of process maturity in the business and in organisations to prepare for potentially exponential changes.

A visual enterprise process framework is a handy communication tool to showcase complex groups of activities from a helicopter view. It can have levels of detail, from the first [the purpose of the enterprise's existence) to the sixth (specific elements of an operational activity] (APQC, 2022a, b).

With the support of technology, enterprise processes and different levels of detail can be stored online as living, breathing documentation. They show how business activities align with the organisational purpose, as the up- and downstream effects create commercial value for the end customers. This view is crucial for the ESG scope three risk assessment of the entire lifecycle of the value chain.

Disruption brings opportunities to create with fewer restrictions. An idea for a new way of doing business needs to sit with commercial activities. To map with innovation, business activities require clear headspace and an empty drawing space.

The status quo should not define the future. As indicated earlier, the term 'clean headspace' refers to clearing past and present biases and preconceptions. A canvas filled with current activities leaves no room for future possibilities. The empty drawing space policy applies to sustainable development in the tropical region.

Starting with purpose and strategy, the renewal of the vision or mission statement is the highest level of the process map. Regardless of the approach, there should be a clear vision of the end goal.

With the vision comes the supporting functions. These can be separated into departments in traditional businesses: sales and marketing, production or service operation, customer services, financial resources, human resources, assets and technologies management. In start-ups, departmental boundaries blur, with multiple functions resting in a single department. Some activities may be automated with technologies or outsourced to other service providers to focus on core activities. Clarity and focus on functions and processes help leaders streamline priorities and rapidly deliver solutions.

5.3.6 Fire

A spark is a little thing, yet it may kindle the world. – Martin Farquhar Tupper. (Tupper, n.d.)

Organisations that do good by being socially responsible, ethical and caring for the environment are closer to their customers' hearts. Caring for the safety and well-being of workers, minimising the impact on our environment and the subsequent implications for future generations are increasingly important elements in corporate decision-making processes.

An IBM-led survey completed in 2020 found that 81% of respondents identified as either value-driven or purpose-driven consumers looking for products and services aligned with their values. Some 57% of respondents were willing to change their buying behaviours to reduce negative environmental impact (Haller et al., 2020).

Similarly, a PwC Consumer Insights Survey found that 50% of participants are becoming more eco-friendly. Their survey also reported that an average of 80% of consumers in South East Asia and 67.5% of consumers in the Middle East reported being significantly more environmentally conscious (PricewaterhouseCoopers, 2021b). Sustainable products and services that are good for the environment are in greater demand.

The tropical region has a rosy economic forecast. With an economic outlook of 5.7% growth projection in 2022 and projected growth of more than 6% in Asia by the International Monetary Fund (IMF), it is increasingly important to identify changing consumer preferences in the global regions (IMF, 2021).

A shift in consumer and customer preferences means organisations in the Tropics need to focus on profit, as well as people and the planet (Elkington, 2018). Adapting this new thinking means the business and operations are likely to align closely with the values of their customers and key stakeholders.

A vision is an aspiration, a mental image that paints desired outcomes. A manufacturing business may have the foresight to drive social and environmental sustainability through its products. Those desires formulate a vision of the future for the enterprise and inform its strategy.

The vision and strategy are the steering mechanism for the sustainable future of a new initiative: a heartfelt vision and meaningful purpose across the end-to-end supply chain fuel the growth and speed of innovation.

Technology and the disruption of business models challenge traditional organisations to remain competitive. It is no different in space. The cost of designing and building rockets is traditionally astronomical and restricted by government agencies.

In the early 2000s, several visionary entrepreneurs disrupted the market by launching space services. Elon Musk founded SpaceX in 2002 with a vision of expanding human civilisation into space (SpaceX, 2022). Richard Branson established Virgin Galactic in 2004, saying that travelling and exploring space will enable 'the unique ability to shift perspectives, technology, and even our trajectory as a species' (Virgin Galactic, n.d.).

In 2006, Peter Beck, a New Zealander who spent his childhood making homemade rockets in a country town, founded Rocket Lab, a startup satellite launching company. Despite his love of rocket making, Beck has a vision of democratising space, seeking 'open access to space to improve life on Earth' (Beck, n.d.).

Environmental data helps scientists research and understand changes in the earth's atmosphere, land and ocean. However, collecting environmental data comes with challenges. First, it is impossible or costly to collect data physically in a human-prohibitive environment. Second, the coverage of data collected is limited, restricting our ability to understand the complete picture of an issue around the globe. And third, even if enough data was gathered from various stations, it becomes outdated if it is not processed and analysed in time.

Satellite technology has helped resolve several of these issues by providing ongoing monitoring of the planet from a distance, covering previously unreachable areas and feeding the data back to earth for processing (Medina, 2010).

Before the 2000s, accessing space was only possible by giant players such as NASA and billionaires. Peter Beck started the first commercial aerospace company in the Southern Hemisphere in his youth, creating and testing homemade rockets. His high school counsellor was concerned about his career choice as it 'didn't fit any predefined boxes' and was seen as 'absurdly unachievable' (Hendery, 2017), so Beck went to work in a household appliance company as a tool-making apprentice. He maintained his passion by conducting after-hours tests of his rockets in Auckland's Industrial Research Ltd., which later became Callaghan Innovation.

Beck and the team designed and developed their rocket technology using 3D printing for parts and established a full launching service for commercial clients. Gaining support through seed funding in Silicon Valley, the New Zealand government and other investors, Rocket Lab has since launched 150+ satellites into orbit. The company was publicly listed on the Nasdaq in 2021 with a pro forma enterprise value of $4.1 billion (Etherington, 2021). NASA is a client of Rocket Lab.

The example of Beck and Rocket Lab demonstrates that a heartfelt vision with grit and passion activates customers' support and investment in achieving the 'absurdly unachievable'.

5.4 Conclusion

> The credit belongs to the man who is actually in the arena, whose face is marred by dust and sweat and blood; who strives valiantly; who errs, who comes short again and again, because there is no effort without error and shortcoming; but who does actually strive to do the deeds. – Theodore Roosevelt (Roosevelt, 1910).

The word *challenge* shares similarities with an Asian fruit, the durian, or king of fruits, which has a distinctively strong fragrance and flavour. Some people look for it, while others avoid it.

There is no such option to avoid life's challenges. As the Tropics recover from the pandemic, there will be no foreseeable shortage of issues. It is wise to prepare and grow our capacity to face the expected and the unexpected. Fear is normal, but when flipped, it becomes excitement. It can be exciting to tackle workplace and even larger ecosystem challenges.

The key difference with a team of innovators is the ability to challenge the status quo with a shared purpose despite differing perspectives and understanding. With faith in a vision and the ability to implement it, innovation is essential to embedding sustainability in the Tropics.

Engaging and mobilising a diverse community of supply chain, logistics and manufacturing organisations with a shared vision will foster collaboration between the public and private sectors in resolving some of the world's biggest sustainability challenges.

Collective wisdom through cooperation will see the region's economic sustainability and social well-being thrive. With a shared goal of prosperity and implementation actions, communities and places will be empowered and transformed.

References

Abdi, Y., Li, X., & Càmara-Turull, X. (2021). Exploring the impact of sustainability (ESG) disclosure on firm value and financial performance (FP) in airline industry: The moderating role of size and age. *Environment, Development and Sustainability, 24*(4), 5052–5079. https://doi.org/10.1007/s10668-021-01649-w

Agency. (2023, February 11). *Plastic in paradise: Bali is struggling with mountains of rubbish*. The Star. https://www.thestar.com.my/lifestyle/people/2023/02/11/plastic-in-paradise-bali-is-struggling-with-mountains-of-rubbish

Antivachis, N. A., & Angelis, V. (2015). Network organizations: The question of governance. *Procedia – Social and Behavioral Sciences, 175*, 584–592. https://doi.org/10.1016/j.sbspro.2015.01.1241

APQC. (2022a, May 23). *What is the process of standardization?* https://www.apqc.org/blog/what-process-standardization

APQC. (2022b, October 10). *APQC Process Classification Framework (PCF) – Cross Industry – Excel Version 7.2.1.* https://www.apqc.org/resource-library/resource-listing/apqc-process-classification-framework-pcf-cross-industry-excel-7

ASEAN Secretariat. (2021). *ASEAN regional action plan for combating marine debris in the ASEAN member states (2021–2025).* Association of Southeast Asian Nations. https://asean.org/wp-content/uploads/2021/09/FINAL_210524-ASEAN-RAP-Summary.pdf

Auto, H. (2021, November 17). *Cities are not only tackling Covid-19, but its pollution, too.* The Straits Times. Retrieved October 1, 2022, from https://www.straitstimes.com/world/europe/cities-are-not-only-tackling-covid-19-but-its-pollution-too

Balls, A. (2001, June). *Why tropical countries are underdeveloped.* NBER. Retrieved October 9, 2022, from https://www.nber.org/digest/jun01/why-tropical-countries-are-underdeveloped

Barhate, B., Hirudayaraj, M., Gunasekara, N., Mellado, M., Alizadeh, A., & Abadi, M. (2021). Crisis within a crisis: Migrant workers' predicament during COVID-19 lockdown and the role of non-profit organizations in India. *Indian Journal of Human Development, 15*(1), 151–164. https://doi.org/10.1177/0973703021997624

Bates, R. H., Coatsworth, J. H., & Williamson, J. G. (2007). Lost decades: Postindependence performance in Latin America and Africa. *The Journal of Economic History, 67*(4), 917–943. https://doi.org/10.1017/s0022050707000447

Beck, P. (n.d.). *Rocket Lab|from idea to orbit.* New Zealand Story. Retrieved October 10, 2022, from https://www.nzstory.govt.nz/stories/from-idea-to-orbit-rocket-lab/

Beck, K., Beedle, M., Van Bennekum, A., Cockburn, A., Cunningham, W., Fowler, M., Grenning, J., Highsmith, J., Hunt, A., Jeffries, R., Kern, J., Marick, B., Martin, R. C., Mellor, S., Schwaber, K., Sutherland, J., & Thomas, D. (2001). *Principles behind the Agile Manifesto.* https://agilemanifesto.org/principles.html

Berkhout, A. J., Hartmann, D., Van Der Duin, P., & Ortt, R. (2006). Innovating the innovation process. *International Journal of Technology Management, 34*(3/4), 390. https://doi.org/10.1504/ijtm.2006.009466

Bovey, W. H., & Hede, A. (2001). Resistance to organizational change: The role of cognitive and affective processes. *Leadership & Organization Development Journal, 22*(8), 372–382. https://doi.org/10.1108/01437730110410099

Callaghan Innovation. (2022, November 18). *Manufacturing & Industry 4.0.* https://www.callaghaninnovation.govt.nz/industry-4

Campbell, A. (2019, February 7). *Why good leaders make bad decisions.* Harvard Business Review. https://hbr.org/2009/02/why-good-leaders-make-bad-decisions

De Bono, E. (1985). *Six thinking hats: An essential approach to business management* (Revised and Updated). Little Brown and Company.

De Silva, R., Bayliss, K., Riste, L., & Chew-Graham, C. A. (2013). Diagnosing chronic fatigue syndrome in south Asians: Lessons from a secondary analysis of a UK qualitative study. *Journal of Family Medicine and Primary Care, 2*(3), 277–282(PMC3902687). https://doi.org/10.4103/2249-4863.120765

Edwards, K. A., Classen, G. A., & Schroten, E. H. J. (1983). The water resource in tropical Africa and its exploitation. *ILCA research report no. 6 international livestock Centre for Africa, 6.* https://cgspace.cgiar.org/rest/rest/bitstreams/88e59f9a-8a9a-4cb3-8ee8-d25f313c7987/retrieve

Elkington, J. (2018, September 13). *25 years ago I coined the phrase "Triple Bottom Line."* Here's why it's time to rethink it. Harvard Business Review. https://hbr.org/2018/06/25-years-ago-i-coined-the-phrase-triple-bottom-line-heres-why-im-giving-up-on-it

Etherington, D. (2021, March 1). *Rocket Lab to go public via SPAC at valuation of $4.1 billion.* TechCrunch. Retrieved October 10, 2022, from https://techcrunch.com/2021/03/01/rocket-lab-to-go-public-via-spac-at-valuation-of-4-1-billion/

European Union – European Commission. (n.d.). Corporate sustainability reporting. Finance. https://finance.ec.europa.eu/capital-markets-union-and-financial-markets/company-reporting-and-auditing/company-reporting/corporate-sustainability-reporting_en

Fava, F. M. (2022, June 9). *Plastic pollution in the ocean: Data, facts, consequences*. Ocean Literacy Portal. Retrieved October 8, 2022, from https://oceanliteracy.unesco.org/plastic-pollution-ocean/

Flinn, J. (2022). *Greensight: The sustainability guide for company directors*. McCrae Boulevard Publishing.

Fordham, A. E., & Robinson, G. M. (2018). Mapping meanings of corporate social responsibility – An Australian case study. *International Journal of Corporate Social Responsibility, 3*(1). https://doi.org/10.1186/s40991-018-0036-1

Frothingham, M. B. (2021, October 6). *Fight, flight, freeze, or fawn: How we respond to threats*. Retrieved October 9, 2022, from https://www.simplypsychology.org/fight-flight-freeze-fawn.html

Gallup, Inc. (2022, September 23). *State of the global workplace report – Gallup*. Gallup.com. Retrieved October 3, 2022, from https://www.gallup.com/workplace/349484/state-of-the-global-workplace-2022-report.aspx

Gillan, S. L., Koch, A., & Starks, L. T. (2020, September 9). Firms and social responsibility: A Review of ESG and CSR research in corporate finance. https://sites.pitt.edu/~awkoch/CSR%20review%20JCF.pdf

Haller, K., Lee, J., & Cheung, J. (2020, June). *2020 consumers driving change*. IBM. https://www.ibm.com/thought-leadership/institute-business-value/report/consumer-2020

Hanh, T. N. (2011). *Peace is every breath: A practice for our busy lives* (First Printing). HarperOne.

Hanh, T. N. (n.d.). *Key teachings*. Plum Village. Retrieved October 8, 2022, from https://plumvillage.org/thich-nhat-hanh/key-teachings/

Harmsworth, G. R., & Awatere, S. (2013). Indigenous māori knowledge and perspectives of ecosystems. In *Ecosystem Services in New Zealand – Conditions and Trends* (pp. 74–286). Manaaki Whenua Press. https://www.researchgate.net/publication/258423762_Harmsworth_GR_Awatere_S_2013_Indigenous_Maori_knowledge_and_perspectives_of_ecosystems_In_Dymond_JR_ed_Ecosystem_services_in_New_Zealand_-_conditions_and_trends_Manaaki_Whenua_Press_Lincoln_New_Zealan

Hendery, S. (2017, June 30). *National Portrait: Peter Beck – NZ space pioneer once mocked for his vision*. Stuff. Retrieved October 10, 2022, from https://www.stuff.co.nz/business/industries/93375532/national-portrait-peter-beck%2D%2Dspace-pioneer

Hodgkinson, G. P., & Healey, M. P. (2008). Cognition in organizations. *Annual Review of Psychology, 59*(1), 387–417. https://doi.org/10.1146/annurev.psych.59.103006.093612

Hondzel, C. D., & Gulliksen, M. S. (2015). Culture and creativity: Examining variations in divergent thinking within Norwegian and Canadian communities. SAGE Open, 5 1–13. https://doi.org/10.1177/2158244015611448

Hwang, C. (2016). Unbundled bargains: Multi-agreement dealmaking in complex mergers and acquisitions. *University of Pennsylvania Law Review, 164*(6), 1403–1451. https://scholarship.law.upenn.edu/cgi/viewcontent.cgi?article=9529&context=penn_law_review

IMF. (2021, October 15). *Regional economic outlook for Asia and Pacific,* October 2021. https://www.imf.org/en/Publications/REO/APAC/Issues/2021/10/15/regional-economic-outlook-for-asia-and-pacific-october-2021

Jackson, R. H., & Rosberg, C. G. (1985). Democracy in tropical Africa: Democracy versus autocracy in African politics. *Journal of International Affairs, 38*(2), 293–305. https://www.jstor.org/stable/24356915?read-now=1#page_scan_tab_contents

James Cook University. (2022). COVID-19 in the tropics – A– state of the tropics report 2022. *A State of the Tropics Report*. https://www.jcu.edu.au/__data/assets/pdf_file/0003/1973703/SOTT-Report-2022_web.pdf

James Cook University Australia. (2020). *State of the Tropics – Urbanisation*. Retrieved October 6, 2022, from https://www.jcu.edu.au/state-of-the-tropics/earth-system-snapshot/urbanisation2

Japanese Zen Buddhist Philosophy (Stanford Encyclopedia of Philosophy). (2019, July 31). Retrieved October 9, 2022, from https://plato.stanford.edu/entries/japanese-zen/

Jowf, A. G., Ahmed, Z. T., An, N., Reijnders, R. A., Ambrosino, E., Rutten, B. P. F., De Nijs, L., & Eijssen, L. M. T. (2022, May). A public health perspective of post-traumatic stress disorder. MDPI. Retrieved October 9, 2022, from https://www.mdpi.com/1660-4601/19/11/6474/htm

Kain, M., & Hinojosa, V. (2020, April). *Ancestral wisdom and COVID-19*. UN Sustainable Development Knowledge Platform. Retrieved September 30, 2022, from https://sustainabledevelopment.un.org/content/documents/26117Dr_Cunningham_Article.pdf

Kaya, M. (2013). The effect of six thinking hats on student success in teaching subjects related to sustainable development in geography classes. *Educational Sciences: Theory & Practice, 13*(2), 1134–1139. http://files.eric.ed.gov/fulltext/EJ1017274.pdf

Kniberg, H., & Ivarsson, A. (2012, October). *ScalingAgile@Spotify: With Tribes, Squads, Chapters & Guilds*. http://www.agileleanhouse.com. Retrieved February 12, 2023, from http://www.agileleanhouse.com/lib/lib/People/HenrikKniberg/SpotifyScaling.pdf

Kuo, K., Yu, H., Lu, W., & Le, T. (2022). Sustainability and corporate performance: Moderating role of environmental, social, and governance Investments in the Transportation Sector. *Sustainability, 14*(7), 4095. https://doi.org/10.3390/su14074095

Lebreton, L. C. M. (2017, June 7). River plastic emissions to the world's oceans. *Nature*. Retrieved October 1, 2022, from https://www.nature.com/articles/ncomms15611

Lu, Y., Jingjing, Y., Lu, X., Su, C., Zhang, Y., Wang, C., Cao, X., Li, Q., Su, J., Ittekkot, V., Garbutt, R. M., Bush, S. R., Fletcher, S. P., Wagey, T., Kachur, A., & Sweijd, N. (2018). Major threats of pollution and climate change to global coastal ecosystems and enhanced management for sustainability. *Environmental Pollution, 239*, 670–680. https://doi.org/10.1016/j.envpol.2018.04.016

Maslow, A. H. (1943). A theory of human motivation. *Psychological Review, 50*, 370–396. https://link.springer.com/referenceworkentry/10.1007/978-0-387-79061-9_1720

Mbokazi, A. J. (2006). Hypertension: Common patient presentations in the developing world. *CME: Your SA Journal of CPD, 24*(5), 232–236. https://journals.co.za/doi/10.10520/EJC63137

Medina, M. (2010, August). *How things work: Environmental satellites – Our world*. Retrieved October 10, 2022, from https://ourworld.unu.edu/en/how-things-work-environmental-satellites

Meyer, M. A., & Kamaka, M. L. (2019). New, old wisdom—Sprituality, creativity and science reimagined: Ancestral wisdom for these times. *Educational Perspectives, 50*(1), 45–53. https://files.eric.ed.gov/fulltext/EJ1217472.pdf

Munduate, L., & Gravenhorst, K. M. B. (2003). Power dynamics and organisational change: An introduction. *Applied Psychology, 52*(1), 1–13. https://doi.org/10.1111/1464-0597.00120

Munier, D. A. (2021, September 28). The 6Fs of trauma responses. *NeuroClastic*. Retrieved October 9, 2022, from https://neuroclastic.com/the-6fs-of-trauma-responses/

Newman, C., Rand, J., Tarp, F., & Trifkovic, N. (2020). Corporate social responsibility in a competitive business environment. *The Journal of Development Studies, 56*(8), 1455–1472. https://doi.org/10.1080/00220388.2019.1694144

Niyommaneerat, W., Suwanteep, K., & Chavalparit, O. (2023). Sustainability indicators to achieve a circular economy: A case study of renewable energy and plastic waste recycling corporate social responsibility (CSR) projects in Thailand. *Journal of Cleaner Production, 391*, 136203. https://www.sciencedirect.com/science/article/abs/pii/S095965262300361X

Noji, T. (2019). *Toyota Monogatari* (X. Chan, Trans.; 1st ed.). EcoTrend Publications.

NZ Transport Agency. (2019, March 12). *Hackathon looks for ways to get solo drivers into new travel behaviours*. Waka Kotahi NZ Transport Agency. Retrieved October 6, 2022, from https://www.nzta.govt.nz/media-releases/hackathon-looks-for-ways-to-get-solo-drivers-into-new-travel-behaviours/

Oxford Economics. (2021, April). *How business leaders can raise their Digital IQ*. PwC. https://www.pwc.com/us/en/tech-effect/cloud/digital-iq.html

Patel, M., Swift, S., & Digesu, A. (2021). Mental health among clinicians: What do we know and what can we do? *International Urogynecology Journal, 32*(5), 1055–1059. https://doi.org/10.1007/s00192-021-04805-y

Pieris, A., & King, S. (2017). Tropical zone: People, practices and pedagogies. *Fabrications, 27*(2), 131–133. https://doi.org/10.1080/10331867.2017.1327788

PricewaterhouseCoopers. (2021a, March). *Auckland Transport's COVID-19 response review.* Auckland Transport. https://at.govt.nz/media/1985826/at-covid-19-response-review-final-report.pdf

PricewaterhouseCoopers. (2021b, June). *PwC's global consumer insights survey 2021.* PwC. https://www.pwc.com/gx/en/consumer-markets/consumer-insights-survey/2021/gcis-june-2021.pdf

Process Excellence Network. (2022, November 29). *PEX Report 2023 global state of process excellence.* https://www.processexcellencenetwork.com/business-transformation/reports/pex-report-global-state-process-excellence

Raudenbush, D. T. (2012). Race and interactions on public transportation: Social cohesion and the production of common norms and a collective black identity. *Symbolic Interaction, 35*(4), 456–473. https://doi.org/10.1002/symb.36

Roosevelt, T. (1910). *Man in the arena.* TR Center. Retrieved November 9, 2022, from https://www.theodorerooseveltcenter.org/Learn-About-TR/TR-Encyclopedia/Culture-and-Society/Man-in-the-Arena.aspx

Rust, E. G. (1919). Centralization versus decentralization in management: Modern manufacturing. A partnership of idealism and common sense. *The Annals of the American Academy of Political and Social Science, 85*, 100–109. https://www.jstor.org/stable/1013936

Sadiq, M., Adil, M., & Paul, J. (2021). An innovation resistance theory perspective on purchase of eco-friendly cosmetics. *Journal of Retailing and Consumer Services, 59*, 102369. https://doi.org/10.1016/j.jretconser.2020.102369

Sarfraz, Z., Sarfraz, A., Iftikar, H. M., & Akhund, R. (2021). Is COVID-19 pushing us to the fifth industrial revolution (society 5.0)? *Pakistan Journal of Medical Sciences, 37*(2), 591. https://doi.org/10.12669/pjms.37.2.3387

Saxena, A., Singh, R., Gehlot, A., Akram, S. V., Twala, B., Singh, A., Montero, E. C., & Priyadarshi, N. (2022). Technologies empowered environmental, social, and governance (ESG): An industry 4.0 landscape. *Sustainability, 15*(1), 309. https://doi.org/10.3390/su15010309

Shao, Y., Zhang, C., Zhou, J., Gu, T., & Yuan, Y. (2019). How does culture shape creativity? A mini-review. *Frontiers in Psychology, 10*, 1219. https://doi.org/10.3389/fpsyg.2019.01219

Sharma, S., Kundu, A., Basu, S., Shetti, N. P., & Aminabhavi, T. M. (2020). Sustainable environmental management and related biofuel technologies. *Journal of Environmental Management, 273*, 111096. https://doi.org/10.1016/j.jenvman.2020.111096

Silva, J. A. (2022). Implementation and integration of sustainability in the water industry: A systematic literature review. *Sustainability, 14*(23), 15919. https://doi.org/10.3390/su142315919

Smith, N. (2017, January 29). *Why Latin America and Africa struggle to grow.* BQ Prime. https://www.bqprime.com/amp/markets/why-latin-america-and-africa-struggle-to-grow

Smith, P. D. (2018, February 22). *A Monk's guide to a clean house and mind review – Buddhist housekeeping.* The Guardian. Retrieved October 26, 2022, from https://www.theguardian.com/books/2018/jan/05/a-monks-guide-to-a-clean-house-and-mind-review-shoukei-matsumoto-buddhist

Sondh, K. (2021, April). *In the 5th Industrial Revolution, creativity must meet technology.* https://blog.oxfordeconomics.com/world-post-covid/in-the-5th-industrial-revolution-creativity-must-meet-technology

SpaceX. (2022). *Mission.* Retrieved October 10, 2022, from https://www.spacex.com/mission/

Stuckenbruck, L. C. (1979, September). *The matrix organization.* Project Management Institute. https://www.pmi.org/learning/library/matrix-organization-structure-reason-evolution-1837

Trim, J. N. (2020). *Ancestral wisdom and spiritual practices for healing: Decolonizing feminist theory and pedagogy.* ScholarWorks @ Georgia State University. Retrieved October 1, 2022, from https://scholarworks.gsu.edu/wsi_theses/80/

Tuckman, B. W. (1965). Developmental sequence in small groups. *Psychological Bulletin, 63*(6), 384–399.

Tupper, M. F. (n.d.). *A quote by Martin Farquhar Tupper*. https://www.goodreads.com/quotes/537430-a-spark-is-a-little-thing-yet-it-may-kindle

UNECE. (2021, February 25). *Countries endorse UNECE Roadmap to strengthen harmonization of Intelligent Transport Systems | UNECE*. https://unece.org/sustainable-development/press/countries-endorse-unece-roadmap-strengthen-harmonization-intelligent

United Nations – CEPAL. (1999, December). *Open regionalism in Asia Pacific and Latin America: A survey of the literature*. www.cepal.org. https://www.cepal.org/sites/default/files/publication/files/4380/S9900674_es.pdf

United Nations Environment Programme. (n.d.). *Where does waste go on a small island?* UNEP. https://www.unep.org/news-and-stories/story/where-does-waste-go-small-island

United Nations Industrial Development Organization [UNIDO]. (n.d.). *What is CSR?* https://www.unido.org/our-focus/advancing-economic-competitiveness/competitive-trade-capacities-and-corporate-responsibility/corporate-social-responsibility-market-integration/what-csr

Vallance, S., Perkins, H. C., & Dixon, J. E. (2011). What is social sustainability? A clarification of concepts. *Geoforum, 42*(3), 342–348. https://doi.org/10.1016/j.geoforum.2011.01.002

Van Trotsenburg, A., & Lim, J. H. (2022, July 22). *Turning the tide on plastic pollution through regional collaboration in Southeast Asia*. World Bank Blogs. Retrieved September 28, 2022, from https://blogs.worldbank.org/eastasiapacific/turning-tide-plastic-pollution-through-regional-collaboration-southeast-asia

Vervaeke, J. (2013, July 20). *Neuroenlightenment: John Vervaeke at TEDxUofT* [Video]. TEDx University of Toronto. https://www.youtube.com/watch?v=qKvRUfZ_u1o

Virgin Galactic. (n.d.). *The Spaceline for earth*. Virgin.com. Retrieved October 10, 2022, from https://www.virgin.com/virgin-companies/virgin-galactic

Vitalari, N., & Shaughnessy, H. (2012). *The elastic Enterprise: The new manifesto for business revolution*. Telemachus Press, LLC.

Waka Kotahi NZ Transport Agency. (n.d.-a). *Benchmarking Sustainable Urban Mobility*. Retrieved October 6, 2022, from https://www.nzta.govt.nz/assets/resources/sustainable-urban-mobility-benchmarking/sustainable-urban-mobility-benchmarking-report.pdf

Waka Kotahi NZ Transport Agency. (n.d.-b). *Keeping cities moving | Waka Kotahi NZ Transport Agency*. Retrieved October 6, 2022, from https://www.nzta.govt.nz/walking-cycling-and-public-transport/keeping-cities-moving/

Wansink, B., & Sobal, J. (2007). Mindless eating: The 200 daily food decisions we overlook. *Sage Journals, 39*(1), 106–123. https://journals.sagepub.com/doi/abs/10.1177/0013916506295573

World Bank Group. (2022, June 27). *World Bank approves US>0 million regional Grant for ASEAN to combat marine plastic pollution in Southeast Asia*. World Bank. Retrieved October 1, 2022, from https://www.worldbank.org/en/news/press-release/2022/06/22/world-bank-approves-us-20-million-regional-grant-for-asean-to-combat-marine-plastic-pollution-in-southeast-asia

World Health Organization. (2022, June 17). *World mental Health report*. Retrieved October 3, 2022, from https://www.who.int/teams/mental-health-and-substance-use/world-mental-health-report

Yang, J. (2022, September 29). *From concept to practice: Digital twins to City twins*. Harvard Data-Smart City Solutions. https://datasmart.ash.harvard.edu/concept-practice-digital-twins-city-twins

Yip, C. W. K. (2022). *Power up: How to improve productivity and Innovation*. C Why International Ltd.

Chapter 6
Exploring the Role of Trust, Competence, and Likability in Fostering Workplace Relations

Smita Singh and Patrick K. F. Lin

Abstract Undergraduate participants (N = 240) learned about the competence (low *vs.* high) and likability (low *vs.* high) of a possible working partner and indicated their trust and attraction toward the partner. Results showed that work attraction was higher towards a likable work partner than a competent one, indicating that the effect of likability was superior to that of competence. Furthermore, trust completely mediated the likability-work attraction link but not the competence-work attraction link, indicating that work attraction was due to the partner's likability via trust activation. Finally, the theoretical implications of mediators for likability and competence are discussed in the present study.

Keywords Trust · Competence · Likability · Workplace relations · Mediator · Attraction · Coworker

6.1 Introduction

It is crucial to like one's workplace. A well-liked workplace can be summed up as a nurturing environment where mutual admiration is the norm. Coworkers here share a supportive, helpful, and cooperative relationship. Ethical organisational leadership is linked with positive employee relations (Jha & Singh, 2019). Such relationships are established when leaders influence collaboration and engagement and facilitate *Camaraderie* at work (p. 155; Burchell & Robin, 2011). Camaraderie brings meaningfulness to work relations. This can be referred to as critical social capital in the workplace. Putnam (2000) explains social capital as "connections among individuals, social networks, and the norms of reciprocity and trustworthiness that arise from them." Trust is, therefore, fundamental for work relations

S. Singh (✉) · P. K. F. Lin
School of Social and Health Sciences, James Cook University, Singapore, Singapore
e-mail: smita.singh@jcu.edu.au; patrick.lin@jcu.edu.au

E. L. Eijdenberg et al. (eds.), *Innovation-Driven Business and Sustainability in the Tropics*, https://doi.org/10.1007/978-981-99-2909-2_6

to thrive. Trusting coworkers brings authenticity to work relationships, enhances social networks (Stolle & Rochon, 1998), and positively relates to social well-being (Klein, 2013).

6.1.1 Warmth and Competence in the Judgments of Others

As established in social cognition literature, trust falls under the warmth dimension of social judgment. The warmth dimension also encompasses empathy, benevolence, sincerity, friendliness, likability, and morality (Fiske et al., 2007; Abele et al., 2008). While warmth (communion) is considered fundamental in establishing any social relations, competence (agentic), which is the second dimension of social judgment, is deemed necessary, as it captures our evaluation of others' capabilities in terms of their skills, expertise, or talent to achieve success (Fiske et al., 2007).

Warmth and competence dimensions have a significant historical foundation, especially in group relations and organisational settings. Bales (1950) categorized leadership into these two dimensions socio-emotional (warmth-oriented) and task (competence) oriented. These two dimensions are also important in voters' judgement of election outcomes or party leaders' evaluations (Cornwell et al., 2015; Ferreira Da Silva & Costa, 2019; Todorov et al., 2005). In a study by Wojciszke et al. (2009), working professionals were asked to form impressions of their work supervisors. Results indicated these impressions centered on the dimensions of warmth and competence. In addition, past studies have shown that people are attracted to strangers (Willis, 1978), colleagues (Watson et al., 2004), friends (Baron, 1985), and romantic partners (Donnellan et al., 2005) who possess the competence- and warm-related traits.

To sum up, warmth and competence are universal in person or group perception and ubiquitous in every domain. Warmth underlies one's intent, guiding us in our evaluation of a possible friend or foe (Fiske et al., 2007). Often reported, warmth judgment is more important than competence, as it has a more significant impact on our perceptions of others (Wojciszke et al., 2009), as these are considered to be more beneficial for others, consistent with the 'other-profitable trait' concept by Peeters and Czapinski (1990) and is also more stable (Kenworthy & Tausch, 2008). However, when we have self-profit in mind, competence becomes more important than warmth (Damodaran et al., 2017).

6.1.1.1 Competence Versus Likability

Casciaro and Lobo (2005) studied work relationships in the West. Results from various work setting (banking, small and medium business, information technology, and government sector) showed that people were most attracted to the "lovable star" (i.e., a colleague high in competence and likability) and most repulsed by the "incompetent jerk (i.e., a colleague low in competence and likability). Interestingly, when people want to have the job done, they prefer the "lovable fool" (i.e., a colleague low in competence but high in likability) to the "competent jerk" (i.e., a colleague high in competence but low in likability). Casciaro and Lobo (2005) explained the dominance of likability over competence in work attraction by stating,

> ... if someone is strongly disliked, it's almost irrelevant whether or not she is competent; people won't want to work with her anyway. By contrast, if someone is liked, his colleagues seek out every bit of competence he has to offer a little extra likability goes a longer way than a little extra competence in making someone desirable to work with (p. 94).

However, such conclusions from survey studies had two weaknesses: (1) The direction of causality was uncertain, and (2) the meaning of competence and likability was ambiguous to participants. To overcome these two problems, Singh and Tor (2008) experimentally manipulated competence and likability in a 2 × 2 between-participant design and defined competence as the "general intellectual capability of the individual" and likability as "how much others enjoyed being around that particular individual" (p. 9). Eighty participants were randomly assigned to one of the four conditions. Then, they examined the competence and likability levels of the working partner and answered the 10-item attraction questionnaire (Montoya & Horton, 2004; Singh et al., 2008). Results from Singh and Tor's experiment were consistent with Casciaro and Lobo's (2005) findings. Thus, work attraction is driven by likability (i.e., lovable fool) and not competence (i.e., competent jerk), reinstating the preference for lovable fools.

Work-related relationships often comprise affective components (Roethlisberger & Dickson, 1939). In Casciaro and Lobo's (2008) study, social network data from employees of different organisational backgrounds (academic institutions, entrepreneurial computers, and information technology firms) indicated that even for task-related networking, people needed 'active liking' (p. 678). Negative affect toward a target was a dominant factor for rejecting a competent resource. To seek out a coworker, s/he has to be liked. So, affect, the warmth aspect of judgment precedes work interaction.

Trust in the Judgment of Competence and Likability

Trust is imperative in any relationship. For example, trust in work relations entails "...others will not take advantage of me" (Porter et al., 1975, p. 497). Recent studies of close relationships have also found that trust is an important mediator in interpersonal attraction (e.g., Cottrell et al., 2007; Montoya & Insko, 2008; Singh et al., 2009, 2015; Singh, et al., 2017a; Wojciszke et al., 2009).

Interpersonal attraction studies of other information-attraction links such as similar *vs.* dissimilar attitudes (Byrne, 1971; Singh et al., 2007b), warmth *vs.* cold traits (Fiske et al., 2007; Wojciszke, 2005), good *vs.* bad evaluations (Blead et al., 1973; Byrne & Clore, 1970; Wentura et al., 2000), other-profitable *vs.* self-profitable traits (Abele & Wojciszke, 2007; Peeters & Czapinski, 1990; Vonk, 1999), and communal *vs.* agency dimensions (Buhrmester, 1996; Wojciszke et al., 2009) have also found that trust is a mediator in these attraction links (Rempel et al., 1985; Rempel et al., 2001; Wieselquist, 2009; Wieselquist et al., 1999). In Wojciszke et al. (2009) study, for example, Polish university students were presented with positive and negative communal (e.g., forgiving, helpful, unkind, egoistic) and agency (e.g., organised, efficient, thoughtless, ambitionless) traits of a target person and asked to respond to the measure of trust, status potential, attraction, and respect. Mediation and path analysis results showed that the status potential mediated the impact of agency traits on respect, but communal traits-attraction was mediated by trust.

Singh et al. (2009) also found trust to mediate the information-attraction link. In their Study 2, participants were given profiles of their working partner that showed the partner's self-profitable (e.g., intelligent *vs.* unintelligent) and other-profitable (e.g., sincere *vs.* irresponsible) traits in the typical bogus stranger paradigm (Byrne, 1961). They were asked to form an impression of the partners. Results showed that trust completely mediated the other-profitable trait-attraction relationship but partially mediated the self-profitable trait-attraction relationship. Trust has emerged as a mediator in the attitude similarity-attraction link. Trust was studied along with other variables like respect, positive affect, inferred attraction, and validation. Trust in the partner emerged as one of the strongest mediators (Singh et al., 2015; Singh, Wegener, et al., 2017b). Thus, trust can be considered a possible mediator in the competence-attraction and likability-attraction links.

In work-related domains, warmth, which consists of trust and likability, is seen as imperative for effective leadership practices (see Cuddy et al., 2011). For example, Falvo et al. (2016) investigated the association between employees' basic needs and leader's perceived warmth and competence. There was a dominance of warmth over competence. Further, the supervisor was perceived as supportive, friendly, and trustworthy, fostering a high organisational commitment among employees. The findings of Oleszkiewicz and Lachowicz-Tabaczek (2016) further highlight the importance of social dimensions of warmth and competence in organisational settings. Competence and warmth measures have influenced managers' respect, liking, and trust. A warm manager was trusted, liked, and respected by the coworkers more than the cold one. A competent supervisor was more respected than an incompetent supervisor. However, this study did not establish a distinction among the constructs of liking, trust, and respect. Furthermore, trust is important in organisational setting for reinforcing positive employee well-being and performance outcomes (Baptiste, 2008). In a study by Rubel et al. (2018), trust in management was found to be a significant mediator between high-commitment human resource management and individual performance outcome.

As indicated in the discussion above, trust has been a significant intervening variable driving positive organizational outcomes. Therefore, it is imperative to assess its importance in establishing work relationships. In this study, we explore the importance of trust in the likability versus competence-work attraction link. Specifically, we examine how trust functions in a competent coworker rather than a lovable coworker.

6.2 Present Study

Casciaro and Lobo's (2005) results indicated that work colleagues could be divided into four archetypes based on their high and low levels of competence and likability. Given the preceding evidence on the importance of trust, we hypothesized that (Hypothesis 1) trust would mediate the likability-work attraction relationship fully, (Hypothesis 2) but the competence-work attraction relationship partially. Our rationale was that likability is a hot-affect-driven variable (Singh et al., 2007a) and is conceptually closer to the *other-profitable* and *communal* attributes. Hence, likability is more important than competence. Further, because of this supremacy of likability over competence (Casciaro & Lobo, 2005; Singh & Tor, 2008), we believe that the 'lovable star' (i.e., individual high on likability and competence) will be more attractive than a 'lovable-fool' (i.e., individual high on likability but low in competence) or a 'competent-jerks' (i.e., individuals low in likability and high in competence); however, the lovable-star and lovable-fool will be equally trusted.

6.2.1 Method

6.2.1.1 Participants

An a priori power analysis was conducted. We targeted a medium effect size with .90 power. Hence, 240 psychology undergraduates (163 women, 77 men, $M_{age} = 23.96$, $SD = 7.21$)) from James Cook University Singapore campus were recruited to participate in the "partner and work attraction study" in partial fulfillment of their course requirements.

6.2.1.2 Design

The design was a 2 (likability: high *vs.* low) x 2 (competence: high *vs.* low) x 2 (order of information presentation: competence-likability order *vs.* likability-competence ordering) between-participants factorial. Participants were randomly assigned to one of the eight conditions (*n*s = 30 per cell).

6.2.1.3 Materials

Each participant received a set of questionnaires that contained information about (a) the possible coworker's competence and likability levels and (b) the Impression Formation Scale (IFS). Partner's likability and competence information were counterbalanced to control for order effects.

Partner's profile

The partner's levels of competence and likability were indicated by two bell-shaped curves. For example, a lovable star would have the bell shape curve that the partner's competence would be +2 above the general population and likability would be +2 above the general population, and a competent jerk would have the bell shape curve that the partner's competence is +2 above general population and likability is −2 below the general population. Figure 6.1 demonstrates the sample of a competent jerk. The definitions of competence and likability used in the present study were identical to those in Singh and Tor (2008).

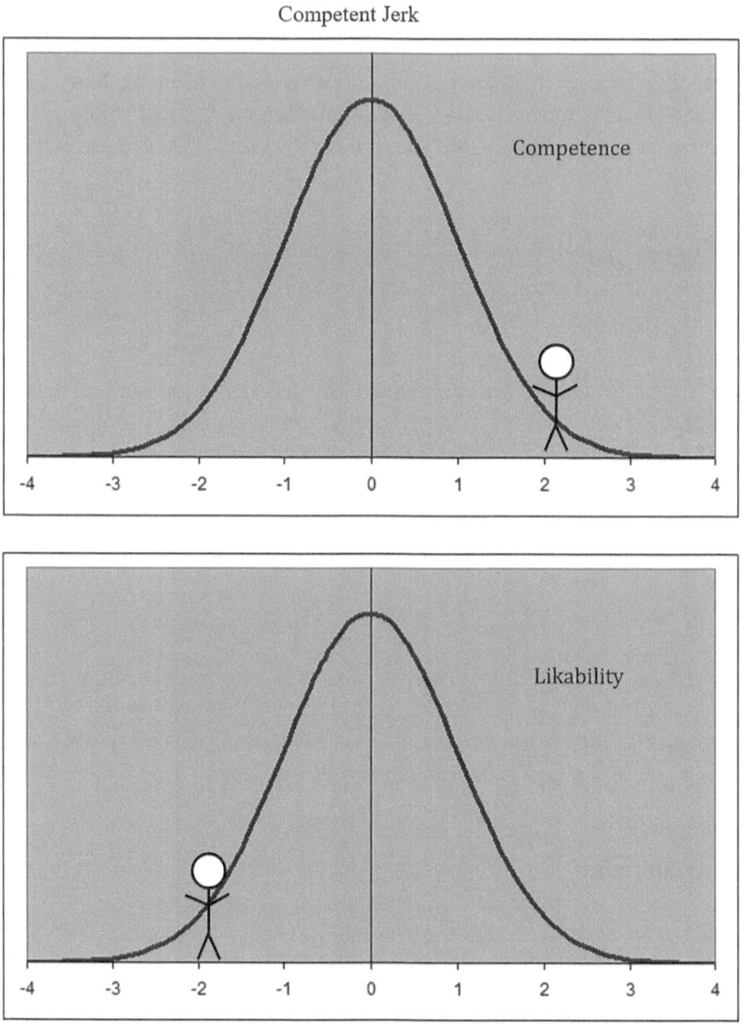

Fig. 6.1 Sample of competent Jerk working partner: The bell shape curve indicates the partner's competence is +2 above general population and Likability is −2 below general population

IFS

IFS consisted of six trust items (e.g., *My interaction partner would look out for my interest*) (Singh et al., 2009), eight work attraction items (e.g., *I look forward to working on the upcoming task with my future interaction partner*) (Singh et al., 2007a), and six filler items (e.g., *This interaction partner is someone I would consider reliable*). The filler items were interspersed with the trust and work attraction items. However, the trust items always preceded the work attraction ones.

6.2.1.4 Procedure

The study first obtained ethical clearance from the human research ethics committee (HREC) at James Cook University (H7113). Participants were invited to the research lab and made to believe that they would be working together with an unknown partner on a cooperative task (i.e., related to their university course). They were told to read through the partner's information carefully as this person could help him/her to succeed in future task. After they had done so, two questions of manipulation checks (i.e., do you think this person is likable and do you think this person is competent) were given on 7-point scales (*1 = extremely below average, 7 = extremely above average*) to make sure that participants understood their partners level of competence and likableness in the bell shape curves. Then, they were asked to form an impression of the partner and record their responses (i.e., IFS) on 7-point scale (1 = *strongly disagree*, 7 = *strongly agree)*. The experiment ended with debriefing, and the participants were informed there was no cooperative task in the study.

6.2.2 Results

6.2.2.1 Factor Analysis and Reliability

To reconfirm the construct distinction between trust and work attraction, we conducted a principal component factor analysis with varimax rotation was conducted for the IFS. Assumptions for the factor analysis were met: the Kaiser-Meyer-Olkin (KMO) index was .93, and Bartlett's Test of Sphericity was significantly different ($p < .001$). As indicated in Table 6.1, trust and work attraction items in the IFS were two distinct factors. The six trust items tapped the participants' belief that the partner was *benevolent, reliable,* and *unselfish* (Gambetta, 1988; Montoya & Insko, 2008; Wojciszke et al., 2009), and the eight items of work attraction asked for the participant's intention to interact with the person, know the person more, and work with the person and hence tapped *work attraction* (Michinov & Monteil, 2002; Montoya & Insko, 2008). In addition, Cronbach's alpha reliability of *trust* and *work* attraction were .83 and .92, respectively.

Table 6.1 Principal component factor analysis in trust and work attraction items: Varimax rotation (N = 240)

Items	Factor 1	Factor 2
Factor 1: Trust		
T01: My interaction partner would look out for my interest.	0.30	**0.79**
T02: In any upcoming task, this interaction partner would act benevolent towards me	0.12	**0.81**
T06: This interaction partner would make me feel secure	0.35	**0.74**
T07: I would find this interaction partner to be a dependable person	0.46	**0.63**
T08: I would expect this interaction partner to play fair with me	0.39	**0.63**
T10: I expect to be able to confide in this interaction partner.	0.47	**0.55**
Factor 2: Work attraction		
A01: I would like to meet my future interaction partner.	**0.83**	0.23
A02: I look forward to meeting my future interaction partner.	**0.80**	0.32
A03: I would enjoy my future interaction partner's company.	**0.61**	0.29
A04: I would like my future interaction partner.	**0.65**	0.50
A05: I would like to get to know this person better.	**0.78**	0.29
A06: I look forward to working on the upcoming task with my future interaction partner.	**0.68**	0.47
A09: I would like to be with my interaction partner.	**0.65**	0.44
A10: I would enjoy discussing controversial topics with my future interaction partner.	**0.70**	0.19

6.2.2.2 Manipulation Checks

We used independent-sample *t*-tests to check whether the manipulations were successful. Competence was rated as higher when it was high ($M = 5.23$, $SD = 0.83$) than low ($M = 2.66$, $SD = 0.79$), $t(238) = 24.60$, $p < .001$. Likewise, likability was greater when it was high ($M = 5.23$, $SD = 0.79$) than low ($M = 2.62$, $SD = 0.75$), $t(238) = 26.44$, $p < .001$. Competence and likability were successfully manipulated in the study, and high and low levels of competence and likability were perceived as uniformly distant.

6.2.2.3 Preliminary Analysis

Two separate 2 (competence: high vs. low) × 2 (Likability: high vs. low) x 2 (order of information presentation: competence-likability order *vs.* likability-competence order) between-subjects analysis of variance (ANOVA) were conducted on attraction and trust. The results showed that the order of information presentation had no significant difference in trust and work attraction, $Fs(1, 232) < 0.13$, $ps > .72$, $\eta^2s < .005$. Since the effect of the order of information presentation had no impact on the study, it was removed for further analysis.

6.2.2.4 Main Analysis

Two separate 2 (competence: high vs. low) × 2 (Likability: high vs. low) between ANOVAs were performed, and the results revealed that when trust as the dependent variable (DV), high competence ($M = 4.08$, $SD = 0.95$) had a higher score than low competence ($M = 3.56$, $SD = 1.26$), $F(1, 236) = 21.83$, $p < .001$, $\eta^2 = .09$, and high Likability ($M = 4.50$, $SD = 0.80$) had a higher score than low Likability ($M = 3.13$, $SD = 1.02$), $F(1, 236) = 152.20$, $p < .001$, $\eta^2 = .39$.

Similarly, when work attraction is the DV, high competence ($M = 4.46$, $SD = 1.05$) had a higher score than low competence ($M = 3.81$, $SD = 1.13$), $F(1, 236) = 29.19$, $p < .001$, $\eta^2 = .11$, and high likability ($M = 4.71$, $SD = 0.84$) had a higher score than low Likability ($M = 3.56$, $SD = 1.11$), $F(1, 236) = 93.28$, $p < .001$, $\eta^2 = .28$.

The ANOVAs indicated that (1) high was always stronger than low in both competence and likability manipulations and (2) the effect of likability was always more superior than that of competence in both trust (i.e., $\eta^2 = .09 < \eta^2 = .39$) and work attraction (i.e.,$\eta^2 = .11 < \eta^2 = .28$).

Interaction Effect of Competence × Likability

The non-interaction effect in work attraction, $F(1, 236) = 1.44$, $p = .23$, $\eta^2 = .006$ and the interaction effect in trust, $F(1, 236) = 15.37$, $p < .001$, $\eta^2 = .06$ between competence x likability indicated that competence and likability were independent of each other in work attraction (Fig. 6.2, right graph), and the additive of convergent pattern in trust was due to the presence of high Likability (Fig. 6.2, left graph). Simply said, the likability effect added to the impact of competence (regardless of the level of competence).

To determine the differences between competent-jerk, lovable-fool, and lovable star, separated dummy coding was used in assigning the groups (i.e., competent-jerk

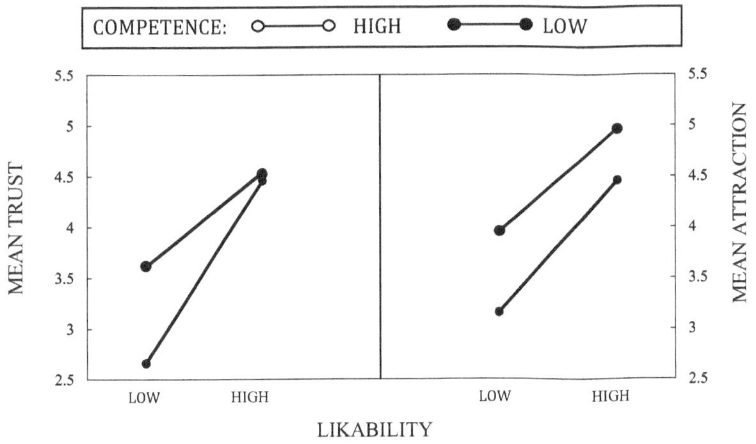

Fig. 6.2 The interaction effect of competence x likability in Trust is presented on the left and the non-interaction effect of competence x Likability in attraction is presented on the right side of the figure

coded as 0 *vs.* lovable-fool coded as 1; lovable-fool coded as 0 *vs.* lovable-star coded as 1). The first set of independent-sample *t*-tests results indicated that loveable-fool ($M = 4.46$, $SD = 0.89$) was more attracted, $t(118) = 2.79$, $p = .006$ than competent-jerk ($M = 3.95$, $SD = 1.10$) and lovable-fool ($M = 4.46$, $SD = 0.85$) was also more trusted than competent-jerk ($M = 3.61$, $SD = 0.94$), $t(118) = 5.10$, $p < .001$. More importantly, the second set of independent-samples *t*-tests results revealed that loveable-star ($M = 4.97$, $SD = 0.72$) was more attracted than lovable-fool ($M = 4.46$, $SD = 0.89$), $t(118) = 3.42$, $p = .001$, but lovable-star ($M = 4.54$, $SD = 0.71$) was equally trusted as a lovable fool ($M = 4.46$, $SD = 0.85$), $t(118) = 0.57$, $p = .57$. These results suggested that (1) lovable-star was the most preferred, lovable-fool was second preferred, and competent-jerk was least preferred in work attraction (Casciaro & Lobo, 2005; Singh & Tor, 2008), and (2) positivity bias occurred in Trust: Regardless of the levels of competence, likability was a more important determinant for Trust.

Mediation Analyses

Three separate mediation analyses were conducted by SPSS macro Model 4 (Hayes, 2012) to test Hypotheses 1 and 2. With work attraction as the DV, trust as the MV, likability, competence, and interaction (likability x competence). For clarity purposes, we presented only when likability is the main predictor in Fig. 6.3. Following the mediation model (Baron & Kenny, 1986), the macro simultaneously tested: (a) the effect of IV on the MV (i.e., mediator), (b) the effect of MV on the DV, (c) the total effect of IV on the DV, and (c') the direct effect of the IV on the DV when the MV was entered the model. The bias-corrected 95% CIs around the indirect effect of the IV through an MV (i.e., (a) x (b) = (c) – (c')) was also tested in the macro via the 5000 bootstrap re-sampling. If the biased corrected 95% CIs of the indirect effect from the bootstrap re-sampling excluded zero, then the MV was adjudged

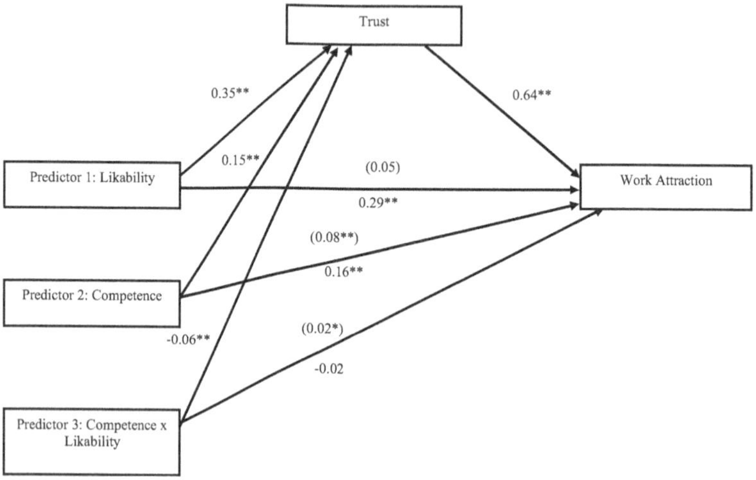

Fig. 6.3 The information-trust-attraction relationships

significant. Otherwise, the MV was considered nonsignificant (Williams & MacKinnon, 2008). In addition, complete and partial mediation when c' was nonsignificant and significant, respectively. All these calculations yielded unstandardized coefficients.

When likability was the main predictor, competence and the interaction were the covariates, likability predicted trust, (a) = 0.34, $t = 11.51$, $p < .001$, and work attraction, (c) = 0.29, $t = 9.13$, $p < .001$, and trust predicted work attraction, (b) = 0.74, $t = 14.25$, $p < .001$. The indirect effect of likability via trust was 0.25 and significantly excluded zero, 95% CIs: 0.20 to 0.31. The direct effect of likability on attraction was nonsignificant, (c') = 0.04, $t = 1.12$, $p = .26$. Therefore, trust was the mediator and completely mediated the likability-work attraction link. Hypothesis 1 was supported.

In contrast, when competence was the main predictor, likability and the interaction were the covariates, competence predicted trust, (a) = 0.13, $t = 3.59$, $p < .001$, and work attraction, (c) = 0.16, $t = 4.58$, $p < .001$, and trust predicted work attraction, (b) = 0.74, $t = 14.25$, $p < .001$. The indirect effect of competence via trust was 0.10 and was significantly excluding zero, 95% CIs: 0.06 to 0.15. The direct effect of competence on work attraction was significant, (c') = 0.06, $t = 2.77$, $p = .006$. Trust was one of the potential mediators and partially mediated the competence-work attraction link. Hypothesis 2 was supported.

Recall that likability had a more substantial impact than competence in work attraction. Our mediation result further showed that when the interaction (Likability x competence) was the main predictor, likability and competence were the covariates, interaction predicted trust, (a) = −0.05, $t = -3.92$, $p < .001$, but not work attraction, (c) = −0.02, $t = -1.20$, $p = .23$, and trust predicted work attraction, (b) = 0.74, $t = 14.25$, $p < .001$. The indirect effect of interaction via trust was −0.04 and was significantly excluding zero, 95% CIs: −0.06 to −0.02. On the other hand, the direct effect of the interaction on work attraction was significant, (c') = 0.02, $t = 1.94$, $p = .05$. Altogether, these mediations suggested that trust could function as a mediator when likability and competence were the main IVs. However, due to the reverse effect of direct effect to the total effect, the trust would be considered as a suppressor when the interaction (Likability x competence) is the main IV (MacKinnon et al., 2007).

Additional Mediation Analyses

To further understand how (and why) trust functioned as a suppressor when the likability interacted with competence, we did two additional mediation analyses to examine only lovable-fool and competent-jerk on work attraction via trust.

The results showed that lovable-fool predicted trust, (a) = 0.86, $t = 5.29$, $p < .001$, and work attraction, (c) = 0.44, $t = 2.60$, $p = .01$, and trust predicted work attraction, (b) = 0.82, $t = 19.90$, $p < .001$. The indirect effect of lovable-fool via trust was 0.70 and was significantly greater than zero, 95% CIs: 0.47 to 0.97. The direct effect of lovable fool on work attraction was significant, (c') = −0.27, $t = -2.45$, $p = .02$ (Fig. 6.4a). However, the effects of competent jerk were not significant on trust, (a) = −.28, $t = -1.63$, $p = .11$, and on work attraction (c) = −.24, $t = -1.44$, $p = .15$.

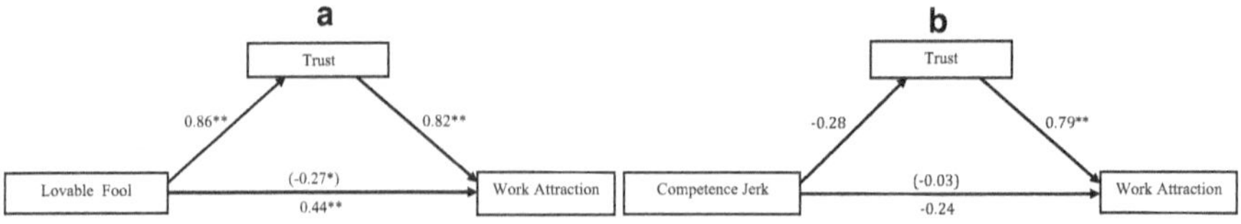

Fig. 6.4 The information-trust-attraction relationships of (**a**): Lovable fool-trust-attraction link; (**b**): Competent jerk-trust-attraction link.

Trust did not qualify as a mediator in the competent jerk-work attraction link (Fig. 6.4b). The ambivalent mediation effect of trust in the interaction between likability and competence could be because (a) trust was one of the potential mediators for lovable-fool, but not a mediator for a competent-jerk and (b) the mediating effect of trust was canceled out when both likability and competence were interacted (MacKinnon et al., 2007).

6.2.3 *Discussion*

The current study aimed to examine the mediational effect of trust in the work attraction relationship. Specifically, we believed that trust would completely mediate the likability-work attraction relationship, but it only partially mediates the competence-work attraction relationship. Due to the importance of likability over competence in work attraction (e.g., Singh & Tor, 2008), we further examined the interaction between likability and competence. We found that trust mediated the lovable fool-work attraction link but not the competent jerk-work attraction link.

6.2.3.1 Key Findings

The present study obtained four key findings. First, it established the construct distinction of trust and work attraction. Second, it confirmed the previous literature and indicated the preference for likability (Casciaro & Lobo, 2005) by showing the importance of likability over competence in work attraction (Singh & Tor, 2008). Third, the results indicated that high likability had an additive effect on driving workplace relations. Such positivity bias in trust could be seen in the convergent pattern but not in the parallel pattern in work attraction, as shown in Fig. 6.2. Fourth, regardless of the working partner's competence or incompetence, likability has an enhancing effect on competence.

In contrast, though likability was more important than competence, likability and competence were independent of each other in work attraction. This resonates closely with folk intuition and past literature, which has asserted a trade-off between likability and competence (Cuddy, 2009). This demonstration indicated that the most important attribute in Trust at work relationship was the partner's Likability, and his/her competence was simply a bonus (Casciaro & Lobo, 2005) or avoiding negative affect is imperative to increase cohesiveness and so to build work-related ties, coworker's warm traits would be preferred over his abilities (Casciaro & Lobo, 2008). Lastly, our mediation results demonstrated one novel role of Trust: The main effects of likability and competence on work attraction were not only *mediated* by trust but the interaction between them was also *suppressed* by trust. Recall that trust completely mediated the likability-work attraction relationship (Hypothesis 1) and partially mediated the competence-work attraction relationship (Hypothesis 2). However, when interaction was the main predictor of work attraction, trust suppressed the relationship. We further found that trust only partially mediated lovable-fool on work attraction but did not mediate competent-jerk. Trust as a mediator can be treated as a *facilitator* and an *inhibitor* in the information-trust-attraction relationships. As trust and work attraction are distinct constructs, these mediation results indicated that the interaction in trust had suppressed the interaction in work attraction.

6.2.3.2 Implications

Our study puts forth a comprehensive theoretical model for understanding workplace relations. The likability of a coworker is imperative. The present study showed that the effect of likability on work attraction was fully mediated via trust, but the competence-work attraction link was only partially mediated by trust. So it is worth highlighting from our finding that trust is predominantly associated with likability than with competency. A likable coworker is trusted automatically. Trust also means that the working partner will look after one's interest. With our results, we can say that this is a key driver for work relations. As stated earlier, trust brings positivity and meaningfulness to work. It adds belongingness and builds camaraderie at the workplace. For a nurturant work environment these are crucial and hence considered social capital (Hauser et al., 2016).

Results from the study imply that certain variables (i.e., IVs) are strongly attached to some particular mediator(s). More specifically, the hot-affect of other-profitable (and communion) type of variables such as kind, helpful, sincere, and likability robustly predict the activation of trust; therefore, trust always fully mediates the hot-affect of other-profitable/communal-attraction link (e.g., Singh et al., 2009; Wojciszke et al., 2009). Conversely, the cold-cognition of self-profitable (and agency) type of factors such as intelligence, confidence, organised, and competence are not strongly attached to trust; thus, trust only partially mediated the competence-work attraction relationship in the present study. Simply said, a more specific mediator or mediators is/are attached to the cold-cognition of self-profitable (and agency) type of variables.

In addition, our results emphasize strong characteristics of trust; that is, it may not be universally superior across every work-related domain, and therefore, it may not be wrong to consider it context-driven. So in situations where cohesiveness and low risks are involved, workers would prefer a *likable* coworker than an *able* coworker (Damodaran et al., 2017). However, the reverse would be true in opposite contexts. Belmi and Pfeffer's (2018) research, based on three studies ($N = 993$) indicated that in a context where economic returns are dependent on a coworker, the preference for competence would be high. Results showed that workers in more *reward interdependent* conditions indicated a higher priority for competent coworkers than sociable ones.

Similarly, in another recent research, we also found that if the task outcome had (a) a monetary reward to the participant or (b) affecting their status (e.g., GPA, position in an organisation), trust would have different mediational effect in work attraction link (Lin, Singh, & Tan, in preparation). Furthermore, the mediational effect of trust became uncertain in work relationships when the interaction partner's credibility was introduced, and/or the participants were economically self-sufficient (Lin, Singh, Chan, Choo, & Hsiao, in preparation). Hence, trust could have different impacts (as a mediator) depending on the independent variables connected to it. Another important contribution is that trust, attraction, and competence are reinstated as distinct constructs (Singh & Tor, 2008; Singh et al., 2009; Singh et al., 2015). The current work shows that trust is distinct from competence and emerged as the complete mediator for the likability and attraction link.

If trust is not the "designated mediator" in the competence-work attraction link, what other potential mediators exist? Previous studies have indicated that partner's respect (Singh et al., 2009), cognitive evaluation (Montoya & Horton, 2004), and status potential (Wojciszke et al., 2009) seemed to be the other potential mediators in the cold cognition of self-profitable-attraction relationship. Therefore, it is unwise only to consider one mediator in the attraction paradigm (Singh et al., 2007b).

According to Singh et al. (2007b) study on multiple mediators in the similarity-attraction link, the outcomes of the attraction link were strongly related to the number of mediators measured in the link. The results showed that when positive affect was introduced alone and with other mediators (i.e., cognitive evaluation and inferred attraction), the mediating effect of positive affect was significantly different. When it was alone, positive affect had a partial mediating effect in the similarity-attraction link. However, when positive affect was measured after and before inferred attraction in the multiple mediator design, it had no mediating impact in the former. It had a reverse mediating effect later in the similarity-attraction relationship.

6.2.3.3 Future Directions and Limitations

In the present study, there was only one mediator, trust, introduced in the work attraction link. Though trust completely mediated the likability-attraction link, the lack of mediating effect in the competence-attraction relationship suggested that other mediators were missing from the design. Therefore, when we introduce the multiple mediator design (Singh et al., 2007a), it is likely to find the specific mediator in the competence-attraction relationship. More importantly, we can identify each predictor's specific mediator in the attraction paradigm using the multiple mediator design. Thus, to show the complete picture of the mediation effect in the competence-attraction link, other potential mediators (i.e., respect, cognitive evaluation, and status) need to be considered as well.

The participants in this study lacked work experience in an organisational setting. However, in our research, student participants were assigned the role of organisational workers; it will be of merit to see whether their reactions are similar to participants with work experience. In addition, participants with work experience will have information about coworkers and an understanding of day-to-day organisational communication. This could be crucial information; therefore, future studies should include a sample of working employees as an additional participant pool.

6.2.3.4 Conclusion

Two conclusions can be drawn from the present study. First, it is confirmed that likability is superior to competence in building workplace relations. Second, trust is a complete mediator in the likability-attraction link and only a partial mediator in the competence-attraction relationship. Hence, trust is more crucial for a likable coworker.

References

Abele, A., & Wojciszke, B. (2007). Agency and communion from the perspective of self and others. *Journal of Personality and Social Psychology, 93*, 751–763. https://doi.org/10.1037/0022-3514.93.5.751

Abele, A. E., Cuddy, A. J. C., Judd, C. M., & Yzerbyt, V. Y. (2008). Fundamental dimensions of social judgment. *European Journal of Social Psychology, 38*(7), 1063–1065. https://doi.org/10.1002/ejsp.574

Bales, R. F. (1950). A set of categories for the analysis of small group interaction. *American Sociological Review, 15*, 257–263.

Baptiste, N. R. (2008). Tightening the link between employee well- being at work and performance: A new dimension for HRM. *Management Decision, 46*(2), 284–309.

Baron, R. A. (1985). Effects of negative ions on interpersonal attraction: Evidence for intensification. *Journal of Personality and Social Psychology, 52*, 547–553. https://doi.org/10.1037/0022-3514.52.3.547

Baron, R. M., & Kenny, D. A. (1986). The moderator-mediator variable distinction in social psychological research: Conceptual, strategic, and statistical considerations. *Journal of Personality and Social Psychology, 51*, 1173–1182. https://doi.org/10.1037/0022-3514.51.6.1173

Belmi, P., & Pfeffer, J. (2018). The effect of economic consequences on social judgment and choice: Reward interdependence and the preference for sociability versus competence. *Journal of Organisational Behaviour, 39*, 990–1007. https://doi.org/10.1002/job.2274

Blead, P. R., Bell, P. A., & Byrne, D. (1973). Prior induce affect and sex difference in attraction. *Memory and Cognition, 1*, 435–438.

Buhrmester, D. (1996). Need fulfillment, interpersonal competence, and the developmental contexts of early adolescent friendship. In W. M. Bukowski, A. F. Newcomb, & W. W. Hartup (Eds.), *The company they keep: Friendship in childhood and adolescence* (pp. 158–185). Cambridge University Press.

Burchell, M., & Robin, J. (2011). *The great workplace: How to build it, how to keep it, and why it matters* (1st ed.). Jossey-Bass.
Byrne, D. (1961). Interpersonal attraction and attitude similarity. *Journal of Abnormal and Social Psychology, 62*, 713–715.
Byrne, D. (1971). *The attraction paradigm*. Academic.
Byrne, D., & Clore, G. L. (1970). A reinforcement model of evaluative responses. *Personality: An International Journal, 1*, 103–128.
Casciaro, T., & Lobo, M. S. (2005). Competent jerks, lovable fools, and the formation of social networks. *Harvard Business Review, 83*, 92–99.
Casciaro, T., & Lobo, M. S. (2008). When competence is irrelevant: The role of interpersonal affect in task-related ties. *Administrative Science Quarterly, 53*, 655–684. https://doi.org/10.2189/asqu.53.4.655
Cornwell, J. F. M., Bajger, A. T., & Higgins, E. T. (2015). Judging political hearts and minds: How political dynamics drive social judgments. *Personality & Social Psychology Bulletin, 41*(8), 1053–1068. https://doi.org/10.1177/0146167215589720
Cottrell, C. A., Neuberg, S. L., & Li, N. P. (2007). What do people desire in others? A sociofunctional perspective on the importance of different valued characteristics. *Journal of Personality and Social Psychology, 92*, 208–231. https://doi.org/10.1037/0022-3514.92.2.208
Cuddy, A. J. C. (2009). Just because I'm nice, don't assume I'm dumb. *Harvard Business Review, 87*(2).
Cuddy, A. J., Glick, P., & Beninger, A. (2011). The dynamics of warmth and competence judgments, and their outcomes in organisations. *Research Organisational Behaviour, 31*, 73–98. https://doi.org/10.1016/j.riob.2011.10.004
Damodaran, A., Shulruf, B., & Jones, P. (2017). 'Trust' versus 'competency' in the workplace. *Medical Education, 51*, 338–338. https://doi.org/10.1111/medu.13203
Donnellan, M. B., Larsen-Rife, D., & Conger, R. D. (2005). Personality, family history, and competence in early adult romantic relationships. *Journal of Personality and Social Psychology, 88*, 562–576. https://doi.org/10.1037/0022-3514.88.3.562
Falvo, R., Capozza, D., Bernardo, G. A. D., & Manganelli, M. (2016). Attributions of competence and warmth to the leader and employees' organisational commitment: The mediation role of the satisfaction of basic needs. *Testing, Psychometrics, Methodology in Applied Psychology, 23*, 203–213. https://doi.org/10.4473/TPM23.2.5
Ferreira Da Silva, F., & Costa, P. (2019). Do we need warm leaders? Exploratory study of the role of voter evaluations of leaders' traits on turnout in seven European countries. *European Journal of Political Research, 58*(1), 117–140. https://doi.org/10.1111/1475-6765.12273
Fiske, S. T., Cuddy, A. J. C., & Glick, P. (2007). Universal dimensions of social cognition: Warmth and competence. *Trends in Cognitive Sciences, 11*, 77–83. https://doi.org/10.1016/j.tics.2006.11.005
Gambetta, D. (ed.). (1988). *Trust. Making and breaking cooperative relations*. Basil Blackwell.
Hauser, C., Perkmann, U., Puntscher, S., Walde, J., & Tappeiner, G. (2016). Trust works! Sources and effects of social capital in the workplace. *Social Indicators Research, 128*(2), 589–608. https://doi.org/10.1007/s11205-015-1045-z
Hayes, A. F. (2012). *Process: A versatile computational tool for observed variable mediation, moderation, and conditional process modeling*. Retrieved from http://www.afhayes.com/public/process2012.pdf
Heider, F. (1958). *The psychology of interpersonal relations*. Wiley.
Jha, J. K., & Singh, M. (2019). Exploring the mechanisms of influence of ethical leadership on employment relations. *IIMB Management Review, 31*(4), 385–395.
Judd, C., James-Hawkins, L., Yzerbyt, V., & Kashima, Y. (2005). Fundamental dimensions of social judgment: Understanding the relations between judgments of competence and warmth. *Journal of Personality and Social Psychology, 89*, 899–913. https://doi.org/10.1037/0022-3514.89.6.899
Kenworthy, J. B., & Tausch, N. (2008). Expectations about the accuracy and stability of warmth versus competence traits: An intergroup analysis. *European Journal of Social Psychology, 38*(7), 1121–1129. https://doi.org/10.1002/ejsp.543

Klein, C. (2013). Social capital or social cohesion: What matters for subjective Well-being? *Social Indicators Research, 110*(3), 891–911. https://doi.org/10.1007/s11205-011-9963-x

Lin, P. K. F., Singh, S., Chan, V., Choo, J., & Hsiao, B. (2020a). The role of traits, *Trust, credibility, and respect in interpersonal attraction*. Manuscript under preparation.

Lin, P. K. F., Singh, S., & Tan, N. (2020b). Moderating effect of situational factors on warmth, competency and trust in work attraction.. Manuscript under preparation.

MacKinnon, D. P., Fairchild, A. J., & Fritz, M. S. (2007). Mediation analysis. *Annual Review of Psychology 58*, 593–614. https://doi.org/10.1146/annurev.psych.58.110405.085542

Michinov, E., & Monteil, N. (2002). The similarity-attraction relationship revisited: Divergence between the affective and behavioural facets of attraction. *European Journal of Social Psychology, 32*, 485–500. https://doi.org/10.1002/ejsp.104

Montoya, R. M., & Horton, R. S. (2004). On the importance of cognitive evaluation as a determinant of interpersonal attraction. *Journal of Personality and Social Psychology, 86*, 696–712. https://doi.org/10.1037/0022-3514.86.5.696

Montoya, R. M., & Insko, C. A. (2008). Toward a more complete understanding of the reciprocity of liking effect. *European Journal of Social Psychology, 38*, 477–498. https://doi.org/10.1002/ejsp.431

Oleszkiewicz, A., & Lachowicz-Tabaczek, K. (2016). Perceived competence and warmth influence respect, liking and trust in work relations. *Polish Psychological Bulletin, 47*, 431–435. https://dx.doi.org.elibrary.jcu.edu.au/10.1515/ppb-2016-0050

Peeters, G., & Czapinski, J. (1990). Positive-negative asymmetry in evaluations: The distinction between affective and informational negative effects. In W. Stroebe & M. Hewstone (Eds.), *European review of social psychology* (Vol. 1, pp. 33–60). Wiley.

Porter, L. W., Lawler, E. E., & Hackman, J. R. (1975). *Behaviour in organisations*. McGraw-Hill.

Putnam, R. D. (2000). *Bowling alone: The crumbling and revival of American community*. Simon & Schuster.

Rempel, J. K., Holmes, J. G., & Zanna, M. P. (1985). Trust in close relationships. *Journal of Personality and Social Psychology, 49*, 95–112. https://doi.org/10.1037/0022-3514.49.1.95

Rempel, J. K., Ross, M., & Holmes, J. G. (2001). Trust and communicated attributions in close relationships. *Journal of Personality and Social Psychology, 81*, 57–64. https://doi.org/10.1037/0022-3514.81.1.57

Roethlisberger, F. J., & Dickson, W. J. (1939). *Management and the worker*. Harvard University Press.

Rubel, M. R. B., Rimi, N. N., Yusliza, M. Y., & Kee, D. M. H. (2018). High commitment human resource management practices and employee service behaviour: Trust in management as mediator. *IIMB Management Review, 30*(4), 316–329.

Singh, R., & Tor, X. L. (2008). The relative effects of competence and likability on interpersonal attraction. *Journal of Social Psychology, 148*, 253–255. https://doi.org/10.3200/SOCP.148.2.253-256

Singh, R., Ho, L. J., Tan, H. L., & Bell, P. A. (2007a). Attitudes, personal evaluations, cognitive evaluation, and interpersonal attraction: On the direct, indirect, and reverse-causal effects. *British Journal of Social Psychology, 46*, 19–42. https://doi.org/10.1348/014466606X104417

Singh, R., Yeo, S. E., Lin, P. K. F., & Tan, L. (2007b). Multiple mediators of the attitude similarity-attraction relationships: Dominance of inferred attraction and subtlety of affect. *Basic and Applied Social Psychology, 29*, 49–62. https://doi.org/10.1080/01973530701331007

Singh, R., Ng, R., Ong, E. L., & Lin, P. K. F. (2008). Different mediators of the age, sex, and attitude similarity effects in interpersonal attraction. *Basic and Applied Social Psychology, 30*, 1–17. https://doi.org/10.1080/01973530701665165

Singh, R., Simons, J. J. P., Young, D. P. C. Y., Sim, B. S. X., Chai, X. T., Singh, S., & Chiou, S. Y. (2009). Trust and respect as mediators of the other- and self-profitable trait effects on interpersonal attraction. *European Journal of Social Psychology, 39*, 1021–1038. https://doi.org/10.1002/ejsp.605

Singh, R., Wegener, D. T., Sankaran, K., Singh, S., Lin, P. K. F., Seow, M. X., et al. (2015). On the importance of trust in interpersonal attraction from attitude similarity. *Journal of Social and Personal Relationships, 32*(6), 829–850. https://doi.org/10.1177/0265407515576993

Singh, R., Tay, Y. Y., & Sankaran, K. (2017a). Causal role of trust in interpersonal attraction from attitude similarity. *Journal of Social and Personal Relationships, 34*(5), 717–731. https://doi.org/10.1177/0265407516656826

Singh, R., Wegener, D. T., Sankaran, K., Bhullar, N., Ang, K. Q. P., Chia, P. J. L., Cheong, X., & Chen, F. (2017b). Attitude similarity and attraction: Validation, positive affect, and trust as sequential mediators. *Personal Relationships, 24*, 203–222. https://doi.org/10.1111/pere.1278

Stolle, D., & Rochon, T. R. (1998). Are all associations alike? Member diversity, associational type, and the creation of social capital. *The American Behavioral Scientist, 42*(1), 47–65. https://doi.org/10.1177/0002764298042001005

Strinić, A., Carlsson, M., & Agerström, J. (2020). Multiple-group membership: Warmth and competence perceptions in the workplace. *Journal of Business and Psychology*. https://doi.org/10.1007/s10869-020-09713-4

Todorov, A., Mandisodza, A. N., Goren, A., & Hall, C. C. (2005). Psychology: Inferences of competence from faces predict election outcomes. *Science (American Association for the Advancement of Science), 308*(5728), 1623–1626. https://doi.org/10.1126/science.1110589

Vonk, R. (1999). Effects of other-profitable and self-profitable on evaluative judgments of behaviours. *European Journal of Social Psychology, 29*, 833–842. https://doi.org/10.1002/ejsp.605

Watson, S., McCracken, M., & Hughes, M. (2004). Scottish visitor attractions: Managerial competence requirements. *Journal of European Industrial Training, 28*, 39–66. https://doi.org/10.1108/03090590410513884

Wei, C., Sun, X., Liu, J., Zhou, C., & Xue, G. (2017). High power distance enhances employees' preference for likable managers: A resource dependency perspective. *Frontiers in Psychology, 7*, 2066. https://doi.org/10.3389/fpsyg.2016.02066

Wentura, D., Rothermund, K., & Bak, P. (2000). Automatic vigilance: The attraction- grabbing power of approach and avoidance-related social information. *Journal of Personality and Social Psychology, 78*, 1024–1037. https://doi.org/10.1037/0022-3514.78.6.102

Wieselquist, J. (2009). Interpersonal forgiveness, trust, and the investment model of commitment. *Journal of Social and Personal Relationships, 26*, 531–548. https://doi.org/10.1177/0265407509347931

Wieselquist, J., Rusbult, C. E., Foster, C. A., & Agnew, C. R. (1999). Commitment, pro-relationship behaviour, and trust in close relationships. *Journal of Personality and Social Psychology, 77*, 942–966. https://doi.org/10.1037/0022-3514.77.5.942

Williams, J., & MacKinnon, D. P. (2008). Resampling and distribution of the product methods for testing indirect effects in complex models. *Structural Equation Modeling, 15*, 23–51. https://doi.org/10.1080/10705510701758166

Willis, T. A. (1978). Perceptions of clients by professional helpers. *Psychological Bulletin, 85*, 968–1000. https://doi.org/10.1037/0033-2909.85.5.968

Wojciszke, B. (2005). Morality and competence in person- and self-perception. *European Review of Social Psychology, 16*(1), 155–188. https://doi-org.elibrary.jcu.edu.au/10.1080/10463280500229619

Wojciszke, B., Abele, A. E., & Baryla, W. (2009). Two dimensions of interpersonal attitudes: Liking depends on communion, respect depends on agency. *European Journal of Social Psychology, 39*, 973–990. https://doi.org/10.1002/ejsp.595

Chapter 7
Detecting Public Speaking Stress via Real-Time Voice Analysis in Virtual Reality: A Review

Arushi, Roberto Dillon, Ai Ni Teoh, and Denise Dillon

Abstract Stress during public speaking is common and adversely affects performance and self-confidence of individuals in various professional contexts. Virtual reality (VR) has been used in psychology and human-computer interaction (HCI) to induce and measure barriers to good public speaking skills, such as anxiety and fear. We reviewed the most significant papers published on major indexed journals across the past 20 years. We outline how minimal research has been conducted to detect stress via auditory means in real time during public speaking. As a measurement criterion, the use of questionnaires and physiological parameters remains prevalent. Furthermore, to induce and provide feedback, past experiments relied on simulated audiences that are either scripted or controlled by outside human agents. In this context, we explore the current complexities, limitations and opportunities for novel systems that can provide more engaging and immersive experiences. Hence, we propose a conceptual framework for the development of a voice analysis-based stress-detection computational algorithmic model that can be integrated into a virtual reality simulation. The implementation of the proposed model would ultimately help users to gradually learn how to overcome their stress in real-time and improve their public speaking performance.

Keywords Virtual reality · Affect sensing and analysis · Nonverbal signals · Real-time feedback system · Voice analysis · Intelligent virtual agents · Signal processing

---

Arushi (✉) · R. Dillon
School of Science and Technology, James Cook University, Singapore, Singapore
e-mail: arushi@my.jcu.edu.au; roberto.dillon@jcu.edu.au

A. N. Teoh · D. Dillon
School of Social and Health Sciences, James Cook University, Singapore, Singapore
e-mail: aini.teoh@jcu.edu.au; denise.dillon@jcu.edu.au

E. L. Eijdenberg et al. (eds.), *Innovation-Driven Business and Sustainability in the Tropics*, https://doi.org/10.1007/978-981-99-2909-2_7

7.1 Introduction

Public speaking is considered a vital skill (Schreiber, 2011). It has several benefits to individuals at various levels, such as rapport building and networking in professional as well as social contexts. The predominant functional state of speakers during public speaking is the experience of stress (Koroleva et al., 2014). Several studies found that public speaking causes and induces excessive stress in speakers and therefore compromises the quality of speech being delivered (Beatty & Behnke, 1991; Dowd et al., 2010; Elfering & Grebner, 2011, 2012; Garcia-Palacios et al., 2002; Georgiades et al., 2000; Gramer & Saria, 2007; Gramer & Sprintschnik, 2008; Kotlyar et al., 2008; Pisanski et al., 2016; Westenberg et al., 2009; Wiemers et al., 2015; Wirtz et al., 2013). According to the American Psychological Association (APA), stress is defined as a physiological or psychological response to any internal or external stressor (American Psychological Association, 2022c). Stress manifests in every system of the body, for example, through heart palpitations, dry mouth, shortness of breath, accelerated speech, and changes in breathing patterns leading to changes in voice (American Psychological Association, 2022c). Although a moderate level of stress is beneficial for optimal performance, high levels of stress lead to fatigue and reduced performance (Dongrui et al., 2010). Stress during public speaking not only impacts speaking ability in large social gatherings, but it also affects daily interpersonal communication skills. Ultimately, it impacts opportunities for learning and growth.

Despite public speaking commonly triggering stress among individuals, it has received relatively little attention in the fields of affective computing and human-computer interaction (HCI). This is possibly due to the limitations and complexities of creating a suitable testing environment. Specifically, little attention has been given to the real-time identification of stress during public speaking. Automatic detection of stress from audio and voice is one of the most challenging tasks because emotions (such as anxiety) and stress are basically indistinguishable in terms of reaction patterns and response to an event (American Psychological Association, 2022a).

In the past, researchers have tested various classification algorithms to analyse human voice for the identification of six basic, distinct categorical emotions, such as happiness, anger, sadness, surprise, disgust, and fear, and other dimensional emotions, such as anxiety, boredom, calmness, and sarcasm (Bitouk et al., 2010; Deng et al., 2013; Kwon et al., 2003; Lin & Wei, 2005; Poorna et al., 2018; Soltani & Ainon, 2007; Zhou et al., 2001). Emotions are fundamental in human nature and impact both verbal and non-verbal vocalisations. Therefore, emotion classification algorithms can be developed by creating emotionally significant events which induce physiological, psychological, and complex behavioural and reactive patterns (American Psychological Association, 2022b). The algorithms discern emotions using voice analysis and extracting specific features that are indicative of affective states. For instance, some studies (Ang et al., 2002; Liscombe et al., 2005; Lugger & Yang, 2007) utilised prosodic features of voice which are essentially non-verbal patterns of tune in speech, such as speaking rate, pitch, energy and pause duration to help detect the speaker's state beyond the literal spoken words. Other studies (Rong et al., 2009; Sanchez et al., 2010; Schuller et al., 2007; Wang et al., 2015) used spectral features which are obtained from the time domain signals (temporal features) through the application of Fourier transforms to describe the signal in the frequency domain.

The process of feature extraction (e.g., prosodic or spectral) for detection/identification of specific emotional/affective state by voice analysis can be a difficult task considering both the event and the environment. Specifically, identifying features to detect stress in real-time during the event of public speaking is a complex and challenging problem to be solved, as the associated physiological changes, such as increased heart rate and blood pressure, are not exclusively indicative of stress experience (Clinton et al., 2017; Kappas et al., 1991; Westenberg et al., 2009) Therefore, stress detection should include changes in voice and breathing patterns (Droppleman & McNair, 1971).

Stress during public speaking can be reduced by participating in training programs as well as receiving social support (Fredrick et al., 2018; Teoh & Hilmert, 2018; Thorsteinsson & James, 1999; Uchino & Garvey, 1997). Furthermore, stress can be detected by organising speaking tasks in laboratory environments, for example, by using recent exponential technologies like Virtual Reality (VR). Application of the latest technologies like VR may help in overcoming limitations and complexities involved in creating an environment to simulate public speaking. Being a human-computer interface designed to immerse users in a simulated environment (Azwar et al., 2016), VR provides a safe space for HCI for various purposes, such as training (Fruchter et al., 2007) and applications in different industries. Since VR has the capability to engineer stress responses to create a more confident public speaker in real life situations, it could therefore be utilised as a training tool to help reduce excessive stress of public speaking in real-time.

This literature review aims to give readers a general overview of the various voice features being used to detect stress, or relatively similar states such as anxiety and fear, using various algorithms. Furthermore, in this review paper we tried to identify how VR has been used to detect various states of anxiety and fear and how the virtual audiences in VR were designed and programmed or trained to give feedback/response to speaker's performance.

7.2 Method for Article Screening

Numerous studies have examined the relationship between the voice and emotions. This review primarily focused on emotion detection from voice and VR for public speaking. Therefore, peer-reviewed articles and book chapters that refer to emotion/affective state detection, public speaking and voice analysis were explored by using ScienceDirect, Web of Science and IEEE Xplore databases. Only English-language publications were selected. Several different searches were conducted for the different topics using various keywords and combinations of keywords.

We conducted the first round of literature search (Search 1) to understand and identify the relationship between emotional/affective state and its effect on voice. The search included keywords *voice and emotion*, *public speaking*, and *virtual reality*. The setting of the timeframe for 50 years yielded important earlier research papers such as by Scherer (1995), Wallbott and Scherer (1986), and Kappas (1991), which were helpful in the basic understanding of the relationship between voice and emotional/affective state in humans. Similarly, some of the research conducted by Slater and his colleagues (1999, 2006) helped elaborate the earlier research methods and experiments related to public speaking in virtual reality. Search 1 resulted in a total of 686 articles. These articles provided us with the necessary introduction to public speaking, voice, emotions, virtual social support, and virtual reality.

Before we made our Search 2, we were fairly confirmed in finding that little research has been conducted to detect stress in real-time by voice analysis. Therefore, our Search 2 focused on speech emotional/affective state recognition models and included keywords *audio and voice analysis*, *speech emotion detection* and *voice stress detection*. A timeframe of 20 years (i.e., 2000–2020) was set for Search 2 to understand the recent research related to affective state detection from voice. This was done mainly to get an overview of application and improvements in emotional state recognition models in the past 20 years. This provided more insights into changes that came in by using machine learning technology for emotion detection. Search 2 resulted in 438 articles.

Items from both searches were screened by using EndNote software (The EndNote Team, 2013) was used to manage the references. After a screening of the total 1124 abstracts and conclusions, 241 articles were selected. Articles which were less than a single page were eliminated, as were commentaries and reflective viewpoints. Furthermore, short papers with no data were excluded. Numerous articles which were not relevant and coherent with our research area were also removed. Research articles without a focus on emotional/affective state detection models, voice analysis features and VR for public speaking were excluded. Taken together, all search and screening methods resulted in a total of 169 articles.

7.3 Results

7.3.1 Voice Analysis

Human voice is capable of conveying emotions through speech (Banse & Scherer, 1996; Darwin & Prodger, 1998; Scherer et al., 1991; Wallbott & Scherer, 1986) and non-speech vocalisations (Cowen et al., 2019). Furthermore, analysis of non-speech vocalisations (voice) and speech has received much recognition during the past decade to detect various emotional/affective states (El Ayadi et al., 2011; Schuller et al., 2011). The state detection process from voice involves various algorithms which require training to work correctly.

An algorithm is a well-defined set of instructions that maps an input to an output using a function. For instance, if a given input is X (e.g., voice features) and we want to know if the output is Y (e.g., specific emotion/affective state), then the function involves mapping the given input X to Y as f(X) = Y. Detecting emotional/affective state via voice analysis also involves some preliminary steps such as preprocessing, signal framing, windowing, detection of voice activity, normalisation, and noise reduction of the data (Hamid, 2018). These steps play an essential role in extracting the specific features of voice capable of identifying different affective states and training the algorithmic models for classifying and recognising emotions.

7.3.2 Voice Features and Emotion Detection

The communication of emotions in humans takes place beyond the literal spoken words, such as in non-verbal patterns of rhythm, timbre, and tone in speech. Overall, many non-lexical patterns can be identified by features such as intensity, fundamental frequency (F_0) and duration of the sounds. The prosodic features, which are a combination of spectral, also identified as frequency-based features and including time-domain features, also known as temporal features, are of paramount importance for detecting affective states have also been discussed in the literature (Mitchell & Ross, 2013).

Temporal features include intensity, which signifies the energy of the sound waves (signal) travelling through the air. It is the representation of a change in the amplitude of speech signals over time. Amplitude here in this process is the displacement of the sound waves produced, which determines the loudness of the voice (Kappas et al., 1991). These features are relatively simple to extract and are easier to interpret than spectral features.

Spectral features specifically include features associated with the fundamental frequency (F_0) such as frequency components, formants, and coefficients. Vibrations of the vocal cords cause F_0, which denotes the lowest oscillation of sound waves to be produced, and it is related to the pitch of voice. F_0 one of the most-used parameters for detecting emotions (Scherer, 1995). The pitch comprises characteristics related to rhythm and tone of the speech. The variation of the F_0 over time yields its other statistical properties and F_0 contour, which can also be used as features (Kamiloğlu et al., 2020). More specifically, formants indicate the location of resonance occurring in any vocal tract. They are particularly described with their specific frequencies, their amplitude at the peak, and their bandwidth. The localisation of these formants' resonance on frequencies causes amplification or attenuation. The resonance of the formants regulates articulated sound quality and are assessed as the peak in the frequency spectrum of the sound (Koolagudi & Rao, 2012). Spectral features are obtained by converting the time-based signals into the frequency domain signals using a Fourier Transform (Kappas et al., 1991; Scherer, 1995).

One of the essential spectral features is the Mel Frequency Cepstral Coefficients (MFCC), which represents the speech signal's short term power spectrum. It is obtained by division of the utterances into segments. Then a short-time discrete Fourier Transform is applied on each segment to convert it into the frequency domain. Next, the Mel filter bank is utilised for the calculation of the number of sub-band energies, which is then followed by taking logarithms and finally the application of inverse Fourier Transform obtains MFCC (Kuchibhotla et al., 2014). Other spectral features include Linear Prediction Cepstral Coefficients (LPCC), Log-Frequency Power Coefficients (LFPC) and Gammatone Frequency Cepstral Coefficients (GFCC) that can be acquired by a Linear Prediction Coefficient (LPC), by measurement of spectral band energies using Fast Fourier Transform and Gammatone filter-bank respectively (Nwe et al., 2003). Furthermore, an algorithm documented by Kaiser (1993) as.

$$\Psi[(n)] = x^2(n) - x(n+1)x(n-1)$$

was also developed to measure the energy from speech by a non-linear process, where $\Psi[]$ is the Teager Energy Operator (TEO), and x(n) represents the sample of a speech signal. TEO has various features, such as TEO decomposed FM (frequency modulation), TEO decomposed FM variation (TEO-FM-Var), and TEO autocorrelation envelope area (TEO-Auto-Env), as well as a critical band based TEO auto-correlation envelope area (TEO-CB-Auto-Env). These features explore the change in the characteristics of energy's airflow of speech under stress (Sun & Moore, 2011). These features can be particularly utilised for detection of stress.

Another set of features called prosodic features are a combination of both temporal and spectral features. For instance, intensity, pitch, F_0, formants and duration are also categorised as prosodic features. Duration is defined as the time to construct vowels and other factors present in speech, such as words. Speech pace, the time duration of voiced, unvoiced, and silenced region and longest voiced speech are some of the commonly used duration related features. Furthermore, some other properties of a voice include shimmer, jitter and harmonics to noise ratio (HNR). These features might also help differentiate the emotions produced in a speech signal. While jitter represents the unevenness of F_0 between successive oscillations, the shimmer is the unevenness of the amplitude. Furthermore, the HNR is the representation of the ratio between periodic to aperiodic components in a voiced speech signal (Li et al., 2007). In Table 7.1, we summarise common voice features used in emotion/affective state detection.

It has been found that listeners can judge five types of emotions – anger, fear, happiness, sadness and sensitivity – with up to 70% accuracy (Juslin & Laukka, 2003). Researchers (Kappas et al., 1991) suggested that emotions such as anger, fear, anxiety, happiness or surprise, which are considered to be high arousal emotions, result in increased intensity as well as a high mean F_0. In comparison, disgust,

Table 7.1 Different types of voice features

Feature	Representation	Example
Temporal features (Time based features)	Features pertaining to intensity	Minimum energy, zero-crossing rate, maximum amplitude
Spectral features (Frequency based features)	Represents the signal in terms of frequency	Fundamental frequency (F_0), formants, pitch, fundamental frequency contour
Mel Frequency Cepstral Coefficients (MFCCs)	Represents short term power spectrum	Linear Prediction Cepstral Coefficients (LPCC), Log-Frequency Power Coefficients (LFPC) and Gammatone Frequency Cepstral Coefficients (GFCC), Linear prediction Coefficient (LPC)
Teager Energy Based features	Represents energy in signal by following a non-linear process	TEO decomposed FM (frequency modulation), TEO decomposed FM variation (TEO-FM-Var), and TEO auto-correlation envelope area (TEO-Auto-Env), as well as a critical band based TEO auto-correlation envelope area (TEO-CB-Auto-Env)
Prosodic Features	Combination of Temporal and Spectral features	Intensity, pitch, F_0, formants, duration Unvoiced and silenced region,
Some other voice features	Represents unevenness of F_0 between successive oscillations	Shimmer
	Represents unevenness in amplitude	Jitter
	Represents representation of the ratio between periodic to aperiodic components in a voiced speech signal	Harmonics to noise ratio (HNR)

and sadness, which are considered to be low arousal emotions, have the opposite effect. Kamiloğlu et al. (2020) suggest that pitch is high for emotions such as amusement, interest, and relief, but moderate for savouring emotions like contentment and pleasure, and low for prosocial emotions such as admiration. Low et al. (2010) used prosodic, spectral voice quality as well as TEO-based features for detecting clinical depression in adolescents. The results showed that TEO-based features, specifically TEO CB AutoEnv, outperformed all other features and all other combinations of features as well.

Despite a range of voice features, most of the early studies in the last decade were focused on analysing the prosodic features including pitch, formant frequencies and intensity (Busso et al., 2009; Nogueiras et al., 2001; Nwe et al., 2003; Schuller et al., 2003a). Recent literature surveys showed extensive use of spectral features and cepstral measurements (e.g., MFCCs), voice quality features including HNR, jitter, or shimmer, and Teager energy operator such as TEO-FM-Var and TEO-CB-Auto-Env (Bhavan et al., 2019; Hao et al., 2020; Semwal et al., 2017).

This might be since various features perform differently in the detection of emotional/affective state based on the newly developed algorithms.

There exist various algorithms for analysing the voice and audio for emotion detection. The most significant ones are the Gaussian Mixture Model (GMM), the Hidden Markov Model (HMM), Support Vector Machines (SVM), Artificial Neural Networks (ANN), the Deep Neural Network (DNN) and the Convolutional Neural Network (CNN) (Hansen & Liu, 2016; Julião et al., 2015; Přibil & Přibilová, 2013; Schuller et al., 2011; Zeng et al., 2019).

7.3.3 Models for Detecting Affective States from Audio and Voice Features

In recent years, the Gaussian Mixture Model (GMM) is one of the well-known models for emotion detection (Anagnostopoulos et al., 2015; Busso et al., 2009; Tashev et al., 2017; Truong & van Leeuwen, 2007). GMMs are efficient in modelling multi-modal distribution that best model any input data, by finding probabilistic cluster assignments (Douglas-Cowie et al., 2007). A GMM uses expectation – maximization [E-M] approach, where it chooses starting guesses for setting location and shape. It repeats the E-M steps until each cluster is connected with a smooth Gaussian model which can be in any form from stretched circular (Fig. 7.1) to even oblong stretched out clusters (Fig. 7.2) (VanderPlas, 2016).

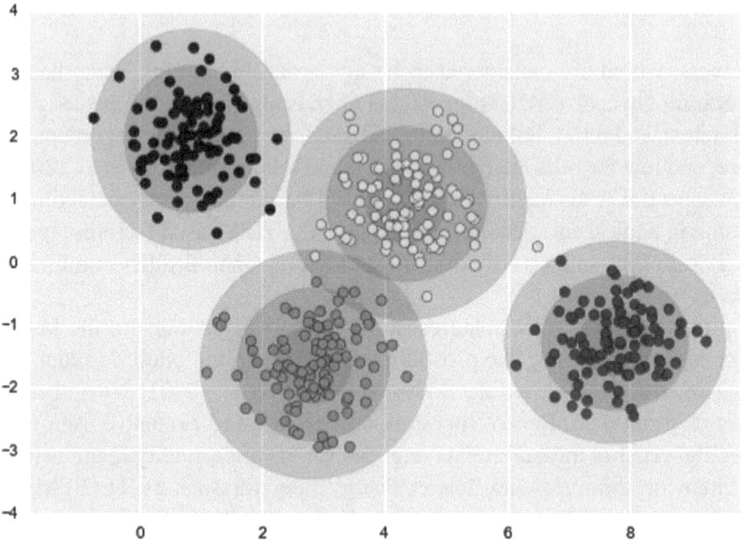

Fig. 7.1 Circular stretched out clusters using GMM

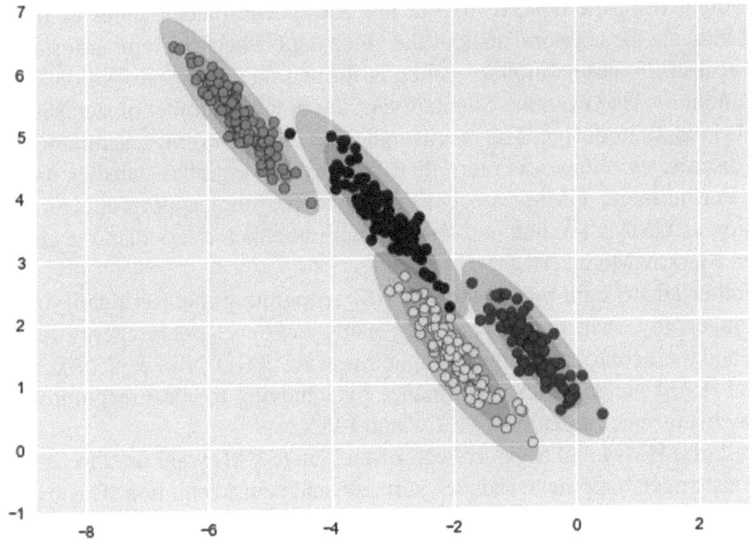

Fig. 7.2 Oblong stretched out clusters using GMM

A group of researchers developed and tested the various GMMs with spectral features such as MFCC, MFCC-low, and pitch. Neiberg et al. combined three different models for recognising emotions. The developed models were tested on voice controlled telephonic service recordings recorded by Swedish company Voice Provider (VP) and on the meeting recordings from the ISL Meeting corpus. The results showed that the combination of developed GMMs based on the spectral features obtained the best results (Neiberg et al., 2006).

In another study, Schuller et al. (2003a) compared two models: GMM and HMM. GMM was used to classify the utterances using global statistics of raw pitch and energy contour. On the other hand, HMM classified the utterances using low-level statistical features (which represent a stationary state of emotions in voice). Each emotion in HMM is modelled by a single state HMM (Casale et al., 2007). The single state HMM is trained by increasing the minimizing distance margin between emotions, and a loss function is used to scale the margin. In comparison to GMMs, the HMM is based on the Markov chain model and in its basic formulation, the Markov chain model states that the future state of any pattern is decided by the current state and not by the past state.

Markov Assumption:

$$P(qi = a \mid q1 \ldots qi-1) = P(qi = a \mid qi-1)$$

Where q1 …qi are the random i states (Martin, 2021).

It is similar to predicting tomorrow's weather based on today's weather only, without looking at the past weather. Furthermore, in HMM, the various states are kept hidden from the observer (Li et al., 2007). The hidden states of the HMM model indicate the temporal state of the voice data, where the temporal state is created because the observation sequence is formed due to its association with each state randomly. However, the calculation of the optimal number of states is an issue of HMM classifier design. The results indicated that the average accuracy in identifying discrete emotions was more than 86% by using global statistics on the features. Furthermore, GMMs are considered to be more appropriate for emotion detection as GMMs training and testing requirements are less than the continuous Hidden Markov Model (HMM).

Another HMM built model showed 70% recognition rate for identifying happiness, anger, joy, fear, disgust, sadness; using low-level pitch, energy features of voice, and their contours of voice (Nogueiras et al., 2001). Nwe et al. (2003) showed that the HMM yields better performance by achieving the best recognition rate of 89% by using spectral features MFCC and LPCC.

Similarly, HMM and Support Vector Machine (SVM) were used to classify five emotions: anger, happiness, sadness, surprise, and neutral emotion. The results from the study showed a 99.5% accuracy rate for HMM whereas SVM obtained an accuracy rate of only 88.9% in recognising the emotions (Lin & Wei, 2005).

However, generally, in contrast to GMM and HMM, the SVM models are more recently used (Bhavan et al., 2019; Bitouk et al., 2010; Hao et al., 2020; Jain et al., 2020; Semwal et al., 2017; Truong & van Leeuwen, 2007; Wang et al., 2015). SVM seems to be promising in many research studies for the classification of stress or not stressed (Barreto et al., 2007). It is used to find the best hyperplane for linearly separable patterns of any given data in an N-dimensional space (where N is number of features) which distinctly classify the data. Hyperplane here refers to the boundaries upon which a decision is made, whereby data falling on either side of the hyperplane can be considered with differed classes. Some of the possible hyperplanes for given data points are shown in Fig. 7.3 (Gandhi, 2018).

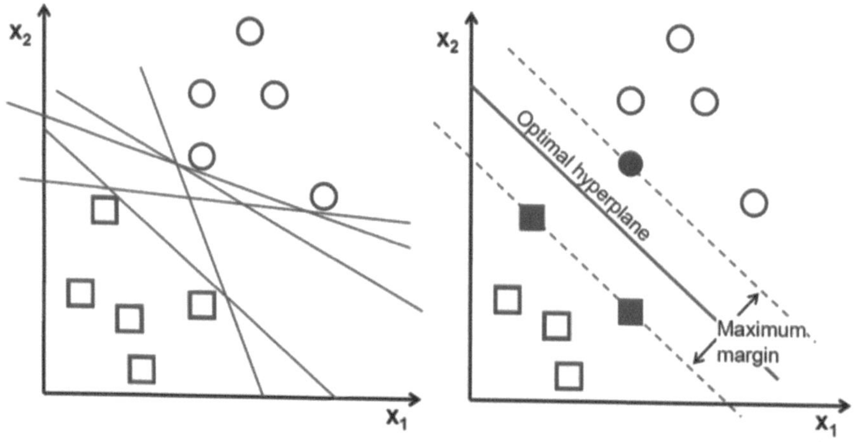

Fig. 7.3 Possible hyperplanes

In case it is not possible to separate the patterns linearly, a kernel function is utilised to map the original data to a new space. However, since there is no particular defined way of choosing the kernel, the separation of transferred features is not guaranteed. Despite this, SVM also offers some specific advantages over the HMM and GMM such as global optimality of training algorithm and memory efficiency, since it uses a subset of training points in the decision-making function (Scikit Learn, 2022).

Similarly, in the study conducted by Hu et al. (2007) GMM supervector based on SVM for classification of emotions using spectral features reported an accuracy rate of 82.5%, while an accuracy rate of 77.9% was obtained by only using GMM.

Bhavan et al. (2019) recognised emotions such as happiness, fear, sadness, anger, disgust, boredom, calm, surprise, and sarcasm on three databases: the Berlin EmoDB (Burkhardt et al., 2005), the Indian Institute of Technology Kharagpur Simulated Emotion Hindi Speech Corpus (IITKGP-SEHSC) (Koolagudi et al., 2009), and the Ryerson Audio-Visual Database of Emotional Speech and Song (RAVDESS) (Livingstone & Russo, 2018). A combination of spectral features was extracted, further processed, and reduced to have the required features set including MFCC, spectral centroids, and MFCC derivatives. The group of researchers then further utilised a bagged ensemble model consisting of SVM with a Gaussian kernel. The results showed an improved accuracy rate of 92.45% (EmoDB), 75.69% (RAVDESS), and 84.11% (IITKGP-SHSC) respectively. Similarly, other researchers (Truong & van Leeuwen, 2007) also used SVM for emotion recognition and found that SVM performs better with acoustic and linguistic features ultimately increasing the recognition of emotions by 8%.

Recently, several new computational models are reported in the literature. This includes the Neural Network for the classification of emotions/affective states from audio (Palo et al., 2015; Soltani & Ainon, 2007). Neural Network or Artificial Neural Network (ANN) consists of an input layer, one or more hidden layers and an output layer as shown in Fig. 7.4.

The layers are made up of nodes, and each layer is connected to the next layer. Once the training of the ANN is completed with raw data, the ANN can be used to classify new data. Each node works based on its own linear regression model, which is composed of input data, weights and a threshold (bias) and an output. Machine Learning (ML) and Deep Learning (a subset of ML), which are part of Artificial Intelligence (AI), are also emerging fields for recognising affective states. Though ANN has various specific advantages over the HMM and GMM it still lacks rules for the optimal setting of ANN topology, and the learning and training makes the classification procedure difficult.

Agarwalla and Sarma used Feed-Forward (FF) network and Deep Neural Network (DNN) approaches to extract relevant data samples from big data space and used them for automatic speech recognition using soft computing techniques for Assamese speech with dialectal variations. The Feed-Forward Network is ANN where the information only moves in one direction without forming a loop between different nodes in layers. The Multi-Layer Perceptron (MLP), which is a Feed-Forward ANN, was configured with inputs to learn emotion classification

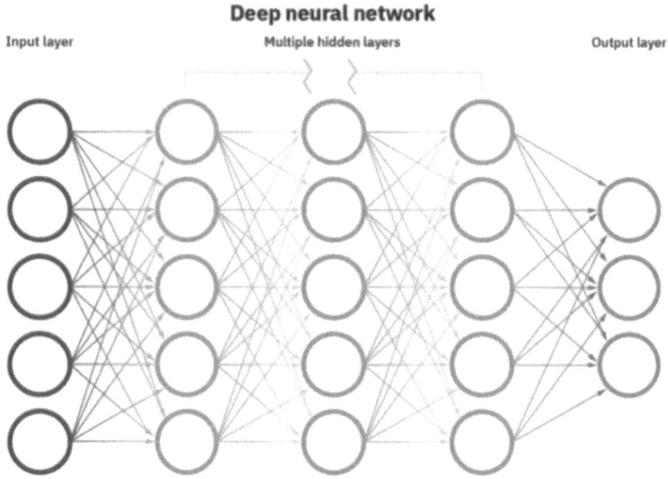

Fig. 7.4 Neural network or artificial neural network (ANN) with layers

information using clustering and manual labelling. The extracted features comprised spectral and prosodic features. The obtained features were applied to Recurrent Neural Network (RNN) and Fully Focused Time Delay Neural Network (FFTDNN) for the evaluation of their performance to recognise mood, dialect, speaker, and gender variations in Assamese speech. Agarwalla and Sarma tested models by considering the recognition rates which were obtained by using confusion matrices and manually calculating time. The results showed that their proposed Machine Learning (ML) based sentence extraction techniques and the composite feature set when used with RNN as a classifier outperformed all other approaches (Agarwalla & Sarma, 2016). The Recurrent Neural Network (RNN) is one of the commonly used deep learning algorithms. RNN is a family of neural networks specialised for sequential data processing and has short term internal memory. Although RNNs use training data to learn similar to other ANNs, they are distinguished as they can also learn from prior given inputs to improve current outputs. Furthermore, RNNs also share their parameters across each network layer and share the same weight within each layer of the network (IBM, 2020). On the other hand, FFTDNN is a multilayer ANN which classify pattens based on shift-invariance, without needing explicit segmentation before classification.

Various deep learning methods contribute to emotion recognition from speech or song. Deep learning involves the creation of algorithms with multiple layers, working similarly to the human brain process of sensing (message travels within many neurons before making a decision). DNN is the hidden network of algorithms as seen in the ANN's middle layers highlighted in turquoise colour in Fig. 7.4. The input data go through different layers of DNN. DNNs then form high-level invariant appropriate features called identifiers from raw input data and then go on to classify audio and voice data for detecting emotions (Bengio et al., 2013). Therefore, DNNs perform very well in ML tasks such as speech recognition (Dahl et al., 2011). In recent years, the performance of the DNN has surpassed the traditional ML algorithms. Furthermore, the feature is automatically selected with the use of deep learning algorithms.

Ooi et al. (2014) used prosodic and spectral features for recognising six different emotions: anger, happiness, sadness, disgust, fear and surprise. The performance of the proposed architecture, which included two main paths, were evaluated on eNTER-FACE'05 (Martin et al., 2006) and RML database (Ryerson Multimedia Research Lab, 2017). It revealed that the Radial Basis Functions Neural Network (RBFNN) was more accurate in recognising emotions than in comparison to RNN. RBFNN transforms the input signal to a different form, that can be fed into the single hidden layer (here called feature vector) to get linear separability.

Hao et al. (2020) used an ensemble visual-audio emotion recognition algorithm to identify different emotions. A multi-task model (which included four sub-models) was built based on the CNN networks which is another type of DNN. The authors performed two different experiments using eNTERFACE database, showing that multi-task CNN recognised 3% over the CNN model in speaker-independent experiments and an average of 2% more over the CNN model in speaker-dependent experiments respectively. The emotion recognition accuracy rate was also reported to be increased to 81.36% in speaker-independent and 78.42% in speaker-dependent experiments.

Issa et al. (2020) used one-dimensional deep CNN. The input features included MFCC, Mel-scale spectrogram, and spectral contrast features. The features were extracted using samples from the Ryerson Audio-Visual Database of Emotional Speech and Song (RAVDESS) (Livingstone & Russo, 2018), Berlin (EMO-DB) (Burkhardt et al., 2005), and Interactive Emotional Dyadic Motion Capture (IEMOCAP) datasets (Busso et al., 2008). They utilized an incremental process to modify initial models to improve classification accuracy. The proposed framework obtained an accuracy rate of 71.61% for RAVDESS, 86.1% for EMO-DB, 95.71% for EMO-DB and 64.3% for IE-MOCAP in speaker-independent audio classification tasks.

We summarise most common algorithms used by researchers for detecting emotions in Table 7.2. Furthermore, most of the research related to emotion recognition and affective state detection has emphasised detection of six universal emotions of disgust, sadness, happiness, fear, anger, and surprise. Moreover, it is quite evident from the table that a vast range of corpora such as SUSAS (Hansen et al., 1997), Emo-DB (Burkhardt et al., 2005) and Interactive emotional dyadic motion capture database (IEMOCAP) (Busso et al., 2008) and Simulated Telegu Speech Corpus (IITKGP-SEHSC) (Koolagudi et al., 2009) are commonly utilised databases for research work.

Few studies extended the research in the area of detecting stress during any stressful event using either non-verbal features (Han et al., 2014, 2018; Pfister & Robinson, 2011) or physiological features (Barreto et al., 2007; Gillespie et al., 2017).

Table 7.2 Various models of emotion detection from the human voice

Algorithms	Features used	Affective states and emotions detected[a]	Performance	Reference
GMM	Fundamental frequency contours, pitch contours	An, Hp, Sd, Bo, Ds, Fr, Pc, El, Sh, Pr, De, In, Co	Over 77% accuracy on three different databases collected at various universities	Busso et al. (2009))
	Spectral features	An, Fr, Ne, Hp, Sd	82.5% accuracy on the dataset collected by hiring participants	Hu et al. (2007))
HMM	MFCC, Pitch, TEO-CB-AUTO-ENV, 16-GA feature, 48-GA feature	Ne, An, Lm, Lo	Increased performance of emotion detection using the 16-GA features on SUSAS database	Casale et al. (2007))
	Pitch, log energy, formant, MFCCs,	Ne, An, St, Lm, Lo	SUSAS using GSVM 90% and 92% for neutral and stress speech, 96.3% of recognition rate obtained by using HMM while 70% was obtained for 4-class style classification	Kwon et al. (2003))
	Prosodic and spectral features	Sr, Jo, An, Fr, Ds, Sd, Ne	70% accuracy on Spanish corpus of INTERFACE Emotional Speech Synthesis Database (Barra Chicote et al. 2008)	Nogueiras et al. (2001))
	Log frequency power coefficients (LFPC)	Lo, and Lu, St Ne	For Burmese:78.5% accuracy For the Mandarin utterance: 75.7% accuracy on the constructed database	Nwe et al. (2003))
SVM	MFCC, LPCC, TEO-AutoCor	An, Ex, Fu, Hp, Ne, Sd	SVM 90.12% on EMO-DB, 83.2% on IEMOCAP	Bandela and Kumar (2019))
			k-NN 89.3% on EMO-DB, 78% on IEMOCAP	
	Energy, pitch, MFCC coefficients, LPCC coefficients and speaker rate	An, Fr, Hp, Sd	90.08% accuracy with Linguistic data consortium (LDC) datasets and of 65.97% with University of Georgia (UGA) datasets	Jain et al. (2020))
			MFCCs features gave an accuracy of 85.085% in comparison to LPCC features accuracy of 73.125%	

(continued)

Table 7.2 (continued)

Algorithms	Features used	Affective states and emotions detected[a]	Performance	Reference
	Fundamental frequency, formant, short-term energy, loudness and (MFCCs) Line Spectral Pairs (LPSs)	Sr, An, Fr, Ds, Hp, Sd, Ne	Accuracy reaches 81.36% and 78.42% in speaker-independent and speaker-dependent experiments conducted on eNTERFACE database (Martin et al., 2006)	Hao et al. (2020))
	MFCCs, Spectral centroids, and MFCC derivatives	Sr, An, Fr, Ds, Hp, Sd, Ne, Sr, Bo, Ne, Ca	An accuracy of: 92.45% on EmoDB 75.69% on RAVDESS and 84.11% on IITKGP-SEHSC	Bhavan et al. (2019))
	Spectral features Prosodic features	An, Fr, Ds, Hp, Sd, Ne	46.1% on LDC 81.3% for Berlin database of German emotional speech	Bitouk et al. (2010))
	Global and local Prosodic features	An, Fr, Ds, Hp, Sd, Sc, Sr	Local prosodic features performed better compared to the global prosodic features on IITKGP-SEHSC	Rao et al. (2013))
	MFCC	St	66.4% on manually collected data	Han et al. (2018))
	Prosodic and spectral features	An, Hp, Sd, Ds, Fr, Su	68.57 by using the RBF neural network	Ooi et al. (2014))
DNN	MFCC feature, pitch related features,	Ex, Hp, Ne, Sd	54.3% average recognition rate	Han et al. (2014))
k-NN	Pitch, spectral features, ZCR, Intensity, MFCCs	Hp, An, Sd, Fr and Ne	66.24% average recognition rate on Chinese emotional data set	Rong et al. (2009))
CNN rectangular kernels	Spectrograms	An, Hp, Sd, Bo, Ds, Fr, Ne	80.79% on Emo-DB and Korean Speech Database	Badshah et al. (2019))
	Chroma gram, spectral contrast features, Mel-scale spectrogram, Tonnetz representation	An, Ca, Ds, Fr, Hp, Ne, Sd, Su	71.61% for RAVDESS 86.1% on EMO-DB 95.71% for EMO-DB and 64.3% for IEMOCAP with 4 classes	Issa et al. (2020))
Hierarchical classifiers	Spectral, prosodic features, mean of the log spectrum	Jo, An, Fr, Ds, Bo, Ne, Sd	An average 71.5% recognition rate on Berlin Emo-DB	Albornoz et al. (2011))

[a]*An* Anger, *Hp* Happiness, *Sd* Sadness, *Bo* Boredom, *Ds* Disgust, *Fr* Fear, *Pc* Panic, *El* Elation, *Sh* Shame, *Pr* Pride, *De* Despair, *In* Interest, *Co* Contempt, *Ne* Neutral, *Ex* Excitement, *Fu* Frustration, *Lo* Lombard, *Lu* Loud, *Sr* Surprise, *Jo* Joy, *Sc* Sarcastic, Here Lombard (Lo) may refer to the Lombard effect in consideration with the database used, the environment in which it was created, and how the researchers applied it in their research

Barreto et al. was one of the limited studies that detected stress by monitoring physiological signals, such as galvanic skin response, temperature of skin, blood pulse volume, and left eye pupil diameter of the subjects, during a determined computer-based, paced Stroop test. The Stroop incongruent segment was considered to be related to the stressed state in participants, while congruent Stroop was linked to a non-stressed state in participants. Twelve out of 32 samples were used to train the classifiers while the remaining 20 samples were used to test the classifiers. All the extracted features of the physiological signals, such as the mean amplitude of the individual blood pulse volume beat and the mean value of pupil diameter, which were expected to increase under stress, were given as the input to various machine learning algorithms, such as Naïve Bayes, Decision Tree, and SVM classifiers, to classify the relaxed versus stressed state in participants (Barreto et al., 2007).

Another study conducted by Han et al. proposed an algorithm to determine the state of stress (stressed or unstressed) via voice features using a binary decision criterion involving two layers of Long Short-Term Memory Recurrent Neural Networks (LSTM-RNN) and a classifier. The authors evaluated the proposed algorithm by obtaining the speech, video, and bio-signal data under stressful (interview of the Korean speaking subjects in English by a foreigner) and non-stressful (comfortable conditions such as watching videos) conditions and surveyed participants about the stress they felt. Based on the survey results and cortisol levels, the speech signals from 25 subjects whose salivary cortisol level changed more than 10% were labelled as stress or non-stress in the database. Additionally, 15 subjects were used to train the model, while five stressed and five un-stressed speech samples from the database were used to test the data. The authors pre-processed the data before extracting the MFCC, which were used to determine stressed and unstressed state from the testing data. The proposed LSTM-RNN with SVM classifier achieved 66.4% accuracy in stress detection (Han et al., 2018).

Furthermore, Pfister and Robinson presented a new classification algorithm to assess public speaking skills. They trained the classifier using the Mind Reading corpus (Junek, 2007) for the detection of both simple and complex emotions. For the classifier to detect the emotions, the authors chose a wide variety of emotions such as joy, interestedness, unfriendliness, excitement, unsureness, and sureness from the Mind Reading corpus. They pre-processed the corpora, extracted the non-verbal features of speech and computed the SVM model. Then, to assess public speaking skills, Pfister and Robinson first retrained the classifier using six labels which are commonly used by professional experts. For this purpose, they asked an experienced speech coach to label 124 one-minute-long speech samples obtained from 31 speakers attending speech coaching. Finally, Pfister and Robinson segmented the live audio, extracted the audio features, and ran the classifiers. For pairwise machine, the results yielded an average cross-validation accuracy of 89% while for the fused machine, 86% of accuracy was obtained. For assessing public speaking skills, the novel application of the classifier achieved 81% cross-validation accuracy and 61% accuracy when performed using a leave-one-speaker-out method (Pfister & Robinson, 2011).

Specifically, stress is common during public speaking. Although public speaking is recognised as an important skill, it has received little attention for real-time voice analysis. This is most possibly due to limitations and complexities involved in creating a suitable testing environment. To overcome this, technologies like VR will be more helpful in creating a public speaking simulation.

7.4 Virtual Reality for Public Speaking

VR has also been utilised for improving public speaking skills (Kimani & Bickmore, 2019; Lister et al., 2010; North et al., 1998; Takac et al., 2019), and other interpersonal skills. The benefit of the VR environment is the immersive experience it brings to users, which provides the experience of learning in a way that is like real-life learning (Azwar et al., 2016; Gavish et al., 2015; Nijholt, 2014). Therefore, learning skills using VR is becoming increasingly popular as well (Dascalu et al., 2017). It is therefore useful in prototyping, scientific visualization, training, engineering, manufacturing, and learning (Dillon et al., 2006; Kassem et al., 2017; Le et al., 2015; Pedro et al., 2016; Schmid Mast et al., 2018).

Researchers have applied VR in various settings, and some of them are summarized in Table 7.3 (Bhagat et al., 2016; Bouchlaghem et al., 2005; Carl et al., 2019; Chittaro & Sioni, 2015; Crocetta et al., 2018; Dechant et al., 2017; Garcia-Palacios et al., 2002; Gebara et al., 2016; Gerardi et al., 2010; Hilfert & König, 2016; Kim et al., 2009; Laver et al., 2015; Levy et al., 2016; Lindner et al., 2019; Manju et al., 2017; Maskey et al., 2014; Miloff et al., 2016; Molina et al., 2014; Motraghi et al., 2014; Mujber et al., 2004; Opriş et al., 2012; Ordaz et al., 2015; Parsons & Rizzo, 2008; Ticknor, 2018, 2019; Valmaggia et al., 2016).

Furthermore, there has been much research interest in using VR to explore feedback strategies to provide social support in a VR environment for public speaking

Table 7.3 Various applications of virtual reality (VR)

Category	Broad applications	Specific applications
Industrial	Gaming Architectural Design Construction Manufacturing Healthcare	Stroke Rehabilitation Diagnostic tool
Educational	Learning	Social Skills Training
General	Overcoming fears Relaxation therapies	Fear of heights Fear of spiders Fear of public speaking
Clinical Psychology	Assessing & treating disorders Complement to standard CBT treatments	Anxiety, Posttraumatic Stress Disorder Schizophrenia Depression Eating disorders

(Brundage & Hancock, 2015; Chollet et al., 2015b). It is reported that psychosocial stress due to public speaking is a common occurrence across the world, which may hinder the quality of the speech delivered (Koroleva et al., 2014; Ruscio et al., 2008). Studies suggest that interactions with virtual entities and their behaviours may be able to elicit both social stress and social support (Kothgassner et al., 2016, 2019; Kotlyar et al., 2008; Pan et al., 2012). Conducting public speaking tasks in a laboratory setting can help in the evaluation of real-life stress and finding ways to overcome it as well (Feldman et al., 2004; Jezova et al., 2016; Owens et al., 2015).

Brundage & Hancock in 2015 investigated VR exposure therapy for treating people who stutter. In their study, ten people who stutter first delivered a speech to a real audience and then, on another day, performed in front of two virtual audience members. The study results indicated that participants had an experience in the virtual setting similar to their experience with the real audience (Brundage & Hancock, 2015). Therefore, VR can be used as a standardised tool for stress (Jönsson et al., 2010) and fear (Powers et al., 2013) induction in real life. Notably, these studies show how people around us, even in a virtual setting, can influence our feelings, behaviour, and performance. In another research study, the authors explored feedback strategies for public speaking by training a virtual audience to be non-interactive (control condition), or to provide direct visual feedback, or non-verbal feedback from non-verbal behaviour such as eye contact and pause fillers (Chollet et al., 2015a; Wörtwein et al., 2015).

Furthermore, research on VR exposure therapy was investigated by Hartanto et al. (2014) to be used for the treatment of anxiety disorders by controlling social stress. The intervention included a one-to-one dialogue session between the speaker and the virtual audience. The participants were exposed to three virtual scenarios of a neutral virtual scene, a blind date condition and a job interview session. The participants' anxiety levels were significantly increased when the social situation changed.

In one of the earliest studies conducted by Slater et al. 1999, studied the psychotherapeutic effects of a virtual environment on social phobia for public speaking. The study had an experimental design of a virtual public scenario with avatars. The avatars displayed random behaviours such as nodding, twitching, and blinking. Avatars could also yawn, clap, and show hostile reactions. Ten graduate students were recruited from University College London (UCL). The participants either gave their speech to the audience on the monitor or were entirely 'immersed' in a VR setting with a headset. Each participant repeated their speech three times. At the first time, the participants faced either a hostile or a friendly audience. At the second time, participants faced whichever audience they did not face during the first speech. At the third time, participants faced an audience with hostile reactions, which eventually become friendly. A participant immersed using the VR headset reported a high co-presence with a hostile audience (felt as though the participant was together with the listeners in real-life) but did not feel as though the audience was interested. This shows that co-presence amplified the situation and a low-interest audience reduced self-rating and increased anxiety in the speaker (Slater et al., 1999).

In a separate study by Slater et al. 2006, therapeutic intervention in VR was used to reduce the fear of public speaking. The experiment included 16 participants with a fear of public speaking and 20 participants with a lower amount of fear of public speaking to give a speech in an empty seminar room in a VR setting. Later, the same room was populated by a neutrally behaving virtual audience of five people. The responses from participants with a fear of public speaking showed a significant increase in signs of anxiety when speaking to the virtual audience in comparison to when speaking to the empty room. In contrast, the participants with a lower amount of fear of public speaking reported no anxiety at all (Slater et al., 2006).

Significant differences were detected between groups undergoing virtual reality therapy (VRT) sessions and a control group, with VRT found to be effective in reducing the fear of public speaking (North et al., 1998). Furthermore, another study showed that a hostile, negative audience scenario generated a strong effect in speakers, regardless of whether the participants feared public speaking. The results suggested that induced anxiety is directly related to the virtual audience's feedback (Pertaub et al., 2001).

A group of researchers developed a virtual character system, which accepts an audio signal's transcription as the input (Pellett & Zaidi, 2019). Based on the analysis of the audio signal received, the system generates an animated performance as output. A framework for virtual reality training to improve public speaking was proposed, which involved assessing the speech using a speech-to-text approach (Marsella et al., 2013), using the Windows dictation recogniser. The speech performance results were shown to speakers at the end of their speech to grade their overall performance. Another more inventive presentation trainer was developed to assess the public speaking performance by giving the user real-time feedback about different aspects of the participant's non-verbal communication. It tracks the participant's voice and body to interpret performance and present an intervention to give feedback to the user (Schneider et al., 2015). In another research study, a group of researchers developed an interface using Google Glass to help people to improve public speaking by automatically detecting the speaker's volume and speaking rate in real time. Based on the speaker's volume and speaking rate, the system provides feedback during the speech (Tanveer et al., 2015).

Similarly, El-Yamri et al., 2019, created a VR system, which included a virtual audience character model. Emotions such as stress elicited in the speaker by the virtual audience character model were analysed using a third-party emotion detection application. The detected emotional states, such as stress and happiness, were weighted using the authors' common sense only. This may not be accurate due to insufficient and unclear in-formation for the basis of common sense used. Moreover, this model lacks a learning process for the virtual agent based on the analysis of voice features and other factors such as physiological parameters. For example, the authors could have detected emotions using VR in real time and/or integrating the developed VR application with another built emotion detection model to analyse voice features and physiological parameters. Based on the detected emotions, the authors could have then given the score to the speaker. This score could have been

Table 7.4 Various relevant studies of public speaking in virtual reality (VR)

Article	Main issue focused on	Task	Responses of virtual audience
Brundage and Hancock (2015))	Affect generation	Speech	Neutral and challenging virtual audience
Chollet et al. (2015b))	Anxiety	Speech	Non-verbal indirect feedback
El-Yamri et al. (2019))	Fear/stress	Speech	Real-time feedback voice tone, gaze, and speech content
Kothgassner et al. (2016, 2019)	Stress	Speech	Real audience, virtual audience, empty virtual lecture hall
Pertaub et al. (2001))	Fear	Speech	Positive, negative comments and behavior
Slater et al., (1999, 2006)	Anxiety	Speech	Positive and negative evaluation feedback
Hartanto et al. (2014))	Stress	One-to-one conversation session	Neutral and conversing audience

used to train the virtual audience to provide real-time feedback to the speaker based on a certain score of speakers (El-Yamri et al., 2019).

Table 7.4 shows some of the relevant studies on public speaking in VR.

Overall, most studies related to public speaking in VR show a lack of clarity in terms of how the affective state of the speaker was determined in real time during the tasks. Furthermore, changes in the speaker's affective state due to the virtual audience's feedback is or was solely understood based either only on self-reported questionnaires or physiological change. An additional way to determine speaker's affective state is to assess emotions in real time by analysing the voice. Interestingly, emotion/affective state detection from voice has unique traits and also common elements shared with the analysis of emotional contents in music, as discussed in one of earlier works by Scherer (1995). Particularly for detection of stress from voice, a approach similar to discussed by Dillon in research conducted can also be investigated (Dillon, 2001, 2003).

In next Sect. 7.5 we will discuss the gaps, opportunities, potential barriers, and suggestions based on the literature survey in more details.

7.5 Discussion

It is well-known and established that communication by speech is a powerful means of human expression and connection. The human voice has proven to be a good indicator of emotional/affective state in several studies (Cowen et al., 2019; Juslin & Laukka, 2003; Mitchell & Ross, 2013). In the areas of HCI and affective computing, recognition of emotions and human affective states is one of the most challenging tasks. Emotions such as anxiety and affective states such as stress are subjective to individuals. Therefore, the development of a detection model depends on the affective state causing event and its application area.

Various models exist and are utilised for analysing the human voice to detect emotions/affective states. Some studies suggested that prosodic features work more appropriately in the identification of emotion with the GMM (Li et al., 2007). Previous research also suggests that the HMM approach achieves a higher recognition rate when detecting happiness, anger, joy, fear, disgust, and sadness using spectral features such as MFCC and LPCC (Nogueiras et al., 2001; Nwe et al., 2003). Furthermore, in a comparison of HMM and SVM to classify five emotions (anger, happiness, sadness, surprise, and neutral emotion), the results showed a 99.5% accuracy rate for HMM, whereas SVM obtained an accuracy rate of only 88.9% in recognizing the emotions (Lin & Wei, 2005). However, other research studies indicate SVM as promising for the classification of stress or not stressed or other states (Barreto et al., 2007; Truong et al., 2012). Other computational models such as Artificial Neural Network (ANN), Recurrent Neural Network (RNN), and Convolutional Neural Network (CNN) are also reported to perform well. However, in recent years, the performance of the Deep Neural Network (DNN) has surpassed the traditional Machine Learning (ML) algorithm (Dahl et al., 2011).

Most of the research related to emotion recognition and affective state detection has emphasized the detection of six universal emotions (i.e., disgust, sadness, happiness, fear, anger, and surprise) using spectral, temporal, and prosodic features (Bhavan et al., 2019; Busso et al., 2009; Hao et al., 2020; Hu et al., 2007; Jain et al., 2020; Nogueiras et al., 2001; Nwe et al., 2003; Ooi et al., 2014; Schuller et al., 2003b; Semwal et al., 2017). Furthermore, the extraction of voice features depends upon emotion or affective state that needs identification. For example, Low et al. (2010) concluded that specifically for the identification of stress, Teager Energy Operators (TEO) based features, and especially the TEO CB AutoEnv, are more effective in comparison to all other types of features. Furthermore, sometimes the voice features may overlap between different emotions, and therefore, it is crucial to extract correct features carefully.

From these studies, it can be inferred that various voice features, and various datasets and models play a different role in emotion recognition and affective state identification. It depends on the dataset we choose the emotion we want to detect, and the preference of algorithm. A combination of carefully extracted features, with a proper noise-free training data set and with the appropriate classification algorithm, is needed to develop an accurate detection model. Once the application of emotion detection is validated within a specific context, it is possible to port it into other settings to detect stressful events of different nature with an improved recognition rate.

7.5.1 Gaps and Opportunities

Public speaking is recognised as an essential skill as well as a cause of stress. Acquiring public speaking skills for the presentation of ideas is important in various professional contexts (Docan-Morgan & Nelson, 2015). It is reported that psychosocial stress due to public speaking is a common occurrence across the world, which hinders the quality of the speech delivered (Koroleva et al., 2014; Ruscio et al., 2008). Although much recent research has been done in the field of emotion detection, not enough research has been carried out to specifically detect stress in the context of a potentially stressful event such as public speaking in real time. More specifically, public speaking has received little attention for real-time stress detection by analysing voice features and physiological parameters. Very few studies have extended research to the matter of detecting stress during any potentially stressful event using either non-verbal features (Han et al., 2018; Pfister & Robinson, 2011) or physiological features (Barreto et al., 2007; Gillespie et al., 2017) or self-reported indices (Bandela & Kumar, 2019).

For example, Pfister and Robinson (2011) utilised non-verbal features to detect the affective state and apply it to assess public speaking only, leaving out the physiological parameters. The accuracy of this method of detecting stress may not be high because of the restriction to just non-verbal features, leaving out the physiological parameters in the context of public speaking.

In another example, in the study conducted by El-Yamri et al. (2019) where the authors created a VR system, which included a virtual audience character model. Stress elicited in a speaker was identified and analysed using a third-party affective state detection application. Furthermore, the emotional states of the speaker were weighted using the authors' common sense only. This is not an appropriate and accurate option due to insufficient and unclear information for the basis of 'common sense' used, which can be culturally dependent and hence could potentially bias the recognition of certain emotions over others. Moreover, this model lacks a learning process for the virtual agent based on the analysis of voice features and other factors such as physiological features. Also, knowing how the virtual audience were made to work can help in improving the experiment and real-time feedback to the speaker during public speaking.

The literature review points out that real-time stress detection in the areas of affective computing and HCI has not received much attention, and this is possibly due to the limitations and complexities in creating a suitable testing environment for stress during public speaking. While conducting public speaking tasks in a laboratory setting can help in the evaluation of real-life stress (Jezova et al., 2016), technologies like VR can be employed to create a simulation for public speaking. Previous studies have also indicated that interactions with virtual entities are able to elicit social stress. It can also be inferred from research that VR can be used to provide Virtual Social Support (VSS) during a stressful activity (Kothgassner et al., 2019). In this regard, research has been carried out using VR to examine the effects of VSS for public speaking (Chollet et al., 2015a, b; El-Yamri et al., 2019; Hartanto et al., 2014; Pertaub et al., 2001; Slater et al., 1999, 2006). However, most of the research (e.g., (Barreto et al., 2007; Hartanto et al., 2014; Slater et al., 2006)) related to VR for public speaking focused on testing the effects of virtual audience behaviour on a speaker's anxiety and fear of public speaking by only measuring the speaker's physiological parameters such as heart rate or blood pressure. Despite being important indices to emotional experience, changes in heart rate and blood pressure are not exclusively indicative of specific emotional experience. The research could have been improved by detecting emotions from speakers' voices, which could have made the detection of stress more accurate since the human voice is a powerful channel to convey emotions and this has not been done using VR before as accurately as it could be done.

Based on the gaps identified, we propose the development of a stress detection model. This model would be able to analyse the voice of users in real time. The selected voice features to develop the stress detection model will be correlated to the physiological parameters of stress such as heart rate and blood pressure as well as psychological results obtained from self-reported questionnaires such as stress arousal checklist (Cox & Mackay, 1985) and the task specific anxiety checklist.

After getting ethics approvals from Human Research Ethics Committee (HREC), data collection will begin following the steps mentioned in Fig. 7.5, and next, the first step would be to analyse the self-reported responses in pre- and post-test questionnaires for each condition for all speakers (Fig. 7.6). We will then check the corresponding heart-rate readings and blood pressure readings of the participants for both VR scenarios. If both the psychological responses and physiological responses indicate that the person was stressed during public speaking in VR, we will proceed to extract the voice features, which will be counted as our stressed voice data. On the other hand, the speeches provided by participants who did not show signs of stress during their speech will be kept as our confident voice data set. Once the features of voice are extracted, we will evaluate various algorithms and choose the one that can provide us with the best accuracy for developing the stress detection model.

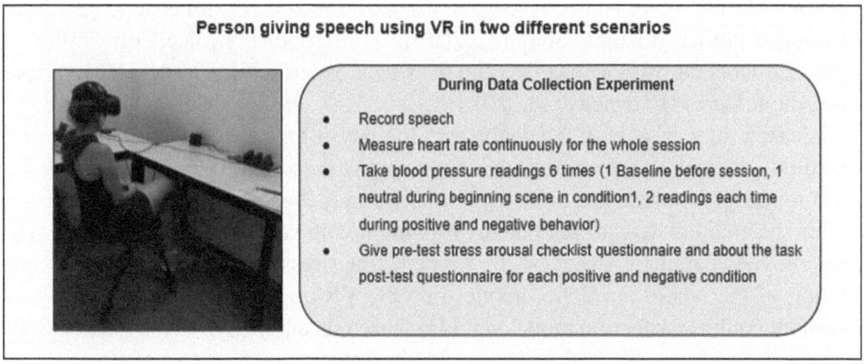

Fig. 7.5 Pilot test being conducted before the actual data collection to validate the experimental setup

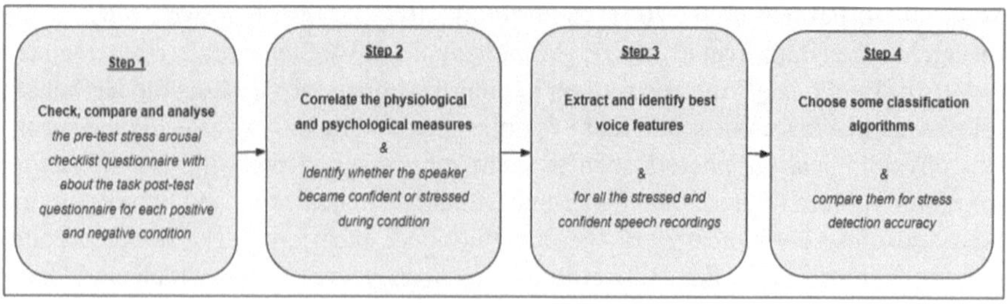

Fig. 7.6 Steps in development of stress detection model to be integrated in VR application

The developed stress detection model will then be integrated or connected to a virtual audience in the VR application to provide real-time feedback in two modes (social supportive and realistic feedback mode) (Fig. 7.7).

This would allow users to practice their public speaking in social supportive mode (when less certain about their speaking abilities) or they could choose to practice in realistic feedback mode (when sure about their public speaking skills and wanting to check their performance). This will allow users to gradually learn to overcome stress caused by public speaking and therefore improve their public speaking skills.

7.5.2 Potential Barriers and Solutions

Several issues may arise in the implementation procedure of the suggestion presented in Sect. 7.5.1. For example, there may be barriers in the development software for extraction and analysis of all necessary voice features. Issues may also arise if we want to analyse the physiological parameters of stress in real time. We can start by pre-processing of recorded voice data, followed by extracting the spectral features of voice such as frequency contours, and prosodic features using Python libraries like My Voice Analysis (Shabahi, 2020), LibROSA (McFee et al., 2015) or pyAudioAnalysis (Giannakopoulos, 2015). Furthermore, if needed, similar to approach labelled by Batrinca, we can also seek expert advice in deciding various prosodic features (Batrinca et al., 2013).

In case issues arise with the analysis of the physiological parameters of stress in real time, we can also develop another application to record the physiological parameters separately for analysis of stress levels. We may then try to combine the results within the emotion detection model by training it with voice features combined with physiological parameters specifically for detecting stress. This would allow the integration of the whole developed model into the VR application using TensorFlow. The built emotion detection model would be based on analysis of voice features such as prosodic features, spectral features, and physiological parameters of stress.

This model could be used to train the virtual audience present in the VR application using the Machine Learning Agents SDK (ML-Agents) using various machine

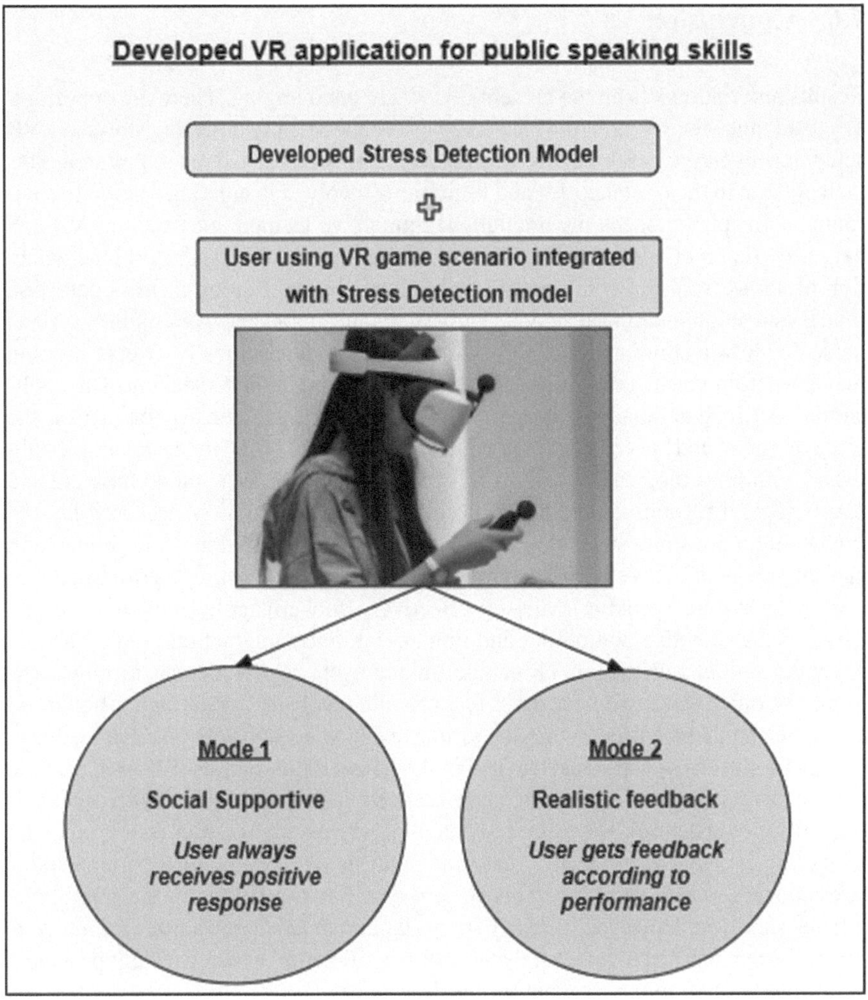

Fig. 7.7 VR game application for improving public speaking skills

learning methods such as reinforcement learning. This would allow the virtual agents to provide real-time feedback to the speaker with respect to voice and physiological features.

Therefore, analysis of stress elicited in a public speaker by a virtual audience should be accomplished by using stress detection models in VR. Furthermore, the developed stress detection model combined with voice analysis and physiological symptoms of stress could be used to train the virtual audience in real time to provide feedback. From the research surveyed here, it is evident that stress detection models in VR have not yet been utilised for providing real-time feedback based on both voice analysis and physiological symptoms.

7.6 Conclusion

Results and findings from the present review are encouraging. There are opportunities to advance the research in voice analysis for specifically detecting stress in a VR setup during public speaking. Limited research has been carried out in this area. This is likely due to the complexities and limitations involved in creating a suitable environment for public speaking simulation. Immersive technologies such as VR can help provide an effective environment for this very purpose. Therefore, the detection of stress from the voice should be explored by developing a stress-detection model and implementing it in VR. Particularly in this paper, we emphasised and presented how a computational algorithmic model that specifically detects stress in real-time from voice could be developed for improving public speaking. The application will include analysis of prosodic features such as intensity, frequency, the pitch of voice, and spectral features which are identified based on correlation established with physiological symptoms of stress such as heart rate, blood pressure and psychological responses obtained from questionnaires. We also discussed how to implement a real-time stress detection model in VR for additional user immersion and engagement. Thereby, overcoming the limitation of testing environment for improving public speaking skills by effectively and efficiently reducing the gap between the affective computing and human-computer interaction fields. Last, an engaging virtual audience in VR can be trained using reinforcement learning techniques or other ways to detect stress and provide feedback in real time. The virtual audience can then be used to provide virtual social support where positive feedback is triggered whenever stress is detected in the voice of the speaker. This will provide the speaker an opportunity to practice in a safe environment without any risk of feeling judged or criticised. However, the potential barriers include analysis of prosodic features of voice and especially real-time analysis of physiological parameters of stress during public speaking. This review also has limitations in the number of articles surveyed. However, it clearly shows that there are opportunities for integrating real-time audio and voice analysis within a VR setup, which can help provide a valid training tool to improve public speaking skills.

References

Agarwalla, S., & Sarma, K. K. (2016). Machine learning based sample extraction for automatic speech recognition using dialectal Assamese speech. *Neural Networks, 78*, 97–111.

Albornoz, E. M., Milone, D. H., & Rufiner, H. L. (2011). Spoken emotion recognition using hierarchical classifiers. *Computer Speech & Language, 25*(3), 25.

American Psychological Association. (2022a). Anxiety. In *APA dictionary*. Retrieved 7/2/2022, from https://dictionary.apa.org/anxiety

American Psychological Association. (2022b). Emotion. In *APA dictionary*. https://dictionary.apa.org/emotion

American Psychological Association. (2022c). Stress. In *APA dictionary* https://dictionary.apa.org/stress

Anagnostopoulos, C.-N., Iliou, T., & Giannoukos, I. (2015). Features and classifiers for emotion recognition from speech: A survey from 2000 to 2011. *Artificial Intelligence Review, 43*(2), 155–177.

Ang, J., Dhillon, R., Krupski, A., Shriberg, E., & Stolcke, A. (2002). Prosody-based automatic detection of annoyance and frustration in human-computer dialog. *Interspeech.*

Azwar, H., Alam, N., Kazmi, B., Zain-ul-abidin, S., & Khan, S. A. (2016). Virtual reality based immersion systems. *International Journal of Technology and Research, 4*(4), 82–84. http://jcu.summon.serialssolutions.com/2.0.0/link/0/eLvHCXMwpV07T8MwED71scD-Ao4B4FJSNKciuX8mEUkhFpRahJCB1qhLHQWJIefX_c6aOWhhYWLx4SHSXfL7vf-HcfABtcEf8XJmimCDWhYbJCj1chzQNd6UDjUvKwrH42zK2KC21rjHN3g5Lf0F0ut-M2aI22XAj1VIMn165tvdaTsfasT1WhD16otIR3rDuP7h2Sdd0HEpk5Sro-HeFmfuQBntwnPzbNOk_V70crMtZz2q8V9vuAc7Lub0otVHsg8tU_esXLMr7ejB9sZUwgO4fBon2WM08ZI4moyzmTeM0vjWG0-ncWLN7KWzNIun6SFkozi7ufOdnoKPhzKSRKRWouTFIBBKEU5JTgskL7kQduqYDhUzVBotJM8ly_WgwsWUghZVKZQ2lB1Bp17U5hg8rQjJjRIFwwgMA6gwrwJuZw8ybQqu5An0G4PM3T_xMV9b4_Tv7TPYwrBErkrm-tD5fF-ac2ijGy6cN78AJO2vbg

Badshah, A. M., Rahim, N., Ullah, N., Ahmad, J., Muhammad, K., Lee, M. Y., Kwon, S., & Baik, S. W. (2019). Deep features-based speech emotion recognition for smart affective services. *Multimedia Tools and Applications, 78*(5), 5571–5589. https://doi.org/10.1007/s11042-017-5292-7

Bandela, S. R., & Kumar, T. K. (2019). Speech emotion recognition using semi-NMF feature optimization. *Turkish Journal of Electrical Engineering and Computer Sciences, 27*(5), 3741–3757. https://doi.org/10.3906/elk-1903-121

Banse, R., & Scherer, K. R. (1996). Acoustic profiles in vocal emotion expression. *Journal of Personality and Social Psychology, 70*(3), 614.

Barreto, A., Zhai, J., & Adjouadi, M. (2007). *Non-intrusive physiological monitoring for automated stress detection in human-computer interaction*. Springer.

Batrinca, L., Stratou, G., Shapiro, A., Morency, L.-P., & Scherer, S. (2013). Cicero-towards a multimodal virtual audience platform for public speaking training. In *International workshop on intelligent virtual agents.*

Beatty, M. J., & Behnke, R. R. (1991). Effects of public speaking trait anxiety and intensity of speaking task on heart rate during performance. *Human Communication Research, 18*(2), 147–176. https://doi.org/10.1111/j.1468-2958.1991.tb00542.x

Bengio, Y., Courville, A., & Vincent, P. (2013). Representation learning: A review and new perspectives. *IEEE Transactions on Pattern Analysis and Machine Intelligence, 35*(8), 1798–1828. https://doi.org/10.1109/TPAMI.2013.50

Bhagat, K. K., Liou, W.-K., & Chang, C.-Y. (2016). A cost-effective interactive 3D virtual reality system applied to military live firing training. *Virtual Reality, 20*(2), 127–140. https://doi.org/10.1007/s10055-016-0284-x

Bhavan, A., Chauhan, P., Hitkul, & Shah, R. R. (2019). Bagged Support Vector Machines For Emotion Recognition From Speech. *Knowledge-Based Systems, 184*, 104886.

Bitouk, D., Verma, R., & Nenkova, A. (2010). Class-level spectral features for emotion recognition. *Speech Communication, 52*(7-8), 613–625.

Bouchlaghem, D., Shang, H., Whyte, J., & Ganah, A. (2005). Visualisation in architecture, engineering and construction (AEC). *Automation in Construction, 14*(3), 287–295. https://doi.org/10.1016/j.autcon.2004.08.012

Brundage, S. B., & Hancock, A. B. (2015). Real enough: Using virtual public speaking environments to evoke feelings and behaviors targeted in stuttering assessment and treatment. *American Journal of Speech-Language Pathology, 24*(2), 139–149. https://doi.org/10.1044/2014_AJSLP-14-0087

Burkhardt, F., Paeschke, A., Rolfes, M., Sendlmeier, W. F., & Weiss, B. (2005). A database of German emotional speech. *Interspeech.*

Busso, C., Bulut, M., Lee, C.-C., Kazemzadeh, A., Mower, E., Kim, S., Chang, J. N., Lee, S., & Narayanan, S. S. (2008). IEMOCAP: Interactive emotional dyadic motion capture database. *Language Resources and Evaluation, 42*(4), 335–359.

Busso, C., Lee, S., & Narayanan, S. (2009). Analysis of emotionally salient aspects of fundamental frequency for emotion detection. *IEEE Transactions on Audio, Speech, and Language Processing, 17*(4), 582–596. https://doi.org/10.1109/TASL.2008.2009578

Carl, E., Stein, A. T., Levihn-Coon, A., Pogue, J. R., Rothbaum, B., Emmelkamp, P., Asmundson, G. J. G., Carlbring, P., Powers, M. B., & Stockholms, u., Samhällsvetenskapliga, f., Psykologiska, i., & Klinisk, p. (2019). Virtual reality exposure therapy for anxiety and related disorders: A meta-analysis of randomized controlled trials. *Journal of Anxiety Disorders, 61*, 27–36. https://doi.org/10.1016/j.janxdis.2018.08.003

Casale, S., Russo, A., & Serrano, S. (2007). Multistyle classification of speech under stress using feature subset selection based on genetic algorithms. *Speech Communication, 49*(10–11), 801–810. https://doi.org/10.1016/j.specom.2007.04.012

Chittaro, L., & Sioni, R. (2015). Serious games for emergency preparedness: Evaluation of an interactive vs. a non-interactive simulation of a terror attack. *Computers in Human Behavior, 50*, 508–519. https://doi.org/10.1016/j.chb.2015.03.074

Chollet, M., Stefanov, K., Prendinger, H., & Scherer, S. (2015a). *Public speaking training with a multimodal interactive virtual audience framework – Demonstration.*

Chollet, M., Wörtwein, T., Morency, L.-P., Shapiro, A., & Scherer, S. (2015b). Exploring feedback strategies to improve public speaking: An interactive virtual audience framework. In *Proceedings of the 2015 ACM international joint conference on pervasive and ubiquitous computing*. Osaka, Japan. https://doi-org.elibrary.jcu.edu.au/10.1145/2750858.2806060

Clinton, E., Cookson, G., Brown, S., & Woods, D. (2017). The stress of public speaking increases cortisol levels in undergraduates: Is increased preparation really the best remedy? *In Vivo, 38*(2).

Cowen, A. S., Elfenbein, H. A., Laukka, P., & Keltner, D. (2019). Mapping 24 emotions conveyed by brief human vocalization. *American Psychologist, 74*(6), 698.

Cox, T., & Mackay, C. (1985). The measurement of self-reported stress and arousal. *British journal of psychology, 76*(2), 183–186.

Crocetta, T. B., de Araújo, L. V., Guarnieri, R., Massetti, T., Ferreira, F. H. I. B., de Abreu, L. C., & de Mello Monteiro, C. B. (2018). Virtual reality software package for implementing motor learning and rehabilitation experiments. *Virtual Reality, 22*(3), 199–209. https://doi.org/10.1007/s10055-017-0323-2

Dahl, G. E., Yu, D., Deng, L., & Acero, A. (2011). Context-dependent pre-trained deep neural networks for large-vocabulary speech recognition. *IEEE transactions on audio, speech, and language processing, 20*(1), 30–42.

Darwin, C., & Prodger, P. (1998). *The expression of the emotions in man and animals*. Oxford University Press.

Dascalu, M.-I., Bagis, S., Nitu, M., Ferche, O.-M., & Alin Dragos Bogdan, M. (2017). Experiential learning VR system for studying computer architecture. *Romanian Journal of Human – Computer Interaction, 10*(3), 197–215. http://jcu.summon.serialssolutions.com/2.0.0/link/0/eLvHCXMwpV1LawIxEB50vXhpFVv6sDLQ82qSjVv3VLQonqRI6VXc2awgZe3L_2_GTVB78NJzIAyZybznG4BIdUX4RyfoJOsnudCUajkwgkQqU2OjryRfmphInw7M1c2FPBrj2O215F51ZxvirHmPu30kGzzx_PkV8h4prre6pRpVqNm_KFUAtdF49jr3MsboK9ZnYa-YN52ENhoSp2pYOdsyuYSVJ8P4DOCatscTOgfUxn8R24AL537isJSXJlRM0YKRxzu2v_0DHeLqCt_nWOKZo3VskRsOeSQK_R4IHB7VIK7gcTJ-e5mGnqyFE9KfxYGm6BqCYlOYG8CItI2AVJzJp1QvBQ3ymHIyfeJALSFxC-1zN92dP76HumK7uO93bUPw-701D1C1z9pxjNoB6Cuspg

Dechant, M., Trimpl, S., Wolff, C., Mühlberger, A., & Shiban, Y. (2017). Potential of virtual reality as a diagnostic tool for social anxiety: A pilot study. *Computers in Human Behavior, 76*, 128–134. https://doi.org/10.1016/j.chb.2017.07.005

Deng, J., Zhang, Z., Marchi, E., & Schuller, B. (2013). Sparse autoencoder-based feature transfer learning for speech emotion recognition. In *2013 humaine association conference on affective computing and intelligent interaction.*

Dillon, R. (2001). Extracting audio cues in real time to understand musical expressiveness. In *Proceedings "Current research directions in computer music", MOSART Workshop.* Barcelona, Spain.

Dillon, R. (2003). A statistical approach to expressive intention recognition in violin performances. In *Proceedings of the Stockholm Music Acoustics Conference (SMAC'03) Stockholm.*

Dillon, R., Wong, G., & Ang, R. (2006). Virtual orchestra: An immersive computer game for fun and education. In *Proceedings of the 2006 International conference on Game research and development.*

Docan-Morgan, T., & Nelson, L. L. (2015). Chapter 11: The benefits and necessity of public speaking education – Tony Docan-Morgan & Laura L. Nelson. In *Public Speaking for the Curious.* https://www.researchgate.net/publication/332974615_The_Benefits_and_Necessity_of_Public_Speaking_Education

Dongrui, W., Courtney, C. G., Lance, B. J., Narayanan, S. S., Dawson, M. E., Oie, K. S., & Parsons, T. D. (2010). Optimal arousal identification and classification for affective computing using physiological signals: Virtual reality stroop task. *IEEE Transactions on Affective Computing, 1*(2), 109–118. https://doi.org/10.1109/T-AFFC.2010.12

Douglas-Cowie, E., Cowie, R., Sneddon, I., Cox, C., Lowry, O., Mcrorie, M., Martin, J.-C., Devillers, L., Abrilian, S., & Batliner, A. (2007). The HUMAINE database: Addressing the collection and annotation of naturalistic and induced emotional data. In *International conference on affective computing and intelligent interaction.*

Dowd, H., Dowd, H., Zautra, A., Zautra, A., Hogan, M., & Hogan, M. (2010). Emotion, stress, and cardiovascular response: An experimental test of models of positive and negative affect. *International Journal of Behavioral Medicine, 17*(3), 189–194. https://doi.org/10.1007/s12529-009-9063-3

Droppleman, L. F., & McNair, D. M. (1971). An experimental analog of public speaking. *Journal of Consulting and Clinical Psychology, 36*(1), 91.

El Ayadi, M., Kamel, M. S., & Karray, F. (2011). Survey on speech emotion recognition: Features, classification schemes, and databases. *Pattern Recognition, 44*(3), 572–587. https://doi.org/10.1016/j.patcog.2010.09.020

Elfering, A., & Grebner, S. (2011). Ambulatory assessment of skin conductivity during first thesis presentation: Lower self-confidence predicts prolonged stress response. *Applied Psychophysiology and Biofeedback, 36*(2), 93–99. https://doi.org/10.1007/s10484-011-9152-3

Elfering, A., & Grebner, S. (2012). Getting used to academic public speaking: Global self-esteem predicts habituation in blood pressure response to repeated thesis presentations. *Applied Psychophysiology and Biofeedback, 37*(2), 109–120. https://doi.org/10.1007/s10484-012-9184-3

El-Yamri, M., Romero-Hernandez, A., Gonzalez-Riojo, M., & Manero, B. (2019). Designing a VR game for public speaking based on speakers features: A case study. *Smart Learning Environments, 6*(1), 1–15. https://doi.org/10.1186/s40561-019-0094-1

Feldman, P. J., Cohen, S., Hamrick, N., & Lepore, S. J. (2004). Psychological stress, appraisal, emotion and cardiovascular response in a public speaking task. *Psychology & Health, 19*(3), 353–368. https://doi.org/10.1080/0887044042000193497

Fredrick, S. S., Demaray, M. K., Malecki, C. K., & Dorio, N. B. (2018). Can social support buffer the association between depression and suicidal ideation in adolescent boys and girls? *Psychology in the Schools, 55*(5), 490–505.

Fruchter, R., Reidsma, D., op den Akker, H. J. A., Nishida, T., Rienks, R. J., Rosenberg, D., Poppe, R. W., Nijholt, A., Heylen, D. K. J., & Zwiers, J. (2007). Virtual meeting rooms: From observation to simulation. *AI & Society, 22*(1, suppl./2), 133–144. https://doi.org/10.1007/s00146-007-0129-y

Gandhi, R. (2018). *Support vector machine—Introduction to machine learning algorithms*. Retrieved 7/2/2022, from https://towardsdatascience.com/support-vector-machine-introduction-to-machine-learning-algorithms-934a444fca47
Garcia-Palacios, A., Hoffman, H., Carlin, A., Furness, T. A., & Botella, C. (2002). Virtual reality in the treatment of Spider Phobia: A controlled study. *Behaviour research and therapy, 40*(9), 983–993. https://doi.org/10.1016/S0005-7967(01)00068-7
Gavish, N., Gutiérrez, T., Webel, S., Rodríguez, J., Peveri, M., Bockholt, U., & Tecchia, F. (2015). Evaluating virtual reality and augmented reality training for industrial maintenance and assembly tasks. *Interactive Learning Environments, 23*(6), 778–798.
Gebara, C. M., Barros-Neto, T. P. D., Gertsenchtein, L., & Lotufo-Neto, F. (2016). Virtual reality exposure using three-dimensional images for the treatment of social Phobia. *Revista brasileira de psiquiatria (Sao Paulo, Brazil: 1999), 38*(1), 24–29. https://doi.org/10.1590/1516-4446-2014-1560
Georgiades, A., Sherwood, A., Gullette, E. C. D., Babyak, M. A., Hinderliter, A., Waugh, R., Tweedy, D., Craighead, L., Bloomer, R., & Blumenthal, J. A. (2000). Effects of exercise and weight loss on mental stress–induced cardiovascular responses in individuals with high blood pressure. *Hypertension: Journal of the American Heart Association, 36*(2), 171–176. https://doi.org/10.1161/01.HYP.36.2.171
Gerardi, M., Cukor, J., Difede, J., Rizzo, A., & Rothbaum, B. O. (2010). Virtual reality exposure therapy for post-traumatic stress disorder and other anxiety disorders. *Current Psychiatry Reports, 12*(4), 298–305. https://doi.org/10.1007/s11920-010-0128-4
Giannakopoulos, T. (2015). pyAudioAnalysis: An open-source python library for audio signal analysis. *PLoS One, 10*(12), e0144610. https://doi.org/10.1371/journal.pone.0144610
Gillespie, S., Moore, E., Laures-Gore, J., Farina, M., Russell, S., Logan, Y. Y., & Ieee. (2017). Detecting stress and depression in adults with aphasia through speech analysis. In *2017 Ieee International conference on acoustics, speech and signal processing* (pp. 5140–5144). <Go to ISI>://WOS:000414286205060.
Gramer, M., & Saria, K. (2007). Effects of social anxiety and evaluative threat on cardiovascular responses to active performance situations. *Biological Psychology, 74*(1), 67–74. https://doi.org/10.1016/j.biopsycho.2006.07.004
Gramer, M., & Sprintschnik, E. (2008). Social anxiety and cardiovascular responses to an evaluative speaking task: The role of stressor anticipation. *Personality and Individual Differences, 44*(2), 371–381. https://doi.org/10.1016/j.paid.2007.08.016
Hamid, O. K. (2018). Frame blocking and windowing speech signal. *Journal of Information, Communication, and Intelligence Systems (JICIS), 4*, 87–94.
Han, K., Yu, D., & Tashev, I. (2014). Speech emotion recognition using deep neural network and extreme learning machine. In *Interspeech 2014*.
Han, H., Byun, K., & Kang, H.-G. (2018). A deep learning-based stress detection algorithm with speech signal. In *AVSU'18 International Multimedia Conference*.
Hansen, J. H. L., & Liu, G. (2016). Unsupervised accent classification for deep data fusion of accent and language information. *Speech Communication, 78*, 19–33. https://doi.org/10.1016/j.specom.2015.12.004
Hansen, J. H., Bou-Ghazale, S. E., Sarikaya, R., & Pellom, B. (1997). Getting started with SUSAS: A speech under simulated and actual stress database. *Eurospeech*.
Hao, M., Cao, W.-H., Liu, Z.-T., Wu, M., & Xiao, P. (2020). Visual-audio emotion recognition based on multi-task and ensemble learning with multiple features. *Neurocomputing, 391*, 42–51.
Hartanto, D., Kampmann, I. L., Morina, N., Emmelkamp, P. G. M., Neerincx, M. A., & Brinkman, W. P. (2014). Controlling social stress in virtual reality environments. *PLoS One, 9*(3), e92804. https://doi.org/10.1371/journal.pone.0092804
Hilfert, T., & König, M. (2016). Low-cost virtual reality environment for engineering and construction. *Visualization in Engineering, 4*(1), 1–18. https://doi.org/10.1186/s40327-015-0031-5
Hu, H., Xu, M., & Wu, W. (2007, April 15–20). GMM Supervector Based SVM with Spectral Features for Speech Emotion Recognition. In *2007 IEEE International conference on acoustics, speech and signal processing – ICASSP '07*.

IBM. (2020). *Recurrent neural networks*. Retrieved 7/2/2022, from https://www.ibm.com/cloud/learn/recurrent-neural-networks

Issa, D., Fatih Demirci, M., & Yazici, A. (2020). Speech emotion recognition with deep convolutional neural networks. *Biomedical Signal Processing and Control, 59*, 101894. https://doi.org/10.1016/j.bspc.2020.101894

Jain, M., Narayan, S., Balaji, P., Bhowmick, A., & Muthu, R. K. (2020). Speech emotion recognition using support vector machine. *arXiv preprint arXiv:2002.07590.*

Jezova, D., Hlavacova, N., Dicko, I., Solarikova, P., & Brezina, I. (2016). Psychosocial stress based on public speech in humans: Is there a real life/laboratory setting cross-adaptation? *Stress, 19*(4), 429–433. https://doi.org/10.1080/10253890.2016.1203416

Jönsson, P., Wallergård, M., Österberg, K., Hansen, Å. M., Johansson, G., & Karlson, B. (2010). Cardiovascular and cortisol reactivity and habituation to a virtual reality version of the Trier Social Stress Test: A pilot study. *Psychoneuroendocrinology, 35*(9), 1397–1403. https://doi.org/10.1016/j.psyneuen.2010.04.003

Julião, M., Silva, J., Aguiar, A., Moniz, H., & Batista, F. (2015). Speech features for discriminating stress using branch and bound wrapper search. In *International Symposium on Languages, Applications and Technologies.*

Junek, W. (2007). Mind reading: The interactive guide to emotions. *Journal of the Canadian Academy of Child and Adolescent Psychiatry, 16*(4), 182.

Juslin, P. N., & Laukka, P. (2003). Communication of emotions in vocal expression and music performance: different channels, same code? *Psychological Bulletin, 129*(5), 770–814. https://doi.org/10.1037/0033-2909.129.5.770

Kaiser, J. F. (1993). Some useful properties of Teager's energy operators. In *1993 IEEE international conference on acoustics, speech, and signal processing.*

Kamiloğlu, R. G., Fischer, A. H., & Sauter, D. A. (2020). Good vibrations: A review of vocal expressions of positive emotions. *Psychonomic Bulletin & Review, 27*(2), 237–265. https://doi.org/10.3758/s13423-019-01701-x

Kappas, A., Hess, U., & Scherer, K. R. (1991). Voice and emotion. In *Fundamentals of nonverbal behavior* (p. 200). Cambridge University Press.

Kassem, M., Benomran, L., & Teizer, J. (2017). Virtual environments for safety learning in construction and engineering: Seeking evidence and identifying gaps for future research. *Visualization in Engineering, 5*(1), 1–15. https://doi.org/10.1186/s40327-017-0054-1

Kim, K., Kim, C.-H., Kim, S.-Y., Roh, D., & Kim, S. I. (2009). Virtual reality for obsessive-compulsive disorder: Past and the future. *Psychiatry Investigation, 6*(3), 115–121. https://doi.org/10.4306/pi.2009.6.3.115

Kimani, E., & Bickmore, T. (2019). Addressing public speaking anxiety in real-time using a virtual public speaking coach and physiological sensors. In *Proceedings of the 19th ACM international conference on intelligent virtual agents*. Paris, France. https://doi-org.elibrary.jcu.edu.au/10.1145/3308532.3329409

Koolagudi, S. G., & Rao, K. S. (2012). Emotion recognition from speech: A review. *International Journal of Speech Technology, 15*(2), 99–117.

Koolagudi, S. G., Maity, S., Kumar, V. A., Chakrabarti, S., & Rao, K. S. (2009). IITKGP-SESC: Speech database for emotion analysis. In *International conference on contemporary computing.*

Koroleva, M., Bakhchina, A., Shyshalov, I., Parin, S. B., & Polevaia, S. A. (2014). Influence of the context of public speaking on human functional state. *International Journal of Psychophysiology, 94*(2), 230–231. https://doi.org/10.1016/j.ijpsycho.2014.08.901

Kothgassner, O. D., Felnhofer, A., Hlavacs, H., Beutl, L., Palme, R., Kryspin-Exner, I., & Glenk, L. M. (2016). Salivary cortisol and cardiovascular reactivity to a public speaking task in a virtual and real-life environment. *Computers in Human Behavior, 62*, 124–135. https://doi.org/10.1016/j.chb.2016.03.081

Kothgassner, O. D., Goreis, A., Kafka, J. X., Kaufmann, M., Atteneder, K., Beutl, L., Hennig-Fast, K., Hlavacs, H., & Felnhofer, A. (2019). Virtual social support buffers stress response: An experimental comparison of real-life and virtual support prior to a social stressor. *Journal of Behavior Therapy and Experimental Psychiatry, 63*, 57–65.

Kotlyar, M., Donahue, C., Thuras, P., Kushner, M. G., O'Gorman, N., Smith, E. A., & Adson, D. E. (2008). Physiological response to a speech stressor presented in a virtual reality environment. *Psychophysiology, 45*(6), 1034–1037. https://doi.org/10.1111/j.1469-8986.2008.00690.x

Kuchibhotla, S., Vankayalapati, H. D., Vaddi, R., & Anne, K. R. (2014). A comparative analysis of classifiers in emotion recognition through acoustic features. *International Journal of Speech Technology, 17*(4), 401–408.

Kwon, O.-W., Chan, K., Hao, J., & Lee, T.-W. (2003). Emotion recognition by speech signals. In *Eighth European conference on speech communication and technology.*

Laver, K. E., George, S., Thomas, S., Deutsch, J. E., & Crotty, M. (2015). Virtual reality for stroke rehabilitation. *The Cochrane Database of Systematic Reviews*, (2), CD008349. https://doi.org/10.1002/14651858.CD008349.pub3

Le, Q. T., Le, Q. T., Pedro, A., Pedro, A., Park, C. S., & Park, C. S. (2015). A social virtual reality based construction safety education system for experiential learning. *Journal of Intelligent & Robotic Systems, 79*(3), 487–506. https://doi.org/10.1007/s10846-014-0112-z

Levy, F., Leboucher, P., Rautureau, G., & Jouvent, R. (2016). E-virtual reality exposure therapy in Acrophobia: A pilot study. *Journal of Telemedicine and Telecare, 22*(4), 215–220. https://doi.org/10.1177/1357633X15598243

Li, X., Tao, J., Johnson, M. T., Soltis, J., Savage, A., Leong, K. M., & Newman, J. D. (2007). Stress and emotion classification using jitter and shimmer features. In *2007 IEEE International conference on acoustics, speech and signal processing-ICASSP'07.*

Lin, Y.-L., & Wei, G. (2005). Speech emotion recognition based on HMM and SVM. In *2005 international conference on machine learning and cybernetics.*

Lindner, P., Miloff, A., Fagernäs, S., Andersen, J., Sigeman, M., Andersson, G., Furmark, T., Carlbring, P., & Linköpings, u., Institutionen för beteendevetenskap och, l., Filosofiska, f., & Psykologi. (2019). Therapist-led and self-led one-session virtual reality exposure therapy for public speaking anxiety with consumer hardware and software: A randomized controlled trial. *Journal of Anxiety Disorders, 61*, 45–54. https://doi.org/10.1016/j.janxdis.2018.07.003

Liscombe, J., Riccardi, G., & Hakkani-Tur, D. (2005). Using context to improve emotion detection in spoken dialog systems. In *The Proceedings of EUROSPEECH 2005.*

Lister, H. A., Piercey, C. D., & Joordens, C. (2010). The effectiveness of 3-D video virtual reality for the treatment of fear of public speaking. *Journal of Cyber Therapy and Rehabilitation, 3*(4), 375. http://jcu.summon.serialssolutions.com/2.0.0/link/0/eLvHCXMwpV1LSwMxEB5avYjgAxXf5OZpbTY7yW4OIkVb6sWC9OahJLOJUKQtffx_k-22Vk-Cl-SSQEgmk2_CfPMBZOKeJ798AupSas-RLKaF48Rtal2IvrQ3ThHhT8IcdNfUmCr5PbrKymmb6XTeKifUagspMEqw5a12_7XzuCWmsXwYxfTSIQWM2oRdoSTGkvov7f7m6yWEhFJUwoJpXmASXmisHfI-NDCr35buIXyul-HWP4AjWm4zdL6rNv5_sUdwUGNQ1l4ZzTE03PgE3oPBsFV2R-0A2cSzLHlmkak3Ce0sUk1YAJkRubMAdlkAj2yTqR6H-3BvYr8qns3mU1eJXZ3CoNsZPPWSWnkh-VAZT7yRKuepUzqAFV5aFMJxnxYcS2eMLpTUWkjDrXIhPvFaWlLOKasRc-JoszPYGU_G7hxYRhgCKqHKNLdoOBVekScnKcZ9mvgF3MUdG8brtJgZMjUrIMyOhamG35t3-eeRV7An6qQTIa5hZzFbuhtohrO7rQwhtr23L_APxyU

Livingstone, S. R., & Russo, F. A. (2018). The Ryerson Audio-Visual Database of Emotional Speech and Song (RAVDESS): A dynamic, multimodal set of facial and vocal expressions in North American English. *PloS One, 13*(5), e0196391.

Low, L.-S. A., Maddage, N. C., Lech, M., Sheeber, L. B., & Allen, N. B. (2010). Detection of clinical depression in adolescents' speech during family interactions. *IEEE Transactions on Biomedical Engineering, 58*(3), 574–586.

Lugger, M., & Yang, B. (2007). The relevance of voice quality features in speaker independent emotion recognition. In *2007 IEEE International conference on acoustics, speech and signal processing-ICASSP'07.*

Manju, T., Padmavathi, S., & Tamilselvi, D. (2017). A rehabilitation therapy for autism spectrum disorder using virtual reality. In *International Conference On Intelligent Information Technologies.*

Marsella, S., Xu, Y., Lhommet, M., Feng, A., Scherer, S., & Shapiro, A. (2013). Virtual character performance from speech. In *Proceedings of the 12th ACM SIGGRAPH/Eurographics symposium on computer animation.*

Martin, D. J. J. H. (2021). *Hidden Markov Models.* https://web.stanford.edu/~jurafsky/slp3/A.pdf

Martin, O., Kotsia, I., Macq, B., & Pitas, I. (2006). The eNTERFACE'05 audio-visual emotion database. In *22nd International Conference on Data Engineering Workshops (ICDEW'06).*

Maskey, M., Lowry, J., Rodgers, J., McConachie, H., & Parr, J. R. (2014). Reducing specific phobia/fear in young people with autism spectrum disorders (ASDs) through a virtual reality environment intervention. *PloS One, 9*(7), e100374. https://doi.org/10.1371/journal.pone.0100374

McFee, B., Raffel, C., Liang, D., Ellis, D. P., McVicar, M., Battenberg, E., & Nieto, O. (2015). librosa: Audio and music signal analysis in python. In *Proceedings of the 14th python in science conference.*

Miloff, A., Lindner, P., Hamilton, W., Reuterskiöld, L., Andersson, G., Carlbring, P., Stockholms, U., Samhällsvetenskapliga, F., Psykologiska, I., & Klinisk, P. (2016). Single-session gamified virtual reality exposure therapy for spider phobia vs. traditional exposure therapy: Study protocol for a randomized controlled non-inferiority trial. *Trials, 17*(1), 60. https://doi.org/10.1186/s13063-016-1171-1

Mitchell, R. L., & Ross, E. D. (2013). Attitudinal prosody: What we know and directions for future study. *Neuroscience & Biobehavioral Reviews, 37*(3), 471–479.

Molina, K. I., Ricci, N. A., de Moraes, S. A., & Perracini, M. R. (2014). Virtual reality using games for improving physical functioning in older adults: A systematic review. *Journal of Neuro Engineering and Rehabilitation, 11*(1), 156. https://doi.org/10.1186/1743-0003-11-156

Motraghi, T. E., Seim, R. W., Meyer, E. C., & Morissette, S. B. (2014). Virtual reality exposure therapy for the treatment of posttraumatic stress disorder: A methodological review using CONSORT guidelines. *Journal of Clinical Psychology, 70*(3), 197–208. https://doi.org/10.1002/jclp.22051

Mujber, T. S., Szecsi, T., & Hashmi, M. S. (2004). Virtual reality applications in manufacturing process simulation. *Journal of materials processing technology, 155*, 1834–1838.

Neiberg, D., Elenius, K., Laskowski, K., & Isca. (2006). *Emotion recognition in spontaneous speech using GMMs.* <Go to ISI>://WOS:000269965900203.

Nijholt, A. (2014). Breaking fresh ground in human-media interaction research. *Frontiers in ICT, 2014.*

Nogueiras, A., Moreno, A., Bonafonte, A., & Mariño, J. B. (2001). Speech emotion recognition using hidden Markov models. In *Seventh European Conference on Speech Communication and Technology.*

North, M. M., North, S. M., & Coble, J. R. (1998). Virtual reality therapy: An effective treatment for the fear of public speaking. *International Journal of Virtual Reality, 3*(3), 1–6. https://doi.org/10.20870/IJVR.1998.3.3.2625

Nwe, T. L., Foo, S. W., & De Silva, L. C. (2003). Detection of stress and emotion in speech using traditional and FFT based log energy features. In *Fourth international conference on information, communications and signal processing, 2003 and the Fourth Pacific Rim conference on multimedia. Proceedings of the 2003 Joint.*

Ooi, C. S., Seng, K. P., Ang, L.-M., & Chew, L. W. (2014). A new approach of audio emotion recognition. *Expert Systems with Applications, 41*(13), 5858–5869. https://doi.org/10.1016/j.eswa.2014.03.026

Opriş, D., Pintea, S., García-Palacios, A., Botella, C., Szamosközi, Ş., & David, D. (2012). Virtual reality exposure therapy in anxiety disorders: A quantitative meta-analysis. *Depression and Anxiety, 29*(2), 85–93. https://doi.org/10.1002/da.20910

Ordaz, N., Romero, D., Gorecky, D., & Siller, H. R. (2015). Serious games and virtual simulator for automotive manufacturing education & training. *Procedia Computer Science, 75*, 267–274. https://doi.org/10.1016/j.procs.2015.12.247

Owens, M. E., Owens, M. E., Beidel, D. C., & Beidel, D. C. (2015). Can virtual reality effectively elicit distress associated with social anxiety disorder? *Journal of Psychopathology and Behavioral Assessment, 37*(2), 296–305. https://doi.org/10.1007/s10862-014-9454-x

Palo, H., Mohanty, M. N., & Chandra, M. (2015). Design of neural network model for emotional speech recognition. In *Artificial intelligence and evolutionary algorithms in engineering systems* (pp. 291–300). Springer.

Pan, X., Gillies, M., Barker, C., Clark, D. M., & Slater, M. (2012). Socially anxious and confident men interact with a forward virtual woman: An experimental study. *PloS One, 7*(4), e32931. https://doi.org/10.1371/journal.pone.0032931

Parsons, T. D., & Rizzo, A. A. (2008). Affective outcomes of virtual reality exposure therapy for anxiety and specific phobias: A meta-analysis. *Journal of Behavior Therapy and Experimental Psychiatry, 39*(3), 250–261.

Pedro, A., Le, Q. T., & Park, C. S. (2016). Framework for integrating safety into construction methods education through interactive virtual reality. *Journal of Professional Issues in Engineering Education and Practice, 142*(2), 4015011. https://doi.org/10.1061/(ASCE)EI.1943-5541.0000261

Pellett, K., & Zaidi, S. F. M. (2019). A framework for virtual reality training to improve public speaking. In *25th ACM symposium on virtual reality software and technology*. Parramatta, NSW, Australia. https://doi-org.elibrary.jcu.edu.au/10.1145/3359996.3364727

Pertaub, D., Slater, M., & Barker, C. (2001). An experiment on fear of public speaking in virtual reality. *Studies in Health Technology and Informatics, 81*, 372–378.

Pfister, T., & Robinson, P. (2011). Real-time recognition of affective states from nonverbal features of speech and its application for public speaking skill analysis. *IEEE Transactions on Affective Computing, 2*(2), 66–78. https://doi.org/10.1109/T-AFFC.2011.8

Pisanski, K., Nowak, J., & Sorokowski, P. (2016). Individual differences in cortisol stress response predict increases in voice pitch during exam stress. *Physiology & Behavior, 163*, 234–238. https://doi.org/10.1016/j.physbeh.2016.05.018

Poorna, S. S., Anuraj, K., & Nair, G. J. (2018). A weight based approach for emotion recognition from speech: An analysis using South Indian languages. In I. Zelinka, R. Senkerik, G. Panda, & P. S. L. Kanthan (Eds.), *Soft computing systems, Icscs 2018* (Vol. 837, pp. 14–24). https://doi.org/10.1007/978-981-13-1936-5_2

Powers, M. B., Briceno, N. F., Gresham, R., Jouriles, E. N., Emmelkamp, P. M. G., & Smits, J. A. J. (2013). Do conversations with virtual avatars increase feelings of social anxiety? *Journal of Anxiety Disorders, 27*(4), 398–403. https://doi.org/10.1016/j.janxdis.2013.03.003

Přibil, J., & Přibilová, A. (2013). Evaluation of influence of spectral and prosodic features on gmm classification of Czech and Slovak emotional speech. *EURASIP Journal on Audio, Speech, and Music Processing, 2013*(1), 1–22. https://doi.org/10.1186/1687-4722-2013-8

Rao, K. S., Rao, K. S., Koolagudi, S. G., Koolagudi, S. G., Vempada, R. R., & Vempada, R. R. (2013). Emotion recognition from speech using global and local prosodic features. *International Journal of Speech Technology, 16*(2), 143–160. https://doi.org/10.1007/s10772-012-9172-2

Rong, J., Li, G., & Chen, Y.-P. P. (2009). Acoustic feature selection for automatic emotion recognition from speech. *Information Processing and Management, 45*(3), 315–328. https://doi.org/10.1016/j.ipm.2008.09.003

Ruscio, A. M., Brown, T. A., Chiu, W. T., Sareen, J., Stein, M. B., & Kessler, R. C. (2008). Social fears and social Phobia in the USA: Results from the national comorbidity survey replication. *Psychological medicine, 38*(1), 15–28. https://doi.org/10.1017/S0033291707001699

Ryerson Multimedia Research Lab., R. U. (2017). *RML emotion database.* http://shachi.org/resources/4965

Sanchez, M. H., Tur, G., Ferrer, L., & Hakkani-Tür, D. (2010). Domain adaptation and compensation for emotion detection. Eleventh Annual Conference of the International Speech Communication Association.

Scherer, K. R. (1995). Expression of emotion in voice and music. *Journal of Voice, 9*(3), 235–248.

Scherer, K. R., Banse, R., Wallbott, H. G., & Goldbeck, T. (1991). Vocal cues in emotion encoding and decoding. *Motivation and Emotion, 15*(2), 123–148. https://doi.org/10.1007/BF00995674

Schmid Mast, M., Kleinlogel, E. P., Tur, B., & Bachmann, M. (2018). The future of interpersonal skills development: Immersive virtual reality training with virtual humans. *Human Resource Development Quarterly, 29*(2), 125–141. https://doi.org/10.1002/hrdq.21307

Schneider, J., Börner, D., Rosmalen, P. V., & Specht, M. (2015). Presentation trainer, your public speaking multimodal coach. In *Proceedings of the 2015 ACM on International Conference on Multimodal Interaction*. Seattle, Washington, USA. https://doi-org.elibrary.jcu.edu.au/10.1145/2818346.2830603

Schreiber, L. (2011). Informative speaking. In The Public Speaking Project (Ed.), *Public speaking. The virtual text* (pp. 15–11).

Schuller, B., Rigoll, G., & Lang, M. (2003a). *Hidden Markov model-based speech emotion recognition* (Vol. 2). https://doi.org/10.1109/ICME.2003.1220939

Schuller, B., Rigoll, G., & Lang, M. (2003b). Hmm-based music retrieval using stereophonic feature information and framelength adaptation. In *2003 International Conference on Multimedia and Expo. ICME'03. Proceedings* (Cat. No. 03TH8698).

Schuller, B., Seppi, D., Batliner, A., Maier, A., & Steidl, S. (2007). Towards more reality in the recognition of emotional speech. In *2007 IEEE international conference on acoustics, speech and signal processing-ICASSP'07*.

Schuller, B., Batliner, A., Steidl, S., & Seppi, D. (2011). Recognising realistic emotions and affect in speech: State of the art and lessons learnt from the first challenge. *Speech Communication, 53*(9), 1062–1087. https://doi.org/10.1016/j.specom.2011.01.011

Scikit Learn. (2022). *Support vector machines*. Retrieved 7/2/2022, from https://scikit-learn.org/stable/modules/svm.html#:~:text=Support%20vector%20machines%20(SVMs)%20are,classification%2C%20regression%20and%20outliers%20detection.&text=Uses%20a%20subset%20of%20training,it%20is%20also%20memory%20efficient

Semwal, N., Kumar, A., & Narayanan, S. (2017). *Automatic speech emotion detection system using multi-domain acoustic feature selection and classification models*. <Go to ISI>://WOS:000411739900003.

Shabahi, S. (2020). *my-voice-analysis 0.7*. https://pypi.org/project/my-voice-analysis/

Slater, M., Pertaub, D.-P., & Steed, A. (1999). Public speaking in virtual reality: Facing an audience of avatars. *IEEE Computer Graphics and Applications, 19*(2), 6–9.

Slater, M., Pertaub, D.-P., Barker, C., & Clark, D. M. (2006). An experimental study on fear of public speaking using a virtual environment. *Cyberpsychology & Behavior, 9*(5), 627–633.

Soltani, K., & Ainon, R. N. (2007). *Speech emotion detection based on neural networks*. <Go to ISI>://WOS:000259439900203.

Sun, R., & Moore, E. (2011). Investigating glottal parameters and teager energy operators in emotion recognition. International Conference on Affective Computing and Intelligent Interaction.

Takac, M., Collett, J., Blom, K. J., Conduit, R., Rehm, I., & De Foe, A. (2019). Public speaking anxiety decreases within repeated virtual reality training sessions. *PloS One, 14*(5), e0216288. https://doi.org/10.1371/journal.pone.0216288

Tanveer, M. I., Lin, E., & Hoque, M. (2015). Rhema: A real-time in-situ intelligent interface to help people with public speaking. In *Proceedings of the 20th international conference on intelligent user interfaces*. Atlanta, Georgia, USA. https://doi-org.elibrary.jcu.edu.au/10.1145/2678025.2701386

Tashev, I. J., Wang, Z. Q., Godin, K., & Ieee. (2017). *Speech emotion recognition based on gaussian mixture models and deep neural networks* 2017 Information Theory and Applications Workshop, <Go to ISI>://WOS:000426450600036.

Teoh, A. N., & Hilmert, C. (2018). Social support as a comfort or an encouragement: A systematic review on the contrasting effects of social support on cardiovascular reactivity. *British Journal of Health Psychology, 23*(4), 1040–1065. https://doi.org/10.1111/bjhp.12337

The EndNote Team. (2013). *EndNote*. In (Version EndNote X9) [64 bit]. Clarivate.

Thorsteinsson, E. B., & James, J. E. (1999). A meta-analysis of the effects of experimental manipulations of social support during laboratory stress. *Psychology & Health, 14*(5), 869–886. https://doi.org/10.1080/08870449908407353

Ticknor, B. (2018). Using virtual reality to treat offenders: An examination. *International Journal of Criminal Justice Sciences, 13*(2), 316–325. http://jcu.summon.serialssolutions.com/2.0.0/link/0/eLvHCXMwpV07T8MwED6VdunCo4B41MoTWyCt09hmQQW1YgJUFRgrxw_EQwmkrQT_nnPiUMrAwpIhGWL5ku8-2_fdB0B7J2HwCxMUZWHXCENjixG3oiu5soorvOhIaLsqmCuLC500xoe7QskCunWm3K75KRIH51GAGfv87T1wPlLuvNWbaqxBw7kt4XKscTG8vh1X6Iy4UMjjXJeaAMmJWMHgGqU-s4w24LEahKn2_57V4qc-Z9mz8V9D3YR1Tz7JoPxatqBm0hY0vzHwswXtUq5LHsyrlbkhx6S6keUv28CLCgNy_5Q72QkZm4LFk3lGJo58khtrC2u62RkZpGT4IV2hjQv9DtyNhpPLq8B7LwRIERGakfYlth9aG2vMcyo0PXdEiOtDpkXsiqyZ4EmfSxkxZAEaaRW-wCQ81kZIai3dhXqapWYPiGJhKA3rJxTpGrItIS2PXKNCqkwSsXgf2tWkTf0PNJsuZ-zg78eH0EQOw8sK2jbU5_nCHMEahqrjQ98p1tlf4p7B7A

Ticknor, B. (2019). Virtual reality and correctional rehabilitation: A game changer. *Criminal Justice and Behavior, 46*(9), 1319–1336. https://doi.org/10.1177/0093854819842588

Truong, K. P., & van Leeuwen, D. A. (2007). Automatic discrimination between laughter and speech. *Speech Communication, 49*(2), 144–158. https://doi.org/10.1016/j.specom.2007.01.001

Truong, K. P., Van Leeuwen, D. A., & De Jong, F. M. (2012). Speech-based recognition of self-reported and observed emotion in a dimensional space. *Speech Communication, 54*(9), 1049–1063.

Uchino, B. N., & Garvey, T. S. (1997). The availability of social support reduces cardiovascular reactivity to acute psychological stress. *Journal of Behavioral Medicine, 20*(1), 15–27. https://doi.org/10.1023/A:1025583012283

Valmaggia, L. R., Latif, L., Kempton, M. J., & Rus-Calafell, M. (2016). Virtual reality in the psychological treatment for mental health problems: An systematic review of recent evidence. *Psychiatry Research, 236*, 189–195. https://doi.org/10.1016/j.psychres.2016.01.015

VanderPlas, J. (2016). Python data science handbook. In *Python data science handbook*. O'Reilly Media, Inc.

Wallbott, H. G., & Scherer, K. R. (1986). How universal and specific is emotional experience? Evidence from 27 countries on five continents. *Information (International Social Science Council), 25*(4), 763–795.

Wang, K., An, N., Li, B. N., Zhang, Y., & Li, L. (2015). Speech emotion recognition using fourier parameters. *IEEE Transactions on affective computing, 6*(1), 69–75.

Westenberg, P. M., Bokhorst, C. L., Miers, A. C., Sumter, S. R., Kallen, V. L., van Pelt, J., & Blöte, A. W. (2009). A prepared speech in front of a pre-recorded audience: Subjective, physiological, and neuroendocrine responses to the leiden public speaking task. *Biological Psychology, 82*(2), 116–124. https://doi.org/10.1016/j.biopsycho.2009.06.005

Wiemers, U. S., Schultheiss, O. C., & Wolf, O. T. (2015). Public speaking in front of an unreceptive audience increases implicit power motivation and its endocrine arousal signature. *Hormones and Behavior, 71*, 69–74. https://doi.org/10.1016/j.yhbeh.2015.04.007

Wirtz, P. H., Ehlert, U., Kottwitz, M. U., La Marca, R., & Semmer, N. K. (2013). Occupational role stress is associated with higher cortisol reactivity to acute stress. *Journal of Occupational Health Psychology, 18*(2), 121–131. https://doi.org/10.1037/a0031802

Wörtwein, T., Chollet, M., Schauerte, B., Morency, L.-P., Stiefelhagen, R., & Scherer, S. (2015). Multimodal public speaking performance assessment. In *Proceedings of the 2015 ACM on International Conference on Multimodal Interaction*. Seattle, Washington, USA. https://doi--org.elibrary.jcu.edu.au/10.1145/2818346.2820762

Zeng, Y., Mao, H., Peng, D., & Yi, Z. (2019). Spectrogram based multi-task audio classification. *Multimedia Tools and Applications, 78*(3), 3705–3722. https://doi.org/10.1007/s11042-017-5539-3

Zhou, G., Hansen, J. H., & Kaiser, J. F. (2001). Nonlinear feature based classification of speech under stress. *IEEE Transactions on Speech and Audio Processing, 9*(3), 201–216.

Chapter 8
Understanding Bias in Recruitment Decision Making: The Impact of Work/Life Experiences in Responding to Diverse Job Candidates

Shane Whitfield and Jacob Wood

Abstract Workplaces have become increasingly diverse as accessibility, acceptance, migration, and societal expectation have grown – but does this mean that everyone has an equal opportunity to have their skills and qualifications recognised, access to meaningful employment, and career progression opportunities? Through better recognising how experience may influence decision making during recruitment, this study will support the development of tools, techniques, practices, and policies that reduce discrimination, enhance innovation, and ensure workplaces are both welcoming and benefitting from what diversity offers. Using data gathered through a questionnaire, this exploratory study conducted within the Aotearoa New Zealand social service sector, has considered the impacts of work/life experiences and demography on decision making during a recruitment process – focused on characteristics of diversity. Our research shows links between experience and decision making, noting people with more experience of diversity appeared less likely to be influenced by diverse characteristics when making recruitment decisions. It also highlighted the apparent impact of diversity-based training on perceptions of diversity, and where recruitment bias was evident toward people with disability and those who have gathered their experience or qualifications overseas.

Keywords Recruitment · Diversity · Decision making · Experience · Aotearoa New Zealand

S. Whitfield
Southern Institute of Technology, Invercargill, New Zealand
e-mail: 2020001368@student.sit.ac.nz

J. Wood (✉)
James Cook University, Singapore, Singapore
e-mail: jacob.wood@jcu.edu.au

E. L. Eijdenberg et al. (eds.), *Innovation-Driven Business and Sustainability in the Tropics*, https://doi.org/10.1007/978-981-99-2909-2_8

8.1 Introduction

Global migration, technological advances, social change, and pro-diversity movements have led to a significantly different workforce supply chain to what existed even 20 years ago (Noon, 2018). Workplaces have become more diverse as accessibility, acceptance, migration, and expectation have increased – but does this mean that everyone has an equal opportunity to have their skills and qualifications recognised, access to meaningful employment, and career progression opportunities? This burgeoning workforce diversity asks employers to think differently about recruitment, maximising potential, maintaining harmony, professional development, understanding difference, and ultimately keeping people safe from discrimination (Ali et al., 2015). Mid-twentieth century economic theory suggested that discrimination in the workplace would be all but eliminated within a generation (Pager et al., 2009), however most pundits would now acknowledge that rather than a workplace revolution, employers have simply found new ways to discriminate (Pager et al., 2009).

Literature and research show that workplace diversity has not only steadily increased over the past few decades but will continue to expand, as employers become more cognisant of inclusiveness and harnessing the power that diversity offers a business (Combs & Nadkarni, 2005; Garnero et al., 2014; Hitchcock et al., 2016; Mensah & Sommers, 2016; Lang, 2020). Yet multiple reports and studies indicate that diverse candidates still struggle with some of the most basic employment rights – often experiencing workplace discrimination, lower pay, fewer career progression opportunities, and recruitment bias (Haar, 2022; OECD, 2020; Pager et al., 2009; Tan, 2021; Yeung, 2017).

Through the continuing discourse around equity, diversity, and inclusion (Oswick & Noon, 2014), societal awareness and expectation for positive change and fair treatment has grown. Companies, academia, and governments have grappled with a range of strategies to try and mitigate the inequity that diverse candidates experience in the workplace, including policy initiatives (Lang, 2020), use of algorithms during recruitment (Parasurama & Sedoc, 2021), diversity based training (Chang et al., 2019), and affirmative action practices (Combs & Nadkarni, 2005) – all of which appear to have limited success particularly when used in isolation of each other (Lang, 2020).

This exploratory study has focused on the recruitment process – specifically the identification of influences on decisions made during recruitment, thereby creating better understanding of the continuing prevalence of discrimination at this stage of employment.Adding to previous social servce sector based studies focused on HR and employment conditions in New Zealand (Tan et al., 2019, 2021; Tan & Yeap, 2022), this study will note links between life experiences and views on diverse candidates during a recruitment process – with suggestions for potential areas for further study discussed. Therefore, the aim of this study is to understand bias in recruitment decision making through identifying the impact of work/life experiences in response to diverse job candidates. We seek to address this specific research question, do work/life experiences impact perceptions of diverse candidates during a recruitment process? To answer this question, we have developed two key objectives, these include (1) Ascertain whether people with more diverse life experiences perceive diverse candidates more positively; and (2) Determine whether people with more work experience, including involvement in recruitment, perceive diverse candidates more positively.

The rest of the study is as follows. In Sect. 8.2 we provide a detailed assessment of relevant empirical literature. Section 8.3 details the methodological approaches utilised in this study before Sect. 8.4 provides a clear description of the results and subsequent areas of discussion. Finally, in Sect. 8.5, a series of key conclusions are then drawn with some important recommendations made.

8.2 Literature Review

8.2.1 Equity, Diversity, and Inclusion – An Evolving Discourse

Oswick and Noon (2014) contend that modern-day discourse around diversity and inclusion can trace its roots back to early thinking and conversations around equity. Essentially, suggest Oswick and Noon (2014), the trend toward pro-diversity rhetoric emerged from the realisation that diversity in the workplace would steadily increase over time – so to manage and maximise this potential, workplaces would need to adapt their policies and practices to suit (Oswick & Noon, 2014). Oswick and Noon (2014) note however that a major issue within the equity discourse was that it problematised difference – making it something that needed resolving rather than a positive phenomenon. This in turn led to social strategies such as affirmative action and positive discrimination – policy approaches where minority population groups were given preferential treatment to facilitate opportunities they may have otherwise not achieved (Hitchcock et al., 2016; Mensah & Sommers, 2016; Oswick & Noon, 2014). To this day multiple jurisdictions continue to apply affirmative action practices to resolve equity issues, and arguably this approach has provided the platform for equal rights movements and other proactive challenges of the status quo (Hitchcock et al., 2016).

The literature also speaks to multiple examples of the negative consequences of affirmative action policy, such as the direct reference to the differences between people causing these to be highlighted as the problem; the resentment created amongst some populations toward other groups, which then leads to further discrimination; the watering down of identity for people with diverse characteristics, created by an expectation to conform; the formation of new class layers within minority groups that still exclude more disadvantaged cohorts; and its universal application with minimal consideration of cultural or domestic structures (Combs & Nadkarni, 2005; Hitchcock et al., 2016; Lang, 2020; Oswick & Noon, 2014; Yeung, 2017). Therefore, while affirmative action may help get people through the door it does not reduce the layers of discrimination they experience on the other side (Oswick & Noon, 2014).

From equity discourse emerged the diversity conversation – where diversity began to be described as a benefit to communities and workplaces rather than as a problem to solve (Lang, 2020; Oswick & Noon, 2014). Garnero et al. (2014) describe managing diversity as a transfer of experience and knowledge between different groups that supports the understanding of ethnic, gender, cultural and other influences on how we behave. This description is built on the premise that bias and discrimination is more commonly driven by simple ignorance toward others, which then triggers othering behaviour and exclusion due to misunderstanding or even fear (Garnero et al., 2014; Oswick & Noon, 2014).

Much literature espouses the benefits of diversity as numerous and broad reaching including increased innovation; new perspectives on issues and solutions; a more accepting and harmonious workforce; expanded talent and workforce pools; and interestingly diverse businesses are viewed more favourably by prospective consumers, partners, and employees (Combs & Nadkarni, 2005; Garnero et al., 2014; Guillaume et al., 2017; Hitchcock et al., 2016). There are similarly multiple accounts of the challenges that diversity may bring to the workplace and communities, such as a sense of loss of purpose which then lowers morale; miscommunication that leads to misunderstanding and highlighting of differences; actions and behaviours that confirm preconceived stereotypes; and all these things leading to conflict situations (Guillaume et al., 2017; Hitchcock et al., 2016; Oswick & Noon, 2014).

Following on from diversity comes the modern day discourse of inclusion – where previously diversity practices spoke to recognising, understanding and managing differences between people (Combs & Nadkarni, 2005; Garnero et al., 2014; Guillaume et al., 2017; Hitchcock et al., 2016; Lang, 2020), inclusion is much more about engaging with the potential that diversity offers, combining this with appropriate management and policy, to ensure that everyone wins – including those within the majority (Oswick & Noon, 2014). It is arguable that inclusion and diversity are interdependent on each other, and policy that reflects a celebration of difference and supports everyone being able to find a space that accommodates them within their workplace is key (Oswick & Noon, 2014). It should be noted that this management approach still has the potential to reinforce structures that suit the majority and does not necessarily ensure that everyone has an equitable opportunity to get to the table in the first place (Oswick &Noon, 2014).

8.2.2 Diversity in the Workplace – A Double Edged Sword?

The positive benefits of a more diverse workplace have been discussed across many aspects within the literature, these positive aspects have included: Lang (2020) suggesting that elected officials and public servants are more likely to be trusted when they better represent the demographics of the constituents they serve; Dietz et al.

(2015) contending that diverse employees in customer facing roles connect more easily to a broader demographic of consumers; and Garnero et al. (2014) noting that the perspectives introduced by diverse employees aides critical thinking in the workplace, as people start to view and understand challenges from different angles. It is also broadly noted that diversity can bring challenges for the workforce including exacerbating stereotypes, a drop in efficiency and productivity, miscommunication and misunderstanding, a loss of purpose and increased anxiety, and of course an increase in discriminatory and bias behaviour driven by much of the above (Combs & Nadkarni, 2005; Dietz et al., 2015; Garnero et al., 2014; Pager et al., 2009). Another key factor addressed within the literature is the issue of recruitment bias. Derous and Ryan (2018) contend that bias is widespread and furthermore, that it is often an unconscious process where recruiters tend to unknowingly lean toward applicants that are more like themselves; somewhat worryingly they further demonstrate that it is unlikely that many regular HR practices and tools can fully address these concerns (Derous & Ryan, 2018). Also of note in their research is the finding that when a candidate is a strong fit or indeed a weak fit for the role, bias is less influential because the decision is relatively straight forward, however, when there are several similar candidates, the recruiter will likely subconsciously prefer someone more like themself (Derous & Ryan, 2018).

Gender bias is also broadly discussed in the literature (Carlsson & Eriksson, 2019; Kazim et al., 2021; Parasurama & Sedoc, 2021). One example of this is where genders are often stereotyped to specified parts of the workforce, what Carlsson and Eriksson (2019) refer to as occupational segregation. Aside from bias they also suggested this phenomenon could be linked to the availability of women in the workforce, and that as women could be more likely to have experienced gender bias, they may favour female recruits – and this may even be a conscious decision (Carlsson & Eriksson, 2019). Another recruitment bias challenge, as noted by Dietz et al. (2015), is skill discounting, whereby education and employment experience gained from overseas is seen as less desirable than their domestic equivalents. Additionally suggest Dietz et al. (2015), some recruiters may in fact feel intimidated by someone from a minority group who is highly qualified and so seek to underpin their supposed superiority by favouring their ingroup.

While arguably gender and ethnicity bias may be more well researched, there are certainly other forms of bias that can be equally disruptive for some groups. Turek and Henkens (2020) discuss the barriers that impact workers over the age of 50 years seeking employment, in particular perceptions around the skillsets of this demographic including their openness to new learning, their physical abilities, lack of tech skills, and general productivity. L'Horty et al. (2022) considered the prevalence of recruitment bias against people with a disability compared to other common factors associated with discrimination in France – ethnicity, place of residence, and gender. Their study noted that overall people with disabilities typically experience higher rates of poverty and job insecurity, alongside lower wages. In their investigation of differences between treatment of applications from both disabled and non-disabled job applicants Ravaud et al. (1992) found that while both cohorts received a similar number of responses, the disabled applicant was far less likely to receive a positive response compared to their able-bodied peers, this was further compounded for applicants with lower or no qualifications – a particular issue, suggest Ravaud et al. (1992), given rates of higher level qualifications are lower within this cohort.

8.2.3 *Strategies to Counter Recruitment Bias*

Multiple tools and techniques have been developed to counteract bias, however some have been found to exacerbate the issue, such as automated systems where candidates are screened by algorithms without human input and yet are still shown to have bias tendancies (Parasurama & Sedoc, 2021). Diversity focused policy however continues to be broadly applied in many workplaces – the success of which is often dependent on it being supported by appropriate training (Garnero et al., 2014; Lang, 2020; Oswick & Noon, 2014); the organisation modelling strong leadership, boundaries, and expectations (Derous & Ryan, 2018; Lang, 2020); and when the organisation has diversity within its workforce already or when there is a higher level of public scrutiny such as in government (Ali et al., 2015; Lang, 2020). Another policy approach has been that of social investment where funding is targeted toward specific groups to help them better adjust to new environments – such as supporting migrant workers in a new country (Bonoli, 2020).

Perhaps the most widely discussed strategy to combat bias and discrimination is that of diversity-based training – these trainings come in multiple forms such as online and classroom based, varying lengths, and both organisationally internal or external formats (Alhejj et al., 2016; Chang et al., 2019; Ehkre et al., 2020; Noon, 2018). Seeking out diversity training is generally driven by wanting to change perceptions of difference, maximise potential, build inclusiveness, or address discrimination issues (Cavaleros et al., 2002; Ehkre et al., 2020). The principle being that once people better understand the nature of bias and where their biases may exist, they can more readily address this for themselves (Noon, 2018). Of course as with other approaches there has been much discussion around the effectiveness of diversity training, with many studies noting training resulted in limited attitudinal or behavioural change and were often too abstract (Chang et al., 2019), that learning diminished over time without concerted follow up (Bezrukova et al., 2016), training was often of poor quality (Alhejj et al., 2016), and that as recognising your bias may then require you to also recognise and address your social advantage, some may be reluctant to make this change (Noon, 2018).

8.3 Methodology

This study uses a survey questionnaire as the primary data collection source. Before conducting the study, Human Ethics approval was sought and given by the Southern Institute of Technology, in New Zealand. The questionnaire was designed to gather important data and information about the respondents, including attribute [demographic information about the respondents], which allows for links to be made between outcomes and particular groups; opinion variables [how the respondent feels about something], which can again be linked to attributes; and behavioural variables [what the respondent has done or would do in a situation] which can then be linked to the first two variables in the discussion (Udemy, 2021b).

The questionnaire is seeking to replicate recruitment decisions that are as close to reality as possible and in doing so has included a range of question types to keep the respondent engaged, these include list questions [respondents can choose as many as apply from a list], category questions [where one choice from a list is required], and rating questions [where respondents rate their feelings or opinion on something] (Udemy, 2021b). The questionnaire has also used open ended response questions to provide an opportunity to share further detail, acknowledging that respondents may not share all their thoughts and that this format can be harder to code – however the mixed question format allows for a range of quantitative and qualitative data to be gathered (Saunders et al., 2019; Udemy, 2021b).

The questionnaire was developed and distributed using SurveyMonkey. This tool was used for its functionality, familiarity with a range of respondents, and ease of access. The survey was shared as an online link, with an accompanying information letter, through the distribution email lists of a regional social service provider network [the region within which the researcher is based, this distribution list is open access however recipients, and therefore respondents, were anonymous to the researcher] and the researcher's employer [a nationally focused social service organisation, permission was granted by the employer for the survey to be shared]. Recipients were also encouraged to share the link with others should they wish. The survey was distributed in August 2022 and was left open until an adequate number of responses was attained.

Participants have been drawn from the social service sector. This sector was chosen due to its diversity, ease of access to particpants, and as a cohort that can be considered as socially aware and active. Given the sector's diversity [such as ethnicity, education, employer, gender, and age], the sample has met the definitional requirements of heterogeneity and the sample size of 74 responses speaks to the validity expectations of the complex nature of the topics discussed (Udemy, 2021a). The survey was shared via specific distribution lists, and although participants were invited to share the survey further, to maintain anonymity there is no way to ascertain how far the survey went beyond the initial mailout. This means that the sample gathered is non-probability based, as not all members of the population [employees within the social sector] will have received the survey (Udemy, 2021a).

Within the non-probability sampling methodology, the study sits across three common sampling methods – convenience, volunteer, and snowball sampling (Saunders et al., 2019; Udemy, 2021a). The study has used a convenience sample as the researcher has used existing access to networks to support distribution of the survey (Udemy, 2021a). Volunteer sampling has been utilised as the survey was shared through a distribution network and recipients were asked to volunteer their participation (Udemy, 2021a). Finally, as all corners of the potential population are

Table 8.1 Sample characteristics

Total participants	Age	Gender	Ethnicity[a]	Lived overseas	Education
74	29% – under 35 years 45% – 35–50 years 26% – 50+ years	71% – Female 29% – Male	Pākehā[b] – 60% Māori[c] – 19% European – 18% Middle Eastern – 7% Pacific – 5% Other – 4% Asian – 3% Latin American – 1%	47% Yes 53% No	72% – degree level or higher

[a]Participants could indicate more than one ethnicity
[b]Indigenous term for New Zealand European
[c]Indigenous New Zealander

not able to be reached through the chosen channels, participants were encouraged to further share the survey request, creating a snowball sampling effect (Udemy, 2021a) (Table 8.1).

8.4 Findings and Analysis

The survey questions sought to understand respondent perceptions and their impacts on diversity from four different viewpoints. Firstly, participants were asked questions that highlighted *influence*, that is, does this diversity characteristic influence your perception of a candidate [it was not asking whether the influence was positive or negative]. The second section then asked the participant to identify their positive *preference* based on a list of characteristics. Thirdly, participants were asked about how they felt about *expectations* that diverse candidates may have within the workplace. Finally, participants were asked to rate the importance of *diverse perspectives* in undertaking some common elements of team functioning and management.

8.4.1 Training, Policy, and Diversity

Of the 74 study participants, 46 [62.1%] had not completed any kind of diversity related training. 36 participants [48.7%] indicated that their organisation had some form of diversity related policy while 8 [10.8%] stated that they did not, 30 [40.5%] respondents were unsure. Interestingly 19 of the respondents that noted a policy was in place, had also not received any diversity-based training. Participants were further asked how well they felt they understood what their policy requires of them,

Table 8.2 Training participation versus total influence

	Influenced	Neutral	Not influenced	Prefer not to say
Yes	14.3%	25.9%	59.8%	0%
No	19.6%	27.7%	52.2%	0.5%

overall, it was found that there was little difference between participant responses for those that had a policy and those that did not or were unsure.

Influence Responses – Training

Table 8.2 shows the total level of influence, neutrality, and/or no influence compared to training participation for respondents, across the eight questions that focused on influence. These questions included responses around workplace gender diversity, same sex relationships, disability, overseas experience and qualifications, English as a second language, and parents returning to the workforce. To support data presentation, we have combined influenced [likely and very likely] responses together and not influenced [unlikely and very unlikely] responses together.

The data demonstrates somedifference in influence [5.3%] between those participants who have completed training and those that have not. The table further shows differences in all response fields, indicating the likely impact of diversity training.

The gap was particularly large between the trained [*T*] and untrained [*UT*] cohorts for workplace gender diversity and disability that requires support – where gender data showed $T = 10.7\%$ influence versus $UT = 21.7\%$; and disability showed $T = 17.9\%$ influence versus $UT = 37\%$.

Preference Responses – Training

Preference questions asked respondents to make a choice between characteristics to indicate any preference they may have when needing to decide between two evenly matched candidates. The topics covered included where candidates studied, physical ability, faith practices, gender, age, and citizenship status. Respondents were also able to select the 'prefer not to say' option and could add comments should they wish. As previously canvassed 37.9% of respondents have participated in training [*T*] and 62.1% had not [*UT*].

The data shows a gap between the trained and untrained cohorts, that is, the *UT* cohort were more likely to indicate a preference. Other results of similar note included both cohorts demonstrating a preference towards candidates that studied in New Zealand or at least in an English-speaking country; and a preference toward candidates with citizenship and/or visa permanence (see Table 8.3 below). Some comments attached to these responses provided further clarity around their thinking – such as the need for understanding of the New Zealand context, and that English competence was important for the role types they hire for. Several comments noted that they did not consider the categories as particularly important either way and would typically see things from a bigger perspective. A third theme indicated people had demonstrated preference or bias toward certain groups, for example, some people appeared to find working with diversity more troublesome and so avoided "...hassles and [the] need to accommodate to different experiences,

Table 8.3 Training participation versus preference responses

	Studied in New Zealand	Studied in English speaking country	They qualified at an Institution you have not heard of	Prefer not to say
T	42.9%	17.8%	3.6%	35.7%
UT	58.7%	30.4%	0%	10.9%
	NZ citizen or permanent resident	**Work visa**	**Student visa**	**Prefer not to say**
T	64.3%	3.6%	3.6%	28.6%
UT	73.9%	8.7%	0%	17.4%

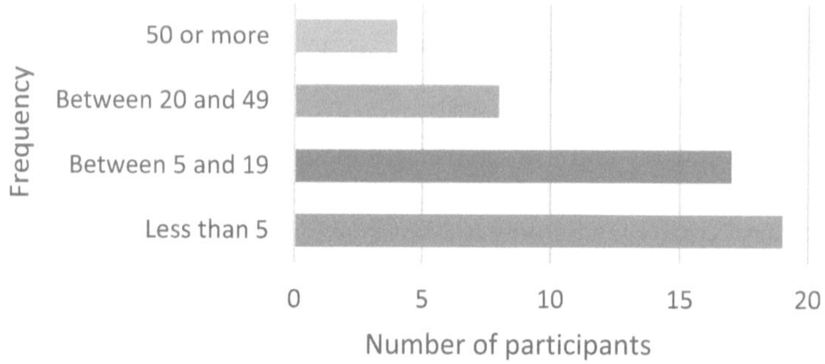

Fig. 8.1 Frequency of participation in recruitment processes

cultures…"; while others preferred candidates from certain ethnicities or genders as they may be better suited to working with their clients [alongside the required skills and experience].

8.4.2 *Recruitment Experience and Organisational Level*

48 [64.9%] respondents reported having participated in a recruitment process during their career, the frequency of which is shown in Fig. 8.1 below.

Influence Responses – Recruitment Experience

It appeared that being part of a recruitment process alone made minimal impact in terms of influence on decision making. However, the more experienced in recruitment the participant was, the more likely they appeared to have an opinion, be it either influenced or not. This was most evident in the 50+ cohort which responded with zero neutrality for 3 out of the 8 influence-based questions. Further to this, the table below shows that overall, the less experienced the respondent was in recruitment, the less likely they appeared to be influenced by characteristics of diversity (Table 8.4).

Table 8.4 Number of recruitments versus total influence

	Influenced	Neutral	Not Influenced	Prefer not to Say
< 5	13.2%	33.5%	53.3%	0%
5–19	16.9%	32.3%	50.8%	0%
20–49	23.4%	20.3%	54.7%	1.6%
50+	28.1%	21.9%	50%	0%

Table 8.5 Number of recruitments versus preference responses

	They are 10 years younger than you	You are a similar age	They are 10 years older than you	Prefer not to say
< 5	15.8%	42.1%	5.3%	36.8%
5–19	11.8%	23.5%	5.9%	58.8%%
20–49	0%	25%	0%	75%
50+	50%	0%	0%	50%

Preference Responses – Recruitment Experience

When it comes to showing a preference between similar candidates, overall, those with recruitment experience tended to show stronger views on what they were seeking and/or what they prefer. In something of a contrast to the findings on influence however, the more experienced the respondent became in recruitment the less likely they appeared to show a preference when choosing between similar candidates (Table 8.5).

8.4.3 *Life Experience Responses*

Figure 8.2 shows that some 47.3% of respondents have lived overseas with 45.7% of this group having lived outside of New Zealand for less than 5 years.

Figure 8.3 highlights the self-reported frequency with which participants interacted with people who display some common characteristics of diversity. It shows that for example on average 21 of the participants interacted with at least 6 [out of 9 possibilities] different characteristics monthly.

Influence Responses – Interacting with Diversity

Respondents were asked to report whether they frequently [monthly] interacted with people that expressed characteristics of diversity. The 9 common characteristics they could choose from included English as a second language, disability, gender diversity, same sex relationships, age diversity, born outside of New Zealand, and faith diversity. Seven respondents reported interactions with all 9 characteristics monthly whereas one respondent reported just 2 interactions per month.

To support statistical robustness the cohort was split into 5 or less interactions per month [27] and 5 or more interactions per month [47]. Table 8.6 below indicates

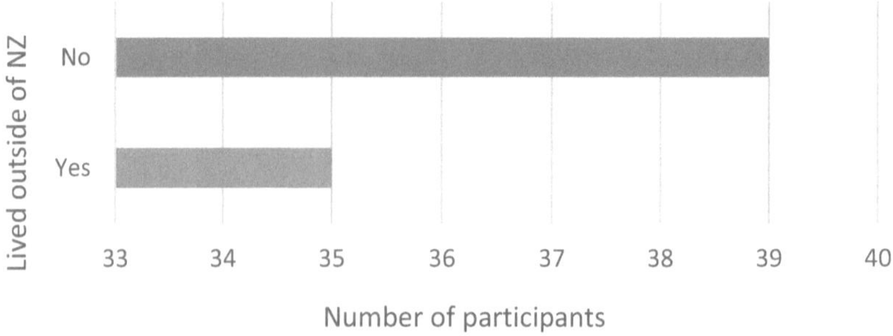

Fig. 8.2 Lived outside of New Zealand responses (individuals)

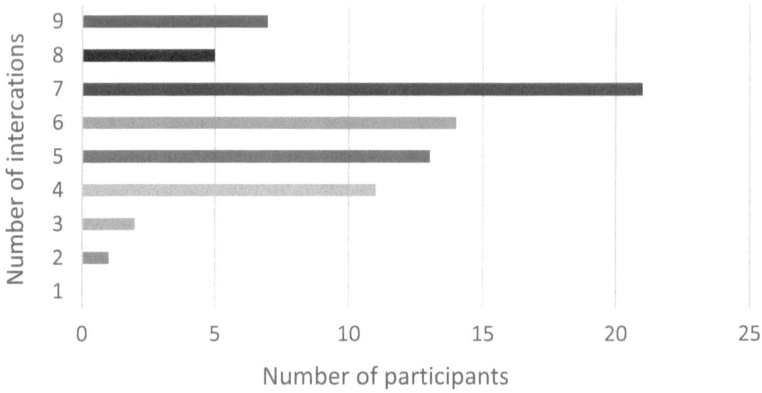

Fig. 8.3 Reported number of regular interactions with characteristics of diversity

Table 8.6 Monthly interaction with diversity versus total influence

	Influenced	Neutral	Not influenced	Prefer not to say
< 5 interactions	20.8%	31.9%	46.8%	0.5%
5 > interactions	14.9%	24.2%	60.6%	0.3%

that the more interaction respondents had with diversity, the less likely they appeared to be influenced by it during recruitment.

Time Overseas

Comparing the influence and preference responses to time spent overseas showed little significant difference, however both question areas that implied ethnic diversity showed that those who had not lived overseas appeared to favor less diverse characteristics.

8.4.4 Expectation Responses

Expectation questions were seeking responses that demonstrated how the respondent felt about particular expectations that employees from diverse backgrounds may bring with them into the workplace. Again, we have combined supportive [agree and strongly agree] responses together and not supportive [disagree and strongly disagree] responses together. Overall respondents appeared generally supportive of the expectations diverse employees may have. Interestingly the expectation that elicited the least supportiveness was time off to attend Pride week celebrations (Table 8.7).

Teamwork Responses

This final set of questions sought responses that indicated how the participants felt about diverse perspectives when it comes to activity that requires teamwork. These included tasks that require working to a tight deadline, creative work, and decision making. Overwhelmingly respondents felt that whether team members thought the same as them or differently made little difference to achieving tasks in the workplace. One set of responses that stood out however was those given to the question around working as a team to complete a task where both thinking the same and thinking differently responses rose significantly (see Table 8.8 below).

Narrative Responses

8.4.5 Training

Respondents that had participated in diversity-based training were invited to share narrative reflections on the content of the sessions. Most respondents noted that trainings were typically part of their workplace either as mandatory induction or as part of additional professional development. Some had done multiple trainings, and many commented that the usefulness of the training(s) was variable. A large proportion of the comments noted session content that reflected the unique New Zealand context around the Te Tiriti O Waitangi and bi-culturalism, others reflected general bias training, while there were also infrequent references to disability and gender

Table 8.7 Supportiveness of time off to attend Pride celebrations

	Supportive	Neutral	Not supportive
Total	71.6%	12.2%	16.2%

Table 8.8 What is important when working as a team to complete a task

	Think the same	Think differently	Neither is important
Total	13.5%	22.9%	63.6%

issues. Typically, the sessions appeared to focus on historical context, shared experience, and understanding of difference.

8.4.6 *Policy*

Similarly, respondents that reported a diversity focused policy were encouraged to share reflections on what this contained. Many responses reflected inclusiveness of all people as a prominent feature of their policy and further strong references were made to Te Tiriti and the New Zealand context. Some responses noted that the policy formed part of their induction but did not really feature in their day-to-day work – some even suggested the policy was something for HR to worry about rather than themselves. A final note was that several respondents knew there was a policy somewhere amongst their documents, but they could not readily find it or recall what was in it.

Demography
Gender, age, and ethnicity data was gathered for all the survey participants and comparison was completed across both influence and preference responses – with areas of note highlighted below (See Figs. 8.4, 8.5, and 8.6).

Age Responses
Generally, the comparison data showed consistency across most of the age ranges when it came to influence responses. Of note however was that the 50+ years age bracket appeared both more influenced by diversity characteristics and substantially more neutral when responding to the survey.

Another area of interest came in the comparison of age and the influence of a candidate with a disability that requires support. The results demonstrated the largest response in the 'influenced' category from across this section for the two younger age brackets – and substantially so for the 35–50 years age range. A final point of note from consideration of influence was that while having English as a second

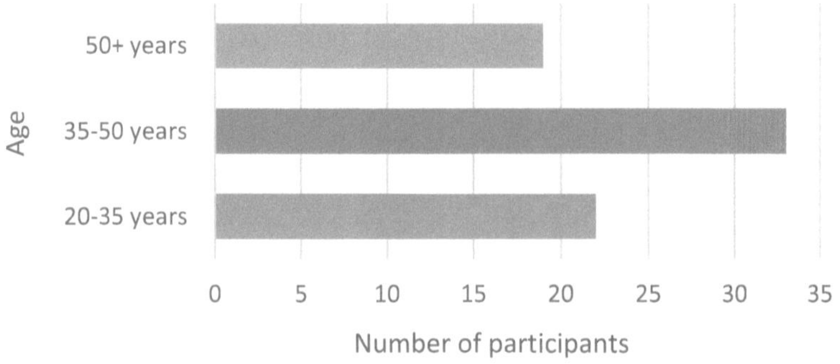

Fig. 8.4 Number of participants in each age bracket

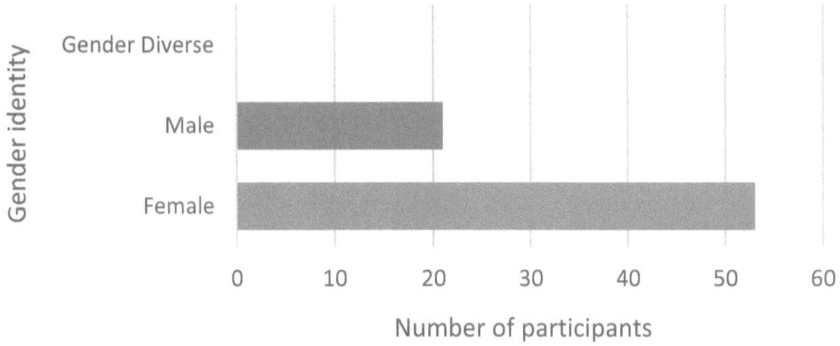

Fig. 8.5 Gender of participants

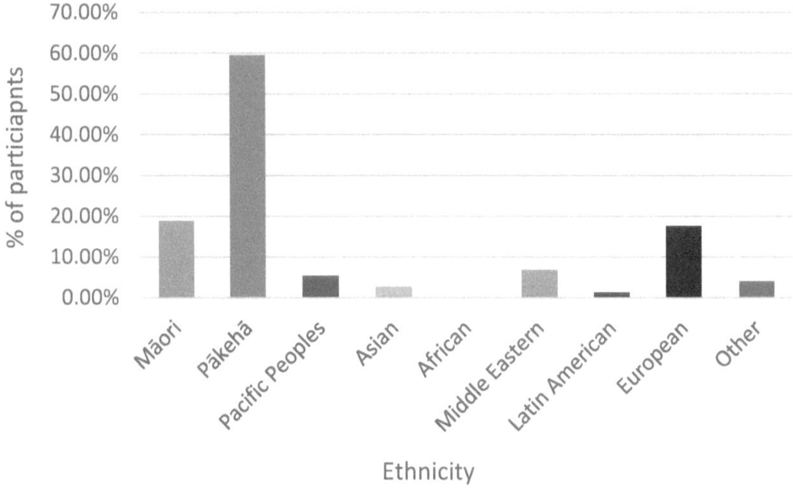

Fig. 8.6 Participant ethnicity

language was not seen as particularly influential, having work experience and/or qualifications obtained from overseas did see a spike in apparent influence for both the younger age brackets.

When it came to preference responses and age, as expected the same areas of note emerged in the data – for example around place of study. One area of interest was the results that showed some 42.4% of respondents aged between 35 and 50 years preferred candidates the same age as them over someone older or younger. Overall, however the 'prefer not to say' option was the highest selected response across all areas and even more so for those aged 50+ years. Finally in consideration of expectation responses the younger age groups appeared to show more comfort with the expectations of diverse candidates across all areas, while there were no differences of note amongst comparison of age groups and the teamwork responses (Table 8.9).

Table 8.9 Age responses versus total influence

	Influenced	Neutral	Not influenced	Prefer not to say
20–35 years	18.7%	25%	55.7%	0.6%
35–50 years	15.5%	21.2%	62.9%	0.4%
50+ years	19.7%	39.5%	40.8%	0%

Gender Responses

When it came to influence responses, there was very little separating the genders across all the areas shown although overall, males showed slightly less influence and more neutrality. Interestingly when it came to preference there was substantial difference in almost every area surveyed although these results can be somewhat tempered by the impact of proportionality. Overall, within the expectation responses, male participants appearedless likely to be accepting of diverse expectations. However, on the flip side male respondents generally demonstrated that diverse perspectives were more important when it came to teamwork responses.

Ethnicity

8.4.7 Discussion

The overarching focus of this research has been to understand whether work/life experiences have an impact on perceptions of diversity during a recruitment process.

The first objective of the present study is to identify if recruiters with more diverse life experiences perceive diverse candidates more positively. The study gathered data around the frequency of respondent interactions with diversity and compared this to how they responded to questions focused on the level of influence a characteristic of diversity would have in their decision making.

The evidence gathered demonstrates links between a participant's experience of interacting with diversity and their perceptions of diversity during recruitment decision making. The data has shown that people who regularly interact with a broader range of diversity appeared less likely to be influenced by candidates that present with diverse characteristics during recruitment. These findings are consistent with Life Course Theory and the recognition of how life experience impacts on our decision-making, assumptions, and perceptions of others (Tomlinson et al., 2018). Furthermore, these findings align with Liu et al. (2021) who contend that our experiences of different groups will impact recruitment decision making, and this may be a positive or negative phenomenon. This experiential learning is supported by the findings of both Garnero et al. (2014) and Oswick and Noon (2014) who note that often discrimination is based on a lack of knowledge about difference.

The second objective of this study was to examine links between work experience and perceptions of diversity. Data was gathered around experiences of recruitment and organisational level, as well as understanding of policy and participation in diversity-based training.

While arguably less stark than with life experiences, there was some difference evident between participant experience levels and their responses. For example, those that had less recruitment experience in the workplace typically showed higher rates of neutrality and appeared less influenced by characteristics of diversity. Conversely those who had been in roles longer appeared much more likely to be influenced by said characteristics. These results may be down to less experienced employees having less entrenched views about what may or may not work in an organisation, they may be less decisive, or it may simply be that they are more open minded in their views. Similarly having stronger views around diversity and recruitment may be a signal of wishing to maintain a status quo or having become assimilated with a particular organisational view. The findings can be seen as consistent with the idea of professional social matching as espoused by Koivunen et al. (2019) where recruiters seek out a match between the candidate and the organisational culture, to support them into the role and make the transition for existing staff more harmonious.

A second noteworthy finding within the results was the positive impact that participation in diversity training appeared to have for participants and their potential openness to diversity. While narrative responses reported a level of variability in the quality and relevance of training, [as noted in multiple previous studies (Alhejj et al., 2016; Bezrukova et al., 2016; Cavaleros et al., 2002; Chang et al., 2019; Ehkre et al., 2020; Noon, 2018)], there was nonetheless evidence to indicate that training [regardless of perceived quality] did have a positive influence on recruitment decision making. Alongside this was the arguably expected results showing that diversity policy was relatively unknown, misunderstood, or poorly recognised within many workplaces – affirming the concerns raised by multiple authors in relation to the gap between what policy says and what people do (Noon & Ogbonna, 2021; Powell, 1998; Stafsudd, 2003).

Across all question areas it was evident that same sex relationships elicited the strongest number of 'not influenced' responses, closely followed by questions relating to age, gender, and parenting. Interestingly the same sex question was also the only area in which the 'prefer not to answer' response was chosen, perhaps indicating a view was held but not shared. This type of approach is consistent with the phenomenon of providing socially acceptable answers rather than expressing your true view on something (Saunders et al., 2019). However, in general terms, the high rates of 'not influenced' responses in relation to all these characteristic areas could also be indicative of an increased level of social acceptance.

Multiple examples of bias toward some aspects of diversity were identified in the data, and these are highly consistent with many studies – including direct ethnic discrimination such as those reported by Pager et al. (2009) and Derous and Ryan (2018); discounting of skills based on where someone gained their education or experience such as those highlighted by Dietz et al. (2015); and bias against disability, as identified by L'Horty et al. (2022) and Ravaud et al. (1992). Conversely there was little evidence of gender or age bias in the results – inconsistent with findings presented around gender Carlsson and Eriksson (2019), Kazim et al. (2021) and Parasurama and Sedoc (2021); or regarding age such as noted by Turek and

Henkens (2020). It should be noted however that some 71% of respondents identified as female, which likely skewed these results somewhat in terms of gender bias – this being consistent with the suggestion of Carlsson and Eriksson (2019) that women may favour female recruits.

It would also appear from the data that where the respondent [in acting as the hypothetical recruiter] may be required to make additional effort to accommodate diversity, they were more likely to respond as being influenced by the characteristic – for example when considering changes to a workspace to accommodate a disability or where communication may be more challenging when interacting with someone for whom English is a second language. This was also supported by some of the narrative responses where participants overtly noted that at times accommodating diversity can be seen as an added 'hassle' for employers.

8.5 Concluding Remarks

The aim of this research was to support better identification and understanding of the relationship between work/life experiences and decision making during a recruitment process. The problem that the study was addressing is directly related to the numerous research accounts, and anecdotal evidence, that points to the ongoing discrimination and bias experienced by minority groups at various points during their employment and working journey (Haar, 2022; OECD, 2020; Pager et al., 2009; Tan, 2021; Yeung, 2017).

While this study has identified interesting links between decision making and experience, it should be noted that the sample size was restricted by time constraints and was therefore less than ideal. Given the exploratory nature of the study however it would be appropriate for future studies to identify points of note and expand on these with larger and more diverse sample sizes.

With data drawn from a questionnaire that was distributed to 74 participants, our analysis has identified several key findings, these include:

1. Links were demonstrated between life experience and perceptions of diversity. Similarly, however, findings also noted that recruiters who had been in a role for less than two years tended toward more open-minded practice and there was little difference in perceptions between hierarchal levels. Rather than recruitment decision making relying on a few senior level staff, organisations should consider using a broader approach to recruitment such as through using newer or more junior staff on panels; using people external to the organisation on panels; ensuring panel diversity; or using a range of processes to support decision making rather than just interviews – these could include time on the job, written exercises, and client feedback.
2. It was evident that diversity-based training made a difference in perceptions and that many participants acknowledged poor knowledge of their current policies. It is recommended that much stronger links between training, practice, and policy

are established – and that this is revisited on a regular basis for staff so that they understand their significance, practice in appropriate ways, and stay abreast of changes. Alongside this may be opportunities to build experience of diversity such as team building exercises, secondments to other workplaces, or volunteering in the community.

3. The final recommendation of this study recognises that employers typically see organisational fit as critical to employment, often more so than the skills required for the role. This approach can lead to ambiguous processes and candidates being required to meet standards that they are not aware of. Therefore, it is recommended that organisations are far more explicit in their advertising and other recruitment tools regarding the type of person they are seeking. Doing this will support people in applying for the right roles; support employers in making their recruitment processes clearer and more consistent; and will allow potential candidates to make more informed choices about employers, their values, and the type of role they are expected to take in an organisation.

In conclusion, the journey to gaining meaningful employment can be long and fraught for many people who may struggle to find a workplace where their diversity is both accepted and valued. This study has sought to identify links between work/life experience and perceptions of diversity with the view to making that journey more achievable, to support employers to apply more inclusive practices, and to help add to the discourse around addressing bias and discrimination.

Through understanding the historical discourse of equity, diversity, and inclusion (Oswick & Noon, 2014) we were able to position the study within a societal context where diversity continues to have a mixed reception in workplaces, where unemployment and underemployment within the diverse workforce is unacceptably high, where discrimination and bias is still rife, and ultimately where businesses are missing out on the potential that diverse perspectives can bring them (Lang, 2020). Then, through acknowledgment of Life Course Theory, the study further considered the phenomenon of decision making and how this is often underpinned by work/life experiences (Tomlinson et al., 2018).

Using a range of literature, this study has highlighted the ongoing impacts of recruitment bias toward diverse candidates – including experiences of ethnic minorities (Derous & Ryan, 2018; Pager et al., 2009), gender bias (Carlsson & Eriksson, 2019; Kazim et al., 2021; Parasurama & Sedoc, 2021), ageism (Turek & Henkens, 2020), and disability (L'Horty et al., 2022; Ravaud et al., 1992). The study also explored the broad range of strategies that continue to be tried to address the concerns raised above – particularly training and policy initiatives (Alhejj et al., 2016; Ali et al., 2015; Bezrukova et al., 2016; Bonoli, 2020; Cavaleros et al., 2002; Chang et al., 2019; Derous & Ryan, 2018; Ehkre et al., 2020; Garnero et al., 2014; Hitchcock et al., 2016; Lang, 2020; Oswick & Noon, 2014).

Aligned with the literature, the findings showed links between participant responses and the objectives of the study including indicating the relationship between work/life experience and perceptions of diversity, as well as emphasising the presence of bias towards some forms of diversity. This study has also recommended how these findings may be of use within the Applied Management field including areas for future study and comparison, as well as how training, policy, and recruitment practices could be strengthened to support a more equitable process.

Ultimately there is no need for the employment journey of diverse candidates to be so challenging. Through using openminded and inclusive practices; acknowledging and mitigating bias; developing and maintaining equity focused policy; and being honest and clear about what kind of fit you need for your organisation, businesses can thrive through the benefits that diversity can bring – and when diverse employees feel a sense of belonging, inclusion, and value in their work, they get to thrive too.

References

Alhejj, H., Garavan, T., Carbery, R., O'Brien, F., & McGuire, D. (2016). Diversity training programme outcomes: A systematic review. *Human Resource Development Quarterly, 27*(1), 96–149. https://doi.org/10.1002/hrdq.21221

Ali, M., Metz, I., & Kulik, C. (2015). Retaining a diverse workforce: The impact of gender-focused human resource management. *Human Resource Management Journal, 25*(4), 580–599.

Bezrukova, K., Spell, C., Perry, J., & Jehn, K. (2016). A meta-analytical integration of over 40 years of research on diversity training evaluation. *Psychological Bulletin, 11*, 1227–1274.

Bonoli, G. (2020). Immigrant integration and social investment. *Journal of European Social Policy, 30*(5), 616–627. https://doi.org/10.1177/0958928720950619

Carlsson, M. & Eriksson, S. (2019). In-group gender bias in hiring: Real-world evidence. *Economic Letters, 185*, 108686. https://doi.org/10.1016/j.econlet.2019.108686

Cavaleros, C., Van Vuuren, L., & Visser, D. (2002). The effectiveness of a diversity awareness education programme. *SA Journal of Industrial Psychology, 28*(3), 50–621.

Chang, E., Milkman, K., Gromet, D., Rebele, R., Massey, C., Duckworth, A., & Grant, A. (2019). The mixed effects of online diversity training. *Proceedings of the National Academy of Sciences, 116*(16), 7778–7783.

Combs, G., & Nadkarni, S. (2005). The tale of two cultures: Attitudes towards affirmative action in the United States and India. *Journal of World Business, 40*(2), 158–171.

Derous, E., & Ryan, A. (2018). When your resume is (not) turning you down: Modelling ethnic bias in resume screening. *Human Resource Management Journal, 29*, 113–130.

Dietz, J., Joshi, C., Esses, V., Hamilton, L., & Gabarrot, F. (2015). The skill paradox: Explaining and reducing employment discrimination against skilled immigrants. *International Journal of Human Resource Management, 26*(10), 1318–1334. https://doi.org/10.1080/09585192.2014.990398

Ehkre, F., Ashoee, A., Steffens, M., & Louvet, E. (2020). A brief diversity training: Raising awareness of ingroup privilege to improve attitudes towards disadvantaged outgroups. *International Journal of Psychology, 55*(5), 732–742.

Garnero, A., Kampelmann, S., & Rycx, F. (2014). The heterogeneous effects of workforce diversity on productivity, wages and profits. *Industrial Relations: A Journal of Economy and Society, 53*(3), 430–477. https://doi.org/10.1111/irel.12064

Guillaume, Y., Dawson, J., Otaye-Ebede, L., Woods, S., & West, M. (2017). Harnessing demographic differences in organizations: What moderates the effects of workplace diversity? *Journal of Organizational Behaviour, 38*, 276–303.

Haar, J. (2022). The future of the Māori workforce is now. *Human Resources, 27*(2). https://issuu.com/hrnz.magazine/docs/2022_hrnz_winter_magazine_issuu/s/15982485

Hitchcock, J., Smuts, M., Alon, S., & Sharmani, P. (2016). The big question: Is affirmative action necessary to overcome institutional racism? *World Policy Journal, 33*(1), 1–4.

Kazim, E., Koshiyama, A. S., Hilliard, A., & Polle, R. (2021). Systematizing audit in algorithmic recruitment. *Journal of Intelligence, 9*(46). https://doi.org/10.3390/jintelligence9030046

Koivunen, S., Olsson, T., Olshannikova, E., & Lindberg, A. (2019). Understanding decision-making in recruitment: Opportunities and challenges for information technology. In *Proceedings of the ACM on human-computer interaction* 3(GROUP), 1–22. https://doi.org/10.1145/3361123

L'Horty, Y., Mahmoudi, N., Petit, P., & Wolff, F. (2022). Is disability more discriminatory in hiring than ethnicity, address, or gender? Evidence from a multi-criteria correspondence experiment. *Social Science & Medicine, 303*. https://doi.org/10.1016/j.socscimed.2022.114990

Lang, C. (2020). Workforce diversity policies in practice: Driver and barriers in local administrations. *Ethnic and Racial Studies, 43*(11), 1961–1980. https://doi.org/10.1080/01419870.2020.1754444

Liu, S., Kent, C., & Briscoe, J. (2021). Self-protecting motivation, indexed by self-threat, modifies retrieval-induced-forgetting and confidence in employment decision bias against out-group targets. *Cognitive Research: Principles and Implications, 6*(77). https://doi.org/10.1186/s41235-021-00334-w

Mensah, M., & Sommers, B. (2016). The policy argument for healthcare workforce diversity. *Journal of General Internal Medicine, 31*(11), 1369–1372.

Noon, M. (2018). Pointless diversity training: Unconscious bias, new racism and agency. *Work, Employment and Society, 32*(1), 198–209.

Noon, M., & Ogbonna, E. (2021). Controlling management to deliver diversity and inclusion: Prospects and limits. *Human Resource Management Journal, 31*(3), 619–638. https://doi-org.ezproxy.sit.ac.nz/10.1111/1748-8583.12332

Organisation for Economic Co-Operation and Development. (2020). *All hands in? Making diversity work for all.* OECD Publishing. https://doi.org/10.1787/efb14583-en

Oswick, C., & Noon, M. (2014). Discourses of diversity, equality and inclusion: Trenchant formulations or transient fashions? *British Journal of Management, 25*(1), 22–39. https://doi.org/10.1111/j.1467-8551.2012.00830.x

Pager, D., Western, B., & Bonikowski, B. (2009). Discrimination in a low-wage labour market: A field experiment. *American Sociological Review, 74*(5), 777–799.

Parasurama, P., & Sedoc, J. (2021). *Gendered language in resumes and its implications for algorithmic bias in hiring* (arXiv – Computer Science). Cornell University. https://doi.org/10.48550/arXiv.2112.08910

Powell, G. (1998). Reinforcing and extending today's organisations: The simultaneous pursuits of person-organisation fit and diversity. *Organisational Dynamics, 26*(3), 50–61.

Ravaud, J., Madiot, B., & Ville, I. (1992). Discrimination towards disabled people seeking employment. *Social Science & Medicine, 35*(8), 951–958.

Saunders, M., Lewis, P., & Thornhill, A. (2019). *Research methods for business students* (8th ed.). Pearson.

Stafsudd, A. M. (2003). Recruitment policy vs. recruitment process: Espoused theory and theory-in-use. *Academy of Management Proceedings*, G1–G6. https://doi-org.ezproxy.sit.ac.nz/10.5465/AMBPP.2003.13792975

Tan, L. (2021). *Teacher makes 200 job applications, but still can't get permanent work: "Is it because I'm Muslim?"*. Retrieved from https://www.nzherald.co.nz/nz/teacher-makes-200-job-applications-but-still-cant-get-permanent-work-is-it-because-im-muslim/DMP7VI67AUV62GSBEIQ5RIOXEA/

Tan, K.-L., & Yeap, P. F. (2022). The impact of work engagement and meaningful work to alleviate job burnout among social workers in New Zealand. *Management Decision, 60*(11), 3042–3065. https://doi.org/10.1108/MD-05-2021-0689

Tan, K.-L., Lew, T.-Y., & Sim, A. K. S. (2019). Is meaningful work the silver bullet? Perspectives of the social workers. *Journal of Asia Business Studies, 13*(4), 612–632. https://doi.org/10.1108/JABS-09-2018-0267

Tan, K.-L., Lew, T.-Y., & Sim, A. K. S. (2021). Effect of work engagement on meaningful work and psychological capital: Perspectives from social workers in New Zealand. *Employee Relations, 43*(3), 807–826. https://doi.org/10.1108/ER-11-2019-0433

Tomlinson, J., Baird, M., Berg, P., & Cooper, R. (2018). Flexible careers across the life course: Advancing theory, research and practice. *Human Relations, 71*(1), 4–22. https://doi.org/10.1177/0018726717733313

Turek, K., & Henkens, K. (2020). How skill requirements affect the likelihood of recruitment of older workers in Poland: The indirect role of age stereotypes. *Work, Employment and Society, 34*(4), 550–570. https://doi.org/10.1177/0950017019847943

Udemy. (2021a). *Research methods for business students: Non-probability sampling techniques* [Video]. Udemy Inc. https://www.udemy.com/course/research-methods-for-business-students/learn/lecture/4893696#learning-tools

Udemy. (2021b). *Research methods for business students: Collecting primary data through questionnaires* [Video]. Udemy Inc. https://www.udemy.com/course/research-methods-for-business-students/learn/lecture/4915174#learning-tools

Yeung, S. (2017). *Redrawing lines in the sand? An examination of discrimination patterns within New Zealand.* Unpublished Masters thesis, Auckland University of Technology.

Chapter 9
Spiritual Tourism: A Review and Synthesis

Eva Lang, Alexander Josiassen, and Florian Kock

Abstract While traditionally interlinked with religiosity, spirituality is today used more broadly to include esoteric, mystic, and New Age beliefs and practices that centre on the individualistic search for meaning and purpose. Spiritual well-being, an outcome of spiritual experiences, has been linked to feelings of inner harmony and direction and thus to reduced stress and higher levels of life satisfaction. Tourism scholars have acknowledged the potential of tourism to provide spiritual experiences and thereby contribute to consumers' well-being (e.g., Moal-Ulvoas G, Ann Tour Res 66:151–158, 2017). However, academics' and tourism managers' understanding and ability to leverage spirituality is considerably limited by two key shortcomings. Firstly, there is a lack of consensus regarding the definition of spiritual tourism, resulting in substantial conceptual ambiguity. Second, researchers disagree on the boundaries between religious and spiritual tourism, which has further complicated the understanding of the concept. These shortcomings leave tourism practitioners ill-equipped to understand and leverage the growing interest in spiritual tourism (Moufakkir O and Noureddine S, Ann Tour Res 70:108–119, 2018; Vada S et al, Tour Manag Perspect 33:100631, 2020). Setting out to address these shortcomings, the present study systematically reviews the body of literature on spiritual tourism and synthesizes the findings along central research themes. Anchored in this review, the study also advances a more nuanced, and much needed, delimitation between religiosity and spirituality in tourism. Based on the findings, the authors identify gaps in the current literature on spiritual tourism and suggest avenues for future research.

E. Lang (✉) · F. Kock
Copenhagen Business School, Frederiksberg, Denmark
e-mail: ekl.marktg@cbs.dk; fk.marktg@cbs.dk

A. Josiassen
Copenhagen Business School, Frederiksberg, Denmark

James Cook University, Singapore, Singapore
e-mail: aj.marktg@cbs.dk

E. L. Eijdenberg et al. (eds.), *Innovation-Driven Business and Sustainability in the Tropics*, https://doi.org/10.1007/978-981-99-2909-2_9

Keywords Spiritual tourism · Well-being · Spirituality · Religiousness · Positive psychology

9.1 Spiritual Tourism: Review, Synthesis, and Future Directions

Tourism's contribution to travellers' overall life satisfaction is a growing stream of research (e.g., Puczkó & Smith, 2012; Sirgy et al., 2011; Vada et al., 2020). Over the last few decades, tourism scholars have demonstrated that leisure travel can enhance well-being and quality of life (for a review, see Uysal et al., 2016), making tourism a vital resource in times of major challenges (Miao et al., 2022; Walton, 2009).

In this context, research has shown an increasing interest in the nexus of tourism, well-being, and spirituality. Among academics and practitioners, it is widely acknowledged that the quest for spiritual enlightenment constitutes an important driver of tourism (e.g., Puczkó & Smith, 2012). In fact, there is evidence of a growth in travel motivated by spiritual reasons (Buzinde et al., 2014). Spirituality in tourism has been the theme of many tourism conferences (The World Academy of Science [WASET], 2022) including by the World Tourism Organization (2015), as well as gained traction in pop culture, as exemplified by Gilbert's (2007) bestseller *Eat, Pray, Love*.

Spiritual tourism has been described as "a self-conscious project" directed toward improving individuals' "sense of well-being" (Norman, 2011, p. 203). In other words, spiritual tourism captures "a variety of tourism practices or behaviours that tourists understand to contribute to their own sense of meaning, purpose, and identity, and/or are seen as beneficial for the individual's health or well-being" (Norman & Pokorny, 2017, p. 203). Over the past few decades, tourism research has invested considerable empirical effort to investigate various aspects of spiritual tourism (e.g., Kato & Progano, 2017; Moufakkir & Noureddine, 2018), such as nature-based tourism (e.g., Sharpley & Jepson, 2011) or meditation retreats (Wang et al., 2021). Tourism scholars have contended that spiritual tourism can enhance tourists' spiritual well-being and inner harmony, thereby contributing to individuals' overall life satisfaction (e.g., Moufakkir & Noureddine, 2018; Sirgy et al., 2011). Moreover, spiritual tourism has been argued to contribute to tourists' quality of life by providing restorative experiences, thus calming anxiety and distress (Lin & Hsieh, 2022).

Despite the flourishing interest in spiritual tourism, the current state of knowledge is unsatisfactory for several reasons. Primarily, the conceptual meaning of spirituality is ambiguous and unclear (de Meezenbroek et al., 2012), which in turn has resulted in a lack of consensus regarding the definition of spiritual tourism (Moufakkir & Noureddine, 2018). As such, a great deal of extant research is focused on a specific manifestation of spiritual tourism (e.g., Kato & Progano, 2017; Moufakkir & Noureddine, 2018), whereas the efforts to consolidate these findings and advance a more general understanding of the construct are limited. A detrimental result of the conceptual ambiguity is a lack of comparability across studies. Further complicating knowledge development in the area, there is a blurring of the boundaries between religious and spiritual tourism, with some scholars using the terms interchangeably (Collins-Kreiner, 2020; Wang & Blasco, 2022). Related thereto, tourism studies typically approach spiritual tourism from a religious point of view (e.g., Buzinde et al., 2014; Hall, 2006; Terzidou et al., 2018), although phenomenological insights reveal that tourists often perceive spirituality as distinct from religious beliefs (e.g., Sharpley & Jepson, 2011; Willson et al., 2013).

Against this background, the present study aims to systematically review (Palmatier et al., 2018) extant knowledge in the field of spiritual tourism and identify promising avenues for future research. As a fundamental part thereof, we discuss the delimitation of spiritual and religious tourism to delineate the theoretical boundaries of the two phenomena. A systematic literature review of the field is appropriate in at least three respects: (1) to synthesize the obtained findings based on two research questions, namely 'How do spiritual tourism experiences materialize?,' and 'How does tourism facilitate spirituality?', (2) to identify and address the disagreements in the extant literature; and (3) to outline what is known about spiritual tourism and where gaps exist for future research (Palmatier et al., 2018). This study thus adds to the existing literature in several ways. First, by providing an integrated overview of the attained knowledge, we advance a more general understanding of spiritual tourism that is not tied to a specific context. Second, we alleviate some of the conceptual ambiguity regarding the concept of spiritual tourism by discussing the disagreements in the extant literature. Third, we devise a future research agenda to facilitate a constructive extension of past research. To the best of our knowledge, there has to date not been conducted any review of the growing body of literature on spiritual tourism. By filling this void, we make a timely contribution and provide a solid foundation for future empirical and theoretical research on spiritual tourism.

9.2 Background and Conceptual Definition

Before exposing the aspects of spiritual tourism that have been addressed by the extant literature, we first elaborate on the conceptual basis of the construct. The conceptual ambiguity surrounding the concept of spiritual tourism is anchored in at least two key issues, namely its internal and external ambiguity. Internal ambiguity refers to the poor understanding of the nature of spiritual tourism, which is arguably related to the fuzziness of the concept of spirituality itself (Sheldrake, 2009; Zinnbauer et al., 1997). Scholars have reiterated the complexity of spirituality and the difficulty in deriving an encompassing and consensual definition (de Meezenbroek et al., 2012). Moufakkir and Noureddine (2018) conclude that "it is apparently impossible to arrive at a consensus on its definition" (p. 109; see also Willson et al., 2013). Despite the lack of a widely recognized definition, several contributions identify the essence of spirituality as a search for meaning in life (e.g., Reed, 1992; Sharpley & Jepson, 2011; Sheldrake, 2009; Willson et al., 2013). In keeping with this, Wang and Blasco (2022) have described spiritual tourism as "a form of tourism focusing on secular spiritual fulfilment and betterment" (p. 2). Similarly, Collins-Kreiner (2010) suggest that spiritual journeys are characterized by a quest for a sense of new meaning in life.

External ambiguity refers to the difficulty of delimiting spiritual tourism from religious tourism, an endeavour that is significantly hampered by the interrelatedness of spirituality and religion. Historically, spirituality has been understood as an aspect of religiosity, pertaining to the personal relationship with the divine (Singleton, 2017; Zinnbauer et al., 1997). With the secularization of Western societies, spirituality has become increasingly disconnected from Christian religion and more popular as an individual phenomenon (Sheldrake, 2009; Zinnbauer et al., 1997). In the wake of this disconnection, the concept of spirituality broadened to include esoteric, mystical, and New Age beliefs and practices such as reincarnation (Houtman & Aupers, 2007; Zinnbauer et al., 1997).

The extant literature offers two perspectives on the contemporary delineation of spirituality and religion. According to one perspective, secular societies conceive religion as confined to institutional elements and spirituality as concerned with the individualistic search for meaning and purpose (Heelas & Woodhead, 2005; Paloutzian & Park, 2014; Zinnbauer et al., 1997). As per Heelas and Woodhead (2005), secular societies are witnessing a turn away from institutionalized religion "towards a life lived by reference to one's own subjective experiences" (p. 2). Pursuant to this perspective, modern spiritual beliefs differ from religious beliefs in that meaning is sought within the self rather than from an external source in the form of a institutionally based belief system (Houtman & Aupers, 2007; Singleton, 2017). Since the focus is on the subjective experience, modern spiritual beliefs may incorporate traditions and ideas from different milieus, provided they are considered spiritual by the individual (Heelas & Woodhead, 2005; Houtman & Aupers, 2007). In this sense, spirituality has been referred to as "do-it-yourself religion" (Houtman & Aupers, 2007, p. 306) or "self-styled spiritualities" (Singleton, 2017, p. 50).

However, not all scholarly work reflects what Houtman and Aupers (2007) term a "post-Christian spirituality" (p. 305). Another perspective evident in the associated body of literature maintains the conception of spirituality as an aspect of religion (e.g., Hall, 2006; Nilsson & Tesfahuney, 2016). Nilsson and Tesfahuney (2016), for instance, claim that religiosity has undergone a post-secular transformation and is contemporarily re-gaining prominence in the public sphere in a new form. "Post-secular religiosity often consists of personal/individual faith, that has to do more with questions of existence, meaning and fulfilment, rather than faith sanctioned by the expectations and obligations of institutionalized religion" (Nilsson & Tesfahuney, 2016, p. 21). While Nilsson and Tesfahuney (2016) thus view spiritual aspects as an inherent and essential part of post-secular religiosity, they also consider these as necessarily shaped by religious traditions and meanings (see also Hill et al., 2000).

Against the backdrop of this discussion, spirituality has also been examined from the perspective of pilgrimage. While traditionally placed within the broader category of religious tourism (Digance, 2003; Holman, 2011), scholars suggest that contemporary pilgrimage is becoming underpinned by modern secular motives focused on spiritual growth rather than religious traditions (e.g., Digance, 2003; Fedele, 2013; Nilsson & Tesfahuney, 2016). In fact, Kim et al.'s (2016) study on pilgrimage along the Camino de Santiago route reveals that most pilgrims travel for spiritual motives (45,2%), followed by religious motives (27,9%). This finding accords well with Moufahim and Lichrou's (2019) conceptualization of pilgrimage as a quest for a spiritual authentic self (p. 329), which serves to affirm and strengthen pilgrims' religious identity (p. 330). Similarly, investigating pilgrimage tourism in India, Buzinde et al. (2014) identify spiritual connectivity and spiritual knowledge attainment as the two main motivations among pilgrims. However, the qualitative insights suggest that attending the pilgrimage is also interpreted as a religious experience (Buzinde et al., 2014). As evident from these studies, contemporary pilgrimage may be considered both as a manifestation of spiritual as well as religious tourism.

In an attempt to delineate spiritual and religious tourism, Holman (2011) suggested that religious tourism is motivated by religious reasons and typically characterized by groups of travellers with similar beliefs (see also Rinschede, 1992). By contrast, spiritual tourism is characterized by a "primary motivation (…) for an individualistic, spiritual and/or transformational experience" (Holman, 2011, p. 91) that is detached from the context of a specific religion. Yet others (e.g., Hall, 2006) argue that religious experiences constitute a central element of spiritual tourism. Hall's (2006) definition of spiritual tourism echoes the concept of a post-secular religiosity "that opens up new spaces for the articulation of faith and the exercise of belief" (Nilsson & Tesfahuney, 2016, p. 21).

It is worth mentioning that qualitative insights into tourists' travel motivations do indeed reflect these different interpretations. Fedele's (2013) ethnographic study describes tourists travelling to Catholic pilgrimage sites who do not identify themselves as practising Christians but instead consider themselves spiritual. Likewise, Sharpley and Jepson (2011) outline that "people may have what they consider or understand to be spiritual experiences even though they may not hold religious beliefs, or a belief in a supreme power or God" (p. 55). On the other hand, others conceive of spiritual tourism explicitly as a religious experience (Moal-Ulvoas, 2017).

Following Stausberg (2014), spiritual tourism may thus be located as "both within and beyond" (p. 355) religious tourism. In other words, spiritual tourism encompasses a variety of ideas that may be drawn eclectically from religious traditions as well as other, non-religious inspirations. Crucially, the focus of spiritual tourism is on the individual and his or her exploration of questions of existence, meaning, and fulfilment (Nilsson & Tesfahuney, 2016, p. 21). As opposed to religious tourists, who travel to traditional pilgrimage centres such as Rome, Jerusalem, and Mecca (Rinschede, 1992), spiritual tourism destinations may therefore include secular sites, "such as war memorials, natural landscapes or places related to celebrities" (Kato & Progano, 2017, p. 245). Furthermore, tourism scholars have pointed to the deliberate quest for spiritual fulfilment as an important element of spiritual tourism (e.g., Kujawa, 2017; Moal-Ulvoas & Taylor, 2014; Willson et al., 2013). Singleton (2017), for instance, views spiritual tourism as "a deliberate effort to use places apart from home as a means [sic] achieve spiritual growth" (p. 51). Such intent distinguishes spiritual tourism from travel for the mere pleasure of the foreign and unknown (Singleton, 2017). This is echoed by Moufakkir and Noureddine (2018) who distinguish between authentic spiritual tourists – those who seek spiritual fulfilment through their travel – and casual spiritual tourists – who may experience spirituality while travelling but lack the deliberate intention to do so.

Having discussed the conceptual background of spiritual tourism, we now address two main perspectives from which tourism scholars have examined spiritual tourism.

9.3 How Do Spiritual Tourism Experiences Materialize?

Much of the attention evident in the extant literature has been directed toward tourists' subjective experience of spirituality. Spiritual experiences are centred on the quest for meaning in life and therefore resemble a process of meaning creation (Moal-Ulvoas & Taylor, 2014). Researchers (e.g., Willson et al., 2013) concur that experiencing spirituality materializes as a sense of transcendence, denoting "an individual's capacity to step out of his/her immediate perception of time and space and to view life from a larger, more objective perspective" (Piedmont, 1999, p. 986). Many authors agree that self-transcendence manifests as a sense of connectedness or oneness with three meaningful dimensions, namely the self, the other (including nature, animals, or other people), and a higher power (e.g., de Meezenbroek et al., 2012; Moal-Ulvoas, 2017; Reed, 1992; Sirgy et al., 2011; Willson et al., 2013)..

In keeping with this, qualitative insights into spiritual tourism journeys testify to experiences of self-discovery, self-development, and self-actualization (e.g., Buzinde et al., 2014; Komppula & Gartner, 2013; Moufakkir & Noureddine, 2018; Singleton, 2017; Willson et al., 2013). Nilsson and Tesfahuney (2016) suggest that spiritual experiences spark a "deep sense of being, an inner peace and the feeling of existential harmony" (p. 22). This is supported by Moufakkir and Noureddine's (2018) study that identifies the feeling of existential authenticity, a sense of being true to oneself, as a manifestation of spirituality in the Sahara desert. "Being able to listen to one's self" (Moufakkir & Noureddine, 2018, p. 116) is therefore considered both a catalyst of spirituality and an experience of spirituality itself (see also Buzinde et al., 2014; Jiang et al., 2018). Relatedly, scholars have pointed to feelings of internal refreshment, self-renewal and rejuvenation of the soul as a manifestation of spirituality while travelling (Buzinde et al., 2014; Moufakkir & Noureddine, 2018).

The qualitative insights into spiritual tourism journeys have also shed light on tourists' feelings of connectedness with nature. Sharpley and Jepson's (2011) seminal paper on nature-based tourism in rural areas illustrates that tourists "find the natural environment (…) spiritually uplifting" (p. 64). In particular, spirituality is found to be experienced as "feelings of being part of something bigger and infinite; the sense of a greater power and the appreciation of creation" (Sharpley & Jepson, 2011, p 64), which can provide a sense of meaning. These insights are consistent with other studies indicating that tourists experience spiritual fulfilment by becoming aware of the sacredness of natural environments (e.g., Jarratt & Sharpley, 2017; Moufakkir & Noureddine, 2018). In particular, the authenticity of natural spaces appears to support tourists' quest for their authentic selves (Moufakkir & Noureddine, 2018). Furthermore, academics have suggested that natural landscapes are conducive to spiritual inspiration by increasing individuals' sensory awareness and facilitating a state of 'flow' (Moufakkir & Noureddine, 2018; Sharpley & Jepson, 2011). As such, natural landscapes "[allow] for greater connectivity with and immersion in the natural surroundings" (Sharpley & Jepson, 2011, p. 58), which in itself can offer a meaningful experience.

To a lesser extent, tourism studies have also documented feelings of connectedness with other people as a source of spiritual growth. For example, Willson et al.'s (2013) phenomenological research illustrates how interpersonal experiences with unfamiliar people can be spiritually inspiring, by opening up a new perspective on life. In a similar vein, Moal-Ulvoas and Taylor (2014) describe how travelling allows to "compare one's life to that of visited populations" (p. 456), oftentimes poorer ones. Such encounters can therefore lead to an appreciation of one's own life, thus giving life new meaning.

Finally, it is also evident that spiritual tourism experiences may encompass feelings of connectedness with a higher power or God. For example, Andriotis (2009) quotes a visitor to Mount Athos who describes a sense of connection with God evoked by the physical qualities of the natural landscape. Similarly, Jiang et al. (2018) find that their study participants perceive the beauty of the landscape as "symbolic of the godhead" (p. 196). These insights correspond with the findings of Moufakkir and Noureddine (2018) that indicate how contemporary spiritual tourists' may particularly find God in nature.

9.4 How Does Tourism Facilitate Spirituality?

Another perspective evident in the associated body of literature approaches spiritual tourism from the perspective of how tourism contributes to travellers' spiritual experiences. Within this research stream, scholars have argued that tourism provides individuals with the conditions for spiritual fulfilment for at least two reasons.

First, tourism offers a temporary interruption of the daily routine and thus provides a suitable context for reflection and introspection (Cheer et al., 2017; Moal-Ulvoas, 2017). As found by Moal-Ulvoas and Taylor (2014), travelling is "a context that frees [the] mind" (p. 458). The relief from the everyday stresses of modern life can strengthen travellers' receptivity to new impulses, which in turn are vital to finding new meaning in life (Moal-Ulvoas & Taylor, 2014). Relatedly, tourism scholars have shed light on the experience of solitude as an important catalyst of spirituality while travelling (e.g., Andriotis, 2009; Moal-Ulvoas & Taylor, 2014; Moufakkir & Noureddine, 2018; Sharpley & Jepson, 2011). As such, the remoteness provided by certain natural environments such as the desert (Moufakkir & Noureddine, 2018) or rural areas (Sharpley & Jepson, 2011) has been considered conducive to finding new meaning in life.

Second, a great deal of research within this stream has devoted special attention to the role of place and the symbolism associated with places. Over the past decades, tourism scholars have examined the spiritual value provided by various locations, especially natural areas. Sharpley and Jepson (2011), for instance, explored tourists' experience of the English Lake District and concluded that the natural environment can evoke deep emotional and spiritual responses. In particular, the study shows that the challenges that natural environments can impose are perceived as generating meaning (Sharpley & Jepson, 2011). This is consistent with Willson et al.'s (2013) portrait of a traveller who interprets climbing Machu Picchu as analogous to the challenges in her life (p. 159). In line with these findings, scholars have supported the potential of nature-based tourism to provide spiritual significance (e.g., Moal-Ulvoas, 2017; Wang & Blasco, 2022).

In a related vein, Wang et al. (2021) found that not only the landscape but also the "spiritual vibrations" (p. 6) felt at a place may constitute key aspects of tourists' spiritual experiences. These spiritual vibrations correspond with what Nilsson and Tesfahuney (2016) refer to as a "sense of revelation" (p. 22) inherent in some places. As per Nilsson and Tesfahuney (2016), such places are experienced as providing spiritual energy and may therefore be considered holy by tourists. Correspondingly, tourism scholars have testified to the spiritual value provided by heritage sites (Laing et al., 2014) as well as dark tourism places (Zheng et al., 2020).

9.5 Conclusion

There is good reason to expect that spiritual tourism will be a central topic for both academics and tourism managers in the coming years (Buzinde et al., 2014; WASET, 2022). Advancing the understanding and conceptual basis of the phenomenon is thus timely and much needed. The present study has therefore taken a first step toward alleviating some of the ambiguity regarding the concept of spiritual tourism.

We have reviewed the relevant literature and synthesized the findings along central research themes. In doing so, we have identified the search for meaning in life as the essence of spirituality (Reed, 1992; Sharpley & Jepson, 2011) and motive behind spiritual tourism (Collins-Kreiner, 2010). Crucially, spiritual tourism is focused on the individual and his or her unique interpretation of spiritual fulfilment (Nilsson & Tesfahuney, 2016). Thus, we find that spiritual tourism encompasses a variety of activities and destinations that may be related to distinct sources of inspiration for meaning (Kato & Progano, 2017). Moreover, we have discussed the interrelatedness of spirituality and religion and outlined the two perspectives on the delineation of these concepts evident in the literature. A key takeaway from this discussion is that spiritual tourism expands beyond the traditional boundaries of religiosity (Nilsson & Tesfahuney, 2016). Whether spiritual travels are characterized by religious elements or not may therefore ultimately be a matter of each tourist's personal interpretation.

Considerable research has been devoted to tourists' subjective experience of spirituality. We find that spiritual experiences manifest as feelings of connectedness with self-transcendent dimensions (Willson et al., 2013). More specifically, studies show that tourists experience spiritual fulfilment through becoming connected with their inner self, with others, as well as with a higher power or God. In particular, we note that nature is conceived of as a key source of meaning (Moufakkir & Noureddine, 2018; Sharpley & Jepson, 2011).

Thus, research indicates that nature-based environments are a valuable vehicle for tourism to cater to the growing interest in spiritual tourism (e.g., Moal-Ulvoas, 2017). In addition, we conclude that tourism provides a range of conditions that are conducive to spiritual experiences (e.g., Moal-Ulvoas & Taylor, 2014). We call future research to contribute to this burgeoning stream of research. For tourism managers, understanding the factors that promote spiritual experiences while travelling is vital in order to leverage them accordingly.

We further note that more research is needed into the characteristics of tourists who travel for spiritual purposes. In a seminal paper, Moal-Ulvoas (2017) found that senior travellers constitute an important target group for spiritual tourism. To the best of our knowledge, there have been no subsequent efforts to add to these findings.Finally, despite the growing number of studies in recent years, we also encourage further research into the distinct types of spiritual tourism and spiritual tourism destinations. Much of the attention evident has been directed toward nature-based areas (e.g., Sharpley & Jepson, 2011). However, more recent research has begun to broaden this perspective to include other spiritually energizing places (e.g., Zheng et al., 2020). Given the subjective interpretation of spiritual experiences, we believe this to be fertile ground for future research.

References

Andriotis, K. (2009). Sacred site experience. A phenomenological study. *Annals of Tourism Research, 36*(1), 64–84. https://doi.org/10.1016/j.annals.2008.10.003

Buzinde, C. N., Kalavar, J. M., Kohli, N., & Manuel-Navarrete, D. (2014). Emic understandings of Kumbh Mela pilgrimage experiences. *Annals of Tourism Research, 49*, 1–18. https://doi.org/10.1016/j.annals.2014.08.001

Cheer, J. M., Belhassen, Y., & Kujawa, J. (2017). The search for spirituality in tourism: Toward a conceptual framework for spiritual tourism. *Tourism Management Perspectives, 24*, 252–256. https://doi.org/10.1016/j.tmp.2017.07.018

Collins-Kreiner, N. (2010). Researching pilgrimage: Continuity and transformations. *Annals of Tourism Research, 37*(2), 440–456. https://doi.org/10.1016/j.annals.2009.10.016

Collins-Kreiner, N. (2020). Religion and tourism: A diverse and fragmented field in need of a holistic agenda. *Annals of Tourism Research, 82*, 102892. https://doi.org/10.1016/j.annals.2020.102892

de Meezenbroek, E. J., Garssen, B., van den Berg, M., van Dierendonck, D., Visser, A., & Schaufeli, W. B. (2012). Measuring spirituality as a universal human experience: A review of spirituality questionnaires. *Journal of Religion and Health, 51*(2), 336–354. https://doi.org/10.1007/s10943-010-9376-1

Digance, J. (2003). Pilgrimage at contested sites. *Annals of Tourism Research, 30*(1), 143–159. https://doi.org/10.1016/S0160-7383(02)00028-2

Fedele, A. (2013). *Looking for Mary Magdalene: Alternative pilgrimage and ritual creativity at Catholic shrines in France*. Oxford University Press.

Gilbert, E. (2007). *Eat, pray, love: One woman's search for everything*. A&C Black.

Hall, M. C. (2006). Travel and journeying on the sea of faith: Perspectives from religious humanism. In D. J. Timothy & D. H. Olsen (Eds.), *Tourism, religion and spiritual journeys*. Routledge.

Heelas, P., & Woodhead, L. (2005). *The spiritual revolution: Why religion is giving way to spirituality*. Blackwell.

Hill, P. C., Pargament, K. I., Hood, R. W., Mccullough, M. E., Swyers, J. P., Larson, D. B., & Zinnbauer, B. J. (2000). Conceptualizing religion and spirituality: Points of commonality, points of departure. *Journal for the Theory of Social Behaviour, 30*(1), 51–77. https://doi.org/10.1111/1468-5914.00119

Holman, C. (2011). Surfing for a shaman: Analyzing an ayahuasca website. *Annals of Tourism Research, 38*(1), 90–109. https://doi.org/10.1016/j.annals.2010.05.005

Houtman, D., & Aupers, S. (2007). The spiritual turn and the decline of tradition: The spread of post-Christian spirituality in 14 Western Countries, 1981–2000. *Journal for the Scientific Study of Religion, 46*(3), 305–320. https://doi.org/10.1111/j.1468-5906.2007.00360.x

Jarratt, D., & Sharpley, R. (2017). Tourists at the seaside: Exploring the spiritual dimension. *Tourist Studies, 17*(4), 349–368. https://doi.org/10.1177/1468797616687560

Jiang, T., Ryan, C., & Zhang, C. (2018). The spiritual or secular tourist? The experience of Zen meditation in Chinese temples. *Tourism Management, 65*, 187–199. https://doi.org/10.1016/j.tourman.2017.10.008

Kato, K., & Progano, R. N. (2017). Spiritual (walking) tourism as a foundation for sustainable destination development: Kumano-kodo pilgrimage, Wakayama, Japan. *Tourism Management Perspectives, 24*, 243–251. https://doi.org/10.1016/j.tmp.2017.07.017

Kim, B., Kim, S. S., & King, B. (2016). The sacred and the profane: Identifying pilgrim traveler value orientations using means-end theory. *Tourism Management, 56*, 142–155. https://doi.org/10.1016/j.tourman.2016.04.003

Komppula, R., & Gartner, W. C. (2013). Hunting as a travel experience: An auto-ethnographic study of hunting tourism in Finland and the USA. *Tourism Management, 35*, 168–180. https://doi.org/10.1016/j.tourman.2012.06.014

Kujawa, J. (2017). Spiritual tourism as a quest. *Tourism Management Perspectives, 24*, 193–200. https://doi.org/10.1016/j.tmp.2017.07.011

Laing, J., Wheeler, F., Reeves, K., & Frost, W. (2014). Assessing the experiential value of heritage assets: A case study of a Chinese heritage precinct, Bendigo, Australia. *Tourism Management, 40*, 180–192. https://doi.org/10.1016/j.tourman.2013.06.004

Lin, L. P. (Lynn), & Hsieh, W. K. (2022). Exploring how perceived resilience and restoration affected the wellbeing of Matsu pilgrims during COVID-19. *Tourism Management, 90*, 104473. https://doi.org/10.1016/j.tourman.2021.104473

Miao, L., Im, J., So, K. K. F., & Cao, Y. (2022). Post-pandemic and post-traumatic tourism behavior. *Annals of Tourism Research, 95*, 103410. https://doi.org/10.1016/j.annals.2022.103410

Moal-Ulvoas, G. (2017). Positive emotions and spirituality in older travelers. *Annals of Tourism Research, 66*, 151–158. https://doi.org/10.1016/j.annals.2017.07.020

Moal-Ulvoas, G., & Taylor, V. A. (2014). The spiritual benefits of travel for senior tourists. *Journal of Consumer Behaviour, 13*(6), 453–462. https://doi.org/10.1002/cb.v13.6; https://doi.org/10.1002/cb.1495

Moufahim, M., & Lichrou, M. (2019). Pilgrimage, consumption and rituals: Spiritual authenticity in a Shia Muslim pilgrimage. *Tourism Management, 70*(August 2018), 322–332. https://doi.org/10.1002/cb.v13.610.1002/cb.1495

Moufakkir, O., & Noureddine, S. (2018). Examining the spirituality of spiritual tourists: A Sahara desert experience. *Annals of Tourism Research, 70*, 108–119. https://doi.org/10.1016/j.annals.2017.09.003

Nilsson, M., & Tesfahuney, M. (2016). Performing the "post-secular" in Santiago de Compostela. *Annals of Tourism Research, 57*, 18–30. https://doi.org/10.1016/j.annals.2015.11.001

Norman, A. (2011). *Spiritual tourism: Travel and religious practice in western society*. Bloomsbury Publishing.

Norman, A., & Pokorny, J. J. (2017). Meditation retreats: Spiritual tourism well-being interventions. *Tourism Management Perspectives, 24*, 201–207. https://doi.org/10.1016/j.tmp.2017.07.012

Palmatier, R. W., Houston, M. B., & Hulland, J. (2018). Review articles: Purpose, process, and structure. *Journal of the Academy of Marketing Science, 46*(1), 1–5. https://doi.org/10.1007/s11747-017-0563-4

Paloutzian, R. F., & Park, C. L. (2014). *Handbook of the psychology of religion and spirituality*. Guilford Publications.

Piedmont, R. (1999). Does spirituality represent the sixth factor of personality? Spiritual transcendence and the five-factor model. *Journal of Personality, 67*(6), 985–1013.

Puczkó, L., & Smith, M. (2012). An analysis of tourism QOL domains from the demand side. In *Handbook of tourism and quality-of-life research* (pp. 263–277). Springer.

Reed, P. G. (1992). An emerging paradigm for the investigation of spirituality in nursing. *Research in Nursing and Health, 15*, 349–357.

Rinschede, G. (1992). Forms of religious tourism. *Annals of Tourism Research, 19*(1), 51–67. https://doi.org/10.1016/0160-7383(92)90106-Y

Sharpley, R., & Jepson, D. (2011). Rural tourism: A spiritual experience? *Annals of Tourism Research, 38*(1), 52–71. https://doi.org/10.1016/j.annals.2010.05.002

Sheldrake, P. (2009). *A brief history of spirituality*. John Wiley & Sons.

Singleton, A. (2017). The summer of the spirits: Spiritual tourism to America's foremost village of spirit mediums. *Annals of Tourism Research, 67*, 48–57. https://doi.org/10.1016/j.annals.2017.08.002

Sirgy, M. J., Kruger, P. S., Lee, D. J., & Yu, G. B. (2011). How does a travel trip affect tourists' life satisfaction? *Journal of Travel Research, 50*(3), 261–275. https://doi.org/10.1177/0047287510362784

Stausberg, M. (2014). Religion and spirituality in tourism. In A. A. Lew, C. M. Hall, & A. M. Williams (Eds.), *The Wiley Blackwell companion to tourism* (pp. 349–360). Wiley.

Terzidou, M., Scarles, C., & Saunders, M. N. K. (2018). The complexities of religious tourism motivations: Sacred places, vows and visions. *Annals of Tourism Research, 70*, 54–65. https://doi.org/10.1016/j.annals.2018.02.011

The World Academy of Science. (2022). ICSTED 2022: 16. *International conference on spiritual tourism and economic development*. Waset.Org. https://waset.org/spiritual-tourism-and-economic-development-conference-in-november-2022-in-paris

Uysal, M., Sirgy, M. J., Woo, E., & Kim, H. L. (2016). Quality of life (QOL) and well-being research in tourism. *Tourism Management, 53*, 244–261. https://doi.org/10.1016/j.tourman.2015.07.013

Vada, S., Prentice, C., Scott, N., & Hsiao, A. (2020). Positive psychology and tourist well-being: A systematic literature review. *Tourism Management Perspectives, 33*, 100631. https://doi.org/10.1016/j.tmp.2019.100631

Walton, J. K. (2009). Prospects in tourism history: Evolution, state of play and future developments. *Tourism Management, 30*(6), 783–793. https://doi.org/10.1016/j.tourman.2009.05.010

Wang, S., & Blasco, D. (2022). East meets West: Spiritual tourism in Chinese protected areas. *Annals of Tourism Research Empirical Insights, 3*(1), 100035. https://doi.org/10.1016/j.annale.2022.100035

Wang, Y. C., Chen, P. J., Shi, H., & Shi, W. (2021). Travel for mindfulness through Zen retreat experience: A case study at Donghua Zen Temple. *Tourism Management, 83*(September 2020), 104211. https://doi.org/10.1016/j.tourman.2020.104211

Willson, G. B., McIntosh, A. J., & Zahra, A. L. (2013). Tourism and spirituality: A phenomenological analysis. *Annals of Tourism Research, 42*, 150–168. https://doi.org/10.1016/j.annals.2013.01.016

World Tourism Organization [WASET]. (2015). *First UNWTO International Conference on Spiritual Tourism for Sustainable Development – Ninh Binh Province, Viet Nam, 21–22 November 2013*. https://doi.org/10.18111/9789284416738

Zheng, C., Zhang, J., Qiu, M., Guo, Y., & Zhang, H. (2020). From mixed emotional experience to spiritual meaning: Learning in dark tourism places. *Tourism Geographies, 22*(1), 105–126. https://doi.org/10.1080/14616688.2019.1618903

Zinnbauer, B. J., Pargament, K. I., Cole, B., Rye, M. S., Butter, E. M., Belavich, T. G., Hipp, K. M., Scott, A. B., & Kadar, J. L. (1997). Religion and spirituality: Unfuzzying the fuzzy. *Journal for the Scientific Study of Religion, 36*(4), 549. https://doi.org/10.2307/1387689

Chapter 10
Gender-Inclusive, Sustainable, Frugal and Innovative Methods in Succession Planning for Indian Small and Medium Enterprises Family-Owned Businesses

Pooja Alfred Arambhan, Jireh Hooi Inn Seow, and Bhanu Ranjan

Abstract India has recently recorded the fastest economic growth among all the major world economies, making the country the fifth-largest economy in the world. Eighty-nine percent of India's gross domestic product is contributed by family-owned businesses (FoBs) that employ 75% of the workforce. Still, there exists a gaping void in the participation of women in top leadership positions, and gender inequality remains a key development issue. Furthermore, the recent COVID-19 global pandemic has aggravated sustainability challenges for these Small & Medium Enterprises (SME) FoBs, with increased importance given to succession planning in the aftermath of the COVID-19 crisis. As a result, FoBs are forced to adopt frugal innovative methods for inter-generational sustainability. The authors conducted a systematic literature review between 2019–2022 to delve into the various innovative methods adopted by SME FoBs and their implications on gender inclusivity as a key human capital to propose suitable recommendations and bridge the prevalent gender gap to improve India's 124th position out of 190 countries on the Gender Inequality Index as rated by the World Bank (2022).

Keywords Family business · Gender · Succession planning · Innovation · Small and medium enterprise

P. A. Arambhan (✉)
S P Jain School of Global Management, Mumbai, India
e-mail: pooja.ds21dba001@spjain.org

J. H. I. Seow
Innovation and Entrepreneurship Centre (i2e), Singapore, Singapore

S P Jain School of Global Management, Singapore, Singapore
e-mail: jireh.seowhi@spjain.org

B. Ranjan
S P Jain School of Global Management, Singapore, Singapore
e-mail: bhanu.ranjan@spjain.org

E. L. Eijdenberg et al. (eds.), *Innovation-Driven Business and Sustainability in the Tropics*, https://doi.org/10.1007/978-981-99-2909-2_10

10.1 Introduction

Despite the effects of the COVID-19 pandemic, India has risen to be the fifth-largest global economy and has been accorded the status of being the fastest-growing economy worldwide. In light of the unprecedented challenges rattling the global economic and social systems, this performance draws our attention to the 'backbone of our economy' – the Family-owned Business (FoB) (Munagapati, 2018, p. 1).

As drivers of economic growth, they have contributed to 70% of the Indian gross domestic product (Bennedsen et al., 2022), ensuring their inter-generational survival becomes imperative. Empirical research has identified that the intergenerational survivability of FoBs is bleak, with only 30% surviving to the second generation (Oudah et al., 2018) and 13% making it to the third (Chahal & Sharma, 2020).

The grounded economic underpinnings of FoBs uniquely make them the largest source of employment generation in the private sector, employing 75% of the Indian workforce and ranking the country third after China and the USA by the number of family firms. Perhaps unsurprisingly, the country also boasts having the second largest number of small and medium enterprises (SMEs) globally, of which most are family-owned (Arambhan & Seetharaman, 2022).

Extant literature has identified the various challenges associated with succession in FoBs and their impact on performance and intergenerational survivability while acknowledging their notable significance to the socio-economic conditions of countries. However, despite the acknowledgement of their contributions to society, research on succession remains scant, even though it is one of the top five topics of family business research (Khoury et al., 2021).

The authors draw specific attention to leverage the 'demographic window of opportunity as India faces a youth bulge' according to the United Nations Population Fund Projections 2022, which highlights 54% of the population below the age of 25 (Arambhan & Seetharaman, 2022). The striking feature is that the Indian population will be one of the youngest in the world until 2030.

In the ever-expanding digital landscape further propelled by social distancing norms and work-from-home restrictions by the pandemic, the authors attempt to bridge the development issues faced by most of the youth population by addressing gender disparity and the intergenerational survival of FoBs for the socio-economic transformation and upliftment of the country.

10.2 Literature Review

10.2.1 Family-Owned Businesses

Studies focused on family businesses in Asia have drawn immense interest in recent times owing to their success on the global scale. Several scholars have attempted to define a family business but have failed to reach a consensus on a universal definition owing to the heterogeneous nature of family businesses (Bhatti, 2021).

This paper adopts the definition of a family business as one in which the ownership, management, control and decision making is directly or indirectly within the family (Liu, 2020).

Family-owned businesses are an inter-mutual overlap between the business and family and represent the most common type of global organisational structure (Chukwuma et al., 2021). The business's success is determined by the interaction of these structural overlaps and how they relate to each other over time (Labaki et al., 2019).

The salient characteristics that distinguish them from their non-family corporate counterparts can be attributed to their reduced layers of management, traditional value system, strong internal and external social networks (Zapata-Cantu et al., 2022) and the prioritisation of socio-emotional wealth (SEW), which could be viewed as both their strengths or their weaknesses (Swab et al., 2020).

The pandemic revealed the strength of some FoBs in how they swiftly responded and adapted to the new normal exhibited by the market's changing demands, owing to their proximity to business processes and management and strong internal and external social ties (Song et al., 2022). Not all of them were able to realign their business models and restructure their offerings to respond to supply chain disruptions and the evolving needs and demands of the customer to affirm organisational resilience (Mihotić et al., 2022).

Empirical research has notably pointed out the resilient nature of FoBs (Moyer, 2020). However, numerous definitions may be used to define resilience owing to the diverse nature of family businesses (Jaskiewicz & Dyer, 2017) and the measurability of their unique outcomes of resilience. Some authors also highlight the succession intentions of FoBs that characterise their resilience (Mihotić et al., 2022). This study adopts the definition of resilience as how FoBs achieve a resilient outcome as they respond to adversity or crisis and their steps towards a positive trajectory encompassing their agility and adaptive capability (Hillmann & Guenther, 2021).

10.3 Succession Planning

Several scholars have highlighted the critical nature of succession, which assumes graver importance in the aftermath of the COVID-19 pandemic that has changed the business landscape (Song et al., 2022).

The definition of succession as 'a process in which new owners, from within or outside the owner family, enter the business as owners and add new capital and resources that have consequences for firm processes and outcomes such as innovation, entrepreneurial orientation and growth' (Nordqvist et al., 2013, p.1990) best suits the focus of this study.

Succession brings with it significant changes to the structure of the organisation and makes businesses more susceptible to failure during this multi-phased process (Arambhan & Seetharaman, 2022).

The founding generations' intransigence to disengage their emotions from the business and make room for future planning with the incoming generation is often the blockade to succession (Nwuke et al., 2020). This connection to the business has been identified through the stewardship theory (Chundu et al., 2021), where the family and business are often inseparable in the minds of the founders. The coexistence of the founders' values systems along with the long-term goals of the business can stir up some turbulence in FoBs (Erdogan et al., 2020). Therefore, the interaction between the business and family assumes increased significance when two or more family members work concurrently in the business (Haynes et al., 2021).

The common oversight of unprioritized succession (Rajan et al., 2020) has now taken on a new avatar in view of the geopolitical tremors of the pandemic. The crisis highlighted the economic, social and environmental impact businesses have on the economy and the obvious uncertainty of life, drawing urgent focus inwards towards intergenerational survivability (Abiri-Franklin & Olugasa, 2022).

A worrying pre-pandemic statistic shows that, despite 60% of FoBs exhibiting an intent to pass on their legacy to the next generation, only 21% of FoBs have a formal well-documented succession plan, and a further 31% have made no preparations for succession (Rajan et al., 2020).

This represents the traditional implicit understanding that the next generation will carry the legacy forward, often ignoring the willingness of the successor (Dorairajan & Bangur, 2020), their commitment and preparedness to carry forward the business (Mokhber et al., 2017) and their skill sets and capabilities to do so (Byrne et al., 2019).

10.4 Sustainability

Sustainability can be attributed to the strategic intent of the business and draws focus in this study, as it addresses major issues of inequality, the repercussions of the macroeconomic crisis and the depletion of resources, which leads to the direction of frugal innovation.

The authors adopt the opinion of Oudah et al. (2018, p. 7) to narrow down the definition of sustainability as the 'significant contribution of strategic planning to the success and long-term survival of family businesses. Strategic planning both establishes the business's scope and long-term goals and adopts resources and competencies in changing environments to achieve the required scope and goals'.

Extant literature also suggests that the various stages of succession lead to avenues for innovation (Wong, n.d.) and share similarities in their natures of both being continuous processes rather than a one-time effort (Porfírio et al., 2020).

A large portion of twentieth-century research points to familial traditions and religious belief systems that may have a significant influence on the sustainability of the business (LeCounte, 2022). Although from the resource-based perspective, culture has an exacting influence on the competitive advantage of a family business (Balabram, 2022). The deep roots of tradition become a hindrance to innovation

(Bouncken & Schmitt, n.d.). This is further buttressed by agency theory that highlights the underinvestment of FoBs in innovation due to their strong need to protect the legacy and socio-emotional wealth of the business (Becerra et al., 2020). Conversely, Rondi et al. (2019) credit FoBs as being among the most innovative globally despite their conservativeness and traditions.

Innovation, therefore, becomes a key component for the sustainability of FoBs from the micro-perspective to tackle uncertainties, such as the global awakening of the pandemic (Liaqat et al. 2021).

To drive organisational and individual value, a sustainability mindset becomes a decisive factor in a disruptive environment, which helps sustenance during calmer periods of business. This would translate to deep diving into a business's processes to eliminate those elements or resources that can be simplified without compromising output or customer value.

Survival is conditional on staying relevant and up to date, lending direction to traditional FoBs being more amenable to the technological advancements and innovations the younger generation can offer. This, coupled with the trust and internal and external social capital garnered by the legacy business, is a sustainably winning combination that hits the sweet spot of competence and traditional values and ethics. Research suggests that SMEs are more conducive to embracing frugal innovative methods by capitalising on their relatively leaner organisational structures than non-family businesses. However, fewer family firms acknowledge the importance of innovation.

With the aim of leveraging the strengths of the incoming generation by empowering their most valuable assets, their employees (Balabram, 2022), SME FoBs can take firm steps towards cost saving and a progressive business strategy.

In a dynamic digital-based economy, the Technology Acceptance Model assumes priority to capitalise on the prior IT knowledge of the successor generation and ensure minimisation of pushback from employees by imparting relevant training on its benefits and developing increased internal employee capabilities (Haynes et al., 2021).

Scholars have noted several differences between family businesses and their non-family counterparts, of which their reluctance to invest in research and development (R&D) and innovation is common across literature even though their salient characteristics exhibit strong innovation potential (Jocic et al., 2021). Their conservativeness to risk-taking and innovation has contributed to their resilience and solvency due to their increased cash reserves with reduced leverage ratios that allow room for flexibility (Le Breton-Miller & Miller, 2022). Nevertheless, with organisational structures being challenged virtually and digitally in a disrupted global environment, developing a competitive advantage through a long-term view of technological innovation assumes increased importance to be able to gain significant opportunities (Song et al., 2022).

Therefore, business model innovation becomes imperative to maintain a competitive advantage that is also financially viable to make a social and environmental impact (Gregori & Holzmann, 2020).

This gives rise to the need to relook at the traditional business models of FoBs to make room for digitisation by way of processes and technologies and appropriate strategic implementation methods to challenge the status quo (Bouncken & Schmitt, n.d.).

10.5 Gender Inclusivity

Gender inclusivity forms part of the United Nations (UN) Sustainable Development Goals (SDG) with a focus on providing equal opportunity and empowering the participation of women devoid of discrimination (United Nations Women, 2018). Several scholars have delved into how larger organisations adopt SDGs for economic development but fail to investigate their role in SME structures (Bauweraerts et al., 2022).

Although government regulatory mechanisms have been enacted to bolster the participation of women and address the gender disparity in listed entities in the enactment of the Companies Act 2013, gender diversity remains elusive.

Indian SME FoBs are deeply rooted in a tradition stemming from the erstwhile joint-family system (Tyagi et al., 2021) that is undergoing changes due to mutations in family structures. Family-owned businesses are also influenced by the socio-cultural environment, which distinguishes them from their non-family counterparts(Ganguly, 2020).

The undercurrents of familial relationships between men and women within a family business shine a light on FoBs falling prey to gender bias (Soost & Moog, 2019). The role of women is still stereotyped as domestic responsibilities, limiting their avenues for roles within the family business (Nguyen et al., 2021).

Gender disparity is a consequence of a systemic void across social institutions (Nguyen et al., 2021) that must be addressed to chart the course for the undergoing demographic transition of a country to create opportunities for women to thrive in business.

The saplings of gender inequality are perpetuated in the practice of primogeniture, overlooking merit-based succession by choosing a successor and transferring the business, assets and inheritance depending on the birth order, often to the first-born male heir (Kubíček & Machek, 2019). This issue of gender-based discrimination on property-related discrimination is still prevalent despite India being a signatory to the UN Convention on the Elimination of all Forms of Discrimination Against Women that its parliament ratified in 1993. There are still conflicting views on the discrimination of women and the violation of their fundamental rights in Articles 14 and 15 (1) of the Constitution of India (Damle & Shah, n.d.).

There is an acknowledgement that the societal prejudices of gendered roles have overshadowed the competencies of women, limiting them to domestic responsibilities and overlooking their qualifications and skills that is often superior to that of their male counterparts in SME FoBs environments, yet automatically exclude them from top management positions (Chahal & Sharma, 2020).

Evidence points to the early socialisation of male heirs to the business involving dinner table discussions imprinting the expectations of gender-tinted roles on the heirs from a young age (Gimenez-Jimenez et al., 2021).

Although many authors have addressed the loyalty of employees to FoBs, employee retention still stands out as a major challenge (Vardaman et al., 2018). Employees look beyond the compensatory package to prioritise work–life balance and equitable organisations in the era of quiet quitting, immediately drawing significant attention to the culture of FoBs.

As the lines between the family and business are often blurred in SME structures, making them intricately intertwined social units (Labaki et al., 2019), the traditions and values that are embodied by the founder seamlessly flow into that of the organisation (Ramachandran & Antony, 2020).

A participative and inclusive culture that embodies the employee buy-in (Tabor & Vardaman, n.d.) demonstrates respect for their opinions and their perception of a positive and higher rating of culture with greater engagement with the leadership (Sull & Sull, n.d.).

10.6 Research Problems and Questions

The prevalent gaps in extant literature lend impetus to this study:

1. What is the impact of the COVID-19 pandemic on SME FoB innovation? (Jocic et al., 2021)
2. What are the challenges to gender inclusivity in SME FoBs in an uncertain environment posed by the pandemic? (Haynes et al., 2021)
3. What is the benefit of proactive succession planning on the sustainability of the business? (Chahal & Sharma, 2020)

10.7 Research Objectives

1. To identify frugal innovative methods for SME FoBs
2. To propose gender-inclusive methods for succession planning
3. To identify factors that positively affect the sustainability of SME FoBs

10.8 Methodology and Approach

For this ethnographic study, the authors reviewed high-quality secondary data consisting of 82 studies carried out between 2019–2022, sourced from various databases, SCOPUS and Google Scholar (Hlady-Rispal et al., 2021). Following this, a

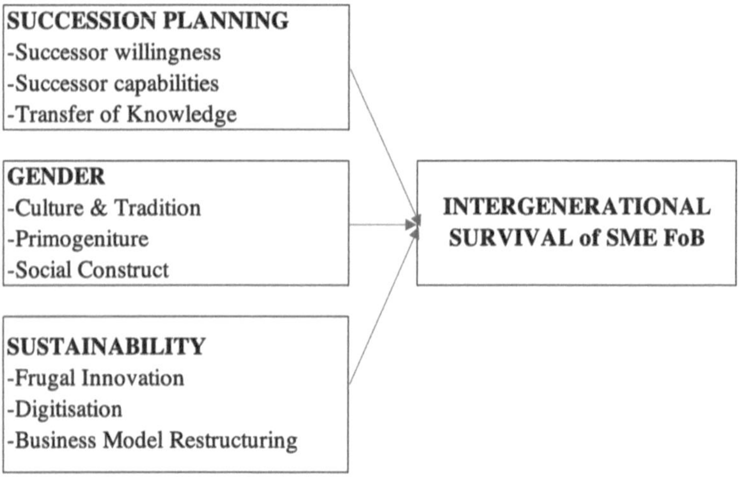

Fig. 10.1 Research framework

research framework was developed to delve deeper into the gender-inclusive, sustainable and frugal methods employed by SME FoBs.

10.9 Research Framework (Fig 10.1)

10.10 Discussion, Analysis and Outcomes

10.10.1 Proposition 1: Frugal Innovation with Business Model Restructuring Positively Impacts the Sustainability of the Business

Many scholars believe that multi-generational involvement in an FoB is not only an obvious indicator of successful succession but also paves the path for increased avenues for innovation (LeCounte, 2022). The tacit knowledge accumulated through the multiple generations position SME FoBs with a distinctive competitive advantage against their non-family counterparts.

The shockwaves of the pandemic revealed that family businesses that adopted a long-term orientation were able to tide through the disruptions of the pandemic by allowing room for innovation, exhibiting their resilient core competencies and strong social ties (Le Breton-Miller & Miller, 2022).

Frugal innovation requires businesses to go back to the drawing board and reassess the entire ecosystem of their go-to-market strategy, product development and business process. It represents a change in mindset to be able to identify those areas that are resource intensive to do away with them or simplify the system to be able to deliver more value at lesser costs without compromising on the firm's output.

To achieve higher volumes at reduced rates, it becomes incumbent on the business to explore the different digital marketplaces that have emerged as a repercussion of the pandemic that lower the barriers to entry, providing an avenue to seize newer opportunities. This opens possibilities for adopting digital technologies as presented by social media, mobile and data analytics. Proactive digitisation includes various 'combinations of information, computing, communication and connectivity or technology enabled by those' (Bouncken & Schmitt, n.d. p. 2).

The Indian government has recognised the need for digital adoption by increasing its telecommunications expenditure and issuing new telecom spectrum licenses. Consequently, the country boasts the second-highest global internet connectivity, with over 700 million users recorded in 2020, of which 79% of usage is from smartphones. The digital literacy that the usage represents, combined with the demographic dividend with a median age of 28 years, is an open avenue for digital workforce participation.

10.10.2 Proposition 2: Gender Inclusivity Bolsters the Participation of Women as an Avenue of Social and Economic Upliftment Addressing the United Nations Sustainable Development Goals

McCoy and Elwood (2009) opine that organisational resilience is determined by the psychological contract of how employees perceive they are treated, shining a spotlight on the importance of creating an equitable and ethical organisation (Hillmann & Guenther, 2021). A gender-balanced leadership team significantly impacts the performance of the business and results in favourable sustainability reporting (Nguyen et al., 2021).

Intergenerational survivability in a highly digitised and outspoken world is dependent on the amalgamation of global diversity, community and society. Extant literature has identified the exclusion of women from long-term succession goals as one of the common reasons for the unsustainability of FoBs. (Abiri-Franklin & Olugasa, 2022).

The presence of female representation in top management positions at the SME level not only poses encouragement to women that they have the skills to be able to lead despite societal bias but also renders a trickle-down effect within the organisation. Female-led FoBs exhibit a distinctive leadership style, as they are known to be less autocratic and more transformational, by empowering individuals to identify new opportunities for growth and exhibiting a collaborative work environment

(Calabrò et al., 2020).Haynes et al. (2021) posit an interesting dimension that couples who give adequate precedence to satisfaction in their interpersonal relationships in their business and family have a higher chance of better business performance in terms of profitability.

10.11 Proposition 3: Succession Planning Reduces Vulnerabilities to Uncertain Macroeconomic Changes Reinforcing the Long-Term Goal of a business's Inter-Generation Succession

A continuous mindful process of intentional succession planning reduces the insecurities of loss of employment and lack of clarity while addressing the issues of the pace of organisational change (Sull & Sull, n.d.). Proactive succession planning is critical to the continuity of the business and involves well-thought-out strategies for replacing key personnel that cushions the organisation in an uncertain macroeconomic environment (Abiri-Franklin & Olugasa, 2022). Intergenerational survivability is dependent on the innovative ability of FoBs to create and transfer knowledge across generations (Zybura et al., 2021).

Therefore, FoBs must adopt a long-term orientation to develop agility and better responsiveness to macroeconomic uncertainties (Fendri & Nguyen, 2019). To do so, they must acknowledge the importance of strategic succession planning by anticipating the potential threats that could disrupt operations and put survival at stake. Organisations need to be adequately protected from sudden shocks, such as the pandemic or the untimely demise of a founder, and be prepared to keep the firm close-knit and the culture intact in an era of remote working (Lévesque & Subramanian, 2022).

10.12 Implications for Theory and Practice

The authors suggest practical implications for SME FoBs, irrespective of generation, to challenge the status quo and disrupt long-standing familial traditions by reflecting inwards for increased self-awareness. Doing this could be instrumental in managing the complexities of a changing business environment for leadership development, and it encourages equitable decision-making for the survivability of the business.

In the scholarly field of family psychotherapy, the intergenerational legacy transfer is a conscious or unconscious driver of the family business's heritage. This is ingrained in an organisation's belief system and culture, guiding the behaviours of those associated with the FoB subsystem that remain unchallenged by them across generations (Labaki et al., 2019). In other words, in the backdrop of a traditional

SME FoB, the collective institutionalised practices of the older generation lend course for subsequent generations to follow (Erdogan et al., 2020). The practice of primogeniture and gender discrimination that besets SME FoB can be potentially damaging to the survivability of the business and the economy of a country (Abiri-Franklin & Olugasa, 2022).

To avoid jeopardising the business's future by making a sub-optimal choice of successor, the inclusion of daughters in the future planning and involvement of a business must gain momentum in SMEs in India (Haynes et al., 2021). This represents a shift in outdated mindsets from the simplest social unit of the family that can be embodied by society at large.

The past casts a strong shadow on the present and future of a business and, accordingly, is in urgent need of adapting to the lifecycle of businesses while streamlining itself to embody the heightened awareness of diversity, equity and inclusion that the socio-economic environment currently represents.

The inherent skill sets that women bring to businesses highlight the need at the family level to shift the traditional generational mindset to put women on an equal footing and promote best practices to minimise gender biases (Calabrò et al., 2020).

Maintaining tradition and investing in innovation may conceptually seem contradictory; they represent essential elements for family firm survival to avoid decision paralysis and the conundrum of preserving tradition to safeguard legacy and pursuing innovation to maintain relevancy and competitiveness (Erdogan et al., 2020).

The prioritisation of investing in innovation and training employees to be future-ready in the digital era has a significant positive impact on the bottom line of the business and intergenerational survivability and avenues for employment and upskilling (Ikechukwu & Enudu, 2022). This new normal calls for a renewed approach to traditional business models that are able to adopt frugal innovative methods to maximise existing resources for an increased competitive advantage in an era of digital transformation. This requires SME FoBs to view innovation from a micro-perspective to not lose out on smaller businesses being more technologically adaptive. This study calls the attention of SME FoBs to reprioritise resources for R&D and innovation by leveraging the ability of the younger generation and marrying the willingness of the founding generation, which are key conditions for remaining relevant and ensuring intergenerational value (Zulfiqar et al., 2022).

Maintaining the balance of organisational and employee resilience due to their strong interconnectedness is imperative to avoid any hindrances to change. Should the balance tip towards the latter (Hillmann & Guenther, 2021), there is a need for proactive succession planning. The authors call upon SME FoB leaders to adopt a collaborative approach to problem solving, especially in the face of uncertainties, by leveraging their social capital to be more inclusive and strategically plan for future opportunities and eventualities (Mihotić et al., 2022).

10.13 Limitations and Scope for Future Research

Research into family businesses (Bennedsen et al., 2022), though nascent, is primarily focused on the West and often ignores India, which leaves room for scholars to investigate and address the fragmented studies.

The authors ascribe the limitations of this study to the scarcity of research on new industry entrants in the digital landscape (George et al., 2020) and their abilities of digital adoption depending on the type of industry. This will be an interesting direction for future research that may employ quantitative techniques to build on the recommendations of this study (Calabrò et al., 2021).

Future research may also adopt a longitudinal method to gain better insight of SME FoB by measuring their productivity through the adoption of innovation and the causal relationships on the variables identified in this study(Becerra et al., 2020). Additionally, scholars could further delve into the pace of innovation adoption and business model restructuring in different industries and their impact on long term survivability and family social capital(Gimenez-Jimenez et al., 2021).

The authors adopted a binary view of gender in their recommendations. Therefore, they urge further research to include a broader definition to represent diversity and inclusion with a non-binary lens.

Although the authors have taken cognisance of the heterogeneous nature of family firms, this research is not free of the bias of the implicit underpinnings of nuclear family structures (Jaskiewicz & Dyer, 2017).

10.14 Conclusion

This study underscores+ the importance of gender inclusivity during the early socialisation of the next generation of FoBs (Calabrò et al., 2020). This ensures the commitment of the next generation and highlights equitable and responsible decision-making by FoBs, which are the most common type of business structure globally (Bhatti, 2021).

Most SMEs have perished due to a lack of succession planning, especially in light of the crisis that the pandemic presented (Corrales-Villegas et al., 2019). Needless to say, a well-documented, strategic succession plan enacted prior to any untimely event or crisis ensures the transgenerational continuity of a business (Cater et al., 2019) while ensuring family relationship stability (LeCounte, 2022).

The SME FoBs will be positioned at a distinct competitive advantage if they are able to streamline the tacit knowledge, experience and skills accumulated through the multiple generations in contributing harmoniously towards their long-term business goals.

Growth cannot be achieved with leadership that does not involve men and women or combine the complementary skill sets of both to create a holistic environment of gender diversity, strong family values and opportunities for social and economic upliftment (Calabrò et al., 2020).

In the backdrop of a looming recession, organisations are mothballing to optimise resources and reduce costs to grapple with the setbacks the pandemic presented due to global lockdowns. The sustainability of FoBs becomes a 'compelling strategy' to not just increase the bottom line but also leverage and retain existing human capital, ensure gender diversity and maintain goodwill (Chundu et al., 2021, p.2).

References

Abiri-Franklin, S., & Olugasa, O. (2022). Succession planning and women inclusion in family businesses. *Business Perspective Review, 4*(1), 41–50. https://doi.org/10.38157/bpr.v4i1.424

Arambhan, P. A., & Seetharaman, A. (2022). Perceptions of succession planning in family-owned businesses. *Journal of the International Council for Small Business, 3*, 1–13. https://doi.org/10.1080/26437015.2022.2098079

Balabram, E. (2022). Brazil: Family firm's culture and values promote sustainable economic growth. In N. Birdthistle & R. Hales (Eds.), *Family Businesses on a Mission* (pp. 35–52). Emerald Publishing Limited. https://doi.org/10.1108/978-1-80382-487-120221004

Bauweraerts, J., Arzubiaga, U., & Diaz-Moriana, V. (2022). Going greener, performing better? The case of private family firms. *Research in International Business and Finance, 63*, 101784. https://doi.org/10.1016/j.ribaf.2022.101784

Becerra, M., Cruz, C., & Graves, C. (2020). Innovation in family firms: The relative effects of wealth concentration versus family-centered goals. *Family Business Review, 33*(4), 372–392. https://doi.org/10.1177/0894486520953700

Bennedsen, M., Lu, Y., & Mehrotra, V. (2022). A survey of asian family business research*. *Asia-Pacific Journal of Financial Studies, 51*(1), 7–43. https://doi.org/10.1111/ajfs.12363

Bhatti, H. S. (2021). The antecedents of the family businesses and family-owned smes. *SSRN Electronic Journal, 4*, 27–52. https://doi.org/10.2139/ssrn.4095717

Bouncken, R., & Schmitt, F. (n.d.). SME family firms and strategic digital transformation: Inverting dualisms related to overconfidence and centralization. *Journal of Small Business Strategy, 32*, 17.

Byrne, J., Fattoum, S., & Thébaud, S. (2019). A suitable boy? Gendered roles and hierarchies in family business succession. *European Management Review, 16*(3), 579–596. https://doi.org/10.1111/emre.12298

Calabrò, A., Fedy, M. J., Yeung, K., & McGinness, T. (2020). *The power of women in family business*. In *26*. KPMG, STEP Project for Family Entperpising.

Calabrò, A., Frank, H., Minichilli, A., & Suess-Reyes, J. (2021). Business families in times of crises: The backbone of family firm resilience and continuity. *Journal of Family Business Strategy, 12*(2), 100442. https://doi.org/10.1016/j.jfbs.2021.100442

Cater, J. J., Young, M., & Alderson, K. (2019). Contributions and constraints to continuity in Mexican-American family firms. *Journal of Family Business Management, 9*(2), 175–200.

Chahal, H., & Sharma, A. K. (2020). Family business in India: Performance, challenges and improvement measures. *Journal of New Business Ventures, 1*(1–2), 9–30. https://doi.org/10.1177/2632962X20960824

Chukwuma, I. O., Abua, B. O., & Ojonugwa, J. (2021). Succession planning; A discourse to refining organizational posterity. *South Asian Research Journal of Business and Management, 3*, 9.

Chundu, M., Njobo, J., & Kurebwa, J. (2021). Sustainability of family-owned businesses in the Willowvale industrial area of Harare, Zimbabwe. *American Journal of Industrial and Business Management, 11*(05), 461–480. https://doi.org/10.4236/ajibm.2021.115029

Corrales-Villegas, S. A., Ochoa-Jiménez, S., & Jacobo-Hernández, C. A. (2019). Leadership in the family business in relation to the desirable attributes for the successor: Evidence from Mexico. *European Journal of Family Business, 8*(2), 117–128. https://doi.org/10.24310/ejfbe-jfb.v8i2.5193

Damle, D., & Shah, A. (n.d.). *Bringing gender equality in the Hindu Succession Act: An overdue reform*. 5.

Dorairajan, S., & Bangur, D. P. (2020). Structural working towards successful succession planning in Indian family businesses. *Journal of Emerging Technologies and Innovative Research (JETIR), 7*(11), 4.

Erdogan, I., Rondi, E., & De Massis, A. (2020). Managing the tradition and innovation paradox in family firms: a family imprinting perspective. *Entrepreneurship Theory and Practice, 44*(1), 20–54. https://doi.org/10.1177/1042258719839712

Fendri, C., & Nguyen, P. (2019). Secrets of succession: How one family business reached the ninth generation. *Journal of Business Strategy, 40*(5), 12–20. https://doi.org/10.1108/JBS-08-2018-0130

Ganguly, A. (2020). HR dynamics in family-managed businesses in India. *NHRD Network Journal, 13*(1), 48–61. https://doi.org/10.1177/2631454119894742

George, G., Lakhani, K. R., & Puranam, P. (2020). What has changed? The impact of covid pandemic on the technology and innovation management research agenda. *Journal of Management Studies, 57*(8), 1754–1758. https://doi.org/10.1111/joms.12634

Gimenez-Jimenez, D., Edelman, L. F., Minola, T., Calabrò, A., & Cassia, L. (2021). An intergeneration solidarity perspective on succession intentions in family firms. *Entrepreneurship Theory and Practice, 45*(4), 740–766. https://doi.org/10.1177/1042258720956384

Gregori, P., & Holzmann, P. (2020). Digital sustainable entrepreneurship: A business model perspective on embedding digital technologies for social and environmental value creation. *Journal of Cleaner Production, 272*, 122817. https://doi.org/10.1016/j.jclepro.2020.122817

Haynes, G., Marshall, M., Lee, Y., Zuiker, V., Jasper, C. R., Sydnor, S., Valdivia, C., Masuo, D., Niehm, L., & Wiatt, R. (2021). Family business research: Reviewing the past, contemplating the future. *Journal of Family and Economic Issues, 42*(S1), 70–83. https://doi.org/10.1007/s10834-020-09732-6

Hillmann, J., & Guenther, E. (2021). Organizational resilience: A valuable construct for management research? *International Journal of Management Reviews, 23*(1), 7–44. https://doi.org/10.1111/ijmr.12239

Hlady-Rispal, M., Fayolle, A., & Gartner, W. B. (2021). In search of creative qualitative methods to capture current entrepreneurship research challenges. *Journal of Small Business Management, 59*(5), 887–912. https://doi.org/10.1080/00472778.2020.1865541

Ikechukwu, U. F., & Enudu, T. O. (2022). Succession planning and the performance of family owned business in enugu state. *Advance Journal of Management and Social Sciences, 6*(04), 29. https://aspjournals.org/Journals/index.php/ajmss/index

Jaskiewicz, P., & Dyer, W. G. (2017). Addressing the elephant in the room: Disentangling family heterogeneity to advance family business research. *Family Business Review, 30*(2), 111–118. https://doi.org/10.1177/0894486517700469

Jocic, M. R., Morris, M. H., & Kuratko, D. F. (2021). Familiness and innovation outcomes in family firms: The mediating role of entrepreneurial orientation. *Journal of Small Business Management*, 1–33. https://doi.org/10.1080/00472778.2020.1861284

Khoury, G., Eid, N., & Khoury, E. N. (2021). Family business trans-generational succession in extreme contexts: A socio-emotional wealth perspective. *International Journal of Entrepreneurship and Small Business, X*, 28.

Kubíček, A., & Machek, O. (2019). Gender-related factors in family business succession: A systematic literature review. *Review of Managerial Science, 13*(5), 963–1002. https://doi.org/10.1007/s11846-018-0278-z

Labaki, R., Bernhard, F., & Cailluet, L. (2019). The Strategic Use of Historical Narratives in the Family Business. In E. Memili & C. Dibrell (Eds.), *The Palgrave handbook of heterogeneity among family firms* (pp. 531–553). Springer International Publishing. https://doi.org/10.1007/978-3-319-77676-7_20

Le Breton-Miller, I., & Miller, D. (2022). Family businesses under COVID-19: Inspiring models – Sometimes. *Journal of Family Business Strategy, 13*(2), 100452. https://doi.org/10.1016/j.jfbs.2021.100452

LeCounte, J. F. (2022). Founder-CEOs: Succession planning for the success, growth, and legacy of family firms. *Journal of Small Business Management, 60*(3), 616–633. https://doi.org/10.1080/00472778.2020.1725814

Lévesque, M., & Subramanian, A. M. (2022). Family firm succession through the lens of technology intelligence. *Journal of Family Business Strategy, 13*(2), 100485. https://doi.org/10.1016/j.jfbs.2022.100485

Liaqat, M. U., Haron, A. J., & Bhatti, H. S. (2021). The effect of succession on family business innovation and leadership: Case analysis of Australia SMEs. *Hypothesis, 10*(2), 1–8.

Liu, H. (2020). Innovation of family business management mode under the environment of big data and artificial intelligence. *Journal of Physics: Conference Series, 1533*(3), 032060. https://doi.org/10.1088/1742-6596/1533/3/032060

McCoy, J., & Elwood, A. (2009). Human factors in organisational resilience: Implications of breaking the psychological contract. *Journal of Business Continuity & Emergency Planning, 3*(4), 368–375.

Mihotić, L., Raynard, M., & Sinčić Ćorić, D. (2022). Bouncing forward or bouncing back? How family firms enact resilience in times of crisis. *Journal of Family Business Management, 13*, 68–86. https://doi.org/10.1108/JFBM-03-2022-0047

Mokhber, M., Gi Gi, T., Abdul Rasid, S. Z., Vakilbashi, A., Mohd Zamil, N., & Woon Seng, Y. (2017). Succession planning and family business performance in SMEs. *Journal of Management Development, 36*(3), 330–347. https://doi.org/10.1108/JMD-12-2015-0171

Moyer, S. (2020). *What family businesses need to adapt to a crisis* (p. 7). Harvard Business Review.

Munagapati, B. R. (2018). Analyzing family-owned sme's & study the factors influencing them. *International Journal of Civil Engineering and Technology (IJCIET), 9*, 11.

Nguyen, M.-H., Nguyen, H. T. T., Le, T.-T., Luong, A.-P., & Vuong, Q.-H. (2021). Gender issues in family business research: A bibliometric scoping review. *Journal of Asian Business and Economic Studies, ahead-of-print* (ahead-of-print). https://doi.org/10.1108/JABES-01-2021-0014

Nordqvist, M., Wennberg, K., Bau, M., & Hellerstedt, K. (2013). An entrepreneurial process perspective on succession in family firms. *Small Business Economics, 40*(4), 1087–1122.

Nwuke, O., Nwoye, C., & Onoyima, N. (2020). Family businesses, succession and survival strategies. In *Indigenous African Enterprise* (Vol. 26, pp. 59–71). Emerald Publishing Limited.

Oudah, M., Jabeen, F., & Dixon, C. (2018). Determinants linked to family business sustainability in the UAE: An AHP approach. *Sustainability, 10*(1), 246. https://doi.org/10.3390/su10010246

Porfírio, J. A., Felício, J. A., & Carrilho, T. (2020). Family business succession: Analysis of the drivers of success based on entrepreneurship theory. *Journal of Business Research, 115*, 250–257. https://doi.org/10.1016/j.jbusres.2019.11.054

Rajan, S., Ganesh, P., & Mehra, N. (2020). Human capital: The key to the longevity of a family business. *NHRD Network Journal, 13*(1), 12–24. https://doi.org/10.1177/2631454119894761

Ramachandran, K., & Antony, S. P. (2020). Decision-making processes in Indian joint families and their implications for HR professionals. *NHRD Network Journal, 13*(1), 62–72. https://doi.org/10.1177/2631454119900426

Rondi, E., De Massis, A., & Kotlar, J. (2019). Unlocking innovation potential: A typology of family business innovation postures and the critical role of the family system. *Journal of Family Business Strategy, 10*(4), 100236. https://doi.org/10.1016/j.jfbs.2017.12.001

Song, S., Zhou, L., Sindakis, S., Aggarwal, S., & Chen, C. (2022). *The impact of intergenerational succession intention on family firm's innovation strategy: Evidence from China* [Preprint]. Social Sciences. https://doi.org/10.20944/preprints202204.0237.v1

Soost, C., & Moog, P. (2019). Gender and organizational performance in business succession. *Journal of Small Business & Entrepreneurship, 33*, 93–122. https://doi.org/10.1080/08276331.2019.1692765

Sull, D., & Sull, C. (n.d.). 10 things your corporate culture needs to get right. *Mit Sloan Management Review, 9*.

Swab, R. G., Sherlock, C., Markin, E., & Dibrell, C. (2020). "SEW" what do we know and where do we go? A Review of socioemotional wealth and a way forward. *Family Business Review, 33*(4), 424–445. https://doi.org/10.1177/0894486520961938

Tabor, W., & Vardaman, J. (n.d.). *The key to successful succession planning for family businesses* (p. 4). Harvard Business Review.

Tyagi, N., Shukla, G., & Singh, P. (2021). In I. L.-P. Dana, N. Sharma, & S. R. Acharya (Eds.), *Asia-Pacific Business Series A woman's perspective of entrepreneurship in MSME family businesses* (Vol. 11, pp. 87–107). WORLD SCIENTIFIC. https://doi.org/10.1142/9789811212741_0005

United Nations Women. (2018). *Turning Promises Into Action: Gender Equality in the 2030 Agenda for Sustainable Development*. UN. https://doi.org/10.18356/917ed83e-en

Vardaman, J. M., Allen, D. G., & Rogers, B. L. (2018). We are friends but are we family? Organizational identification and nonfamily employee turnover. *Entrepreneurship Theory and Practice, 42*(2), 290–309. https://doi.org/10.1177/1042258717749235

Wong, L. K. K. (n.d.). *The impact of global crisis on innovation and succession on family business from a socioemotional wealth perspective* (p. 106). Singapore Management University.

Zapata-Cantu, L., Sanguino, R., Barroso, A., & Nicola-Gavrilă, L. (2022). Family business adapting a new digital-based economy: Opportunities and challenges for future research. *Journal of the Knowledge Economy*. https://doi.org/10.1007/s13132-021-00871-1

Zulfiqar, M., Huo, W., Wu, S., Chen, S., Elahi, E., & Yousaf, M. U. (2022). Behavioural psychology of unique family firms toward R&D Investment in the Digital Era: The role of ownership discrepancy. *Frontiers in Psychology, 13*, 928447. https://doi.org/10.3389/fpsyg.2022.928447

Zybura, J., Zybura, N., Ahrens, J.-P., & Woywode, M. (2021). Innovation in the post-succession phase of family firms: Family CEO successors and leadership constellations as resources. *Journal of Family Business Strategy, 12*(2), 100336. https://doi.org/10.1016/j.jfbs.2020.100336

Chapter 11
Market Power Analysis on Shrimp Import from Tropical Asia: The Korean Case

Dae Eui Kim and Song Soo Lim

Abstract Shrimp is the most highly traded seafood product in the world. While tropical Asia is the leader in shrimp aquaculture and wild harvest, developed economies account for the lion's share of global shrimp imports. Studies show market power issues arise from trade imbalances, regulatory standards, and the non-competitive structure of the market. Market power is largely defined as the ability to alter prices away from competitive levels or affect product quality and trade requirements. A market power analysis would provide insight into the extent to which trade liberalization and market dominance have improved the global shrimp trade. Focusing on food safety regulation and quarantine standards in Korea, this study aims to perform a market power analysis on shrimp imports from tropical Asia, including Vietnam, Thailand, and Malaysia. A residual supply approach is adopted to estimate the buyer power of the importer. Using a monthly panel dataset, the residual supply model contains key factors contributing to market power's potential exercise. The results show that, Korea has market power for shrimp from Thailand and Malaysia. On the other hand, an interesting point is that Korea has no market power over Vietnam, which is accounted for more than half of the import share in Korea. However, the degree of Korean market power has been shown relatively low compared to the prior study.

Keywords Market power · Shrimp trade · Tropical Asia · Residual supply model

---

D. E. Kim · S. S. Lim (✉)
Department of Food and Resource Economics, Korea University, Seoul, South Korea
e-mail: es992306@korea.ac.kr; songsoo@korea.ac.kr

E. L. Eijdenberg et al. (eds.), *Innovation-Driven Business and Sustainability in the Tropics*, https://doi.org/10.1007/978-981-99-2909-2_11

11.1 Introduction

Shrimp is the most highly traded seafood product in the world and export value accounted for 16% of global seafood exports in 2016 (FAO, 2018; Garlock et al., 2020; Yang et al., 2021). While tropical Asia is the leader in shrimp aquaculture and wild harvest, developed economies account for the lion's share of global shrimp imports. The major markets for tropical Asia shrimp are in Japan, the United States, and Europe, while the Asia-Pacific region is home to the majority of shrimp producers (Honculada Primavera, 1994). Global shrimp fishery and aquaculture production were approximately 7.1 million tons in 2020[1], With China producing the most (2.3 million tons), followed by India (930,000 tons), and Vietnam (900,000 tons). Indonesia, Thailand, Bangladesh, Myanmar, Philippines, Malaysia, Iran, and Saudi Arabia were among the top 15 producing countries, with the rest coming from South America (e.g. Ecuador, Mexico, Brazil, and Venezuela). Except for China and India, the production of seven tropical Asia countries has marked up about 35% of global shrimp production, surpassing the production of China.

Shrimp was traditionally consumed primarily by consumers in high-income markets such as North America, Europe, and Japan. However, as the economic level of emerging economies such as China rises, also rises shrimp consumers from other countries quickly. According to the FAO, Korea, after the United States, China, Japan, Spain, and France, is the sixth largest shrimp importer in the world. Shrimp imports in Korea totaled around $730 million in 2020, accounting for 3.2% of the global shrimp trade and Vietnam accounts for roughly half the total import in Korea. Between 2014 and 2019, the amount of fresh, chilled, and frozen shrimp imported to Korea increased by 35.5%, from about 43,000 to 58,000 tons. The top exporter of shrimp to Korea is Vietnam as of 2019, followed by Malaysia, Ecuador, and China. The top exporter in 2014 was Vietnam, which was followed by China, Ecuador, and Malaysia. The most notable shift is that China has slightly slipped from the top spot, and exports from Peru have significantly increased as a result of the signing of the Korea-Peru FTA. An interesting change to point out is, The influence of tropical Asia countries has been standing out gradually in the export market to Korea.

However, increased exports do not always result in only positive outcomes. World organization for animal health (OIE) is taking steps to combat diseases with high contagiousness to prevent the spread of diseases internationally that may occur due to the increase in fisheries trade. As of 2020, 182 countries are OIE members and these nations are identifying diseases that pose a threat because of their high contagiousness and making testing for these diseases mandatory in international fisheries trade.

[1] Fish species of statistics: Banana prawn, Blue shrimp, Brine shrimp, Brine shrimps nei, Caramote prawn, Common prawn, Eastern king prawn, Eastern school shrimp, Fleshy prawn, Freshwater prawns, shrimps nei, Giant river prawn, Giant tiger prawn, Green tiger prawn, Indian white prawn, Kuruma prawn, Lion's paw, Monkey river prawn, Monsoon river prawn, Palaemonid shrimps nei, Penaeus shrimps nei, River prawns nei, Southern white shrimp, Speckled shrimp, and Whiteleg shrimp. (Source: FishstatJ)

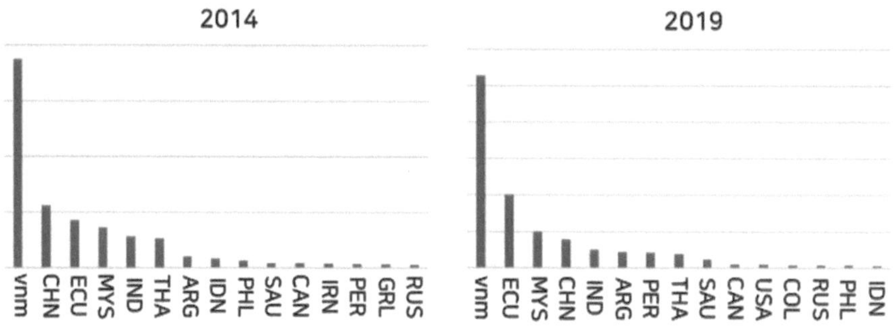

Source: UN COMTRADE

Fig. 11.1 The trend of shrimp import in Korea. (Source: UN COMTRADE)

Korea, which became a member of the OIE in 1953, also continues to conduct quarantine inspections on imported shrimp. The ministry of oceans and fisheries of Korea (MOF) has been conducting 100% precise quarantine since 2008 for live shrimp with a high risk of disease transmission and has expanded the scope of the inspection until frozen and refrigerated shrimp from April 2018. Despite the strengthened regulation, In May 2019, When frozen imported shrimp cases from Vietnam were tested, more than a third of them were found to have viruses. Questions then arise, how does the regulation of Korea affect shrimp exporting countries? Second, does Korea have the buyer power to demand compliance from them? To this end, this study will examine the effectiveness of measures to strengthen quarantine in shrimp imports. If Korea has market power due to large imports, it could give exporters incentives to improve the safety of shrimp production. However, if Korea has no market power, the effect of the import regulations will be a shift in trade patterns and the costs associated with the regulation will be carried by domestic consumers in the form of higher prices and lower shrimp consumption. This paper thereupon estimates whether Korea has buyer power for shrimp by using a residual supply equation. This empirical model targets the main export countries(e.g. Vietnam, Thailand, and Malaysia) to Korean market power for the shrimp import market (Fig. 11.1).

11.2 Literature Review

The inverse residual demand model or the inverse residual supply model were widely used in prior research to examine market power (Carter et al., 1999; Goldberg & Knetter, 1999; Poosiripinyo & Reed, 2005). Table 11.1 shows prior studies of market power applied to various products across countries. While past studies have mainly used the residual demand elasticity (RDE) model to analyze the market power exercised by major exporters such as the US, Russia, and Europe, a few studies used the residual supply elasticity (RSE) model. Song (2006) examined the market power of

Table 11.1 Studies for analysing market power

Study	Product	Exporter	Importer	RDE model	RSE model	Method
Goldberg and Knetter (1999)	Beer	Germany	U.S. Canada France U.K.	−0.065 −0.14 −0.44 −0.21		3SLS
Carter et al. (1999)	Wheat	U.S Canada Australia	Japan	−0.93*** −0.49 −0.08		2SLS
Yang Seung Ryong and Lee Won-Jin (2001)	Wheat Corn	U.S Canada Australia U.S. China	Korea	−0.384** −0.146*** −0.142** −0.054 −0.032		SUR
Cho Gue-Dae et al. (2002)	Wheat	U.S.	Indonesia Japan Korea Malaysia Philippine Singapore	−0.004 −0.112 −0.614*** −0.121*** −0.838*** −0.160***		SUR
Reed and Saghaian (2004)	Beef	Australia Canada New Zealand The U.S.	Japan	−0.117** −0.171** −0.187*** −0.322***		SUR
Poosiripinyo and Reed (2005)	Chicken	Brazil China Thailand The U.S.	Japan	−0.253*** −0.108 −0.081 −0.229***		GLS
Song (2006)	Soybean	U.S	China	−0.040***	0.13	3SLS
Andersen et al. (2008)	Dried salted pod	Norway	Portugal	−0.173***	0.105	3SLS
Felt et al. (2010)	Pork 1st period 2nd period	Denmark Canada U.S. Denmark Canada U.S.	Japan Japan	−0.02* −0.05* 0.01 −0.01 −0.04* −0.10*		GMM
Mulik and Crespi (2011)	Basmati rice 1st period 2nd period	India India	U.S. U.K. Kuwait U.S. U.K. Kuwait	1.2% 27.33% 13.84% 2.31% 19.12% 5.69%		3SLS
Yamaura (2011)	Non-GM soybean	U.S.	Japan	−0.220*	0.04	3SLS

(continued)

Table 11.1 (continued)

Study	Product	Exporter	Importer	RDE model	RSE model	Method
Yamaura (2011)	Non-GM soybean	U.S.	Japan	−0.330***	0.06	3SLS
Pall et al. (2014)	wheat	Russia	Albania Azerbaijan Egypt Georgia Greece Lebanon Mongolia Syria	−0.0883* −0.1723 −0.0048 −0.0730* −0.0527*** −0.0564 −0.2497 −0.0543		IVPPML
Silveria and Resende (2017)	niobium (steel)	Brazi	U.S.	−0.500***		2SLS
Uhl and Perekhozhuk (2018)	wheat	Russia	Egypt Turkey	−0.005 −0.135***		GMM
Son and Lim (2019)	Non-GM soybean GM soybean	U.S. U.S.	Korea Korea	−0.0918** −0.1416*	−0.353 −0.0599	2SLS
Fang and Asche (2021)	Frozen shrimp King crab Tuna	U.S. U.S. U.S.	Thailand Ecuador Indonesia India Russia Thailand Ecuador Vietnam		0.636*** 0.0522 0.736*** 0.679*** 0.944*** 0.912*** −0.379 0.847***	2SLS

Note: *, **, and *** indicate 10%, 5%, and 1% significance levels, respectively
Source: Yamaura (2012), Son and Lim (2019) and Authors' compilation

Chinese soybean in the U.S. import market, and Andersen et al. (2008) analyzed the market power of Portuguese dried salted pod in the Norway import market using RSE. In addition Yamaura (2012) and Son and Lim (2019) analyzed for RSE model for Non-GM soybean and GM-soybean in the Japanese and Korean import markets respectively. Although they could not statistically significant results in their analysis, we could get the meaningful empirical work idea from their studies.

According to residual supply elasticity models, the market is assumed to have an oligopoly structure. Limiting the quantity allows the specific importing firm to exert market power, which can obtain an excessive profit. The structure is assumed for the residual supply of an importing firm as the gap between the market supply and the demand by other competing firms (Son & Lim, 2019). Moreover, this study can be compared to those of the study by Yingkai Fang et al., which examines the market power of the U.S. as an importer of frozen shrimp, king crab, and tuna. They postulated that whether or not the U.S. has market power when importing fishery products would determine how effectively the U.S.'s SIMP would reduce IUU fishing. They examined major seafood exporters such as Russia, Thailand, Ecuador, and

Vietnam and discovered that the U.S. has statistically significant buyer power in each import market.

11.3 Empirical Model Specification and Data

The residual supply model is a simpler specification to use in the empirical work because its parameters can be estimated as a single linear equation in many cases (Fang & Asche, 2021). The residual supply equation to be estimated is given as:

$$lnP_{IM\_t}^{KR\_EX} = \alpha + \delta lnQ_{IM\_t}^{KR\_EX} + \beta_k \sum_{i=1}^{k} lnS_t^{EX} + \gamma_k \sum_{i=1}^{k} lnD_t^{KR} + \varepsilon_t$$

where $P_{IM}^{KR\_EX}$ is the import price to Korea in exporting countries' currency and $Q_{IM}^{KR\_EX}$ is the quantity of shrimp imported. S_t^{EX} is a vector of exogenous supply shifters in the exporting country in year t, including labor force ($Labor^{EX}$) and oil price ($Oil\ price^{EX}$). The vector D_t^{KR} represents the exogenous demand shifter in year t and the average income of household in Korea ($Income^{KR}$) was used in the estimation. The data on price and quantity were collected from Korea customs service trade statistics. The trade data for analysis was organized by product by using the harmonized tariff schedule (HTS) 6-digit codes.[2]

The issue in estimating the supply equation is the endogeneity of explanatory variables. This happens as a result of the supply curve's error term having an impact on quantity $Q_{IM}^{KR\_EX}$, one of the explanatory variables. Therefore, $Q_{IM}^{KR\_EX}$ cannot be regarded as an exogenous variable like other variables. To solve this endogeneity issue, the Two-Stage Least Square (2SLS) method, which uses instrument variables, should be applied. The instrument variable should be related to the endogenous variable closely but should not be correlated with the error term. To this end, $Prod^{EX}$ was used as an instrument variable in this study. While the level of production is related to the export quantity in the exporting country, the import price – which is the CIF price that includes freight and insurance cost – is closely related to external shocks such as freight rate fluctuation. Verification of instrument variable selection is based on weak instrument variable tests and correlation results between problem variables. $Labor^{EX}$ and $Oil\ price^{EX}$ are exogenous supply shifters in the exporting country, Former represents the labor force and the latter represents diesel prices in exporting countries. Also as an exogenous demand shifter, $Income^{KR}$ represents the average income of a household in Korea. ER_{KR}^{US}, ER_{KR}^{JP} and ER_{KR}^{EU} are real exchange rates between competitive importing countries and Korea. The data covers the period from January 2012 to December 2021 and it consists of monthly data. Table 11.2 describes the model variables and sources of data. Table 11.3 shows descriptive statistics of variables.

[2] HTS 6-digit codes: 030616, 030617, 030619, 030635, 030636, 030639, 030695, 030699

Table 11.2 Description of variables and data sources

Variable	Description	Source
$P_{IM}^{KR\_EX}$	Import price to Korea in the exporting countries' currency	Korea Customs Service Trade Statistics
$Q_{IM}^{KR\_EX}$	Import quantity to Korea	Korea Customs Service Trade Statistics
$Prod^{EX}$	Fishery and Aquaculture Production of Shrimp in Exporting Countries	FAO FishStatJ
$Labor^{EX}$	Labor Force in the Exporting Countries	ILO
$Oilprice^{EX}$	Diesel Price in Exporting Countries	U.S. Energy Informantion Administeration (EIA)
$Income^{KR}$	Average Income of Household in Korea	KOSTAT
ER_{KR}^{US}	Real Exchange Rate between U.S. and Korea	Pacific Exchange Rate Service
ER_{KR}^{JP}	Real Exchange Rate between Japan and Korea	Pacific Exchange Rate Service
ER_{KR}^{EU}	Real Exchange Rate between Europe and Korea	Pacific Exchange Rate Service

Table 11.3 Summary statistics of variables

Variable	Unit	Mean	Std. Dev.	Min	Max
P_{IM}^{KRVM}	Dong/Tonnes	182,801.5	30,885.35	102,925.9	254,687.2
P_{IM}^{KRTH}	Baht/Tonnes	352.6018	26.45476	291.4968	421.141
P_{IM}^{KRMS}	Ringgit/Tonnes	35.4381	3.275863	28.4431	43.83833
Q_{IM}^{KRVM}	Tonnes	2136.004	980.4342	553.1	4662.4
Q_{IM}^{KRTH}	Tonnes	226.5233	69.72722	99.2	404.1
Q_{IM}^{KRMS}	Tonnes	351.0433	104.2516	134.6	604.3
$Prod^{VM}$	Tonnes	56,840.37	15,872.06	27,076.33	80,323.52
$Prod^{TH}$	Tonnes	34,284.15	1417.368	31,750.08	35,721.75
$Prod^{MS}$	Tonnes	4050.791	230.8507	3839.558	4467.135
$Oilprice^{VM}$	Dong	56,642.1	24,075.51	22,554.65	123,747.8
$Oilprice^{TH}$	Baht	82.12094	34.47	32.13961	139.4652
$Oilprice^{MS}$	Ringgit	10.64642	4.429725	4.115177	17.74859
$Labor^{MS}$	Persons	31,573.89	865.4343	30,310.06	32,791.24
$Income^{KR}$	Won	3,951,992	185,964	3,617,217	4,290,934
ER_{KR}^{US}	US$/Won	0.000875	3.13E-05	0.000814	0.000937
ER_{KR}^{JP}	Yen/Won	0.095945	0.004257	0.087236	0.104134
ER_{KR}^{EU}	Euro/Won	0.000761	2.43E-05	0.000712	0.000825

Estimate δ yields an inverse residual supply elasticity in the Korean market. If δ is positive and statistically significant, Korea has the market power over the exporting countries in the shrimp import market. Otherwise, Korea cannot exercise market power and give exporting countries incentives to comply with the regulation.

11.4 Results

Table 11.4 shows estimated results for the RSE model using the 2SLS method to exporting countries respectively. To reflect seasonal variation, the equations contain seasonal dummies. But individual coefficients are not reported for brevity.

While Korea has shown to exercise no power to price Vietnam shrimp export, the market power against Thailand and Malaysia existed. Quantity variables for Korea turned out to be statistically significant in imported shrimp from Thailand and Malaysia. The former coefficient is 0.25 and the latter is 0.12. The coefficients of oil price variables showed a positive relationship with import prices in Thailand and Malaysia RSE models. The income variables have shown a negative relationship with import prices except for the RSE model of Thailand. In other words, The increase in household income in Korea decreases the prices of imported shrimp from Vietnam and Malaysia. According to the results, the real exchange rate between Korea and other competitive importing countries could have explained Korea's import prices in the Vietnam RSE model only. Although a strong Korean Won against the U.S. dollar Vietnam does not expand its export to Korea and prefers its export to the U.S. instead. At the bottom of Table 11.4, R^2 represents the explanatory power of the model respectively and the Durbin-Watson statistic shows that there is no autocorrelation in the error term.

Table 11.5 shows the elasticity estimation results of the prior study analysing the RSE model. Most outcomes not only found no market power of importer but also confirmed no statistical significance. Only Fang and Asche (2021) have found the market power of importing countries. The U.S. has a market power for frozen shrimp from Thailand and the elasticity has shown 0.63. In addition, the market power elasticity of the U.S. for Indonesia and India is 0.73 and 0.67 respectively. Like the U.S., the empirical results in this study show that Korea has market power for shrimp from Thailand and Malaysia. On the other hand, an interesting point is that Korea has no market power over Vietnam, which is accounted for more than half of the import share in Korea. However, the degree of Korean market power has been shown relatively low compared to the prior study by Fang and Asche (2021). The market power elasticity of Korea for imported shrimp is 0.15 on average in three exporting countries while the elasticity of the U.S. is close to 0.7 on average.

Table 11.4 Estimation results of RSE models

Variable	Vietnam	Thailand	Malaysia
$\ln Q_{IM}^{KR\_EX}$	0.0939 (0.1042)	0.2524*** (0.0634)	0.1222* (0.0705)
$\ln Income^{KR}$	−2.1587*** (0.7108)	0.7282* (0.3841)	−1.7926*** (0.5706)
$\ln Oilprice^{EX}$	0.0336 (0.0305)	0.0519** (0.0226)	0.0616** (0.0249)
$\ln Labor^{EX}$			2.4982*** (0.8513)
$\ln ER_{KR}^{US}$	0.9458** (0.3755)		−0.4405 (0.6367)
$\ln ER_{KR}^{EU}$	−0.3416 (0.3908)	0.1588 (0.6165)	−0.6339 (0.4353)
$\ln ER_{KR}^{JP}$			−0.6189 (0.4936)
Constant	47.9616*** (8.0246)	−5.7411 (3.5563)	−5.0467 (6.7992)
Seasonality	YES	YES	NO
R-squared	0.3862	0.2675	0.5224
DW	0.7202	2.1244	1.9019
Weak Instrument	42.6311	18.5437	15.1927

Note: *, **, and *** indicate 10%, 5%, and 1% significance levels, respectively. Values in parentheses are standard errors

Table 11.5 Comparison elasticities of RSE estimation with previous studies

Study	Product	Importer	Exporter	Elasticity
Song (2006)	Soybean	China	U.S.	0.13
Andersen et al. (2008)	Dried salted pod	Portugal	Norway	0.105
Yamaura (2011)	Non-GM soybean	Japan	U.S.	0.04
Yamaura (2012)	Non-GM soybean	Japan	U.S.	0.06
Son and Lim (2019)	Non-GM soybean	Korea	U.S.	−0.353
	GM soybean	Korea	U.S.	−0.0599
Fang and Asche (2021)	Frozen shrimp	U.S.	Thailand Ecuador Indonesia India	0.636*** 0.0522 0.736*** 0.679***
	King crab	U.S.	Russia	0.944***
	Tuna	U.S.	Thailand Ecuador Vietnam	0.912*** −0.379 0.847***
This study (2022)	Shrimp	Korea	Vietnam Thailand Malaysia	0.0939 0.2524*** 0.1222*

Source: Authors

11.5 Conclusion

The aquaculture industry in tropical Asia is facing significant challenges that threaten the long-term sustainability of the industry and negatively impact the livelihoods of millions of small-scale farmers. These challenges contain disease outbreaks, labor issues, water pollution, etc. (ASIC, 2016). For example, outbreaks of yellow head disease (YHD) caused by a yellow head virus (YHV) and white spot disease (WSD) caused by white spot syndrome virus (WSSV) since 1992 and 1994, respectively, have negatively impacted the growth and sustainability of shrimp industry in Thailand (Booyaratpalin, 1999). Also, a serious shrimp disease outbreak causing high mortalities in giant tiger prawn and whiteleg shrimp that was later called acute hepatopancreatic necrosis disease (AHPND) was officially documented in Soc Trang province in southern Vietnam in April 2011 and it cause production decreases significantly (T.L. DANG et al., 2018). To overcome these issues, Countries leading shrimp farming are taking steps to improve the safety of shrimp production. And those attempts could be accelerated with strong requirements of importing countries.

A market power analysis can provide insight into the extent to which trade liberalization and market dominance have improved the global shrimp trade. Focusing on food safety regulation and quarantine standards in Korea, this study has targeted to perform a market power analysis on shrimp imports from tropical Asia. If the buyer country wields significant market power, the exporting country will have limited access to alternative markets, and strengthening quarantine regulations will provide strong incentives for them to improve product safety in order to comply with the standard. In contrast, if Korea lacks the power to control import prices, producers in exporting countries will simply change the countries to which they export their goods, and Korean consumers will be burdened with all associated costs with increasing prices.

The empirical results show that Korea cannot wield market power over Vietnam in imported shrimp. Although Korea has market power over Thailand and Malaysia, the elasticities are relatively low compared to the elasticities of the U.S. reported by previous studies. These results offer us simple implications. Unlike the U.S., the quarantine regulations of Korea to import safe shrimp cannot give strong incentives to improve the level of safety production in these countries overall. The case that infectious shrimp were still exported from Vietnam even after Korea strengthened quarantine may be a limitation of the regulation of importing countries without market power. However, these findings still give the policymaker in Korea insights to reconsider policy directions. It is challenging to ensure the effectiveness of regulations if market dominance by a country is not taken into account because the largest import market share does not necessarily lead to a market dominance existence. Therefore, Korea should effort that develop diversified export countries and deter the quarantine loophole to supply safe shrimp to their citizens ahead.

References

Andersen, T. B., Asche, F., & Roll, K. H. (2008). *Oligopoly and oligopsony power in concentrated supply chains* (ISIAC Working Paper, No. 08-1). University of Rhode Island.

ASIC. (2016). *The Southeast Asian Shrimp Aquaculture Improvement Protocol Draft #5 Prepared by the: Steering Committee – Southeast Asian Shrimp Aquaculture Improvement Protocol June, ASIC, 2016*

Booyaratpalin, S. (1999). Viral diseases of farmed shrimp-present status and future research. In P.T. Smith (Ed.) *Towards sustainable shrimp culture in Thailand and the region* (pp. 80–81). Proceedings of a workshop held at Hat Yai, Songkhla, Thailand, 28 October–1 November 1996

Carter, C. A., MacLarean, D., & Yilmaz, A. (1999). *How competitive is the world wheat market* (Working Paper, No. 99–002). University of California.

Cho, G.-D., Jin, H.-J., & Koo, W.-W. (2002). *Measuring the market power of the U.S. wheat exporters in Asian countries: An issue about adjustment of nominal exchange rate when using as a cost shifter*. The American Agricultural Economics Association conference, Long Beach, CA.

DANG, T. L., PHAM, A. T., & PHAN, T. V. (2018). Acute Hepatopancreatic Necrosis Disease (AHPND) in Vietnam. *Asian Fisheries Science, 31S*(2018), 274–282.

Fang, Y., & Asche, F. (2021). Can U.S. import regulations reduce IUU fishing and improve production practices in aquaculture? *Ecological Economics, 187*, 107084.

FAO. (2018). *The State of World Fisheries and Aquaculture 2018 – Meeting the sustainable development goals*. Food and Agricultural Organization. Licence: CC BY-NC-SA 3.0 IGO. [Google Scholar].

Felt, M. H., Gervais, J. P., & Laure, B. (2010). Market power and import bans: The case of Japanese pork imports. *Agribusiness, 27*(1), 47–61.

Garlock, T., Asche, F., Anderson, J. L., Bjørndal, T., Kumar, G., Lorenzen, K., et al. (2020). A global blue revolution: Aquaculture growth across regions, species, and countries. *Reviews in Fisheries Science & Aquaculture, 28*(1), 107–116. https://doi.org/10.1080/23308249.2019.1678111. [Taylor & Francis Online], [Web of Science ®], [Google Scholar]

Goldberg, P. K., & Knetter, M. M. (1999). Measuring the intensity of competition in export markets. *Journal of International Economics, 47*(1), 27–60.

Honculada Primavera, J. (1994). *Shrimp farming in the Asia-Pacific: Environmental and trade issues and regional cooperation, trade and environment, September 25*. https://nautilus.org/trade-and-environment/shrimp-farming-in-the-asia-pacific-environmental-and-trade-issues-and-regional-cooperation-4/

Mulik, K., & Crespi, J. M. (2011). Geographical indications and the trade related intellectual property rights agreement (TRIPS): A case study of Basmati rice exports. *Journal of Agricultural & Food Industrial Organization, 9*(1), 4.

Pall, Z. O., Perekhozhuk, T., Glauben, S., Prehn, S., & Teuber, R. (2014). Residual demand measures of market power of Russian wheat exporters. *Agricultural Economics, 45*(3), 381–391.

Poosiripinyo, R., & Reed, M. (2005). Measuring market power in the Japanese chicken meat market. *Journal of International Agricultural Trade and Development, 1*(2), 135–148.

Reed, M. R., & Saghaian, H. S. (2004). Measuring the intensity of competition in the Japanese beef market. *Journal of Agricultural and Applied Economics, 36*(1), 113–121.

Silveria, J. W., & Resende, M. (2017). *Competition in the international niobium market: An econometric study (CESifo working paper series, no. 6715)*. Munich Society for the Promotion of Economic Research – CESifo GmbH.

Son, E.-A., & Lim, S. S. (2019). Market power of genetically modified soybeans traded between the United States and Korea. *Journal of Korea Trade, 23*(6), 131–144. https://doi.org/10.35611/jkt.2019.23.6.131

Song, B. (2006). *Market power and competitive analysis of China's soybean import market* (Doctoral Dissertation), Lexington. University of Kentucky

Uhl, M. K., & Perekhozhuk, O. (2018). Russian market power in international wheat exports: Evidence from a residual demand elasticity analysis. *Journal of Agricultural & Food Industrial Organization, 17*(2), 1–13.

Yamaura, K. (2011). Market power of the Japanese Non-GM soybean import market: The U.S. exporters vs. Japanese importers. *Asian Journal of Agriculture and Rural Development, 1*(4), 80–89.

Yamaura, K. (2012). World market of vertical differentiated agricultural commodities: A case of soybean markets (Doctoral Dissertation), Manhattan. Kansas State University

Yang, S.-R., & Lee, W.-J. (2001). *Exporters' market power in agricultural import markets in Korea*. The American Agricultural Economics Association Annual Meeting, Chicago, IL.

Yang, B., Anderson, J., & Fang, Y. (2021). Trade duration of Chinese shrimp exports. *Aquaculture Economics & Management, 25*(3), 260–274.

Chapter 12
Coastal Tourism and Sustainability: A Case Study of East Midnapur District, West Bengal, India

Priyanka Ghosh and Tania Chakravarty

Abstract Coastal tourism can be defined as a process in which tourists visit people and places along the coasts as well as experience natural and cultural resources in a coastal environment. Since the second half of the twentieth century, development of tourism along the coastline especially in tropical countries have drastically altered the delicate ecological balance of the coastal regions. With a total coastline of 7,516.6 km and 170 million people living in the coastal region, coastal tourism is becoming a fast-developing component of overall tourism industry in India. At present Digha, Shankarpur, Mandarmani, Tajpur are some of the most popular tourist destinations in West Bengal, India. Situated on the coast of East Midnapur District, West Bengal, these sites fall under the Coastal Regulation Zone I (CRZ-I) which is extremely vulnerable to coastal erosion. From 1950s the government of West Bengal actively promoted Digha as a tourist spot. As the popularity of Digha increased, the nearby beach of Shankarpur also started attracting tourists' attention. On the other hand, Mandarmani and Tajpur remained relatively unknown until 1990s. Both of these sites have developed into well-known tourist sites in the past two decades. This has been associated with a boom in hotel and seaside resort development leading to a drastic change in land use patterns. Today, the website of West Bengal Government Tourism Department promotes Tajpur as 'one of the most hidden beaches of India.' Interestingly, the elements of attraction mentioned in the website for Tajpur – virgin beach, natural vegetation, red crabs and moderate to little tourist presence – were previously applicable to Digha, Shankarpur and Mandarmani. This brings us to the question of the impact of tourism development on land use-land cover of the coastal areas of East Midnapur. This paper examines the transformation of East Midnapur coastal belt as a tourist destination by studying land use data from various available literature. Collation of these data can provide a better understanding of the impact of tourism on East Midnapur and offer sustainable solutions in managing tourism-related investments along the coast of West Bengal.

P. Ghosh (✉) · T. Chakravarty
VISH, VIT-AP, Amaravati, Andhra Pradesh, India
e-mail: priyanka.ghosh@vitap.ac.in; tania.c@vitap.ac.in

E. L. Eijdenberg et al. (eds.), *Innovation-Driven Business and Sustainability in the Tropics*, https://doi.org/10.1007/978-981-99-2909-2_12

Keywords Coastal tourism · CRZ Act · East Midnapur · Sustainable tourism · India

12.1 Introduction

At present tourism is one of the fastest growing industries in the world and coastal zones are one of the prime choices for tourist spots. Globally, travel and tourism industry generate 10.3% GDP and provides jobs to 333 million people. Although the travel and tourism industry suffered a loss of total **US$ 4.9 trillion** in 2020 due to Covid-19 pandemic, the GDP increased by **US$1 trillion (+21.7% rise)** in 2021 (Economic Impacts Report, World Travel and Tourism Council, 2022). For developing countries like India, tourism industry is a significant source of foreign exchange. In 2019, tourism contributed 7% of India's total GDP (USD 212.8 billion). In 2020 due to Covid-19 pandemic, the travel and tourism industry only contributed 4.3% of India's GDP. As post-pandemic restrictions were slowly lifted, the industry bounced back and the GDP increased to 5.8%. As a labor-intensive industry, tourism creates direct employment opportunities for India's 32 million population (World Travel and Tourism Council, 2022 Annual Research: Key Highlights). According to the Travel and Tourism Competitive Index (TTCI), India is ranked 34th among the world's 140 most attractive countries for tourism (Ghosh, 2022). India's tourism policy in 2002 earmarked tourism as an important economic sector. Emphasis was especially put on domestic tourism, improving India's tourism potential in the global market, and develop tourism products. However, the challenge remains to develop India's tourism potential into a sustainable form.

12.2 Literature Review

Coastal tourism can be defined as a process in which tourists visit people and places along the coasts as well as experience natural and cultural resources in a coastal environment (Miller et al., 2011). Around 40% of world's population or 2.4 billion people live within 100 km of the coastline (United Nation, 2017) who are dependent on coastal tourism besides other professions such as fishing and agriculture. In the early twentieth century, specific geographical locations along the Mediterranean coast came to be well-known tourists' destinations. Such destinations were popular for their scenic beauty, warm temperature, sand and sea (Battilani & Rodriguez, 2021). In recent times, tourist consumption pattern has changed and associated infrastructure and amenities have become an integral part of coastal tourism. For instance, the growth of coastal tourism is clearly visible from the annual increase in whale watching diving certification between 1967 and 1990 (Ghosh, 2011). Since the 1990s, cruise tourism has become one of the fastest growing components of coastal tourism. Although initial growth of cruise tourism was mostly concentrated in North America, a significant growth has occurred in other parts of the world such as in Australia and New Zealand (Klein, 2011). India has also ventured into the growing market of cruise tourism and in 2017 the country's first cruise ship docked in Mumbai port (Manoharan & James, 2021). Popularity of cruise tourism has led to building of huge ships capable of accommodating large number of people (Klein, 2011). Such tourism related activities leave enormous human footprint on coastal areas – land and water. These human footprints include illegal infrastructure, waste dump, carbon and oil emissions that causes bio-diversity loss and geo-morphological changes along the coast.

In India, coastal tourism emerged in states like Kerala, Karnataka, Goa and West Bengal from 1960s (Fernandes, 2016). The shoreline of West Bengal stretches across a length of 350 km. Tourism along the coast of West Bengal is concentrated in two districts: South 24 Parganas and East Midnapur. The deltaic region of South 24 Parganas comprises of the ecologically sensitive mangrove forests of the Sundarbans. On the other hand, the coastline of East Midnapur is known for its straightness, flatness, and compactness (Das & Dandapath, 2014). Geomorphologically, it is a meso-tidal coastal plain with sand dunes and clay tidal flats (Ibid.). Coastal tourism in West Bengal has been actively backed by the state government from 1960s onwards. Today, tourism along East Midnapur coast is primarily centered in and around Digha, Shankarpur, Tajpur, and Mandarmani. Tourism activities in these sites are often managed by big hotel conglomerates and business concerns displacing and alienating the local communities in their own lands. This brings us to the dichotomy between the economic benefits of tourism and its impact on land-use patterns of coastal zones.

Although tourism in coastal areas is usually seen in a positive light in terms of creating economic opportunities, there are several negative consequences which affect coastal communities and their livelihoods (Ghosh, 2011). Geophysical phenomena such as coastal erosion and accretion and high-water events associated with tides are often aggravated by tourism activities (Barman, 2014). Coastal regions are also subject to extreme natural hazards: cyclonic storms and associated storm surges, extreme wind events, tsunamis etc. resulting in severe economic damages, loss of cultivable land and loss of lives, both human and animal (Ghosh, 2011; Garrod & Wilson, 2003). For instance, in 2008, typhoon Morakot devastated several tourist resorts in Taiwan leading to a huge loss for the country's tourism industry (Tsai et al., 2012).

Since 1991 the government of India constituted the Coastal Regulation Zones (CRZ) Notification for the purpose of conserving and protecting the coastal areas and marine waters in India. The CRZ applies to the land area from High Tide Line (HTL) to 500 meters on the landward side along the seafront. As per the CRZ notification, the entire coastal region of India is divided into four zones (Coastal Regulation Zone Notification 2011, Ministry of Environment, Forest and Climate Change, Government of India). CRZ-I includes ecologically sensitives areas such as mangroves, coral reefs, sand dunes, biologically active mudflats, salt marshes, intertidal zones, and nesting grounds for birds and marine creatures. CRZ-II constitutes built up areas located near shore lines within existing municipal limits or other legally designated urban areas. CRZ-III constitutes relatively undisturbed rural areas that does not fall under CRZ-II. Such areas are divided into two categories CRZ-III A and CRZ-III B. CRZ-III A comprises of densely populated areas with more than 2,161 people per sq. km. and CRZ-III B includes areas with a population density less than 2,161 people per sq. km. CRZ-III A and CRZ-III B areas are earmarked as "no development zones" up to 50 meters and 200 meters respectively from the HTL on the landward side. CRZ-IV deals with the water area. The water area and the sea bed area between the Low Tide Line (LTL) up to 12 nautical miles on the seaward side constitutes CRZ-IV A. CRZ-IV B protects estuarine areas under tidal influence. The CRZ notifications prohibit the following activities:

1. Industrial activities including manufacturing and processing
2. Manufacturing, processing, and disposal of hazardous substances
3. Land reclamation and obstruction of natural course of sea water
4. Discharge of untreated industrial, urban and human waste
5. Mining of sand and rocks
6. Altering active sand dunes
7. Undertaking port activities in highly eroding areas along the coast
8. Withdrawing of ground water

Although the aforementioned activities are not permitted in CRZ areas, exceptions are made when approved by Coastal Zone Management Plan (CZMP). Ecotourism activities, laying of pipelines, construction of roads and other public infrastructure are allowed in CRZ-IA upon completion of proper environmental impact assessment and when permitted by Ministry of Environment, Forest and Climate Change. In the intertidal areas of CRZ-IB, land reclamation is allowed only in case of certain activities such as foreshore facilities including ports, harbors, jetties and bridges. In No Development Zone (NDZ) of CRZ-III, no construction is allowed except repair and reconstruction of existing structures. Tourism related temporary facilities such as washrooms, drinking water facilities, change rooms etc. are permitted in NDZ and beaches of CRZ-III if those are set up at a minimum distance of 10 m from the HTL and approved in the CZMP. Beyond the NDZ in CRZ-III, fishing communities are allowed to participate in tourism activities by providing "home stay" to the visitors. Extraction of groundwater is usually prohibited within 200 meters of HTL. However, it is only permitted for the need of the local communities from wells by manual means. CRZ-IV allows traditional fishing activities, building of ports, exploration of oil, natural gas and minerals as approved by corresponding government authorities.

Coastal zones provide a unique site for understanding the linkages between socio-economic and natural systems. From 1980s onwards, the coastal belt of East Midnapur has developed into a popular tourist region in various stages leading to massive changes in land use land cover (LULC) patterns. This paper intends to study these changes by focusing on four study sites – Digha, Shankarpur, Tajpur and Mandarmani from 1990 to 2005. Through this changes, it examines the impact of tourism development on coastal land use pattern.

12.3 Study Sites

12.3.1 Digha-Shankurpur

Located 187 km southwest of Calcutta, Digha, originally known as Beerkul village, was discovered by the British in the late eighteenth century. In 1780, the first Governor General of India, Warren Hastings described Digha as the 'Brighton of East' in a letter to his wife. In 1923, British tourist John Frank Smith settled in Digha. After India's independence, Smith convinced the first Chief Minister of West Bengal Dr. Bidhan Chandra Roy to develop Digha as a tourist destination. The site features uniformly sloping beaches – made up of fine-grained sand and silt – bound by dune cliffs on the landward side. The beautiful beaches adorned by casuarinas, shallow sea (about 1 mile from the beach) and calm water facilitating swimming activities – all made Digha a very popular sea-side tourist destination. Digha comprises two beaches – New Digha and Old Digha – the former built 2 km away from the latter to avoid crowding of Old Digha. At present, both sites show a thick cover of built environment consisting of hotels, resorts and restaurants. However, Digha has been subjected to constant beach erosion over the last 140 years. British colonial surveyors and cartographers recorded this phenomenon and Survey of India maps show that 970 m of beach has been lost to the sea between 1877 to 1933 (Bandyopadhyay & Mukerjee, 2009). A more recent study undertaken in 1970 noted that geo-morphological phenomena like beach lowering and beach erosion are active at the Digha site (Ibid.). A 3.7 km dyke was constructed between 1972–1982, to prevent coastal erosion but the situation could not be rectified. Beach lowering could not be stopped and beach erosion is still continuing at a rate of 15–20 cm per year (Ibid.).

Shankarpur is located 14 km east of Digha and known as "twin beach of Digha". It became an alternative to the overcrowded Digha beaches and attracted tourists for its relatively clean water, white sand and fishing harbour. But beach lowering in the eastern part of Digha mohana poses a great risk to Shankarpur and the economic activities (fishing, tourism) carried out in the region.

At present Digha-Shankarpur Development Authority (DSDA), Urban Development Department, Government of West Bengal is responsible for the overall development of Digha and its adjoining areas. Digha Planning Authority was established in 1990 which included 16 mouzas as its planning area. By 2003, its area was extended upto 42 mouzas covering 8,752.63 acres as its planning area. These mouzas fall under Digha Police Station & Ramnagar Police Station. On 14th March, 1993, Digha Planning Authority was transformed into Digha Development Authority (DSDA Official Website).

12.3.2 Tajpur-Mandarmani

Tajpur is a relatively new tourist site in the East Midnapur district. It is famous for its tamarisk trees, red crabs and fishing harbor (Department of Tourism, Government of West Bengal). Adjacent to Tajpur, Mandarmani is a seaside beach resort and is 170 km away from Kolkata. The closest city is Contai, situated 17 km away and the closest market is located at Dadanpatrabar, 10 km away (Ibid.). Although the registered population of the Mandarmani village is a mere 507 (as per census 2011), the seasonal population of the area fluctuates due to its importance as a marine fishing and tourist destination. Since its first mention in the topographical survey map of 1956, Mandarmani has developed very fast from a fishing village to a seaside resort village. Being close to Digha, Mandarmani gained its popularity as a "weekend budget destination" and became well known for its beaches and sand dunes that rise to a heigh of 13 m (Ghosh, 2020, 54).

12.4 Methodology

This research paper is primarily based on data collected through remote sensing. The merit of using remote sensing and GIS techniques lies in: 1) A larger stretch of the East Midnapur coastline can be visualized more efficiently (USGS); 2) Land use changes over a stipulated period of time (long term, short term, and/or seasonal) can be studied more accurately (Samanta & Paul, 2016).

Initially, the area of interest (AOI) for the Digha and Tajpur-Mandarmani regions were delineated from a Digha Shankarpur Development Authority (DSDA) map and vectorized mouza boundaries acquired from the DSDA office and India Water Resources Information System (https://indiawris.gov.in/wris/#/) respectively. Thereafter, two Landsat 5 images dated 03/03/2005 and 22/02/1990 were downloaded from the United States Geological Survey (USGS) website (https://earthexplorer.usgs.gov/). The pre-monsoon season was chosen to have lesser cloud cover. After downloading, the images had undergone through several preprocessing regarding geometric correction, radiometric calibration and atmospheric correction using ENVI 5.3. The radiometric correction was performed on the satellite dataset by converting the digital number (DN) values into the top of atmosphere (TOA) radiance values and then it was again transformed into the bottom of atmosphere (BOA) reflectance product. As the selected study region is occupied with the built-ups, the dark matter subtraction method had been used to perform the necessary atmospheric correction (Campbell 1993; Chavez 1988). The process of Geometric correction was also performed on the geospatial data sets using the collected GCPs from the field survey. After this pre-processing, the AOIs clipped from the images were classified for landuse and landcover (LULC) using the Support Vector Machine (SVM) algorithm in ENVI 5.3. The LULC classes for both areas were selected based on the prior analysis and the classification scheme proposed by National

Remote Sensing Centre (NRSC) (Mitra et. al. 2020). Among the selected classes, while, the built-up area covered all of the impervious landscapes, the waterbody represented waterbodies such as sea, river and canal. The aquafarm and saltpans exhibited the artificially created lands for fish cultivation and salt production along with dried aquafarms respectively. Open mangroves were the pioneer mangrove found in the riverbanks and other vegetation were the natural vegetation cover of this region, excluding mangroves and plantation. Casuarina plantation and cropland were classified here along with other vegetation which is found encircling the croplands. Lastly, bare earth included the beach and the fallow lands. The accuracy of this image classification was further assessed by the error matrices using the 55 pre-collected GCPs using Google Earth. These GCPs were allotted in a stratified random manner to the different LULC classes for checking the classification accuracy without any biases (Shalaby and Tateishi 2007).

12.5 Results and Discussion

Today, Digha and Shankarpur are some of the most important tourist sites in East Midnapur District, West Bengal. The massive tourist development has led to drastic changes in LULC patterns of Digha-Shankarpur. This study has compared two maps of 1990 and 2005 to understand the LULC changes of this region (Fig. 12.1). Due to aggradation, the beach area increased from 2.690 sq km to 3.049 sq km between 1990–2005. Increased tourists' activities and population pressure have led to an increase settlement area from 0.204 sq km to 0.280 sq km. The vegetation cover of this region shows an interesting pattern due to governmental interventions from time to time. The area under open mangrove has increased from 0.139 sq km to 0.580 sq km between 1990–2005. However, other vegetation which excludes open mangroves and plantation displays a decline from 3.123 sq km to 2.400 sq km in the same period. Before the rapid development of Digha-Shankarpur as a tourist

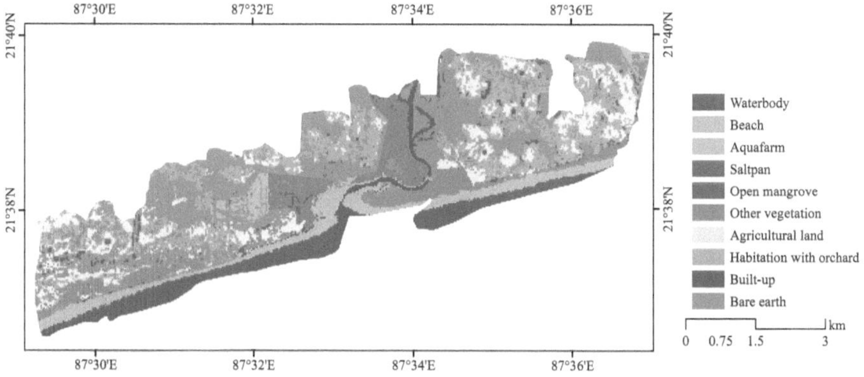

Fig. 12.1 Land Use Land Cover (LULC) Map of Digha-Shankarpur, 1990

site, agriculture was the primary economic activity of the region. Agricultural land has increased from 4.063 to 6.773 sq km between 1990–2005. This could be explained by expansion of agricultural land due to destruction of natural vegetation. Salt pan has remarkably decreased from 1990 to 2005 (1.988–0.508 sq km). In contrast, land use under aquafarms shows a significant increase from 0.692 sq. km. to 2.025 sq km (Fig. 12.2).

12 villages have been studied for the LULC of Tajpur-Mandarmani belt. Of them, Chadapur, Bherichauli, Jaldah, Bera Khana and Tajpur mouzas fall under Tajpur tourism belt. Mandarmani, Silampur, Sonamuhi, Dadanpatrabar, Rania, Mania and Dakshin Purushottampur fall under Mandarmani tourism belt. As per 1990 LULC (Fig. 12.3), Tajpur-Mandarmani area shows 4.662 sq km (14.06% of total area) under agricultural use. Aquafarm and waterbodies cover 7.126 sq km and 1.257 sq km respectively. Built up covers only 0.070 sq km (0.212%) whereas beach covers an area of 3.922 sq km.

LULC in 2005 (Fig. 12.4) shows land under agricultural use has increased to 5.797 sq km (17.489%). Aquafarm and waterbodies occupy 8.013 sq km and 1.235

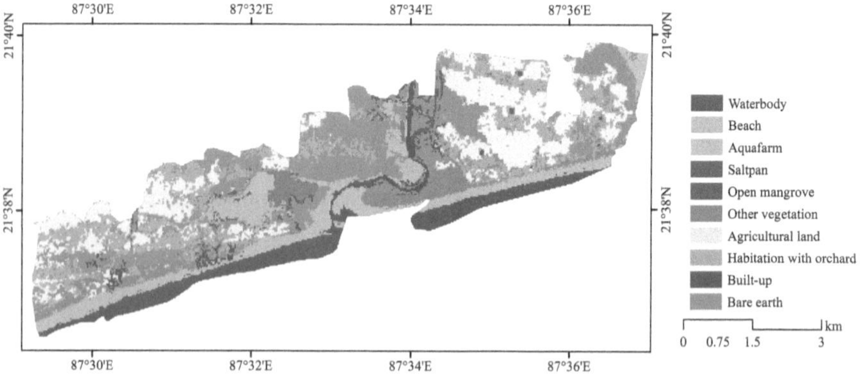

Fig. 12.2 Land Use Land Cover (LULC) Map of Digha-Shankarpur, 2005

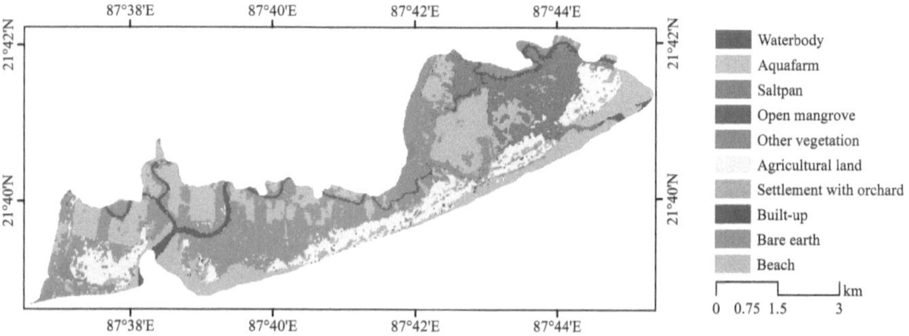

Fig. 12.3 Land Use Land Cover (LULC) Map of Tajpur-Mandarmani, 1990

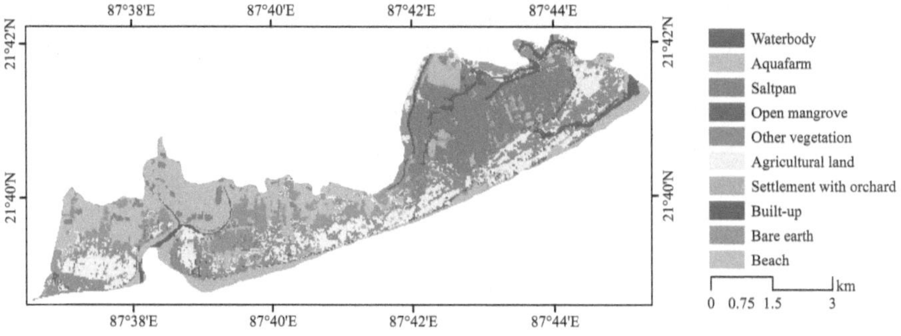

Fig. 12.4 Land Use Land Cover (LULC) Map of Tajpur-Mandarmani, 2005

sq km. Built up has increased to 0.294 sq km (0.888%) whereas beach area decreased to 2.071 sq km (6.246%). Areas under open mangrove has increased from 0.286 sq km to 0.337 sq km between 1990–2005. The increase in built up area can be explained by the building of hotels, resorts, eateries, markets, roads etc. The percentage increase in built up areas from 1990 to 2005 is 0.212 to 0.888. The increase in built-up areas is related to tourism activities and is concentrated in certain mouzas such as Dadanpatrabar, Tajpur, Sonamuhi and Silampur (Saha & Paul, 2021).

In the past two decades, both Tajpur and Mandarmani have transformed into well-known tourist sites due to its virgin beaches, natural vegetation, and relatively pollution free environment. However, increased tourists' presence has led to rapid development of tourism related enterprises along the coast. A number of hotels, resorts, shops and other settlements have come up in the past years. This in turn led to massive change in LULC pattern in the region (Saha & Paul, 2021). Sand dunes were flattened to build hotels and resorts. Agricultural lands and natural vegetation cover were transformed into similar tourism related establishments. Such anthropogenic impact has severe environmental consequences on the coastal ecology of Tajpur-Mandarmani. Some of the consequences are: landscape fragmentation, vegetation degeneration, destruction of dune ecology, coastal erosion and pollution, loss of biodiversity, loss of habitat of local flora and fauna (Ibid.).

The major issues that are being faced in coastal zones of Digha-Shankarpur-Tajpur-Mandarmani are as follows:

1. **Damages incurred through coastal hazards like erosion, tropical storms, and cyclones:** Coastal erosion is a major issue along the Digha shoreline. A combination of various factors like concentration of sea waves energy in Digha-Shankarpur sector, depletion of beach sediments by longshore drifts and construction of dams in the catchment area of River Subarnarekha, are responsible for this coastal erosion. A 3.7 km sea dyke was constructed by the Government of West Bengal along the Digha shoreline in 1972–82 to protect the resorts from the coastal erosion (Bandyopadhyay & Mukerjee, 2009). However, this dyke has been proven inadequate. Tropical storms and cyclones like Amphan (May 2022) also lead to severe damages to human lives and properties.

2. **Loss of biodiversity:** Aggressive construction of tourism facilities resulted into the loss of biodiversity in the area. For example, Digha-Shankarpur, Tajpur-Mandarmani are home to various species of crabs including the horseshoe crabs. However, scientists have observed these crab species are moving towards Orissa due to construction along the Digha beaches and changes in sand texture (Banerjee & Chatterjee, 2022). Hence, beach restoration and stopping of anthropogenic activities at the breeding grounds of crabs are needs of the hour.
3. **Violation of CRZ notifications:** Mouzas like Tajpur, Jaladha, Chandapur, Berakhana, Mandarmani, Silampur, Sonamuhi, Dadanpatrabar fall under CRZ-IA. By 2012, several hotels came up at Tajpur-Mandarmani violating coastal regulations. A survey was conducted by Block Development and Block Land Officers in May 2014 which identified 19 illegally constructed hotels within 200 meters of HTL at Mandarmani. Finally, four of these 19 hotels were demolished by East Midnapur Administration (The Telegraph, 2022) Further, none of the hotels has been registered under the State Pollution Control Board or the West Bengal Coastal Management Zone Authority. Building Plans and sale of lands were authorized by the local Panchayat who lacked the legal authority to do so (Bera, 2013). In defense, the local Gram Panchayat had argued that the state government has failed to map and delineate the CRZ area properly. Between 2005 and 2013, the local Gram Panchayat approved the construction of 135 resorts at Tajpur-Mandarmani.
4. **Change in Land Use Pattern:** Both Digha-Shankarpur and Tajpur-Mandarmani areas have undergone massive LULC changes in the last 30 years. A steady decrease in sand dunes and agricultural land has been observed in both regions, whereas a steady increase in built-up areas and aquafarms have been found. This shows the impacts of anthropogenic activities on LULC pattern in the East Midnapur coastal region. Natural vegetation cover in Tajpur-Mandarmani has decreased, but it has increased in Digha-Shankarpur due to government plantation initiatives.
5. **Environmental Pollution:** Tourism related activities have led to significant pollution in the coastal areas. At present, there are over 500 hotels in Digha-Shankarpur area which produce considerable amount of anthropogenic waste coming from various sources. Solid waste such as kitchen waste, recyclable newspapers, various types of bottles, carry bags, plastics etc., contribute to 12.33 to 25.46 MT in weight during normal day and peak day of a tourist season (Mondal, 2017). Water sample analysis from coastal sea of Digha-Shankarpur areas shows that this waste water often finds its way into the sea. In addition, use of fertilizers and chemicals in agricultural lands and aquafarms lead to pollution of sea water, rivers and creeks (Integrated Coastal Zone Management Project, Govt. of West Bengal).
6. **Problems of livelihoods support for local communities**: Hotels and resorts in this region are mostly owned and operated by outsiders who do not reside in the region. Local communities are often reduced to support staff in these establishments. Additionally, construction of hotels and resorts had contributed to beach erosion leading to reduction of fish-landing centers. At Mandarmani, the fish

landing center has reduced from 16 hectares to 10 hectares between 2003 to 2013. This has devastating effects on the fishing communities of Mandarmani (Bera, 2013).

12.6 Conclusion

This paper has charted the LULC in Digha-Shankarpur-Tajpur-Mandarmani areas since 1990s. It has been observed that tourism activities, population pressure and resultant environmental impacts have played an important role in the above mentioned LULC changes. Several measures can be taken to alleviate the adverse impact of tourism development on coastal ecosystem and local communities. A sustainable tourism development plan should involve local communities as stakeholders. Prioritizing homestay over hotel stay can generate income opportunities for local population. Environmental pollution can be checked by banning of single-use plastics and proper waste management (Mondal, 2017). Development of tourism facilities and construction of sea walls and different types of breakers (e.g., spilling breakers, surging breakers) along the East Midnapur coast should be done as per the behavior of the beach (Samanta & Paul, 2016). In conclusion, long term sustainable tourism development in this region would require cooperation among various departments of state government, private investors and local communities.

References

Bandyopadhyay, S., & Mukerjee, D.. (2009). Coastal erosion and its management at Digha, Medinipur, West Bengal. In *Geomorphology of India*: 287–302

Banerjee, K., & Chatterjee, P. (2022). *Bengal's horseshoe crabs in dire need of protection.* http://www.millenniumpost.in/sundaypost/inland/bengals-horseshoe-crabs-in-dire-need-of-protection-497378

Barman, B. (2014). *Effects of coastal erosion on the fishing community livelihoods: A focus on the east Midnapore coast, West Bengal: a study of the present to understand the future in the era of climate change.* Project report. School of Habitat Studies: Tata Institute of Social Sciences, Mumbai

Battilani, P., & Rodriguez, C. L. (2021). *Coastal tourism in southern Europe in the XXth century: New economy and material culture*. Peter Lang.

Bera, S. (2013, January 31). Playing with sea: Flouting laws, over 90 hotels have mushroomed on what once was a pristine beach in West Bengal. *Down To Earth.* https://www.downtoearth.org.in/coverage/playing-with-sea-40050

Das, R., & Dandapath, P. (2014). Existence and experience of Purba Medinipur Coastal Belt on its Morpho-dynamic journey with the distinctive geology and geomorphology. *International Journal of Science and Research, 3*(6), 1242–1251.

Department of Tourism, Government of West Bengal. (2022). *Tajpur.* https://wbtourism.gov.in/destination/place/digha

Digha-Shankarpur Development Authority (DSDA). http://www.dsda.org.in/index.php

Fernandes, P. (2016, September 27). Goa's tourism journey began with baby steps. *The Times of India*. https://timesofindia.indiatimes.com/city/goa/goas-tourism-journey-began-with-baby-steps/articleshow/54533058.cms#:~:text=Tourists%20started%20arriving%20in%20Goa,megalith%20of%20tourism%20was%20built

Garrod, B., & Wilson, J. C. (Eds.). (2003). *Marine ecotourism: Issues and experiences*. Channel View Publications.

Ghosh, D. (2020). Designing for resilience: Housing for fishermen community at Mandarmani, West Bengal. Unpublished thesis. Department of Architecture, School of Planning and Architecture, Bhopal

Ghosh, P. (2022). India. In A. Gohar (Ed.), *Tourism governance: A critical discourse on a global industry* (pp. 85–96). De Gruyter Oldenbourg. https://doi.org/10.1515/9783110638141-006

Government of West Bengal. Integrated Coastal Zone Management Project. Accessed 14 Nov 2022. https://www.iczmpwb.org/main/index.php

Klein, R. A. (2011). Responsible cruise tourism: issues of cruise tourism and sustainability. *Journal of Hospitality and Tourism Management, 18*, 107–116. https://doi.org/10.1375/jhtm.18.1.107

Manoharan, D., & James, S.. (2021, March 17). Cruise tourism in India: Sailing into troubled waters. *Down To Earth*. http://dspace.jgu.edu.in:8080/jspui/bitstream/10739/4716/1/Cruise%20tourism%20in%20India.pdf

Miller, M., Auyong, J., & Hadley, N. (2011). *Sustainable coastal tourism: Challenges for management, planning, and education*. https://nsgl.gso.uri.edu/washu/washuw99003/1-Introduction_Miller.pdf

Mitra, S., Roy, A. K., & Tamang, L. (2020). Assessing the status of changing channel regimes of Balason and Mahananda River in the sub-Himalayan West Bengal, India. *Earth Systems and Environment, 4*(2), 409–425.

Mondal, G. (2017). Solid waste management: A case study of Digha, Purba Medinipur, West Bengal. *Indian Journal of Spatial Science, 8*(2), 8–14.

Pal, B., Samanta, S., & Pal, D. K. (2012). Morphometric and hydrological analysis and mapping for Watut watershed using remote sensing and GIS techniques. *The International Journal of Advanced Engineering Technology, 2*(1), 357–368.

Saha, J., & Paul, S. (2021). An insight on land use and land cover change due to tourism growth in coastal area and its environmental consequences from West Bengal, India. *Spatial Information Research, 29*(4), 577–592.

Samanta, S., & Paul, S. K. (2016). Geospatial analysis of shoreline and land use/land cover changes through remote sensing and GIS techniques. *Modeling Earth Systems and Environment, 2*, 1–8. https://doi.org/10.1007/s40808-016-0180-0

The Telegraph. (2022, November 15). Mandarmani demolition. *The Telegraph*. https://www.telegraphindia.com/west-bengal/mandarmani-demolition/cid/1319275

Tsai, H. T., Tseng, C. J., Tzeng, S. Y., Wu, T. J., & Day, J. D. (2012). The impacts of natural hazards on Taiwan's tourism industry. *Natural Hazards, 62*, 83–91. https://doi.org/10.1007/s11069-011-0034-z

United Nations. (2017, June 5–9). *Factsheet: People and oceans*. The ocean conference, New York. Accessed 15 Oct 2022. https://www.un.org/sustainabledevelopment/wp-content/uploads/2017/05/Ocean-fact-sheet-package.pdf

United States Geological Survey. (2022). https://www.usgs.gov/

World Travel and Tourism Council. (2022). *Economic Impact Reports*. Accessed 14 Nov 2022. https://wttc.org/research/economic-impact

Chapter 13
An Internet of Things Conceptual Model and User Experience Design for Forest Hiking Systems in the Tropics Tourism

Jusak Jusak and Randy Zhu

Abstract Tourism activities in the tropics region are significantly different from other parts of the world due to its distinctive features such as a mean annual temperature of 25 degrees Celsius, an abundance of sunshine, heavy precipitation which occasionally can induce monsoonal rainfall, high levels of humidity, dense vegetation of the rainforest, and diverse marine life. Although forest hiking has become one of the attractive interests in this wide area, the liveliness of enjoying a jungle walk might be discouraged by fear of getting lost, fear of unreachable locations by emergency vehicles, and fear of natural disasters which might lead to unpredictable subject anxiety. In this paper, we propose a conceptual model of the Internet of Things (IoT) system to support a forest hiking tourism experience. It consists of three functional sub-systems i.e., environmental monitoring sensors, tracking and tracing beacons, and early warning sensors. We propose to employ Long Range Wide Area Network (LoRaWAN) architecture and communication protocols to deal with long-distance data transmission. The proposed system can provide benefits for online operational monitoring and tracking visitors' movements to quickly detect any disruption in the field such as missing persons. The system can also be used as an early warning system when a disaster like a landslide, tsunami, wildfire, volcano eruption, or flood takes place. Several other aspects related to the security, privacy, and interoperability of the proposed system will be addressed to achieve its optimum functionality. The proposed system including both hardware and software interface will be designed and developed using co-design methods. The iterative process and stakeholder engagements used in the co-design may lead to systems that are more acceptable and relevant to the needs of an individual in a unique environment like the tropics forest.

Keywords Internet of things · Co-design · Usability · Forest hiking · Tropics tourism · Tracking and tracing · Early warning system · User experience design

---

J. Jusak (✉) · R. Zhu
School of Science and Technology, James Cook University Singapore, Singapore, Singapore
e-mail: Jusak.jusak@jcu.edu.au; Randy.zhu@jcu.edu.au

E. L. Eijdenberg et al. (eds.), *Innovation-Driven Business and Sustainability in the Tropics*, https://doi.org/10.1007/978-981-99-2909-2_13

13.1 Introduction

Tropics region is widely known as areas geographically located between latitude 23 degrees 30 minutes north of the Equator and the same amount latitude in the south of the Equator. This area has some distinctive features such as a mean annual temperature of 25 degrees Celsius, an abundance of sunshine, heavy precipitation which occasionally can induce Monsoonal rainfall, high levels of humidity, dense vegetation of the rainforest, and diverse marine life (Pearce, 2009). A study in (FAO, 2020) showed that 45% of the world forest areas are in the tropical climatic domain. For these reasons, the nature of tourism in this area driven by its specific climate and environmental conditions is therefore dominated by many outdoor activities such as city tours, hiking and climbing (Chhetri et al., 2004), combined wet jungle walk and local community visit (Pabel et al., 2017), and others.

Forest hiking is currently gaining interest among tourists for its positive impact on physical health and mind. It was claimed that this type of hiking or commonly called jungle walking has positive effects to improve human heart and vascular functions (Farrow & Washburn, 2019; Tsao et al., 2022). From tourism point of view, forest hiking can also be combined with other advantages such as for educational purposes that include several activities related to enhancing visitors' awareness and behavior toward the conservation and education of tropical forests (Amici et al., 2022). Besides, several countries are actively promoting the indigenous tourism experience as part of national programs for increasing people's consciousness about native culture (Salazar-Sepúlveda et al., 2022). For example, Australia, rich with its aboriginal culture uses this activity to enrich visitors' appreciation about oral histories, artifacts, rock art, and dance of the local people (Pabel et al., 2017).

The proliferation of the Internet of Things (IoT) technology in the last decade has sprung many opportunities for the tourism industry (Novera et al., 2022; Wise & Heidari, 2019). These tiny devices sense physical measurements such as the crowdedness of an area, the number of pollutant gas, energy consumption, etc., and transmit the data through wireless communication to an application server using the Internet protocol. With the help of this data, a lot of useful information associated with tourism management can be produced, for instance, traffic monitoring, tourist behavior analysis, smart tour guide, and also disaster warning. Several works of literatures show the important role of IoT devices in creating smart tourism in the context of smart cities where communication infrastructure is readily available (Nitti et al., 2017; Tripathy et al., 2018). On the other hand, there is only a limited number of papers describing the implementation of IoT technology in rural area tourism mainly due to difficulties to provide robust and good quality wireless communication systems. Examples of successful implementation of IoT for rural area tourism can be seen in (Ko et al., 2022; Masohor et al., 2020).

The information gathered and analysed by the IoT sensors can be transmitted to forest hikers through smart devices like their smartphones or wearables. Research conducted by Anderson et al. (2017) suggests that about 95% of forest hikers have their smartphones with them throughout the hike. The use of a curated information system can be beneficial in numerous ways: It can be used as a warning system, navigating guide, or emergency support to enhance the safety of the hikers. Hikers can also create their personalised hike itinerary and hiking experience through the integration with other technologies such as big data, artificial intelligence (AI), virtual reality/augmented reality, and other technologies (Ko et al., 2022). This can lead to an increase in computing interaction during the hike where it was previously absent, changing these activities in both subtle and obvious ways that may affect safety and the hiking experience. There is a vast corpus of related work in the area of designing systems to support people while navigating in outdoor environments (Cheverst et al., 2015; Daiber et al., 2017; Ladha et al., 2013) however, limited research has looked into the area of computing design considerations specifically for hikers.

In this paper, we present an IoT conceptual model for deploying a tourism monitoring and tracking system for specific applications in a forest hiking system. It embodies sensors to retrieve physical data measurements which are embedded in point of interest (POI) devices (i.e., sensor node). The data acquisition module in the model can be customised to include various environmental monitoring sensors, tracking and tracing devices, and early warning system sensors. A real-time early warning system is essential for visitors in the area when a disaster like landslide, tsunami, and flood take place. The other important part included in the model is the network infrastructure model assisted by communication protocols to deal with the vast amount of data and low latency transmission suitable for rural area deployment. The paper also discusses functional issues such as secure consumer data for maintaining user security and privacy as well as interoperability of devices and communication protocols.

We highlight the contributions of the paper as follows. We develop an IoT conceptual model as a building block for the forest hiking monitoring system. And for a guideline in establishing the whole proposed system, we introduce co-design methods that will involve stakeholders in an iterative process. As far as the study carried out, there have been only a limited number of literature covering IoT-based systems for forest hiking use cases in the tropics environment. The root cause of the arduous implementation of IoT systems in this rural area tourism is the scarce radio connection availability. Here, we propose a model based on the LoRaWAN architecture as a communication backbone to overcome this hurdle.

13.2 Literature Review

In this part, we will survey several works in IoT-based smart tourism encompassing its conceptual view and real implementation. Several conceptual views have been proposed on the establishment of a modern tourism industry that is expected to provide a more comfortable environment, easy-to-use tools, easy-to-find locations, robust and integrated monitoring systems with handheld devices. Hence, the term smart tourism is coined. One of the disruptive technologies which will have a direct benefit to this smart tourism concept is the deployment of IoT systems incorporating sensors to retrieve real-time data on its actual location and with that, customers and service management can observe and experience real-time updates surrounding the site.

Smart tourism conceptual models in various contexts had been proposed in several papers. For example, the work by Hu (2022) offers a theoretical model of rural smart tourism service by taking personalised recommendations as data input. Then, by using the collected data, the model employed machine learning algorithms to produce a set of tourism destinations based on the domain adaptation. The paper claimed that optimum tourist recommendations can be presented by examining the relationship between the target user and other users. Furthermore, a study performed by Ribeiro et al. (2022) underlines a creation of a platform for exploring tourist destinations in low-density rural areas. These low-density territories are usually marked by their characteristics such as tourism attractions being located in scattered places and lack of support infrastructure that make them difficult to be reached. Therefore, a platform that will be able to provide adequate information for these specific regions is urgently needed. Similarly, a study by Maquera et al. (2022) proposed a concept of an intelligent platform for community-based rural tourism in Peru. The works had been carried on by using the business canvas model to integrate the expected outcomes of the proposed framework. However, the paper underlined the role of knowledge in the local community, e.g., customs, culture, and heritage during development of the proposed model.

Despite the expected paramount role of IoT systems in the future of tourism, their implementation in rural regions such as those in a large forest and mountainous landscapes are currently facing a major hurdle in providing radio communications. Communication infrastructure deployed in these remote areas is generally not as massive as its urban counterparts mainly due to a lack of economic benefits in such a low population density (Zhang et al., 2021). As such, there are only a limited number of works in the IoT infrastructure development, performance analysis, and implementations available in the attempt to enhance tourism activities in these rural regions. For example, a study performed on Jeju island, South Korea, showed a real development of a smart location-based IoT system to help tourists to collect real-time information about location and weather (Ko et al., 2022). Tourists obtained information by using a provided app that is connected to a Bluetooth beacon during their walking tours. Other studies emphasised on the performance of radio communication deployed in these geographical areas and showed possibilities the use of the LoRa (Long Range) and Zigbee technologies in rocky and mountainous environments (Olasupo, 2019). On the other hand, a study by Wang et al. (2020) evaluated the use of the next generation 5G radio communication to assist the development of smart tourism infrastructure.

There are also several works outlining the potential use of a tracking system as an additional feature for the IoT-based rural smart tourism system. For example, devices equipped with radio frequency identification (RFID) can be used to store data at every checkpoint along the hiking trails as a means of visitor tracking (Masohor et al., 2020). Additionally, previous work (D'Antonio et al., 2022) showed the concept of using a global positioning system (GPS) tracking system to record off-trail visitors' behavior.

13.3 Methods

The architectural model of our proposed system is developed based on the established LoRa network bearing advantages such as a low-power wireless communication system intended to operate over long distances, running on top of an unlicensed spectrum, and resistance against noise due to its spread spectrum modulation (Sun et al., 2022). Furthermore, because of its broad acceptance by industries and standard bodies, we foresight that LoRa communications might lead the development of smart tourism which span across a large rural area in the future.

The conceptual model described in this part consisted of four building blocks, owing to the general LoRaWAN architecture, i.e., end devices, concentrators, network servers, and cloud-based application servers as shown in Fig. 13.1. The end devices equipped with specific sensors perform data gathering from the

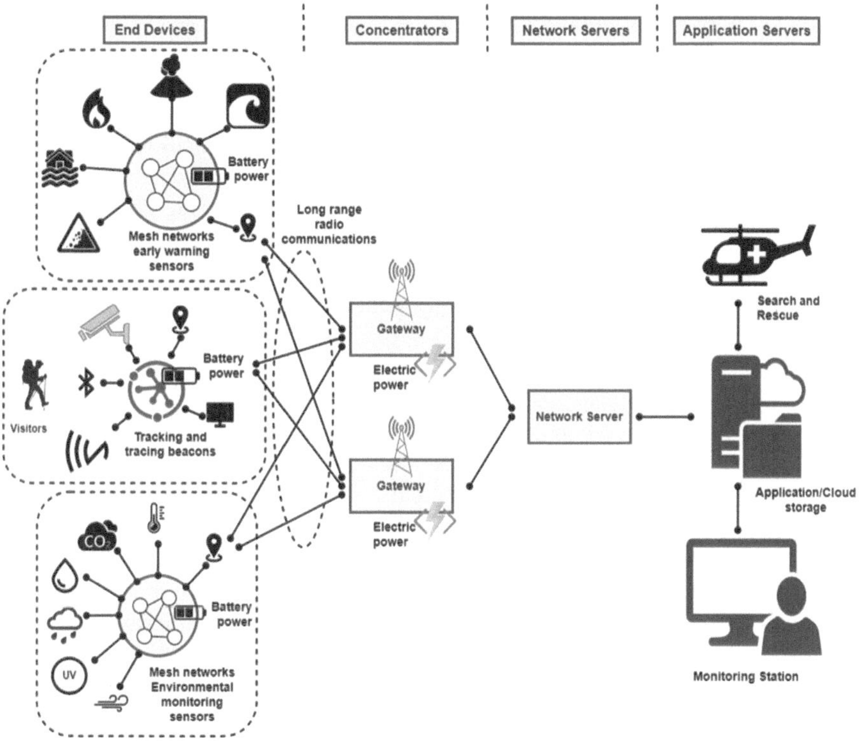

Fig. 13.1 Generic network diagram of the IoT-based forest hiking system

environment. Concentrators act as gateways that manage connections from end devices to network servers over the Internet. These gateways work concurrently with network servers to manage end devices on each point of interest and to handle communications between them. On the other hand, the cloud-based application servers do much of the duties of the application layer to provide user interface and payload encryption/decryption. The Search and Rescue team is an important entity in this model to support the entire tourism area when an emergency takes place, henceforth, real-time and accurate information about location, type of disaster, and other supporting environmental data should be readily available for them. Figure 13.2 shows a data flow diagram of the IoT-based system for forest hiking.

13.3.1 End Devices

To assist the deployment of forest hiking systems in the tropical environment, we classified the end devices into three functional sub-systems i.e., environmental monitoring sensors, tracking and tracing beacons, and early warning sensors. In addition to that, a GPS sensor should be affixed to each of the end devices in each category as a location identification tool.

The environmental monitoring sensors capture real-time status of an environment useful for preliminary information before deciding on hiking and walking tracks, for example, temperature, humidity, carbon dioxide (CO2) level, rain, ultraviolet (UV) level, and wind speed. The devices will continuously report these data to the pertaining monitoring systems as a long-term trend history of the area and as a future decision-support tool. Upon receiving the environmental data, the monitoring system shall push this information to all tracking and tracing beacons in the form of a waterproof display to supply visitors who arrive at each of the checkpoint with the current condition of the area surrounding. Table 13.1 shows detail of sensors and their function suitable for tropics conditions for both the environmental monitoring sensors and the early warning system sensors.

Tracking and tracing beacons are sub-systems deployed in several POIs which act as visitors' checkpoints and environmental condition displays. Each tracking and tracing beacon may comprise devices such as a camera to capture visitors' image only (video streaming might not be available due to the scarce wireless communication resources), Bluetooth, Near Field Communication (NFC), and a waterproof monitor display. Table 13.2 elaborates the functions of each sub-system device. With these tracking and tracing beacons, visitors who arrive at a particular checkpoint will be registered and recorded through their validated devices and a snapshot of visitors' presence. The beacon stations subsequently transmit these data to the application servers. In this way, the monitoring stations will have adequate data and information to be able to track and trace visitors' movements to quickly detect any disruption in the spots such as traffic collision and a missing person.

Early warning devices provide critical information (for all parties in this model) about several possible natural disasters in the covered area, for example, tsunami,

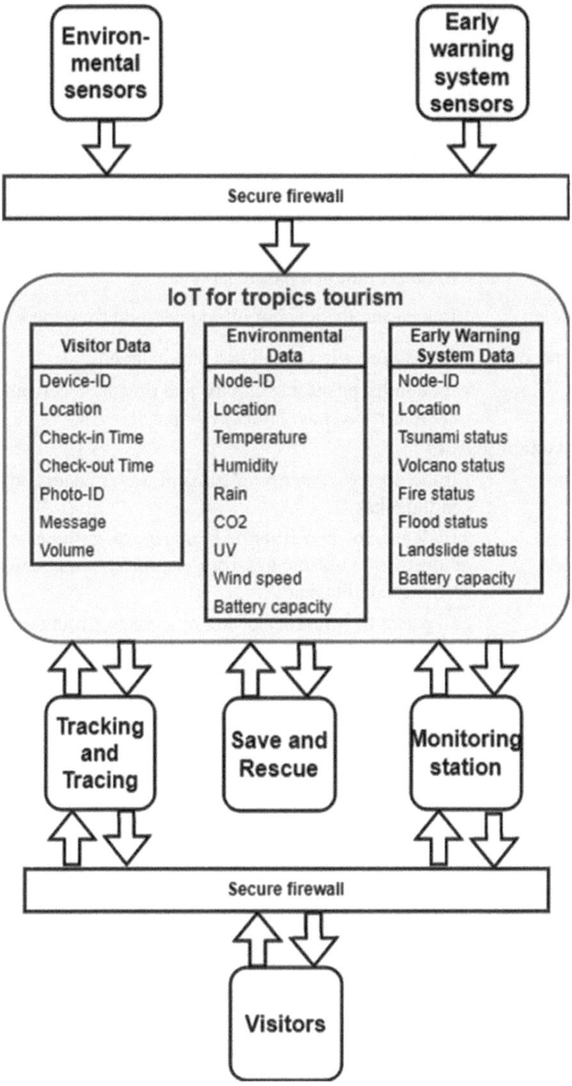

Fig. 13.2 Data flow diagram of the IoT-based forest hiking system

volcano eruption, wildfire (forest fire), flood, or landslide that might occur. Detail of the natural disasters sensors is shown in Table 13.2. When any one of these disasters take place, sensors will be triggered to generate report and location for application servers. Next, the monitoring system will forward this information to the Search and Rescue team and broadcast a warning to all tracking and tracing beacon stations.

Table 13.1 Possible environmental monitoring and early warning system sensors suitable for tropics environment

Symbol	Type of sensors	Purpose
Environmental monitoring sensors		
	Temperature	To measure temperature surrounding the area
	Humidity	To measure relative humidity of the air surrounding the area
	Carbon dioxide (CO2)	To measure the level of carbon dioxide gas surrounding the area
	Rain	To detect rain in a particular area
	Ultraviolet	To measure the level of ultraviolet light from the sun
	Wind speed	To measure wind speed in a particular area
	GPS	To identify position, velocity, and time by receiving data from the satellite-based navigation system
Early warning system sensors		
	Tsunami	To detect the existence of tsunami waves generated by undersea earthquakes
	Volcano eruption	To detect volcano eruption by means of earthquakes, ground movement, volcanic gas, rock chemistry, water chemistry, and remote satellite analysis
	Wildfire	To detect the presence of fire or smoke surrounding the area
	Flood	To detect the level of water in a particular area
	Landslide	To detect noise created by soil movement or measure changes in the length (soil gap) due to soil movement
	GPS	To identify position, velocity, and time by receiving data from the satellite-based navigation system

Table 13.2 Tracking and tracing beacons: devices and purposes

Symbol	Devices	Purpose
	Camera	To capture visitors' image
	Bluetooth	To capture visitors' device ID
	NFC	To capture visitors' device ID
	Monitor display	To display environmental status and early warning alerts surrounding the area
	GPS	To identify position, velocity, and time by receiving data from the satellite-based navigation system

13.3.2 LoRa and LoRaWAN Networks

Low-Power Wide-Area Networks (LPWANs) are wireless communication protocols developed for energy-constrained devices such as those in our IoT-based forest hiking system. The protocol was designed specifically to allow data transmission of long-range communications at a low bit rate (ranges from 0.3 to 37.5 kbps) in exchange for low energy consumption. One of the competing LPWAN technology that has broad industry support compared to other schemes is the LoRaWAN. The term LoRa refers to the physical radio communication modulation based on the chirp spread spectrum techniques, while LoRaWAN is a bundle of data link protocols built on top of LoRa. Advantages of utilising LoRa for long-range radio communications in our use case are: (i) LoRa operates in the unlicensed frequency band lower than 1 GHz, (ii) it has low power energy consumption, (iii) its spread spectrum modulation resulting in robust signal against interference and noise, and (iv) it can cover transmission distance range up to 15 km in rural areas or 5 km in urban areas.

The general architecture of LoRaWAN is shown in Fig. 13.1. We have adopted this standard architecture to provide maximum benefits to our proposed model and maintain interoperability among devices. As can be seen in the figure, end devices may consist of many sensor nodes deployed in various locations. Thus, the end devices may communicate with the network server via available gateways in their coverage. In this structure, a gateway acts as a bridge between end devices, network servers, and application servers over a backhaul interface e.g., Internet or cellular communications. Moreover, gateways and network servers also retain an important role to coordinate all nodes in its network for data transmission synchronisation under an access control technique to avoid packet collision. This function was specifically defined in LoRaWAN as the Medium Access Control (MAC) operation that guarantees the best communication performances for multiple connections end devices to a gateway.

In the LoRaWAN realm, end devices are categorised in three classes depending on how these end devices apply scheduling schemes in receiving their downlink (from network servers to end devices) traffic. Class A (ALOHA) communications is the default class for all end devices in which an end device can start transmitting uplink (from end devices to network servers) data at any moment. Once the uplink transmission is completed the device then opens two short downlink windows. In Class B (Beacon), an end device can only open a receive window and transmit data between a periodic time-synchronised beacon signal defined by the network server. Class C (Continue) is the most energy consuming scheme compared to the other two classes. In this class, an end device constantly listens to downlink signals from the network server unless they are transmitting data.

We justify that deployment of LoRaWAN in our use case should employ mixed-class schemes for the end devices. End devices in the environmental monitoring sensors and early warning system sensors blocks should adopt Class A to get the advantage of its low energy consumption. Additionally, these two blocks of end devices do not necessarily produce a huge amount of uplink data traffic making them suitable for the Class A category. To sustain long-distance operation, it might be more efficient for these two blocks to use mesh network architecture that will extend their reachability through multi-hop communications (Berto et al., 2021). On the other hand, end devices in the tracking and tracing beacon block which will require extensive both uplink and downlink data transmission should implement Class C. This block might be equipped with a solar panel power source to maintain hourly operation of these end devices.

13.3.3 Co-design

Co-design is a methodological approach that includes stakeholders, such as potential users and the community in the design process (Fuad-Luke, 2013). The iterative process in the co-design approach allows the system designers and participants to make fine-grained adjustments to the system functionalities and interface design as the project progresses intending to improve User Experience (UX) (Lee, 2008; Steen et al., 2011). The use of co-design can lead to solutions that are more acceptable and relevant to the needs of an individual in a unique environment. Stakeholders go through a recursive phase of problematising, experiencing, and solutioning via workshops. This pragmatic approach allows the system designer and participants (hikers) to learn and adjust the requirements of the solution through each cycle (de Couvreur & Goossens, 2011). The recursive workshops also aim to incorporate human-centred design and activity-centred design (Rizzo, 2011), creating solutions that are applicable to their environment.

We propose a series of seven co-design workshops that iterates through three co-design cycles to design an IoT hiker system as shown in Fig. 13.3.

Workshops use qualitative methods like group discussions, sketching, mind mapping, and reflection to collect data. Data can be analysed using thematic analysis and key themes can be shared and discussed in the follow-up workshop. The group may then make new or amendments to the system design based on the themes. Table 13.3 shows the activities and aims of each workshop.

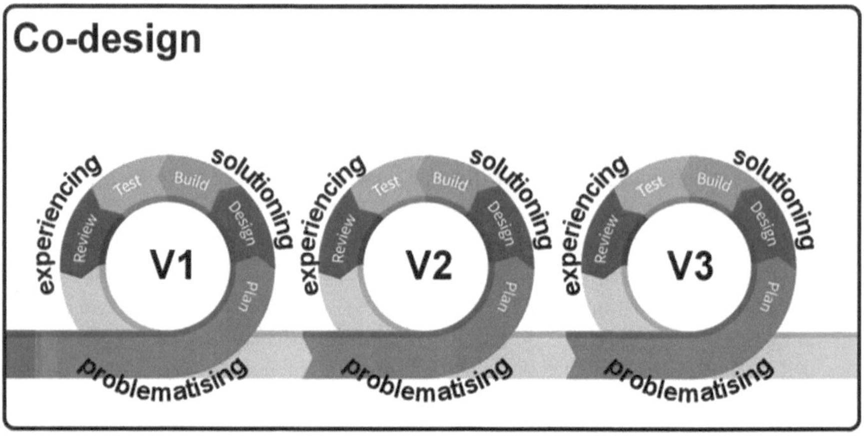

Fig. 13.3 Co-design framework

Table 13.3 Summary of co-design activities

Co-design stage	Activities	Aims
Iteration One		
WS1	Group discussion Sketching Reflection	Familiarise with co-design activities Co-design nature of the system (hardware and software requirements)
Break (1 month)		Designer develops prototype
WS2	Group discussion Mind Mapping Sketching Reflection	Install prototype Introduce the user testing process
Break (1 month)		Participants' test system (field trial)
Iteration two		
WS3	Group discussion Mind Mapping Sketching Reflection	Review key system features Improve UX through interface design
Break (1 month)		Designer continues to develop prototype Participants test system (field trial)
WS4	Group discussion Mind Mapping Sketching Reflection	Receive software updates
Break (1 month)		Participants test software (field trial)
Iteration Three		
WS5	Group discussion Mind Mapping Sketching Reflection	Prepare for system release Review UX through interface design
Break (1month)		The designer continues to develop the system Participants' test software (field trial)
WS6	Group discussion Mind Mapping Sketching Reflection	Receive system updates Prepare for system release
Break (1month)		Participants' test system (field trial)
WS7	Group discussion Mind Mapping Reflection	Review co-designers experiences

13.4 Discussion and Recommendation

In this part, we will elaborate on message exchange interaction between entities in our proposed model through a sequence flow diagram. Followed by discussions about security and data privacy which should be upheld by the system in its full operation, interoperability of devices that construct the overall system, challenges in applying the duty cycle to minimise interference with other devices, user experience design, and recommendation for future applications.

The sequence flow diagram of our proposed IoT-based for forest hiking system is shown in Fig. 13.4. It started with visitor registration of his/her device identification (ID) such as Medium Access Control (MAC) address, International Mobile Equipment Identity (IMEI) number, or Electronic Serial Number (ESN) number to the monitoring station. With this registration procedure before entering the forest hiking area, the monitor station can observe the movement of each visitor through his/her attendance at every checkpoint. Here, checkpoints are located in all tracking and tracing beacons shown in Fig. 13.1.

Environmental monitoring sensors and early warning sensors will periodically send their updated data to the monitoring station. Subsequently, the monitoring station will broadcast environmental and warning status to the tracking and tracing beacons to be displayed. Therefore, visitors who arrive at the checkpoint will be able to perceive the surrounding status in the forest hiking area. At the same time, devices will automatically detect visitors' attendance at a certain checkpoint through Bluetooth or NFC devices capturing their device ID and an image screenshot taken

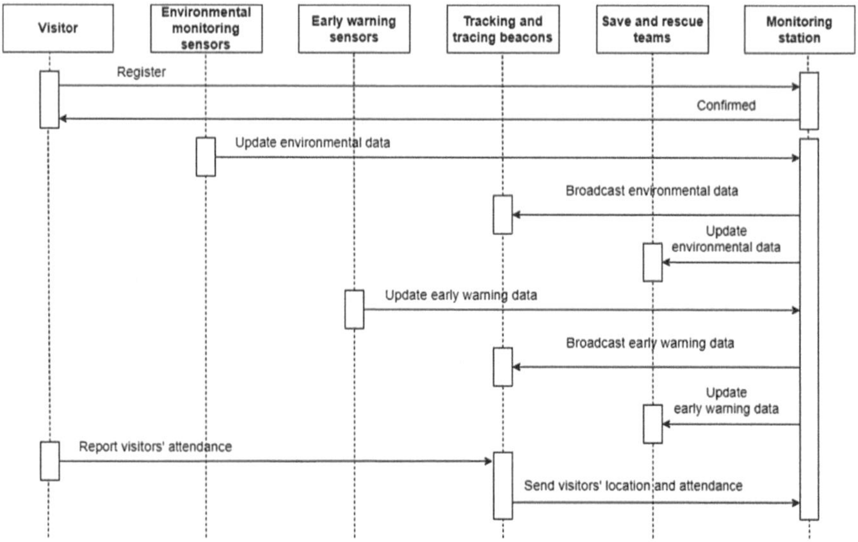

Fig. 13.4 Sequence flow diagram of the IoT-based forest hiking system

by a camera. Finally, tracking and tracing beacons will upload the visitor attendance information and location to the monitoring stations.

13.4.1 Security and Privacy

Physical nature of IoT devices brings about consequences for overall system security. As the spearhead of data collection, its limitation in terms of processing capability, memory, and operating system might be manipulated as the first point of attack. In our forest hiking system, the main points of attack are including the monitor station where visitors register their device ID at the first time before embarking on their journey and the tracking and tracing beacon devices where visitors report their attendance at a certain checkpoint. Possible attacks at these points are malicious code injection leading to a denial of service, false data injection, sleep deprivation, and node capturing (Hassija et al., 2019). Other parts of the system are also prone to security incidents with the same degree of severity, for example, side-channel attacks, eavesdropping, and interference attacks through the environmental monitoring and early warning system devices. Furthermore, device vandalism and thieving are other common types of system disruption as devices are located outdoors.

On the other hand, privacy is associated with data confidentiality and integrity that should be maintained rigorously in the system. Data theft and data leaks might lead to the unpleasant advertisements, and email phishing toward visitors in the future. Therefore, we recommend removing visitors' device IDs from the system database after visitors complete the journey and depart from the site. This way will minimise the risk of data theft.

13.4.2 Interoperability

The vast development of IoT devices, infrastructure, and platforms in the last decades has led to the emergence of interoperability issues needed to be addressed carefully. Such cautious actions might be applied to the design of sensor nodes that might encompass several types of sensor and microcontroller products produced by various vendors. For example, some type of microcontrollers has LoRa support embedded on the same board while others require separate LoRa module with different serial interface standards to be configured for transmitting and receiving data. In our proposed model, LoRa and LoRaWAN protocols are adopted as wireless communications backbone that connects various IoT devices in scattered locations to the application server. The fact that broad industry and standard bodies are currently supporting the LoRa and LoRaWAN protocols might minimised interoperability issues in the development of the IoT-based forest hiking system in our model.

13.4.3 LoRaWAN Duty Cycle

The duty cycle (DC) specifies the period of time allowed for the radio devices to occupy a channel during transmission. Enforcement of the DC in some countries is mainly motivated by the fact that LoRa devices utilise the unlicensed spectrum frequency and it has the ability to reach a large distance range. Therefore, the DC can be viewed as an instrument to protect this free spectrum sharing from interfering with each other (i.e., fair use policy). For example, devices in Europe apply DC limitations to conform with the regulations issued by the European Telecommunications Standards Institute (ETSI). The DC is commonly set to 1% per channel. In other words, if a channel applies a DC of 1%, the total amount of time the device allowed for transmitting data on that channel must not exceed 36 seconds per hour. It is obvious that the amount of DC is considerably small compared to what is required in our forest hiking model, particularly for transmitting data from tracking and tracing beacons to the application servers. When the number of visitors is raising, the DC restriction might discourage the effectiveness of the proposed model. Therefore, to address this issue we recommend operating LoRa devices with the capability to run on several channels. Applying a channel scheduling algorithm to manage data transmission on the tracking and tracing beacon devices will be advantageous to overcome the DC limitation.

13.4.4 User Experience Design

Usability is a concept that looks into the fulfillment of functional requirements and relates to whether a product or service is fit for purpose, i.e., fit to be used (Jordan, 2020). Usability is commonly associated with UX (User Experience) since UX reflects a person's overall experience in using a product or service. Each person has their ways of accomplishing design tasks, depending on their capabilities, characteristics, and the situated environment. It is necessary and important to understand these elements to design solutions with them.

Although hiking is commonly associated with low risk and challenges, however, fatal accidents do occur when the associated risks connected with hiking are misjudged (Scholl-Grissemann et al., 2022). A system designed for hikers would have to consider the environment and the activities the hikers would be in while using the system. In addition, interaction with the hiking system may be obtrusive and affect the overall hiking experience (Anderson & Jones, 2020).

13.5 Conclusion

In this paper, we proposed a conceptual model of an IoT system to support an establishment of smart forest hiking tourism. The proposed conceptual model is projected to enrich a limited number of literatures on the implementation of IoT technology in rural area tourism. The model consists of three functional sub-systems i.e., environmental monitoring sensors, tracking and tracing beacons, and early warning sensors. The environmental monitoring sensors have the main function to capture real-time status of an environment, such as temperature, humidity, carbon dioxide (CO2) level, rain, ultraviolet (UV) level, and wind speed. The tracking and tracing beacons are sub-systems deployed in several POIs which act as visitors' checkpoints and environmental condition displays. Early warning devices provide critical information (for all parties in this model) about several possible natural disasters in the covered area, for example, tsunami, volcano eruption, wildfire (forest fire), flood, or landslide that might occur. To deal with long-distance data transmission in the rural area that is often becoming a hurdle to cover a forest site, we propose to employ Long Range Wide Area Network (LoRaWAN) architecture and communication protocols. We also addressed some critical aspects such as security, privacy, and interoperability of the model to achieve its optimum upcoming implementation. Finally, we discussed the computing design considerations for hikers to improve the user experience for future realisation.

References

Amici, A. A., Nadkarni, N. M., Lackey, N. Q., & Bricker, K. S. (2022). Conservation, education, and adventure tourism: A case study of adventure parks as potential venues for communication in Monteverde, Costa Rica. *Journal of Ecotourism, 21*(3), 230–245. https://doi.org/10.1080/14724049.2021.1933503

Anderson, Z., & Jones, M. (2020). Rethinking the role of a Mobile computing in recreational hiking. In *HCI outdoors: Theory, design, methods and applications* (pp. 291–305). Springer. https://doi.org/10.1007/978-3-030-45289-6_16

Anderson, Z., Lusk, C., & Jones, M. D. (2017). Towards understanding hikers' technology preferences. In *UbiComp/ISWC 2017 – Adjunct proceedings of the 2017 ACM international joint conference on pervasive and ubiquitous computing and proceedings of the 2017 ACM international symposium on wearable computers* (pp. 1–4). https://doi.org/10.1145/3123024.3123089

Berto, R., Napoletano, P., & Savi, M. (2021). Alora-based mesh network for peer-to-peer long-range communication. *Sensors, 21*(13). https://doi.org/10.3390/s21134314

Cheverst, K., Do, T. V., & Fitton, D. (2015). Supporting the mobile in-situ authoring of locative media in rural places: Design and expert evaluation of the SMAT app. *International Journal of Handheld Computing Research (IJHCR), 6*(1), 1–19.

Chhetri, P., Arrowsmith, C., & Jackson, M. (2004). Determining hiking experiences in nature-based tourist destinations. *Tourism Management, 25*(1), 31–43. https://doi.org/10.1016/S0261-5177(03)00057-8

D'Antonio, A., Monz, C. A., Crabb, B., Baggio, J. A., & Howe, P. D. (2022). Proof of concept study using GPS-based tracking data to build agent-based models of visitors' off-trail behavior in nature-based tourism settings. *Applied Geography, 147*, 102771. https://doi.org/10.1016/j.apgeog.2022.102771

Daiber, F., Jones, M., Wiehr, F., Cheverst, K., Kosmalla, F., & Häkkilä, J. (2017). UbiMount – 2nd workshop on ubiquitous computing in the mountains. In *UbiComp/ISWC 2017 – Adjunct proceedings of the 2017 ACM international joint conference on pervasive and ubiquitous computing and proceedings of the 2017 ACM international symposium on wearable computers* (pp. 1022–1026). https://doi.org/10.1145/3123024.3124462

de Couvreur, L., & Goossens, R. (2011). Design for (every) one: Co-creation as a bridge between universal design and rehabilitation engineering. *CoDesign, 7*(2), 107–121.

FAO. (2020). Global Forest Resources Assessment 2020: Key Findings. In *Global forest resources assessment 2020*. FAO. https://doi.org/10.4060/ca8753en

Farrow, M. R., & Washburn, K. (2019). A review of field experiments on the effect of Forest bathing on anxiety and heart rate variability. *Global Advances in Health and Medicine, 8*, 216495611984865. https://doi.org/10.1177/2164956119848654

Fuad-Luke, A. (2013). *Design activism: Beautiful strangeness for a sustainable world*. Routledge.

Hassija, V., Chamola, V., Saxena, V., Jain, D., Goyal, P., & Sikdar, B. (2019). A survey on IoT security: Application areas, security threats, and solution architectures. *IEEE Access, 7*, 82721–82743). Institute of Electrical and Electronics Engineers Inc. https://doi.org/10.1109/ACCESS.2019.2924045

Hu, X. (2022). Optimization of rural smart tourism service model with internet of things. *Security and Communication Networks, 2022*, 1–10. https://doi.org/10.1155/2022/6004728

Jordan, P. W. (2020). *An introduction to usability*. CRC Press.

Ko, T.-S., Kim, B.-J., & Jwa, J.-W. (2022). Smart tourism information system and IoT data collection devices for location-based tourism and tourist safety services. *International Journal of Advanced Culture Technology, 10*(1), 310–406. https://doi.org/10.17703/IJACT.2022.10.1.310

Ladha, C., Hammerla, N. Y., Olivier, P., & Plötz, T. (2013). ClimbAX: Skill assessment for climbing enthusiasts. In *UbiComp 2013 – Proceedings of the 2013 ACM international joint conference on pervasive and ubiquitous computing* (pp. 235–244). https://doi.org/10.1145/2493432.2493492

Lee, Y. (2008). Design participation tactics: The challenges and new roles for designers in the co-design process. *Co-Design, 4*(1), 31–50.

Maquera, G., da Costa, B. B. F., Mendoza, Ó., Salinas, R. A., & Haddad, A. N. (2022). Intelligent digital platform for community-based rural tourism—A novel concept development in Peru. *Sustainability (Switzerland), 14*(13). https://doi.org/10.3390/su14137907

Masohor, S. M. A. S., Bakar, M. Z. H. A., Yamin, W. S. A. W., Wahab, M. H. A., Ahmad, M. S., Ma'Radzi, A. A., Ibrahim, T. N. T., & Choon, C. C. (2020). Tracking system using RFID for hiking activity with IoT technology. *Journal of Physics: Conference Series, 1529*(5), 052030. https://doi.org/10.1088/1742-6596/1529/5/052030

Nitti, M., Pilloni, V., Giusto, D., & Popescu, V. (2017). IoT architecture for a sustainable tourism application in a smart city environment. *Mobile Information Systems, 2017*, 1–9. https://doi.org/10.1155/2017/9201640

Novera, C. N., Ahmed, Z., Kushol, R., Wanke, P., & Azad, M. A. K. (2022). Internet of Things (IoT) in smart tourism: A literature review. *Spanish Journal of Marketing – ESIC, 26*, 325–344. https://doi.org/10.1108/sjme-03-2022-0035

Olasupo, T. O. (2019). Wireless communication modeling for the deployment of tiny IoT devices in rocky and mountainous environments. *IEEE Sensors Letters, 3*(7), 1–4. https://doi.org/10.1109/LSENS.2019.2918331

Pabel, A., Prideaux, B., & Thompson, M. (2017). Tourists' preferences with Indigenous tourism experiences in the Wet Tropics of Queensland, Australia. *Journal of Hospitality and Tourism Management, 31*, 142–151. https://doi.org/10.1016/j.jhtm.2016.11.004

Pearce, P. L. (2009). Tourism research and the tropics: Further horizons. *Tourism Recreation Research, 34*(2), 107–121. https://doi.org/10.1080/02508281.2009.11081583

Ribeiro, F., Metrolho, J., & Cabral, S. (2022). IoT technologies to promote tourism experiences in low-density territories. In *2022 17th Iberian conference on information systems and technologies (CISTI)* (pp. 1–7). https://doi.org/10.23919/CISTI54924.2022.9820237

Rizzo, F. (2011). 12. Co-design versus user Centred design: Framing the differences. *Notes on Doctoral Research in Design. Contributions from the Politecnico Di Milano*, 125–135

Salazar-Sepúlveda, G., Vega-Muñoz, A., Contreras-Barraza, N., Zada, M., & Adsuar, J. C. (2022). Indigenous forestry tourism dimensions: A systematic review. *Forests, 13*(2). MDPI. https://doi.org/10.3390/f13020298

Scholl-Grissemann, U., Peters, M., Bichler, B. F., & Happ, E. (2022). Hiking tourism: Educating hikers through the interpretation of on-site information and predicting precautionary behavior. *Tourism Review*, ahead-of-print

Steen, M., Manschot, M., & de Koning, N. (2011). Benefits of co-design in service design projects. *International Journal of Design, 5*(2).

Sun, Z., Yang, H., Liu, K., Yin, Z., Li, Z., & Xu, W. (2022). Recent advances in LoRa: A Comprehensive Survey. *ACM Transactions on Sensor Networks*. https://doi.org/10.1145/3543856

Tripathy, A. K., Tripathy, P. K., Ray, N. K., & Mohanty, S. P. (2018). ITour: The future of smart tourism: An IoT framework for the independent mobility of tourists in smart cities. *IEEE Consumer Electronics Magazine, 7*(3), 32–37. https://doi.org/10.1109/MCE.2018.2797758

Tsao, T. M., Hwang, J. S., Lin, S. T., Wu, C., Tsai, M. J., & Su, T. C. (2022). Forest bathing is better than walking in Urban Park: Comparison of cardiac and vascular function between urban and Forest parks. *International Journal of Environmental Research and Public Health, 19*(6). https://doi.org/10.3390/ijerph19063451

Wang, W., Kumar, N., Chen, J., Gong, Z., Kong, X., Wei, W., & Gao, H. (2020). Realizing the potential of internet of things for smart tourism with 5G and AI. *IEEE Network, 34*(6), 295–301. https://doi.org/10.1109/MNET.011.2000250

Wise, N., & Heidari, H. (2019). Developing smart tourism destinations with the internet of things. In *Big data and innovation in tourism, travel, and hospitality: Managerial approaches, techniques, and applications* (pp. 21–29). Springer Singapore. https://doi.org/10.1007/978-981-13-6339-9_2

Zhang, Y., Love, D. J., Krogmeier, J. v., Anderson, C. R., Heath, R. W., & Buckmaster, D. R. (2021). Challenges and opportunities of future rural wireless communications. *IEEE Communications Magazine, 59*(12), 16–22. https://doi.org/10.1109/MCOM.001.2100280

Chapter 14
Spatial Characteristics and Driving Mechanism of Hainan Tourism Development Under the COVID-19 Epidemic

Fenggui Chen, Jinlong Jiang, Yuhuan Jiang, Chao Zhang, Qingsheng Li, and Jianwei Wu

Abstract Tourism plays an important role in promoting economic growth, employment, government revenue and national income. Due to the influence of economic development level, resource distribution, regional transportation infrastructure and other factors, the unbalanced development of regional tourism has always existed. However, at present, there is little research on the driving mechanism of tourism development. As the largest island completely located in the tropical area of China, Hainan has rich tourism resources, unique cultural customs and favorable conditions for developing tourism, and its tourism output value accounts for a high proportion of GDP. The outbreak of COVID-19 at the end of 2019 caused the global tourism industry to slow down and cool down, which also had a great impact on the development of tourism in Hainan. Due to the influence of COVID-19 epidemic, there are obvious differences in tourism development in Hainan island. Therefore, it is particularly important to study the driving factors and driving mechanisms of tourism development differences in Hainan island, which can provide favorable support for Hainan island to put forward reasonable and effective policies. In this study, an analytical framework of spatial difference-driving factors-driving mechanism is constructed, which provides a framework for the study of spatial heterogeneity of tourism development. The findings are as follows: ①In 2020, the total tourism revenue of Hainan decreased by 17.48%, and the total number of domestic and foreign tourists decreased by 22.33%. After February, the number of domestic overnight visitors showed a gradual recovery, and inbound tourism has been in a downturn. ②There are obvious regional differences in tourism in Hainan, with Sanya and Haikou as the north and south poles. In 2020, the number of tourists from them accounted for nearly 60% of the island. ③Analysis of the driving factors of regional differences in tourism in Hainan, and two major factors affecting the spatial differences of tourism are obtained, namely, resource and economic factor and

F. Chen (✉) · J. Jiang (✉) · Y. Jiang · C. Zhang · Q. Li · J. Wu
Third Institute of oceanography, Ministry of Natural Resources, Xiamen, China
e-mail: chenfenggui@tio.org.cn; jiangjinlong@tio.org.cn

E. L. Eijdenberg et al. (eds.), *Innovation-Driven Business and Sustainability in the Tropics*, https://doi.org/10.1007/978-981-99-2909-2_14

urban population density factor. ④Through the analysis of driving mechanism, it is found that resources and economic factor has the most important influence on the spatial difference of tourism. For every increase of one unit, the number of overnight visitors in various cities increases by 0.991 units. Under the epidemic situation, although it is a difficult period for the whole industry to develop, it can also be seen that while the international tourism market is severely frustrated, the development potential of the domestic market is huge. In the future, there is much to be done to promote regional coordinated development by optimizing the spatial layout.

Keywords COVID-19 epidemic · Driving mechanism · Hainan island · Index system · Spatial difference analysis

14.1 Introduction

After the Second World War, the tourism industry developed rapidly, and the number of international tourists increased from 0.25 billion in 1950 to 1.5 billion in 2019 (UNWTO, 2020). Tourism plays an important role in promoting economic growth, employment, government revenue and national income (Haddock-Fraser & Hampton, 2012). The era characteristics of the great development of world tourism have promoted the climax of island tourism development and construction. As a typical leisure and holiday tourism, marine tourism has great development space and potential, and has become one of the fastest growing activities of tourism (Luck, 2008). The rapid development of marine tourism has significantly changed the islands and coastal areas (Miller & Auyong, 1991). At present, the international island resorts are mainly distributed in the tropics and subtropics, where appropriate climatic factors and good regional resources give the island unique advantages for development. Tourism has become a major sector in the Indian Ocean, the Caribbean Sea and the whole Asia-Pacific region. Some economies think that tourism accounts for more than 50% of GDP and is a major source of direct employment (Hampton & Jeyacheya, 2013). In China, since the reform and opening up, the tourism industry has achieved great-leap-forward development, with the number of inbound tourists increasing from 1,809,200 in 1978 to 145 million in 2019, an increase of more than 70 times. In 2019, the number of domestic tourists in China reached 6.006 billion, and the total tourism revenue was 6.63 trillion yuan. The comprehensive contribution of tourism to GDP was 10.94 trillion yuan, accounting for 11.05% of the total GDP (China News Network, 2019).

The development of tourism is easily affected by public safety emergencies, such as major infectious diseases. The Coronavirus disease in 2019 (COVID-19) is an ongoing epidemic disease, which was declared a global epidemic by the World Health Organization (WHO) on March 11th, 2020 (Chirwa et al., 2021). This pandemic has constituted one of the most destructive global crises in recent times, surpassing the outbreak of severe acute respiratory syndrome (SARS) in 2003 and

Middle East respiratory syndrome (MERS) in 2012 (Baldwin & Di Mauro, 2020; Huynh, 2020; Ruiz-Estrada et al., 2020). The number of deaths and infections related to COVID-19 has increased exponentially. Health systems in most countries are under great pressure, and the common goal is to flatten the COVID-19 curve (Karabulut et al., 2020; Sohn et al., 2021). COVID-19 crisis has forever changed the way that individuals, communities and organizations around the world manage their plans and operations (Gabriel-Campos et al., 2021), and has had a significant impact on global economic growth. One year after being declared a global epidemic, many countries are still struggling to cope with the devastating impact of the epidemic on many economic sectors, and tourism is the most seriously affected among all major economic sectors (Gabriel-Campos et al., 2021). The Travel & Tourism sector suffered a loss of almost US$4.5 trillion to reach US$4.7 trillion in 2020, with the contribution to GDP dropping by a staggering 49.1% compared to 2019; 62 million jobs were lost, representing a drop of 18.5% (World Travel & Tourism Council Organization (WTTC), 2021). The threat of job losses persists as many jobs are currently supported by government retention schemes and reduced hours, which without a full recovery of Travel & Tourism could be lost.

The destruction of the COVID-19 epidemic highlighted the fragility of tourism. Tourism is the most seriously affected by this kind of influence, and it needs a carefully planned strategy to reduce this influence (Yeh, 2020). Shao et al. (2020) made a preliminary exploration of China's tourism recovery policy in the COVID-19 era, emphasizing that effective and pragmatic policies are necessary and key to improve tourism after the epidemic, and found that the policy priorities of tourism recovery in different areas of China are different. Samarathunga and Gamage (2020) introduced alternative tourism as a beneficial remedy to develop tourism during the COVID-19 epidemic, that is, focusing on health tourism, agricultural tourism and eco-tourism. Due to the lack of international tourists, domestic tourism has become the largest part of tourism in most countries, and the main consumer groups of local tourism have also changed (Sohn et al., 2021). Tourists' willingness and habits to travel have been affected accordingly, and new changes have taken place in tourism demand (Gyimóthy et al., 2022). COVID-19 has become an external factor that can't be ignored, and the regional difference of its impact on tourism needs further empirical test (Zhang & Yuan, 2022). City is the main carrier of tourism economic growth, and also the basic place of tourism activities (Koodsela et al., 2019). Different cities have great differences in tourism development and recovery level due to their own conditions. It is of great significance to accurately understand the differences in the affected degree of epidemic situation in different places, and to find out the driving factors and driving mechanisms of these differences, so as to formulate the corresponding recovery policies in a targeted way, and to promote the all-round development of regional tourism. As the largest island completely located in the tropical area of China, Hainan has abundant tourism resources, unique cultural customs and favorable conditions for the development of tourism (Zhang & Ju, 2021), and its tourism output value accounts for a high proportion of GDP. However, there are obvious differences among Hainan's tourism affected by the COVID-19 epidemic. Therefore, this study chooses Hainan as a case area to analyze the development characteristics of tourism under the COVID-19 epidemic from two dimensions of time and space, and measures its driving mechanism by constructing the index system of driving factors of spatial differences in tourism development, using SPSS, EXCELL and ARCGIS software to carry out factor analysis and multiple regression analysis.

14.2 Literature Review

14.2.1 Spatial Difference of Tourism Industry

Tourism is a real global force for economic growth and development, promoting the creation of more and better employment opportunities and becoming a catalyst for innovation and entrepreneurship (UNWTO, 2019). Due to the influence of economic development level, resource distribution, regional transportation infrastructure and other factors, the unbalanced development of regional tourism has always existed (Wang & Xia, 2018). Priskin (2001) constructed a natural resources evaluation index system with 29 indexes from four aspects: attraction, accessibility, infrastructure condition and environmental degradation, and evaluated the natural resources of the midwest islands in Australia. Shi et al. (2012) used principal component analysis to analyze the development level of tourism economy, and revealed the regional differences of tourism economy of 14 prefecture-level cities in Gansu Province. Wei et al. (2022) investigated the seasonal changes of night light images in 122 counties (cities, districts) in Hunan Province and their correlation with tourism, revealing the geographical and spatial differences of tourism activities. Zhang and Yuan (2022) collected the tourism network attention of 337 prefecture-level cities in China from 2018 to 2021 through data mining, and analyzed the temporal and spatial evolution characteristics and regional differences of urban tourism network attention in China by using seasonal concentration index, Zipf model and Dagum Gini coefficient. Some scholars also pay attention to the spatial structure of island tourism resources. Zhang and Ju (2021) investigated the quantity and types of tourism resources in Hainan Island, China, and analyzed the spatial pattern of tourism resources in Hainan Island from the perspective of spatial variation and spatial correlation. However, it is not enough to make a comprehensive and quantitative study on the factors that affect the development of tourism in nature, society and economy. Especially in the context of the epidemic situation in COVID-19, it is particularly important to study the differential driving factors and driving mechanisms of tourism development, which can provide favorable support for putting forward reasonable and effective policies.

14.2.2 Site Description

Hainan Island is the second largest island in China. It faces Leizhou Peninsula in Guangdong Province across Qiongzhou Strait in the north, Qinzhou City in Guangxi Zhuang Autonomous Region in China and Vietnam in the west across Beibu Gulf. This land is a pear-shaped oval with a long axis from northeast to southwest, covering an area of over 30,000 square kilometers.

As a tropical island, Hainan is located in the internationally recognized golden holiday tourism belt in the world. Its ecological environment is first-class in China, and its marine tourism resources are extremely rich and unique. The highest point of Hainan Island is Wuzhishan in the middle, and it descends to the periphery step by step (Zhang et al., 2022). It has a large sea area, many islands and reefs, long coastline and beaches, and the biological landscapes such as coral, mangroves and seaweed beds are precious and rare. In 2019, the total tourism revenue was 105.78 billion yuan, accounting for 19.92% of the region's GDP, far higher than the global average (6.61%) and China average (11.05%) (Zhang & Ju, 2021). In the past decade, the total revenue of tourism industry has been increasing continuously, and its proportion in GDP has steadily increased. The development of marine tourism is dominated by coastal and inshore islands, and as a whole, it has formed a marine tourism product format that focuses on leisure, sightseeing and vacation. In recent years, new formats such as marine sports, cruise ships and yachts have gradually emerged, and marine tourism has also expanded from coastal areas to distant seas. The COVID-19 epidemic at the end of 2019 caused the global tourism to slow down and cool down (Chirwa et al., 2021) which also had a great impact on the development of Hainan tourism.

14.3 Material and Methods

14.3.1 Data Sources

The data used in this study comes from Hainan Statistical Yearbook 2021 published on the website of Hainan Provincial People's Government of China, including data on tourism development, resource conditions, economic conditions and social conditions of Haikou, Sanya, qionghai city, Wanning, Wenchang, Lingshui, Wuzhishan, Ding 'an, Tunchang, Qiongzhong, Baoting, Baisha, Danzhou, Dongfang, Chengmai, Lingao and Lingao counties under the jurisdiction of Hainan Province. Information on the number of tourists, overnight tourists, domestic tourists and inbound tourists from January 2020 to December 2020 in each city (or county) of Hainan is obtained from the website of Hainan Tourism, Culture, Radio, Film and Sports Department (http://lwt.hainan.gov.cn/).

14.3.2 Methodology

14.3.2.1 Spatial Difference Analysis of Tourism Industry

A tourist is a traveler who travels to a destination outside his usual environment in less than one year for the main purpose of staying (business, leisure or other personal purposes, not being employed by a resident entity in the visited country or place).[1] We generally use statistical indicators, such as the number of tourists and tourism income, to evaluate and quantify the impact of tourism activities (Wei et al., 2022). The number of overnight visitors is regarded as the core indicator of tourism statistics. Therefore, in this study, the number of overnight visitors in various cities and counties in Hainan island is used to reflect the tourism development in various places, and the gap between 2019 and 2020 is used to reflect the changes in various places.

14.3.2.2 Factorial Analysis

The relationship between supply and demand of tourism is affected by the development conditions of tourism, such as resource endowment, infrastructure, traffic conditions and market scope. These conditions have different degrees of urban heterogeneity, which will inevitably lead to the spatial imbalance of tourism economic activities in various cities. There are obvious spatial differences between tourism resources and tourism economy in Hainan Island. Previous studies have shown that the number of hotels, the proportion of tertiary industry in GDP and regional population are the most important factors affecting the distribution of tourism resources, while the density of road network, the number of hotels, GDP per capita, the proportion of tertiary industry in GDP, regional population and the number of tourism resources have a significant impact on the tourism economy of Hainan Island (Zhang & Ju, 2021). Based on the above analysis, this study selected 10 related indicators, such as resources, economy and society, from the factors that affect the spatial differences of tourism development in Hainan, as shown in Table 14.1.

In order to eliminate the influence of different dimensions, each index data is standardized, and it is used as the data source for quantitative analysis of spatial difference driving force of tourism development in Hainan. The factor analysis is carried out by the "maximum variance orthogonal rotation method", and the factor is extracted according to the principle that the characteristic root is greater than 1.0.

[1] International Recommendations for Tourism Statistics 2008

Table 14.1 Driving force index of spatial difference of tourism development in Hainan

Type of indicator	Name of indicator
Resource factor	Number of tourist attractions(x_1), number of beds in tourist hotels(x_2)
Economic factor	GDP(x_3), per capita GDP(x_4), output value of tertiary industry(x_5), proportion of tertiary industry(x_6)
Social factor	Tertiary resident population(x_7), City population density(x_8), per capita disposable income(x_9), proportion of employees in tertiary industry(x_{10})

14.3.2.3 Analysis of Driving Mechanism

In order to clarify the quantitative relationship between each driving factor and tourism development, the driving mechanism is analyzed. Specifically, the standardized data of each driving factor of 18 cities (or counties) in Hainan island are substituted into each factor expression to calculate the factor score matrix; Standardize the number of overnight visitors in 18 cities (or counties) in Hainan island in 2020 to get another matrix; With the number of overnight visitors as the dependent variable and the driving factors (F_1, F_2) as the independent variables, a multiple regression model of the number of overnight visitors and the driving factors is obtained.

14.4 Results

14.4.1 Spatio-Temporal Characteristics of Hainan Tourism Under the COVID-19 Epidemic

14.4.1.1 Characteristics of Hainan Tourism Development Under COVID-19

Under the influence of COVID-19 epidemic, Hainan's tourism industry has been greatly affected. In 2020, the total tourism revenue of Hainan was 87.286 billion yuan, a year-on-year decrease of 17.48%, and the total number of domestic and foreign tourists received was 64.5509 million, a year-on-year decrease of 22.33%. By analyzing the change of the number of tourists every month, we found that: (1) In February, when the epidemic broke out in an all-round way, the number of tourists in Hainan showed a cliff-like decline. (2) After February, the number of domestic overnight visitors showed a gradual recovery. By August, the year-on-year growth of domestic overnight visitors had been positive, and it gradually entered a state of recovery. (3) The number of inbound overnight visitors has been in a downturn since February, as shown in Fig. 14.1. This is directly related to the proper control of COVID-19 epidemic in China and the tourists' confidence in domestic tourism soon. The rebound in the number of domestic overnight visitors reflects that

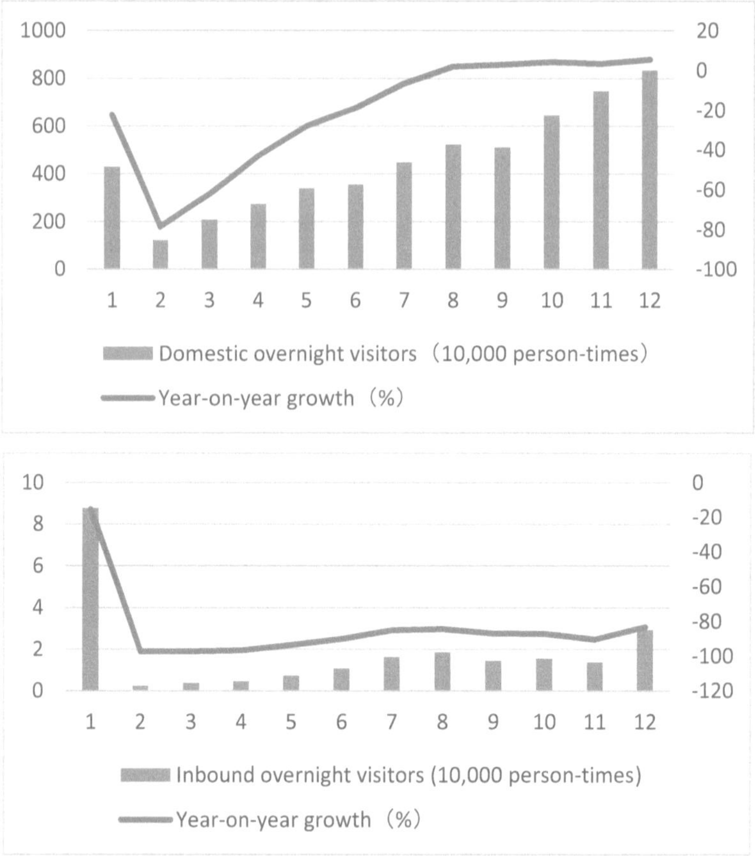

Fig. 14.1 Comparison of domestic overnight visitors and inbound overnight visitors in Hainan in 2020

the COVID-19 epidemic in China was properly controlled, and tourists soon regained confidence in domestic tourism.

Further analysis of the tourist sources in Hainan island shows that the tourists in Hainan island mainly come from domestic tourists, and the proportion of overseas tourists is very small. Before the outbreak of COVID-19, the proportion of inbound overnight visitors hovered around 2%. In 2020, under the impact of COVID-19, the proportion of inbound overnight visitors was only 0.41%, as shown in Fig. 14.2. For Hainan island, even though the number of overseas tourists fluctuates greatly, its contribution to the total amount is small, which will not affect the growth trend of the total number of tourists in Hainan island until 2019. Under the impact of the COVID-19 epidemic in 2020, the number of domestic tourists dropped sharply, resulting in a decrease in the total number of tourists. The daily leisure tourism demand of Hainan residents is small, and the tourism industry mainly serves tourists from other provinces.

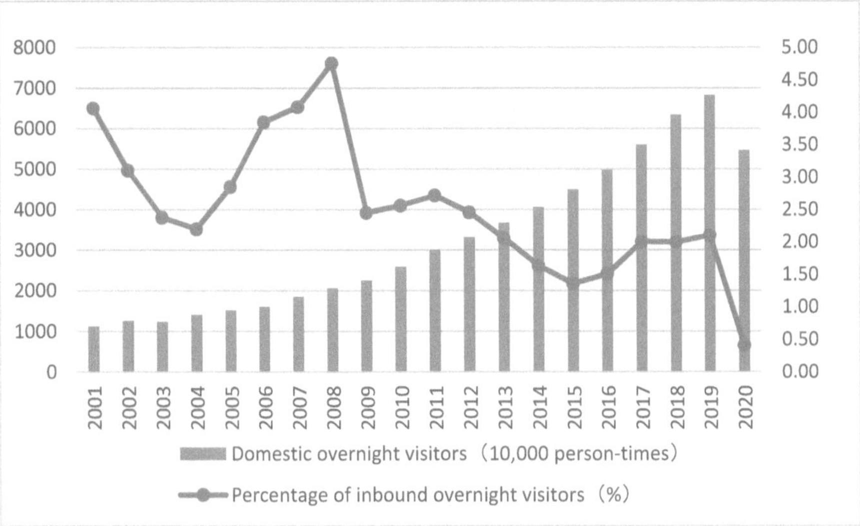

Fig. 14.2 The number of overnight visitors and the proportion of inbound overnight visitors from 2001 to 2020

14.4.1.2 Spatial Differences of Tourism Development in Hainan Under COVID-19

For a long time, the tourism industry in Hainan has been developing steadily with Sanya and Haikou as the north and south poles and other cities and counties. Haikou, located in the north of the island, is the financial, political, social and transportation hub of the region. Sanya, located at the southernmost tip of Hainan, has become the most popular tropical resort city in China (Xie, 2022). After the outbreak of the epidemic in COVID-19, the tourism industry of all cities (or counties) has been impacted. As can be seen from Fig. 14.2, the tourism industry in Hainan island under the COVID-19 epidemic in 2020 has not changed this pattern. Sanya and Haikou have the largest number of overnight visitors, reaching 17.55 million and 13.4 million respectively. Wenchang, Qionghai, Wanning and Lingshui, four cities and counties in the east, are located in the second echelon, with over 2.5 million overnight visitors. Except Danzhou, the number of overnight visitors in the central and western cities and counties is less than 2.5 million, especially Anding, Tunchang and Baisha in the middle, with the lowest number of visitors, no more than 500,000.

According to the difference between the number of overnight visitors received by each city (or county) in 2020 and the previous year, the tourism recovery level can be divided into five levels, among which Danzhou, Dongfang, Ledong, Baisha and Wenchang are the first, and the number of overnight visitors decreases by no more than 10% compared with the previous year; Qionghai, Lingshui, Tunchang, Chengmai and Lingao are in the second grade, with a decline of 10–20%; Sanya and Haikou are in the third grade, down by 24.1% and 23.3% respectively, and

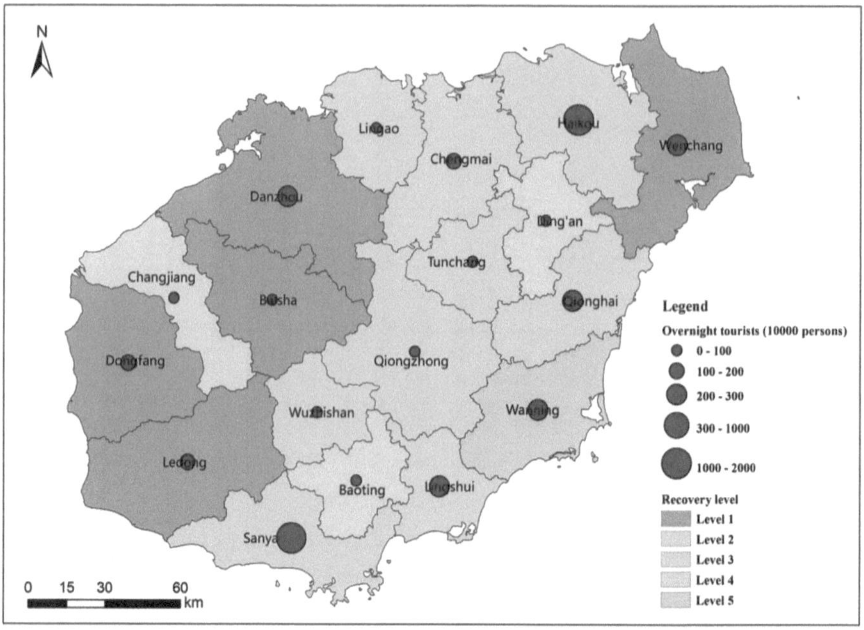

Fig. 14.3 The difference of overnight visitors and the distribution of tourism recovery level in Hainan island in 2020

Wuzhishan City and Qiongzhong County are also in the third grade; Anding, Baoting and Changjiang counties are located in the fourth grade, with a decline of 30–40%; Wanning is the region where the number of overnight tourists in the island has dropped the most, with a drop rate of 51.7%, and its tourism recovery level is ranked as the fifth grade (Fig. 14.3).

14.4.2 Driving Factors of Spatial Differences of Hainan Tourism under the COVID-19 Epidemic

As can be seen from Table 14.2, the cumulative variance contribution rate of the two factors reaches 80.414%, which can fully reflect the driving force information of Hainan tourism spatial differences represented by the original indicators. It is acceptable and scientific to extract the two factors, and the load of the two factors is shown in Table 14.3.

As can be seen from Table 14.2 and Table 14.3, the elgenvalue of the first factor (F_1) is 6.974, and the variance contribution rate is 69.739%. Nine variables, such as indexes x_1, x_2, x_3, x_4, x_5, x_6, x_7, x_9 and x_{10}, have the largest positive load on the common factor of F_1, which is positively correlated with F_1. Because the nine variables highly related to F_1 include all resource factors and economic factors, F_1 can be

Table 14.2 The elgenvalues and variances contribution rate

	Elgenvalue	Variances contribution rate (%)	Cumulative variance contribution rate(%)
F_1	6.974	69.739	69.739
F_2	1.067	10.675	80.414

Table 14.3 The loading matrix of factors

		Loading matrix of factors	
Type of indicator	Name of indicator	F_1	F_2
Resource factor	X_1	0.922	0.029
	X_2	0.881	0.018
Economic factor	X_3	0.928	−0.014
	X_4	0.715	0.256
	X_5	0.923	−0.002
	X_6	0.817	−0.033
Social factor	X_7	0.890	−0.084
	X_8	0.068	0.984
	X_9	0.907	−0.145
	X_{10}	0.915	−0.049

named as resource and economic factor. The factor score function calculated according to the regression algorithm is:

$$F_1 = 0.132x_1 + 0.126x_2 + 0.133x_3 + 0.103x_4 + 0.132x_5 + 0.117x_6 + 0.128x_7 + 0.01x_8 + 0.13x_9 + 0.131x_{10}.$$

The elgenvalue of the second factor (F_2) is 1.067, and the variance contribution rate is 10.675%. Index x_8 has the maximum load on F_2, which is positively correlated with F_2. Because there is only one index positively related to F_2, namely x_8, F_2 is named as the urban population density factor. The factor score function calculated according to the regression algorithm is:

$$F_2=0.027x_1+0.016x_2–0.013x_{3+}0.24x_4–0.002x_5–0.031x_6–0.079x_7+0.922x_8–0.136x_9–0.046x_{10}.$$

From the above quantitative analysis, it can be concluded that the driving factors of spatial differences of tourism in Hainan under the COVID-19 epidemic are resource and economic factor and urban population density factor.

14.4.3 Driving Mechanism of Spatial Difference of Hainan Tourism under the COVID-19 Epidemic

Through the above analysis, the regression model of Hainan tourism spatial difference under COVID-19 epidemic situation is obtained.

$Y = -0.115 + 0.991F_1 - 0.008F_2$.

Judging from the coefficient R^2 of regression equation is 0.895, two factors can explain 89.5% of Hainan's tourism spatial difference information, which indicates that these two factors have great influence on Hainan's tourism spatial difference under the epidemic situation of COVID-19. Moreover, the P value of variance analysis of regression model is 0.000, which is less than 0.05 significant level, indicating that the overall revealed variation of regression model has reached a significant level. First of all, judging from the coefficient of each influencing factor in the regression equation, the two factors have different effects on tourism development in different cities. The influence of resources and economic factor is the most important. For every increase of one unit, the number of overnight visitors in various cities increases by 0.991 units. The urban population density factor has a negative influence on the operation, and for every increase of one unit, the number of overnight visitors in various cities decreases by 0.008 units. The influence of resources and economic factor on the development of tourism industry has an absolute advantage. Secondly, judging from the coefficient symbols of the influencing factors in the regression equation, the influence of resources and economic factor on the development of tourism industry is positive, while the influence of urban population density factor on the development of tourism industry is negative.

14.5 Discussion and Conclusion

The main academic contributions of this research include the following three points: Firstly, the analysis framework of spatial differences-driving factors-driving mechanism is constructed, which provides a thinking framework for the research of spatial heterogeneity of tourism development. Tourism economic activities are characterized by spatial disequilibrium, so how to comprehensively and quantitatively study the reasons behind it is of great significance. This study rationalizes the analysis ideas of spatial differences by constructing an analysis framework of spatial differences-driving factors-driving mechanisms. Secondly, on the basis of constructing the index system of resource-economy-society driving factors in an all-round way, through factor analysis, two major factors that influence the spatial difference of tourism are obtained, namely, resource and economy factors and urban population density factors. Thirdly, through the analysis of driving mechanism, it is found that resources and economic factors have the most important influence on the spatial difference of tourism. For every increase of one unit, the number of overnight visitors in various cities increases by 0.991 units.

Under the influence of COVID-19 epidemic, Hainan's tourism industry has been greatly affected. In 2020, the total tourism revenue of Hainan island decreased by 17.48% year-on-year, and the total number of domestic and foreign tourists decreased by 22.33% year-on-year. After February, the number of domestic overnight visitors showed a gradual recovery. By August, the year-on-year growth of domestic overnight visitors had been positive, and it gradually entered a state of recovery. The number of overnight visitors has been in a low state since February. Further analysis of the tourist sources in Hainan island shows that the tourists in Hainan island mainly come from domestic tourists, and the proportion of overseas tourists is very small. Before the outbreak of COVID-19, the proportion of inbound overnight visitors hovered around 2%. Therefore, expanding the domestic market is the most important thing in the future.

There are obvious regional differences in Hainan's tourism. Sanya and Haikou are the north and south poles. In 2020, the number of their tourists accounted for nearly 60% of the total in the island. Under the epidemic situation, although it is a difficult development period for the whole industry (Yeh, 2020), it can also be seen that while the international tourism market is severely frustrated, the development potential of the domestic market is huge. Through the above analysis, we know that the driving factors of regional differences in tourism in Hainan are resources and economic factors. Therefore, there is still much to be done to promote regional coordinated development by optimizing the spatial layout in the future. Hainan is the first batch of pilot provinces for all-for-one tourism in China. All-for-one tourism is a new concept and model in tourism, that is, regional tourism is planned and constructed as a whole tourist area. By giving full play to Hainan's location and resource advantages, effectively integrating resources and coordinating resources, transportation, products and services, the overall development of Hainan's tourism industry and regional coordination will be promoted.

Tourism is very sensitive and easily affected by meteorological disasters, geological disasters and infectious diseases. In particular, the COVID-19 epidemic has caused unprecedented public panic (Zheng et al., 2021), which has a long-term impact on global economic flows, tourism and everyone (Gajic et al., 2023). During the epidemic, tourists' willingness and habits to travel have been affected accordingly, and new changes have taken place in tourism demand (Gyimóthy et al., 2022). In order to cope with these challenges, tourism organizations need to adapt to the ever-changing environment to achieve continuous resilience (Lengnick-Hall et al., 2011; Jiang et al., 2021). Resilience is used to describe the ability of a system to resist and respond to crises and disasters. Specifically, it refers to "the ability of a system to absorb interference and reorganization when it experiences changes, so that it still maintains basically the same functions, structures, characteristics and feedback" (Walker et al., 2004; Guo et al., 2018). At present, under the influence of COVID-19 epidemic, tourism has been greatly affected. How to fully consider the resilience of tourism? The measures of "integrating resources to expand the domestic market" put forward above are to think about the resilience of tourism, that is, to adjust the organization and structure of tourism activities in time to cope with the current crisis.

References

Baldwin, R., & Di Mauro, B. W. (2020). *Economics in the time of COVID-19*. Centre for Economic Policy Research.

China News Network. The total number of inbound and outbound tourists of 2019 in China was 300 million, a year-on-year increase of 3.1%. https://baijiahao.baidu.com/s?id=1660774105220595490&wfr=spider&for=pc

Chirwa, P. W., Kamwi, J. M., Kabia, G., Makhubele, L., Sagona, W., Matakala, N., et al. (2021). The impacts of covid-19 on the sustainable management of the forestry sector in southern Africa. *International Forestry Review, 23*(3), 298–308.

Gabriel-Campos, E., Werner-Masters, K., Cordova-Buiza, F., & Paucar-Caceres, A. (2021). Community eco-tourism in rural Peru: Resilience and adaptive capacities to the Covid-19 pandemic and climate change. *Journal of Hospitality and Tourism Management, 48*, 416–427.

Gajic, T., Petrovic, M. D., Blešic, I., Radovanovic, M. M., & Syromiatnikova, J. A. (2023). The power of fears in the travel decision—Covid-19 against lack of money. *Journal of Tourism Futures, 9*(1), 62–83

Guo, Y., Zhang, J., Zhang, Y., & Zheng, C. (2018). Catalyst or barrier? The influence of place attachment on perceived community resilience in tourism destinations. *Sustainability, 10*(7), 2347.

Gyimóthy, S., Braun, E., & Zenker, S. (2022). Travel-at-home: Paradoxical effects of a pandemic threat on domestic tourism. *Tourism Management, 93*, 104613.

Haddock-Fraser, J., & Hampton, M. P. (2012). Multistakeholder values on the sustainability of dive tourism: Case studies of Sipadan and Perhentian Islands, Malaysia. *Tourism Analysis, 17*(1), 27–41.

Hampton, M. P., & Jeyacheya, J. (2013). *Tourism and inclusive growth in small Island developing states*. The Commonwealth Secretariat.

Huynh, T. L. D. (2020). The COVID-19 risk perception: A survey on socio-economics and media attention. *Economics Bulletin., 40*(1), 758–764.

Jiang, Y., Ritchie, B. W., & Verreynne, M.-L. (2021). Developing disaster resilience: A processual and reflective approach. *Tourism Management, 87*, 104374.

Karabulut, G., Bilgin, M. H., Demir, E., & Doker, A. C. (2020). How pandemics affect tourism: International evidence. *Annals of Tourism Research, 2020*(84), 102991.

Koodsela, W., Dong, H., & Sukpatch, K. (2019). A holistic conceptual framework into practice-based on urban tourism toward sustainable development in Thailand. *Sustainability, 11*, 7152.

Lengnick-Hall, C. A., Beck, T. E., & Lengnick-Hall, M. L. (2011). Developing a capacity for organizational resilience through strategic human resource management. *Human Resource Management Review, 21*(3), 243–255.

Luck, M. (2008). *Encyclopedia of tourism and recreation in marine environments*. CABI.

Miller, M. L., & Auyong, J. (1991). Coastal zone tourism: A potent force affecting environment and society. *Marine Policy, 15*(2), 75–99.

Priskin, J. (2001). Assessment of natural resources for nature-based tourism: The case of the central coast region of Western Australia. *Tourism Management, 22*(6), 637–648.

Ruiz-Estrada, M. A., Park, D., & Lee, M. (2020, July). *The evaluation of the final impact of Wuhan COVID-19 on trade, tourism, transport, and electricity consumption of China*. Available: https://ssrn.com/abstract=3551093

Samarathunga, W., & Gamage, D.. (2020). Alternative tourism as an alternate to mass tourism during the post-COVID-19 recovery phase: The case of Sri Lanka

Shao, Y., Hu, Z., Luo, M., Huo, T., & Zhao, Q. (2020). *What is the policy focus for tourism recovery after the outbreak of COVID-19? A co-word analysis Current Issues in Tourism*. (pp. 1–6). Springer International Publishing.

Shi, P., Wang, Z., & Li, W. (2012). Spatial-temporal pattern of tourism economic differences in Gansu Province. *Applied Mechanics and Materials, 137*, 335–343.

Sohn, J. I., Alakshendra, A., Kim, H. J., Kim, K. H., & Kim, H. D. (2021). Understanding the new characteristics and development strategies of coastal tourism for post-COVID-19: A case study in Korea. *Sustainability, 13*(13), 7408.

United Nations World Tourism Organization. (2020). International tourism growth continues to outpace the global economy

Van der Merwe, P., Saayman, A., & Jacobs, C. (2021). Assessing the economic impact of COVID-19 on the private wildlife industry of South Africa. *Global Ecology and Conservation, 28*, e01633.

Walker, B., Holling, C. S., Carpenter, S. R., & Kinzig, A. (2004). Resilience, adaptability and transformability in social-ecological systems. *Ecological and Society., 9*(2), 5.

Wang, J., & Xia, J. (2018). Study on the spatial network structure of the tourism economy in China and its influencing factors: Investigation of QAP method. *Tourism Tribune, 33*, 13–25.

Wei, J., Zhong, Y., & Fan, J. (2022). Estimating the spatial heterogeneity and seasonal differences of the contribution of tourism industry activities to night light index by POI. *Sustainability, 14*, 692.

World Tourism Organization. (2019). *International tourism highlights*, (2019th ed., pp. 2). UNWTO.

World Travel and Tourism Council. (2021). *Economic Impact Reports*. https://wttc.org/Research/Economic-Impact

Xie, X. (2022). Analysis of spatial and temporal differences in China's provincial tourism economy based on parallel data model and IoT applications wireless communications and mobile computing, 1431345

Yeh, S.-S. (2020). Tourism recovery strategy against COVID-19 pandemic. *Tourism Recreation Research*, 1–7.

Zhang, S., & Ju, H. (2021). The regional differences and influencing factors of tourism development on Hainan Island, China. *PLoSONE, 16*(10), e0258407.

Zhang, G., & Yuan, H. (2022). Spatio-temporal evolution characteristics and spatial differences in urban tourism network attention in China: Based on the Baidu index. *Sustainability, 14*, 13252.

Zhang, T., Wang, Y., Zhang, S., & Wang, Y. (2022). An estimation and development model of tourism resource values at the township scale on Hainan Island, China. *Plos ONE, 17*(1), e0262837.

Zheng, D., Luo, Q., & Ritchie, B. W. (2021). Afraid to travel after COVID-19? Self-protection, coping and resilience against pandemic 'travel fear'. *Tourism Management, 83*, 104261.

Chapter 15
A Conceptual Framework for Supporting High-Value Innovation in the Large Medical Technology Industry

Hemant Vilas Belsare, Jireh Hooi Inn Seow, and C. J. Meadows

Abstract This paper proposes a conceptual framework that identifies internal and external elements that support high-value innovation in the large medical technology industry in North America, Europe, and Asia. While there are several types of innovations, including open, closed, incremental, sustaining, radical, and disruptive, this study focuses on high-value innovation. High-value innovation involves the pursuit of differentiation, cost, quality, and scalability, all at the same time. The traditional approach to market differentiation is to pick between the contrast of higher-value and lower-cost, but when low-cost, high-value, high-quality, and scalability are effectively integrated, this is regarded a movement toward attaining high-value innovation. So far, there is lack of literature on the factors that drive high-value innovation in large medical technology enterprises. There are very few studies on how new insights might be leveraged to develop effective responses to the internal and external environmental factors of innovation so as to inform the top management of the large medical technology industry. As such, this study aims to provide new insights into successful responses to internal and external environmental factors of high-value innovation to the top management of such firms. This model is based on a systematic literature review of most relevant ABDC journal publications and unstructured interviews with management and professionals in the large medical technology industry. Future research on confirming this conceptual framework as well as discovering the most and least influential factors of high-value innovation will involve the formal collection and analyses of empirical data.

Keywords Innovation · Medical technology industry · Large firms · Business model · Entrepreneurship orientation

H. V. Belsare (✉)
SP Jain School of Global Management, Sydney, Australia
e-mail: hemant.ds20dba029@spjain.org

J. H. I. Seow · C. J. Meadows
SP Jain School of Global Management, HortPark, Singapore
e-mail: jireh.seowhi@spjain.org; cj.meadows@spjain.org

E. L. Eijdenberg et al. (eds.), *Innovation-Driven Business and Sustainability in the Tropics*, https://doi.org/10.1007/978-981-99-2909-2_15

15.1 Introduction

That global healthcare expenditure is on the rise is no secret. With longer life expectancies creating a higher geriatric population, an increased demand for high-performing medical technology has been witnessed across the board. As a result, there will be a greater need for cutting-edge medical technology (Medtech). More stringent regulations, especially in the U.S. and European markets, forces medical-device makers to release complex products that include cutting-edge technology and innovations that emerged from the cross-pollinating applications from one sector to another (Boisseau et al., 2020).

Because of the intense competition in the Medtech industry, businesses in this sector will need to regularly revamp their product lines in order to keep up with the market and establish themselves as leaders in the healthcare system. The healthcare industry is evolving into one where prices and purchases are determined by the results they provide. Consequently, there is more competitiveness and closer assessment of technological developments (Malodia et al., 2020).

More than 40% of companies concentrate their innovation efforts on product performance, increasing value through complementary services, enhancing the services they provide, and fostering compelling customer interactions. In one of research conducted in EU in 2018 related to innovation, 80% of respondents stated that their company will increase innovation investments over the next 2 years' time-frame. Simply increasing innovation budgets will not be sufficient to become innovative in the new era and in volatility, uncertainty, complexity, and ambiguity (VUCA) world. The combination of numerous types of innovation, the implementation of suitable innovation strategies and methods, and the integration of digital technologies into companies will be decisive. It's a need that innovation must be embedded into the DNA of organizations and shall not be just limited about experimenting with new technologies or focusing on product features and performance (Deloitte, 2018).

The market for medical devices is expected to expand rapidly in the next years, with yearly sales increasing by more than 5% worldwide to approximately US$800 billion by 2030 (KPMG, 2019). Figure 15.1 represents global Medtech industry sales forecast to 2030, shows year vs US revenue in billion dollars with compound annual growth rate (CAGR). These forecasts reflect the growing need for cutting-edge products and services as the incidence of lifestyle-related disorders rises and the vast untapped potential in both established and developing economies, especially China and India, is unlocked by economic growth (KPMG, 2019).

Despite these seemingly promising possibilities, the Medtech industry is plagued by a persistent downward pressure on price due to governments throughout the globe frantically wanting to decrease the cost of healthcare.

These changes create a predicament for medical device businesses, which have traditionally prioritized production and research and development (R&D), but increasingly find their profit margins eroded by rising healthcare costs and shifting payment policies. This brings in innovation at healthcare within Medtech industry

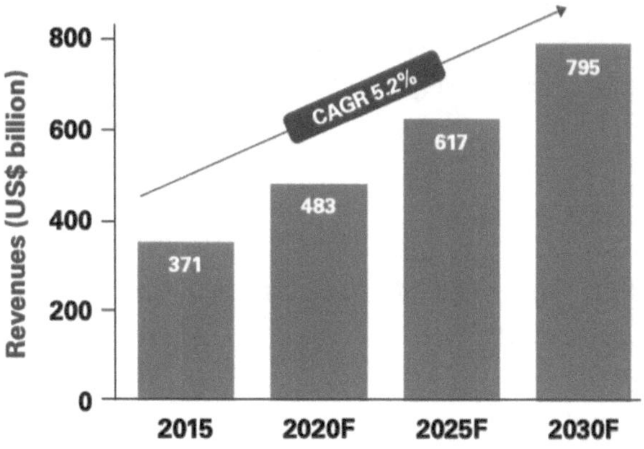

Fig. 15.1 Global Medtech industry sales forecast to 2030

at forefront to accomplish the goals by overcoming challenges of cost, budget, quality, speed, agility, and volume delivery with satisfaction to the customers.

Healthcare innovation enhances efficacy, quality, sustainability, safety, or cost (Marone et al., 2020). Many healthcare practitioners throughout the globe are using innovative strategies to enhance diagnosis, treatment alternatives, preventative education, and community access to services. Patients require new solutions to diagnose and treat severe chronic and acute illnesses, improve healthcare access and cost, and promote health equality for marginalized groups (Marone et al., 2020). Innovators approach these problems to enhance clinical, economic, and social health outcomes for patients, providers, and healthcare systems.

This paper investigates impact of innovation and related factors which are critical to the large firm in the MedTech industry. The aim of this research is to study a med-tech innovation process. This research implies a scrutiny of the possibilities and limitations of innovation in making contributions to the large MedTech firms.

A key research gap exists:

- in the mobilisation of large firm's internal and external determinants to create high-value innovation impact in MedTech industry to meet unmet consumer requirements and accomplish corporate growth performance.
- as, so far, the research has concentrated on the possibility for innovation in a wide range of fields within SMEs, rather than specifically in the MedTech within large firms.
- as very little has been written on high-value innovation in MedTech industry about large firms in North America, Europe, Asia.

Real value is the new success mantra, prevention the preferable healthcare result, and intellect the new significant advantage by utilizing high-value innovation framework. This article will describe how large Medtech companies can innovate following a high-value innovation strategy which is a differentiator with key elements considering speed, cost, quality, and scale or volume. This will support large

Medtech companies to examine current organizations and rethink business and operational paradigms, in several areas including product, marketing, processes, business and service innovation (Boisseau et al., 2020).

15.2 Literature Review

15.2.1 The Definition of Medtech and the Background of the Industry

Medtech, or medical technology, is any kind of technology, be it a product, device, service, or solution that improves human health, including preventing, diagnosing, monitoring, and treating diseases (Nyåkern, 2020).

The Medtech business covers more than 500,000 items, from needles to high-cost and complex medical devices or electrocardiographs. As per the World Health Organization (WHO), it incorporates all instruments, apparatuses, and materials that are intended for indicative as well as restorative purposes to screen, treat, predict, or ease illness, wounds/diseases and that don't rigorously accomplish their activity by pharmacological, immunological, or metabolic means. These all devices are recognized in four categories of items dependent on complexity: disposables (needles, needles, swathes, careful gloves, and so forth), clinical and surgical instruments (dental instruments, dialysis, defibrillators, and so on), therapeutic devices (man-made created parts, 3D prints, hearing devices, inserts, and so on) and symptomatic and imaging devices (ultrasound, electrocardiographs, X-ray, X-beams, etc.) (Baharun et al., 2019).

The Medtech business is exceptionally inventive. Medtech items ordinarily have a lifecycle of just 18 months to 2 years. Like different ventures, increasing expenses (of the medical care framework overall) have compelled for new procedures as far as creation and acquirement Area choices, aside from costs, accessibility of workforce and distance to the market are likewise influenced by guidelines. With expanding item complexity, the administrative necessities are a lot stricter. This is related with higher vertical grouping or integration, and it is one reason why numerous exercises are kept in-house. The Medtech area additionally faces a few difficulties, especially those related with shifts in repayment, buyer strengthening, and computerized enablement.

15.2.2 Definition of High-Value Innovation for Research

High-value innovation is the simultaneous pursuit of differentiation, low cost, quality and scalability. The conventional approach to market differentiation is to choose between higher value and lower cost. But when successfully combined the low cost, high value, high quality and scalable, which to be considered as movement of needle towards achieving high-value innovation.

Innovation is the predilection of organizations to inducement in and support inquisitiveness, novel thoughts, imaginative cycles, and examinations that lead to new items or new innovative products or processes. Imaginativeness can likewise be viewed as inventive annihilation, specifically the pathway towards creativity which can disrupt economic situations and animate new interest from contenders. Innovation is a thought, practice or item that is acknowledged and acknowledged as something new by an individual or groups to be taken on for development in product, process, marketing, organization management. Innovation can be described as newness, either novel actions or novel uses of established practices, better approaches to support execution as far as sales, productivity, and market share in an association (Asemokha et al., 2019).

High-value innovation concept is quite far from the open, closed, sustenance, incremental radical, and disruptive innovation. High-value innovation brings in multiple aspects such as quality, cost, value differentiator, speed or agility and scale of volume without compromising traditional ways of either between cost or quality.

15.2.3 Conceptual Framework

The thorough review of the existing literature helped to identify the research gaps and to determine six independent variables and their sub-variables. The research framework arrived at through the literature review is provided in the Fig. 15.2 as shown below.

The Fig. 15.2 is a framework which illustrates the relationship between the identified input independent variables (the six variables mentioned on the left side of the figure), namely – research and development, business management system, entrepreneurship orientation and dynamics, business process management, product portfolio management, product portfolio management, service delivery and management and the benefits they could generate for large Medtech companies. Impact of determinants of the high-value innovation in Medtech industry is the dependent variable research process and which is shown at the center of the Fig. 15.2. At the right side of the Fig. 15.2, which represents the outcomes/measures with reference to each input independent variables.

This research framework developed from the research gaps, which in-turn helped to build the research objectives and research questions along with the hypothesis to test the overall framework.

Following are the specific internal and external determinants of the high-value innovation.

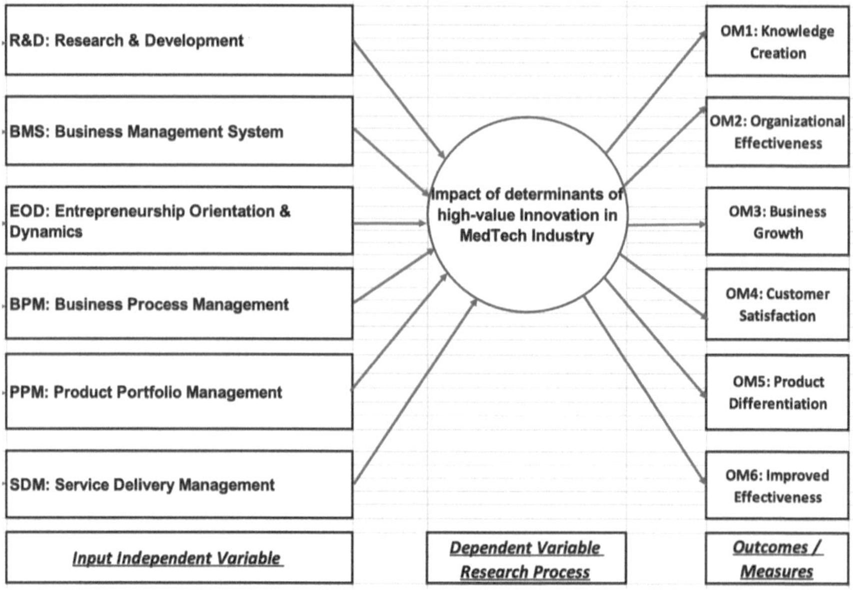

Fig. 15.2 Conceptual research framework for high-value innovation

15.2.4 Determinants of High-Value Innovation

15.2.4.1 Research and Development

R&D in medical technology is responding with new products and services to the changing landscape of healthcare. R&D is also finding new approaches to innovation by searching broadly for ideas that can be implemented in the healthcare industry as new solutions. Collaboration among governments, companies, universities, clinicians, and investors is a necessary feature for these new approaches to be successful. They also anticipate an increasing emphasis on open innovation, that facilitates cooperation in research and development among companies from a wide range of industries (Schuhmacher et al., 2018).

The Medtech ecosystem is changing, and rapid technological advancements are opening new avenues for progress in the healthcare industry (Espinoza et al., 2020). Meaningful innovation can take many forms, such as a novel approach to making a product useful to applying a growing technology to a real-world problem. In this scenario, investing in research and development acquires greater significance as it is focused on transformative innovation to develop breakthrough solutions or products to solve unmet market demands (Schuhmacher et al., 2018).

Companies also use mergers, acquisitions, and partnerships as forms of R&D. By merger and acquisitions (M&A) organization benefits from each other's talent and expertise (Marone et al., 2020). Based in on the literature review for this study research and development can be further sub divided ion to elements of digitalization and emerging business model, new product development, sustainability, technology and advancement, and innovation capabilities as sub independent variables (Kalita, 2017).

15.2.4.2 Business Management System

Business management system includes provisions and methodologies utilized by the organization to guarantee that it can satisfy the undertakings needed to accomplish its goals and objectives (Cantwell, 2021). These goals and objectives cover numerous parts of the association's tasks (organizational, business model innovation, economic success, safety, product quality, customer connections, administrative and administrative conformance, and associate engagements) (Winterhalter et al., 2017).

Within overall management structure, system aspects an organizational innovation is a very impotent parameter for the growth of the medical technology companies (Halfmann et al., 2019). Innovation in work environment include the execution of new strategies for distributing roles and responsibilities and for dynamic decision making among organization's associates for the division of work inside and between organization's activities (Tohmo & Storhammar, 2019).

The board framework support as a construction for the way toward interpreting a thought or idea into invention and development into a decent product and services that makes organization worth. Quality management system, Regulatory with ISO, FDA, CFDA, etc. are the prominent and inherent part of the management system in Medtech product industry despite small or large organization (Winterhalter et al., 2017). This is considered as non-technical innovation development, which is the execution of another firm's technique in the firm business practice, work area association or outer relations. It incorporates the creation of information, advancement and advertising, and the presentation of another, updated, or significantly improvement in the labour and products delivered to the public. Business management system can be studied further by categorizing them into sub-independent variables such as organizational behaviour, specificity and talent management, quality management, growth mindset and leadership, firms values and behaviour, learning and development (L&D) (Fitriati et al., 2020).

15.2.4.3 Business Process Management

Process Management majorly signifies alignment of the various processes of the organization in perspective towards supporting innovation practices which helps organization's alignment towards innovation and strategic goals. Developing process, educating managers and associates of the organization in the direction of the expected outcome for the customer satisfaction (Cantwell, 2021). Process innovation plays instrumental role within this environment. Process innovation management also gives perspective on how products or services are developed, managed, and distributed. This also means that looking holistically towards the entire process system towards automation for manufacturing and digitization and many more areas (Ha et al., 2018).

Further process management is broken into various sub-independent variable based on the literature review conducted: operational transformation and delivery, process performance and analysis, implementation process open innovation, dynamic capabilities, standard and regulations, and compliance (Kalita, 2017). Within overall larger frame of process management probable settings that can favor the deployment of open innovation in firms, by collaboration, M&As, knowledge transfer, distribution of information between establishments, approaching of investors, and legal motivation for innovation (Gama et al., 2019).

15.2.4.4 Product Portfolio Management

Product management is very instrumental in managing the end-to-end product portfolio for the key outcome to the organization which may include product differentiator over competition and many more attributes (Expósito & Sanchis-Llopis, 2019). Bringing product differentiation can be achieved by product innovation. Product management cuts across many functions like research and development medical affairs quality and regulatory manufacturing and generally ownership stays within marketing with some overlap with respective heads of the R&D (Markovic et al., 2021). Product innovation is one of the key elements of product management it can come through various channels few of the channels could be complaint handling for the existing product understanding unmet need of the customer understanding improvement opportunity within the existing processes or defining forward thinking to identify and deploy what customer may want to do with the product in future (De Oliveira et al., 2019).

Firms annual strategic review is key area leverage for overall project management activities. Annual strategic review encompass is all attributes including budget finance head count competencies capabilities investments an expected return. Product management can be categorized into two high level groups, first one to name is inbound development which is nothing but product development and outbound development which is nothing but product marketing department (Mennens et al., 2018). Inorganic and organic product development is part of the portfolio decision making capabilities based on the information available from the technical scouting, white papers, and market research and reports.

Furthermore, product management has been broken down into more sub independent variables such as product life cycle management and sustenance engineering, customer experience, product innovation and analytics and product cost, timeline, quality, and scale (CTQS).

15.2.4.5 Service Delivery and Management

Service delivery is taking a huge leap in maintaining products and managing end to end product lifecycle management. Some of the products designed for 15 years of life and considering service strategy at the time of product development has very relevant inputs to consider. Service strategy hover on the selection of the components, design of the assembly, selection of the processes, application into account at very early stage of the development (Mugogo & Salau, 2020). Service strategy also help in building product cost architecture from gross profit to service margins. Customers looks at service plan and cost associated with the plans while making decisions to buy between competition (Mennens et al., 2018). Based on the funding availability customers viewpoint keeps hovering on high product cost and less service plans and/or comparatively less upfront investment but go for higher service plans (Mazumdar-Shaw, 2018). Also, several innovative service business models have been evolving within environment by sub-contracting the model purchase and pay by usages in actual. New models also have substantial gain but with higher usage cost vs lower or zero basis investment (Trosman et al., 2017).

Furthermore, service delivery management has been broken down into more sub independent variables such as service ecosystem approach, reshaping and reconfigurations, service process, servitization (systemic and relational nature of service innovation), and remote service design and automation.

15.2.4.6 Entrepreneurship Orientation and Dynamics

Entrepreneurship orientation or marketing innovation and performance is an instrumental key factor on the growth in medical technology. Several aspects of market are into key consideration for innovation such as – economics, B2B openness, business demography, effective adoption, outbound innovation, entrepreneurial orientation, emerging market etc. (Ribau et al., 2017). The organization's performance can be evaluated through sales revenue, market share, profitability, competitive advantage, customer satisfaction and loyalty (Saunila, 2017). It's understood from some of the research which demonstrated that entrepreneurial orientation which had a significant constructive effect on business model innovation (Peter et al., 2020). In addition, study can broaden the understanding of the organization's capability to develop innovative ideas which help organization to achieve their innovation goals (Sriboonlue & Puangpronpitag, 2019).

Territorial development framework are potential conditions that can support the execution of open advancement in large Medtech companies, by participation, organizations, mechanical exchanges, sharing of information among public and private foundations, and legitimate upgrade for advancement (Malodia et al., 2020). The financial impacts might depict diversely particularly for each geography, separately area in North America, Europe, and Asia etc. Furthermore, thus study can be fundamentally pointed towards exactly inspecting the interrelated connections that exist among different builds (i.e., brand direction, brand trust, brand value, innovation, execution, and financial capabilities) (Afriyie et al., 2018). This will likewise add to new knowledge/information on the space of medical care and technology domain, and support to distinguish the prominent influences on the economy and promoting innovation perspective (Davide, 2021).

15.2.5 Research Methodology

This study used mixed method research methodology. First phase of study has involved a detailed critical literature review from the secondary sources exploring methodically plethora of articles published in leading international publications. A detailed mapping of the research gap, problem, questions, objectives, and hypothesis are done.

Secondary data gathered from an in-depth literature review of quality academic journals, which aid in recognizing scope for future research and lead to the identification of a dependent variable and five independent variables. Numerous literature studies, industry reports, and proceedings are used for this study. The information and data are gathered from sources like ProQuest, Ebscohost, Google scholar, and research gate. McKinsey, Deloitte, HBR, and Gartner reports are used for an extensive understanding of the current market scope and future needs of the company and customer. Literature contributed by international researchers published in A grade and peer-evaluated globally recognized journals mostly listed in ISI Thomson (Clarivate analytics) was reviewed and referenced appropriately. All latest and time-honored articles are reviewed and part of the literature review for this research. Quality, significance, and practicality principles are strictly followed while literature survey which is the major strength of the research.

Concurrently, there were 10 unstructured interviews conducted successfully. Participants were from large firms Medtech industry who are CEOs, CXOs, executives, managers, associates, and their stake holders and spread across continents of North America, Europe and Asia. Each interview was focused for approximately about 30 to 40 minutes duration of time with pre-planned appointment of an interviewee. E-mail appointment letter were sent to confirm the participation and the mode of interview. There were about 5–6 questions asked to the each of the interviewee. Few questions were prepared in advance in relation to a topic which researcher wished to cover. This nature of conversation allowed for spontaneity and for questions to develop during the course of the interview, which are based on the interviewees' responses. Unstructured interviews helped while hypotheses were developed and being open discovering new or shifting viewpoints. Also, it helped in seeking descriptive data, and being ready to ask questions that will deepen and contextualize initial thoughts and hypotheses. Post processing was conducted by coding/decoding the written scripting of an interview and relating to the outcome of the literature review for finalizing the conceptual framework.

First phase outcome is formation of the research model or construct based on the detailed critical literature review from the secondary sources and exploratory interviews conducted with industry experts globally.

The second phase of the research is to test and validate the established model which involves developing a questionnaire incorporating all variables as established from critical literature review and exploratory interviews. This is part of second phase of the research which is explained as in the future scope section.

15.3 Benefits of the Research – Outcome Measurements

Having looked at the independent variables and their sub-variables that the research study identified, the following section provides the outcome measures and the benefits of the research through the dependent variable as high-value innovation in large Medtech industry. A detailed study is performed to develop a conceptual framework, which as demonstrated in Fig. 15.2. Based on the conceptual framework and solution, significance of R&D in core innovation capabilities will be implicit to the CEOs and CXOs of the firm for the knowledge creation. This study will also be facilitated by bringing focus on business process management in gaining customer satisfaction and by exploring business management system for organizational effectiveness for the large Medtech organizations. Deep understanding of the Service delivery and management elements supports to bring improved effectiveness in the service operations end to end (AlQershi et al., 2018). Entrepreneurship orientation and dynamics and product portfolio management gives business growth and product differentiation to the enhanced differentiated portfolio.

15.4 Future Scope and Limitation

Future scope and as a next step, the influence of each variable will be tested for identifying the impact of external and internal determinants for large Medtech industry in North America, Asia, and Europe regions. This research and the framework have six objectives pertaining to the six independent variables: R&D, business management system, entrepreneurship orientation and dynamics, business process management, product portfolio management, service delivery and management. This research paper instituted six benefits or outcome measures which are understood by studying, impact of determinants of high-value innovation in Medtech industry, which are: knowledge creation, organizational effectiveness, business growth, customer satisfaction, product differentiation, and improved effectiveness.

This framework has some limitations, one of them is that it can only be applied for large Medtech companies; thus, this framework would not be applicable to small and medium enterprises within the Medtech industry or any company outside of the

Medtech industry without further study of the internal and external determinants considering potential differences and market dynamics.

15.5 Conclusion

This model is established based on a mixed research methodology. Large firms in medical technology industry will be benefited from this research by understanding the critical factors from innovation perspective. This will inform strategic decision at many levels within the medical technology industry including entrepreneurs, incumbent firms, investors, and technology transfer offices. This shall help them to re-focus and improvise their overall innovation practices to achieve high value innovation within their organization. As second part of the study, this framework needs further testing and validation. Post validity of the framework this research will include managerial implications and strategic recommendations taking into account the impact of determinants on high value innovation in large Medtech industry. This model can be used by large Medtech organization, based on the most and the least significant external and internal environments determinants impacting high-value innovation. This research could help the large firms enjoy benefits in building a very strong innovation pipeline, before moving rapidly on projects to gain momentum into the product development phase.

References

Afriyie, S., Duo, J., & Musah, A.-A. I. (2018). The nexus between innovation types and marketing performance of SMEs in an emerging economy: The mediating role of knowledge sharing. *Journal of Economics, Management and Trade, 21*(10), 1–22. https://doi.org/10.9734/jemt/2018/44223

AlQershi, N., Abas, Z., & Mohd Mokhtar, S. S. (2018). Strategic innovations driver for SME performance in Yemen. *Journal of Technology and Operations Management, 13*(1), 30–41. https://doi.org/10.32890/jtom2018.13.1.4

Asemokha, A., Musona, J., Torkkeli, L., & Saarenketo, S. (2019). Business model innovation and entrepreneurial orientation relationships in SMEs: Implications for international performance. *Journal of International Entrepreneurship, 17*(3), 425–453. https://doi.org/10.1007/s10843-019-00254-3

Baharun, R., Mi, T. J., Streimikiene, D., Mardani, A., Shakeel, J., & Nitsenko, V. (2019). Innovation in healthcare performance among private brand's healthcare services in small and medium-sized enterprises (Smes). *Acta Polytechnica Hungarica, 16*(5), 151–172. https://doi.org/10.12700/APH.16.5.2019.5.9

Boisseau, P., Küttel, O., Draaisma, A., & Condoluci, G. (2020). Innovation in medical technologies. *MedTech Europe*, 1–34.

Cantwell, J. (2021). A study of the impact of managerial innovation on SME performance in Africa: The case of Cameroon. *A Journal of Economics and Social Research, 7*(1), 1–38. https://doi.org/10.1093/oxfordhb/9780199286805.003.0020

Davide, M. (2021). The drivers of SME innovation in the regions of the EU. *Research Policy, 50*. https://doi.org/10.1016/j.respol.2021.104316

De Oliveira, L. S., Soares Echeveste, M. E., Cortimiglia, M. N., & Gularte, A. C. (2019). Open innovation in regional innovation systems: Assessment of critical success factors for implementation in SMEs. *Journal of the Knowledge Economy, 10*(4), 1597–1619. https://doi.org/10.1007/s13132-019-00619-y

Deloitte. (2018, November 1–15). *The Deloitte Innovation Survey: The case of Greece.*

Espinoza, J., Cooper, K., Afari, N., Shah, P., Batchu, S., & Bar-Cohen, Y. (2020). Innovation in Paediatric medical devices: Proceedings from the west coast consortium for Technology & Innovation in Paediatrics 2019 annual stakeholder summit. *JMIR Biomedical Engineering, 5*(1), e17467. https://doi.org/10.2196/17467

Expósito, A., & Sanchis-Llopis, J. A. (2019). The relationship between types of innovation and SMEs' performance: A multi-dimensional empirical assessment. *Eurasian Business Review, 9*(2), 115–135.

Fitriati, T. K., Purwana, D., & Buchdadi, A. D. (2020). The role of innovation in improving small medium enterprise (SME) performance. *International Journal of Innovation, Creativity and Change, 11*(2), 232–250.

Gama, F., Frishammar, J., & Parida, V. (2019). Idea generation and open innovation in SMEs: When does market-based collaboration pay off most? *Creativity and Innovation Management, 28*(1), 113–123. https://doi.org/10.1111/caim.12274

Ha, S.-T., Lo, M.-C., Mohamad, A. A., & Ramayah, T. (2018). Determinants of innovation performance among SMEs: Moderating effect of entrepreneurial orientation. *Global Business & Management Research, 10*(2), 241–252. https://search.ebscohost.com/login.aspx?direct=true&db=bth&AN=133000727&site=ehost-live

Halfmann, S. S. G., Evangelatos, N., Kweyu, E., Devilliers, C., Steinhausen, K., Van Der Merwe, A., & Brand, A. (2019). The creation and management of Innovations in healthcare and ICT: The European and African experience. *Public Health Genomics, 21*(5–6), 197–206. https://doi.org/10.1159/000499853

Kalita, A. (2017). The innovation performance of Russian SMEs: The role of internal factors and the external transition context. *Journal of Business Management, 13*, 20–39.

KPMG. (2019, December). KPMG report on medical device outlook to 2030. *ISSUE*. https://issuu.com/healthcaresalesandmarketingmagazine/docs/hsm_201911_v4/s/10791943

Malodia, S., Gupta, S., & Jaiswal, A. K. (2020). Reverse innovation: A conceptual framework. *Journal of the Academy of Marketing Science, 48*(5), 1009–1029. https://doi.org/10.1007/s11747-019-00703-4

Markovic, S., Koporcic, N., Arslanagic-Kalajdzic, M., Kadic-Maglajlic, S., Bagherzadeh, M., & Islam, N. (2021). Business-to-business open innovation: COVID-19 lessons for small and medium-sized enterprises from emerging markets. *Technological Forecasting and Social Change, 170*, 120883. https://doi.org/10.1016/j.techfore.2021.120883

Marone, L., Onofrio, R., & Masella, C. (2020). The Italian case of Lecco innovation living lab: Stakeholders' needs and activities to contribute to the technological innovation process in healthcare. *Sustainability (Switzerland), 12*(24), 1–15. https://doi.org/10.3390/su122410266

Mazumdar-Shaw, K. (2018). Leveraging affordable innovation to tackle India's healthcare challenge. *IIMB Management Review, 30*(1), 37–50. https://doi.org/10.1016/j.iimb.2017.11.003

Mennens, K., Van Gils, A., Odekerken-Schröder, G., & Letterie, W. (2018). Exploring antecedents of service innovation performance in manufacturing SMEs. *International Small Business Journal: Researching Entrepreneurship, 36*(5), 500–520. https://doi.org/10.1177/0266242617749687

Mugogo, M., & Salau, A. (2020). Barriers to SME innovation for performance: Evidence from Zimbabwe. *International Journal of Education and Research, 8*(11), 45–58.

Nyåkern, M., (2020, June). What is MedTech?. AKRN Consulting. https://akrnconsulting.com/what-is-medtech/

Peter, L., Hajek, L., Maresova, P., Augustynek, M., & Penhaker, M. (2020). Medical devices: Regulation, risk classification, and open innovation. *Journal of Open Innovation: Technology, Market, and Complexity, 6*(2). https://doi.org/10.3390/JOITMC6020042

Ribau, C. P., Moreira, A. C., & Raposo, M. (2017). SMEs innovation capabilities and export performance: An entrepreneurial orientation view. *Journal of Business Economics and Management, 18*(5), 920–934. https://doi.org/10.3846/16111699.2017.1352534

Saunila, M. (2017). Understanding innovation performance measurement in SMEs. *Measuring Business Excellence, 21*(1), 1–16. https://doi.org/10.1108/MBE-01-2016-0005

Schuhmacher, A., Gassmann, O., McCracken, N., & Hinder, M. (2018). Open innovation and external sources of innovation. An opportunity to fuel the R&D pipeline and enhance decision making? *Journal of Translational Medicine, 16*(1), 1–14. https://doi.org/10.1186/s12967-018-1499-2

Sriboonlue, P., & Puangpronpitag, S. (2019). Towards innovative SMEs: An empirical study of regional small and medium Enterprises in Thailand. *Procedia Computer Science, 158*, 819–825. https://doi.org/10.1016/j.procs.2019.09.119

Tohmo, T., & Storhammar, E. (2019). Innovations and growth: Evidence from Finnish SMEs. *Journal of Enterprising Culture, 27*(03), 229–257. https://doi.org/10.1142/s0218495819500092

Trosman, J. R., Weldon, C. B., Douglas, M. P., Deverka, P. A., Watkins, J. B., & Phillips, K. A. (2017). Decision making on medical innovations in a changing health care environment: Insights from accountable care organizations and payers on personalized medicine and other technologies. *Value in Health, 20*(1), 40–46. https://doi.org/10.1016/j.jval.2016.09.2402

Winterhalter, S., Zeschky, M. B., Neumann, L., & Gassmann, O. (2017). Business models for frugal innovation in emerging markets: The case of the medical device and laboratory equipment industry. *Technovation, 66–67*, 3–13. https://doi.org/10.1016/j.technovation.2017.07.002

Chapter 16
Small Businesses Beyond Resilience: A Functional Structure Approach to the Growth of Small Businesses in India

Vijay Bijlani, Jireh Hooi Inn Seow, and Muniza Askari

Abstract India aimed to become a US$5 trillion economy and create additional 50 million employment opportunities. Small businesses contribute only 28 percent to total This industry and India's GDP have the potential to expand more quickly. As such, the key question leading this research has been *how can small businesses in India scale up?* Small businesses are classified as micro, small, and medium enterprises and 110 million people in India are working in small businesses. This research employed participatory action research as a methodology with the researcher collecting the data being a practicing consultant to the small businesses. The research was conducted in a manufacturing small business engaged in power transmission motor belts. The results indicate that strengthening company resilience and giving small enterprises the tools, they need to recover from the COVID-19 epidemic requires adjustments in organizational cohesion and cooperation, flexibility, and resource management. Small enterprises might display creative and sensitive responses to the shifting market conditions. Nonetheless, for their efforts to be successful, small businesses must create and implement functional strategies and methods that are congruent. The research significantly contributed in the growth of motor belts unit and laid a foundation for other small businesses to follow the approach of growth through building functional structures.

Keywords Entrepreneurs · Small businesses · Functional structures · The Covid-19 pandemic · Resilience · Enterprise growth

---

V. Bijlani (✉) · M. Askari
S P Jain School of Global Management, Singapore, Singapore
e-mail: vijay.dj19dba011@spjain.org; muniza.askari@spjain.org

J. H. I. Seow
Innovation and Entrepreneurship Centre (i2e), Singapore, Singapore

S P Jain School of Global Management, Singapore, Singapore
e-mail: jireh.seowhi@spjain.org

E. L. Eijdenberg et al. (eds.), *Innovation-Driven Business and Sustainability in the Tropics*, https://doi.org/10.1007/978-981-99-2909-2_16

16.1 Introduction

Defining Small Businesses: Until, 2019, small businesses in India were defined based on only investments made in plants and machinery by such enterprises. To make this easier, the Government of India initiated a proposal to define small businesses based on the annual sales turnover that these enterprises post. As per the notification for small businesses, annual sales turnover slabs will also be included in the new definition (Reserve Bank of India, July 2020). The World Bank defines small businesses when any two out of the three criteria are met from employee strength, asset size, or annual sales. The definition of small businesses, also called as MSMEs (micro, small and medium enterprises) differs across economies due to uniqueness in small businesses themselves as well as the country-specific problems (Reserve Bank of India, MSME Report June 2019).

Significance of small businesses: Manufacturing, Trade, and Services are the three vital business activities other than the agricultural sector. With low capital requirements, the small business sector in India creates employment opportunities for 110.99 million people (Dun and Bradstreet, 2018). Asian Development Bank (ADB), 2015 data states that the employer contribution of small business enterprises is as high as 88% in the Republic of Korea and 80% in Thailand. Small businesses in Bangladesh, Cambodia, and Japan have 75%, 72%, and 70% share respectively. Similarly, Singapore is at 68%, China and Malaysia both have a 65% share, and the Philippines at 64%. Out of the 410 million people employed in India (Centre for Monitoring Indian Economy, February 2022), small businesses in India contribute only close to 27.5% of employment.

Research gap: According to the Dun and Bradstreet Report (Leading SMEs of India, 2018), India has emerged as one of the high-growth economies globally. The development of the small businesses sector will help India to make a mark as a manufacturing hub, along with fostering the development of new entrepreneurs. Micro enterprises account for 99.47% of the total estimated MSMEs whereas small and medium enterprises put together are 0.53%. With this economic context and significance, the present research is motivated toward the growth of small businesses from micro to small enterprises, small to medium enterprises, and medium to full large-scale enterprises in India.

On the whole, it will be favourable to probe how one of the world's fastest-growing economies can accelerate a vital sector, MSME. All businesses have to go through typical stages in the development stage and because of the different characteristics of each stage, the transition from one to the next is often accompanied by an internal or external crisis.

Research Objective: The COVID-19 pandemic has had a significant impact on a number of enterprises worldwide (Brammer et al., 2020; Donthu & Gustafsson, 2020). Smaller, more susceptible companies were threatened with closure or other severe economic upheavals. (Belitski et al., 2021; Khlystova et al., 2022; Torrès et al., 2021). The findings suggest that improving organisational cohesiveness and cooperation, adaptability, and resource management are required by small businesses to recover from the COVID-19 epidemic (Hadjielias et al., 2022). Very few companies that succeeds expands and scale up. In the growth stage of a small business, the organization structure should be functional and centralized (Mel & Richard, 1987). Therefore, the objective of this research is to discover how does functional structures in a small business affect its business growth and this research is likely to add to the knowledge in the domain of small business management.

16.2 Literature Review

Why small businesses remain small: Largely, business start-ups exit within the initial decade, and surviving ones remain small (Ryan et al., 2014). To improve the start-up process, the five main elements that are vital are a business model, customer development, a viable product, perseverance, and a market opportunity (Dean & Marc, 2020). Adequate capital, good bookkeeping practices, industry experience, management education and expertise, business planning process, professional advisors, timely launches of products and services, marketing abilities, and certain vintage will increase the prospect of growth for small businesses (Bimal & Sugata, 2019). Smaller businesses do not provide fringe benefits, not even health insurance. The education level of small business owners gives them an understanding of productivity drivers and makes them value healthy and happy workers (Jayachandran & David, 1998).

Human capital and organizational challenges: According to *Routledge Revivals Report* (1995) despite small businesses growing importance in the 1990s, the industry was oblivious of the human and organizational challenges to the growth of smaller-scale enterprises. Formal human resources policies and small firms' performance are positively related. The family-managed business practices lessen the prospect of businesses adopting formal human resource practices to engage with employees. Family loyalty and the success of the family business are more important to the employees of these companies than meeting individual demands (Thang & Scott, 2004). Yanqing et al. (2017) saw a positive association between formalized people management practices and small businesses' performance, measured by financial performance and labor productivity. Their study suggests that firms with low job satisfaction can improve small firms' performance by introducing human resource management policies. Lack of human capital and locational limitations force women entrepreneurs to choose to operate in informal enterprises (Mirela et al., 2019). When the quality of human capital increases in a sports organization, the chances of survival and success are higher. The newly founded firms and established firms both can succeed and grow if they keep the human capital stock high (Giovanni et al., 2018). Adaptability, involvement, mission, and consistency are dimensions of organizational culture. Information acquisition, behavioral and cognitive is the dimension of organizational learning (Hasliza et al., 2019).

Clearly defined roles and performance: It further states that a lack of clearly defined roles is not conducive to growth. There exists a strong relationship between small businesses' performance with market orientation and emphasis on growth or differentiation strategy (Alfred, 2000). Family characteristics drive performance and other business aspects of the firms. (Pramodita et al., 2020). Individuals' learning and competence are enhanced by entrepreneurial activities which promote freedom to perform and create opportunities (Nadav et al., 2019).

Training and development: Small businesses view human resource training as a requirement of the competitive business context and the entrepreneurs' business growth strategy (Philip, 2008). Training influences growth in small manufacturing businesses. The businesses intending to grow and having inclination towards training people will grow faster and will perform better than those that do not. A confident workforce is better equipped to adapt to changing work practices, routines, and resources (Jane, 2006).

Managerial capabilities: Those small businesses which have higher managerial values, entrepreneurial proactiveness, innovation, and risk-taking, deliver better performance. SMEs outperform with these attitudes when compared to those who do not exhibit these attitudes (Timothy et al., 2019). By improving employee awareness and training, lean Kaizen implementation eliminates rework time, reduces inventory levels and lead time, improves productivity, enhances product quality, and thereby increases the overall productivity of small businesses (Sunil et al., 2018). de Teresa and Peter (2009) state that to encourage learning, knowledge should flow seamlessly and thereby reduce entrepreneurial risk.

Financial capabilities: The problems faced by small businesses are similar enough to have a general growth model useful to manage a small business (Mel & Richard, 1987). Yet, financial issues restrict efforts to develop and grow, which poses a threat to the life cycle of businesses that can't timely scale up to the appropriate levels (Fedra & Sukru, 2011). At the early stage of the firms, need support for start-up capital is required, along with capacity. Such capital can be made available from public or private institutions, or NGO sources, and the administration has to reward these sources who come forward to support in the form of tax breaks for donations. Access to microcredit leads to a marginal increase in business size, in the case of loans taken for expanding existing businesses (Manuela et al., 2015). During the times of the Great Recession years, small firms are unable to switch between bank lenders without any cost implications (Michael et al., 2020). Microfinance has a limited role to play in the growth and profitability of rural businesses (Abhijit et al., 2015). Entrepreneurs have to largely finance their businesses with their capital. With productivity growth in the business and a small increase in capital, entrepreneurs enhance saving to self-finance new investments in the business (Damiano, 2014).

Growth oriented strategic approach: small firms that follow strategic processes, grow. The owners led small firms to use promising strategies, making their workers part of the small firms' decision-making, planning, and scanning the environment (Abdela & Idris, 2019). The graduating point from a small to medium size firm is the 50 full-time equivalent workforce size with sustainable systems (John et al., 2004). Businesses with a dedicated development strategy will have a business plan, and growth-oriented businesses will demonstrate a greater predisposition to do so.

An expansion strategy is necessary to grow the consumer base. Either from financial institutions or business consulting firms, the firms look for outside assistance in developing a plan. The owner-growth manager's orientation is positively associated with having a business strategy. The traits of the owner-managers determine whether the small company has a business plan or not (Suzanne et al., 2006). Ajay et al. (2006) expanded in their review that how a medium-sized firm, which believed that they never had a strategy ever, adopted different approaches such as classical, evolutionary, processual, and systemic.

External factors: small businesses need support from agencies, policymakers, skills development initiatives, financial facilitation programs, and ease of doing business environment (Neneh & Avan, 2013). Small businesses' capacity to contribute to the Indian economy is constrained by a number of issues. According to the Expert Committee on MSME's 2019 Report (1) the implementation of institutional and policy changes, (2) the facilitation of formalisation and accelerating growth, (3) the resolution of infrastructure issues, (4) the support of capacity development, (5) the facilitation of credit and risk financing, (6) the facilitation of increased delivery and standardisation of underwriting, and (7) the facilitation of links between both the market and portals for public procurement are among the biggest challenges.

Entrepreneurs' choices and mindset: entrepreneurs and founders, who are of middle-age, represent the high-growth firms and younger counterparts do not represent this particular subset (Pierre et al., 2020). Personalized consulting sessions from role models foster more growth for micro-entrepreneurs with limited experience (Jeanne et al., 2018). In their study, Patricia et al. (2017) found that most entrepreneurs showed persistence in their psychological as well as emotional functioning after the collapse of their business. The study questioned the idea that rehabilitation is necessary after an enterprise fails. Physiological changes in the body are referred to as allostatic load. Longer the duration of self-employment leads to higher wear-and-tear of the entrepreneurs (Pankaj et al., 2019). The four I's of the entrepreneurship model prove that firms fail because of a lack of transparency, communication, trust, and organizational culture. At the outset, the collective entrepreneurial team awareness exists only till the 'initial' stage, i.e., while entering a project. The shared vision notion becomes more fragmented as the process progresses. The communication gap starts becoming evident and once co-entrepreneurs, start finding it difficult to relate with the original vision. The lack of transparency also leads to entrepreneurs' obscuring personal agendas from one another (Anthony, 2019). Consumer discrimination poses minority founders with more challenges and leads to their firms' underperformance. This leads to price discounting, where the founder's ethnicity determines the price that a consumer would pay for a product. If consumers are made aware that their product is made for a broad audience and not just for other minorities, the founders of the companies can lessen the level of bias and raise their revenue in order to create an equal opportunity for their businesses (Peter & Venkat, 2019).

For this research: the author conducted this research in the premises of a small business engaged in the manufacturing of power transmission motor belts as a consulting research practitioner. The unit was a micro enterprise and the manufacturing process of the small business was first studied to understand all the stages to convert different raw materials to a finished product. During the research, various internal documents and standard operating procedures were referred to establish the link between various functions and sections on the shopfloor.

Theoretical basis and framework: Systematic Theory possibly be stated in a normal or regular language, without having a formal structured calculus as its main purpose is to capture and simplify the element of an activity for which the imposition of rules is regarded as theoretically basic. However quite often than not the symbolic representation may be deployed which represents as an ad hoc coding method and not as a ratification (Freese, 1980). Anecdote and theory have very different meanings: lighthearted versus somber, specific versus all-encompassing, brief versus expansive. Through overcoming these oppositions, anecdotal theory creates theory with wit and reasoning that celebrates the strange detail of real experience. All theories involve tales, and theorists must take note of the minor everyday narratives that theory quite frequently suppresses (Jane, 2002). The researcher-practitioner intends to propose a theory defined empirically from the findings of this research.

16.3 Methodology

Qualitative approach: In qualitative research, there are a variety of important research approaches, including ethnography, case studies, and action research. Grounded theory somewhat overlaps each of the aforementioned methodologies (Locke, 2001). A group of procedures known as action research are ways of conducting research in which the researcher actually takes action. Action research is a sort of participatory research that depends on the direct involvement of the researcher and practitioner (Reason & Bradbury, 2001).

Action research: The author came to the conclusion that action research was the most appropriate methodology for this research study through the qualitative methodologies of ethnography, grounded theory, case study research, and action research, with participatory action research being applied in the initial exploratory phase. Ethnography does not include an action component; hence it did not meet the researcher's criteria or directly answer the research question. While agreeing that the aim of grounded theory is to provide practitioners with aspects that are beneficial over scenarios they experience on a regular basis (Glaser and Strauss cited in Locke, 2001), Because it lacked an action component, this methodology was rejected as the standard for research. Grounded theory researchers do not share action researchers' commitments to organizational transformation or to partnering with study subjects in the enquiry process (Locke, 2001). Due to the absence of the execution component, the case study research methodology was also disqualified as the primary research methodology. When the relevant behaviors cannot be changed, case study research is used to observe research circumstances (Yin, 1994), thus was not appropriate for a study that sought to improve a current work environment.

Nonetheless, considering that action research is somewhat dependent on a researcher's observations to provide "a comprehensive grasp of the context of the research and the processes being enacted," certain case study research components were deemed pertinent to the proposed research study (Morris and Wood as cited in Saunders, 2003). Principally, action research was selected as the prime research methodology, because it answers both requirements of action and research. The researcher in the present study is a consulting practitioner, where real-time actions are taken in real-life assignments and bring a body of knowledge to the research. It is therefore action research best suited for the present research.

Applications of action research: Unilever's Food Business, which began in Holland and moved on to Asia, is one of the most intriguing examples of action research in the workplace. When Tex Gunning, the company's then-president, took over the Dutch food company in 1995, it was in financial crisis with outdated plants, quality problems, and dwindling profits. This is when the reform programme got underway. Gunning gathered approximately 10,000 garbage pallets from several locations into a sizable warehouse in order to affect a turnaround. Together with quality specialists and production staff, the manager and their cost accountants rode buses from three local factories to the location. A total of 1600 workers surveyed the aisles of spoiled goods, calculated the enormous financial loss, and considered the waste of their own time and abilities. After this powerful alarm, there were angry outbursts, introspection, and confrontation. Finally, there was an admission of the first steps towards a new course of action. (as cited in the Sage Handbook of Action Research, Reason & Bradbury, 2001).

Participatory Action Research: Since PAR is multidisciplinary and multifaceted, no one viewpoint can be considered authoritative or authentic. Contextualizing research requires participation and action. The roles of the researchers and researchers switch during dialogue, resulting in a mutual growth in knowledge and understanding of people's concerns. The students analysed how the researcher's presence affected the study situation and questioned the researcher's position. The political philosophy that workers and peasants should create the country was in line with PAR. The university's chief education officer was impressed by the students' altered views and advised using the strategy in all university departments while students were working as research assistants (Swantz, 1976 as cited in Reason & Bradbury, 2001). According to Alfredo Molano, nobody ever invented or discovered PAR; rather, it was the result of a conflict between precise scientific explanations and rough reality helpers. (Molano, 1998). Traditional sympathetic participation, in which the researcher puts themselves in the researcher's shoes, proved insufficient for Falls Borda. The researcher had to participate fully in the process under study, gaining an insider's perspective while being conscious of the fact that he or she belonged to a different class or social group (Reason & Bradbury, 2001). PAR must be incorporated into the process of producing knowledge; it cannot simply be participatory practise. As it is in several parts of the world already, PAR can be considered as a necessary component of professional training (Swantz, 1976 as cited in Reason & Bradbury, 2001).

PAR applied in a small business / manufacturing unit: In the year 2020, Indian manufacturing units saw a surge in demand for alternate domestic products due to disruption in imports. A similar situation was faced by a power transmission motor belts company in India, specifically for v-belts. The manufacturing unit, with a total strength of 90 workers and supervisors was flushed with orders but the production output was lagging way behind to meet the growing customers' demand. The lead time to service orders went as high as 40–50 days, resulting in irate customers. To tackle this problem, a practitioner consultant, the author of this research, was brought in by the management. The practitioner committed 2 days of the week and was physically present in the factory premises. After having intensive interactions with the management for the 2 weeks, participatory action research was proposed and undertaken for the research for this thesis also commenced.

On-the-shopfloor: The broad guideline of the PAR was to understand the problems that were deterring the growth of the business by being with the workers on the shopfloor. To do that, for the next 6 weeks, the practitioner reported to the shop floor, like all workers at 08:00 am. The entire process was toured repetitively to understand the gaps which led to a loss of production. Fals Borda noted that the researcher had to participate fully in the process of his or her study while keeping in mind that he or she represented a different class or social group (Reason & Bradbury, 2001). The research practitioner became a part of the workers' community, even to the extent of dressing in uniform as they did. The data was collected by conducting morning shop-floor meetings with the supervisors, discussing individual previous day's outputs with some of the workers, production reports, and the manufacturing unit's installed CCTV units. The stage-wise raw material flow on the shop flow, machines adjacencies, and demarcation of the sections were also reviewed to evaluate the workflow. Basis the inputs during the PAR and by bringing the domain expertise of management by the research practitioner, the functional classification of each department in the manufacturing unit was initiated. A framework of one-man-one-machine-one-priority was set to clearly define and demark the purpose of the resources deployed.

16.4 Findings

Manufacturing process shortcomings and interventions: The starting point of this participatory action research was the research problem of *how could this small enterprise in India scale up?* The small business engaged in the manufacturing of power transmission motor belts, facing the problem of seizing the growth opportunity, became the representative small business for this research. In this case, despite of being fully resourced with machines, materials, and manpower, the lead time to serve the customers was 40–50 days. The management problem from the enterprise was that they are unable to pinpoint the core reason for orders not getting translated into sales. The measurement matrix was the output of the operations function, for different stages of the manufacturing process.

The manufacturing process of one particular type of belt, V-belts, is mentioned below (Fig. 16.1).

The existing Operations Function's structure, before intervention is explained in the below-mentioned diagram (Fig. 16.2).

The comments mentioned in red are the shortcomings, identified on the shop floor.

The second, third, and fourth stages of the process mentioned below namely, Double Drum, Sleeve Slitting, and Making were identified as points of intervention or where the research practitioner mediated (Fig. 16.3).

The weekend PAR intervention was started from mid-October 2020 onwards and functional structure inputs were introduced, as mentioned in the diagram below, points 1 to 7 (Fig. 16.4).

After four weekends of intervention, the output was measured on daily basis. The formats of the production reports are as follows (Table. 16.1).

The consolidated monthly output of all three stages of manufacturing is mentioned in the below diagram (Fig. 16.5).

Double Drum, Sleeves Slitting, and Making saw an improvement of 16%, 67%, and 10% output respectively. This top 10 customers' sales contribution improved by 15% on a year-on-year basis. This gave confidence to the management and the team

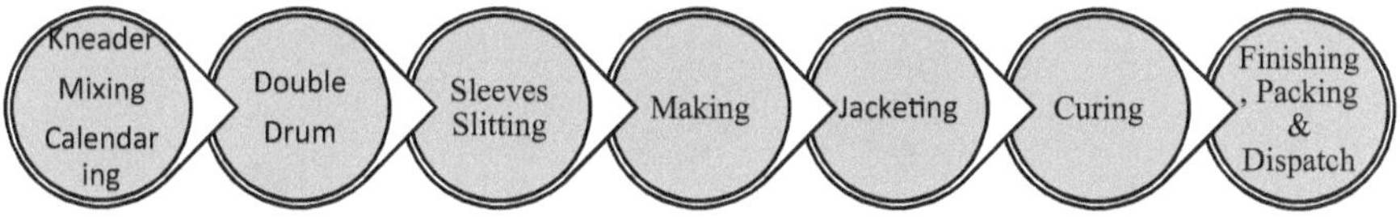

Fig. 16.1 V-belts manufacturing process, assimilated from the internal documents

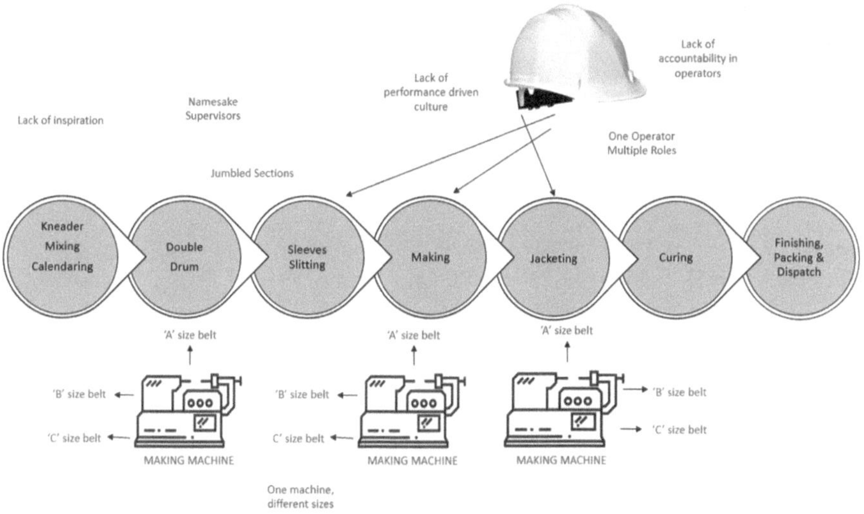

Fig. 16.2 Operations function structure before intervention, assimilated from internal documents of the manufacturing unit

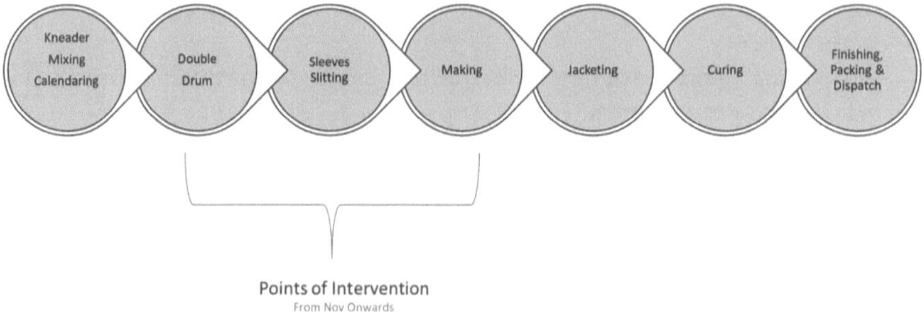

Fig. 16.3 Operations function structure, points of intervention

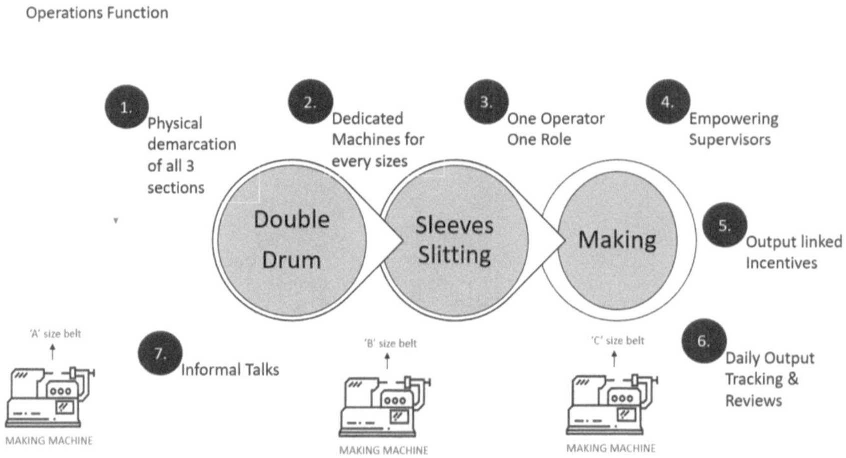

Fig. 16.4 Operations function structure, after the intervention

both, that with the existing resources and better functional structuring, higher output can be achieved and this small manufacturing enterprise planned for a 50% growth in the business for the subsequent financial year; FY2021–22.

Year	FY20	FY21*	FY22^
Turn Over (mn $)	1.70	1.73	2.40
Top 10 Customers	54%	69%	100%

*10 months of operations due to 2 months of national lockdown

^Plan for this financial year

From the PAR it was evident that undefined functional structures and small businesses' growth are related (Fig. 16.6).

The anecdotal theory derived from the research: is titled as 'Theory of Under Organized'. This implies that small-medium enterprises are organized to some extent functionally and once the definite functional structures are implemented;

Table 16.1 Section-wise daily output after the intervention; internal document of the manufacturing unit

Date	Section	Size		Actual qty		Date	Section	Size		Actual qty		Date	Section	Size		Actual qty
01.12.2020	C	355	2.96	2.96		02.12.2020	B	113	1	1.00		03.12.2020	B	105	1	1.00
01.12.2020	C	350	2.92	2.92		02.12.2020	B	115	1	1.00		03.12.2020	B	105	1	1.00
01.12.2020	C	345	2.88	2.88		02.12.2020	B	168	1.40	1.40		03.12.2020	B	72	1	1.00
01.12.2020	C	335	2.79	2.79		02.12.2020	B	71	1	1.00		03.12.2020	B	72	1	1.00
01.12.2020	C	330	2.75	2.75		02.12.2020	B	72	1	1.00		03.12.2020	B	72	1	1.00
01.12.2020	C	325	2.71	2.71		02.12.2020	B	72	1	1.00		03.12.2020	B	72	1	1.00
01.12.2020	C	320	2.67	2.67		02.12.2020	B	72	1	1.00		03.12.2020	B	82	1	1.00
01.12.2020	C	72	1	1.00		02.12.2020	B	72	1	1.00		03.12.2020	B	83	1	1.00
01.12.2020	SPB	88	1	1.00		02.12.2020	B	154	1.28	1.28		03.12.2020	B	84	1	1.00
01.12.2020	C	80	1	1.00		02.12.2020	B	128	1.07	1.07		03.12.2020	B	84	1	1.00
01.12.2020	B	125	1.04	1.04		02.12.2020	B	124	1.03	1.03		03.12.2020	B	72	1	1.00
01.12.2020	B	125	1.04	1.04		02.12.2020	B	138	1.15	1.15		03.12.2020	A	76	1	1.00
01.12.2020	B	130	1.08	1.08		02.12.2020	B	110	1	1.00		03.12.2020	A	76	1	1.00
01.12.2020	B	130	1.08	1.08		02.12.2020	B	106	1	1.00		03.12.2020	A	76	1	1.00
01.12.2020	B	132	1.10	1.10		02.12.2020	B	101	1	1.00		03.12.2020	A	76	1	1.00
01.12.2020	B	132	1.10	1.10		02.12.2020	B	60	1	1.00		03.12.2020	A	76	1	1.00
01.12.2020	B	150	1.25	1.25		02.12.2020	B	60	1	1.00		03.12.2020	A	76	1	1.00
01.12.2020	B	150	1.25	1.25		02.12.2020	B	58	1	1.00		03.12.2020	A	76	1	1.00
01.12.2020	B	152	1.27	1.27		02.12.2020	B	58	1	1.00		03.12.2020	A	76	1	1.00
01.12.2020	B	111	1	1.00		02.12.2020	B	58	1	1.00		03.12.2020	A	76	1	1.00
01.12.2020	B	113	1	1.00		02.12.2020	B	58	1	1.00		03.12.2020	A	76	1	1.00

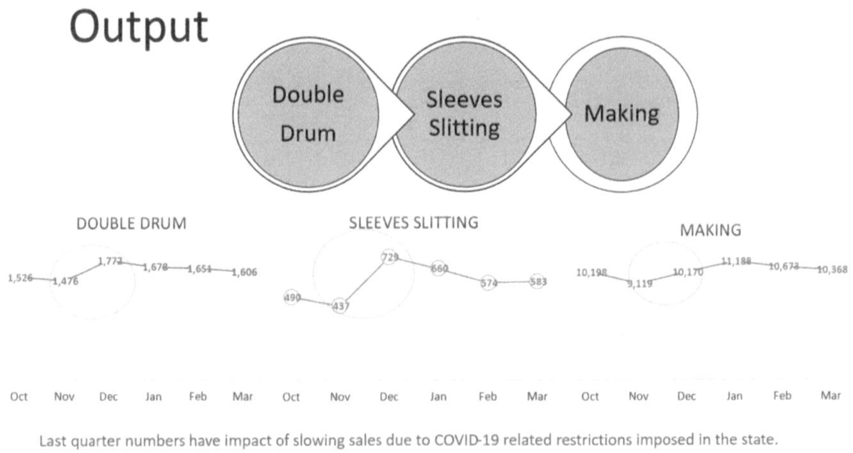

Fig. 16.5 Output results after the intervention

Fig. 16.6 Model before validations

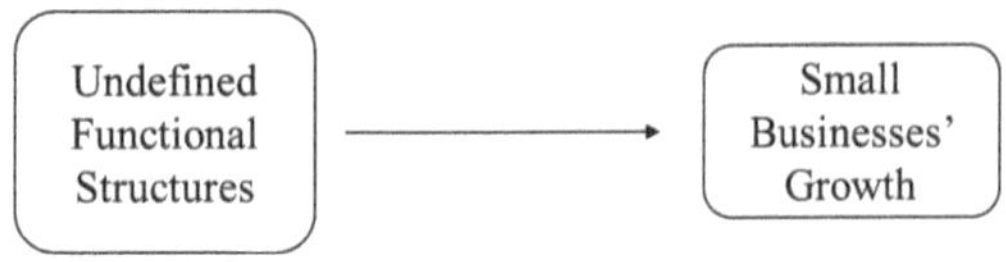

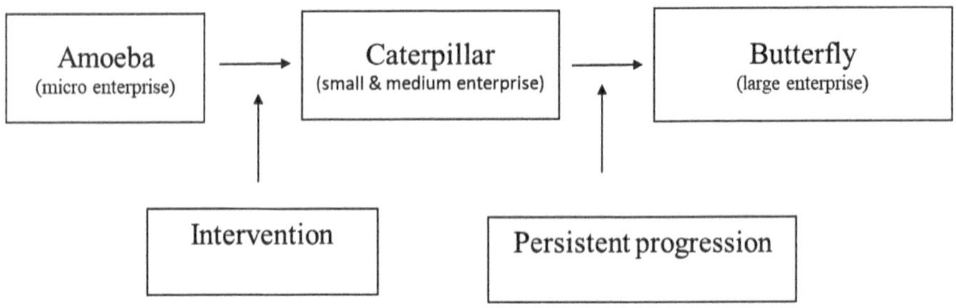

Fig. 16.7 The theory of under-organized

their enterprises achieve higher growth. The theory is further explained through a pictorial representation, where the analogy is linked to organisms (Fig. 16.7).

From participatory action research, it can be inferred that the small enterprise which is considered in the scope of the study, has shown significant growth in performance after the functional structure intervention. Before the intervention, the resources were rotated between different departments to get the jobs on hand completed, very similar to an amoeba, where all the body parts are temporary, and used for specific tasks. After the intervention, all the resources were assigned to specific roles and thereby yielding higher results.

This leads to the conclusion that when a small enterprise graduates from the behavior of an amoeba to a caterpillar, which is denoted in the theory as a system that has fixed parts with predefined roles for better results. Furthermore, the theory borrows the natural progression of caterpillar to butterfly as an anecdote to explain the growth of an enterprise from a medium-scale to a large.

16.5 Concluding Discussion

Overall: The missing middle problem implies that over time, micro firms have not succeeded in expanding into smaller and medium-sized businesses, and so on (Krueger, 2009). In India's endeavour to grow to a US$5 trillion economy and create additional 50 million employment opportunities (Reserve Bank of India, 2020), the small businesses have the potential to scale up quickly. The key question that this research has aimed to answer is *how can small businesses in India scale up?* This research employed participatory action research in a small manufacturing business and took a functional structure approach to help the small business grow.

The research: was conducted in a manufacturing unit of a power transmission motor belts. The results of participatory action research linked the growth of small businesses with functional structures. The structure of functions of operations was a factor that impacted the growth of small businesses. A theory was built by the practicing researcher and named as Theory of Under Organised, anecdotally linking an amoeba's progression, from a small enterprise, to a caterpillar, a medium enterprise was established. This progression was proved in the action research conducted by the practicing researcher through interventions. And once the leap is taken, the next transition, through persistence, for a medium enterprise, denoted as a caterpillar, is to a butterfly, represented as a large grown enterprise. From participatory action research, it can be inferred that the small enterprise which is considered in the scope of the study, has shown significant growth in performance after the functional structure intervention. Before the intervention, the resources were rotated between different departments to get the jobs on hand completed, very similar to an amoeba, where all the body parts are temporary, and used for specific tasks. After the intervention, all the resources were assigned to specific roles and thereby yielding higher results. This leads to the conclusion that when a small enterprise graduates from the behavior of an amoeba to a caterpillar, which is denoted in the theory as a system that has fixed parts with predefined roles for better results. Furthermore, the theory borrows the natural progression of caterpillar to butterfly as an anecdote to explain the growth of an enterprise from a medium-scale to a large. Thereby the research makes an attempt to address the problem of missing middle and sets a foundation for small businesses to grow with a functional structure approach.

Contribution to practice and further research: On August 15, 2015, a new economic vision for India was unveiled. Its main goal was to unleash the nation's vast entrepreneurial potential and give Indians the tools they need to develop their ideas into viable businesses. The Start-up India initiative was established by the Indian government with the goals of creating a robust ecosystem in the areas of ease of doing business, provide financial support and incentives, collaboration with academia, and incubation (Start-up India Report, 2020). The finding of the research will contribute to the accelerators' scope of the Start-up India initiative, where enterprises will be guided and structured in the infancy stage.

The research findings will be significant inputs to the Office of the Development Commissioner (small businesses), under the Ministry of MSME, to formulate the policy governing small businesses in India, and to design schemes and programs for the development of the small businesses Sector. The National Institute for Entrepreneurship and Small Business Development (NIESBUD) provides Management Consultancy and conducts training programs through Entrepreneurship Development Programmes (EDP) for small businesses to improve their managerial proficiency. The proposed study is significant as it is focused on finding ways to enable present entrepreneurs to structure their enterprises and likewise draw a roadmap for future entrepreneurs. The findings may help in clusters of Directorate of Industries or policymaking at the national level. Moreover, the findings may also be incorporated into the curriculum by academia.

The further research can be expanded to other functions of a small business such as marketing, legal, and information technology. The theory can also be tested in a trading or a services small business. It will also be interesting to learn if any large enterprises swayed away from their functional structures approach and witnessed any negative growth.

References

Abdela, C., & Idris, K. (2019). Strategic process and small venture growth: The moderating role of environmental scanning and owner-CEO. *Journal of Small Business Strategy, 29*(3), 60–77. Middle Tennessee State University.

Abhijit, B., Esther, D., Rachel, G., & Cynthia, K. (2015). The miracle of microfinance? Evidence from a randomized evaluation. *American Economic Journal: Applied Economics, 7*(1), 22–53. American Economic Association.

Ajay, B., Steven, H., & David, W. (2006). A multiparadigmatic perspective of strategy, a case study of an ethnic family firm. *International Small Business Journal, 24*(5), 515–537. Sage Publication.

Alfred, P. (2000). Market orientation and other potential influences on performance in small and medium-sized manufacturing firms. *Journal of Small Business Management, 38*(1), 48–67. Researchgate.

Anthony, L. (2019). The 4Is of entrepreneurship - a study of the entrepreneurial perspectives behind a failed large-scale distributed research infrastructure. *Entrepreneurship Research Journal, 9*, 20170115. Walter de Gruyter.

Belitski, M., Guenther, C., Kritikos, A. S., & Thurik, R. (2021). Economic effects of the COVID-19 pandemic on entrepreneurship and small businesses. *Small Business Economics, 58*, 1–17.

Bimal, N., & Sugata, N. (2019). Prediction model of success or failure for small business in north East India. *Journal of Management, 6*(1), 197–201. IAME Publication.

Brammer, S., Branicki, L., & Linnenluecke, M. K. (2020). COVID-19, Societalization, and the future of business in society. *Academy of Management Perspectives, 34*(4), 493–507.

Centre for Monitoring Indian Economy Pvt. Ltd. (2022). *Centre for Monitoring Indian Economy Pvt. Ltd.* https://unemploymentinindia.cmie.com/

Damiano, S. (2014). Growth and capital flow with risky entrepreneurship. *American Economic Journal: Macroeconomics, 6*(3), 102–123. American Economic Association.

de Teresa, V., & Peter, N. (2009). Knowledge and innovation: The strings between global and local dimensions of sustainable growth. *Entrepreneurship and Regional Development, 21*(4), 441–455. Taylor and Francis Group.

Dean, S., & Marc, G. (2020). The lean startup framework: Closing the academic practitioner divide. *Entrepreneurship Theory and Practice, 45*, 1–31. Sage Publications.

Donthu, N., & Gustafsson, A. (2020). Effects of COVID-19 on business and research. *Journal of Business Research, 117*, 284–289.

Dun and Bradstreet. (2018). *Leading SMEs of India Report*, Dun and Bradstreet Information Services India Pvt. Ltd https://www.dnb.co.in/events/sme-awards/Publications/2018.pdf

Fedra, E., & Sukru, E. (2011). Functional strategies and practices of small medium-sized family businesses. *International Journal of Islamic and Middle Eastern Finance and Management, 4*, 174–185. Emerald Group Publishing Limited.

Freese, L. (1980). Formal theorizing. *Annual Reviews Inc, 6*, 187–212.

Giovanni, R., Claudio, E., Federico, F., & Antonio, P. (2018). Entrepreneurship and human Capital in Professional Sport: A longitudinal analysis of the Italian soccer league. *Entrepreneurship Theory and Practice, 42*(1), 70–93. Sage Publications.

Hadjielias, E., Christofi, M., & Tarba, S. (2022). Contextualizing small business resilience during the COVID-19 pandemic: Evidence from small business owner-managers. *Small Business Economics, 59*, 1351–1380. https://doi.org/10.1007/s11187-021-00588-0

Hasliza, A. H., Noor, A., Alan, G., & Ramayah, T. (2019). Innovation culture in SMEs – The importance of organizational culture, org learning, and market orientation. *Entrepreneurship Research Journal*. Walter de Gruyter.

Jane, G. (2002). *Anecdotal theory*. Duke University Press.

Jane, B. (2006). Training and performance in small firms. *International Small Business Journal, 24*(6), 635–660. Sage Publications.

Jayachandran, V., & David, K. (1998). Fringe benefits provision by rural small businesses. *American Journal of Agricultural Economics, 80*(May 1998), 360–368. Oxford University Press.

Jeanne, L., Julio, R., & Jose, T. (2018). Role models or individual consulting. *American Economic Journal: Applied Economics., 10*(4), 222–245.

John, S., Celia, S., Anna, W., David, P., & Simon, H. (2004). Franchising as a small business growth strategy, a resource-based view of organizational development. *International Small Business Journal, 22*(6), 539–559. Sage Publications.

Khlystova, O., Kalyuzhnova, Y., & Belitski, M. (2022). The impact of the COVID-19 pandemic on the creative industries: A literature review and future research agenda. *Journal of Business Research, 139*, 1192–1210.

Krueger, A. (2009). *The missing middle*. Indian Council for Research on International Research Economic Relations.

Locke, K. D. (2001). *Grounded theory in management research*. Sage Publications Ltd.

Manuela, A., Dean, K., & Jonathan, Z. (2015). Microcredit impacts – Evidence from a randomized microcredit program placement experiment by Compartamos Banco. *American Economic Journal: Applied Economics, 7*(1), 151–182. American Economic Association.

Mel, S., & Richard, B. (1987). *Five stages of growth in small business*. Long Range Plan.

Michael, G., Alexandre, M., & Hoai-Luu, N. (2020). Do credit market shocks affect the real economy – quasi-experimental evidence from the great recession and Normal economic times. *American Economic Journal: Economic Policy, 12*(1), 200–225. American Economic Association.

Mirela, X., Adrian, M., & Shova, K. (2019). Value of formalization for women entrepreneurs in developing contexts: A review and research agenda. *International Journal of Management Reviews, 21*, 3–23. BAM and John Wiley and Sons.
Molano, A. (1998). Cartagena revisited twenty years on. In O. F. Borda (Ed.), *People's participation: Challenges ahead* (pp. 3–10). Conciencias, IEPRI, TM Editores.
Nadav, S., Boris, N., & Joakim, W. (2019). Entrepreneurship and well-being: The role of psychological autonomy, competence, and relatedness. *Journal of Business Venturing, 34*(2019), 105875. Elsevier Inc.
Neneh, N., & Avan, S. (2013). Will promoting more typical SME start-ups increase job creation in South Africa? *African Journal of Business Management, 7*(31), 3043–3051.
Pankaj, P., Marcus, W., & Trenton, W. (2019). Self-employment and allostatic load. *Journal of Business Venturing, 34*(2019), 731–751. Elsevier Inc.
Patricia, C., Simta, S., & Kathryn, P. (2017). Entrepreneurial resilience and venture failure. *International Small Business Journal: Researching Entrepreneurship, 35*(6), 687–708. Sage Publications.
Peter, Y., & Venkat, K. (2019). Discounted: The effect of founder race on the price of new products. *Journal of Business Venturing, 34*(2019), 389–412. Elsevier Inc.
Philip, H. (2008). Regulating the 'animal spirits' of entrepreneurs. *International Small Business Journal, 26*(2), 181–206. Sage Publications.
Pierre, A., Benjamin, J., Daniel, K., & Javier, M. (2020). Age and high-growth entrepreneurship. *American Economic Reviews: Insights, 2*(1), 65–82. American Economic Association.
Pramodita, S., James, C., Jess, C., & Lloyd, S. (2020). Family firm behaviors from a psychological perspective. *Entrepreneurship Theory and Practice, 44*(1), 3–19. Sage Publications.
Reason, P., & Bradbury, H. (Eds.). (2001). *Handbook of action research: Participative inquiry and practice*. Sage.
Reserve Bank of India. (2019). *Reserve Bank of India Report* https://rbidocs.rbi.org.in/rdocs/AnnualReport/PDFs/0RBIAR201920DA64F97C6E7B48848E6DEA06D531BADF.PDF
Reserve Bank of India. (2020). *Reserve Bank of India Report* https://rbidocs.rbi.org.in/rdocs/AnnualReport/PDFs/0RBIAR202021_F49F9833694E84C16AAD01BE48F53F6A2.PDF
Routledge Revivals. (1995). *Corporate Realities – The dynamics of large and small organizations*, Routledge Revivals report.
Ryan, D., John, H., Ron, J., & Javier, M. (2014). The role of entrepreneurship in US job creation and economic dynamism. *Journal of Economic Perspectives, 28*(3), 3–24. American Economic Association.
Saunders, M. (2003). *Research methods for business students* (3rd ed.). Pearson Education Limited.
Start-up India. (2020): *Start-up India Report* https://www.startupindia.gov.in/content/dam/invest-india/Templates/public/5_years_Achievement_report%20_%20PRINT.pdf
Sunil, K., Ashwani, D., & Bhim, S. (2018). Lean-Kaizen implementation a roadmap for identifying continuous improvement opportunities in Indian small and medium-sized enterprises. *Journal of Engineering, Design, and Technology, 16*(1), 143–160. Emerald Publishing Limited.
Suzanne, R., Doug, W. H., & Perry, W. (2006). Owner-managers and business planning in the small firms. *International Small Business Journal, 24*(5), 496–514. Sage Publications.
Swantz, M.-L. (1976). Research in action in Dar es Salaam. *Overseas Universities, 22*, 19–22.
Thang, N., & Scott, B. (2004). A study of the formality of HRM practices in SMEs in Vietnam. *International Small Business Journal, 22*, 595–618. Sage Publications.
Timothy, P., John, F., & James, W. (2019). The interplay of strategic orientation and its influence on SME performance. *Journal of Small Business Strategy, 29*(3), 46–59. Middle Tennessee State University.
Torrès, O., Benzari, A., Fisch, C., Mukerjee, J., Swalhi, A., & Thurik, R. (2021). Risk of burnout in French entrepreneurs during the COVID-19 crisis. *Small Business Economics, 58*, 717–739.
Yanqing, L., George, S., & Stewart, J. (2017). Human resource practices, employee attitudes, and small firm performance. *International Small Business Journal, 35*(4), 470–494.
Yin, R. K. (1994). *Case study research: Designs and methods* (2nd ed.). Sage Publications Inc.

Chapter 17
A Conceptual Framework for Impact of Artificial Intelligence and Machine Learning (AIML) in Drug Development Within Pharmaceutical Industry

Mugdha Hemant Belsare and Josip Burusic

Abstract A conceptual framework is proposed within the scope of this study, which focuses on determining impact of AI in drug discoveries in pharmaceutical industry in India region. This is achieved by identifying internal and external determinants which are most significant to the success of the AI in Pharma. In the pharmaceutical sector, lowering prices and speeding up the development of new drugs has become a demanding and pressing issue. The pharmaceutical industry is expanding at a lightning speed in the pandemic time frame. The global pharmaceutical business is on the verge of a new paradigm, as rapid advances in artificial intelligence bring up the possibility of producing more effective drugs faster and at a lower cost. Artificial intelligence has the potential to revolutionize pharmaceutical industry as AI and new deep learning techniques have opened the pathway for modern drug development. Machine learning is a branch of AI that comprises the compilation of mathematical formulae and advanced statistics that researchers use through algorithms to solve real-world issues. AI has the potential to increase drug approval rates, lower development costs, accelerate the delivery of pharmaceuticals to patients and assist patients in complying to their treatment regimens. AI technology has a promising future in drug development, but the disparity across the domains is a significant blocking point, which this framework shall help to understand based on the internal and external determinants. This model is based on systematic literature review of most relevant ABDC journal publications. Developed conceptual framework will be helpful to the CEO, CXOs, business leaders and managers of the Pharma companies, while making strategic decision and action plan for execution. This shall help to gain the knowledge proactively acquired and deeply tested to implement and enjoy the results in making strong decisions. Using the most

M. H. Belsare (✉)
Swiss School of Business and Management, Geneva, Switzerland
e-mail: mugdha@ssbm.ch

J. Burusic
Institute of Social Sciences Ivo Pilar and Prof, University of Zagreb, Zagreb, Croatia
e-mail: josip.burusic@ssbm.ch

E. L. Eijdenberg et al. (eds.), *Innovation-Driven Business and Sustainability in the Tropics*, https://doi.org/10.1007/978-981-99-2909-2_17

cutting-edge AI-based technologies not only shortens the time it takes for items to reach the market, but also raises product quality, ensures worker safety, maximises resource utilisation, and reduces production costs, which are the focus areas from the conceptual framework. Future research on confirming the conceptual framework, identifying most and least impactful factors, will involve formal collection and analysis of empirical data.

Keywords Pharmaceuticals · Artificial Intelligence (AI) · Machine Learning (ML) · Drug discovery · Healthcare

17.1 Introduction

Artificial intelligence refers to the development of algorithms for tasks such as pattern recognition and data interpretation. There has been an increase in the use of AI in pharmaceutical technology in recent years. Several pharma companies have formed partnerships with AI firms as a result of the widespread interest in applying AI methods to the drug development process. AI is just recently beginning to gain traction in a variety of fields, but the pharmaceutical business is already reaping significant benefits. AI has been effectively applied in several pharmaceutical domains, such as drug research and development, drug repurposing, boosting pharmaceutical productivity, clinical trials, etc., to reduce human effort and speed up the process of achieving objectives.

Machine learning has resulted in a significant shift in the pharmaceutical industry's research and development departments (Dara et al., 2022). The pharmaceutical industry has already been under pressure as a result of lower new medication output, higher research and development expenses, the present economic recession, and stricter regulatory standards. Developing a new drug is a complicated, expensive, and time-consuming process that costs an average of 2.6 billion US dollars and takes around 12 years (Deng et al., 2022). The pharmaceutical industry is also grappling with high attrition rates in new drug approvals (Mak & Pichika, 2019). There is very high demand of developing new drugs for several diseases in shorter amount of time and accurate in treatment. This need brings huge pressure on drug development on pharma industry and it has seen that AIML has a high potential to enter in these areas and bring the wonders to meet unmet needs of the customers.

This research will focus on determining impact of AI in drug discoveries in pharmaceutical industry in India region by identifying internal and external determinants which are most significant to the success of the AI in Pharma.

India's pharmaceutical industry has grown to become a major force worldwide. The market for its products is projected to grow to $120 billion by the year 2030. It has an extensive record of accomplishments. Invest India reports that India provides 62% of the world's need for vaccinations and has a 20% stake in the amount of generic pharmaceuticals sold throughout the world (60,000 generic products in 60 therapeutic categories). Also, it manufactures more vaccines than any other company in the world (Lu, 2021).

Numerous factors, including government efforts and supporting legislation, contribute to the country's competitive edge in the pharmaceutical industry. The India Brand Equity Foundation (IBEF) adds that the affordable cost of manufacturing and R&D increases the productivity of Indian pharma businesses, making their exports more competitive. Increasing health insurance coverage and robust economic development, according to the IBEF, are additional factors that bode well for the country's healthcare budget. Increased spending on research and development (R&D) and mergers and acquisitions by the business sector is also highlighted (Lu, 2021).

Considering advances in the fusion technology, application in drug discovery, advances and needs of application of AI in drug discovery makes it significantly important to research internal and external determinants for application of AI in drug discovery together in India region. Machine learning and deep learning have brought up new options for medication research and development. AI might enhance medication approval rates, cut development costs, speed up drug delivery, and help patients adhere to treatment regimens. Taconic Biosciences said medication development is expensive and time-consuming. Drug development costs $2.8 billion. AI and machine learning are useful throughout drug research. Healthcare AI start-ups received almost $2 billion in 2020 utilising AI to simplify medication manufacture, collecting some of the largest amounts relative to other healthcare AI start-ups.

Therefore, the topic of study is necessary since it highlights how technologies are shaping the pharmaceutical industry and future of pharma. It is essential to study as it may enable to understand the technological adoption in every stage of the drug development. Moreover, since technology adoption differs along with the different sectors in the pharma industry, it becomes novel to understand this topic.

17.2 Literature Review

Artificial intelligence is an up-and coming tool in drug development in Pharma industry. Artificial intelligence has the potential to significantly contribute to the further incorporation of the developed drug in the appropriate dosage form and to its optimization, in addition to facilitating rapid decision-making, which accelerates production of better-quality products and ensures batch-to-batch consistency. The product's safety and effectiveness must be confirmed via clinical studies, and AI can help with this.Additionally, AI can help with market research and analysis, allowing for more accurate product positioning and pricing. Artificial intelligence is driving the fourth industrial revolution and has the potential to stop the production of unstable drugs. There are various projects to apply AI to change the present drug development process.

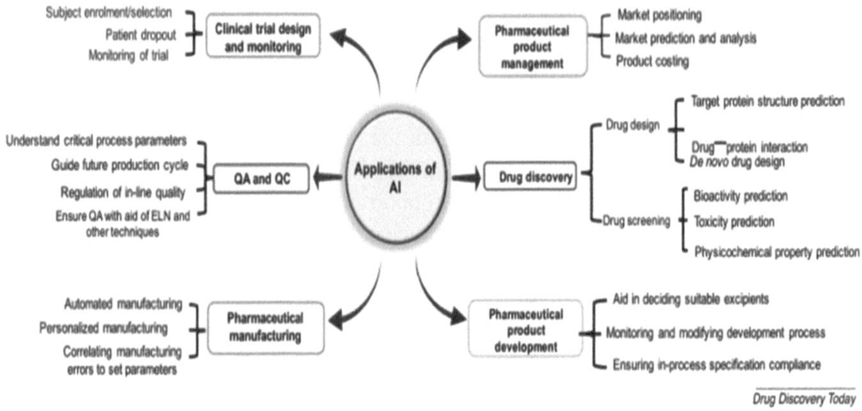

Fig. 17.1 Applications of AI in pharma. (Paul et al., 2021)

17.2.1 AI in Pharma

AI can help with rational medication design (Duch et al., 2007), decision making, determining the correct treatment for a patient, including tailored medicines, and managing clinical data for future drug research (Blasiak et al., 2020).

Applications of AI in different subfields of the pharmaceutical industry, from drug discovery to pharmaceutical product management (Paul et al., 2021). Figure 17.1 summarises the many uses of AI in the pharmaceutical industry. AI and ML does not only help in R&D but for marketing too within pharma companies. To help marketing executives allocate resources for maximum market share gain, reverse poor sales and anticipate where to make investments, Eularis developed an AI platform called E-VAI that employs ML algorithms alongside an intuitive user interface to generate analytical roadmaps based on competitors, key stakeholders, and current market share (Blasiak et al., 2020).

17.2.2 AI in Drug Discovery and Development

The expanding number of AI and Machine learning start-ups, Pharma alliances with AI platforms and articles and reviews documenting applications, their success, and obstacles show AI's growing relevance in drug research and development (Liebman, 2022). Researchers and professionals are interested in artificial intelligence as a path to achieving the requisite advancement in the pharma industry. However, little research has been done on the impact of AI and how it can be used to improve industries (Kulkov, 2021).

Figure 17.2 shows AI drug discovery applications. (Mak & Pichika, 2019). Artificial intelligence could identify hit and lead compounds, as well as evaluate and optimise drug targets (Mak & Pichika, 2019), (Sellwood, 2018).

There are three phases where AI is employed in drug discovery which are; Phase-1 in which the drug development process involves reviewing and interpreting existing literature and studying how prospective medicines interact with targets. In Phase-2, during preclinical research, possible therapeutic targets are explored in animal models. AI might help trials go more smoothly and assist researchers to forecast a drug's animal model interaction much faster. Whereas, in Phase-3, after preclinical development and FDA approval, researchers test the medication on humans. This procedure is the most time-consuming and costly in medication production (Paul et al., 2021).

AI can assist monitor clinical trials by collecting more data quicker and by customising the trial experience. AI can discover molecules fast and at a fifth of the expense of previous approaches (Gupta, 2021). The epidemic has been a great illustration of worldwide capacity to collaborate and use collective expertise in order to achieve a common goal of coming up with a solution rapidly (Bloom, 2021). There is a need of a drive to transform the traditional drug development process by integrating data, AI technology and a patient-centric approach. The global pharmaceutical industry is on the verge of a technological revolution as rapid advances in artificial intelligence open the possibility of developing more effective drugs faster and at a lower cost.

For drug development, a wide range of experimental data, whether chemical, transcriptomic, or genomic, is easily accessible. Summarizing the large volume of biological data available into appropriate models in order to truly understand the complete process of diseases appears to be becoming exceedingly challenging. However, in order to speed up the process of developing effective drugs, advancements in systems biology and machine learning are already being made. Drug

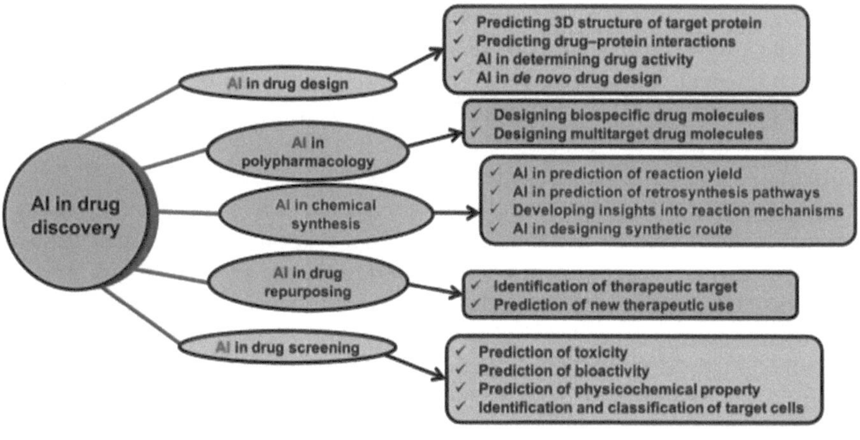

Fig. 17.2 AI in drug discovery. (Mak & Pichika, 2019)

discovery, drug testing, and drug repurposing are three major relevant and interrelated concerns that can all be automated. Developments in pharmaceutical business processes influenced by AI are significant, although they have not been well investigated. In the pharmaceutical industry, there are not many successful AI implementations (Hessler & Baringhaus, 2018).

17.2.3 Conceptual Framework

Conceptual framework is an analytical technique used in this research to provide a full grasp of the subject matter to the CEOs, CXOs, business leaders, managers, and associates of the Pharma companies. In this study, the conceptual framework is used to describe the major variables to be researched and their interactions in the way concepts are organised to fulfil the aim of a research study, with explanation being the most prevalent approach. Literature review is part of this conceptual framework. Survey of literature has provided ample amount data including various research gaps, future scope and opportunities, and various independent and sub-independent variables which impacts the dependent variables in the contract.

This framework helped to put together all relevant information and present the unexplored impactful internal and external determinants on this research topic. Thorough literature review has been conducted on the research topic with latest articles from ABDC journals. Meticulous literature review gave inputs on the research method, dependent variables, sub independent variables, dependent variables, research gaps and future scope. Based on the gathered data, the next steps taken were to find the individualised factors that are discussed in the literature, and then to analyse the connection between those factors. This supported to form a diagram or a flowchart to complete the conceptual framework.

Based on the literature review, appropriate conceptual framework is designed for this research. The framework shows the connects within dependent variable and independent variables as a part of construct. As indicated by literature review and research gaps mentioned below, there is a lack of a theoretical framework, to guide research on identifying factors impacting AI implementation in drug development in pharma industries. This study to utilize a version of the independent variables to construct a preliminary conceptual framework which will be validated through quantitative research to formulate research hypothesis.

As per survey of literature, some of the key internal factors for research are quality management system, research & development, talent & culture management, and budget/finance management where as some of the key external factors are standard & compliance and market dynamics. These each independent variables or factors will have sub-independent variables further (Fig. 17.3).

In the future, AI technology is predicted to cover all aspects of newer drug discovery and development as more medical data is accumulated and more efficient AI algorithms are developed, and therefore become a widespread computer-aided drug

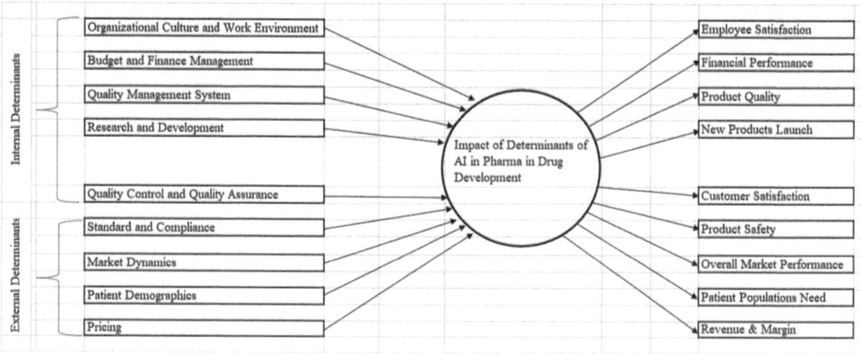

Fig. 17.3 Conceptual framework of AI in pharma industry in drug development

design approach. (Bender & Cortes-Ciriano, 2021). Drug development is still at the early stage of adopting new and emerging experimental and computational technologies. The process might be revolutionized as a result of remarkable advances in computer power combined with innovations in AI technology. Because of rising R&D expenditures and decreased efficiency, the pharmaceutical industry is now having difficulty in maintaining its drug development programs. One of the major issues is determining whether these technologies should be used to improve the existing pipeline and processes or whether there is a true possibility to re-engineer the processes in light of these technologies (Bender & Cortes-Ciriano, 2021).

To effectively improve the area, we must first get a deeper understanding of biology and then create data containing a signal of relevance in a hypothesis-driven way, which is tied to both efficacy and safety end objectives. Conveyed in another way, we need to advance better candidates into the clinic, enhance target validation, improve patient recruitment, and advance how clinical trials are run in order to forecast medication effectiveness and safety with the necessary quality, then at a lower cost and faster pace.

Artificial intelligence approaches have a lot of potential for improving the process in terms of clinical significance and cost by using computational and reasoning techniques, but their success will be dependent on combining the appropriate question with the correct technology (Deng et al., 2022). Considering the strengths of AI in Pharma and few identified research gaps and future scope, developing research construct to identify the impact of external and internal determinants which signifies process relevance within drug development. From survey of literature, its understood that, in most cases, pharmacists follow strict protocols while developing new medications. But recently, there has been a shift in both theory and practise toward using AI in drug development to boost productivity or provide treatments for illnesses that have so far been intractable. However, there is still no study that examines AI-based drug development research from a macro level. It is surprising that there hasn't been more study into the use of AI in the pharmaceutical industry, given its relevance and promise. Based on a bibliometric examination of all relevant works and the links between algorithms, institutions, nations, and financial sponsors, this study intended to fill this knowledge vacuum (Karger & Kureljusic, 2022).

Literature review provided research gaps and future scope in the several areas such as, areas of AI and ML in drug discovery which are related to the various unexplored, unexperimented internal and external determinants of the application of AI for the drug development and formation of the conceptual research framework which enables successful implementation of application AIML in regular practice in Pharma industry. Hence, based on the literature review, research gaps and future scope, the key proposed research questions and objectives are arrived for drug development within Pharma industry:

17.2.4 Research Questions

- How AI and ML can be best implemented for drug development in the Pharma Industry?
- How external environmental determinants influence drug development in Pharma industry?
- How internal environmental determinants influence drug development in Pharma industry?

17.2.5 Research Objectives

- To identify key factors, various opportunities exist in the pharma industry for fast drug development
- To provide new insight into the development activities of the market
- To gain better understanding of Pharma industries development capabilities and process in drug development

Based on the literature review following internal and external determinants were identified which can influence implementation of AI and ML in pharma industry for drug development phase. There determinants are considered as independent variables of the defined construct whereas dependent variable is impact of AI and ML in drug development in pharma industry.

17.2.6 Internal Determinants

The factors which are in control of the firm or company are called as internal determinants. Below are the internal determinants which impact application of AI in drug discovery.

17.2.6.1 Quality Management System

Within the QMS framework, AI is an invaluable resource that will likely continue at the front of digitalization, leading the pharmaceutical sector into the 4.0 era. The pharmaceutical sector is now inflexible, reactive rather than proactive, and delayed due to the application of Good Manufacturing Practice standards in line with US FDA, MHRA, and other regulatory organisations. The incorporation of new technology into established procedures will allow for more agility and responsiveness to market changes, as well as the capacity to foresee and prevent any problems (Kumar, 2022).

As AI becomes more prevalent in the manufacturing sector, we may anticipate an increase in quality control and a consequent reduction in the requirement for product recalls and corrective measures after items have left the factory. Artificial intelligence will revolutionise quality control in the pharmaceutical industry, one digitalized manufacturing facility at a time.

17.2.6.2 Research & Development

In the last 10 years, AI and ML have emerged as the cutting-edge technology most expected to revolutionize the pharmaceutical R&D industry (R&D). Part of the impetus for this is the dissolution of barriers to large-scale data collecting and processing brought about by recent breakthrough developments in computer technology. Meanwhile, the expense of researching, developing, and delivering new medicines to market and to patients has skyrocketed. AI/ML approaches are attractive to the pharmaceutical sector because of their automated nature, predictive capabilities, and the projected gain in efficiency that results from taking use of these features. The planning, execution, and analysis of clinical trials are the most recent steps in the drug development process to see beneficial disruption from AI and ML. As we go toward a future in which AI/ML is increasingly included into R&D, it is crucial to get beyond the associated buzz-words and noise (Kolluri et al., 2022).

17.2.6.3 Organizational Culture and Work Engagement

Literature review shows that the pharmaceutical business has workforce concerns worldwide. Although the pharmaceutical business has lower turnover rates than others, the expense is higher. Authors who have studied the pharmaceutical sector have different opinions. Nafisa Shahin (2017) says when a research expert quits an organisation, product development is delayed and talent is lost. Pharmaceutical reps depart with client ties. Jindal et al. (2016) find that organisations with more engaged workers had lower attrition rates, better productivity and greater customer satisfaction. Hussin et al. (2016) claim pharmaceutical enterprises are supporting their human capital, which drives innovation, by focusing on employee happiness, working environment, organisational support, respect and continual growth. These considerations, among others, drive pharmaceutical professionals to persist (Vijayakumar & John, 2018).

17.2.6.4 Budget/Finance Management

A company's budget is a set of estimates and predictions detailing how it will arrange and utilise its resources during each stage of the drug development process to accomplish its strategic goals. Managers' ability to plan and control costs throughout the project's R&D phase is greatly enhanced by the use of budgets. Budgeting is essential for all pharmaceutical businesses, no matter their size, since it requires the establishment of clear goals, the recording of actual outcomes, and the assessment of efficacy. The goal of this consideration is to assess the state of R&D budgeting processes in the pharmaceutical industry and to provide recommendations for improving these procedures so that businesses may create more efficient budgets and budget reports (Ngoc & Oanh, 2019).

17.2.6.5 Quality Control and Quality Assurance

Obtaining the ideal mix of raw materials and finished product requires a delicate balancing act involving many factors (Gams, 2014). Keeping the goods consistent from batch to batch and conducting quality assurance checks on them both involve human intervention. This demonstrates the pressing necessity for the introduction of AI right now, even if it may not be the optimal strategy in all circumstances (Rantanen & Khinast, 2015). To better comprehend the key operation and specific criteria that regulate the ultimate quality of the pharmaceutical product, the FDA updated the cGMP with a "Quality by Design" approach (Aksu, 2013).

Preliminary data from manufacturing batches was evaluated, and decision trees were created, using a mix of human and AI labour by Gams et al. The operators then interpreted these into rules to use in the future as a basis for the production cycle (Gams, 2014). As an indication of theophylline pellets' consistency from batch to batch, Goh et al. used ANN to examine dissolution profiles, and their results accurately predicted the tested formulation's dissolution with an error of 8% (Goh, 2002).

Artificial intelligence may be used to control in-line manufacturing processes so that final products meet quality standards (Aksu, 2013). Freeze-drying processes are monitored using ANNs, which employ a hybrid of self-adaptive evolution, local search, and backpropagation methods. For a given set of working parameters, this may be used to foretell the temperature and desiccated-cake thickness later (t + t), which can then be used to monitor the final product's quality (Drăgoi, 2013).

17.2.7 External Determinants

The factors which are out of control of the firm or company are called as external determinants. Below are the external determinants which impacts application of AI in drug discovery.

17.2.7.1 Market Dynamics

Artificial intelligence has the potential to revolutionise the drug discovery process by drastically shortening the R&D timetable, reducing drug development costs, and speeding up the approval process. Asia-Pacific AI in Drug Discovery Market Industry is expected to account for USD 3424.04 MN by 2029. Drug repurposing studies may benefit from AI technology as well (Data Bridge Market Research, 2022).

Figure 17.4, shows AI in Drug Discovery Market (Data Bridge Market Research, 2022), with full view of applications, indications, offerings, end users, technologies, drug types and companies involved in the development of software and technologies. The nation portion of the research includes market-impacting variables and regulatory changes that affect current and future market trends. New sales, replacement sales, nation demographics, regulatory activities, and import-export taxes are utilised to anticipate country markets. Also discussed are the existence and availability of Asia-Pacific brands, their problems owing to big or limited competition from local and domestic brands, and the influence of sales channels (Data Bridge Market Research, 2022).

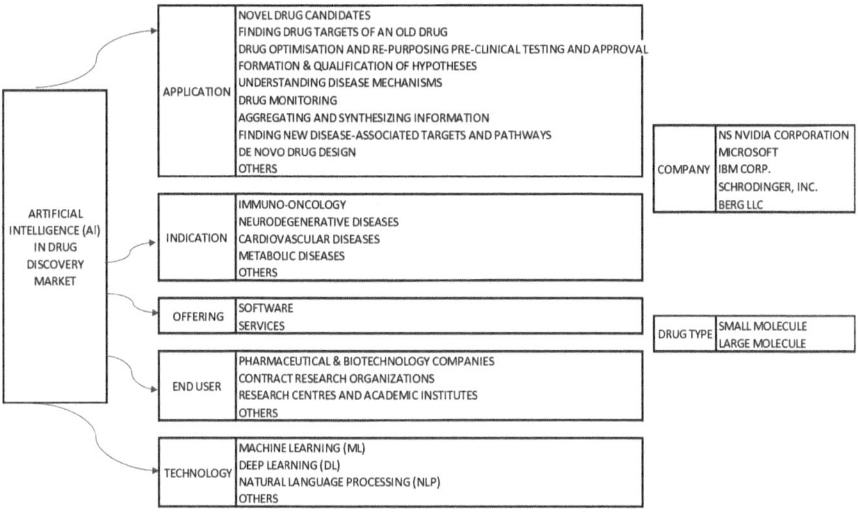

Fig. 17.4 AI in drug discovery market. (Data Bridge Market Research, 2022)

17.2.7.2 Standard & Compliance

Pharmaceutical firms are dynamic. Changes in FDA and EMA rules have enhanced the need of regulatory compliance management for pharma makers. Pharma businesses must adjust their compliance methods to comply with new rules and anti-corruption legislation. The US FDA controls global regulatory action, requiring pharma & life sciences corporations to detect quality concerns before affecting production.

17.2.7.3 Pricing

Pricing is an extremely important factor for stakeholders, companies, and customers. Pricing determines success rate and speed at which particular drug spreads and supports patients after quality. Novel gene therapies and cures are straining health care budgets due to their high up-front costs and value.

For patients, payers, and governments to afford pharmaceuticals, aging and shifting demographics have put pressure on health care systems, while novel gene treatments and cures are straining finances. In rising nations, the middle class expects superior health care and novel therapies. These reasons have raised emphasis on the cost of medications, and some governments, payers, patient organisations, and other stakeholders are working to cut pharmaceutical prices via legislation and/or other ways (Pfizer, 2017).

Pharma firms, especially in India, must restructure their quality and compliance structure to adhere to growing regulatory norms. With the FDA and other agencies expanding compliance requirements, organisations should take a holistic approach and make compliance part of their company strategy. Effective training, regular communication, frequent assessments, and top-management support are needed. As part of their commitment to quality and compliance, companies should implement strong internal controls. Regulators must link country-specific regulatory frameworks with global norms to harmonise requirements and boost company efficiency. Government regulates pharmaceuticals. Pharma is heavily controlled. Global political instability impacts Pharma businesses' ability to operate in various nations as governments adopt pharmaceutical rules and regulations.

An investment in pharmaceuticals helps prevent expensive health care interventions, improves patient quality of life, and boosts worker productivity. We consider several criteria while pricing drugs. We also try to make our medicines inexpensive for patients, payers, and governments, given their importance to the health care system (Pfizer, 2017).

17.2.7.4 Patient Demographics

Changes in food, urbanisation, and exercise habits, together with rising life expectancy, are increasing the incidence of non-communicable diseases (NCDs) such as cancer, cardiovascular disease, and diabetes. Chronic illnesses are hard to cure, therefore pharmaceutical firms must develop new drugs and vaccines. These elements provide new challenges to improve and lengthen lives, but also strain health care professionals and lawmakers (Pfizer, 2017).1 in 4, individuals outside Africa will be over 60 by 2050 and Chronic illnesses will cause almost 3 out of 4 deaths globally by 2020.

17.3 Discussion

The use of artificial intelligence and machine learning in computer-assisted drug development has its own set of issues and advantages (Selvaraj et al., 2022). For finding the novel ways to treat the diseases that are currently incurable, the application of AI in Drug development has lot of potential. But no doubt that there is a requirement of constant improvement of AI platforms. On the other hand, poor management of data is also one of the reasons of failure of AI. Therefore, there is a need for the pharmaceutical companies with extensive AI knowledge in order to create the databases and integrate them with AI-assisted drug development. Experts believe that AI will revolutionize the pharmaceutical industry and the way new drugs are discovered. Through screening, evaluation, and treatment suggestions, AI has the potential to improve the quality of care for specialties and rare diseases.

AI's relevance in drug research and development is evolving as AI and machine learning start-ups, Pharma collaborations with AI platforms, and studies and reviews on applications, their success, and challenges increase (Liebman, 2022).

As per survey of literature, its understood that, there are following research gaps existing which are clearly, the future opportunities to focus research upon:

- There has been very little written on identifying and exploring impact of determinants in implementation of AI within drug discoveries in Pharma industries in India.
- As, so far, the research has concentrated on certain possibilities of AI in drug discoveries for developing algorithms for various processes within drug development for pharma companies.
- In the mobilisation of firm's external determinants to create high-value impact in Pharma industry to meet unmet consumer needs and accomplish corporate growth performance
- In the mobilisation of firm's internal determinants to create high-value impact in Pharma industry to meet unmet consumer needs and accomplish corporate growth performance

- Exploration of various AI implementation practices in satisfying unmet needs such as, shortening drug discoveries developmental cycle, to predict drug efficacy and safety with the desired quality at decreased cost and increased speed in Pharma industry

In the days before artificial intelligence, regulation was affected by cutting-edge technology such as genetic engineering, gene-based pharmaceuticals, and stem cell research (Sharma & Manchikanti, 2021).

Ethical considerations are one of the most important parts of the research. Ethical standards and considerations are upheld throughout entire research process. Researcher has ethical responsibilities for conduct of research and transparency. This comprises research design, data gathering and analysis, and data sharing and publication.

17.4 Conclusion

The drug development process is extremely complex, requiring specialized expertise in a wide range of domains (biology, chemistry, and medicine are the few to name). Secondly, compelling evidence is required for decision-making in the drug discovery process. (Kim et al., 2020). Despite of all these, several researchers have demonstrated that AI technology has a promising future in drug development. But, the disparity across the domains is a significant blocking point.

The rise in the number of start-ups in the healthcare technology space may be explained by the fact that AI is constantly being developed alongside remarkable tools that aim to reduce the difficulties pharmaceutical companies face, which in turn affects the drug development process and the product's entire lifecycle (Chan, 2019). The health sector is in dire need of substantial overhauls, since it is currently plagued by a variety of critical challenges, such as the rising price of medications and treatments. Incorporating AI into the production of pharmaceuticals will allow for the creation of individualised drugs that meet the needs of each patient in terms of dosage, timing of release, and other factors (Rantanen & Khinast, 2015). Using the most cutting-edge AI-based technologies not only shortens the time it takes for items to reach the market, but also raises product quality, ensures worker safety, maximises resource utilisation, and reduces production costs (Jämsä-Jounela, 2007).

Concerns of using these technologies include employment losses and the necessity for rigorous AI legislation. These devices are meant to simplify labour, not replace people (Davenport & Ronanki, 2018). AI can help with hit compound discovery, synthesis method recommendations, chemical structure prediction, and drug–target interactions. As of 2021, the total value of the drug discovery market was estimated to be about $74.96 billion (Drug Discovery Market, 2022). Even with these huge budgets, the FDA has approved comparatively a small percentage of proposed new medications (Monika, 2022). The current medication development process is long and costly, controlled by multinational pharmaceutical corporations, and dependent on inhumane animal experiments.

The development of more effective strategies for finding new therapeutics is a global priority. The healthcare industry is seeing a transformation thanks to recent developments in artificial intelligence, machine learning, and innovative organ modelling (Gupta, 2021). Newer, more efficient, and more trustworthy approaches are being used by the pharmaceutical sector.

AI may help incorporate a developed medicine into the right dosage form and optimise it, as well as assist in rapid decision-making, resulting to speedier manufacturing of better-quality goods with batch-to-batch consistency. AI can help prove the product's safety and effectiveness in clinical trials and ensure correct placement and pricing via market research and prediction. While there are no AI-based medications on the market and implementation issues exist In the not-too-distant future, artificial intelligence will unquestionably develop into a tool that is impossible to managed without for pharmaceutical business.

AI professionals will need to understand drug discovery data and develop relevant and interpretable algorithms to explain modes of action to support future decision making. The most essential thing for both organizations is to be interested in collaborating and communicate actively in order to build a concrete foundation for a new revolution in drug development. The analysis of this research has been able to suggest a decent beginning point for bridging the gap and support identifying conceptual framework with internal and external determinants of the Pharma industry within AI environment for drug development in India. As a next step of this research this model will be tested and confirmed for India region.

17.5 Future Scope

This model can also be tested for other region for identifying significance of the relevant internal and external determinants and co relating studies done within India. This model can also be tested with mixed research method to see if any more observations can contribute to the model.

References

Aksu, B. (2013). A quality by design approach using artificial intelligence techniques to control the critical quality attributes of Ramipril tablets manufactured by wet granulation. *Pharmaceutical Development and Technology, 18*, 236–245.

Bender, A., & Cortes-Ciriano, I. (2021). Artificial intelligence in drug discovery: What is realistic, what are illusions? Part 2: A discussion of chemical and biological data. *Drug Discovery Today, 26*(4), 1040–1052. https://doi.org/10.1016/j.drudis.2020.11.037

Blasiak, A., Khong, J., & Kee, T. (2020). CURATE. AI: Optimizing personalized medicine with artificial intelligence. *SLAS Technology, 25*(2), 95–105. https://doi.org/10.1177/2472630319890316. Epub 2019 Nov 26.

Bloom, B. (2021). Building the future of drug discovery. *Drug Discovery Today, 26*(4), 863–864. https://doi.org/10.1016/j.drudis.2021.01.032

Bonam, S. R., et al. (2021). Role of pharmaceutical sciences in future drug discovery. *Future Drug Discovery, 3*(3). https://doi.org/10.4155/fdd-2021-0005

Chan, H. S. (2019). Advancing drug discovery via artificial intelligence. *Trends in Pharmacological Sciences, 40*(8), 592–604.

Dara, S., et al. (2022). *Machine learning in drug discovery: A review, artificial intelligence review*. Springer. https://doi.org/10.1007/s10462-021-10058-4

Data Bridge Market Research. (2022). *Artificial Intelligence (AI) in drug discovery market size, scope & industry overview by 2029*. https://www.databridgemarketresearch.com/reports/global-artificial-intelligence-ai-in-drugdiscovery-market

Davenport, T. H., & Ronanki, R. (2018). Artificial intelligence for the real world. *Harvard Business Review, 96*, 108–116.

Deng, J., et al. (2022). Artificial intelligence in drug discovery: Applications and techniques. *Briefings in Bioinformatics, 23*(1), 1–65. https://doi.org/10.1093/bib/bbab430

Drăgoi, E. N. (2013). On the use of artificial neural networks to monitor a pharmaceutical freeze-drying process. *Drying Technology, 31*, 72–81.

Drug Discovery Market. (2022). By drug type: Small molecule and large molecule; by end user: Pharmaceutical Companies, CRO, Others; By Technology: High throughput screening, pharmacogenomics, combinatorial chemistry, nanotechnology, other technologies). *Global Industry Analysis, Size, Share, Growth, Trends, Regional Outlook, and Forecast* 2021–2030. Report Code: 1464

Duch, W., Swaminathan, K., & Meller, J. (2007). Artificial intelligence approaches for rational drug design and discovery. *Current Pharmaceutical Design, 13*(14), 1497–1508. https://doi.org/10.2174/138161207780765954

Gams, M. (2014). Integrating artificial and human intelligence into tablet production process. *AAPS PharmSciTech., 15*, 1447–1453.

Goh, W. Y. (2002). Application of a recurrent neural network to prediction of drug dissolution profiles. *Neural Computing and Applications, 10*, 311–317.

Gupta, J. (2021). *The power of artificial intelligence in drug discovery*. Indiaai.gov.in. https://indiaai.gov.in/article/thepower-of-artificial-intelligence-in-drug-discovery

Hessler, G., & Baringhaus, K. H. (2018). Artificial intelligence in drug design. *Molecules, 23*(10). https://doi.org/10.3390/molecules23102520

Hussin, H., et al. (2016, April). Employee retention in the pharmaceutical companies: Case of Lebanon. *IOSR Journal of Business and Management (IOSR-JBM)., 18*(4), 58–75. e-ISSN: 2278-487X, p-ISSN: 2319-7668.

Jämsä-Jounela, S.-L. (2007). Future trends in process automation. *The Annual Review of Control, 31*, 211–220.

Jindal, P., et al. (2016). Employee engagement; Tool of talent retention: Study of a pharmaceutical company. *SDMIMD Journal of Management*. https://doi.org/10.18311/sdmimd/2017/18024. Print ISSN: 0976-0652 Online ISSN 2320-7906.

Karger, E., & Kureljusic, M. (2022). Using artificial intelligence for drug discovery: A bibliometric study and future Research agenda. *Pharmaceuticals, 15*, 1492. https://doi.org/10.3390/ph15121492

Kim, H., et al. (2020). Artificial intelligence in drug discovery: A comprehensive review of data-driven and machine learning approaches. *Biotechnology and Bioprocess Engineering, 25*(6), 895–930. https://doi.org/10.1007/s12257-020-0049-y

Kolluri, S., Lin, J., Liu, R., Zhang, Y., & Zhang, W. (2022). Machine learning and artificial intelligence in pharmaceutical Research and Development: A review. *The AAPS journal, 24*(1), 19. https://doi.org/10.1208/s12248-021-00644-3

Kulkov, I. (2021). The role of artificial intelligence in business transformation: A case of pharmaceutical companies. *Technology in Society, 66*(June), 101629. https://doi.org/10.1016/j.techsoc.2021.101629

Kumar, S. (2022, March 7). *Integration of artificial intelligence and machine learning in quality management systems*. AmpleLogic | Pharma Quality Solutions. https://amplelogic.com/integration-of-artificial-intelligence-andmachine-learning-in-quality-management-systems

Liebman, M. (2022). The role of artificial intelligence in drug discovery and development. *Chemistry International, 44*(1), 16–19. https://doi.org/10.1515/ci-2022-0105

Lu, R. (2021, Spring). Drug discovery and India: The future looks bright. *Drug Discovery World (DDW), 22*(2). https://www.ddw-online.com/drug-discovery-and-india-the-future-looks-bright-10649-202104/

Mak, K. K., & Pichika, M. R. (2019). Artificial intelligence in drug development: Present status and future prospects. *Drug Discovery Today, 24*(3), 773–780. https://doi.org/10.1016/j.drudis.2018.11.014

Markets & Markets. (2022). Global Artificial Intelligence (AI) in Drug discovery market – Industry trends and forecast to 2029

Monika, G. (2022). *The future of drug discovery: AI, simulated organs, and no more mice*. Wevolver. https://www.wevolver.com/article/the-future-of-drug-discovery-ai-simulated-organs-and-no-more-mice

Nafisa, S. (2017, September). A study of employee retention in the pharmaceuticals sector in Ranchi City. *International Journal of Engineering Technology Science and Research IJETSR, 4*(9). www.ijetsr.com ISSN 2394-3386.

Ngoc, B. T., & Oanh, L. T. T. (2019). Budgeting for management functions in the pharmaceutical enterprises. *SSRG International Journal of Economics and Management Studies, 6*(11), 34–43. https://doi.org/10.14445/23939125/IJEMS-V6I11P105

Paul, D., Sanap, G., Shenoy, S., Kalyane, D., Kalia, K., & Tekade, R. K. (2021). Artificial intelligence in drug discovery and development. *Drug Discovery Today, 26*(1), 80–93. https://doi.org/10.1016/j.drudis.2020.10.010

Pfizer Annual Review. (2017). *Understanding the external environment*. https://www.pfizer.com/files/investors/financial_reports/annual_reports/2017/our-business-ourpurpose/understanding-the-external-environment/index.html

Rantanen, J., & Khinast, J. (2015). The future of pharmaceutical manufacturing sciences. *Journal of Pharmaceutical Sciences, 104*, 3612–3638.

Sellwood, M. A. (2018). Artificial intelligence in drug discovery. *Future Science, 10*, 2025–2028.

Selvaraj, C., Chandra, I., & Singh, S. K. (2022). Artificial intelligence and machine learning approaches for drug design: Challenges and opportunities for the pharmaceutical industries. *Molecular Diversity, 26*(3), 1893–1913. https://doi.org/10.1007/s11030-021-10326-z

Sharma, K., & Manchikanti, P. (2021, December). Regulation of artificial intelligence in drug discovery and health care. *Biotechnology Law Report, 39*(5). https://doi.org/10.1089/blr.2020.29183.ks

Vijayakumar, S., & John, G. (2018). Organisational excellence in the pharmaceutical industry. *International Journal for Research in Engineering Application & Management (IJREAM), 04*(09), 649–652. https://doi.org/10.18231/2454-9150.2018.1260

Vyas, M. (2018). Artificial intelligence: The beginning of a new era in pharmacy profession. *Asian Journal of Pharmaceutics, 12*, 72–76.

Chapter 18
Exploring Employee Engagement in the New Zealand Healthcare Industry During the COVID-19 Pandemic

Erlita Cabal-Roberts and Jacob Wood

Abstract Our research examines employee engagement in the New Zealand healthcare industry during the COVID-19 pandemic. Our qualitative study examines 17 management staff (2 Chief Executive Officers and 15 Managers) employed in healthcare organizations across New Zealand. Our study specifically addressed the negative impacts of the COVID-19 pandemic on employee engagement, the factors that diminish organisational commitment and strategies that boost employee engagement in the New Zealand healthcare industry during the COVID pandemic. Following an interpretivist approach, this research examined the different workplace realities of 17 research participants. Semi-structured interviews were then conducted as the primary basis of data collection. The results of which were then interpreted using thematic analysis as this research sought to identify emerging themes and patterns around factors that affect employee engagement. Our results showed that the pandemic had negative impacts on employee engagement among healthcare employees in New Zealand. Burnout associated with overwhelming job demands, extended work hours, and staffing shortages diminished organisational commitment. In order to address these issues, open communication, appreciation, authentic leadership, succession planning, and a positive organisational culture were found to be effective in boosting employee engagement.

Keywords Employee engagement · Healthcare industry · COVID-19 pandemic · New Zealand

---

E. Cabal-Roberts
Southern Institute of Technology, Invercargill, New Zealand
e-mail: robertserlita@gmail.com

J. Wood (✉)
James Cook University, Singapore, Singapore
e-mail: jacob.wood@jcu.edu.au

E. L. Eijdenberg et al. (eds.), *Innovation-Driven Business and Sustainability in the Tropics*, https://doi.org/10.1007/978-981-99-2909-2_18

18.1 Introduction

The COVID-19 pandemic has altered people's lives all over the world. It has challenged businesses of all sizes to respond and adapt to the changes and forced management to think outside the box. Amid shock and disbelief, business leaders were confronted with the reality of having to make quick decisions in finding ways to keep their finances afloat and implement strategies to keep business operations going despite the high level of uncertainty. The unthinkable happened: closing of borders, different phases of lockdowns, social distancing, contact tracing protocols, and a myriad of precautions set by the government. Managers realised that forward thinking and the development of new strategies were needed. A failure to respond to the crisis could quickly cause reduced profits (or no profit at all), which could eventually lead to the closure of many small businesses around the world. Due to this, some workers unfortunately lost their jobs, while some were given opportunities to work from home. Among those who are affected by the rapid changes were the medical professionals; with the pandemic having a huge impact on the healthcare industry. As healthcare workers serve in the frontlines, risking their lives and that of their families, they experienced job stress, while also being confronted with the need to cope with challenges both personal and professional.

Unlike other employees who are able to transition immediately to a home office set-up, medical professionals are required to work onsite to care for their patients. Burnout, which involves physical and emotional exhaustion and disengagement is common among medical professionals and is a catalyst for healthcare workers wanting to leave their profession (Chakrabarti & Markless, 2022). As the demand for healthcare workers continues to rise, competition amongst healthcare companies also continues to increase. To ensure that healthcare workers do not venture into other opportunities elsewhere, business leaders must pay attention to an important factor in organisational success – employee engagement.

What the clinical workforce goes through on a day-to-day basis during this pandemic is beyond difficult to put into words. Given this complex dynamic, there is an urgent need to assess the health and well-being of healthcare workers. As they sacrifice a lot in putting their patients' welfare first, employers in the healthcare industry must take responsibility to ensure that their medical staff are appropriately cared for in the workplace. After all, a robust healthcare facility is not possible without a healthy clinical workforce.

Given the myriad of negative impacts of the pandemic on healthcare workers and the steady rise of healthcare workers experiencing burnout, there is no better time for this study than now. In order to address this critical issue, our key research objectives for our study are:

1. To assess the impact of the COVID-19 pandemic on employee engagement in the New Zealand healthcare industry.
2. To identify factors that diminished organisational commitment of employees in the New Zealand healthcare industry during the COVID-19 pandemic.

3. To explore strategies that improved employee engagement in the New Zealand healthcare industry during the COVID-19 pandemic.

The rest of the study is as follows. Section 18.2 provides an assessment of the relevant contemporary literature on employee engagement, from a predominately New Zealand healthcare perspective. Section 18.3 outlines the methodological approach adopted for this research, while Sect. 18.4 details our key findings and areas of important discussion. Finally, Section 18.5 draws a series of concluding remarks and outlines areas of future potential research.

18.2 Literature Review

Kahn (1990) defined employee engagement as an employees' ability to be their full selves at work, which propels themselves towards achieving their full potential both in personal and professional spheres. Engagement is often associated with an employee's level of satisfaction with their job role and team. A study by Benjamin (2020) found that employees who are engaged are those that love what they do, are experiencing work-life balance, are led by effective leaders and possess values, which are aligned to that of the organisation they work for. High levels of job performance can be achieved by fostering employee engagement (Gruman & Saks, 2011; Kim et al., 2016; Wood et al., 2016, 2020). Managers are the key drivers of employee engagement. It is imperative that they know how to maintain staff organisational commitment to ensure that employees are willing to perform their best and work for the organisation's goals, and not just work for the paycheck. If getting paid is the only motivation in completing work assigned to them, it is easy for workers to venture elsewhere for greener pastures, a risk that should be mitigated by the management.

Sheraton et al. (2020) found that the COVID-19 pandemic triggered psychological impacts on healthcare workers such as depression, anxiety, insomnia, and work-related stress. Although the negative effects of the pandemic were experienced by everyone in varying degrees, healthcare professionals were more susceptible to it because their primary role involves facing the unknown head-on. It is greatly concerning that the risk of trauma and suicidal tendencies are particularly high among healthcare workers. Many are already physically and mentally worn-out due to increased job demands caused by issues of decreased staffing, intensified feelings of hopelessness and frustration as they are faced with the conflicting decision whether to prioritise providing care for their patients or protecting themselves and their loved-ones (Kinman et al., 2020). Shoja et al. (2020) stated that healthcare workers became more vulnerable to mental health issues during the pandemic because their workload was significantly higher than that of other professionals. Poor staff engagement in medical services has negative impacts on quality healthcare delivery, which leads to serious risks to both patients and staff (Chandrasiri, 2017). In a fast-paced healthcare environment, burnout happens when there is lack of employee and work engagement (Kim & Oh, 2012).

Providing direct care to COVID patients while desiring to be present for their families during times of uncertainty led the clinical workforce to feelings of fear and despair (Wu et al., 2020). As if experiencing psychological stress is not enough, there was also the added burden of having to wear facemasks all the time. A study by Purushothaman et al. (2021) revealed that healthcare workers suffer from prolonged use of facemasks as it leads to not only nasal discomfort but also to more serious issues such as cardio-respiratory strain and increased risk of infection. Wearing full personal protective equipment (PPE) is exhausting and adds to the overwhelming emotional distress experienced by healthcare workers. Choudhury et al. (2020) explored the physiological effects that are associated with the prolonged wearing of PPE among healthcare workers. They found that it can cause major adverse effects such as fatigue, headache, increased heart rate and a rise in blood pressure.

Healthcare workers suffered from post-traumatic stress disorder (PTSD) as they witnessed numerous deaths of COVID patients, so urgent organisational support is crucial in applying coping strategies to improve physiological safety (Zhou et al., 2021). Severe stress and anxiety hinder health workers' ability to provide efficient and safe patient care in a timely way, so it is important to protect their well-being because they are the most valuable resource in combatting the pandemic (Armitage & Nellums, 2020). When the health and well-being of healthcare workers are jeopardised, there can be increases in absenteeism, which then leads to productivity loss, directly affecting the welfare of the patients that require their care (Yaghoubi et al., 2021). Frontline healthcare workers also experienced ethical challenges and moral distress during the pandemic which caused acute stress and a number of post-traumatic symptoms (Aymerich et al., 2022). Moreover, work restrictions caused by isolation, lockdown, and social distancing protocols decreased the opportunity for primary healthcare workers to access support systems that could have been an excellent coping strategy (Shi et al., 2022). Emotional exhaustion among healthcare workers was caused by time pressure and unmanageable workloads (Wang et al., 2021).

A Singapore-based study by Tan et al. (2020) revealed that healthcare workers suffer from mild to severe depression, anxiety, and fear as they battle against the COVID-19 pandemic. Several studies found that the COVID-19 pandemic caused significant negative impacts on the mental health of healthcare workers (García-Fernández et al., 2022; Gupta et al., 2021; Lasalvia et al., 2020; Rodríguez-Rey et al., 2020). This is alarming, as these factors hinder employee engagement. Yuan et al. (2021) posited that there is a need to not only improve workplace conditions for healthcare workplaces, but to also set realistic goals and expectations that avoid employee disengagement. Shreffler et al. (2020) recognised that a lack of employee engagement is one of the hindrances in the implementation of strategies to improve the well-being of healthcare workers. There is a need for urgent interventions to improve the health and well-being of healthcare workers so that they can continue to perform their vital function while mitigating psychosocial risks (de Moura Villela et al., 2021).

Literature on employee engagement in the New Zealand healthcare industry specifically throughout the COVID-19 pandemic is scarce. Haar (2022) explored the drivers of burnout among New Zealand workers and attributed long hours of work as one of the major causes. Participants from his New Zealand study are from different industries and are not specific to the healthcare sector. Burholt et al. (2022) examined the well-being of older people's caregivers in New Zealand during the COVID-19 pandemic and found that there is insufficient access to support care services during the pandemic. The study does not include the clinical and non-clinical workforce in New Zealand; as it mainly focused on the caregiving sector.

Holroyd et al. (2022) assessed the effects of COVID-19 lockdowns on community healthcare workers in New Zealand and found that the significant health risks faced by the nurses, midwives, and community-based carers caused overwhelming stress, anxiety, and loneliness which remained prevalent even after the lockdowns were lifted. Bell et al. (2020) provided similar findings; New Zealand healthcare workers were found to be more susceptible to mental and physical health risks than non-essential workers. Both studies explored the ill effects of the pandemic on health workers' well-being; however, employee engagement was not explored in-depth.

Parr et al. (2020) explored the issue of engagement by examining 252 participants that were employed as registered nurses, enrolled nurses, healthcare assistants, and administrative staff of two hospitals in New Zealand. Their study found that improved patient experience can be achieved through organisational support and a high-quality leader-member relationship. A study focused on finding a solution in the recruitment and retention issues of New Zealand nurses found that supportive leadership and a workplace culture that encourages collaboration are vital in fostering engagement among nurses, allowing them to thrive in the workplace (Moloney et al., 2018).

Our research sought to address the empirical gap that exists on employee engagement from a New Zealand healthcare sector perspective. Moreover, very little is known of the employee engagement experiences of healthcare workers employed in the industry during the COVID-19 pandemic. Our results provide a mechanism by which New Zealand healthcare organisations can re-examine their workplace policies, organisational culture, leadership styles, manager-employee relationships, and communication styles.

18.3 Methodology

Following an interpretivist approach, this research examined the different workplace realities of the research participants (healthcare workers who hold management positions in the New Zealand healthcare industry) around employee engagement during the COVID-19 pandemic. This philosophical principle complements the research topic and corresponds to the beliefs and values that guide the overall design of this study.

Given that the COVID pandemic is a new phenomenon, an exploratory approach is appropriate for this study. A single data collection technique known as the mono method qualitative study is utilised in this research with semi-structed interviews conducted as the primary basis of data collection. Adhabi and Anozie (2017) asserted that semi-structured interviews have unique features that make them superior – they are functional, can explore reality by unfolding the meaning behind people's experiences, offer flexibility for participants to express themselves based on how well they know a topic rather than just ticking boxes. This qualitative approach represents the most appropriate means of delving into the employee engagement experiences of our participants. Our collected data was then interpreted using thematic analysis as this research involves identifying emerging themes and patterns around factors that affect employee engagement. Purposive sampling is used in the sample selection process. The 17 research participants interviewed for the study were all employed in management positions within the New Zealand healthcare industry. In order to stage the interviews, our study received formal ethical approval from the Southern Institute of Technology's Human Research Ethics Committee, based out of Invercargill, New Zealand.

18.4 Findings and Discussion

From the interviews that were conducted, we found that all participants confirmed that although burnout was already present before the pandemic due to the nature of their role in a fast-paced healthcare environment, the level of burnout experienced was felt more strongly during the COVID-19 pandemic.

> People are a lot more tired and a lot less willing to engage in extra activities beyond work. There is exacerbated tiredness. There are situations where we thought that we might be able to have a holiday and then suddenly, we got people off with COVID, holidays get postponed or at other times people were going on holiday. However, we were in lockdown, and as such there is no point going on holiday and locked down when we cannot go anywhere so we would end up coming back to work instead of taking a break. COVID created a whole extra layer of work. – Participant A.

Furthermore, Participant D contended that there were no real positive effects associated with employee engagement during the pandemic, stating that:

> Our staff lived through stress, even our non-clinical workforce is very exhausted. Our reception team were verbally abused to the point of tears by upset patients, clients are dealing with their own stressors caused by the pandemic and sometimes they take it out on staff. I have seen my staff lose the glitter in their eyes. They need to pause and breathe.

Participant F shared the same sentiments, stating that:

> Having to treat COVID patients is really wearing down our healthcare workers, add to that how some patients treat our medical staff poorly. We understand that there can be some

> frustrations with not knowing how things are working during the pandemic, but patients need to understand staff are also going through a lot. Some patients get irritated with the added COVID pre-screening questions before they are allowed to enter our practice.

Participant P expressed similar concerns:

> Employee stress is high, staff burnout is prevalent. Even if we listen to them and try to react as best as we can, we just do not have the staff to cover. And the expectation from the community has been frankly, nasty, and unreasonable. Not only our staff are fighting a battle to keep a level of service available, but when they hear from patients all kinds of negative foul language, it adds to the pressure.

Participant E confirmed that staff are complaining due to burnout, by stating that:

> Some staff are affected by COVID and so we rely on those who are not affected to do some double shifts. There is too much work to do so even the healthy ones could no longer deliver. COVID has forced a lifestyle change in our workers and it has been very tough for everyone.

Participant G raised the same concern, stating:

> There has been some need to work weekends as well, we felt the need to work weekends due to workload issues. There is real fatigue. There is the burden of extra work.

Similarly, Participant H explained:

> The expectation is for you to do more on the same salary. For those of us who are expected to go above and beyond over the COVID period with any emergency response, initially, everyone jumps around and must go the extra mile. But that reaches a limit. And when it goes on for a long time, you become very tired and disengaged.

Participant I commented:

> There is this feeling of enough is enough. The government needs to hear that we are not going to see extra patients, we have been working short-staffed for a long time. We are in a crisis; the bigger picture is the government needs to be looking at how they will fund this.

Participant J stated:

> There is a lot of extra pressure on general practice. Some flu patients are sicker than COVID patients are, but we were asked to intensely manage COVID patients, which is taking up a lot of resource.

Despite the enormous challenges brought about by the pandemic, three participants thought that COVID had a positive impact on employee engagement. Participant C shared:

> Our engagement went up during the pandemic. Our relationships have become stronger during tough times. People either break or they really make it work. In our team, when the world turns against us, we unite, we look after each other because we are all going through challenging times.

When asked about the factors that diminish organisational commitment, they all linked back to burnout, overwhelming work demands, and lack of resources to perform their role, and the need for better pay and benefits.

> Some key staff members are really pushing, they are over giving, even though they need to pull back and look after themselves. They need to be given some recovery time to maintain commitment. – Participant L

> Staff need mental health days, over and above the requirement for sick days. – Participant M

> Healthcare professionals in New Zealand should be paid better, so that we do not lose them to Australia or to other parts of the world. – Participant P

When asked about the strategies that are proven to be effective in enhancing employee engagement, it is apparent that little things go a long way.

> We provide opportunities to get together and share a meal. Informal moments are as important as formal performance appraisals. – Participant A

> It is easy to go around catching people doing something wrong. The job is to go and catch people doing something right. It is important to acknowledge when staff are doing a great job. Managing a team is relational, as well as functional. Performance should be ongoing; it should be a constant dialogue. – Participant C

> Keeping the communication flowing is key. We have a job board, and a joke board. Everybody put jokes up on so that we do not just focus on work stuff, we keep the laughter going in the workplace. – Participant D

> I think the secret to success in engagement is when the leadership team are also moving from the front; putting themselves in a position where they are doing the dangerous work as well, making sure that they are no strangers to their own business, that they are prepared to do what they ask staff to do. – Participant G

> You need to act with integrity; to be honest and when you promise you must deliver, you must be present and visible to the team. – Participant H

> It is important to foster a team culture where staff are being listened to. – Participant K

> We promote and develop employees professionally. It is important for staff to have something to look forward to in their career. – Participant N

> More time off would be great if only we could afford it; a good rest is what everyone really needs. – Participant Q

Findings from this study reinforce the theoretical frameworks, which guided this research. Participants have confirmed that a healthy employer-employee relationship and adequate resources can foster engagement and impact staff organisational commitment.

It is important to highlight that only 6 out of 17 participants utilise an employee engagement survey in their workplace. This shows that New Zealand healthcare organisations need to pay much greater attention to their staff and do more to actively engage with employees. A deterioration in the level of employee engagement that is experienced by staff has financial consequences; therefore, it is crucial to make this a part of an organisation's strategic plan. A well-executed employee engagement survey, should be one that acts on employee feedback, provides opportunities for organisations to re-examine their strategies and a chance to improve fundamental processes which affects financial outcomes (Hills, 2022).

Based on the findings of this study, there are several strategies that can be introduced that boost employee engagement. These are outlined below:

1. *Open Communication* – Communication is the lifeblood of any organisation, much more so in healthcare. Without it, a seamless workflow would be difficult, if not impossible. It is prevalent from our findings that an open-door policy is crucial in maintaining engagement. The managers who were interviewed confirmed that staff value being listened to and that they need a safe work environment wherein honest discussion is encouraged. Fostering positive employee communication behaviour invites team participation, which enhances employee engagement (Kang & Sung, 2017).
2. *Appreciation/Recognition* – Whether it be giving free meals, vouchers to cafes, pay increases, staff bonuses, or simple words of gratitude, the bottom line is, employees thrive in a workplace where their work contribution is recognized and rewarded. A higher level of engagement is achieved when leaders proactively support and celebrate team successes (Xu & Helena, 2011). Sincere appreciation holds immense power; it boosts employee morale and enhances their commitment towards continuously striving to do their best at every task assigned to them (Turaga, 2022).
3. *Authentic Leadership* – Leaders and managers must model the work ethics that they want to see from their staff. They must be ready to roll up their sleeves and do their part. As what one of the participants said, "We as managers need to use the 'walking in their shoes' concept. We should be representing every level of the business." Leaders can be more influential when they lead from the front. Authentic leadership enables meaningfulness of work, motivates followers to work towards the achievement of organisational goals, and creates a positive impact to employee engagement (Winton et al., 2022).
4. *Training and Development Support/Succession Planning* – Employees do not want to remain stagnant. Opportunities for career progression is always welcomed. This is one of the most effective staff retention strategies. An organisation's success depends on its willingness to invest in continuously upskilling and reskilling its employees and equipping them to perform their role more efficiently. Employees who are provided with proper training become more immersed in their role, which positively affects their work performance (Rakatu et al., 2022).
5. *Positive Organisational Culture* – If an organisation only focuses on outputs, be it profits or the achievement of work targets, but fails to cultivate a positive culture in the workplace, chances are, organisational commitment lessens. One of the participants shared, "We keep the laughter going, it keeps us motivated no matter how difficult our tasks can become." An efficient work culture is a significant enabler of employee engagement, it empowers employees to align their

values to that of the organisation's goals and mission (Srimulyani & Hermanto, 2022).

18.5 Conclusion

This research represents the first of its kind to examine employee engagement in the New Zealand healthcare industry during the COVID-19 pandemic. Using a qualitative approach, 17 management staff (2 Chief Executive Officers and 15 Managers) employed in healthcare organizations across New Zealand were interviewed. At the heart of our study, we sought to better understand the ways in which the COVID-19 pandemic had impacted employee engagement, the factors that diminish organisational commitment, and from this develop a series of strategies that seek to improve the way in which healthcare industry engages with its staff.

From our research, we found that the key issue that needs to be urgently addressed is the nationwide shortage of healthcare workers that exists in New Zealand. The current workforce is stretched and has had to work beyond their capacity, which then leads employees leaving due to burnout. Our study showed that the factors that diminish organisational commitment are all linked to burnout, increased workload, and unreasonable job demands and lack of resources caused by healthcare workforce crisis. In particular, as Participant L emphasised:

> We have advertised for nearly two years now, and we still do not have the right staffing for nurses. There are many general practitioners that are not too far from retiring. Who will replace them? To think that the primary health care has a very important role in the community, and yet we are undervalued.

Ultimately, the New Zealand government has a huge role to play in addressing healthcare staffing shortages. There is an urgent need to accelerate funding support to devise more workforce strategies to assist healthcare workers. Focusing on the well-being of healthcare workers is as important as prioritising high quality patient care delivery, if not more. The saying, "You cannot pour from an empty cup" is applicable here. To continuously be able to provide high quality healthcare services to patients, healthcare professionals must be cared for too, and they deserve so much more.

The COVID-19 pandemic has certainly taken a toll on everyone, and the healthcare workers are the ones battling on the frontlines. Most of them are fighting silent battles. They are depleted, over-fatigued, physically, emotionally, and mentally drained. Their voices should not remain unheard. The COVID pandemic created huge negative impact on employee engagement in the New Zealand healthcare industry.

The healthcare workforce in New Zealand is in a crisis. There is a need for the New Zealand government to develop strategies that would generate healthcare workforce sustainability. More initiatives need to be provided towards supporting medical students during their training and in absorbing them into New Zealand healthcare organisations. Moreover, the existing healthcare workers must be supported as they are experiencing severe fatigue and are vulnerable to physical and mental health issues due to overwhelming job demands. If the workforce crisis is not resolved, those in the healthcare sector will continue to experience severe fatigue, which is detrimental to their health and the health of the patients they are looking after. A healthy healthcare organisation requires a healthy workforce.

18.5.1 Future Areas of Research

Expanding the research population to include subordinates in the New Zealand healthcare organisation and not just the management team may reveal new insights around employee engagement strategies. It would be interesting to find out whether the common themes that emerged from this research would be similar to the perspectives of the employees who do not belong to the leadership team. The industry analysis of this research confirmed that New Zealand is in a health workforce crisis and part of the reason is that most healthcare workers move to Australia. Further research could be done with New Zealand trained doctors and nurses who prefer to work in Australia as the research participants. This would potentially provide valuable insights into what the New Zealand healthcare sector can do better to keep New Zealand's healthcare workforce sustainable. Insights shared by the participants regarding their own definition of employee engagement and the measurement of it revealed that employee engagement is individualistic. A case study within one healthcare organisation in New Zealand is recommended as it may allow an in-depth investigation of how employee engagement is distinct to a particular organisation and may provide insight into the different applicable strategies in engaging employees with a more specific approach. The literature review in this study revealed that there are serious financial consequences when employees are disengaged. Further research could be done on the economic implications of not engaging employees. It would be interesting to study how low productivity impacts financial outcomes. Disengaged employees tend to leave so it would be helpful to explore the associated financial implications of high staff turnover such as the cost in hiring new staff, onboarding process, training, and unfulfilled tasks due to role vacancies.

References

Adhabi, E., & Anozie, C. B. (2017). Literature review for the type of interview in qualitative research. *International Journal of Education., 9*. https://doi.org/10.5296/ije.v9i3.11483

Armitage, R., & Nellums, L. B. (2020). Protecting health workers' mental health during COVID-19. *Public Health, 185*(18), 18. https://doi.org/10.1016/j.puhe.2020.05.044

Aymerich, C., Pedruzo, B., Pérez, J. L., Laborda, M., Herrero, J., Blanco, J., Blanco, J., Gonzalo, M., Lucia, A., Estevez, O., Fernandez, M., de Pablo, G. S., Catalan, A., & González-Torres,

M. Á. (2022). Covid-19 pandemic effects on health workers' mental health: Systematic review and meta-analysis. *European Psychiatry, 65*(1). https://doi.org/10.1192/j.eurpsy.2022.1

Bell, C., Williman, J., Beaglehole, B., Stanley, J., Jenkins, M., Gendall, P., Rapsey, C., & Every-Palmer, S. (2020). Challenges facing essential workers: A cross-sectional survey of the subjective mental health and Well-being of New Zealand healthcare and 'other' essential workers during the COVID-19 lockdown. *BMJ Open, 11*, e048107. https://doi.org/10.1136/bmjopen-2020-048107

Benjamin, L. (2020). *Achieving the dream through a screen: Exploring employee engagement and commitment in virtual environments* (Master of science in organizational dynamics theses, University of Pennsylvania, Philadelphia, Pennsylvania). Penn Libraries. https://repository.upenn.edu/od_theses_msod/103

Burholt, V., Balmer, D., Balmer, D., Frey, R., Meha, P., Parsons, J., Roberts, M., Simpson, M. L., Wiles, J., Moema Gregorzewski, R. F., Gregorzewski, M., Moema Gregorzewski, J. P., Moema Gregorzewski, M. R., Moema Gregorzewski Mary, L. S., Moema Gregorzewski, J. W., Moema Gregorzewski, M. G., Moema Gregorzewski, T. P., & Reddy, R. (2022). Health equity and wellbeing among older people's caregivers in New Zealand during COVID-19: Protocol for a qualitative study. *PLoS One, 17*(7). https://doi.org/10.1371/journal.pone.0271114

Chakrabarti, R., & Markless, S. (2022). More than burnout: Qualitative study on understanding attrition among senior obstetrics and Gynaecology UK-based trainees. *BMJ Open, 12*(2), e055280. https://doi.org/10.1136/bmjopen-2021-055280

Chandrasiri, S. (2017). An ideal hospital: Is leading a workforce engagement strategy the key to tackling bullying, harassment and discrimination in surgical practice? *Leadership in Health Services, 30*(3), 263–271. https://www.proquest.com/docview/1917620310/fulltext/E66939650B14400BPQ/1?accountid=46872

Choudhury, A., Singh, M., Khurana, D. K., Mustafi, S. M., Ganapathy, U., Kumar, A., & Sharma, S. (2020). Effects of N95 FFP and PPE in healthcare workers in COVID intensive care unit: A prospective cohort study. *Indian Journal of Critical Care Medicine, 24*(12), 1169–1173. https://doi.org/10.5005/jp-journals-10071-23671

de Moura Villela, E. F., López, R. V. M., Sato, A. P. S., de Oliveira, F. M., Waldman, E. A., den Bergh, R. V., Fodjo, J. N. S., & Colebunders, R. (2021). COVID-19 outbreak in Brazil: Adherence to national preventive measures and impact on people's lives, an online survey. *BMC Public Health, 21*(152), 1–10. https://doi.org/10.1186/s12889-021-10222-z

García-Fernández, L., Romero-Ferreiro, V., López-Roldán, P. D., Padilla, S., Calero-Sierra, I., Monzó-García, M., Pérez-Martín, J., & Rodriguez-Jimenez, R. (2022). Mental health impact of COVID-19 pandemic on Spanish healthcare workers. *Psychological Medicine, 52*(1), 195–197. https://doi.org/10.1017/S0033291720002019

Gruman, J. A., & Saks, A. M. (2011). Performance management and employee engagement. *Human Resource Management Review, 21*(2), 123–136. https://doi.org/10.1016/j.hrmr.2010.09.004

Gupta, N., Dhamija, S., Patil, J., & Chaudhari, B. (2021). Impact of COVID-19 pandemic on healthcare workers. *Industrial Psychiatry Journal, 30*(3), 282–284. https://doi.org/10.4103/0972-6748.328830

Haar, J. (2022). Burnt to a crisp? Understanding drivers of burnout amongst New Zealand workers. *Evidence – Based HRM, 10*(2), 174–188. https://doi.org/10.1108/EBHRM-07-2021-0132

Hills, L. D. A. (2022). Improving your workplace experience to increase employee productivity and engagement. *The Journal of Medical Practice Management:MPM, 37*(5), 234–239. https://www.proquest.com/docview/2702262478/25B156600CEF42D6PQ/10?accountid=46872

Holroyd, E., Long, N. J., Nayantara, S. A., Sharyn, G. D., Deckert, A., Fehoko, E., Laws, M., Martin-Anatias, N., Simpson, N., Sterling, R., Trnka, S., & Tunufa'i, L. (2022). Community healthcare workers' experiences during and after COVID-19 lockdown: A qualitative study from Aotearoa New Zealand. *Health & Social Care in the Community, 30*(5). https://doi.org/10.1111/hsc.13720

Kahn, W. A. (1990). Psychological conditions of personal engagement and disengagement at work. *The Academy of Management Journal, 33*, 692–724. https://doi.org/10.2307/256287

Kang, M., & Sung, M. (2017). How symmetrical employee communication leads to employee engagement and positive employee communication behaviors. *Journal of Communication Management, 21*(1), 82–102. https://doi.org/10.1108/JCOM-04-2016-0026

Kim, S., & Oh, J. (2012). Employee emotional response toward healthcare organization's service recovery efforts and its influences on service recovery performance. *Service Business, 6*(3), 297–321. https://doi.org/10.1007/s11628-012-0137-y

Kim, W., Khan, F. G., Wood, J., & Mahmood, M. T. (2016). Employee engagement for sustainable organizations: Keyword analysis using social network analysis and burst detection approach. *Sustainability, 8*(631), 1–11.

Kinman, G., Teoh, K., & Harriss, A. (2020). Supporting the Well-being of healthcare workers during and after COVID-19. *Occupational Medicine, 70*(5), 294–296. https://doi.org/10.1093/occmed/kqaa096

Lasalvia, A., Bonetto, C., Porru, S., Carta, A., Tardivo, S., Bovo, C., Ruggeri, M., & Amaddeo, F. (2020). Psychological impact of COVID-19 pandemic on healthcare workers in a highly burdened area of north-East Italy. *Epidemiology and Psychiatric Sciences, 29*. https://doi.org/10.1017/S2045796020001158

Moloney, W., Gorman, D., Parsons, M., & Cheung, G. (2018). How to keep registered nurses working in New Zealand even as economic conditions improve. *Human Resources for Health, 16*, 45. https://doi.org/10.1186/s12960-018-0312-x

Parr, J. M., Teo, S., & Koziol-McLain, J. (2020). A quest for quality care: Exploration of a model of leadership relationships, work engagement, and patient outcomes. *Leading Global Nursing Research., 77*, 207–220. https://doi.org/10.1111/jan.14583

Purushothaman, P. K., Priyangha, E., & Vaidhyswaran, R. (2021). Effects of prolonged use of facemask on healthcare workers in tertiary care hospital during COVID-19 pandemic. *Indian Journal of Otolaryngology and Head & Neck Surgery, 73*, 59–65. https://doi.org/10.1007/s12070-020-02124-0

Rakatu, V. L., Chandra, A. K., & Soma, M. K. (2022). Employee engagement, job performance, turnover intention and workplace culture: A comparative study of private and public sector banks in Chhattisgarh †. *IUP Journal of Organizational Behavior, 21*(2), 117–140. https://www.proquest.com/docview/2676142975/8194C47F726344CAPQ/19?accountid=46872

Rodríguez-Rey, R., Garrido-Hernansaiz, H., & Bueno-Guerra, N. (2020). Working in the times of COVID-19. Psychological impact of the pandemic in frontline workers in Spain. *International Journal of Environmental Research and Public Health, 17*(21), 8149. https://doi.org/10.3390/ijerph17218149

Sheraton, M., Deo, N., Dutt, T., Salim, S., Hall-Flavin, D., & Rahul, K. (2020). Psychological effects of the COVID-19 pandemic on healthcare workers globally: A systematic review. *Psychiatry Research, 292*, 113360. https://doi.org/10.1016/j.psychres.2020.113360

Shi, L. S. B., Xu, R. H., & Chen, D. X. (2022). The impact of COVID-19-related work stress on the mental health of primary healthcare workers: The mediating effects of social support and resilience. *Frontiers in Psychology, 12*. https://doi.org/10.3389/fpsyg.2021.800183

Shoja, E., Aghamohammadi, V., Bazyar, H., Moghaddam, H. R., Nasiri, K., Dashti, M., Choupani, A., Garaee, M., Aliasgharzadeh, S., & Asgari, A. (2020). Covid-19 effects on the workload of Iranian healthcare workers. *BMC Public Health, 20*, 1636. https://doi.org/10.1186/s12889-020-09743-w

Shreffler, J., Petrey, J., & Huecker, M. (2020). The impact of COVID-19 on healthcare worker wellness: A scoping review. *Western Journal of Emergency Medicine, 21*(5), 1059. https://doi.org/10.5811/westjem.2020.7.48684

Srimulyani, V. A., & Hermanto, Y. B. (2022). Organizational culture as a mediator of credible leadership influence on work engagement: Empirical studies in private hospitals in East Java, Indonesia. *Humanities & Social Sciences Communications, 9*(1). https://doi.org/10.1057/s41599-022-01289-z

Tan, B. Y. Q., Chew, N. W. S., Lee, G. K. H., Jing, M., Goh, Y., Yeo, L. L. L., Zhang, K., Chin, H. K., Ahmad, A., Khan, F. A., Shanmugam, G. N., Chan, B. P. L., Sunny, S., Chandra, B.,

Ong, J. J. Y., Paliwal, P. R., Wong, L. Y. H., Sagayanathan, R., Chen, J. T., Ng, A. Y. Y., Teoh, H. L., Ho, C. S., Ho, R. C., & Sharma, V. K. (2020). Psychological impact of the COVID-19 pandemic on health care workers in Singapore. *Annals of Internal Medicine, 173*, 317–320. https://doi.org/10.7326/M20-1083

Turaga, R. (2022). The power of appreciation. *IUP Journal of Soft Skills, 16*(2), 52–57. https://www.proquest.com/docview/2704059168/4D052757084C4D18PQ/7?accountid=46872

Wang, H., Zhou, X., Jia, X., Song, C., Luo, X., Zhang, H., Wu, H., & Ye, J. (2021). Emotional exhaustion in front-line healthcare workers during the COVID-19 pandemic in Wuhan, China: The effects of time pressure, social sharing and cognitive appraisal. *BMC Public Health, 21*, 829. https://doi.org/10.1186/s12889-021-10891-w

Winton, B. G., Whittington, J. L., & Meskelis, S. (2022). Authentic leadership: Making meaning and building engagement. *European Business Review, 34*(5), 689–705. https://doi.org/10.1108/EBR-01-2022-0020

Wood, J., Khan, F. G., & Kim, W. (2016). Work engagement in organizations: A social network analysis of the domain. *Scientometrics, 109*(1), 317–336.

Wood, J., Park, J., Kim, W., & Oh, J. (2020). The relationship between work engagement and work-life balance in organizations: A review of the empirical research. *Human Resource Development Review, 19*(3), 240–262.

Wu, P. E., Styra, R., & Gold, W. L. (2020). Mitigating the psychological effects of COVID-10 on health care workers. *Canadian Medical Association Journal, 192*(17), E459–E460. https://doi.org/10.1503/cmaj.200519

Xu, J., & Helena, C. T. (2011). How can leaders achieve high employee engagement? *Leadership & Organization Development Journal, 32*(4), 399–416. https://doi.org/10.1108/01437731111134661

Yaghoubi, M., Salimi, M., & Meskarpour-Amiri, M. (2021). Systematic review of productivity loss among healthcare workers due to Covid-19. *The International Journal of Health Planning and Management, 37*(1), 94–111. https://doi.org/10.1002/hpm.3351

Yuan, Z., Yu, D., Zhao, H., Wang, Y., Jiang, W., Chen, D., Liu, X., & Li, X. (2021). Burnout of healthcare workers based on the effort-reward imbalance model: A cross-sectional study in China. *International Journal of Public Health, 66*. https://doi.org/10.3389/ijph.2021.599831

Zhou, T., Guan, R., & Sun, L. (2021). Perceived organizational support and PTSD symptoms of frontline healthcare workers in the outbreak of COVID-19 in Wuhan: The mediating effects of self-efficacy and coping strategies. *Applied Psychology: Health and Well-being, 13*(4), 745–760. https://doi.org/10.1111/aphw.12267

Chapter 19
Contemporary Employability Norms for Guest-Facing Hospitality Workers: Some Empirical Evidence During Covid-19

Nicolas Hepp, Riley Lynn Starling, Greta Elbracht, Miriam Sneha Rajkumar, Win Khant, and Pengji Wang

Abstract The Covid-19 pandemic has disrupted industries and now poses uncertainties regarding the skills necessary for employability in a peri- and post-pandemic landscape. With limited options to work remotely, the hospitality industry has been especially perilous and forced to adapt. This research is informed by a thorough literature review into employability in hospitality and theories on employability in the pandemic. This study seeks to address the need for empirical evidence of contemporary employability norms through interviews of 14 hospitality workers and content analysis of 2700 hospitality job advertisements from 158 different hotels and hotel groups. The findings of the job advertisements are compared with the interviews to reveal teamwork, communication, prioritization of guest experience, positivity, and flexibility as the top employability qualities. The paper argues that the top interview skills, like patience and emotional intelligence, should also be

N. Hepp (✉)
Independent Academic, AviAlliance, Düsseldorf, Germany
e-mail: nicolas.hepp@my.jcu.edu.au

R. L. Starling
Independent Academic, Swiss Asia Finanical Services, Singapore, Singapore
e-mail: rileystarling@gmail.com

G. Elbracht
Independent Academic, Cunard Line, Southampton, United Kingdom
e-mail: g.elbracht@gmx.de

M. S. Rajkumar
Independent Academic, Rakuten Symphony Singapore Pte. Ltd., Singapore, Singapore
e-mail: miriamsnehar@yahoo.com

W. Khant
Independent Academic, Phoe La Min Shopping Center, Hpa-An, Myanmar
e-mail: winkhant.446@gmail.com

P. Wang
JCU Singapore Business School, James Cook University, Singapore, Singapore
e-mail: pengji.wang@jcu.edu.au

E. L. Eijdenberg et al. (eds.), *Innovation-Driven Business and Sustainability in the Tropics*, https://doi.org/10.1007/978-981-99-2909-2_19

emphasized as they are not explicit in the job advertisements, which can be mistaken for a comprehensive description of employability qualities. The key skills mentioned in interviews are adaptability, patience, emotional intelligence, and innovation. The exploratory nature of this paper leaves many opportunities for further research, and meaningful implications for stakeholders.

Keywords Tourism & hospitality industry · Employability norms · Job advertisements · Content analysis · COVID-19 impact on employment

19.1 Introduction

The Covid-19 pandemic, which became a global crisis in early 2020, has caused chaos in industries around the globe, changed people's daily routines, and disrupted working conditions. As a result, there have been changes in the employability norms for what can be considered a peri-covid work environment (Eurico et al., 2015; Tiwari et al., 2020). While industries such as Information Technology or global supply chains operations received attention on the threats and opportunities that developed from the pandemic (Hobbs, 2020), the essentiality and sustainability of the hospitality and tourism industry is under-researched. The industry had to rapidly shift its focus by re-utilising the available resources and capabilities to meet constantly evolving consumer needs during the pandemic and keep the businesses running.

Hospitality workers face constant challenges in acquiring skills demanded by the employers to maintain their employability (Sisson & Adams, 2013; Yang et al., 2015). Front-of-house workers are especially vulnerable insofar as they cannot work remotely (Shobha & Johnson, 2021) and are also the most prone to workplace bullying from customers (Page et al., 2018). They now need to obtain an updated set of skills and abilities, to enhance their competency in the peri-covid labour market for better employability. Employability is the skills, attributes, and traits required to gain, maintain, and move between inter- and intra-organization positions, with acknowledgement that this package of qualities is dynamic due to ever changing customer and industry needs (Adeyinka-Ojo, 2018; Chen et al., 2021; Dhaliwal & Misra, 2020; Eurico et al., 2015; Wilson-Wünsch et al., 2015).

Scholarly, though there is existing literature on the skills, abilities, and knowledge necessary for employability in the hospitality and tourism industry (Dhaliwal & Misra, 2020; Weber et al., 2020; Yang et al., 2015), there have been limited opportunities to thoroughly investigate how these evolve, especially in the context of a global pandemic. There is not any article featuring an empirical approach to peri-covid employability in the hospitality industry.

To address this urgent yet underexplored gap, this project investigates the essential qualities for employment in the hospitality and tourism sector. The focus is narrowed towards front-of-house workers as they are considered 'essential workers' who do not have the option to transition to remote work. The research methods used in this study are job advertisement content analysis compared against interviews with hospitality employees. This method both revealed the necessary skills and abilities for employability and was useful in evaluating the accuracy of job advertisements.

The findings enrich the understanding of the employability norms by comparing the explicit employer demands with interviews. The gap reveals employability expectations that are not mentioned in job advertisements. The findings offer meaningful implications for employers, educators, job seekers, and other researchers aiming to address gaps in this topic.

19.2 Literature Review

19.2.1 Defining Employability

Employability has been defined in different ways, with an absence of a consistent and institutionally agreed upon definition. Adeyinka-Ojo (2018) defines employability as "basic skills and attributes necessary for securing, keeping and performing well at the workplace" (p. 48). This definition is broad, to the extent it covers endless skills and attributes; those which help one secure a job position are not necessarily the same that will define the strong performance in that position. It is also dubious to describe these skills as 'basic', as depending on the position, skills and attributes required for employability can be highly specialized (Wilson-Wünsch et al., 2015). Dhaliwal and Misra (2020) also struggle to find an unanimous definition of employability but synthesize eight distinct definitions into one: "the inculcation of knowledge, skills, and abilities that help to enter in a profession and help to remain employment afterward" (p. 21). This definition has similar problems to Adeyinka-Ojo (2018) in its failure to distinguish between the components of employability and its conflation of the skills that get one hired with the skills that allow for continued success.

Eurico et al. (2015) regard employability less as a profile of skills and attributes, positing instead that it is intrinsically linked to the identity of the prospective employee. They define employability as "based on an individual's ability to adapt to the professional needs and recent dynamics of new labour markets, and it is directly linked to the ability to find and maintain employment" (p. 32). The exceptional point made in this definition is that employability is a dynamic concept; what is a valid, desired skill set and/or personality in 1995 may no longer be the paradigm in 2020. The Covid-19 pandemic has illustrated that a catastrophic event has the capacity to drastically change the dynamics of the labour market in a matter of weeks (Hite & McDonald, 2020; Shobha & Johnson, 2021). Chen et al. (2021) build on Eurico et al. (2015)'s definition, giving more attention to the ongoing acquisition and honing of skills. To them, employability is "the ability of the individual to gain the first employment, maintain it and move between positions within the same organization, transfer to other jobs if required and obtain a sustainable job" (p. 2). Though still a broad definition, its acknowledgement of the dynamism of employability renders it the preferred definition for the sake of this research. This research will work with a composite definition of employability: the skills, attributes, and traits required to gain, maintain, and move between inter and intra-organization positions, with acknowledgement that this package of qualities is dynamic due to ever changing customer and industry needs.

The boundaries between skills, attributes, knowledge, and abilities are not clear, with some studies considering emotional skills to be attributes (Chapman & Lovell, 2006; Nyanjom & Wilkins, 2021), and even the discussion of knowledge as a skill (Wilson-Wünsch et al., 2015). Given this inability of prior literature to agree on what is a skill versus an attribute versus an ability, and the overwhelming support for emotional attributes, or 'soft skills', being of utmost importance for employability in the hospitality industry (Adeyinka-Ojo, 2018; Chalupa & Chadt, 2021; Chapman & Lovell, 2006; Dhaliwal & Misra, 2020; Weber et al., 2020), all these components will be discussed together as *employability qualities*. Emotional labour, technical skills, experience, and education can all be considered in the quest to understand employability qualities. Though the following study focuses on the hospitality industry, gaps between the employability qualities taught in pedagogical realms and those demanded by the professional community are found in many industries, from agriculture (Robinson, 2006) to environmental science (Stewart, 2021), to marketing and finance (Bennett, 2002).

19.2.2 Dimensions and Measurements of Employability

While it is easy to consider all employability qualities together, it is necessary to draw some lines: not necessarily those between skills versus attributes, but rather to create categories of these employability qualities. The KSA (knowledge, skills, and abilities) framework, referenced in a job advertisement analysis in Kang and Ritzhaupt (2015), is a useful tool to measure the competencies of employees. They define *knowledge* as "an organized body of information", *skills* as "the proficient application of knowledge and process to a task", and *ability* as "the capacity to perform an activity" (Kang & Ritzhaupt, 2015, p. 2).

Hard and soft skills can be considered as subsets of the skills component. Hard skills are explicitly taught, and generally are distinct to a limited range of positions or industries (Gruzdev et al., 2018). Examples of hard skills include mastery of software, speaking a foreign language, or technical skills, like those expected of culinary professionals or chemists. Soft skills are those less measurable, and maybe more difficult to teach, skills, like empathy, communication, self-efficacy, and innovation (Chan, 2010; Dhaliwal & Misra, 2020; Slåtten & Mehmetoglu, 2014; Tiwari et al., 2020). These skills are also sometimes referred to as 'people skills' and are especially important in guest-facing positions (Sisson & Adams, 2013; Wilks & Hemsworth, 2012). The gap between the soft skills required by employers and those that graduates possess is ubiquitous in the literature (Chen et al., 2021; Weber et al., 2020; Yang et al., 2015). Historically, hard skills were prioritized over soft skills, but as the workforce becomes increasingly educated and therefore well-versed in industry-specific hard skills, it is the transferable soft skills that distinguish a job seeker from her competitors (Bennett, 2002; Dhaliwal & Misra, 2020; Gruzdev et al., 2018).

The KSA framework is a useful categorization but does not differentiate between KSAs required for entry versus those required for continuous employment. A study comparing the importance versus employee performance of soft skills found there are consistent mismatches between employer expectation and employee competence in knowledge, skills, and abilities (Weber et al., 2020). One solution for addressing this gap is work experience as part of education: internships have a considerable effect on employability, as the internship experience enhances the students' knowledge and skills (Chen et al., 2021). The focus of Chen et al.'s study is on the relationship between career intention and career retention. Retention implies employability: a student who intends to, and successfully goes into, the hospitality industry, can be considered to have the necessary qualities for employability. Though Chen et al. (2021)'s definition of competency includes 'hard' skills like foreign language proficiency and computer skills, they also consider soft skills like leadership, innovation, and adaptability.

The aforementioned studies provide a useful lens through which to consider employability qualities. The KSA framework is especially useful as the three categories offer clear definitions in distinguishing among employability qualities. Chen et al. (2021)'s findings are not particularly useful for *measuring* employability, however, do challenge earlier literature that constrains the concept of employability to only soft and hard skills (Bennett, 2002; Chapman & Lovell, 2006). It is clear that employability goes beyond a skillset and supports the authors' decision to use a definition of employability that takes a more holistic perspective as opposed to looking at skills and knowledge alone.

19.2.3 Employability During Covid-19

Before the Covid-19 pandemic, employability norms for hospitality workers have been widely examined from the curriculum management perspective. For example, Lin (2002) analysed the courses and required competencies and found that accounting, marketing, foreign language, communication, and quality management are more important in hospitality education. Baum (2002) noted the employer expectations of graduates and that communication and people skills, as well as problem solving are the mostly expected skills by employers for graduates from hospitality programs. Mayo and Thomas-Haysbert (2005), by surveying participants of the Council on Hotels, Restaurants, and Institutional Education Conference (CHRIE), reported that the top competencies essential for hospitality management graduates include listening skills, ability to manage subordinates and revenue, a passion for service, ability to handle, plan and conduct meetings and events, and knowledge of legal issues. Tesone and Ricci (2006) identified entry-level competencies for hospitality managers, such as team work spirits, effective listening, verbal and writing skills, ability to project a professional image and empathize with guest experience.

Griffin (2020) conducted a survey with 264 participants from industry and university faculty and reported critical thinking skills was rated the top-rated KSAs by industry, followed by an overview of the hospitality industry and profession and financial management, while understanding for organizational and management theory, as well as legal environment is the least important. In contrast, faculties perceive ethical considerations, critical thinking and overview of industry as the top KSAs, while rating an understanding of economic environment, management theory and information systems as the least important. These findings suggest that the majority of the competences perceived as important before Covid-19 seem to be related to the routine job content.

Covid-19 has drastically altered the employability norms across industries. Employers and employees alike have been forced to grow increasingly resilient and adaptable in the throes of the pandemic (Hite & McDonald, 2020). However, not all industries have been uniformly affected: while many corporate jobs can transition to a work-from-home model with relative ease, this is not true of many hospitality roles, whether food service workers or hotel receptionists. This struggle is further compounded by the hospitality and tourism industry being among the most negatively affected by the Covid-19 pandemic in terms of customer needs and customer volume (Baum & Hai, 2020; Chalupa & Chadt, 2021; Mihailescu & Rinaldi, 2021; Shobha & Johnson, 2021; Stone et al., 2017; Tiwari et al., 2020). It also complicates employee morale and self-efficacy; Baum and Hai (2020) accurately portray the poignance of Covid-19's impact on hospitality culture, describing "social distancing … [as] the very antithesis of our expectations of the experience of hospitality and tourism" (p. 2398).

The inability to transition to a safer, home-based work solution, coupled with the threat of job dissatisfaction and job loss, are both factors that complicate employability in the hospitality industry. Shobha and Johnson (2021) also cite physical and mental health as prerequisites for employability in a Covid-19 environment. Though it is farfetched to consider these as employability qualities, it is a valid point: immunocompromised job seekers, and those lacking in emotional resilience, for whatever reason, may find they are seen as vulnerable and therefore less desirable in the context of employability (Gröschl, 2013). Resilience is also complicated as Covid-19 is likely exacerbating the high prevalence of violence, bullying, and harassment towards employees, which is especially evident in guest-facing positions (Page et al., 2018). If guest tension is heightened because of pandemic stress, it is suspected that the intensity of these outbursts against guest-facing employees has also grown.

19.2.4 Framing the Current Investigation

Though the hospitality industry has been exceptionally hard hit, frontline workers have continued to persevere to accommodate guest needs – from guests in quarantine, to those enjoying 'staycations', or even the few that still need to travel for family or business matters. Despite the wealth of literature on employability norms in the hospitality industry and the growing body of work on how Covid-19 has transformed work environments, nearly all of the hitherto articles write that empirical evidence is still needed in the research on how Covid-19 has changed employability norms in the hospitality industry (Fakunle & Higson, 2021; Nyanjom & Wilkins, 2021). The research herein will investigate, using front-of-house hospitality workers as most emblematic of essential workers who have faced unprecedented levels of adaptability and resilience asked of them, how the pandemic has altered the in-demand employability qualities. Specifically, this study aims to answer the following research questions:

1. What are the required qualities for successful employment as a front-of-house worker in the hospitality and tourism industry during the pandemic?
2. Are there any changes in the required skills and employability norms for employment as a front-of-house worker in the hospitality and tourism industry over the course of the pandemic?

19.3 Research Methods

In this study, employability skills in the hospitality industry are evaluated using a combination of qualitative and quantitative methods. Qualitative data is collected from interviews with participants who have worked in the hospitality industry during the Covid-19 pandemic. Quantitative data is extracted via content analysis on a popular hospitality job portal, Hosco.com.

19.3.1 Content Analysis for Job Postings

19.3.1.1 Data and Sample

Content analysis is a research tool for systematically evaluating the presence of keywords and themes within otherwise unstructured media (Columbia Public Health, 2019). For the purpose of the research, this method was implemented to analyse the job advertisement data collected from www.hosco.com, a global job portal that connects job seekers and employers in the hospitality industry. With the help of the contracted web scraping agency X-Byte, the job portal website was scraped to collect data from these hospitality job postings from 04/10/2021 to 04/01/2022. 2700 listings were collected from 158 different hotels or hotel groups. The dataset contains information about the company, location, job title, job description, requirements, languages, wages, etc.

19.3.1.2 Coding Scheme

The data was prepared for analysis, and later analysed, using Microsoft Excel software. The job levels were categorised into Base Level, Assistant, Associate, Officer, Supervisor, Lead, Manager, Training, and other. The "other" category covers mainly jobs which were posted by a hospitality firm, yet are not guest-facing roles, e.g. HR or IT staff. To provide data matching the research topic, 60 postings for "other" and "training" were excluded.

To test the feasibility of the concept, the skills and employment criteria from Dhaliwal and Misra (2020) were applied, and the 2640 job postings were checked for the appearance of those criteria. Following the proof of concept, the first 20 postings for each job level were scanned for qualities indicating the requirements mentioned in the posting. These were then grouped to 74 qualities, looked for by 466 stem words. For example, the requirement "Adaptability" is looked for by searching the expressions "adaptable", "adapt", and "adaptability", which are then counted as being required if one or more variations are found. This way, the postings were analysed by searching for 466 stem words in 2640 job ads for a total of 1.23 million checks across all job advertisements. The coding was implemented in three steps. First, the 2640 job postings were split among 3 authors to identify the keywords. Second, another author in the team cross-checked the coding scheme developed in the Step 1. Third, in case some coding could not be agreed upon, the fourth author had a discussion and consent was achieved based on the majority's view. This process guarantees the reliability and the quality of the research.

19.3.2 Interviews

19.3.2.1 Data and Sample

Conducting interviews to collect data is a viable and a highly engaged tool during research (McGrath et al., 2019). In a semi-structured interview, the interviewer is able to probe and dig deeper based on interviewees' responses in addition to having a list of predetermined questions (Galletta, 2013).

14 participants for interviews were sourced through convenience and snowball sampling. The criteria for a suitable candidate is being a front-of-house worker, who is currently employed, or has been employed, during the Covid-19 pandemic. Table 19.1 reports demographic information of the interviewees.

Considering the Covid-19 restrictions in place, the interviews were conducted virtually using the Zoom video conferencing platform. Each interview took between 20–45 min. The transcription process for these interviews was conducted in 2 steps. First, the audio file from the Zoom call was run through the Otter.ai platform. Though this same software powers the Zoom auto transcription, it is not as effective when it can't transcribe iteratively. Then, the authors reviewed the transcripts to correct any language that was incorrectly transcribed. These transcriptions are then imported to NVivo for qualitative analysis.

Table 19.1 Demographic information of the interviewees

#	Sector	Position	Gender	Country
Interviewee 1	Hotel	Receptionist/Guest Service Agent	Female	Myanmar
Interviewee 2	Resort	Guest Service Officer	Female	Singapore
Interviewee 3	Cruise	Hostess/Travel Agent	Female	Germany
Interviewee 4	Cruise	Entertainment Hostess	Female	Canada
Interviewee 5	Hotel	Guest Relations Officer	Female	Vietnam
Interviewee 6	Restaurant	Waitress	Female	Germany
Interviewee 7	Restaurant	Chef	Male	India
Interviewee 8	Restaurant	Restaurant Manager	Male	India
Interviewee 9	Restaurant	Restaurant Manager	Female	India
Interviewee 10	Hotel	Bellboy	Male	Myanmar
Interviewee 11	Cruise	Guest Service Officer	Female	Germany
Interviewee 12	Hotel	Receptionist	Female	France
Interviewee 13	Restaurant	Restaurant Manager	Male	Germany
Interviewee 14	Hotel	Reservations Executive	Female	Austria

Using the constant comparison analysis method developed by Corbin and Strauss (2011) the information is broken down by assigning themes and keywords to quotes. Through this coding process, the core themes of the responses are identified as critical qualities required in the hospitality industry. In the initial round of coding, mentions related to knowledge, skills, abilities, and other information perceived as potentially important have been flagged. With each additional interview, new themes were developed, which were then retroactively applied to prior interviews, constantly comparing newer data against that which came before it. In subsequent rounds, the interviews have been coded more meticulously by identifying specific criteria from the job advertisements to determine which of these were also present in the interviews.

To ensure the reliability and validity of the coding process, we followed the three steps. Step 1 was independent coding. Two authors independently coded each set of interview script. Step 2 involves comparing the coding results of the outcome of the Step 1. In Step 3, the disagreement was discussed by including the third author. A final decision was made until at least two of the three authors agreed.

19.4 Results

19.4.1 Job Advertisement Content Analysis

Having the job advertisement data prepared for analysis, the job advertisements were grouped according to job level into "managerial" and "non-managerial" to gain a clearer description of the sample. This also provided a more useful distinction than going based on each individual categories: an assistant can be everything from a low entry level to a role with a certain degree of responsibility – making it difficult to rely on these categorizations. Therefore, the levels Base Level, Assistant, Associate, and Officer were grouped to non-managerial, while Supervisor, Manager, Lead were grouped to managerial. The 74 qualities identified in the job ads were categorized according to the KSA scheme as mentioned before, to allow for a more focused analysis of the criteria (Kang & Ritzhaupt, 2015). By applying the above-mentioned methods to the hosco.com dataset, the following conclusions were drawn from the content analysis.

As Table 19.2 shows of the 2640 postings, 81% were non-managerial positions, which matches the expectation that guest-facing roles are mostly lower-level positions. Furthermore, the higher number (13) of mentioned qualities per posting for the managerial positions matches the expectation of higher requirements for higher level positions (Wilson-Wünsch et al., 2015). Observing the difference in the number of qualities mentioned per job advertisement, the question for the significance of the distribution comes up. Applying the T-test for both job levels led to a p-value <0.01. Therefore, the average mentions of criteria in job ads in managerial versus non-managerial roles are significantly different.

Regarding the geographical distribution, the dataset contains job postings in 711 locations in 70 countries. Roughly 50%, or 1303, job postings were from the United States, followed by 388 from the United Kingdom, and 106 from China. This might result in a bias due to certain criteria being more relevant or requested in the US, for example a higher value of hospitality university degree compared to other countries (Gardini, 2016).

19.4.1.1 Analysis of KSAs Required by Employers

Focusing on the most frequently mentioned KSA statements for the whole dataset, abilities (5893 mentions) are the most mentioned qualities, followed by knowledge (5204), soft skills (5143) and attitudes (4840). Interestingly, physical requirements (3481), like moving objects or walking a lot, are in high demand, too. Keeping the high share of non-managerial postings in mind, experience (1887) and hard skills (1227) are non-surprisingly in lower demand. Work permits (34) were hardly requested, implying a focus on the local workforce. Table 19.3 shows the rankings of the KSA statements within the job levels, which are largely similar, with half of them equal, the remaining half only slight deviation. Remarkably, soft skills are top ranked for managerial positions yet only fourth for non-managers. This implies that the soft skills, especially those related to the "hospitality gene", can be seen as a

Table 19.2 Overview of the postings and mentioned qualities per posting for managerial and non-managerial job postings

	Non-managerial positions	Managerial positions
Job postings	2,143	497
Qualities per posting	10	13

Table 19.3 Ranking of KSA statements for non-managerial and managerial job postings

	Non-managerial	Managerial
Ability	1	2
Attitude	3	4
Experience	6	6
Hard skill	7	7
Knowledge	2	3
Physical	5	5
Soft skill	4	1
Work permit	8	8

Table 19.4 Top ranked qualities per KSA statement per job level. KSA statements appearing in both categories are highlighted in bold and italic

	Rank	Non-managerial	Managerial
Ability	1	***Teamwork***	***Teamwork***
	2	Work Under Pressure	Influence
	3	Productivity	Details
Attitude	1	***Passion***	***Positivity***
	2	***Positivity***	***Passion***
	3	Attitude	Respect
Experience	1	***Guest Experiences***	***Guest Experiences***
	2	***Working Experience***	***Working Experience***
Hard skill	1	Email skills	***Telephone Skills***
	2	***IT Skills***	Financial Decision Making
	3	***Telephone Skills***	***IT Skills***
Knowledge	1	***Hotel Operating Systems***	***Hotel Operating Systems***
	2	***Quality Assurance***	***Quality Assurance***
	3	Cash Handling	Legislation
Physical	1	***Grooming***	***Grooming***
	2	***Move objects***	***Move objects***
	3	***Physical Requirements***	***Physical Requirements***
Soft skill	1	***Communication***	***Leadership***
	2	***Leadership***	Supervision
	3	Listening Skills	***Communication***

requirement for a successful career advancement in the industry (Lounsbury et al., 2012).

On a more detailed level, the most frequently mentioned qualities requested for in the job advertisements for all levels of positions are: Knowledge of hotel operating systems (1756), Quality assurance (1545), Ensuring positive guest experiences (1326), Teamwork (1317) and Passion (1257). Table 19.4 further shows the top three qualities per KSA statement for managerial and non-managerial positions. Unsurprisingly, the above-mentioned top five criteria are relevant for both, the managerial and non-managerial level (Farag & Mouzughi, 2018). Keeping in mind that in the tourism and hospitality industry the focus is on providing a good service and memorable experience to the guest, quality assurance, positivity, passion, and a good physical appearance are basic requirements. Basic working skills like IT and telephone skills are non-surprising as well. Also matching the expectation, on one side the non-managerial job requirements are more focused on running the daily operations, expressed by cash handling and a high productivity. On the other hand, managing staff has a higher focus on a good understanding of the legislative requirements, supervision, and financial decision-making skills when running a department (Novacka et al., 2019).

Although this research has no explicit hypothesis, there was some expectation these advertisements would have noticeable references to Covid-19 protocols and professional conduct; to the contrary, the overwhelming majority (over 96%) of job postings have zero mention of Covid-19. The only mentions of Covid-19 include:

1. Vaccination requirements (already having or receiving upon commencing employment)
2. Workplaces which previously provided meals are no longer doing so due to health concerns
3. Participation in events depends on Covid-19 guidelines
4. Training on hygiene and sanitation
5. Responsibility of ensuring guest and departmental compliance with Covid-19 regulations

One possible reason for this low coverage is that most of the job advertisements come from the United States, a country that has faced a lot of criticism for its mismanagement of the Covid-19 pandemic. However, with the overwhelming presence of Covid-19 in everyday life, it is surprising that it is mentioned in so few job advertisements. This implies that the job advertisements may not be a sufficiently useful measure of how Covid-19 has changed the employability qualities for the hospitality industry. This lends credibility to the decision to conduct interviews to gather in-depth qualitative data on employability qualities.

19.4.2 Results from Interviews

The interview data reveal two overarching themes: (1), challenges identified that have made working in a guest-facing position more difficult due to Covid-19 and the related employability requirements for hospitality workers in a peri-Covid-19 environment. (2), KSAs generally required for front-line workers.

19.4.2.1 Theme 1: Challenges of Covid-19 and the Requirement for Employability

Figure 19.1 illustrate the findings related to the first theme: challenges and the requirement for employability. Regarding the first theme, there is consensus among the interviewees that Covid-19 has created an unfavourable working environment. Major challenges due to Covid-19 include that guests have become ruder, there is uncertainty-induced stress, increasing demands of flexibility, all made worse by ever-changing Covid-19 regulations and rules and the cultural or country-specific differences of those rules. Related to the challenges, frequently changing and country-specific rules require a higher cognitive ability among employees to comprehend the changes quickly. Furthermore, employees are expected to perform tasks outside their position, provide support to their team members as needed, and consequently employees are required to manage their emotions better. Lastly, hospitality workers have also been forced to change their positions and move to other industries. The following provides more detailed discussion about the challenges and the requirement on employability.

19.4.2.2 Rude Guests and the Related Requirement for Employability

Guests in the hospitality industry, especially at higher-income establishments, have the potential to be very rude to, even blatantly bullying, hospitality workers (Page et al., 2018). This phenomenon does not describe all guests. However, it does happen, and the theory of conspicuous consumption suggests that the rude guest will

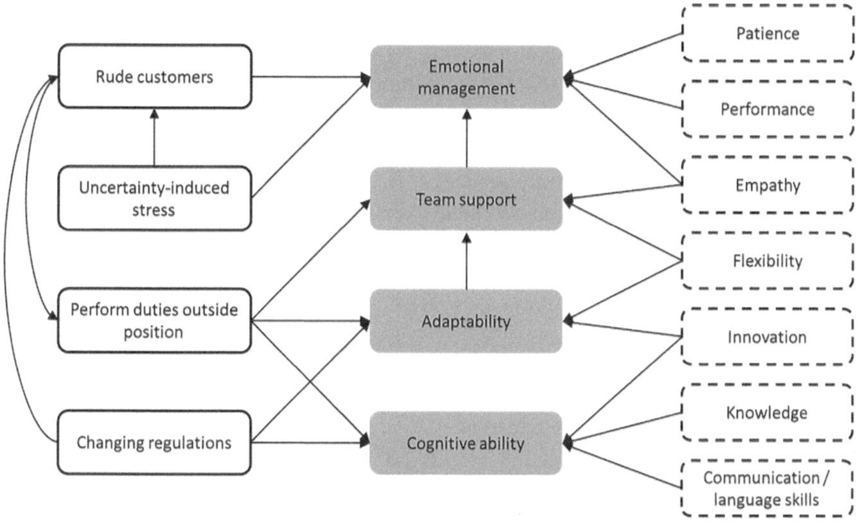

Fig. 19.1 Mind map of the issues found from interviews

continue to be a hallmark of hospitality work (Veblen & Mills, 2017). If the perceived privilege to conspicuously condemn unsatisfactory service is part of the service consumption, an experience to which guests are entitled through their membership in the 'leisure class', then difficult and rude guests will be a constant in the hospitality industry. This theoretical observation is directly corroborated by interview responses: "rich people, you know, they have a certain mentality and they come in, and they don't like to treat you nice." The concept of the difficult guest has been exacerbated by Covid-19, both in the heightened expectations of hospitality experiences after being deprived of them, and as a consequence of the stress of the pandemic:

> People are … not very happy at the moment. So you just have to be extra happy and extra patient with them.… Go that extra mile … pay even more attention to the guests.… For example, going to a restaurant, it's kind of a highlight at the moment because there is not much that you can do. So if you go there, you want your experience to be extra good and not just regular.

Dealing with rude guests, a theme in every interview, requires a high level of self-management and regulating one's emotions. Even 2 years into the pandemic, there are still emotional repercussions,

"[guests are] fed up, they've been stuck in their houses for two plus years" and are expecting the best possible service experience. This means employees must work extra hard not only to provide an exceptional service experience, but also to offset any compromises caused by Covid-19 related regulations (facilities being closed, reduced operating hours, masking requirements, etc.). One coping mechanism is to strengthen the boundary between the self as an employee versus the personal self. Employees are required to have a positive attitude, performing humbleness and politeness, in front of guests, regardless of what is going on in their personal lives. Some find it easiest to build a facade, to perform an artificial self of whom they are cynical, in order to not take the events of the day personally: "it's just a passing moment… if an incident happens, we just pretend like it didn't."

Patience is a major component of hospitality-related emotional intelligence, but is seldom mentioned in the reviewed literature, and it only appears 32 in the job advertisements, barely 1% coverage. It is an ability which can be strengthened and is integral to success in hospitality roles. It is "the top skill … [guests] will be screaming at your face, and you still have to be like, yeah, I understand." In the same way the rude customer will continue to be a problem, hospitality workers will have to continue to deal with "people just going off at service workers and people in the hospitality industry for things that are out of their control." Patience was important pre-Covid-19, has become increasingly critical during Covid-19, and will continue to be essential in the knowledge-skill-ability 'toolkit' of hospitality workers.

19.4.2.3 Changing Regulations and the Related Requirement for Employability

Changing regulations are another component of the unfavourable working environment that make service work more difficult. The regulations related to Covid-19 not only differ across countries, but keep changing and in many occasions not clear cut. This results in both resistance by and enquiries from guests, which heightens the hospitality workers' burden of explaining Covid-19 phenomena to concerned guests. One interviewee working in a water park shared the point:

> the rule on the mask is very questionable ... I've seen a lot of people without masks, but … I understand because it's a water … when someone comes up to you [asking] why are people not wearing masks? I can't answer the question ... And we can't have people monitoring them all the time … In that sense, [the job] got more difficult.

Several qualities required to cope with such uncertain and ever-changing regulations emerged from the reflections of the interviewees. The same interviewee cites the importance of "know[ing] the measures and restrictions put into place really well, like down to the smallest [terms and conditions]. So that when they … attack you, you have something to say back." Owing to the dynamic nature of such knowledge, interviewees also alluded to the importance of cognitive ability in employability, "even if you don't have a degree, you need to be able to pick up skills really fast". This finding is novel: there is a popular sentiment that service jobs are low-skilled, to the contrary, though these roles may not require education, cognitive abilities like fast learning are a key contributor to success. The ability to learn on the job becomes particularly important during the pandemic, when volatility, uncertainty, complexity, and ambiguity dominate.

19.4.2.4 Uncertainty-Induced Stress, Increasing Demands of Flexibility and the Related Requirement for Employability

Employability in the hospitality industry has undoubtedly been made more challenging by the pandemic, as demonstrated in the above quotes, and many of these challenges, like rude guests, are expected to remain, even as the pandemic subsides. The demands on the individual worker cannot happen in social isolation; hospitality workers need a sense of community and support, without this there is a high risk of burnout. Supportive teams are key to employability, even though they don't necessarily fit within the KSA framework.

Team support is essential on two fronts. First, it is indispensable to the training program. All respondents verified that most of the training happens informally, through learning from co-workers, rather than through official programs. Without a strong mentor, it will be difficult to succeed in a hospitality role. Secondly, and arguably more important to employee wellbeing and sustainability, is the role of emotional support. "[Teams] do offer a lot of emotional support because you know, after you get hit with a bad guest, you don't want to be out there anymore". There are higher rates of burnout when employees cannot rely on their peers to support them through difficult guest engagements. Even if it is expected in a service encounter, it is difficult to not take these issues personally. "You definitely need emotional support in the hospitality industry" is a sentiment shared by all respondents. It is not sustainable to act otherwise, "for your own personal mental health … if you try to be a lone wolf, it's going to eat your life.... there are people [without whom] I would have not made it through the contract. I know that, they know that." These statements show the high importance of emotional and team support to be able to sustainably remain in a guest-facing position. Since sustaining a role is included in the definition of employability, the role of the external environment should not go overlooked in discussing employability.

19.4.2.5 Theme 2: KSAs Emerging from Interviews

A second theme emerging from interviews is related to the KSAs generally required for employability of front-line workers in hospitality industry. Figure 19.2 illustrates the top 20 employability qualities mentioned in the interview, as a comparison with those identified from the job advertisement content analysis. Only four of the skills were included in both:

Teamwork is a critical skill in the hospitality industry. The unpredictable nature of working with guests means that team members need to be able to voice when and how they need support from their co-workers. Second, as discussed in the interview findings, team support is crucial to individual resilience and sustainable careers. If the emotional dynamics of a team can be considered part of teamwork as a skill, then there is strong support for teamwork as the top quality in the employability framework.

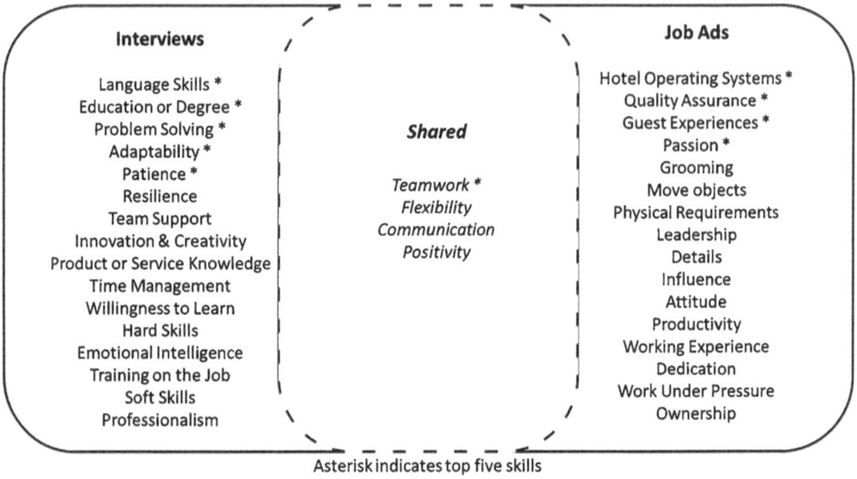

Fig. 19.2 Comparison of qualities from Jobs Ads and Interviews

Flexibility is also a necessity. Hospitality roles are unpredictable, and employees are constantly undertaking unexpected roles (Salem & Abdien, 2017). This finding is particularly noteworthy because there is some admission in the job advertisements that its content does not include all the potential responsibilities of the position.

Communication is undoubtedly essential, both as a pillar of effective teamwork and creating a positive experience for the guest. One interviewee noted that this is also a crucial skill for roles which are not predominantly guest-facing, on the basis there will still be guest-facing interactions, and for successful collaboration with guest-facing co-workers.

Positivity is useful in performing the role of a service worker, insofar as these guest-facing roles require a lot of acting (Goffman, 2002), maintaining a positive disposition is a key component of that performance. Especially during the Covid-19 pandemic, when guests have heightened expectations in the service experience and global morale is low (Thartori et al., 2021), the hospitality worker must be exceptionally positive.

A compelling dynamic is visible when comparing these top four skills. They are all interrelated, especially if a good service can be considered a direct product of mastered employability qualities in a hospitality role. Positivity, as mentioned, is directly related to interactions with guests, as is communication. Communication, and flexibility, are mandated by teamwork.

Figure 19.2 shows that the job advertisements often do not fully depict the criteria that are important to be successful in a position. A few other important skills mentioned in the interviews that do not appear in the job advertisements include:

Adaptability. Adaptability is one of the top mentioned skills in interviews. One of the interviewees made the profound observation that adaptability will be the most important skill going forward. She said, "if you would have asked me that last year, maybe my answer would have been different," but now she is confident that adaptability is the most important skill after working through the pandemic in the hospitality industry. If one has mastered adaptability, one can handle anything that is thrown at them in the workplace; alternative employability frameworks view adaptability as one of three key determinants of employability (Fugate et al., 2004).

Examples of adaptability in Covid-19 include adjusting personal conduct and professional practices to Covid-19 rules and regulations. Quickly learning new sanitation practices, the skill of administering Covid-19 tests, understanding the rapidly changing country and company terms and conditions, and supporting guest queries related to the pandemic all require exceptional adaptability. Adaptability will remain important even once the pandemic subsides: every guest interaction is different: "you have to be quick, a quick thinker. You have to have the ability to adapt because not every day is the same. Every day is different. Every hour is different".

Emotional Intelligence. Emotional intelligence is a broad ability that subsumes many other 'soft skills' like empathy, emotional management, and negotiation (Colfax et al., 2010; Thartori et al., 2021). In the context of the interviews, it was most frequently brought up in relation to managing one's own emotions. The stress of the Covid-19 pandemic renders it more difficult to manage one's emotions when compared with a pre-Covid-19 amount of stress. This stress has several contributing factors, including personal distress, fulfilling work related duties, and managing unruly guests. Emotional intelligence was already an important quality for success in hospitality but must be further developed in order to succeed during the pandemic (Chen et al., 2021).

Language Skills. Language skills came up in almost every interview. That they do not appear in the top skills for job advertisements is likely a limitation of the analysis method. It is possible that many job ads mentioned a desire for multilingual candidates, however rather than specifying as 'multilingual' or 'speaking additional languages', this was specified by the language itself, e.g. German speaking candidates preferred. Nearly all interviewees mentioned the value of speaking an additional language, as a way to more easily communicate with guests, and through this, create a closer bond with the guests and increase the likelihood of customer loyalty.

Innovation and Creativity. Innovation and creativity were rarely mentioned in job advertisements, covering less than 1% of the sample. The understanding from the interviews is that innovation is crucial to success and is supported by adaptability. Additionally, the type of innovation is not the grand-scale, disruptive innovation that has become a buzzword in the modern business environment. Innovation, in the context of front-of-house hospitality work, is the ability to fabricate and communicate answers and solutions to unexpected questions and problems. As mentioned, several times, guests are unpredictable, there are often 'unprecedented' scenarios and no rule book to which the employee can refer. It is up to the employee to gracefully communicate her quickly concocted solutions. Enough years of experience generally equips employees with the necessary knowledge and quick-thinking ability to answer guest enquiries, even those for which there is not a pre-defined answer (Wilson-Wünsch & Plattes, 2014). Unfortunately, operating in the pandemic is a new experience for everyone, so it will be harder to generate these solutions on the spot. It is suspected that dealing with inquisitive guests will become easier as the pandemic endures.

Patience. Because the issue of patience is heavily discussed as part of the interview analysis, this section will focus on a brief exploration as to why 'patience' does not come up in job advertisements. It is likely that patience is a tacit expectation of employers, that any employee applying for a hospitality role understands that patience and the capacity to withstand the stress of a hospitality job are necessities. It is also possible that patience is covered by other criteria, like professionalism, positivity, or 'good at dealing with guests.'

The majority of these top qualities are 'transferable skills': employability qualities which are desirable regardless of position or industry (Bennett, 2002). Arguably, they are all transferable skills; the only dubious quality would be 'guest experience', but even this can be 'transferred' to domestic hospitality contexts or other situations wherein a client should be made to feel comfortable. The top skills in this research differ from those listed in Bennett's (2002) article, which include IT skills and numeracy. This may be because his research did not focus on guest-facing roles, instead on finance, human resource management, and marketing. Another reason for this gap is because his study used exclusively job advertisement data, which the present study suggests is not an adequate measure of in-demand employability qualities. Regardless, the present study has strong support for the argument that personal transferable skills — which is somewhat of a misnomer as 'transferable skills' comprise knowledge, attributes, and attitudes — are more important employability qualities than hard skills.

19.4.2.6 Service Gene and Hospitality Education

One respondent described the importance of the 'service gene' in hospitality work. Its nomenclature suggests it is a capacity for hospitality with which one is born. An alternate, sociological perspective posits that it is learned behaviour. One can be born into a life where she is socialized to have this 'service gene', lived experiences which amount to adaptability, the ability to perform, relative extraversion and the variety of communication skills. For example, women are often socialized more as caretakers relative to their male counterparts, and consequently may find more success in service roles.

Related to the learning perspective, as mentioned in discussing adaptability and the role of a team, there are many aspects of competence in hospitality that cannot be taught during a degree program and must be learned on the job. The interviewees lack consensus on the importance of a degree. One perspective is that the degree is only necessary as a formality, it gets the job candidate past the requirement and may open more doors during the career search, but does not necessarily teach skills, abilities, and theories necessary for success. This belief should be taken with a grain of salt; there is a possibility that knowledge learned in the specific degree, and overall professional competencies developed in a classroom context are taken for granted. There is agreement among participants that the degree, at least as a formality, is necessary to gain access to management roles and more quickly advance in one's hospitality career. The other prevailing perspective on hospitality education is that it does teach valuable transferable skills: organization, time management, communication, attention to detail, teamwork, and critical thinking. However, internships, apprenticeships, regular upskilling, and on-the-job training are paramount to thriving in hospitality roles. A degree alone is not sufficient preparation for strong performance in this industry.

19.5 Conclusion and Implications

This research has addressed its driving questions: what are the necessary skills for employability in the hospitality industry, and have these changed in the Covid-19 environment? The necessary skills, based on job advertisements and an emphasis of interview findings, are predominately transferable skills, including teamwork, communication, positive dispositions, and emotional intelligence. There is a special focus on adaptability, as when adaptability is mastered, a new or more challenging skill, ability, or knowledge can be easily learned by the employee. The research also found, with more support from interviews than from job advertisements, that Covid-19 has altered the necessary knowledge, skills, and abilities for employability in the Covid-19 era. The first takeaway is that many of the hallmark employability qualities of the hospitality industry are much harder as a result of the unfavourable working environment, the key features of which are ruder guests, rapidly changing rules and regulations, and social distancing as the antithesis of the hospitality experience. The other key takeaway is that the knowledge element of the job is more intense in terms of keeping up with, interpreting, and enforcing the changing rules and regulations. The job advertisements highlighted some other Covid-19 related aspects such as vaccination status and some job benefits (like meals) being suspended during to Covid-19, but these do not directly fit into our employability framework.

The results of this exploratory study have meaningful implications for its four key stakeholders: employers, educators, job seekers, and researchers. Employers are strongly encouraged to modify their job advertisements to better reflect the details of the job. Terms like 'guest experience' and 'teamwork' should not be used as a catch-all for 'patient, innovative workers with exceptional emotional management skills' and 'empathetic individuals capable of giving and receiving emotional support to co-workers'. The soft skills that are so essential to employability should be emphasized over the hotel operating systems; it is the soft skills and abilities that take years of experience to develop, these hotel operating systems can be taught in a matter of weeks, therefore they should not be considered the most valuable skill an employee can possess.

Educators should prioritize experiential learning, as so many of these employability qualities are difficult to develop in the classroom. The pedagogical community recognizes the need to prioritize practical training over theoretical knowledge (Dhaliwal & Misra, 2020; Fakunle & Higson, 2021; Nyanjom & Wilkins, 2021; Stone et al., 2017; Yang et al., 2015). This gap is not a Covid-19 related development: hospitality degrees have long been found to not adequately prepare pupils for success in the hospitality industry. However, this is difficult to rectify in a peri-Covid-19 environment: even the classroom development of communication and teamwork are severely undermined by online learning platforms and the isolation associated with remote learning (Gill, 2020). There have been some attempts to work around this, like virtual internships, however there are many transferable skills that are difficult to develop in an online environment, like anticipatory impulses and the ability to delight customers (Bilsland et al., 2020). Educators should reform curriculum to hone students' soft skills and abilities in conjunction with hospitality theory. This should better prepare pupils for employability in the hospitality industry and increase the retention rate if students are getting practical experiences working in hospitality before applying for jobs (Chen et al., 2021).

For employees, current and prospective, this research has provided empirical data on which skills are most essential to your success. This discussion emphasizes the most important qualities as those shared by the job advertisements, and those found only in the interviews; job ad criteria is already understood by employers and employees as the necessary criteria for employability, but this research has found those criteria are not entirely valid.

19.6 Limitations and Opportunities for Further Research

The main limitation of this study concerns the sample size of the interviews. Future comparative studies should, in the interest of research integrity, have more participants. Higher sample sizes align with similar research in tourism and hospitality (Phelan, 2015) and allows to achieve data saturation (Aldiabat & Le Navenec, 2018). It is entirely possible that a full sample would have yielded similar results, however this data cannot be reported with full confidence due to the limited sample size. There are also limitations on the sample of job advertisements. There are only 90 days' worth of data, collected from 4 October 2021–4 January 2022. If larger hotel chains are mass posting job advertisements, the sample could be sensitive to being dominated by one company, corporate culture, or country. These cultural differences, or over-representation of certain hiring postings, could render the data insufficiently representative of the global demand for employability qualities. Recommendations would be to sample over a longer period of time or use quota sampling to achieve a representative sample. Related to the validity of the job advertisement sample is a suggestion for taking this line of research in a more descriptive direction. There is a possibility that the employability qualities discovered in this exploratory study differ according to corporate and national culture (Stoffers et al., 2019). Future studies could take a comparative approach of boutique hotels with larger multinational companies, or also look at differences across countries. Lastly, this study highlighted the insufficiency of job advertisements as a comprehensive measure of employability qualities. Future studies into job advertisements should explore whether this gap is unique to the Hospitality and Tourism industry, or if it is also encountered in other industries, and to what extent?

References

Adeyinka-Ojo, S. (2018). A strategic framework for analysing employability skills deficits in rural hospitality and tourism destinations. *Tourism Management Perspectives, 27*, 47–54. https://doi.org/10.1016/j.tmp.2018.04.005

Aldiabat, K. M., & Le Navenec, C.-L. (2018). Data saturation: The mysterious step in grounded theory methodology. *The Qualitative Report, 23*(1), 245–261.

Baum, T. (2002). Skills and training for the hospitality sector: A review of issues. *Journal of Vocational Education and Training, 54*(3), 343–364.

Baum, T., & Hai, N. T. T. (2020). Hospitality, tourism, human rights and the impact of COVID-19. *International Journal of Contemporary Hospitality Management, 32*(7), 2397–2407. https://doi.org/10.1108/IJCHM-03-2020-0242

Bennett, R. (2002). Employers' demands for personal transferable skills in graduates: A content analysis of 1000 job advertisements and an associated empirical study. *Journal of Vocational Education & Training, 54*, 457–476. https://doi.org/10.1080/13636820200200209

Bilsland, C., Nagy, H., & Smith, P. (2020). Virtual internships and work-integrated learning in hospitality and tourism in a post-COVID-19 world. *International Journal of Work-Integrated Learning, 21*, 425–437.

Chalupa, S., & Chadt, K. (2021). The perception of soft skills and their training at hotel front–Office in Connection to CoVid-19 pandemics. *Tem Journal-Technology Education Management Informatics, 10*(2), 517–521.

Chan, J. K. L. (2010). Enhancing the employability of and level of soft skills within tourism and hospitality graduates in Malaysia: The issues and challenges. *Journal of Tourism, XII*, 1–16.

Chandrachud, A., & Gokhale, M. (2019). Effect of emotional labour on job satisfaction and burnout of restaurant employees. *IAHRW International Journal of Social Sciences Review, 7*(1), 99–102.

Chapman, J., & Lovell, G. (2006). The competency model of hospitality service: Why it doesn't deliver. *International Journal of Contemporary Hospitality Management, 18*, 78–88. https://doi.org/10.1108/09596110610642000

Chen, T.-L., Shen, C.-C., & Gosling, M. (2021). To stay or not to stay? The causal effect of interns' career intention on enhanced employability and retention in the hospitality and tourism industry. *Journal of Hospitality, Leisure, Sport & Tourism Education, 28*, 100305.

Colfax, R. S., Rivera, J. J., & Perez, K. (2010). Applying emotional intelligence (EQ-I) in the workplace: Vital to global business success. *Journal of International Business Research, 9*, 89.

Columbia Public Health. (2019). *Content Analysis. Columbia Public Health.* Retrieved 02.12. from https://www.publichealth.columbia.edu/research/population-health-methods/content-analysis

Corbin, J. M., & Strauss, A. (2011). Grounded theory methodology. In N. K. Denzin & Y. S. Lincoln (Eds.), *Handbook of Qualitattive Research* (pp. 273–285). Sage.

Dhaliwal, R. S., & Misra, P. (2020). Employability skills needed in hospitality industry: A Scopious review. *Asian Journal of Education and Social Studies, 10*(1), 18–34.

Eurico, S. T., Da Silva, J. A. M., & Do Valle, P. O. (2015). A model of graduates′ satisfaction and loyalty in tourism higher education: The role of employability. *Journal of Hospitality, Leisure, Sport & Tourism Education, 16*, 30–42. https://doi.org/10.1016/j.jhlste.2014.07.002

Fakunle, O., & Higson, H. (2021). Interrogating theoretical and empirical approaches to employability in different global regions. *Higher Education Quarterly., 75*, 525–534.

Farag, E., & Mouzughi, Y. (2018). Knowledge-advanced innovative behaviour: A hospitality service perspective. *International Journal of Contemporary Hospitality Management, 30*(1), 197–216. https://doi.org/10.1108/IJCHM-04-2016-0200

Fugate, M., Kinicki, A., & Ashforth, B. (2004). Employability: A psycho-social construct, its dimensions, and applications. *Journal of Vocational Behavior, 65*, 14–38. https://doi.org/10.1016/j.jvb.2003.10.005

Galletta, A. (2013). *Mastering the semi-structured interview and beyond.* New York University Press.

Gardini, M. A. (2016). Zwischen Tradition und Managementmoderne. *Zeitschrift für Tourismuswissenschaft, 8*(1), 3–22.

Gill, R. (2020). Graduate employability skills through online internships and projects during the COVID 19 pandemic: An Australian example. *Journal of Teaching and Learning for Graduate Employability, 11*, 146–158. https://doi.org/10.21153/jtlge2020vol11no1art946

Goffman, E. (2002). Front and Back regions of everyday life (1959). *The Everyday Life.*

Griffin, W. C. (2020). Hospitality faculty: Are we meeting the demands of industry? *Journal of Teaching in Travel & Tourism, 20*(4), 262–283. https://doi.org/10.1080/15313220.2020.1746225

Gröschl, S. (2013). Presumed incapable exploring the validity of negative judgments about persons with disabilities and their employability in hotel operations. *Cornell Hospitality Quarterly, 54*, 114–123. https://doi.org/10.1177/1938965512453082

Gruzdev, M. V., Kuznetsova, I. V., Tarkhanova, I. Y., & Kazakova, E. I. (2018). University graduates' soft skills: The employers' opinion. *European Journal of Contemporary Education, 7*, 690–698. https://doi.org/10.13187/ejced.2018.4.690

Hite, L. M., & McDonald, K. S. (2020). Careers after COVID-19: Challenges and changes. *Human Resource Development International, 23*(4), 427–437. https://doi.org/10.1080/13678868.2020.1779576

Hobbs, J. E. (2020). Food supply chains during the COVID-19 pandemic. *Canadian Journal of Agricultural Economics, 68*(2), 171–176. https://doi.org/10.1111/cjag.12237

Kang, Y., & Ritzhaupt, A. D. (2015). A job announcement analysis of educational technology professional positions: Knowledge, skills, and abilities. *Journal of Educational Technology Systems, 43*(3), 231–256. https://doi.org/10.1177/0047239515570572

Lin, S. C. (2002). Exploring the relationships between hotel management courses and industry required competencies. *Journal of Teaching in Travel & Tourism, 2*(3–4), 81–101. https://doi.org/10.1300/J172v02n03_05

Lounsbury, J. W., Foster, N., Carmody, P. C., Young Kim, J., Gibson, L. W., & Drost, A. W. (2012). Key personality traits and career satisfaction of customer service workers. *Managing Service Quality: An International Journal, 22*(5), 517–536. https://doi.org/10.1108/09604521211281404

Mayo, C. R., & Thomas-Haysbert, C. (2005). Essential competencies needed by hospitality and tourism management graduates as determined by industry professionals and hospitality educators. *Consortium Journal of Hospitality & Tourism, 9*(2), 5–16.

McGrath, C., Palmgren, P. J., & Liljedahl, M. (2019). Twelve tips for conducting qualitative research interviews. *Medical Teacher, 41*(9), 1002–1006.

Mihailescu, R., & Rinaldi, A. (2021). A preliminary evaluation of the impact that the COVID-19 pandemic could have on female employability in the tourism and hospitality sectors in Italy. *Research in Hospitality Management, 11*(2), 165–169. https://doi.org/10.1080/22243534.2021.1917085

Novacka, L., Pícha, K., Navratil, J., Topaloglu, C., & Švec, R. (2019). Adopting environmentally friendly mechanisms in the hotel industry: A perspective of hotel managers in central and eastern European countries. *International Journal of Contemporary Hospitality Management, ahead-of print*(ahead-of-print), 2488–2508. https://doi.org/10.1108/IJCHM-04-2018-0284

Nyanjom, J., & Wilkins, H. (2021). Emotional labor and the hospitality and tourism curriculum: The development and integration of emotion skills. *Journal of Human Resources in Hospitality & Tourism, 20*, 611–631. https://doi.org/10.1080/15332845.2021.1960118

Page, S. J., Bentley, T., Teo, S., & Ladkin, A. (2018). The dark side of high performance human resource practices in the visitor economy. *International Journal of Hospitality Management, 74*, 122–129. https://doi.org/10.1016/j.ijhm.2018.02.016

Phelan, K. V. (2015). Elephants, orphans and HIV/AIDS: Examining the voluntourist experience in Botswana. *Worldwide Hospitality and Tourism Themes., 7*, 127–140. https://doi.org/10.1108/WHATT-12-2014-0049

Ramsey, P. H. (1989). Critical values for Spearman's rank order correlation. *Journal of Educational Statistics, 14*(3), 245–253. https://doi.org/10.3102/10769986014003245

Robinson, J. S. (2006). *Graduates' and employers' perceptions of entry-level employability skills needed by agriculture, food and natural resources graduates*. University of Missouri. https://doi.org/10.32469/10355/4328

Salem, I. E.-B., & Abdien, M. K. (2017). Implementation of employee cross-training during perilous conditions in hotels. *Tourism Management Perspectives, 23*, 68–74. https://doi.org/10.1016/j.tmp.2017.05.005

Shobha, C. V., & Johnson, B. (2021). Employability framework in the post- Covid scenario – A literature review. *Abhigyan (New Delhi), 39*(2), 28. https://elibrary.jcu.edu.au/login?url=https://www.proquest.com/scholarly-journals/employability-framework-post-covid-scenario/docview/2632833624/se-2–36.

Sisson, L. G., & Adams, A. R. (2013). Essential hospitality management competencies: The importance of soft skills. *Journal of Hospitality & Tourism Education, 25*(3), 131–145. https://doi.org/10.1080/10963758.2013.826975

Slåtten, T., & Mehmetoglu, M. (2014). The effects of transformational leadership and perceived creativity on innovation behavior in the hospitality industry. *Journal of Human Resources in Hospitality & Tourism, 14*, 195–219. https://doi.org/10.1080/15332845.2014.955557

Stewart, B. A. (2021). An empirical approach to identifying employability skills required of graduates in the environmental sciences. *Industry and Higher Education, 35*(2), 89–101. https://doi.org/10.1177/0950422220936869

Stoffers, J., Henikx, K., Habets, O., & van der Heijden, B. (2019). Employability and innovative work behaviours in SMEs in a Euroregion: A cross-national comparison between Belgium and The Netherlands. *Personnel Review, 49*(1), 167–187. https://doi.org/10.1108/PR-10-2018-0387

Stone, G. A., Duffy, L. N., Pinckney, H. P., & Templeton-Bradley, R. (2017). Teaching for critical thinking: Preparing hospitality and tourism students for careers in the twenty-first century. *Journal of Teaching in Travel & Tourism, 17*(2), 67–84.

Tesone, D. V., & Ricci, P. (2006). Toward a definition of entry-level job competencies: Hospitality manager perspectives. *International Journal of Hospitality & Tourism Administration, 7*(4), 65–80. https://doi.org/10.1300/J149v07n04_04

Thartori, E., Pastorelli, C., Cirimele, F., Remondi, C., Gerbino, M., Basili, E., Favini, A., Lunetti, C., Fiasconaro, I., & Caprara, G. V. (2021). Exploring the protective function of positivity and regulatory emotional self-efficacy in time of pandemic COVID-19. *International Journal of Environmental Research and Public Health, 18*(24), 13171. https://doi.org/10.3390/ijerph182413171

Tiwari, P., Séraphin, H., & Chowdhary, N. R. (2020). Impacts of COVID-19 on tourism education: Analysis and perspectives. *Journal of Teaching in Travel & Tourism*, 1–26.

Veblen, T., & Mills, C. W. (2017). *The theory of the leisure class*. Routledge.

Weber, M. R., Lee, J., & Crawford, A. (2020). A suggested best practices for enhancing performance of soft skills with entry-level hospitality managers. *Anatolia, 31*(1), 76–87. https://doi.org/10.1080/13032917.2019.1703770

Wilks, D., & Hemsworth, K. (2012). Soft skills as key competencies in hospitality higher education: Matching demand and supply. *Tourism & Management Studies, 17, 131–139.*

Wilson-Wünsch, B., & Plattes, L. (2014). The influence of a service culture on positive guest experience and customer loyalty in luxury hotels in the Middle East. 32nd EuroCHRIE conference" Hospitality and Tourism Futures", Dubai 6–9 October 2014.

Wilson-Wünsch, B., Beausaert, S., Tempelaar, D., & Gijselaers, W. (2015). The making of hospitality managers: The role of knowledge in the development of expertise. *Journal of Human Resources in Hospitality & Tourism, 14*(2), 153–176. https://doi.org/10.1080/15332845.2015.955562

Yang, H., Cheung, C., & Fang, C. C. (2015). An empirical study of hospitality employability skills: Perceptions of entry-level hotel staff in China. *Journal of Hospitality & Tourism Education, 27*(4), 161–170. https://doi.org/10.1080/10963758.2015.1089510

Chapter 20
Impact of Students' Village Residence on the Students Performance and the Host Community: A Study of Federal Polytechnic Bauchi, Nigeria

Usman Yusuf Dutse

Abstract This study is on the impact of students' village residence on students of tertiary institutions performance and the host community. Federal Polytechnic, Bauchi was used for the study, it is located in Gwallameji community about 7 km south of Bauchi metropolis along Dass/Tafawa Balewa road, Nigeria. In the study, questionnaire were administered physically, direct observation and oral interview were used to generate data from the students, staff and people in the community; descriptive survey design, tables and percentages were used to present data. Purposive sampling strategy was used to select the sample. The data collected were analyzed using mean scores to answer the research questions. Any item with less than 2.50 was rejected as having no influence. On the other hand, it was accepted if it was 2.50 and above for having significant impact. It was established that there is significant gap between demand and supply for hostel accommodation in higher institutions and that the increasing reliance on students' village residence outside the institutions has significant negative influence on their academic performance and their social development. It also have its economic impact as it attract different forms of business activities which provides sources of income, and reduces poverty in the host community. However, it was also evident that cult's activities, drugs peddling/consumption and insecurity become prevalent in the host community. Careful and coordinated effort is required on the side of government, schools administration and the community leaders to mitigate these challenges effectively.

Keywords Impact · Students · Village resident · Performance · Host community

---

U. Y. Dutse (✉)
Department of Business Administration and Management, Federal Polytechnic, Bauchi, Nigeria
e-mail: udyusuf@fptb.edu.ng

E. L. Eijdenberg et al. (eds.), *Innovation-Driven Business and Sustainability in the Tropics*, https://doi.org/10.1007/978-981-99-2909-2_20

20.1 Introduction

Nigeria like other countries of the world recognizes education as the major instrument for effecting national development. It is regarded as a catalyst and a means of achieving growth and development, because the socio-economic, political and technological advancement of any nation depends greatly on its educational system. It is recognized as an instrument par excellence for achieving growth, progress and national development, (FRN, 2013). This therefore, underscores the value being placed on the quality and standards which encompasses quality learning, resources inputs, instructional process, manpower capacity development, effective management, monitoring and evaluation as well as quality learning outcome in Nigerian universities. Huge amount of money is invested into the system through budgetary allocations year in year out for the effectiveness of the educational system. Consensus has been reached by stakeholders within the educational system that advanced nations of the world have attained a high level of social, economic, scientific and technological advancement through well planned and implemented educational systems.

Education is the facilitator, the bedrock, the power house and the driving force for the strong socio-economic, political, cultural, healthier and industrial development of a nation as its institutions are the key mechanisms increasingly recognized as wealth and human capital producing industries (Osamwonyi & Iyamu, 2007). The relationship between education and development is well established such that education is a tool that improves productivity, empowerment and health, as well as reduces negative features of life such as child labour, prostitution, crime and other social related vices (Ogeah & Ajalaye, 2014 and Sawyer & Yosuf, 2013).

According to Federal Republic of Nigeria (FRN, 2013), tertiary education is given after secondary education. The goal of higher education in Nigeria has captured in the National Policy on Education of Federal Republic of Nigeria (FRN, 2013) include; the development of individuals through high level relevant manpower training inculcation of proper values for survival of individuals to understand their environment, acquisition of physical and intellectual skills for self-reliance, to promote and encourage scholarship and community service; and promote national and international understanding and interaction, these goals can be achieved through teaching and learning within the framework of tertiary education system which include universities, polytechnics/monotechnics and collages (Angelina and Mahmud, 2012).

Consequent on the above, Universities, Polytechnics and Colleges' enrolments are booming across Nigeria. However, the surge in students' enrolment has not been matched by a corresponding growth in student accommodation. As of date, the vast majority of students in tertiary institutions live in privately rented accommodation. Increase in the number of students admitted into Nigerian tertiary institutions and the corresponding needs for hostel accommodation and facilities are serious challenges facing the governments and school administration. (Najib et al., 2012, 2017; Jansen, 2014).

According to the National Universities Commission (NUC) and as of 2 November 2018, Nigeria has 43 Federal Universities, 47 State Universities, and 75 Private Universities. 27 Federal Polytechnics, 48 State and 61 Private Polytechnics (NBTE, 2019). While In addition, there are 22 Federal Collages, 47 States and 20 Private collages in the country (NCCE, 2018). This information indicates that there is increasing access to tertiary education in Nigeria, while students' enrolment in tertiary institutions is growing at an average of 12% per annum, the provision of new purpose-built students' housing is limited. This is evident in the provision of students' housing which is less than 30% of demand and which in turn, creates opportunities for private developers to invest in the development of students' housing in many cities in Nigeria called off-campus/students village (Ogeah & Ajalaye, 2014).

The term Students' village/Off-campus residence is commonly refers to accommodation which students occupy outside the school premises. Some Authors such as Yusuff (2010) opined that when a student lives on-campus he or she lives in a dormitory or other type of housing on the school's property. He further stresses that off-campus living is usually when the student lives away from campus or in a rented apartment outside school environment. Choi and Chu (2011) are of the view that off-campus residence as a place which is away from (residing outside) the facilities of the institution. Whether such students are staying with their parents, relatives or rented apartment, once it is outside the properties of the institution, they are staying off-campus.

Residential accommodation play a significant role in the academic, social and economic life of students at all tiers of education. Therefore, the issue of students' accommodation should not be neglected be taken for granted by policy makers, parents, and administrators of educational institutions (Agwa et al., 2018). However, with the current challenge of inadequate availability of accommodation facilities on campus, students are compelled to take a house close to the institution to enable them to stay closer leading to the development of students' village. The concentration of students in such areas generate different kind of challenges to the students and the host communities.

20.1.1 Statement of the Problem

Nigeria in line with the National Policy on Education (2013) increase provision for access to education, government at various level of government established several tertiary institutions in strategic locations in the geopolitical zones in the country which serve as engines of development in the nation. The increasing concentration of students has impacted on the physical and socioeconomic development of host communities and the surrounding areas.

Furthermore, students staying off-campus may be facing numerous challenges as a result of little or no control, regulations or surveillance system put in place as it is provided by the management to guide the activities, guard and protect lives and properties of those students living in the school hostels. Such issues include insecurity, inadequate use of school facilities, exposure to cult-related activities and some anti-social activities. All these may affect students' learning habits which in turn may lead to poor academic performance compared to their counterparts on school campuses (Owolabi, 2015),

Similarly, the concentration of students on off-campus basis seem to pose challenges to the host and surrounding communities in the form of cultists activities, poor sanitary conditions, drug abuse and other social vices. It became imperative to investigate the impact of off-campus residence on students and the host community in Gwallameji, Bauchi State, Nigeria.

20.1.2 Purpose of the Study

The purpose of this study was to investigate the impact of off-campus residence on students in tertiary institutions and the host communities in Bauchi State. Specifically, the study sought to:

(i) Assess the gap between demand for hostel accommodation and the available bed space in Federal polytechnic, Bauchi
(ii) Identify the effects of off-campus residence on students of Federal Polytechnic Bauchi
(iii) Examine the impact of off campus students residence on Gwallameji community

20.1.3 Research Questions

The study was guided by the following research questions:

(i) How adequate is the availability of hostel accommodation in relation to the number of registered students in Federal Polytechnic, Bauchi?
(ii) What are the effects of off-campus residence on the performance of students of Federal Polytechnic Bauchi?
(iii) What are the impact of students' off-campus residence on the host community of Gwallameji?

20.1.4 Scope of the Study

The study is to investigate the impact of student's village/off-campus residence on students in tertiary institutions and the host community. Description of the study area for this work is Federal Polytechnic Bauchi that was established by the Federal Government of Nigeria, in 1979. The institution is situated in Gwallameji community about 7 km south of Bauchi metropolis along Dass/Tafawa Balewa highway.

20.2 Research Methodology

For the purpose of this study questionnaire, direct observation and oral interview were used to generate data from the students, staff and people in the community. The work adopted descriptive survey design, tables and percentages were used to present data. A sample of 22 out of 58 private students' hostels in Gwallameji village were randomly selected. 5 students were randomly selected from each of the 22 sampled hostels for distribution of questionnaire, making a total of 110 students. Out of the questionnaire administered 101 were filled and returned. Purposive sampling strategy was use to sampled Final year students due to the fact that, they are the most competent to respond to the questionnaire because of their long stay in off campus residence.

A structured questionnaire was used for data collection. Two set of questionnaire were developed and administered physically; one for off campus students while the other was for members of the host community; interview was coordinated for those that are not literate enough to fill the questionnaire. The questionnaire were divided into Sections A and B, Section A contained items on the personal data of the respondents, while Section B contained four items that were set to sought information on the issues under study. Responses were based on a 4-point scale with the response graded as Strongly Agree (SA) = 4, Agree (A) = 3, Disagree (D) = 2, Strongly Disagree (SD) = 1.

The validity and reliability of the instrument was measured using Cronbach Alpha which yielded a reliability coefficient of 0.79. This indicated high internal consistency. The data collected were analyzed using mean scores to answer the research questions. Any item with less than 2.50 was rejected as having no influence. On the other hand, it was accepted if it was 2.50 and above.

20.3 Empirical Review

Many authors have conducted researches on students' accommodation issues. The following are review of works related to the this study;

The study by Agwa et al. (2018), on the implication of mass off campus students housing adopted a survey and archival research approaches and used descriptive statistics to analyse the data collected. The study revealed that over 75% of the students lived off-campus. This situation has given rise to the mass off-campus student housing phenomenon. Identified implications of this mass off-campus student living included the ever-increasing house rents in the proximate neighborhoods, inadequate security of students' life and properties, lateness to lectures due to poor transportation network, compounding academic stress, and lack of basic infrastructure in the host communities compared to the university's campus.

This study by Ado et al. (2017) examines students' satisfaction with hostel facilities in Kano University of Science and Technology, wudil, Kano State, Nigeria. A multi stage sampling technique was employed where stratified random sampling was used. Structured questionnaire was used in the study and both descriptive statistics and One-way Analysis of Variance (One-way ANOVA) were employed in the data analyses. The findings suggest that students were satisfied with waste collection, internet services, fence, kitchenette, recreation areas, toilets, laundry, drainage systems, privacy, and writing tables in the hostels. However, this are mostly lacking in off campus residence

Angelina and Mahmud (2012) in their work on influence of Off-campus residence on students' academic performance in tertiary institutions in Benue state used mean and standard deviation for data analysis. The findings revealed that insecurity of off-campus residence and inadequate use of school facilities by off-campus residence significantly influences students' academic performance in tertiary institutions.

In a work conducted by Ogeah and Ajalaye (2014), a field survey was carried out with the use of questionnaire. The study reveals that the presence of the students in the host community of Ekosodin has brought significant changes both positively and negatively on the physical and socio economic environment of the village. Although the students enjoy the close proximity between the village and the university, they experience some problems living in the village. These include increase in rent, crime occurrence, and poor supply of water and electricity. Indiscriminate waste disposal and open defecation are also common in such communities.

In their work, Kuh and Hu (2007) states that the problems associated with students living off-campus are numerous. One of the challenges confronted by Nigerian higher institutions is violence which has become a major cause of concern that threatens the peace and security of people in off-campus environment while deterring the developmental pace of Nigerian economy. Today, cultism and cult-related activities, violence, killings, raping and kidnapping have become a recurrent theme in Nigerian campuses and off campuses.

Simon and Francis (2013) observe that government in developing countries are unable to adequately meet the accommodation demand for all public higher institutions due to limited government resources. In Nigeria, the managements of few public tertiary institutions are beginning to partner with private hostel providers to participate in building hostels and halls of residence for students in order to meet the increasing demand for more hostel accommodation facilities on campuses.

Olugun (2006) states that students who stay on-campus stay longer in the library compared to their counterparts who stay off-campus. They visit and borrow textbooks and journals from the university library, while their off-campus counterparts under-utilizing the library facilities. Abu (2010) adds that off-campus students have limited access to university libraries and laboratories as they spend less time on the campus compared to their counterparts. Consequently, their academic performance suffers.

Similarly, Okonkwo (2009) observes that most off-campus students arrive the school lately, thereby missing some lectures. They also find it difficult to even have seat where such facilities are insufficient. This makes most off-campus students find it difficult to catch up with their academic activities, most students that stay on-campus have even better access to light, internet services and textbooks than their off-campus counterparts.

Owolabi (2015) similarly notes that the federal and state governments in Nigeria do not recognize students' on-campus accommodation as housing need, rather as an educational need. Each university was, however, mandated to cover a wide catchment area. Hostel facilities in pubic tertiary institutions in many tertiary institutions throughout the federation are in dire need of attention.

Due to the insufficient availability of bed space on campus, Students of tertiary institutions have to make alternative arrangements by staying off-campus which may lead to challenges to the students; and the concentration of students can have impact on the host community. This have attracted the interest of many researchers but, most of the works reviewed focused more on the effects on students' academic performance without giving attention to the impact on host communities. It is against this background that this study examined the impact of off-campus residence on students and the host community.

20.4 Results and Findings

20.4.1 Registered Students in FPT Bauchi 2013/2014–2018/2019 Sessions

The statistics of registered students' population of Federal Polytechnic, Bauchi for the past 7 years is 77,288 (Male 50,891 and Female 26,297) as shown on Table 20.1. The average total number of registered male students for the 7 academic sessions was 7270 which accounted for 66%. The table also shows that average number of registered female students for the periods were 3756 which represents 34%. This indicates that the male students are higher in number than the female of students for the period under study.

Table 20.1 Records of registered students of Federal Polytechnic, Bauchi (2012–2019)

SN	Session	Male	Female	Total
1	2012/2013	7708	3588	11,296
2	2013/2014	7874	3644	11,518
3	2014/2015	7921	3658	11,579
4	2015/2016	7516	3662	11,178
5	2016/2017	6550	3817	10,467
6	2017/2018	6354	3821	10,175
7	2018/2019	6968	4107	11,075

(Source: FPTB MIS/ICT Center 2020)

20.4.2 *Number of Rooms and Bed Spaces in the Hostel Blocks as at 2019/2020 Session in Federal Polytechnic Bauchi*

The availability of hostel accommodation in the institution is on the basis of 8 hostel blocks where 4 are for male students, which are constitute 88 rooms that provides 528 bed spaces. While the remaining four (4) are for the female counterparts, that has 70 rooms with 310 bed spaces. These shows that the total of number of rooms in the 8 hostel blocks are 158 rooms and the total bed spaces contained in the rooms are 838 as provided in Tables 20.2 and 20.3.

20.4.3 *Determining the Gap Between Student Population and the Number of Student Accommodations on Campus*

It is clearly revealed by the statistics contained in Tables 20.1, 20.2, and 20.3 that there is a wide gap between the number of registered students and the capacity of the available hostel accommodation in Federal Polytechnic, Bauchi. What is available is grossly inadequate compared to the demand by students. The average total number of registered male students for the 7 academic sessions (2013–2019) was 7270 which accounted for 66%. While that of registered female students for the periods were 3756 which represents 34%, making a total of 11,026 students. However, there 8 hostel blocks in the school, 4 for male student with 88 rooms that provides 528 bed spaces; the remaining 4 blocks are for female students, which has 70 rooms that accommodates 318 bed spaces. By implications, there are total of 158 rooms and 846 bed spaces in the campus.

Therefore, there exist an estimated shortage of accommodations of 10,180 in terms of bed spaces, representing about 92.3% of the average student population as sourced from the tables. This indicates that only an average of 7.7% of the student were accommodated in the campus. Consequently, accommodations shortage is the major reason for the mass off-campus student housing phenomenon in the study area.

Table 20.2 Bed spaces in male students hostel (Federal Polytechnic, Bauchi)

SN	Name hall	No. of rooms	Bed space
1.	Mal. Yakubu	24 rooms × 6 spaces	144 spaces
2.	Mal. Buba Yero	24 rooms × 6 spaces	144 spaces
3.	Mal. Manga	24 rooms × 6 spaces	144 spaces
4.	Mal. Zaki	24 rooms × 6 spaces	144 spaces
Total		= 96 rooms	= 528 spaces

(Source: Students Affairs Office FPTB 2021)

Table 20.3 Bed Spaces in Female Hostel (Federal Polytechnic, Bauchi)

SN	Name of hall	No of rooms	Bed space
1.	Block A	18 rooms × 4 spaces	72 spaces + common room = 10 spaces
2.	Block B	18 rooms × 4 spaces	72 spaces
3.	Block C	18 rooms × 4 spaces	72 spaces + common room = 10 spaces
4.	Block D	18 rooms × 4 spaces	72 spaces + common room = 10 spaces
Total		= 70 rooms	= 318 spaces

(Source: Students Affairs Office FPTB 2021)

Table 20.4 Mean ratings on the effects of off-campus residence on students of Federal Polytechnic Bauchi

Item no	Item description	SA	A	D	SD	*M*	Decision
1	Off-campus students mostly come to class late and do not return to school to make use of learning facilities due to distance that affect their academic performance negatively.	133	162	47	63	2.92	Agreed
2	Off-campus students live in unregulated areas that tend to be risky which expose some of them to drugs and alcohol.	97	160	106	56	2.73	Agreed
3	There may be poor sanitary condition and lacking clean drinking water which may affect their health condition and their studies.	65	206	113	21	2.81	Agreed
4	Off-campus students are exposed to cases of rape or harassment and this may affect their studies.	164	166	36	34	3.17	Agreed
5	Off – campus students are often exposed to theft/ burglary attack which takes away their valuables and this may affect their concentration.	120	190	41	49	2.98	Agreed
	Cluster Mean: 2.88						**Agreed**

20.4.4 Mean Rating of the Responses

The results are presented in line with the research questions as follows:

Research Question One: what are the effects of off-campus residence on students of Federal Polytechnic Bauchi?

Table 20.4 showed that the mean ratings of items 1–5 are; 2.87, 2.70, 2.75, 3.15 and 2.95 respectively with corresponding standard deviations of 1.03, 0.97, 0.79, 0.91 and 0.95. The cluster mean of 2.88 was also found to be above the cut-off point of 2.50. This means that distractions associated with off-campus residence influence students' academic performance in Federal Polytechnic, Bauchi.

Table 20.5 Mean rating of the impact of students of Federal Polytechnic, Bauchi staying in off-campus residence on the host communities

Item no	Item description	SA	A	D	SD	*M*	Decision
6	Concentration of Off-campus students have attracted different forms of businesses to the host community which reduces poverty.	150	187	27	36	2.92	Agreed
7	Off-campus students provides source of income to the youths in the community through menial jobs.	143	178	32	37	2.97	Agreed
8	Establishment of the polytechnic have provided easy access to higher education and job opportunities to the youth in the communities.	182	163	30	25	3.06	Agreed
9	Cultist activities, drug peddling and theft/burglary become prevalent in the communities due to concentration of students residing off campus.	121	201	38	40	2.91	Agreed
10	Off-campus students' residence expose the community to indiscriminate waste disposal which lead to blocked drainages, flood and contamination of water sources.	151	140	66	43	2.80	Agreed
	Cluster Mean					**2.93**	**Agreed**

Research Question Two: What are the impact of students' off-campus residence on the host community of Gwallameji?

Table 20.5 showed that the mean ratings of items 6–10 are; 2.92, 2.97, 3.06, 2.91 and 2.80 respectively. The cluster mean of 2.93 was also above the cut-off point of 2.50. This implies that the concentration of students living in off-campus residence have impacted on the socio economic activities of Gwallameji, the host community.

20.5 Discussion of Findings

The findings of this work indicated that there is significant gap between demand and supply for hostel accommodation; what is available is grossly inadequate compared with the number of students admitted. The number of registered students far outnumber the available bed spaces in the institutions. Students' population is changing but number of hostel blocks is static in Federal polytechnic Bauchi. Students are left with no option rather than to move out of campus to look for where to reside in the surrounding communities. This is in line with the findings of Ado et al. (2017) and Sulaiman (2018), which they also agreed that inadequate availability of hostel accommodation lead to concentration of students in off-campus that also resulted to the growing construction of buildings to be used by the students as residence in the communities.

The findings also exposed that the increasing reliance on off-campus residence by students has significant negative influence on their academic performance and their social development in institutions under study. This was attributed to distractions as a result of distance from learning facilities, alcohol /drugs, insecurity, and sickness due to poor environmental hygiene. The finding concur with that of Owolabi (2015) and Sulaiman (2018) who found that there is much risk associated with off campus students as attack by cultist, harassment and threat faced by female students. These has become a major cause of concern to the students, parents, school administrators and leaders of the host communities.

Furthermore, the findings revealed that irregular patronage of learning facilities by students staying in off-campus residence due to distance has significant negative influence on their academic performance. This finding is in line with that of Olatubara and Pike (2012) who also affirms that on-campus students do use laboratory/library facilities more than off-campus students as the former have access to the facilities 24 hours a day and are always challenged when they see other students reading. Abu (2010) reported that off-campus students have limited access to the school library as they spend lesser time on the campus compare to their counterparts and could not come back due to distance as a result, their academic performance suffers. This was also supported by the works of Pascarella and Mable, (2005) and Sawyer and Yosuf (2013).

In addition to the above findings, it was also confirmed that concentration of students due to off campus residence have attracted different forms of business activities into the host community which provides sources of income, and reduces poverty. Establishment of the Polytechnic have provided easy access to higher education and job opportunities for the youth in the community. This findings concur with the work of Angelina and Mahmud (2012) and Akinpelu (2015). However, it was also revealed that cult's activities, drugs peddling/consumption and insecurity become prevalent in the host community due to high concentrations of students living in off-campus residents. That also, exposes the community to open defecation, indiscriminate waste disposal which lead to flood due blockage of drainages and contamination of water sources. This was affirmed by Ogeah and Ajalaye (2014),

20.6 Conclusion

It was established that there is significant gap between demand and supply for hostel accommodation in higher institutions; what is available is grossly inadequate compared with the number of students. Students are left with no option rather than to move out of campus to look for where to reside in the surrounding communities. It was also exposed that the increasing reliance on off-campus residence by students in these institutions has significant negative influence on their academic performance and their social development. It is also evident that concentration of students due to off campus residence have its economic and social consequences; it attract different forms of business activities which provides sources of income, and reduces poverty. Establishment of the polytechnic provide easy access to higher education and job opportunity for the youth in the community. However, it was also evident that cult's activities, drugs peddling/consumption and insecurity become prevalent in the host community. High concentrations of students living in off-campus residents also, exposes the community to open defecation, indiscriminate waste disposal which lead to flood due blockage of drainages and contamination of water sources. Careful and coordinated effort is required on the side of government, schools administration and the community leaders to mitigate these challenges effectively.

20.7 Recommendations

The following recommendations were made in line with the conclusion made:

1. Government at all levels should as a matter of policy provide adequate accommodation for all admitted students in all tertiary institution by extending the intervention of Tertiary Education Trust Fund (TETFund) to the construction of hostel accommodation.
2. Government, School Proprietors and School management of institutions should create an enabling environment that can promote Public-Private-Partnership (PPP) and Build-Operate-and Transfer (BOT) contracts, which will encourage private organizations and individuals to complement government efforts towards provision of hostel accommodation in campuses.
3. The management of institution should dedicate reasonable part of its Internally Generated Revenue (IGR) to building of hostels which can generate additional source of revenue.
4. Urban Development Board should be proactive and take into account the plight of the communities by effectively regulating/controlling the indiscriminate constructions of students' residence by landlords, without any consideration for provisions in the master plan for the layout.
5. The host community should organize a dependable community policing network in collaboration with the Nigeria Police and other security agents for surveillance and information sharing to manage criminality.
6. There is need for collaboration between School Management and Landlords for screening, data generation, monitoring, and information sharing so as to identify criminals among the students.
7. The Federal Mortgage Bank of Nigeria (FMBN) should expand its services to incorporate tertiary institution student housing schemes.
8. Efficient and sustainable transportation system should be arranged to ease movement to and fro the campus for the off –campus students adequately utilize learning facilities in campus.

References

Abu, O. (2010). Sustainable development of higher education in Nigeria. *African Journal of Development Studies, 7*(6), 16–28.

Ado, A., Ado, M. B., & Auwal, I. A. (2017). Students hostel satisfaction with facilities in Kano University of Science and Technology Wudil, Kano State, Nigeria. *Research Journal of Geograhpy, 4*(7), 9.

Agwa, Y. H., Bello, N. A., Abdulraheem, M. O., & Gobwer, N. W. (2018). Implication of mass off-campus students housing at the University of Ilorin, Nigeria. *Ife Research Journal, 16*(1), 75–86.

Akinpelu, O. P. (2015). Students' assessment of hostel facilities in the polytechnic, Ibadan, Ibadan, Nigeria: Realities and Challenges.IISTE. *Research on Humanities and Social Sceinces, 5*(17), 74–81.

Angelina, O, & Mahmud, P. (2012). Impact of out-campus residence on academic performance of students' performance in tertiary institutions in Benue state of Nigeria. *African Journal of Education Management 23*(3).

Choi, T. Y., & Chu, R. (2011). Determinants of hostel gusts: Satisfaction and repeat patronage in the Hong Kong hostel industry. *International Journal of Hospitality Management, 2*(20), 277–297.

Federal Republic of Nigeria (FRN), National Policy on Education. (2013).

Jansen, S. (2014). The impact of the have-want discrepancy on residential satisfaction. *Journal of Environmental Psychology, 40(20), 26–38.*

Kuh, G., & Hu, S. (2007). The effects of students' faculty interaction in the 1990s. *The Review of Higher Education, 24*(3), 309–332.

Najib, N. M., Yusof, N., & Sani, N. M. (2012). The effects of students' socio-physical backgrounds onto satisfaction with student housing facilities. *Procedia – Social and Behavioral Sciences, 62*(2012), 64–74.

Najib, N. M., Yusof, N., & Osman, Z. (2017). The influence of socio-economic backgrounds towards satisfaction with student housing facilities. *International Journal of Social, Management, Economics and Business Engineering, 5*(10), 222–227.

National Board for Technical Education (NBTE) Brochure. (2019).

National Commion for Collages Education (NCCE) Brochure. (2018).

Ogeah, F. N., & Ajalaye, V. (2014). Students off-campus residence and impact on localities: The case of the university of Benin and Ekosodu Village. *Global Journal of Social Sciences, 10*(1 & 2), 37–43.

Okonkwo, Y. (2009). The status of university education in Nigeria. *African Journal of Educational Management, 7*(2), 12–18.

Olugun, R. (2006). Higher education and Nigeria's national development: Challenges for millennium. *Research for Educational Reforms, 7*(9), 6–12.

Osamwonyi, I. O., & Iyamu, I. J. G. (2007). The socio-economic impact of a rural based University in Edo State. In B. A. Chokor & A. O. Ozo (Eds.), *Environment and society in Nigeria* (p. 94). Environment and Behaviour Association of Nigeria (EBAN) University of Lagos.

Owolabi, O. B. (2015). The effects of students' housing on academic performance at the University of Ibadan in Nigerian. *International Journal of Scientific & Engineering Research, 6(3)*, 1118–1132. March-2015 ISSN 2229-5518.

Pike, T. (2012). Sustaining the Development of higher education in Nigeria. *The Review of Higher Education 20*(2)

Sawyer, P. T., & Yosuf, N. (2013). Student satisfaction with hostel facilities in Nigerian polytechnics. *Journal of Facilities Management, 11*(24), *306–322.*

Simon, G. N., & Francis, K. B. (2013). An empirical evaluation of student accommodation quality in higher education. *European Journal of Business and Social Sciences, 1*(12), 164–177. ISSN: 2235-767X.

Sulaiman, Y. (2018). *Spatial analysis of off-campus students housing around the new campus of Bayero university, Kano.*

Yusuff, O. S. (2010). Students' access to housing: A case study of Lagos state university students. *Journal of Sustainable Development, 4*(2), 107–122.

Chapter 21
E-marketing, Technological Capabilities, and Performance of Small and Medium Enterprises in North East Nigeria

Mohammed Lawal Inuwa and Friday Igbadumhe

Abstract Small and Medium Enterprises (SMEs) play a major role in the world economy accounting for humongous economic development and employment growth. On the other hand, the revolution in information technology (IT) and communications has changed the way people conduct business today. Thus, the reinvention of marketing requires a cursory examination of the role of e-marketing and technological capabilities on the performance of SMEs is imperative. A cross-sectional survey was used to collect data from SMEs in Northeast Nigeria, while the Linear Regression model was deployed to test hypotheses. The study found that e-marketing has a significant effect on competitive advantage, Sales volume, customer retention, and market share Furthermore, the technological capabilities of small businesses have proven to be a catalyst to the performance of SMEs in Northeast Nigeria. Beneficiaries of this research include Researchers, Entrepreneurs, Policy makers, and practitioners.

Keywords E-marketing · Technological capabilities · SME · Competitive advantage

21.1 Introduction

Small and medium-sized enterprises (SMEs) play a crucial role in the global economy and are recognized as one of the most important contributors to economic development and job growth. The revolution in information technology (IT) and communications has changed the way people do business today. In recent years,

M. L. Inuwa (✉)
Department of Marketing, Federal Polytechnic Bauchi, Bauchi, Nigeria
e-mail: mlinuwa@fptb.edu.ng

F. Igbadumhe
Department of Management & Accounting, Lead City University, Ibadan, Nigeria
e-mail: igbadumhe.abaye@lcu.edu.ng

E. L. Eijdenberg et al. (eds.), *Innovation-Driven Business and Sustainability in the Tropics*, https://doi.org/10.1007/978-981-99-2909-2_21

more and more companies have turned to the Internet and other electronic media for their marketing efforts, giving electronic marketing (as a new marketing phenomenon and philosophy) a chance to grow in dramatic and dynamic ways (AlBar & Hoque, 2019).

Accordingly, implementing electronic marketing (E-marketing) by SMEs can change both the shape and nature of SMEs all over the world (Pradhan & Nigam, 2018). This is because the growing usage of the Internet and other electronic marketing tools in electronic transactions will not only generate numerous opportunities for SMEs, but also reduce many dangers from both the internal and external environments.

According to the World Bank, SMEs make up most of the world's businesses and make a significant contribution to job creation and global economic growth. Globally, SMEs account for about 90% of businesses and more than 50% of employment, for instance in developing economies, SMEs contribute up to 40% of GDP (Muriithi, 2017). Moreover, the current rush of publications in the field may give the impression that EM can be used in any context, but there is little empirical evidence to support this. Some herald it as the new marketing paradigm. (Eid & El-Gohary, 2013).

Meanwhile, over the past three decades, SMEs were seen as the economic engine that fuels global economic development; they have attracted considerable attention from scholars and practitioners (Min et al., 2021). SMEs are vital to a country's economic development, as a result, the performance of the SME sector is strongly linked to the nation's performance. They bear the greatest responsibility for private sector employment around the world. Therefore, the development of small enterprises has been an important factor in the achievement of development goals such as the reduction of poverty, economic growth and the promotion of democratic societies. (Qashou & Saleh, 2018).

In Nigeria, greater emphasis has been placed on the SME sector and the role that entrepreneurs may play in reshaping the economy, particularly in the current global economic context. (Febriantoro, 2018). One of the efforts to develop and improve the competitiveness of SMEs can be made through internet-based business programs better known as e-commerce, (Permana, 2017; Febriantoro, 2018). The adoption of EM by multinational organizations has to a greater extent, changed the shape and nature of their business all over the world (Iddris & Masud, 2015) The rapid spread of the Internet, the World Wide Web (WWW), and ITs, communication technologies, social media, and computer sciences has generated dynamic new electronic channels for marketing, and most businesses now consider an online presence to be important. (Liang & Huang, 1998).

Although various studies have addressed E-marketing acceptance and adoption by SMEs in developing countries, few of these studies have been conducted in Sub-Saharan Africa (SSA). (Kalu et al., 2017). Similarly, the question of how technological capabilities can strengthen relationships between e-marketing and SME performance remains unanswered. On average, studies tend to focus on the consumer perspective, such as determinants of online buying decisions (Cheung et al., 2009) and deciphering word-of-mouth in social media (Zhang et al., 2012;

Rudansky-Kloppers, 2017; Khanna & Awal, 2019; Dermawan et al., 2020). Based on these identified gaps, this study therefore will examine the role of e-marketing and technological capabilities on SMEs performance in North-eastern Nigeria.

The purpose of this research is to examine the role of technological capabilities in fostering the relationship between e-marketing and the performance of SMEs in North-East Nigeria. Specifically, this current study is anchored on Social Network Theory SNT and the Unified Theory of Acceptance and Use of Technology UTAUT due to their popularity in the literature of studies related to new technology and innovation adoption and acceptance. The SME sector was chosen to be the application sector of the study due to its high-level contribution to the Nigerian economy (Odubanjo, 2000; Nnanna, 2001; Onwumere et al., 2012). The study area's vast population of registered SMEs necessitated the conduct of this research as a good representative random sample could be gathered and the results could be easily applied to the full population. The paper also provides insight into the effect of e -marketing on SME dimensions including competitive advantage, sales performance, customer retention, customer patronage, and market share.

The following section provides a review of relevant literature, study framework, and Hypothesis development. This is followed by a description of the research methodology, while the data analysis is presented alongside a discussion of the research results. Finally, a general discussion, conclusion, and Notions for Future Researchers and Limitations.

21.2 Literature Review

The concept of Small and Medium scale enterprises (SME) is a discourse that continues to occupy the front burner in Nigeria today. Small and medium-sized enterprises (SMEs) are defined and evaluated differently in different countries and by a wide range of sources that report SME data (Perera & Chand, 2015). The number of employees, total net assets, sales, and profits are some of the most commonly used criteria. However, employment is the most commonly used definitional basis, but there are others (Chen & Lien, 2013).

The definition in Nigeria, as in other economies, is based on the size or amount of Asset investment, total annual revenue, and employee count are all factors to consider. Within this context, the classification of businesses as 'medium' or 'small' varies from one economy to the other, as well as from one epoch to the next... (El-Gohary, 2012). In Nigeria, the National Council of Industry, which reports to the Federal Ministry of Industries, revises the classification of SMEs on a regular basis. Other institutions, including the Central Bank of Nigeria and the Nigerian Association of Small-Scale Industries (NASSI), use classifications that differ from those used by the Federal Ministry of Industries. However, when it comes to defining SMEs in terms of asset value, there is more agreement than on any other basis. Because the impact on turnover and the number of people employed is greater than the impact on asset value in the event of an economic downturn (Izediuno et al., 2018). The Committee for Economic Development of the United States of America defines a small business as one that has two or more of the following four characteristics: the owners are also managers, the capital for running the business is supplied, and one individual or a small group holds ownership, the area of business operations is primarily local, and the business is small when compared to other businesses in the field (Haider et al., 2015). Factors that affect the creation and expansion of SMEs in Nigeria. The majority of SMEs fail during the first 5 years of operation. Only roughly 5–10% of early enterprises survive, prosper, and mature because a lower proportion disappears between the sixth and tenth year. Numerous variables have been noted as potential causes of or contributors to their untimely demise. The most significant of these are: insufficient funding; lack of concentration; inadequate market research; excessive concentration on a small number of finished product markets; lack of succession planning; inexperience; improper bookkeeping; lack of proper records; absence of any records; inability to distinguish between business and family or personal finances; lack of business strategy; inability to differentiate between revenue and profit; and inability to engage or employ the right caliber staff, lack of planning, cut-throat competition, lack of official patronage of locally produced goods and services, dumping of foreign goods and over-concentration of decision making on one (key) person, usually the owner (Abdulsaleh & Worthington, 2013).

21.2.1 Challenges of SMEs

A plethora of challenges related to small businesses and reasons for possible failure have been highlighted in the literature. The identified problems include poor planning, hostile Government regulations and interventions, inadequate business marketing approach, poor technical know-how, and a high rate of interest (Gumel, 2017). Tariffs are generally perceived to be more favorable to imported commodities, among other things; limited access to appropriate tools; over-dependence on imported commodities and materials; low demand for products, reducing consumer purchasing power; unbalanced trade practices characterized by the import of inferior goods; poor organizational strength, poor marketing, and information usage; multiple levels of government regulatory agencies, with high levies and taxes.

21.2.1.1 Overview of Electronic Marketing

Globally, advances in information technology have transformed marketing operations and corporate systems. Several companies are using the Internet and other electronic media to undertake marketing operations. As a result, e-marketing has grown and developed as a new marketing concept. E-marketing is a modern business technique that involves the promotion of goods, services, information, and ideas over the Internet and other electronic channels (El-Gohary, 2010). E-marketing is the use of electronic data and applications for planning and executing the conception, distribution, promotion, and pricing of ideas, goods, and services to create exchanges that satisfy individual and organizational goals (Strauss & Frost, 2001). The use of digital media is evolving to manage marketing operations including the management of digital customer data and electronic customer relationship management systems (Smith & Chaffey, 2005). Generally, e-marketing involves the application of the Internet and related digital technologies to achieve marketing objectives.

Electronic marketing (e-marketing) is one of the fastest-growing forms of digital marketing in both developed and developing countries (Kalu et al., 2017). It provides opportunities for business enterprises to attract new customers and reach the existing ones more effectively (Taiminen & Karjaluoto, 2015). E-marketing has been defined by various scholars, for instance, e-marketing is described as the integration of electronic communication technology and traditional marketing media to acquire and deliver services to customers, (Iddris & Ibrahim, 2015). The term e-marketing includes, but is not limited to: digital marketing, internet marketing, online marketing, and social media marketing (Shaltoni et al., 2018). In various business enterprises including Small and Medium Enterprises (SMEs), e-marketing appears to be one of the most significant aspects for achieving competitive advantage through business efficiency and marketing improvement (Chong et al., 2018). Despite the importance of e-marketing to SMEs, the number of SMEs that have adopted e-marketing is still low leading to limited application of the technology (Eze et al., 2020).

21.2.1.2 E-marketing and Competitive Advantage

Marketing, which progressed from the productive perception to the selling and then marketing perception to the social perception, found its applications on the Internet within the context of what has been labeled as "Electronic Marketing", besides, this international network has opened companies with widespread prospects and great prospects to reach consumers across the world (Aljawarneh, 2020). Hence, the increase in global internet users led to the growth of application fields for its use, particularly in the field of commercial marketing (Al-Jarrah & Arafat, 2014), as customers are often dissatisfied with customer service owing to the absence of personal service, entertainment, and social connections experienced in old marketing activities.

Though, Raoofi (2012) counters this fact by arguing that digital marketing offers massive potential benefits to consumers worldwide by providing them with a broader choice and variety of products at lower prices, as well as taking advantage of completely new and many more products, besides product groups such as books and travel packages to consumers who are far from the world's traditional trade hubs. Companies are vying in this period to reach the greatest number of three clients in order to boost their earnings and raise their products, as a big number of these companies' shoulder increasing marketing channels through the use of digital technology (Gregurec & Grd, 2012). Therefore, it is essential to have suitable electronic marketing means for the customer which are based on the environment surrounding it. As a consequence, marketing means have now become elements that characterize the environment surrounding the organizations, affects the volume of sales and profits achieved. Nonetheless, we should bear in mind, the notion that competitive advantage is a relational concept and it is also context-specific, there are possibilities that competitive advantage does not result in a superior firm's performance in an E marketing ecosystem (Ma, 2000; Rose et al., 2010). Following the review, it can be hypothesized that:

> H1: E-marketing has no significant effect on the competitive advantage of SMEs in North-East Nigeria

21.2.1.3 E-marketing and Sales Performance

Previous studies allude that sales technology can enable sales professionals to improve sales performance (Behrman & Perreault Jr, 1982, 1984; Hunter & Perreault 2007). Sales performance is defined as "behavior evaluated in terms of its contribution to the goals of the organization" (Johnston & Marshall, 2006). In the current study, performance measures are an important aspect of measuring productivity and are reflected by competitive advantage, sales performance, customer retention, and Market share. Relationships formed through social media networks can expand the pool of qualified prospects while also improving interactions with current customers, perhaps leading to higher customer retention (Rodriguez et al., 2012). Firms that use social media technology may engage with clients who are comfortable searching for information about products or services that meet their business needs on social media. Using social media to distribute value-added material or provide more effective communication may help organizations better serve current clientele. Social media should have an impact on outcome-based sales success measurements as well. A recent poll of 668 New Zealand small and medium-sized firms found that if a Web presence generated 20% or more of their revenues, those with a social media program outperformed those without a social media presence ("Domainz eBiz Review", 2010). In a survey of financial advisors, those that used social media saw a 19 percent gain in revenue and a 21 percent increase in client base (Mitchell et al., 2010). On the other hand, several studies contradict the previous findings. For instance, Sufian et al. (2020) found that content sharing has no direct influence on sales performance, likewise, there are not very well-established systems to measure the efficiency of e-marketing, therefore, it is difficult to measure sales derived directly from technology (Gilmore et al., 2007). Based on the preceding discussion it can be concluded that e-marketing has a link to sales performance. Therefore, it can be hypothesized that:

H2: E-marketing has no significant effect on the sales performance of SMEs in North-East Nigeria

21.2.1.4 E-marketing and Customer Retention

Online Marketing and indeed E-marketing have been shown to have a positive effect on customer tention. According to Asbari et al. (2021); Indra et al. (2020) The internet is increasingly becoming a medium suitable for connecting long distances. The internet's technological triumph has created a new world order, known as globalization. Various benefits are apparent from the effectiveness of getting the internet extensively embraced by business people for their commercial purposes. Organizations must consider electronic marketing prospects; thus, organizations must understand how to design an appealing website in order to retain their clients.

The facts demonstrate that internet users have increased over the last 15 years and are expected to continue to expand, causing firms, particularly those in the marketing communications section, to pay greater attention to the potential available in cyberspace or the internet. This validates e-marketing and its ability to retain customers (Novitasari et al., 2021; SetiaBakti & Kartika, 2020; Suwandi & HariHadi, 2020). A website can help businesses reach out to potential clients and manage customer relationships. This will undoubtedly function well when the number of visitors to the corporate website grows. The quick development of cyberspace (digital) or online today makes it very worthwhile for a firm to consider immediately building relationships with clients. In the electronic realm, consumer loyalty is also known as e-loyalty and is synonymous with customer retention (Indra et al., 2020; Fahmi et al., 2021; Maryani et al., 2020; Novitasari et al., 2021;SetiaBakti & Kartika, 2020; Suwandi & HariHadi, 2020). Loyal clients are intimately tied to the company's continuity and future good growth. Nonetheless, some studies have found a negative relationship between E-marketing and client retention attributing the success of E-marketing primarily to the support and enhancement of existing marketing techniques and integration with other marketing practices. (Brodie et al., 2007) In a related study, Kassim and Asiah Abdullah (2010) found that trust does not influence directly purchase decisions and authors have not found any link between trust and loyalty in an e-marketing setting. Consequently, this study presents the following hypothesis for testing:

H3: E-marketing has no significant effect on customer retention of SMEs in North-East Nigeria

21.2.1.5 E-marketing and Market Share

Many construction companies are facing lower profit margins as builders slash margins in order to compete. This has a significant impact on small and medium-sized enterprises (SMEs), which are struggling to grow and sustain market share against much larger and better-equipped competitors (Malesev & Cherry, 2021). Traditionally, the residential construction industry has not been a ready adopter of social media and digital marketing, but authors such as Parveen et al. (2014), Stewart and Pavlou (2002), and Quinn et al. (2016) believe digital marketing techniques and greater use of social media can expand brand awareness and achieve more effective business outcomes. Digital marketing techniques and social media offer benefits across all market segments and industries, but they would appear to offer a significant multiplier effect for SMEs in particular, including those in the construction sector. The most obvious benefit of the internet and social media is that they reduce costs by supplementing media spending for a more extensive but bettertargeted audience reach (Paswan, 2018). Housing and construction firms may spend 6–11% of their revenue on traditional advertising each year, although an increasing number of companies are choosing to divert a greater portion of their marketing spend – in some cases, up to 60% – toine marketing (Deloitte, 2018). The internet has greatly improved the ease and effectiveness of purchasing display ads or paid searches (Fulgoni, 2015), while social media have enabled an explosion in no- or low-cost organic marketing, whereby a company creates content and shares it amongst its social media followers (Lipsman et al., 2012). Social media can also be used to boost brand equity by helping to increase brand awareness, extend brand association and improve perceived brand quality (Khajuria & Rachna, 2017). Brand equity, best defined as the measure of brand strength and brand value (Lassar et al., 1995), can be increased by using social media to demonstrate a track record in the industry, the value-add to the consumer, and a positive image by way of community engagement (Yazdanparast et al., 2016). Social media can also be used to establish trustworthiness and an excellent customer experience in an industry plagued by customer complaints (Kim & Ko, 2012). On the other hand, several studies suggest that e-marketing efforts do not positively affect market share. For instance, Thurman (2018) reports that the British National Readership Survey found that, of the time spent with 11 UK national newspaper brands by their British audiences, 88.5% still comes via their print editions, 7.49% via mobiles, and just 4% via PCs. The study reveals that the "share of consumption" (AKA Market share) of UK national newspaper brands is less evenly distributed than commonly understood, conforming better to a logarithmic pattern than a linear one, and that a single brand—The Mail—has close to a 30 percent market share. E-marketing had not positively6 affected market share in this case. Similarly, Jiang et al. (2016) developed a model to predict the market share of online brands. However, despite the success recorded, the model was criticized 3 for its limitations arising from bias in data fitting that influence the simulation model. Another takeaway here is that e-marketing efforts are relational and do not always result in soaring market share. In line with the literature and the aim of this study, the following Hypothesis is formulated

H4: E-marketing has no significant effect on the market share of SMEs in North-East Nigeria

21.2.1.6 Technological Capabilities

Technological competence has been identified as an important factor in a country's economic growth because the success of an enterprise is dependent on the ability to introduce new products over time. There has been little research into technological capability and the internationalization of firms from rising economies such as Russia, India, Brazil, Mexico, and China (Chittor & Ray, 2007; Ménière, 2009; Pillania, 2009).

In many industries, innovation is the key to success. It has the potential to overcome entry obstacles and provide a long-term competitive advantage. A firm's ability to innovate is built, at least in part, on its knowledge base. As a result, management researchers have become more conscious of the significance of company knowledge, particularly technical information, in determining corporate success. Despite its crucial importance, academic academics and practicing managers are hampered by their inability to precisely quantify and appraise a company's technological capabilities.

An intangible asset is a firm's technological capabilities and the store of organizational knowledge that acts as its foundation. As a result, while attempting to judge a firm's technological capabilities, one is required to utilize some kind of proxy, or indicator. (FTC). Various technical indicators have been proposed and used during the previous few decades. However, the validity of these metrics across industries has not been sufficiently validated. As a result, academics and practicing managers may risk employing indicators that are inappropriate in all industrial scenarios. In some businesses, using improper indicators may result in faulty research findings or misleading competition analysis. This research adopts the following as sub-measures of technological capability: IT infrastructure Quality, IT Human Resources Competency, Environmental IT competence, and Business Process Digitization. However, the findings of Al Asheq, 2020 indicate that E-Marketing Orientation, technology, and Learning Capability are strong and significant determinants of online SME performance.

H5: There is no significant effect of technological capabilities on the performance of SMEs in North-East Nigeria

Dependent variable measures: SME Performance adapted from Anne (2020); and Hidayatullah et al. (2019).

To summarize the literature review and the study Hypothesis, the study will put the model in Fig. 21.1 to test.

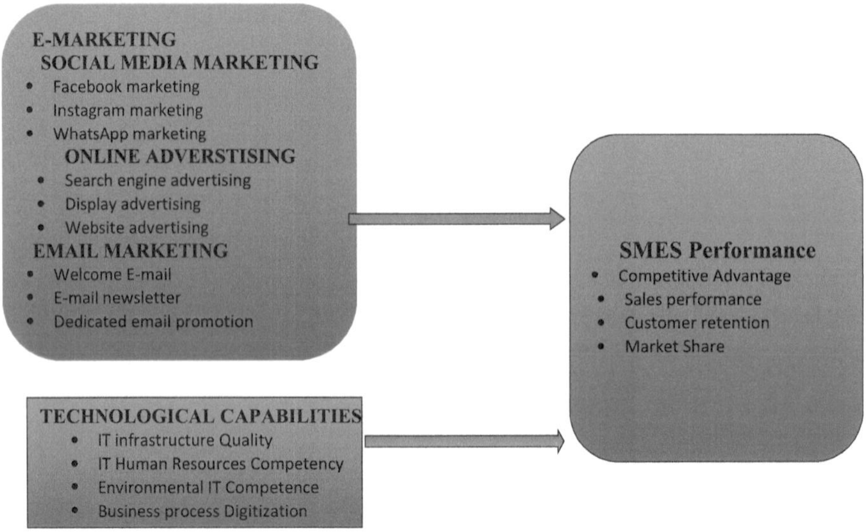

Fig. 21.1 Conceptual model of the study
Source: Independent Variable Measures: E-marketing measures adapted from Onyango (2016); Akyuz and Ibrahim (2020); while The measures for Technological Capabilities are from Antoni, D., Jie, F., & Abareshi, A. (2020)

21.3 Research Methodology

21.3.1 Research Design

A descriptive research design was used for the investigation. A descriptive technique was chosen because of its strength in recognizing and encapsulating major issues, as well as allowing for more extensive and richer decryption of the study's components (ElKordy, 2014). The quantitative approach was used and a cross-sectional survey was opted for because it involves collecting data from a large number of respondents across the parent population over a shorter period.

21.3.2 Population of the study

The population of the study is derived from the SMEDAN/NBS survey of 2021 which states that there are 157,314 registered SMEs in North Eastern Nigeria. The table below provides a breakdown of the population (Table 21.1).

The population of the study comprises the 157,314 SMEs of the North Eastern States of Nigeria which include, Adamawa, Bauchi, Gombe Taraba, Borno, and Yobe States.

Table 21.1 Breakdown of the population

S/N0	State	Number of businesses	Percentages (%)
1	Adamawa	24,940	15.85
2	Bauchi	34,685	22.04
3	Borno	26,479	16.83
4	Gombe	29,930	19.02
5	Taraba	18,855	11.98
6	Yobe	22,425	14.25
	Total	157,314	

Source: SMEDAN/NBS Survey 2021

Table 21.2 Proportionate sample size distribution by states and sample using Krejcie & Morgan, 1970

S/N	States	SME Population
1	Adamawa	24,940
2	Bauchi	34,685
3	Borno	26,479
4	Gombe	29,930
5	Taraba	18,855
6	Yobe	22,425
Total		157,314

Source: Researcher's computational result from SMEDAN and NBS Collaborative Survey, 2021. Therefore, the sample size of 157,314 generated from the Krejcie & Morgan table is 382 SMEs in the study area

21.3.3 Sample and Sampling Techniques

This study used stratified, proportional random and probability sampling methods. Stratified sampling was utilized to divide the population into several strata based on states, and proportionate sampling was used to ascertain the number of SMEs in each stratum. Finally, the sample size was determined by random sampling in each stratum (Asikhia & Naidoo, 2020) (Table 21.2).

21.3.4 Research Instrument Description

The research adapted a questionnaire from previous literature for this study. The work of Hatem Al-Gohary, an authority in E-Marketing was adapted for this study. The questionnaire comprises the following items, E-marketing, Sales performance, and technological capabilities.

21.3.5 Reliability Test

Reliability is a test of the consistency of items when using multiple measurements of variables (Hair et al., 2010) The study adopted the Cronbach alpha to test the reliability of the instrument48 employed. From the table below, the Cronbach alpha values are 0.915, 0.887, and 0.876 for E-marketing, SMEs performance, and technological capabilities respectively. All values exceeded the threshold value of 0.70 required for acceptable reliability. Therefore, we concluded that our instrument is reliable (Table 21.3).

21.3.6 Method of Administration of Instruments

The study-data was collected through the deployment of structured questionnaires. For clarity and a high rate of return of the instrument, self-administration was utilized. While the study employs other secondary sources to compare the paper's findings with existing findings in the field of research.

21.3.7 Data Analysis

The data collected from the participants were analyzed using the Statistical Package for Social Sciences SPSS. The choice of statistical analysis was based on previous literature in articles from reputable Journals which were conducted in comparable scenarios. Thus, linear regression was adopted to draw inferences from the analysis. Result and Discussion.

From Table 21.4 below, when E-marketing was incorporated into the equation, the results indicated that there was a positive correlation coefficient ($\beta = -0.058$ $p < 0.05$), between e-marketing and competitive advantage. Hence, the study rejected the null hypothesis and accepted a significant relationship between e-marketing and competitive advantage.

The results indicated that E- marketing is significant in determining competitive advantage which is consistent with findings from similar previous studies (Kannabiran & Dharmalingam, 2012; Hashim, 2007; Chuang et al., 2009; Wainwright et al., 2005; Tan et al., 2009; Melumad et al., 2019) (Table 21.4).

Table 21.3 Reliability statistics

	Cronbach's Alpha
E-marketing	0.915
SMEs Performance	0.887
Technological capabilities	0.876

Table 21.4 Hypothesis 1: E-marketing has no significant effect on the competitive advantage of SMEs in North-East Nigeria

	Coefficients				
Model	Unstandardized Coefficients		Standardized Coefficients	t	Sig.
	B	Std. Error	Beta		
1 (Constant)	2.227	.108		20.632	.000
Using E-Marketing improves my job performance.	−.043	.038	−.058	−1.140	.255

a. Dependent Variable: Competitive advantage

		Coefficients Unstandardized Coefficients		Standardized Coefficients		
Model		B	Std. Error	Beta	T	Sig.
1	(Constant)	.363	.172		2.113	.035
	With e-marketing, I could be able to achieve my sales target	.115	.055	.129	2.112	.035

Our customers do not like to make
.396 .046 .393 8.612 .000 transactions through the Internet. e-marketing
Contributes to my gross .591 .059 .631 9.930 .000 margin

Table 21.5 Hypothesis 2: E-marketing has no significant effect on the Sales performance of SMEs in North-East Nigeria

The analysis indicates that E-marketing has a significant positive relationship with Sales performance ($\beta = 0.631$, $p < 0.05$), thus, the study rejected the Null hypothesis and accepted the alternative hypothesis that E-marketing plays a significant role in Sales performance. This result agrees with previous research findings of Wang'anya (2018) which found that social media marketing and online advertising had significant positive effects and correlations with the sales performance of SMEs in Lagos State, Nigeria.

Table 21.6 indicates that there was a significant negative correlation coefficient ($\beta = 0.336$, $p < 0.05$) therefore, the H3 was rejected that E-marketing has no significant effect on Customer retention. Although the results revealed that E-marketing influences customer retention, this is not consistent with other similar studies (Adegbuyi et al., 2015).

Table 21.7 below indicates that there was a significant positive correlation coefficient ($\beta = 0.224$, $p < 0.05$) therefore, the H4 was rejected. E-marketing does not play a significant role in the market share. A study by (Kheng, 2018; Adegbuyi et al., 2015) found that social media marketing had a strong correlation with performance. Similarly, El-Gohary (2012) found that website marketing, social media, email marketing, digital marketing, and viral marketing had substantial beneficial effects and relationship with the market share of Malaysia's small and medium-sized family firms.

Coefficient

Model	Unstandardized Coefficients B	Std. Error	Standardized Coefficients Beta	T	Sig.
1 (Constant)	2.616	.175		14.933	.000

Our customers do not trust E-Marketing
tools (e.g. the
.153 .045 .160 3.400 .001
Internet, E-Mail, and Mobile).
Customers usually trust E-Marketing
tools (e.g. the
65 .317 .045 .336 7.044 .000

Table 21.6 Hypothesis 3: E-marketing has no significant effect on Customer retention of SMEs in North-East Nigeria

Coefficients
Unstandardized Standardized
Coefficients Coefficients

Model B Std. Error Beta T Sig. 1 (Constant) 1.949 .149 13.081 .000
We use E-marketing resources to conduct commercial
transactions (e.g., .221 .049 .224 4.429 .000 selling products and accepting payment via web site).
Dependent Variable: Market Share

Table 21.7 Hypothesis 4: E-marketing has no significant effect on the market share of SMEs in North-East Nigeria

The result in Table 21.8 suggests a positive relationship between technological capabilities and SMEs performance. The p-values of all the dependent variables were less than 0.05 level of significance. Thus, the study rejects the hypothesis that there is no significant effect of technological capabilities on the performance of SMEs in North East Nigeria. A study by (Davis et al., 2014) found that technological capacity such as online advert provides feedback that enhances product awareness. In the same vein, (Chen & Lien, 2013) found that online advertising, digital marketing, e-distribution, online marketing research, and email marketing had significant positive effects on performance of telecom industry in Kenya.

Coefficients
Unstandardized Standardized
Coefficients Coefficients
Model B Std. Error Beta t Sig.
1 (Constant) 1.437 .168 8.554 .000
The quality of IT infrastructure affects he relationship -.051 .052 -.060 -.981 .0025
between e-marketing and SMEs performance The competence of human resources in IT
81
affects the relationship .117 .050 .143 2.340 0.000 between e-marketing
and SMEs performance
Environmental IT
competence affects the 1
relationship between e- -.56 .390 -.0105 -1.438 0.000 marketing and SMEs
performance
Business process
digitization affects the
relationship between e- -.59 .445 -0.215 -1.326 0.000 marketing and SMEs
performance
a. Dependent Variable: Performance of SMEs

Table 21.8 Hypothesis 5: There is no significant effect of technological capabilities on the performance of SMEs in North-East Nigeria

21.4 General Discussion

Even though the study provides a comparative discussion of the findings under each of the Hypothesis results. Nonetheless, it is necessary to provide a summarized general discussion. E-marketing exhibited a positive link to the four SME Performance dimensions, and Technological capability was found to reinforce the relationship between E-marketing and SME performance.

Also, noteworthy is that though H3: E-marketing has no significant effect on Customer retention of SMEs in North-East Nigeria was also rejected, the findings contrasted previous similar studies.

The demographic data suggests that the low level of education in the Northeastern region has hindered many businesses from deploying e-marketing tools, thus mitigating the positive effects of e-marketing on SME performance in the study area. Perhaps, the procrastination and lagging attitude of numerous entrepreneurs may account for the delay in the adoption of e-marketing in the study area.

21.5 Conclusion

This study attempted to place empirical evidence upon the Hypotheses suggesting that e-marketing enhances small business performance in terms of competitive advantage, sales performance, customer retention, and market share. It also attempts to examine the role of Technological capability in the performance of SMEs.

Based on the findings arising from the results, it can be concluded that e -marketing has a significant effect on competitive advantage, Sales volume, customer retention, and market share. Consequently, SME performance in North-East Nigeria can be improved through the effective deployment of E-marketing. Furthermore, the technological capabilities of small businesses have proven to be a catalyst to the performance of small business enterprises in Northeast Nigeria.

21.5.1 Notions for Future Researchers and Limitations

There is still a need for further research on E-marketing and the performance of SMEs as a result of conclusions that differ from earlier studies. This study deployed a cross-sectional approach, which may limit the interpretation of the results and mitigate the conclusions of this investigation. There is a need for further studies using a longitudinal approach. Also, this study focuses on the Enterprise perspective, future researchers should explore the customer's perspective. The use of cross-sectional survey does not provide proof of causality, unlike the longitudinal research design. Future researchers should contrast this study's findings with data from customer's perspective.

References

Abdullahi, M. (2016). Challenges affecting the performance of small and medium scale enterprises (smes) in Nigeria. *Journal of Human Capital Development*. Universiti Teknikal Malaysia Melaka, *9*, 1–18.

Abdulsaleh, A. M., & Worthington, A. C. (2013). Small and medium-sized enterprises financing: A review of literature. *International Journal of Business and Management, 8*(14), 36.

Adamu, A., & Ibrahim, M. (2011). *Small and medium scale enterprises (SMEs) and economic growth in Nigeria* (Vol. 2, pp. 80–98). Nasarawa State University.

Adegbuyi, O. A., Akinyele, F. A., & Akinyele, S. T. (2015). Effect of social media marketing on small-scale business performance in Ota-Metropolis, Nigeria. *International Journal of Social Sciences and Management, 2*(3), 2207–2215.

Ahmad, S. Z., Bakar, A. R. A., Faziharudean, M. T., & Zaki, K. A. M. (2014). Information technology for development an empirical study of factors affecting e-commerce adoption among small- and medium-sized enterprises in a developing country: Evidence from Malaysia. *Information Technology For Development, 21*(4), 37–41. https://doi.org/10.21102/026213212.2014.19992061

Ahmed, R. R., Vveinhardt, J., Streimikiene, D., & Awais, M. (2016). Mediating and marketing factors influence the prescription behavior of physicians: An empirical investigation. *Amfiteatru Economic Journal, 18*(41), 153–167.

Akanbi T. A., (2018). An investigative study of challenges facing Nigerian small and medium scale enterprises in the adoption of E-commerce technology. JAME. pp 22–31. Accessed online at www.managementjournal.info on May 21st, 2017.

Al Asheq, A., Tanchi, K. R., Kamruzzaman, M., & Karim, M. M. (2021). The impact of emarketing orientation, technological orientation, and learning capacity on online SME performance. *Innovative Marketing, 17*(3), 168. https://doi.org/10.21511/im.17(3).2021.14

Al-Jarrah, O., & Arafat, A. (2014). Network intrusion detection system using attack behavior classification. In *In 2014 5th international conference on information and communication systems (ICICS)* (pp. 1–6). IEEE.

AlBar, A. M., & Hoque, M. R. (2019). Factors affecting the adoption of information and communication technology in small and medium enterprises: A perspective from rural Saudi Arabia. *Information Technology for Development, 25*(4), 715–738.

Aljawarneh, S. A. (2020). Reviewing and exploring innovative ubiquitous learning tools in higher education. *Journal of Computing in Higher Education, 32*, 57–73.

Antoni, D., Jie, F., & Abareshi, A. (2020). 'Critical factors in information technology capability for enhancing firm's environmental performance: Case of Indonesian ICT sector. *International Journal of Agile Systems and Management, 13*(2), 159–181.

Asbari, M., Dylmoon Hidayat, D., & Purwanto, A. (2021). Managing employee performance: From leadership to readiness for change. *International Journal of Social and Management Studies, 2*(1), 74–85. https://doi.org/10.5555/ijosmas.v2i1.12

Asikhia, O., & Naidoo, V. (2020). SMEs management success determinants and its implications on their performance in South West, Nigeria. *International Journal of Economics and Business Administration, VIII*, 1057.

Bandura, A. (2001). Social cognitive theory an agentic perspective. *Annual Review of Psychology, 52*, 52, 2001–52, 2026.

Behrman, D. N., & Perreault, W. D., Jr. (1982). Measuring the performance of industrial salespersons. *Journal of Business Research, 10*(September), 355–369.

Behrman, D. N., & Perreault, W. D., Jr. (1984). A role stress model of the performance and satisfaction of industrial salespersons. *Journal of Marketing, 48*(4), 9–21.

Brodie, R. J., Winklhofer, H., Coviello, N. E., & Johnston, W. J. (2007). Is e-marketing coming of age? An examination of the penetration of e-marketing and firm performance. *Journal of Interactive Marketing, 21*(1), 2–21. https://doi.org/10.1002/dir.20071

Brown, S. A., Venkatesh, V., & Hoehle, H. (2015). Technology adoption decisions in the household: A seven-model comparison. *Journal of the Association for Information Science and Technology, 669*, 19953–19969.

Casalo, L., Flaviam, C., & Guiraliu, M. (2008). The role of usability and satisfaction in the consumers' commitment to financial services. *International Journal of Electronic Finance, 2*(1), 2008–2031.

Chen, C. C.-W., & Lien, N. N.-H. (2013). Technological opportunism and firm performance: Moderating contexts. *Journal of Business Research, 66*(11), 2218–2225. https://doi.org/10.2116/j.jbusres.2012.02.001

Cheung, C. M. K., Lee, M. K. O., & Thadani, D. R. (2009). The impact of positive electronic word-of-mouth on consumer online purchasing decision. In *World Summit on Knowledge Society* (pp. 501–510). Springer.

Chong, W. K., Man, K. L., & Kim, M. (2018). The impact of e-marketing orientation on performance in Asian SMEs: A B2B perspective. *Enterprise Information Systems, 12*(1), 4–18.

Chuang, M., Yang, Y. S., & Lin, C. T. (2009). Production technology selection: Deploying market requirements, competitive and operational strategies, and manufacturing attributes. *International Journal of Computer Integrated Manufacturing, 22*(4), 345–355.

Chittoor, R., & Ray, S. (2007). Internationalization paths of Indian pharmaceutical firms: A strategic group analysis. Journal of International Management, 13(3): 338–355.

Compeau, D. R., & Higgins, C. A. (2018). Application of social cognitive theory to training for computer skills. *Information Systems Research, 21405*, 206–209.

Davis, R., Piven, I., & Breazeale, M. (2014). Conceptualizing the brand in social media community: The five sources model. *Journal of Retailing and Consumer Services, 21*(4), 468–481.

Deloitte. (2018). *Results by firms & industry characteristics*. Deloitte CMO Survey. Available at: https://cmosurvey.org/wp-content/uploads/sites/15/2018/02/The_CMO_Survey Results_by_Firm_and_Industry_Characteristics-Feb-2018.pdf

Dermawan, A. A., Nasution, H., & Sitepu, M. H. (2020). *The impact of branding on purchasing decision-making in mall shopping and online shopping*. In IOP Conference series: Materials science and engineering, *801*(1) 012146. IOP Publishing. Dissertation, United States International University-Africa.

Domainz eBiz Review. (2010). Domainz, Wellington. (Available at www.domainz.net.nz/ebizreview2010.asp).

Eid, R., & El-Gohary, H. (2013). The impact of E-marketing uses on small business enterprises' marketing success. *The Service Industries Journal, 33*(1), 31–50. https://doi.org/10.21102/028214069.2011.520421300

El-Gohary, H. (2010). E-marketing – A literature review from a small business perspective. *International Journal of Business and Social Science, 1*(1), 214–244.

El-Gohary, H. (2012). Factors affecting E-Marketing adoption and implementation in tourism firms: An empirical investigation of Egyptian small tourism organizations. *Tourism Management, 33*(5), 2136–2149. https://doi.org/10.2116/j.tourman.2011.10.013

ElKordy, M. (2014). The impact of CRM capability dimensions on organizational performance. *European Journal of Business and Social Sciences, 2*, 128–146.

Eze, S. C., Chinedu-Eze, V. C. A., Okike, C. K., & Bello, A. O. (2020). Critical factors influencing the adoption of digital marketing devices by service-oriented microbusinesses in Nigeria: A thematic analysis approach. *Humanities and Social Sciences Communications, 7*(1), 1–14.

Fahmi, K., Mustofa, A., Rochmad, I., Sulastri, E., Wahyuni, I. S., & Irwansyah, I. (2021). Effect of ISO 9001:2015, ISO 14001:2015, and ISO 45001:2018 On operational performance of automotive industries. *Journal of Industrial Engineering & Management Research, 2*(1), 13–25. https://doi.org/10.7777/jiemar.v2i1.110

Farida, N., Naryoso, A., & Yuniawan, A. (2017). Model of relationship marketing and e-commerce in improving marketing performance of Batik SMEs. *JDM (Jurnal Dinamika Manajemen), 8*(1), 20–29.

Febriantoro, W. (2018). Study and strategies to support the development of e-commerce for MSMEs in Indonesia. *Manajerial: Jurnal Manajemen dan Sistem Informasi, 17*(2), 184207.

Fink, D. (2018). Guidelines for the successful adoption of information technology in small and medium enterprises. *International Journal of Information Management, 18*(4), 243–253. https://doi.org/10.2116/S0268-4012(208)00013-9

Fulgoni, G. M. (2015). How brands using social media ignite marketing and drive growth. *Journal of Advertising Research, 9*, 232–238. https://doi.org/10.2501/JAR-2015-004

Ghosh, A., Sufian, A., Sultana, F., Chakrabarti, A., & De, D. (2020). Fundamental concepts of convolutional neural network. In *Recent trends and advances in artificial intelligence and Internet of Things* (pp. 519–567) Springer.

Gilmore, A., Gallagher, D., & Henry, S. (2007). E-marketing and SMEs: Operational lessons for the future. *European Business Review, 19*. https://doi.org/10.1108/09555340710746482

Grandon, E. E., & Pearson, J. M. (2004). Electronic commerce adoption : An empirical study of small and medium US businesses. *Information & Management, 42*(1), 197–216. https://doi.org/10.2116/j.im.2003.12.010

Gregurec, I., & Grd, P. (2012). Search engine optimization (SEO): Website analysis of selected faculties in Croatia. In *Central European conference on information and intelligent systems*. Faculty of Organization and Informatics Varazdin.

Gumel, B. (2017). Critical challenges facing small business enterprises in Nigeria: A literature review. *International Journal of Scientific and Engineering Research, 8*, 796–808.

Haider, Z., Chen, S., & Abbassi, Z. (2015). Adoption of e-government in Pakistan: Demand perspective. *International Journal of Advanced Computer Science and Applications, 6*(5), 203–212. https://doi.org/10.21169/IJACSA.2015.060512

Hair, J. F., Black, W. C., Babin, B. J., & Anderson, R. E. (2010). *Multivariate data analysis* (7th ed.). Pearson.

Hammond, S. C., & Glenn, L. M. (2004). The ancient practice of Chinese social networking: Guanxi and social network theory. *Emergence-Mahwah-Lawrence Erlbaum, 6*(1/2), 24.

Hashim, J. (2007). Information communication technology (ICT) adoption among SME owners in Malaysia. *International Journal of Business and information, 2*(2), 221–240.

Haugh, H., & Robson, P. (2005). Are Scottish firms meeting the ICT challenge? Results from a National Survey of Enterprise. *Entrepreneurship & Regional Development, 17*(3), 205–222. https://doi.org/10.21102/0199217218050009201l1

Hunter, G. K., & Perreault, W. D., Jr. (2007). Making sales technology effective. *Journal of Marketing, 71*(1), 16–34.

Hidayatullah, S., Firdiansjah, A., Patalo, R. G., & Waris, A. (2019). The effect of entrepreneurial marketing and competitive advantage on marketing performance. *International Journal of Scientific and Technology Research, 8*(1), 2207–2181. https://doi.org/10.7777/jiemar.v1i1.29

Iddris, F., & Ibrahim, M. (2015). Examining the relationships between e-Marketing adoption and marketing performance of small and medium enterprises in Ghana. *Journal of Marketing and Consumer Research, 10*, 160–169.

Iddris, F., & Masud, I. (2015). Examining the relationships between e-Marketing adoption and marketing performance of small and medium enterprises in Ghana. *Journal of Marketing and Consumer Research, 10*, 160–169.

Indra, E., Yasir, M., Andrian, A., Sitanggang, D., Sihombing, O., Tamba, S. P., & Sagala, E. (2020, June). Design and implementation of student attendance system based on face recognition by Haar-like features methods. In *2020 3rd international conference on mechanical, electronics, computer, and industrial technology (MECnIT)* (pp. 336–342). IEEE.

Izediuno, O. L., Alice, O. T., & Daniel, O. A. (2018). Analytical review of small and medium scale enterprises in Nigeria. *International Journal of Small Business and Entrepreneurship Research, 6*(2), 32–46.

Jamil, A. H. A., Jusoh, M. S., & Ghani, M. R. A. (2020). The impact of E-marketing on business performance in Northern Malaysia. *International Journal of Business and Management, 4*(5), 55–61.

Jiang, G., Tadikamalla, P. R., Shang, J., & Zhao, L. (2016). Impacts of knowledge on online brand success: An agent-based model for online market share enhancement. *European Journal of Operational Research, 248*(3) ISSN 03772217, 1093–1103.

Johnston, M. W., & Marshall, G. W. (2006). *Churchill/Ford/Walker's sales force management* (8th ed.). McGraw-Hill/Irwin.

Johnston, D. A., Wade, M., & McClean, R. (2007). Does e-business matter to SMEs? A comparison of the financial impacts of internet business solutions on European and North American SMEs. *Journal of Small Business Management, 45*(3), 354–361. https://doi.org/10.1991/j.1980-1991X.2007.00217.x

Kalu, A., Nto, C., & Nwadighoha, E. (2017). Environmental forces as catalysts in electronic-marketing, the 21st century trends in Nigeria. *Singaporean Journal of Business Economics and Management Studies, 5*, 46–56. https://doi.org/10.12816/0037549

Kannabiran, G., & Dharmalingam, P. (2012). Enablers and inhibitors of advanced information technologies adoption by SMEs: An empirical study of auto ancillaries in India. *Journal of Enterprise Information Management, 25*, 186.

Karahanna, E., Straub, D. W., & Chervany, N. L. (2019). Information technology adoption across time: A cross-sectional comparison of pre-adoption and post adoption beliefs. *MIS Quarterly, 23*, 183–213.

Kassim, N., & Asiah Abdullah, N. (2010). The effect of perceived service quality dimensions on customer satisfaction, trust, and loyalty in e-commerce settings: A cross cultural analysis. *Asia Pacific Journal of Marketing and Logistics, 22*(3), 351–371.

Khajuria, I., & Rachna. (2017). Impact of social media brand communications on consumer-based brand equity. *Indian Journal of Commerce and Management Studies, 8*(3), 124–131, Educational Research Multimedia & Publications, India.
Khanna, R., & Awal, G. (2019). Consumer online purchasing decision and its influencing factors in Uttrakhand: An exploratory study of selected districts of Garhwal Division. In *International Conference on Advances in Engineering Science Management & Technology (ICAESMT)-2019*, Uttaranchal University.
Kheng, Y. K. (2018). *Nigerian SMEs marketing innovation performance: Influence of business process management and environmental dynamism*. IJASSH.
Kim, A. J., & Ko, E. (2012). Do social media marketing activities enhance customer equity? *Journal of Business Research, 65*, 1480–1486. https://doi.org/10.1016/j.jbusres.2011.10.014
Korir, E. J. (2020). *E-marketing strategies and performance of registered rated hotels in Nakuru County* [MBA thesis, Kenyatta University, Kenya].
Lassar, W., Mittal, B., & Sharma, A. (1995). Measuring customer-based brand equity. *Journal of Consumer Marketing, 12*, 11–19.
Li, Y. H., (2008). An empirical investigation on the determinants of E-procurement adoption in Chinese manufacturing enterprises. In *2008 International Conference on Management Science and Engineering 15th Annual Conference Proceedings* (pp. 32–37). ICMSE.
Liang, T.-P., & Huang, J.-S. (1998). An empirical study on consumer acceptance of products in electronic markets: a transaction cost model. *Decision Support Systems, 24*(1), 29–43.
Lipsman, A., Mud, G., Rich, M., & Bruich, S. (2012). The power of "like": How brands reach (and influence) fans through social media marketing. *Journal of Advertising Research, 52*(1), 40–52. https://doi.org/10.2501/JAR-52-1-040-522011.10.014
Ma, H. (2000). Competitive advantage and firm performance. *Competitiveness Review: An International Business Journal, 10*(2), 15–32.
Malesev, S., & Cherry, M. (2021). Digital & social media marketing – Growing market share for construction SMEs. *Construction Economics and Building, 21*(1), 65–82.
Maryani, E., Purba, H. H., & Sunadi, S. (2020). Process capability improvement through DMAIC method for Aluminium Alloy wheels casting. *Journal of Industrial Engineering & Management Research, 1*(4), 19–26. https://doi.org/10.7777/jiemar.v1i4.98
Melumad, S., Inman, J. J., & Pham, M. T. (2019). Selectively emotional: How smartphone use changes user-generated content. *Journal of Marketing Research, 56*(2), 259–275.
Ménière, Y. (2009). Technology transfer by CDM projects: A comparison of Brazil, China, India, and Mexico. *Energy Policy, 37*(2), 2023–2031. https://doi.org/10.2116/j.enpol.2008.10.007
Min, Z., Sawang, S., & Kivits, R. A. (2021). Proposing circular economy ecosystem for Chinese SMEs: A systematic review. *International Journal of Environmental Research and Public Health, 18*(5), 2395.
Mitchell, R. W., Wooliscroft, B., & Higham, J. (2010). Sustainable market orientation: A new approach to managing marketing strategy. *Journal of Macromarketing, 30*(2), 160–170.
Molla, A., & Licker, P. S. P. (2005). E-Commerce adoption in developing countries: A model and instrument. *Information & Management, 42*(6), 1999–1999. https://doi.org/10.2116/j.im.2004.09.002
Muriithi, S. M. (2017). African small and medium enterprises (SMEs) contributions, challenges and solutions. *European Journal of Research and Reflection in Management Sciences, 5*(1), 36–48.
Musa, H., Rahim, N., Azmi, F. R., Shibghatullah, A. S., & Othman, N. A. (2016). Social media marketing and online small and medium enterprises performance: Perspective of Malaysian small and medium enterprises. *International Review of Management and Marketing, 6*(70), 1–5.
Mutlu, H. M., & Sürer, A. (2016). Effects of market, e-marketing, and technology orientations on innovativeness and performance in Turkish health organizations. *Health Marketing Quarterly, 33*(2), 95–111.
Mzee, R. M., Ogweno, K. L., & Irene, N. (2015). Factors influencing adoption of E-marketing by Small and Medium Enterprises (SMEs) in Kisumu Municipality. *IOSR Journal of Business and Management, 17*(5), 78–83.

Negm, R. A. (2016). *The value of customer relationship management m the service industry in Egypt*. Walden University.

Nganga, M. W., & Monayo, A. V. (2017). *Electronic customer relationship management strategy and organizational performance of associated motors limited (K) Ltd.* University of Nairobi.

Njau, J. N., & Karugu, W. (2014). Influence of E-marketing on the performance of small and medium enterprises in Kenya: Survey of small and medium enterprises in the manufacturing industry in Kenya. *International Journal of Business & Law Research, 2*(1).

Njuguna N. A., (2017). The effectiveness of online advertisements on consumer decision: A case of radio Africa group limited Nairobi, . Doctoral.

Nnanna, O. J. (2001, July). *Monetary policy framework in Africa: The Nigerian experience*. In A paper presented at the 2001 South African Reserve Bank conference.

Novitasari, D., Asbari, M., & Purwanto, A. (2021). Maximizing employee performance: An analysis of organizational and individual factors. *International Journal of Social and Management Studies, 1*(1), 95–104. https://doi.org/10.5555/ijosmas.v1i1.11

Odubanjo, E. K. (2000). Relevance of small scale enterprises in the development of the Nigerian economy, The Nigeria Bankers. *Journal of the Chartered Institute of Bankers of Nigeria*, 33–34.

Onwumere, J. U. J., Ibe, I. G., Ozoh, F. O., & Mounanu, O. (2012). The impact of financial deepening on economic growth: Evidence from Nigeria. *Research Journal of Finance and Accounting, 3*(10), 64–71.

Pakistan E.S.O. (2015). *Overview of the economy*. Retrieved from http://finance.gov.pk/survey/chapters_15/Overview_of_the_Economy.Pdf

Parveen, F., Jaafar, N. L., & Ainin, S. (2014). Social media usage among businesses: A website content. *Asian Journal of Information Technology, 12*(10), 342–348.

Paswan, A. (2018). Social media marketing strategies. *Journal for Contemporary Research in Management, 1*, 8–12.

Perera, D., & Chand, P. (2015). Issues in the adoption of international financial reporting standards (IFRS) for small and mediumsized enterprises (SMES). *Advances in Accounting, 31*(1), 165–178.

Permana, S. D. H. (2017). E-marketing strategy in game industry with social media using e-business model. *IMC 2016 Proceedings, 1*(1).

Pillania, R. K. (2009). Internationalization and company performance: A study of emerging Russian multinationals. *Multinational Business Review, 17*(2), 157–178. https://doi.org/10.2010/21853215X2002000014

Pradhan, P., & Nigam, D. (2018). Digital marketing and SMES: An identification of research gap via archives of past research. *Journal of Internet Banking and Commerce, 23*(1), 1–14.

Pradhan, P., Nigam, D., & Ck, T. (2018). Digital marketing and SMEs: An identification of research gap via archives of past research. *Journal of Internet Banking and Commerce, 23*(1), 1–14.

Premkumar, G., & Roberts, M. (2019). Adoption of new information technologies in rural small businesses. *Omega: The International Journal of Management Science, 27*(4), 4201–4216. https://doi.org/10.2116/S0305-04215(208)000203-1

Qashou, A., & Saleh, Y. (2018). E-marketing implementation in small and medium-sized restaurants in Palestine. *Arab Economic and Business Journal, 13*(2), 93–110.

Quinn, L., Dibb, S., Simkin, L., Canhoto, A., & Analogbei, M. (2016). Troubled waters: The transformation of marketing in a digital world. *European Journal of Marketing, 50*(12), 2103–2133. https://doi.org/10.1108/EJM-08-2015-0537

Qureshi, S., Keen, P., & Kamal, M. (2010). Business models for development: The global capability sourcing model. In S. Kamel (Ed.), *E-strategies for technological diffusion and adoption: National ICT approaches for socioeconomic development* (pp. 200–214). IGI Publishing.

Rahayu, R., & Day, J. (2015). Determinant factors of E-commerce adoption by SMEs in developing country: Evidence from Indonesia. *Procedia- Social and Behavioral Sciences, 1997*(2015), 208–216. https://doi.org/10.2116/j.sbspro.2015.06.423

Rahim, A., Bakar, A. B. U., & Ahmed, Z. U. (2015). Technology motivation in e-marketing adoption among Malaysian manufacturers. *Journal of Transnational Management, 20*(April), 214–218. https://doi.org/10.21102/19820933300.2015.21319949

Raoofi, M. (2012). Moderating role of e-marketing on the consequences of market orientation in Iranian firms. *Management & Marketing-Craiova, 2*, 301–316.

Ratnasingham, P. (2008). Internet-based EDI trust and security. *Information Management & Computer Security, 6*(1), 33–40.

Raymond, L., Bergeron, F., & Blili, S. (2018). The assimilation of E-business in manufacturing SMEs: Determinants and effects on growth and internationalization. *Electronic Markets, 15*(2), 216–206. https://doi.org/10.21102/2121401212500021520103

Rodriguez, M., Peterson, R. M., & Krishnan, V. (2012). Social media's influence on business-to-business sales performance. *Journal of Personal Selling & Sales Management, 32*(3), 365–378.

Rose, R. C., Abdullah, H., & Ismad, A. I. (2010). A review of the relationship between organizational resources, competitive advantage and performance. *Journal of International Social Research, 3*(11).

Rudansky-Kloppers, S. (2017). Key factors influencing the online buying decision when purchasing products in specific product categories. *African Journal of Science, Technology, Innovation and Development, 9*(1), 43–54.

Saha, P., & Zhao, Y. (2006). Relationship between online service quality and customer satisfaction. A study of internet banking. Retrieved on September 2022 from www.http/epubt.Itu/se 1404 5508/2005/083/LTU-SHU-EX05083.

Saleh, H. (2020). Enhance small-medium enterprises (SMEs) family business in Malaysia through E-marketing strategies. *International Journal of Scientific & Technology Research, 9*(2), 33206–33209.

Saleh, A., Ochi, J. E., & Hussain, M. S. (2018). Comparative costs and returns pattern of small-scale groundnut milling of RMP-12 and Ex-dakar Varieties in Gombe Metropolis, Gombe State Nigeria. *Journal Ekonomi dan Studi Pembangunan, 10*(2), 220230.

Salome, I. O., & Ofunre, I. C. (2019). E-marketing in Nigeria: Benefits, challenges, and strategies. *Journal of Asian Business Strategy, 9*(2), 220–234.

SetiaBakti, C., & Kartika, H. (2020). Analysis of ice cream product quality control with Six Sigma Method. *Journal of Industrial Engineering & Management Research, 1*(1), 63–69.

Setiawan, I., & Purba, H. H. (2020). A systematic literature review of Key Performance Indicators (KPIs) implementation. *Journal of Industrial Engineering & Management Research, 1*(3), 200–208. https://doi.org/10.7777/jiemar.v1i3.79

Shaltoni, A. M., West, D., Alnawas, I., & Shatnawi, T. (2018). Electronic marketing orientation in the small and medium-sized enterprises context. *European Business Review, 30*, 272.

Sheikh, Adnan Ahmed, Naeem Ahmad Rana, Aneeq Inam, Arfan Shahzad, & Hayat Muhammad Awan. (2018). Is e-marketing a source of sustainable business performance? Predicting the role of top management support with various interaction factors. Cogent Business & Management 5(1): 1516487.

Sheikh, A. A., Shahzad, A., & Ishaq, A. K. (2017). The growth of e-marketing in business-to-business industry and its effect on the performance of businesses in Pakistan: Marketing success. *International and Multidisciplinary Journal of Social Sciences, 6*(2), 178–214.

Sidek, S., Mohd Rosli, M., Khadri, N. A. M., Hasbolah, H., Manshar, M., & Abidin, N. M. F. N. Z. (2020). Fortifying small business performance sustainability in the era of IR 4.0: E-marketing as a catalyst of competitive advantages and business performance. *Journal of Critical Reviews, 7*(13), 2143–2155.

Smith, P. R., & Chaffey, D. (2005). *E-marketing excellence-at the heart of E-business*. Butterworth Heinemann.

Stewart, D. W., & Pavlou, P. (2002). From consumer response to active consumer: measuring the effectiveness of interactive media. *Journal of the Academy of Marketing Science, 30*(4), 376–396. https://doi.org/10.1177/009207002236912van

Strauss, J., & Frost, R. (2001). *E-marketing* (2nd ed.). Prentice Hall.

Sufian, A., Ghosh, A., Sadiq, A. S., & Smarandache, F. (2020). A survey on deep transfer learning to edge computing for mitigating the COVID-19 pandemic. *Journal of Systems Architecture, 108*, 101830.

Sunny, E. E., & Abolaji, O. S. (2016). Electronic Customer Relationship Management (E-CRM) and marketing performance: Empirical evidence from Nigeria telecom sector. *British Journal of Economics, Management and Trade, 11*(1), 1–14.

Suwandi, S., & HariHadi, A. (2020). Value analysis method for cost reduction analysis of fuel filter products at PT Duta NichirindoPratama. *Journal of Industrial Engineering and Management Research, 1*(1), 28–36. https://doi.org/10.7777/jiemar.v1i1.22

Taiminen, H. M., & Karjaluoto, H. (2015). The usage of digital marketing channels in SMEs. *Journal of Small Business and Enterprise Development, 22*(4), 633–651.

Tan, M., & Teo, T. (2018). Factors influencing the adoption of the Internet. *International Journal of Electronic Commerce, 2*(3), 5–18. https://doi.org/10.21102/2112110615.21408.203200712

Tan, K. S., Chong, S. C., Lin, B., & Eze, U. C. (2009). *Internet-based ICT adoption: Evidence from Malaysian SMEs* (Vol. 109, p. 224). Industrial Management & Data Systems.

Teo, T. (2007). Organizational characteristics, modes of internet adoption and their impact: a Singapore perspective. *Journal of Global Information Management, 15*(2), 201. https://doi.org/10.4018/jgim.20020240214

Thong, J., & Yap, C. (2015). CEO characteristics, organizational characteristics and information technology adoption in small businesses. *Omega, 23*(4), 429–442. https://doi.org/10.2116/0305-04215(205)00017-I

Thurman, N. (2018). Newspaper consumption in the mobile age. *Journalism Studies, 19*(10), 1409–1429. https://doi.org/10.1080/1461670X.2017.1279028

Valos, M. J., Habibi, F. H., Casidy, R., Driesener, C. B., & Maplestone, V. L. (2016). Exploring the integration of social media within integrated marketing communication frameworks: Perspectives of services marketers. *Marketing Intelligence & Planning, 34*(1), 40.

Venkatesh, V., Thong, J. Y., & Xu, X. (2012). Consumer acceptance and use of information technology: Extending the unified theory of acceptance and use of technology. *MIS Quarterly, 36*, 157–178.

Wainwright, D., Green, G., Mitchell, E., & Yarrow, D. (2005). Towards a framework for benchmarking ICT practice, competence and performance in small firms. *Performance Measurement and Metrics, 6*, 39.

Wang'anya, E. T. (2018). *Supplier & business performance measurement; A study of the Kenyan Restaurant Chains*. Doctoral dissertation. United States International University-Africa.

Wilson, V., & Makau, C. (2018). Online marketing use: Small and Medium Enterprises (SMEs) experience from Kenya. *Orsea Journal, 7*(2), 1–10.

Yazdanparast, A., Joseph, M., & Muniz, F. (2016). Consumer-based brand equity in the 21st century: An examination of the role of social media marketing. *Young Consumers, 17*(3), 243–255. https://doi.org/10.1108/YC-03-2016-00590

Zeithaml, V. A., Berry, C. L., & Parasuraman, A. (1996). The behavioural consequences of service. Quality. *Journal of Marketing, 60*(2), 31–46.

Zhang, J., & Mao, E. (2020). Cash, credit, or phone? An empirical study on the adoption of mobile payments in the United States. *Psychology & Marketing, 3203*, 197–208.

Zhang, Z., Li, X., & Chen, Y. (2012). Deciphering word-of-mouth in social media: Textbased metrics of consumer reviews. *ACM Transactions on Management Information Systems (TMIS), 3*(1), 1–23.

Chapter 22
Last-Mile Delivery Innovations for Parcels Collection in Singapore

Maria Cecilia Rojas Lopez and Hui Shan Loh

Abstract The last-mile delivery industry has been adapting and implementing innovations to enhance its overall service. With the ubiquity of e-commerce, the number of parcels to be delivered rapidly increased. This created logistics and urban-transport challenges, especially in densely urbanised and populated areas – such as Singapore. Singapore, a tropical island country in South East Asia, is steadily becoming an example of a "smart-nation". Since the year 2016, the country has been working to improve the last-mile delivery system. Initial developments included providers "dropping" parcels at shops, transport stations, or selected residences for the customer to collect at their own convenience. Then, other innovations, such as self-collection parcel lockers, began to be implemented. As of 2022, a nationwide parcel locker network – available to all last-mile delivery providers – is available in Singapore. The virtually unmanned and 24–7 available lockers can enhance logistics efficiency, reduce costs due consolidation of goods, reduce failed deliveries, and provide flexibility for customers' parcel collection. This paper presents an overview of Singapore's evolution of last-mile delivery innovations related to parcels collection. A discussion on logistics, urban planning, and sustainability impacts is provided – in relation to the country and how these could be used as learning points in other (tropical) countries for improving last-mile deliveries. Finally, potential innovations are highlighted and future research directions are suggested.

Keywords Parcel collection · Parcel locker · Locker stations · Last-mile delivery · Logistics innovation

M. C. Rojas Lopez (✉) · H. S. Loh
School of Business, Singapore University of Social Sciences, Singapore, Singapore
e-mail: eciliarojas@suss.edu.sg; hsloh@suss.edu.sg

E. L. Eijdenberg et al. (eds.), *Innovation-Driven Business and Sustainability in the Tropics*, https://doi.org/10.1007/978-981-99-2909-2_22

22.1 Introduction

Transport and logistics are fields that are constantly evolving to cater for social and national needs. As cities around the world become more urbanised, the movement of people and goods has increased. In response, infrastructure has to be retrofitted, adapted, and re-planned (Campbell & Van Woensel, 2019; Lagorio et al., 2016). With these adaptations and planning, much consideration is placed on improving lifestyles, enhancing the economy, and positively affecting sustainability. Thus, related research and innovations are necessary. Statistics indicate that urban population in the world would reach 6.3 billion people by the 2050s and that this growth will be concentrated in tropical countries. In the tropics, several developments in infrastructure for different modes of transport have been implemented since around the year 2000. These developments focused on facilitating the movement of goods (i.e. logistics) and boosting economies (SOT, 2017, 2020).

E-commerce has been growing rapidly in Singapore with Singapore's e-commerce market to be worth more than US$5.4 billion by 2025 (Channel News Asia, 2016. The number of parcels delivered in 2021 globally was over 159 billion parcels, which represents an increase of 21% as compared to the previous year (Statista, 2022). As can be seen, the result is a consequential increase in demand for parcel deliveries, posing challenges to the sustainable management of transport in the urban cities. E-commerce modified business to customers (B2C) relations and revolutionised logistics. The final process of delivering the product to the consumer or buyer, it often referred as last-mile deliveries. The traditional last-mile delivery method tends to see road congestion, noise and air pollution, thereby imposing heavy societal costs.

The last-mile delivery is a costly process, it is estimated that more than half of the shipping cost of the product is on last-mile delivery (Lee, 2019). In addition, the process has other operational challenges. Last-mile deliveries impact sustainability, deliveries are often completed by motorised vehicles which in turn can pollute the environment. Moreover, the process can be a tedious and labour-intensive process, whereby smaller individual packages are handled and addresses/locations should be found (Boysen et al., 2021; Suguna et al., 2022). Another challenge of last-mile deliveries is the undelivered packages due to missing information from the seller or due to customer not being home to receive the parcel (Lin et al., 2020).

Planners and researchers have been researching different options to improve the last-mile delivery. Some have proposed the combination of logistic transport with passenger trips for optimal use of space and exiting facilities (Le Pira et al., 2021). There has also been ample discussion on new concepts, such as the use of autonomous vehicles or robots and usage of drones for deliveries. Much of this technology is still being pilot tested and/or slowly implemented (Demir et al., 2022; Sorooshian et al., 2022). Moreover, some innovations in the area are incorporating the concept of "customer self-service", whereby the logistic network and load can be relieved by customers completing (parts of) the last-mile delivery task by collecting parcels on their own (Ma et al., 2022; Zhou et al., 2020; Zurel et al., 2019).

Singapore, a tropical island country in South East Asia, has constantly being considered a leader in economic development and is steadily becoming an example of a "smart-nation" (Lyu & Teo, 2022; SmartNation, 2018). The country has invested in transport and last-mile logistic infrastructure to improve traffic, enhance sustainability, and promote business efficiency and customer satisfaction (Lui, 2022; URA, 2022). E-commerce started to gain popularity in the country around a decade ago, then the number of items bought online – that then needed to be delivered at home – rapidly escalated with the rise of COVID-19 pandemic and related limitations in 2020 (Tang, 2019). This increase put a heavy strain on the last-mile delivery system. It should be noted that demand for deliveries of ready to consume food items/meals is also increasing in the country and this is being taken into consideration under urban logistics (Heng, 2022). Requirements for food deliveries and collection are different than those of parcels, and while innovations are also being made in the area, these are outside the scope of this paper.

This paper aims to explore the potential innovations in parcel collection by way of studying the existing literature and findings from local initiatives on the related developments in Singapore's urban logistics. Parcels collection, in this paper, is referred to users picking-up (collecting) their packages of products (parcels) bought from online shops of through e-commerce platforms, from locations other than the physical store of the good or their registered addresses. Findings and lessons presented herein can be considered by other tropical and non-tropical countries that are aiming to improve their overall urban logistics and/or introducing innovations for parcels collection to alleviate last-mile deliveries. The remaining of this paper is organised as follows; first shopping trends in the country are presented, followed by an overview of urban logistics and last-mile deliveries. Then, innovations for parcel collections are outlined. Finally, a discussion on these developments and what are some lessons to be learned from Singapore concludes the paper.

22.2 Research Background

22.2.1 Shopping Trends in Singapore

Singapore is recognised for being a "shopper's paradise" and its population is well known for its shopping habits. While in previous years, frequenting malls and brick-and-mortar stores was the norm, the trend has shifted towards online shopping (Ho, 2021; Suñga, 2023). With the ubiquitous of the internet and the rise of online shopping websites and apps, more and more consumers have moved to online shopping (MediaOne, 2022). The online shopping trend further increased with the introduction of large international e-commerce companies such as Lazada, Shopee, and Amazon, in 2014, 2015, and 2017 respectively (Lazada, 2022; Shopee, 2022; Today Online, 2017). Furthermore, the movement and interaction limitations due to COVID-19 further impacted e-commerce. Companies were "forced" to become

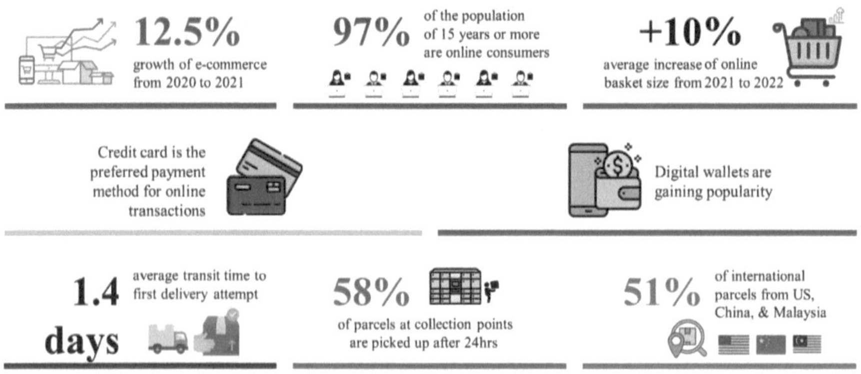

Fig. 22.1 E-commerce in Singapore. (Adapted from: SCA, 2020 and Ting, 2022)

digitally available, thus giving more options to customers to access online stores – ergo, increasing online shopping and number of parcels to be delivered from shops and warehouses to costumers (Wang et al., 2022; Youjin, 2022). It is estimated that 4.3 million habitants in Singapore are online shoppers. This is around 76% of the total population of 5.64 million (DoS, 2022; MediaOne, 2022). Figure 22.1 illustrates some information on Singapore e-shopping trends.

It should be noted that, while local reports do indicate a rise in e-commerce – with a revenue expected to reach 20 billion SGD (14 billion USD) by 2027 (Ganesan, 2022b; Ting, 2022), these also indicate that physical in-store shopping is still very much present in Singapore. Several stores in Singapore have implemented an Online + Offline (O + O) retail approach, creating an omnichannel and investing in in-store experiences as much as in online accessibility and activities (Rodiukova, 2022). Today, online shoppers can be quite demanding on their delivery options. While competitive rates and fast delivery times are a must, the flexibility of parcel collection could make the difference between choosing one provider over the other (Lyu & Teo, 2022; Varma, 2017). The access to online shopping further increased access to products, with many of these purchases being done from overseas. The increase in e-commerce and online shopping weighs on the urban logistics system of the country.

22.2.2 Urban Transport and Last-Mile Delivery

There are various approaches to last-mile deliveries in Singapore. An overview of the urban structure will be introduced to explain the relevance of the different methods of last-mile delivery in Singapore.

Singapore's urban structure plays an important role on the last-mile logistic. Its urban transport system sees much effort invested in the planning and management as it is densely populated. Singapore seeks to create public transport centric towns, with an equal distribution of residential, industrial-commercial-educational, and transport-recreational land uses (Rojas Lopez et al., 2020). This distribution enhances movement of people and fosters dispersion of activities (LTA, 2019; Rojas López & Wong, 2017). Commercial activity centres commonly located at transport hubs (MRT stations and/or bus interchanges).

Singapore has also been investing heavily on infrastructure for active modes of transport and encouraging the use of walking and cycling (Che et al., 2021). In other words, Singapore aims to reduce traffic and maximise operations. In 2017, it was estimated that 15% of the road vehicles in Singapore are delivery vehicles, and that delivery vehicles travel two times more than private cars (Eveland, 2022). As can be seen, Singapore is keen on being a smart and sustainable country.

The mentioned COVID-19 and related increase in parcels, triggered a shortage of delivery slots since early 2020. To address the issue, drivers of taxis and private-hire cars were allowed to conduct deliveries (Ho, 2020). This allowance will continue until March 2023 when it will be reviewed to decide on further action (Yufeng, 2022). It has also been observed that some parcels are being deliveries by greener modes of transport such as bicycles and other personal mobility devices (PMDs). Parcels to be delivered varies in size and value, causing an additional challenge for arranging the deliveries. The Singapore Post (SingPost), the country's postal service provider, has reported that in recent years, as opposed to letters and post-cards, larger e-commerce parcels are gaining ground. This has led Singpost to updrade its overall postal infrastructure and technology (Tan, 2021). The key developments are explained in the subsequent section.

22.3 Parcels Collection in Singapore

22.3.1 Initiatives from Public Sector

In Singapore, there have been several developments or initiatives in terms of parcels collection. An overall timeline illustration is presented in Fig. 22.2. Initial innovations for parcel collection in Singapore were first seen in the year 2013, when SingPost, launched the "Pick Own Parcel Stations" (POP Stations). Herein, SingPost customers who (e)buy items from overseas could have their parcels delivered at one of the automated delivery locker systems that allows customers collect their parcels round the clock. The usage of the locker system service is free and it can be used around the clock. Once parcels are ready for collection, the user receives a notification to collect their parcels within 3 calendar days (Tham, 2013). Upon launching the service, 100 lockers at 5 stations were rolled out, as of 2021, it has been reported that there are 154 POPStations throughout Singapore, of which 125, operates 24–7 (AllSGPromo, 2021; SingPost, 2022a).

Later on in 2016, SingPost decided to expand the POPStations services by adding a locker rental feature. This service was called "Rent-a-POP". Using

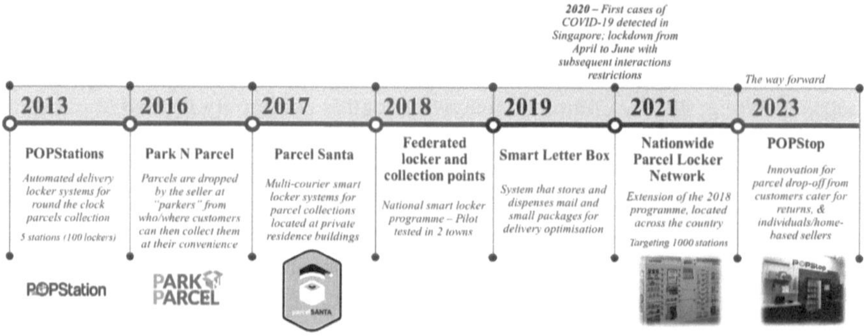

Fig. 22.2 Parcels collection innovations timeline

Rent-a-POP, retailers and consumers could rent a locker for drop-off and later collection (i.e. a seller can rent locker in agreement with the buyer, the seller drop's the parcel here and the buyer can then collect at his/her convenience) (Juanda, 2016; Lee, 2016). However, according to their webpage the service is no longer available at any POPstations as of 2022 (SingPost, 2022b).

22.3.2 *Initiatives from Private Sector*

Developments on parcels collection also came from the private sector in late 2016, when the start-up Park N Parcel launched its online portal. Park N Parcel allowed sellers to drop parcels, that otherwise would be delivered to customers' doorstep, at a "parker". The parker is someone at selected shops, transport stations, or residences (other than the customers'), who picks up the parcel on behalf of the customer. The parcels could then be collected from the parker at a date and/or time of convenience for the customer (PnP, 2022; Tay, 2017; Varma, 2017). Collection dates and time varies depending on the parker. The parcels dropped at parker points should weigh ≤8 kg and measure ≤100 cm of total dimension (Length + Width + Height). The service comes at a cost of 2.5 SGD (Approx. 1.8 USD) per parcel.

Another private start-up, Parcel Santa, launched its services in Singapore in 2017. This was the first company to offer smart locker systems-based services open for all courier companies. These lockers are located at private residence buildings (condominiums) in Singapore and are available for e-commerce parcel deliveries (Parcel Santa, 2022; Yahya, 2017). The system aims to provide convenience for consumers and improve courier services by minimising deliveries. Courier companies that would like to deliver at the lockers, need to register for the service. Collecting parcels from the Parcel Santa lockers is free for customers who reside in condominiums where the lockers are located. Once the parcel is at the locker, customer will receive a One-Time-Password (OTP) or a Quick Response (QR) Code via SMS or email, this is then used on the interactive touchscreen of the locker system to collect the parcel within 48 hours of the notification.

22.3.3 Collaborative Efforts

In 2018, the Infocomm Media Development Authority (IMDA) launched the "Federated Locker and Collection Points Programme" pilot in two towns in Singapore – Bukit Panjang and Pungol (Wong, 2018b). The programme, which was first announced in 2016, focuses on improving overall urban logistics by delivering parcels at smart lockers so these can then be collected by the buyers. Locker stations from several operators were introduced as a single, interoperable network platform. Lockers are located across the selected towns at public residences ground floor open spaces (referred as void decks), transport nodes, and community spaces to better serve the needs of last-mile deliveries in Singapore. The locker network standardises and interchange data for seamless parcel delivery (for sellers) and collection (for buyers). For the pilot, 15 logistics service providers – including Parcel Santa, marketplaces, and online stores agreed to use the lockers and collections points (IMDA Singapore, 2018, 2022). The pilot was set to be for 1 year with possibility to extend it to an additional year (total of 2 years). The programme would then expand nationally with aims to create a clear blueprint for last-mile deliveries that could eventually be offered internationally.

On the same year, SingPost and Park N Parcel joined in partnership for last-mile delivery, bringing the number of parker points (collection points) to over 1600 in the country (The Strait Times, 2018). In addition, SingPost announced a new last-mile platform in partnership with courier services, parcel lockers and collection points in all South-east Asian countries. The integration of these partners will allow sellers to offer the option of receiving purchases through any delivery node in the network (Tay, 2018). Furthermore, a huge e-commerce player in Singapore – Lazada and its logistic service provider Ninja Van, announced a new stablished partnership with 7-Eleven convenience stores for parcel collection points (Wong, 2018a).

Towards the end of 2019 and 2020, with the rise of COVID-19 cases, Singapore (and many other countries) saw a sudden change in shopping, travelling, and other activities patterns. This causes some uncertainties for retailers and logistics providers. An example is Park N Parcel, who shifted towards door-to-door last-mile deliveries (delivering at the doorstep) to minimise human interaction (PnP, 2022). In 2020, understanding that there is an apparent permanent shift toward e-commerce and deliveries in the country, SingPost introduced their smart letterbox. The smart letterbox system stores and dispenses mail and small packages in order to optimise delivery, including those that are to be dropped into POPStations for later collection by the costumer (Tay, 2020).

By early 2021, the IMDA announced the extension of the "Federated Locker and Collection Points Programme" into "The Nationwide Parcel Locker Network". Both initiatives operate in similar ways, being managed by the IMDA and open to virtually all logistic operators, marketplaces, and customers. Refer to Fig. 22.3 for an overview of the process flow when using the network. The network is an alliance between local government and large delivery companies who own lockers and collection points (Lyu & Teo, 2022). It has been identified that commercial lockers cater for 5% of the total parcel volume in Singapore, the network alliance aims to increase accessibility and further alleviate the load on last-mile deliveries. In addition, the programme is also aimed to improve overall society digital reception. At the initial launch, 200 locker stations were made available with aims to reach 1000 within a year (IMDA Singapore, 2022; Ma et al., 2022; Tan, 2021). Within a year of the network alliance, it has been reported that while overall usage of the system is relatively low (average of <15% utilisation rate), logistics partners have reported productivity gains (by 3 to 9 times) and positive feedback has been collected from consumers (Ganesan, 2022a).

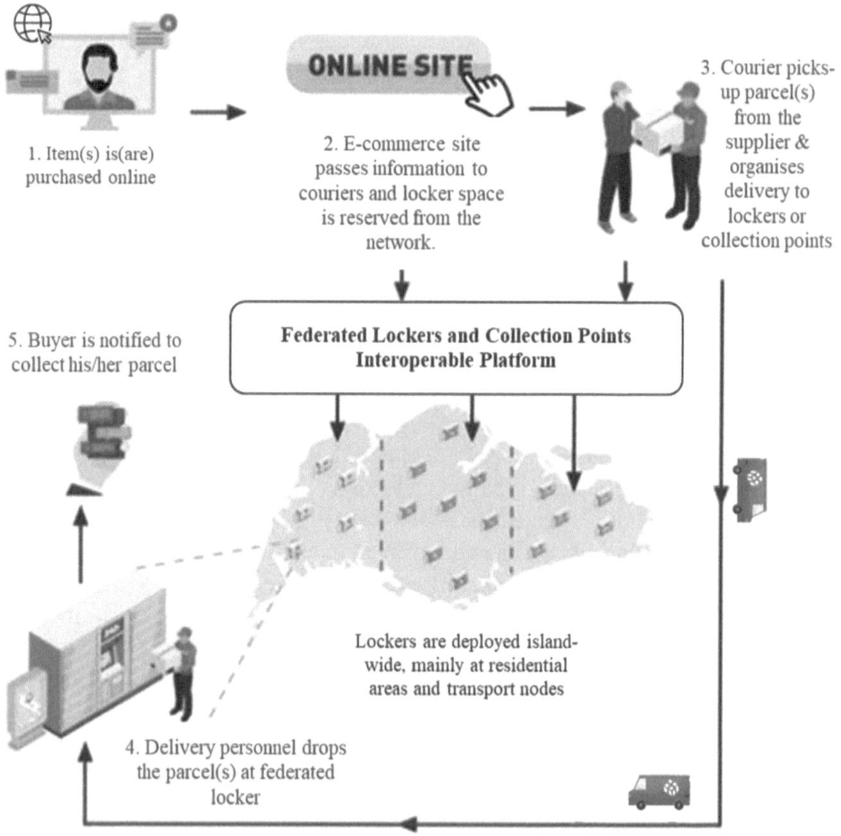

Fig. 22.3 Delivery process flow using the nationwide parcel locker network. (Adapted from: *IMDA Singapore*, 2018)

Furthermore, a latest initiative was announced to be rolled out by 2023. Taking into consideration that there is an increasing rate of returns (reverse logistics) and that several individuals or independent (home-based) sellers are increasingly shipping parcels, an alternative for parcels drop-off will be introduced. The initiative is called POPStop and it is to be combined with POPStations. While this is more focused on improving the first mile deliveries, SingPost overall aim is to provide a holistic service aimed at improving overall urban logistics in the country (Ganesan, 2022b).

22.4 Discussion and Conclusion

As seen, Singapore has been investing much efforts in improving the urban logistics of the county for some time. Initial innovations for parcels collection in the country date approximately a decade back. These innovations are a combination of developments by private companies and public agencies to facilitate parcels collection and alleviate the load on last-mile deliveries. The latest initiative is a nation-wide development, that while a relatively low usage was reported, logistics service providers have seen the benefits and it has helped them improve the last mile delivery. These are positive trends that are expected to further improve, especially considering that locker stations infrastructure is set to last for several years.

There are some points for consideration that are very specific of Singapore. First is the fact that Singapore is a very dense country where the population is mostly living in high rise buildings. This means that lockers located at these residential buildings serve for a high concentration of people. In addition, lockers that are located at transport hubs also serve many as public transport is the most common mode of transport for many in Singapore. This brings two folded benefits. On one hand, convenience for the users, who in the end are the key players that make the decision to use the lockers and on the other hand for delivery service providers as they could provide delivery of several parcels at one particular location, thus reducing required manpower and number of trips (Morganti et al., 2014). This in turn can have positive impacts on the society and environment.

Questions have been raised regarding if usage of lockers could be free of charge only for a particular user group, such as younger population or technology savvy. As mentioned, most of the population in Singapore are online consumers, thus most of them could access the usage lockers without many limitations. In regards to elders and their usage of lockers, some questions are still to be answer as they might have not only technology limitations, but also limited mobility. Overall, Singapore government is working to build a digitally receptive population as well as companies, so that parcels can be delivered at a convenient, fast, and cost-effective rate.

Moreover, the elevated number of parcels that are delivered in Singapore contributes to the usage of parcel lockers and collection points. This is as one buys several packages online, organising oneself to be available to receive every packages might not be possible. Thus, users might have greater preference for lockers and collection points to them picking up they parcels at their convenience. From the logistic and urban point of view, being able to consolidate the increasing number of parcels for delivery at lockers or collection points. As recent research has indicated (Ma et al., 2022; Collins, 2015), it is important to considerate both users and providers perspective for planning, implementing, maintaining, and updating these system. This could help to further increase the overall benefits.

The high levels of security in the country also play a key role in the success of parcel lockers and self-collection (Qiu & Huang, 2013; Zhang et al., 2016). Majority of the lockers are located at public spaces and the high levels of security gives users and delivery providers the assurance that parcels will "remain safe" from the moment when they are dropped at the lockers until they are picked up by the buyer. Nevertheless, safety measures are installed to further enhance security, these are both in terms of technology (surveillance and alarms) and laws that penalise offences (e.g. tampering). Singapore also has relatively high levels of personal security, this in a sense increases accessibility of the lockers, as people would have the opportunity, or would be willing to, collect parcels anytime (even night/dark times). Countries how are considering the implementation of locker stations or aim to improve the usage of the lockers, should consider the levels of security where the lockers are to be located and/or options for improving safety in the area.

Finally, the urban layout and usage of different modes transport in the country should also be considered for successful implementation of parcel lockers. It is important that areas where the lockers and collection points are located are well connected and accessible by different modes of transport. It is particularly important for active modes of transport, as non-accessible or far away lockers might not be widely used. Covering long distances walking or cycling and carrying the collected packages at the same time might not be appalling to users. The weather could also affect usage of parcel lockers. Singapore, as well as many other tropical countries is characterised by humid and hot weather.

22.5 Future Research

The elderly may face limitations when accessing technology, which plays a major role in innovative parcel collection methods. Hence, one possible future research is to cater innovations that are also applicable to the elderly who may be less savvy. Future research may also seek to have tailored measures for residents with less mobility, especially in cities that start to see aging population. There is not much research focusing on the impact of weather on parcels collection and this is an area that could also be further investigated. Additionally, further studies on the relationship between actual/perceived safety and successful usage of parcel lockers could also be conducted.

References

AllSGPromo. (2021, September 15). POPStations Outlets: Opening Hours, Locations and Outlets in Singapore. *AllSGPromo*. https://www.allsgpromo.com/popstations-outlets/

Boysen, N., Fedtke, S., & Schwerdfeger, S. (2021). Last-mile delivery concepts: A survey from an operational research perspective. In *OR Spectrum* (Vol. 43, Issue 1, pp. 1–58). Springer. https://doi.org/10.1007/s00291-020-00607-8

Campbell, A. M., & Van Woensel, T. (2019). Special issue on recent advances in urban transport and logistics through optimization and analytics. *Transportation Science, 53*(1), 1–5. https://doi.org/10.1287/trsc.2018.0882

Channel News Asia (2016). *Singapore e-commerce market to exceed S$7b in 2025*: Report: http://www.channelnewsasia.com/news/business/singapore-e-commerce/2811118.html

Che, M., Wong, Y. D., Lum, K. M., & Rojas Lopez, M. C. (2021). Users' behavioral intention and their behavior: Before-and-after study of "keep left" markings on shared footpaths. *International Journal of Sustainable Transportation*, 1–9. https://doi.org/10.1080/15568318.2021.2015494

Collins, A. T. (2015). *Behavioural influences on the environmental impact of collection / delivery points* (pp. 15–34). Springer International Publishing Switzerland.

Demir, E., Syntetos, A., & Van Woensel, T. (2022). Last mile logistics: Research trends and needs. *IMA Journal of Management Mathematics, 33*(4), 549–561. https://doi.org/10.1093/imaman/dpac006

DoS. (2022). *Population trends 2022*. Department of Statistics, Ministry of Trade & Industry. https://doi.org/10.1038/137158a0

Eveland, J. (2022). Skyline issue 10 – Urban logistics. In *Urban Redevelopment Authority*, Singapore. https://www.ura.gov.sg/Corporate/Resources/Publications/Skyline/Skyline-Issue10/Movinggoods

Ganesan, D. (2022a, July 26). Singapore-wide parcel locker usage low after a year. *The Straits Times*. https://www.straitstimes.com/singapore/low-usage-of-nationwide-delivery-locker-network-but-service-providers-report-productivity-gains.

Ganesan, D. (2022b, October 12). New SingPost facility to be set up at MRT stations for users to send parcels. *The Straits Times*. https://www.straitstimes.com/singapore/new-singpost-facility-to-be-set-up-at-mrt-stations-for-users-to-send-parcels

Heng, M. (2022). Demand for food delivery to stay strong beyond pandemic. *The Straits Times*, 4–6.

Ho, O. (2020, March 29). Taxi, private-hire car drivers allowed to deliver food and groceries to address delivery slot shortage during Covid-19 outbreak. *The Straits Times*, 22–25. https://www.straitstimes.com/singapore/taxi-and-private-hire-car-drivers-to-help-make-grocery-deliveries-to-address-shortage-of

Ho, K. (2021). Three in five Singaporeans say shopping habits have changed since pandemic. *YouGOv*. https://sg.yougov.com/en-sg/news/2021/04/13/over-two-five-singaporeans-report-increased-consum/

IMDA Singapore. (2022). *Federated locker and collection points Programme*. Infocomm Media Development Authority – Singapore. https://www.imda.gov.sg/How-We-Can-Help/urban-logistics/federated-locker-and-collection-points-programme

IMDA Singapore (2018). Fact sheet urban logistics to receive significant boost with last mile delivery via a federated lockers network. In *Infocomm Media Development Authority – Singapore*. https://www.imda.gov.sg/-/media/imda/files/about/media-releases/2018/factsheet_federated-lockers-overview.pdf

Juanda, I. (2016, July 27). *SingPost launches locker rental service for parcel delivery and collection*. Today Online. https://www.todayonline.com/singapore/singposts-launches-locker-rental-service-parcel-delivery-and-collection

Lagorio, A., Pinto, R., & Golini, R. (2016). Research in urban logistics: A systematic literature review. *International Journal of Physical Distribution and Logistics Management, 46*(10), 908–931. https://doi.org/10.1108/IJPDLM-01-2016-0008

Lazada. (2022). *About Lazada*. Lazada. https://doi.org/10.1038/s41583-018-0022-3

Le Pira, M., Tavasszy, L. A., Correia, G. H. d. A., Ignaccolo, M., & Inturri, G. (2021). Opportunities for integration between Mobility as a Service (MaaS) and freight transport: A conceptual model. *Sustainable Cities and Society, 74*(November), 2021–2023. https://doi.org/10.1016/j.scs.2021.103212

Lee, P. (2016, July 27). *SingPost rolls out first islandwide open parcel locker service*. The Edge Markets. https://www.theedgemarkets.com/article/singpost-rolls-out-first-islandwide-open-parcel-locker-service

Lee, C. (2019). The sustainable effort. *Dairy Industries International, 84*(4), 34. https://www.accenture.com/_acnmedia/PDF-153/Accenture-Sustainable-Mile-POV-SG.pdf

Lin, Y. H., Wang, Y., He, D., & Lee, L. H. (2020). Last-mile delivery: Optimal locker location under multinomial logit choice model. *Transportation Research Part E: Logistics and Transportation Review, 142*(Lmd), 1–18. https://doi.org/10.1016/j.tre.2020.102059

LTA. (2019). Land transport master plan 2040. Land Transport Authority. https://www.lta.gov.sg/ltmp2040

Lui, J. (2022, March 19). When your online shopping goes on a wild ride: How parcels are sorted at a logistics facility. *The Straits Times*. https://www.straitstimes.com/life/when-your-online-shopping-goes-on-a-wild-ride

Lyu, G., & Teo, C. P. (2022). Last mile innovation: The case of the locker Alliance network. *Manufacturing and Service Operations Management, 24*(5), 2425–2443. https://doi.org/10.1287/msom.2021.1000

Ma, B., Wong, Y. D., & Teo, C.-C. (2022). Parcel self-collection for urban last-mile deliveries: A review and research agenda with a dual operations-consumer perspective. *Transportation Research Interdisciplinary Perspectives, 16*(June), 100719. https://doi.org/10.1016/j.trip.2022.100719

MediaOne. (2022). *Singapore online shopping trends 2022 the growth of online shopping*. Media One Marketing. https://mediaonemarketing.com.sg/singapore-online-shopping-trends/

Morganti, E., Dablanc, L., & Fortin, F. (2014). Final deliveries for online shopping: The deployment of pickup point networks in urban and suburban areas. *Research in Transportation Business & Management, 11*, 23–31.

Parcel Santa. (2022). *Parcel Santa in the news*. Parcel Santa. https://www.parcelsanta.com/media

PnP. (2022). *About park N parcel*. Park N Parcel. https://www.parknparcel.com.sg/

Qiu, X., & Huang, G. Q. (2013). Supply hub in Industrial Park (SHIP): The value of freight consolidation. *Computers & Industrial Engineering, 65*, 16–27.

Rodiukova, N. (2022, December 6). 2022 Online shopping trends in Singapore. *Storyly*. https://www.storyly.io/post/2022-online-shopping-trends-singapore

Rojas López, M. C., & Wong, Y. D. (2017). Attitudes towards active mobility in Singapore: A qualitative study. *Case Studies on Transport Policy, 5*(4), 662–670. https://doi.org/10.1016/j.cstp.2017.07.002

Rojas Lopez, M. C., Toan, T. D., & Wong, Y. D. (2020). Transitioning different stages of transport planning in urban areas: Experiences of Singapore and Vietnam. In *Lecture Notes in Civil Engineering* (Vol. 54). https://doi.org/10.1007/978-981-15-0802-8_152

SCA. (2020). Parcel monitor: The state of E-commerce in Singapore 2020. *Supply Chain Asia*. https://supplychainasia.org/parcel-monitor-the-state-of-e-commerce-in-singapore-2020/

Shopee. (2022). *Shopee is the leading e-commerce platform in Southeast Asia and Taiwan*. Shopee. https://careers.shopee.sg/about

SingPost. (2022a). *Locate us | Singapore post*. Singapore Post. https://www.singpost.com/locate-us

SingPost. (2022b). *Shopping & POPStation FAQ*. Singapore Post. https://www.singpost.com/support-centre/shop/shopping-popstation

SmartNation. (2018). Transforming Singapore through technology. *Smart nation: The way forward*. smartnation.gov.sg/about-smart-nation/transforming-singapore

Sorooshian, S., Khademi Sharifabad, S., Parsaee, M., & Afshari, A. R. (2022). Toward a modern last-mile delivery: Consequences and obstacles of intelligent technology. *Applied System Innovation, 5*(4), 1–16. https://doi.org/10.3390/asi5040082

SOT. (2017). *Sustainable infrastrucutre in the tropics*. In State of the Tropics Report.

SOT. (2020). *State of the tropics 2020 report*. State of the Tropics Report.

Statista. (2022). *Global parcel shipping volume between 2013 and 2027*. https://www.statista.com/statistics/1139910/parcel-shipping-volume-worldwide/

Suguna, M., Shah, B., Raj, S. K., & Suresh, M. (2022). A study on the influential factors of the last mile delivery projects during Covid-19 era. *Operations Management Research, 15*(1–2), 399–412. https://doi.org/10.1007/s12063-021-00214-y

Suñga, C. A. (2023). 2023 Online shopping trends in Singapore that you must know. In *OOm Shaping Online Future*. https://www.oom.com.sg/2023-online-shopping-trends-in-singapore-that-you-must-know/

Tan, A. (2021, April 5). Nationwide parcel locker network is neutral, accessible to all delivery providers. *The Straits* Times. https://www.straitstimes.com/singapore/consumer/nationwide-parcel-locker-network-is-neutral-accessible-by-all-delivery-providers

Tang, L. W. (2019). *E-commerce in Singapore: An overview of opportunities, challenges and how to get started. 2019*. https://entrepreneurcampfire.com/e-commerce-singapore/

Tay, T. F. (2017, April 7). Not at home when your parcel arrives? No problem. *The Straits Times*. https://www.straitstimes.com/singapore/firms-deliver-with-self-collection-option

Tay, T. F. (2018, November 6). More delivery options with SingPost regional platform. *The Straits Times*. https://www.straitstimes.com/singapore/more-delivery-options-with-singpost-regional-platform

Tay, T. F. (2020, September 12). SingPost to trial smart letterbox system as e-commerce surges. *The Straits Times*. https://www.straitstimes.com/singapore/singpost-to-trial-smart-letterbox-system-as-e-commerce-surges

Tham, I. (2013, April 16). Singapore post launches 24-hour parcel delivery kiosks. *The Straits Times*. https://www.straitstimes.com/singapore/singapore-post-launches-24-hour-parcel-delivery-kiosks

The Strait Times. (2018, November 7). SingPost to add park N parcel collection points to its new last-mile platform. *The Straits Times*. https://www.straitstimes.com/business/companies-markets/singpost-to-add-park-n-parcel-collection-points-to-its-new-last-mile

Ting, C. Y. (2022). *E-commerce sales in Singapore expected to reach $19.6b by 2027, despite slower growth this year*. 1–5. https://www.straitstimes.com/business/e-commerce-sales-in-spore-expected-to-reach-196b-by-2027-despite-slower-growth-this-year

Today Online. (2017, July 27). *Amazon officially launches in Singapore – TODAY*. Today Online. https://www.todayonline.com/singapore/amazon-officially-launches-singapore

URA. (2022). Better and More Efficient Delivery. *Urban Redevelopment Authority, Singapore*. https://www.ura.gov.sg/Corporate/Search-Result?search=deliveryvehicles&category=

Varma, A. (2017, June 18). Easy parcel collection for online shoppers. *The Straits Times*, 1–5. https://www.straitstimes.com/lifestyle/easy-parcel-collection-for-online-shoppers

Wang, X., Wong, Y. D., Chen, T., & Yuen, K. F. (2022). Consumer logistics in contemporary shopping: A synthesised review. *Transport Reviews*, 10–13. https://doi.org/10.1080/01441647.2022.2131010

Wong, D. (2018a, October 19). 350 7-eleven stores to offer parcel pick-up by year end. *The Straits Times*. https://www.straitstimes.com/singapore/350-7-eleven-stores-to-offer-parcel-pick-up-by-year-end

Wong, D. (2018b, December 7). Punggol and Bukit Panjang residents can collect online purchases from lockers at HDB blocks in pilot scheme. *The Straits Times*. https://www.straitstimes.com/singapore/punggol-and-bukit-panjang-residents-can-collect-online-purchases-from-lockers-at-hdb

Yahya, Y. (2017, November 28). Parcel Santa gets delivery into condo residents' hands 24/7. *Business Times* https://www.businesstimes.com.sg/singapore/smes/parcel-santa-gets-delivery-condo-residents-hands-247

Youjin, L. (2022, October 15). *The big read in short: Post-pandemic, shoppers are looking for that little something extra.* Today Online, 1–11. https://www.todayonline.com/big-read/big-read-short-post-pandemic-shoppers-are-looking-little-something-extra-2020191

Yufeng, K. (2022, November 21). Cabbies, private-hire drivers can make deliveries until march. *The Straits Times.* https://www.straitstimes.com/singapore/transport/trial-allowing-cabbies-private-hire-drivers-to-make-deliveries-extended-again

Zhang, W., Uhan, N. A., Dessouky, M. & Toriello, A. (2016). *Cost-sharing mechanism design for freight consolidation among small suppliers.*

Zhou, M., Zhao, L., Kong, N., Campy, K. S., Xu, G., Zhu, G., Cao, X., & Wang, S. (2020). Understanding consumers' behavior to adopt self-service parcel services for last-mile delivery. *Journal of Retailing and Consumer Services, 52*(January), 101911. https://doi.org/10.1016/j.jretconser.2019.101911

Zurel, Ö., Hoyweghen, L. Van, & Braes, S. (2019). Parcel lockers, an answer to the pressure on the last mile delivery? In *New Business and Regulatory Strategies in the Postal Sector*. https://doi.org/10.1007/978-3-030-02937-1

Chapter 23
Scoping the Conveniences of Mobile Money for Micro-entrepreneurs in Kenya

Rael A. Onyango, Emiel L. Eijdenberg, Nelson Obange, and Enno Masurel

Abstract Mobile money is a no-frills mobile phone-based payment instrument, which is widely used in many emerging economies, especially in sub-Saharan Africa. Knowledge of what mobile money means is of great importance for micro-entrepreneurs who operate in the changing digital environments of emerging economies. Little attention has been devoted to contextual studies on mobile money use by micro-entrepreneurs in emerging economies. With this in mind, this study aims to develop a deeper understanding of what mobile money really means to micro-entrepreneurs. We conducted individual interviews with 23 experts on micro-entrepreneurship and experienced entrepreneurs in Kenya, the emerging economy context of this study. Through qualitative analyses, we filtered the data into a number of meaningful takeaways, which are several "conveniences" of using mobile money by micro-entrepreneurs. The findings show that mobile money contains a lot of positive conveniences for micro-entrepreneurs, including convenience for payments, timely updates, savings and, lastly, convenience of obtaining loaning and overdraft facilities. Other than expanding scholarly knowledge, the findings provide useful practical and managerial insights.

R. A. Onyango (✉)
School of Business and Economics, Vrije Universiteit, Amsterdam, The Netherlands

Department of Economics, School of Business and Economics, Maseno University, Maseno, Kenya
e-mail: r.a.onyango@vu.nl

E. L. Eijdenberg
Centre for International Trade and Business in Asia, James Cook University, Singapore, Singapore

N. Obange
Department of Economics, School of Business and Economics, Maseno University, Maseno, Kenya

E. Masurel
School of Business and Economics, Vrije Universiteit, Amsterdam, The Netherlands

E. L. Eijdenberg et al. (eds.), *Innovation-Driven Business and Sustainability in the Tropics*, https://doi.org/10.1007/978-981-99-2909-2_23

Keywords Emerging economy · Entrepreneurship · M-Pesa · Micro-entrepreneurs · Sub-Saharan Africa

23.1 Introduction

Mobile money—a mobile-based financial service considered as "bank in your hand"—is an increasingly promising development in emerging economies. Mobile phone users are able to deposit, send or withdraw money without owning a bank account (Njoroge & Murinde, 2021), thereby reducing the gap between the unbanked and the banked (Prashaant & Sharma, 2015; Hughes & Lonie, 2007). Enterprises in all sectors of emerging economies are widely adopting and using mobile money (Gosavi, 2018; Talom & Tengeh, 2019; Tengeh & Talom, 2020). Currently, mobile money has over 346 million active account users globally with sub-Saharan Africa having the highest number of active account users, 183 million, compared to other regions (Awanis et al., 2022). One of the most widely known mobile money systems called "M-Pesa" ("M" for mobile, while "Pesa" means money in Kiswahili) started in the year 2007 in Kenya (Donovan, 2012; Njoroge & Murinde, 2021). Sub-Saharan Africa, of which Kenya is part, is also noted to be the region in which a considerable share of adults have *only* a mobile money account, rather than a bank or other financial institution account such as a micro-finance account (Demirguc-Kunt et al., 2022). Mobile money thus plays a significant role in emerging economies for enterprises and individuals.

In recent years, researchers have become increasingly interested in mobile money services in relation to the performance of enterprises. For instance, Heyer and Mas (2011) focused on enabling environments for the uptake and scalability of mobile money. Furthermore, a growing stream of studies supports that mobile money use by micro and small businesses leads to a range of benefits such as increased savings; reduced transaction costs; more lines of credit; increased resources available for investments; supplier payments; and general purchases (Beck et al., 2015; Gosavi, 2018; Higgins et al., 2012; Islam et al., 2018; Prashaant & Sharma, 2015). Other studies revealed that mobile money use could also have other direct or indirect positive impacts such as enhanced business innovations, as well as a positive influence on the financial performance of enterprises (Lorenz & Pommet, 2021; Talom & Tengeh, 2019). Such mobile money studies are vital as they may allow enterprises to develop transaction-based business models that are data driven and are useful for the growth and development of enterprises.

Despite valuable earlier research, little attention has been devoted to the background of mobile money use in emerging economies, particularly in terms of what mobile money "means" for micro-entrepreneurs (i.e., those people running micro-enterprises). In regard to this background, the current study pursues the following research question (RQ): *What does mobile money mean for micro-entrepreneurs in an emerging economy?*

Based on individual interviews with 23 experts and micro-entrepreneurs in Kenya, the findings suggest that mobile money appears to be convenient for micro-entrepreneurs beyond facilitating payments (1), viz. it is also convenient for (2) getting real-time updates, for example, micro-entrepreneurs like to visually see their flow of money at a glance; (3) micro-savings and most important; (4) overdraft facilities in addition to piecemeal borrowing. We anticipate that this study will give useful insights for financial technology (hereafter referred to as "fintech") enterprises, financial providers and regulators, policymakers, micro-entrepreneurs, and practitioners. For instance, this study may inform the crafting of impactful contextual policies i.e., savings-led or credit-led mobile money policies. All in all, the meaning of the use of mobile money for micro-entrepreneurs in Kenya, the emerging economy in this study, is convenience, which is operationalized into four different aspects in this paper.

In the next sections, the relevant literature will be discussed, followed by a brief discussion of the applied methods. Subsequently, the findings are presented, followed by the conclusion.

23.2 Reflections on the Literature

23.2.1 Business Financing

Mobile money could be used for financing enterprises, next to personal purposes. Business financing remains to be a key concern for not only micro-entrepreneurs but for policy makers as well. Consequently, we see a number of researchers dedicated to advance this field of business finance research. For instance, a group of researchers has focused on looking at what are the new or potential business finance actors, opportunities and challenges (Block et al., 2018; Giudici et al., 2021; Fatoki, 2014;Hamdan et al., 2022). Another group has focused on studying the effects of various business financing forms used and performance of micro-enterprises (Adusei & Adeleye, 2021; Angeles et al., 2019; Gichuki et al., 2014; Onyango et al., 2022) while other researchers studied business finance trends based on literature reviews (Abdulsaleh & Worthington, 2013; Rao et al., 2021). One of the trends in business financing of micro-enterprises is certainly mobile money, i.e., "bank in your hand" as an innovative tool cited to reduce financial exclusion (Ahmad et al., 2020).

Mobile money has been found to be one of the micro-entrepreneurs' turning points whenever they are financially constrained and cannot obtain finance from credit institutions such as regular banks (Beck et al., 2015; Casey & O'Toole, 2014; Mago & Modiba, 2022). Mixed and inconsistent reactions also exist regarding the role of mobile money in the growth of enterprises (Beck et al., 2015). That is, there is evidence that mobile money increases the availability and access to financial resources by micro-entrepreneurs. This is mainly useful because the micro-enterprise can finance production with more ease if its suppliers provide working capital or the micro-enterprise can sell more if it can alleviate the financial constraints (Ferrando & Mulier, 2013). However, mobile money can also have potential drawbacks especially when micro-entrepreneurs default or do not repay credit. Shrinkage of business financing options for micro-entrepreneurs would be the result. Therefore, mobile money use in emerging economies is a crucial matter worth more research especially concerning the meaning of mobile money for micro-entrepreneurs. We thus conduct this research and aim to contribute to emerging literature on potential and implications of mobile money.

23.2.2 Mobile Money in Emerging Economies

Mobile money is "an electronic system (stores value virtually, payment instrument and channel) that enables financial services (remittance, payments, savings, credit, and insurance) using ubiquitous mobile technology" (David-West et al., 2019, p. 277). It is also an electronic business finance option that enterprises can take advantage of to boost their business through credit facilities (Beck et al., 2015). Hence, it can be concluded that mobile money and financial inclusion are connected to each other. Yet, in emerging economies and particularly in sub-Saharan Africa, financial inclusion is noted to be lagging behind more than in other places (Allen et al., 2014; Demirgüç-Kunt & Klapper, 2012). However, given the rapidly changing technology, mobile money is viewed as a potential tool for reducing financial exclusion gaps in such emerging economies. For instance, Prashaant and Sharma (2015) assert that it is possible for *the unbanked person to be banked* through a mobile money account such as M-Pesa. This is confirmed by statistics that show the share of mobile money accounts has more than doubled between the years 2011 and 2017 in sub-Saharan Africa (Demirgüç-Kunt et al., 2018). Such increase in the share of mobile money accounts makes it even more important to conduct research on mobile money and its potential in the African context (Ahmad et al., 2020). This could add to the contextual evidence and support (Okello & Munene, 2021) that the use of mobile money services can promote convenience to financial services such as payments, savings, and withdrawals in emerging economies.

Furthermore, estimates show that the availability of mobile money increases the productivity of entrepreneurs (Beck et al., 2015). Not only is the availability of mobile money important but its convenience and use are also vital in economies with information asymmetries, credit imperfections and other risks such as stealing of micro-entrepreneurs fiat money (Beck et al., 2015; Jack & Suri, 2014). When the COVID-19 pandemic hit, mobile money enjoyed increased adoption and had a key role in keeping people connected (Demirguc-Kunt et al., 2022). It was a-safe-no-contact-way for enterprises.

One of the first successful and still growing mobile money is Kenya's M-Pesa (Heyer & Mas, 2011; Jack & Suri, 2014). M-Pesa mobile money was originally developed to be a money transfer platform that allows sending money at a low cost across distances (Demombynes & Thegeya, 2012). Over time, mobile money use has gone beyond the remittance of money and keeps on changing with technological changes. Worth noting is that ownership of a mobile phone facilitated the wide use of mobile money in Kenya, about 93% of Kenyan adults are mobile phone users (Demombynes & Thegeya, 2012). Moreover, customers or suppliers require enterprises to adopt mobile money due to convenience (Higgins et al., 2012).

Barriers noted to prevent people from using mobile money include high tariffs, inadequate access to record-keeping and payment-management interfaces, risks, and insecurities such as fraud (Coulibaly, 2021; Higgins et al., 2012). In other studies, gender was found to moderate the relationship between convenient use and the adoption of mobile payment services (Humbani & Wiese, 2018). Specifically, Humbani and Wiese (2018) found that men put more emphasis on the convenience derived from the use of mobile payments than their female counterparts did. Thus, the convenience derived affects their adoption of mobile payment services. Cultural norms are also seen to mediate the relationship between mobile money adoption and usage by micro-enterprises (Heyer & Mas, 2011; Okello & Munene, 2021). For example, where there is cultural pressure to maintain connections with one's ancestral village, mobile money remittances are stronger. Thus, in order to make mobile money ubiquitous, mobile money providers and partners need to keep an eye on mobile money cost, convenience and value-added services beyond the transactions (Heyer & Mas, 2011).

23.3 Micro-Enterprises in the Digital era

One insight about micro-enterprises in the current digital era (i.e., the period of digitalization as a result of technological development) is that most of them do not use funding from formal institutions. Micro-entrepreneurs rely more on funding from non-formal institutions, other value chain actors and mobile money loaning apps. This is because these micro-entrepreneurs often cannot prepare loan applications and/or they lack knowledge/training on financing matters. They hesitate to borrow from formal financial institutions, as the rates are high, and processing time is sometimes longer than those of the other loan providers (Prijadi et al., 2020). Technological development has enabled the emergence of innovative financial services making it possible to have business-to-business (B2B) lending, peer-to-peer lending, invoice factoring, crowdfunding, among others (Block et al., 2018).

Currently, fintech start-ups (i.e., enterprises that have built technology platforms, scoring algorithms, and online marketing strategies to enable financial services such as matching borrowers and lenders; see Desai, 2016) are raising large sums of money, which might have tremendous influence also on financing micro-entrepreneurs (Block et al., 2018). For example, Tala, a mobile money fintech start-up, also referred to as the world's local lender is one of the 2022 Top 50 CNBC disruptors and also known as the next generation of Silicon Valley (CNBC, 2022a). Tala is a common mobile money service that uses a mobile platform to provide access to loans ranging from $10 to around $500 in emerging economies such as India, Mexico, Philippines, and Kenya as well. Tala aims to address gaps in the financial system, especially regarding time spent to go to physical banking locations, money spent on transportation, and lack of credit profile to assess credit worthiness/score. How Tala works is that it uses mobile money services to create a credit profile of the mobile user by looking at their text messages, transaction costs to merchants' and other behavioural data, which is then used to create a risk profile and approve loans within the shortest time (CNBC, 2022b).

The result of such short turnaround time loans or "quickie loans" such as Tala, Fuliza,[1] and Branch loans,[2] issued via mobile money in Kenya, is the increase in digital loans as opposed to traditional loans as shown in Fig. 23.1.

Figure 23.1 shows that digital loans have been increasing overtime from 41.5% in 2014 to 91.2% in 2018; while traditional loans declined from 58.5% in 2014 to 8.8% in 2018. This depicts the importance of the use of mobile money services by micro-entrepreneurs to fill existing financing gaps. Understanding micro-entrepreneurs' perspectives of mobile money requirements in various contexts is thus vital for segmentation and mobile money design for successful entrepreneurship (Davidson & McCarty, 2011).

Digital	41.5%	60.3%	84.1%	83.0%	91.2%
Traditional	58.5%	39.7%	15.9%	17.0%	8.8%

Source: Adopted from Faux (2020)

Fig. 23.1 Share of digital loans in Kenya

[1] Fuliza is an M-Pesa service that allows you to overdraw on your M-Pesa account when you have insufficient funds to complete a transaction (Safaricom, 2022)

[2] Branch loans are digital credit offered to people by Branch fintech start-up based on their personalized smart phone data. No physical documentation is required. Loan amounts vary from 500 to 300,000 Kenyan Shilling (Branch International, 2022). This is approximately USD 4 to USD 2400.

23.4 Methods

23.4.1 Research Context: Kenya

The research context is Kenya, an emerging economy in sub-Saharan Africa. Emerging economies are defined as rapidly growing and volatile economies (Hernandez et al., 2012). Bruton et al. (2013) assert that a dominant concept in the definition of an emerging economy is evolution and change. An emerging economy is also defined as an economy with low to middle per capita income, constitutes 80 percent of the global population and represents about 20 percent of the world economies (Hernandez et al., 2012).

Kenya—one of the fastest growing economies in Africa—has experienced an annual average growth of 4.8% per year from 2015 and 2019 before COVID-19 hit the economy, disrupting many economic activities of the country (World Bank, 2022a). Kenya's population as of 2021 was 54,985,702 with a GDP per capita of USD 2006.8 (World Bank, 2022b). The population in Kenya is mostly found in Nairobi, the capital of Kenya, along lake Victoria and the shores of Indian ocean (Central Intelligence Agency, 2023).

23.4.2 Research Design, Data Collection and Analytical Procedures

This research uses a qualitative approach to offer a fine-grained and in-depth answer to the research question. Precisely, the qualitative approach, as opposed to the quantitative approach, fits the purpose and objective of this study, which is to explore what does mobile money "mean" to micro-entrepreneurs (Creswell & Poth, 2016).

Primary data were collected through semi-structured interviews with 23 experts and experienced entrepreneurs. Ten of the interviewees were females and 13 were males with most of them having at least a university bachelor's education. These experts are highly knowledgeable in the field of mobile money and micro-entrepreneurs, such as micro-finance managers, government directors and officers and experienced entrepreneurs. See Table 23.1 for the respondents' pertinent information.

Unique circumstances such as the consequences of COVID-19 led to four interviews being conducted by phone, one interview on Zoom and the other 18 done physically at respondents' workplaces. The purpose of the study was explained to the respondents before the interviews commenced. Subsequently, consent to voluntarily participate in the interviews as well as consent to do recordings were requested prior to the interviews. Lastly, the anonymity of the interviewees was assured prior to each interview. The interview guide used was developed from extensive literature reviews and in consultation with experts to gain in-depth insights into the meaning of mobile money for micro-entrepreneurs who are active in the fishing industry in

Table 23.1 Pertinent information of the respondents

Interviewee No.	Gender	Age category	Designation as given by the interviewee	Highest completed education	Interview type
1	Female	Early 40 s	Fisheries director, Kisumu County government	University (Master's degree)	Face to face
2	Male	Mid 30 s	Fisheries officer, Kisumu County government	University (Master's degree)	Face to face
3	Male	Late 30 s	Fisheries assistant officer	College diploma	Face to face
4	Male	Early 60 s	Farm Africa fisheries consultant	University (Bachelor's degree)	On phone
5	Male	Early 50 s	Business development officer, agricultural sector development support Programme (ASDSP)	University (Bachelor's degree)	Face to face
6	Male	Late 30 s	Cage farmer, entrepreneur and CEO of Aquarech company	College diploma	Face to face
7	Male	Mid 40 s	Regional manager, Kenya investment authority	University (Master's degree)	Face to face
8	Male	Early 40 s	Managing director, Lake Victoria fish limited	University (Master's degree)	Face to face
9	Male	Mid 30 s	Fisheries consultant and manager at Livingwood consultants limited, Kisumu, Kenya	University (Bachelor's degree)	Face to face
10	Male	Late 30 s	Mastercard foundation	University (Master's degree)	On phone
11	Female	Early 50 s	RAFODE microfinance operations manager	University (Bachelor's degree)	Face to face
12	Female	Mid 30 s	Rafiki microfinance relationship officer	University (Bachelor's degree)	Face to face
13	Male	Late 30 s	Faulu microfinance credit consultant	University (Bachelor's degree)	Face to face
14	Male	Early 40 s	Unitas microfinance branch corporations manager	University (Master's degree)	Face to face
15	Female	Late 20 s	Equity Bank credit monitor officer	University (Bachelor's degree)	On phone

(continued)

Table 23.1 (continued)

Interviewee No.	Gender	Age category	Designation as given by the interviewee	Highest completed education	Interview type
16	Female	Late 30 s	Musoni microfinance branch manager	University (Bachelor's degree)	On phone
17	Female	Early 40 s	ABDP Kisumu-expert	University (Master's degree)	Face to face
18	Female	Mid 40 s	CEO of the incubator nest hub	University (Master's degree)	Zoom
19	Female	Early 30 s	Experienced entrepreneur	Primary education	Face to face
20	Female	Mid 50 s	Experienced entrepreneur	Primary education	Face to face
21	Female	Early 50 s	Experienced entrepreneur	Secondary education	Face to face
22	Male	Mid 50 s	Experienced entrepreneur	College diploma	Face to face
23	Male	Late 20 s	Experienced entrepreneur	College diploma	Face to face

Kisumu, Kenya. This industry was chosen because of the overwhelming presence of micro-enterprises. The interview guide contained several questions that we divided into the following subjects: (A) a description of interviewee's professional identity; (B) sources of financing for micro-entrepreneurs; (C) the "ideal" financial arrangement and parameters, (D) other matters about financial arrangements not covered in (B) and (C); (E) trade credit; and (F) sustainability.

The qualitative data obtained from interviews were transcribed verbatim. Thereafter, transcripts were analyzed iteratively through open coding while paying attention to patterns which helped to build a comprehensive set of categories (Creswell & Poth, 2016), ultimately generating four mobile money convenience themes upon saturation. Coding herein refers to the analytical process by which data segments are categorized and later sorted into themes to develop an understanding of the underlying situation (Charmaz, 2006).

The analytical procedures entailed starting from identifying respondents' quotes and forming first-order codes, which are close to the respondents' quotes. First-order codes were then categorized into second-order codes, and subsequently, they were grouped into aggregated themes (Corbin & Strauss, 1990). Illustrative extended quotes from the analysis are shown in Table 23.2. Coding, interpretation and structuring of data were done according to the "Gioia-method" (Gioia et al., 2013).

Table 23.2 Extended quotes for convenience of mobile money for micro-entrepreneurs

Quote number	Extended quotes
(1)	"I used to engage in the transportation of fish apart from just selling them, but I got an accident while doing that. So nowadays I do not go, I order by making a phone call, pay using M-Pesa and they get transported to where I am." (interviewee 20)
(2)	"The best realistic financial arrangement to grow micro-enterprises is by the use of mobile money. This is because the banks are not easily accessible to them then, the entrepreneurs have mobile phones and use Safaricom, like the M-Pesa platform is highly effective for loan disbursement and loan repayments. It is difficult for fish vendors to come to the bank and do the banking activities given that they spend most time on the beaches and markets, but M-Pesa is very accessible to them." (interviewee 16)
(3)	"On the important financing parameters, the micro-entrepreneurs also look at the mode of payment. As I have just told you, people who use the M-Pesa platform, mostly/frequently, they do not need to come to town to get a bank. So, if you can be able to provide a more flexible way to access and repay a loan like the M-Pesa platform, they appreciate that." (interviewee 16)
(4)	"The best and sustainable way to deliver microcredits at this age, I believe we have digitization. There is mobile banking. Whereby after they have fulfilled all their requirements, they can use e-payments or digital payments or mobile payments. This can be channelled directly to their phones, and they can either pay or bank at their convenience with their phones. It is readily available to each and everyone. I believe 95% of Kenyans are using mobile money." (interviewee 14)
(5)	"We have M-Pesa nowadays and you pay your loans anywhere and get your balances anywhere while computers are monitoring. So, the tools of monitoring are well-equipped. Even Safaricom, you pay your loan, and it gives you your balance, your areas, your due date for the next instalment. So, it trickles from you, as an entrepreneur, to the institution, to the donor. You get your status, the institutions, bank, and the donor also gets their status in real-time, they do not need a report from somewhere." (interviewee 11)
(6)	"The best financial arrangement is one with the ability to have visibility of how a micro-entrepreneur has used their money. For example, they usually have a written book for tracking their money, knowing what their balance is etc. that is why M-Pesa is also used." (interviewee 18)
(7)	"If savings mobilization is done through M-Shwari [a mobile money-based platform], what if someone steals your phone? Someone can also be tempted to withdraw anytime when saving using M-Shwari because it is within your hands. An entrepreneur should go to insurance company and save. Somewhere you cannot access your savings easily." (interviewee 11)
(8)	"Savings can be best done daily through mobile transactions or something like that to the bank…. The model that we use is people having their own ways of saving without really meeting in person. So, everybody has his or her own account and everybody can save at whatever time they wish. In the evening, in the morning, or at whatever time they want because savings are done through the M-Pesa platform. So, because you have your account and the paybill number, you do not need to wait for anyone to remind you that they are supposed to save. So whatever little amount you get daily, you can be able to also save by depositing it in your account." (interviewee 16)

(continued)

Table 23.2 (continued)

Quote number	Extended quotes
(9)	"But even, with saving in banks you can withdraw anytime. The micro-entrepreneurs can be advised to take savings to insurance companies. Because for banks you can withdraw, M-Shwari you can unlock" (interviewee 11)
(10)	"Ways in which a fish seller can be given money is through cash at hand or on a Mobile and it also depends on the amount of money. For example, 50 k Kenyan shillings is not safe to give as cash, but you give them on a mobile phone. Mobile phones are preferred since the seller may fail to use the money immediately and it is more secure on the mobile phone than cash" (interviewee 19)
(11)	"Currently the micro-entrepreneurs are so much in mobile banking whereby they can borrow. Others can borrow in their groups, and then there are those who are developed and have a banking history, they can be enabled through banks. So, it depends on the category, the environment and what someone is engaged in." (interviewee 13)
(12)	"… you are supposed to calculate that instead of being given goods on credit [trade credit] then you trade, you look for your own money. If possible, you can get it from M-Shwari. A bank cannot loan you small amount like 5 k Kenyan shillings. M-Shwari can give you, you can 'Fuliza M-Pesa' and then you do your business" (interviewee 8)
(13)	"Trade credit is cheaper than bank credit because of the processes involved in accessing that bank credit. However, nowadays they have Fuliza, M-Shwari, and all those mobile loans, traders can access to pay you. But you see, the cost of repaying those loans is expensive. If some of these trade credits given to traders have zero interest. Because they take them [fish] at the same price traders are taking them. The only thing is that you rely on their trade history so you might want to extend some goodwill to the trader. So, in turn, they turn out to be cheap because the trader pays zero interest on them, as that is the way it is now. I do not know if the other aggregators charge interest on them. We do not. So, they are cheaper to the person borrowing the fish from you." (interviewee 6)
(14)	"I think the banks do understand the micro-enterprises, they just do not want to take that risk. The risk is just too much to bank on unstructured businesses, and unstructured processes, which for them is something they do not want to take as a risk. That is why up to date we still cannot get bank loans through our phones the same way we do with M-Pesa. They do not have the capacity to take up that kind of risk may be because of government policies regarding the lending, and borrowing process, and having to know the borrower in detail" (Interviewee 18)
(15)	"The best way to deliver micro-credits is through mobile money. That is the easiest right now. Whether direct, yes, because it gives them the responsibility to handle that money and choose to do what they need to do with it and then repay. What we need to improve on is to have mobile money that can deduct payments automatically when they are needed. To create discipline out of it. So, if I get 20k Kenyan Shillings from my M-Shwari, it reaches a day every time I have a certain amount of money in my M-Pesa, and it takes a piecemeal of it. So, I do not have to wait until a month elapses to pay the total amount. I know they tell you that you can repay anytime, but why not structure repayment in such a way it can deduct the lowest amount of money anytime you have some amount in M-Pesa. So mobile money works, it should be just structured in such a way that repayments are done often and not in lumpsum and top-ups to be also possible." (Interviewee 12)

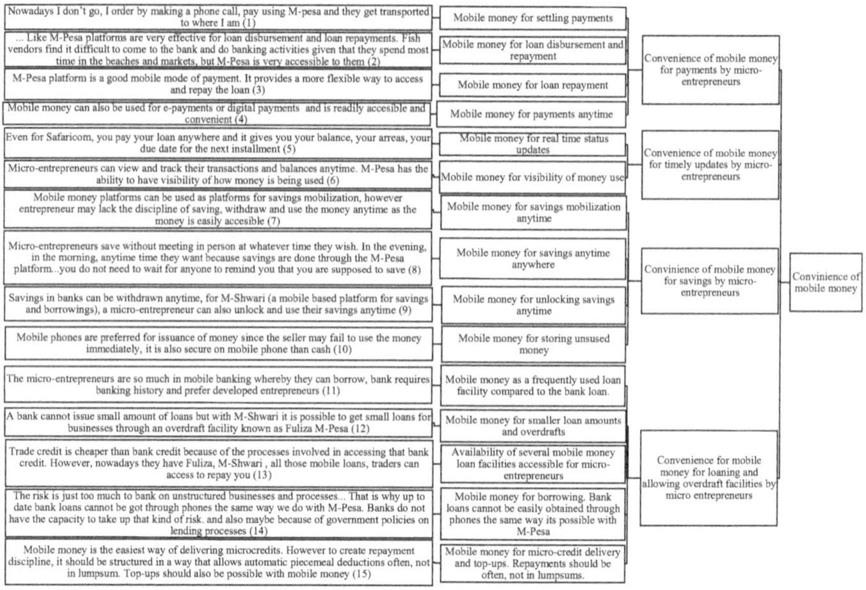

Fig. 23.2 Analyzed data structure: first order codes, second order codes, aggregated dimensions

23.5 Findings

The findings revealed four convenience aspects of the use of mobile money by micro-entrepreneurs: (1) Convenience for payments, (2) Convenience for timely updates, (3) Convenience for savings; and (4) Convenience for loaning and allowing overdraft facilities. These four themes are also shown in Fig. 23.2.

23.5.1 Convenience for Payments

The first aspect of mobile money to micro-entrepreneurs is its convenience for payments. The type of mobile money payments are noted to vary from making payments to suppliers for restocking their businesses or even loan repayments as illustrated by the following quotes:

> Nowadays I don't go, I order by making a phone call, pay using M-Pesa and they get transported to where I am. (Interviewee 20)

> The best realistic financial arrangement to grow micro-enterprises is by the use of mobile money. The banks are not easily accessible to fish vendors, it is difficult for them to come to the bank and do the banking activities given that they spend most time on the beaches and markets, but M-Pesa is very accessible to them. They have mobile phones with M-Pesa platform which is very effective for loan repayments.... (Interviewee 16)

The findings are in line with Higgins et al. (2012) that payments and transactional needs of micro-entrepreneurs are not met by banks. In addition, the convenience of mobile money payments anytime anywhere supports other study results such as for Heyer and Mas (2011) who described the mobile money phenomenon in terms of coverage, simply being able to use mobile money anytime, wherever one happens to be and to send money to anyone, anywhere. The payment convenience anywhere anytime by mobile money users is extremely useful for micro-entrepreneurs as they can now use mobile money beyond the original remittance use.

23.5.2 *Convenience for Timely Updates*

The second theme that emerged from the data analysis was the convenience of mobile money for real time status updates. It was noted that micro-entrepreneurs preferred mobile money due to its convenience in getting frequent and timely updates with regard to their flow of money, loan status and balances. One respondent said:

> The best financial arrangement for micro-entrepreneurs is the one with the ability to have visibility of how money is used. For example, most micro-entrepreneurs usually have a written book for tracking their money… to know what their balance is. It is for this reason that nowadays they prefer and use M-Pesa so much. Viewing and tracking transactions and balances is anytime. (Interviewee 14)

The following response was also given;

> Let us consider the money they borrow within the groups. They usually have a book where one person writes very quickly, this is how much you saved, this is how much you have as a loan, how much you can take as a loan, and how much you can be repaying. At a very quick glance. They quickly check the book and say I have sold this here is my money. You know, and that is it. Same with M-shwari, very quickly they check what is their balance, and how much one is supposed to pay then pay through their M-Pesa number. That is why it is easier for micro-entrepreneurs to use M-Pesa but have still not been able to get a hold of how to use the M-Pesa for business app itself. They don't want all those troubles of separating funds... They just want to be able to work with their own simple M-Pesa, get all the details they need, and pay immediately they get money. They don't have to go and look somewhere as they have their phones and can use them to check on all their balances. (Interviewee 18)

Another respondent also said:

> We have M-Pesa nowadays, you pay your loans anywhere and get your balances anywhere and we have well-equipped monitoring tools. Even Safaricom,[3] you pay your loan and it gives you your balance, your arrears, your due date for the next instalment. So, the status timely updates trickles from you, as an entrepreneur, to the institution, to the donor. You get

[3] Safaricom is one of the telecommunication companies or mobile network operators in Kenya. Safaricom offers mobile telephony, mobile money transfer, consumer electronics, e-commerce, cloud computing, data, music streaming, and fibre optic services. It is the mobile operator behind M-Pesa. More about Safaricom can be found at https://www.safaricom.co.ke/.

> your status, the institutions, bank, and the donor also gets their status real-time, they do not need to wait for a report from somewhere. (Interviewee 11)

These real-time updates are critical in entrepreneurship as micro-entrepreneurs will be able to take advantage of any forthcoming opportunities in a timely manner. Additionally, the convenience of mobile money for real-time status updates may enable tracking of expense and loan details for proper planning and money management practices by micro-entrepreneurs. Most micro-entrepreneurs are not well versed in bookkeeping skills thus the potential of mobile money for real-time updates use is very handy for them.

23.5.3 Convenience for Savings

The third emergent mobile money theme was its convenience for micro-savings purposes. Selected illustrative quotes from respondents include:

> The model that we use is in such a way that it enables having own ways of saving without really meeting in person as everybody has his or her own account and can save at whatever time they wish. In the evening, in the morning, at whatever time they want because savings are done through M-Pesa platform...you do not need to wait for anyone to remind you that you are supposed to save. (Interviewee 16)

> Ways in which a fish seller can be given money is through cash at hand or on a mobile and it also depends on the amount of money. For example, KSh 50k, sometimes you cannot give cash at hand, but you give it to micro-entrepreneurs on a mobile phone. Mobile phones are preferred since the seller may fail to use the money immediately and it is more secure on a mobile phone than cash. (Interviewee 19)

Such statements and micro-savings findings agree with the fact that micro-entrepreneurs could be encouraged to accumulate more savings through simple technologies like "commitment" mobile money savings accounts (Dupas & Robinson, 2013). In Kenya, M-Shwari[4] and M-Kesho[5] are good examples of mobile money accounts linked to M-Pesa and used for saving any amount of money anytime. Worth highlighting also is that low risks and ease of mobile money use have been cited as the greatest reasons for saving through M-Pesa as opposed to traditional repositories. This finding also builds on other studies which show that it is possible to convert cash into e-money for secure overnight storage, a phenomenon

[4] M-Shwari is a savings and loan service mobile-based platform that enables M-Pesa users to save and access credit (Safaricom, 2022).

[5] M-Kesho is a full savings account issued by Equity Bank in Kenya and is fully integrated into the M-Pesa user interface on customers' mobile phones, and is also accessible through Equity Bank's own mobile banking service. Like M-Pesa accounts, M-Kesho accounts have no account opening fees, minimum balances or monthly charges. But unlike M-Pesa accounts, M-Kesho accounts pay interest, do not have a limit on account balances, and are linked to limited emergency credit and insurance facilities (Safaricom, 2022).

termed as secure transport of cash or "self-transport" (Eijkman et al., 2010; Demombynes & Thegeya, 2012).

23.5.4 *Convenience for Loaning and Allowing Overdraft Facilities*

The last emergent theme from the analysis established an interesting convenience of mobile money use, which is, for loaning and overdraft facilities by micro-entrepreneurs. For instance, the responses below were said:

> Currently the micro-entrepreneurs are so much in mobile banking whereby they can easily borrow. The bank requires banking history and prefers developed entrepreneurs. (Interviewee 13)

> I calculate that instead of being given goods on trade credit I look for money. If possible, I get a loan from M-Shwari. Normally, a bank cannot loan you a small amount like KSh 5k but M-Shwari can give you, you can also Fuliza M-Pesa and then you do your business… (Interviewee 8)

Our findings contribute to other studies that micro-entrepreneurs rarely do have opportunities to get loans from banks and other financial providers who require collateral and good credit scores (Beck et al., 2015; Ghimire & Abo, 2013). This leaves the micro-entrepreneurs relying on other business financing options such as mobile money, which do not have a lot of borrowing requirements (Okello & Munene, 2021). As such, micro-entrepreneurs currently prefer to borrow in the form of mobile money since they can take several credits and even overdraft facilities, "quickie loans" at any time for their convenience. Islam et al. (2018) found that the use of mobile phone financial services leads to liquidity increase, reduced transaction costs, and improved credit worthiness which is associated with the positive relationship between mobile money use and micro-enterprises purchase of fixed assets. Therefore, in addition to Okello and Munene (2021), our findings show that indeed the use of mobile money services can promote convenience to financial services such as payments, savings, withdrawals and loans in emerging economies.

23.6 Conclusion

Reiterating the RQ, our findings show that mobile money means convenience to micro-entrepreneurs. In sum, mobile money equals (1) convenience for payments, (2) convenience for timely updates, (3) convenience for savings, and (4) convenience for loaning and allowing overdraft facilities.

This paper sheds new light on the user-friendliness of mobile money. Moreover, the findings contribute to literature on the nexus between mobile money and entrepreneurship as also evident from other studies (Higgins et al., 2012; Koomson et al.,

2022; Islam et al., 2018; Okello & Munene, 2021; Ramayah et al., 2017). Specifically, this study boosts the understanding of mobile money convenience construct by operationalizing convenience into the four abovementioned aspects, hence the theoretical contribution of this paper.

The practical implications are novel insights for finance providers, regulators, policymakers, and micro-entrepreneurs. Specifically, tailored products that enhance micro-entrepreneurs' mobile money savings, mobile money micro-insurance, and other enhanced overdraft facilities can be further developed (Dupas & Robinson, 2013; Koomson et al., 2022; Tengeh & Talom, 2020). This study also contributes to insights that could allow further development of transaction-based business models that are data driven and useful for the growth and development of micro-enterprises.

Notwithstanding the contributions and practical implications of this research, this study has its limitations. This research was purely qualitative, done in one emerging economy (Kenya) and in the Kisumu region only. The study also focused on only one sector (the fishing sector) which may limit the generalization of these mobile money convenience findings for other contexts. These limitations, however, also provide opportunities for future research. We recommend studying the use of mobile money by micro-entrepreneurs in different sectors of the economy as well as other regional contexts, both within and outside Africa. Such studies can be used for cross-context comparison purposes and enable replication of best practices. In addition, we recommend doing a mix of both qualitative and quantitative methods to assess a comprehensive understanding of the use of mobile money by micro-entrepreneurs, including advantages and disadvantages (Molina-Azorín et al., 2012). Lastly, issues relating to violation of private data of mobile money users—especially from those who take loans—are also not thoroughly studied and, henceforth, recommended for future research as well.

References

Abdulsaleh, A. M., & Worthington, A. C. (2013). Small and medium-sized enterprises financing: A review of literature. *International Journal of Business and Management, 8*(14), 36–54. https://doi.org/10.5539/ijbm.v8n14p36

Adusei, M., & Adeleye, N. (2021). Start-up microenterprise financing and financial performance of microfinance institutions. *Journal of Small Business & Entrepreneurship*, 1–24. https://doi.org/10.1080/08276331.2020.1842047

Ahmad, A. H., Green, C., & Jiang, F. (2020). Mobile money, financial inclusion and development: A review with reference to African experience. *Journal of Economic Surveys, 34*(4), 753–792. https://doi.org/10.1111/joes.12372

Allen, F., Carletti, E., Cull, R., Qian, J. Q., Senbet, L., & Valenzuela, P. (2014). The African financial development and financial inclusion gaps. *Journal of African Economies, 23*(5), 614–642. https://doi.org/10.1093/jae/eju015

Angeles, I. T., Calara, M. S., & de Guzman, A. B. (2019). The mediating effect of microfinancing on access to finance and growth of microenterprises: Evidence from The Philippines. *Journal of Global Entrepreneurship Research, 9*(1), 1–16. https://doi.org/10.1186/s40497-019-0150-x

Awanis, A., Lowe, C., Andersson-Manjang, S. K., & Lindsey, D. (2022). State of the industry report on mobile money 2021. GSMA. https://www.gsma.com/sotir/wp-content/uploads/2022/03/GSMA_State_of_the_Industry_2022_English.pdf.

Beck, T., Pamuk, H., Ramrattan, R., & Uras, B. (2015, April 2). *Mobile money, trade credit and economic development: Theory and evidence*. (CentER Discussion Paper; Vol. 2015-023). Center for Economic Research. https://pure.uvt.nl/ws/portalfiles/portal/5712274/2015_023.pdf

Block, J. H., Colombo, M. G., Cumming, D. J., & Vismara, S. (2018). New players in entrepreneurial finance and why they are there. *Small Business Economics, 50*(2), 239–250. https://doi.org/10.1007/s11187-016-9826-6

Branch International. (2022). *Money at the speed of life*. https://branch.co/how-it-works

Bruton, G. D., Filatotchev, I., Si, S., & Wright, M. (2013). Entrepreneurship and strategy in emerging economies. *Strategic Entrepreneurship Journal, 7*(3), 169–180. https://doi.org/10.1002/sej.1159

Casey, E., & O'Toole, C. M. (2014). Bank lending constraints, trade credit and alternative financing during the financial crisis: Evidence from European SMEs. *Journal of Corporate Finance, 27*, 173–193. https://doi.org/10.1016/j.jcorpfin.2014.05.001

Central Intelligence Agency. (2023). *Kenya*. https://www.cia.gov/the-world-factbook/countries/kenya/

Charmaz, K. (2006). *Constructing grounded theory: A practical guide through qualitative analysis*. Sage.

CNBC. (2022a). *The 2022 CNBC disruptor 50 list: Meet the next generation of Silicon Valley*. CNBC. https://www.cnbc.com/2022/05/17/these-are-the-2022-cnbc-disruptor-50-companies.html

CNBC. (2022b, May 17). *CNBC disruptor 50*. CNBC. https://www.cnbc.com/2022/05/17/tala-disruptor-50.html

Corbin, J. M., & Strauss, A. (1990). Grounded theory research: Procedures, canons, and evaluative criteria. *Qualitative Sociology, 13*(1), 3–21. https://doi.org/10.1007/bf00988593

Coulibaly, S. S. (2021). A study of the factors affecting mobile money penetration rates in the West African economic and monetary union (WAEMU) compared with East Africa. *Financial Innovations, 7*(1). https://doi.org/10.1186/s40854-021-00238-0

Creswell, J. W., & Poth, C. N. (2016). *Qualitative inquiry and research design: Choosing among five approaches*. Sage publications.

Davidson, N., & McCarty, Y. (2011). *Driving customer usage of mobile money for the unbanked*. http://gsma.com/mobilefordevelopment/wp-content/uploads/2012/03/drivingcustomerusagefinallowres.pdf.

David-West, O., Iheanachor, N., & Umukoro, I. O. (2019). Mobile money as a frugal innovation for the bottom of the pyramid – Cases of selected African countries. *Africa Journal of Management, 5*(3), 274–302. https://doi.org/10.1080/23322373.2019.1652023

Demirgüç-Kunt, A., & Klapper, L. F. (2012). *Financial inclusion in Africa: An overview*. World Bank policy research working paper no.6088. https://doi.org/10.1596/1813-9450-6088.

Demirgüç-Kunt, A., Klapper, L., Singer, D., & Ansar, S. (2018). *The global findex database 2017: Measuring financial inclusion and the fintech revolution*. https://doi.org/10.1596/978-1-4648-1259-0

Demirguc-Kunt, A., Klapper, L., Singer, D., & Ansar, S. (2022). *The global findex database 2021: Financial inclusion, digital payments, and resilience in the age of COVID-19*. https://doi.org/10.1596/978-1-4648-1897-4.

Demombynes, G., & Thegeya, A. (2012). *Kenya's mobile revolution and the promise of mobile savings*. World Bank policy research working paper No. 5988. https://doi.org/10.1596/1813-9450-5988

Desai, F. (2016). *An inside look at fintech marketplace lenders*. https://www.forbes.com/sites/falgunidesai/2016/02/27/an-inside-look-at-fintech-marketplace-lenders/?sh=39a4481fae73

Donovan, K. (2012). Mobile money for financial inclusion. In World Bank (Ed.), *Information and communications for development 2012: Maximizing mobile* (pp. 61–73). https://doi.org/10.1596/9780821389911_ch04
Dupas, P., & Robinson, J. (2013). Why don't the poor save more? Evidence from health savings experiments. *American Economic Review, 103*(4), 1138–1171. https://doi.org/10.1257/aer.103.4.1138
Eijkman, F., Kendall, J., & Mas, I. (2010). Bridges to cash: The retail end of M-Pesa. *Savings and Development, 34*(2), 219–252.
Fatoki, O. (2014). The financing options for new small and medium enterprises in South Africa. *Mediterranean Journal of Social Sciences, 5*(20), 748–755. https://doi.org/10.5901/mjss.2014.v5n20p748
Ferrando, A., & Mulier, K. (2013). Do firms use the trade credit channel to manage growth? *Journal of Banking & Finance, 37*(8), 3035–3046. https://doi.org/10.1016/j.jbankfin.2013.02.013
Ghimire, B., & Abo, R. (2013). An empirical investigation of Ivorian SMEs access to bank finance: Constraining factors at demand-level. *Journal of Finance and Investment Analysis, 2*(4), 29–55.
Gichuki, C. N., Mulu-Mutuku, M., & Kinuthia, L. N. (2014). Performance of women owned enterprises accessing credit from village credit and savings associations in Kenya. *Journal of Global Entrepreneurship Research, 4*(1), 1–13. https://doi.org/10.1186/s40497-014-0016-1
Gioia, D. A., Corley, K. G., & Hamilton, A. L. (2013). Seeking qualitative rigor in inductive research: Notes on the Gioia methodology. *Organizational Research Methods, 16*(1), 15–31. https://doi.org/10.1177/1094428112452151
Giudici, G., Sannajust, A., & Van Auken, H. E. (2021). Special issue on small business financing: New actors, new opportunities, new challenges. *Journal of Small Business Management, 59*(2), 219–222. https://doi.org/10.1080/00472778.2020.1865540
Gosavi, A. (2018). Can mobile money help firms mitigate the problem of access to finance in eastern sub-Saharan Africa? *Journal of African Business, 19*(3), 343–360. https://doi.org/10.1080/15228916.2017.1396791
Hamdan, J. S., Lehmann-Uschner, K., & Menkhoff, L. (2022). Mobile money, financial inclusion, and unmet opportunities: Evidence from Uganda. *The Journal of Development Studies, 58*(4), 671–691. https://doi.org/10.1080/00220388.2021.1988078
Hernandez, A. M. L., Bolivar, M. P. R., & Munoz, L. A. (2012). Analyzing e-government research in emerging economies: Contextualization and opportunities. In K. J. Bwalya & S. Zulu (Eds.), *Handbook of research on e-government in emerging economies: Adoption, e-participation, and legal frameworks* (pp. 641–663). IGI Global. https://doi.org/10.4018/978-1-4666-0324-0.ch033
Heyer, A., & Mas, I. (2011). Fertile grounds for mobile money: Towards a framework for analysing enabling environments. *Enterprise Development & Microfinance, 22*(1), 30–44. https://doi.org/10.3362/1755-1986.2011.005
Higgins, D., Kendall, J., & Lyon, B. (2012). Mobile money usage patterns of Kenyan small and medium enterprises. *Innovations: Technology, Governance, Globalization, 7*(2), 67–81. https://doi-org.vu-nl.idm.oclc.org/10.1162/INOV_a_00129
Hughes, N., & Lonie, S. (2007). M-PESA: Mobile money for the "unbanked" turning cellphones into 24-hour tellers in Kenya. *Innovations: Technology, Governance, Globalization, 2*(1–2), 63–81. https://doi.org/10.1162/itgg.2007.2.1-2.63
Humbani, M., & Wiese, M. (2018). A cashless society for all: Determining consumers' readiness to adopt mobile payment services. *Journal of African Business, 19*(3), 409–429. https://doi.org/10.1080/15228916.2017.1396792
Islam, A., Muzi, S., & Meza, J. L. R. (2018). Does mobile money use increase firms' investment? Evidence from enterprise surveys in Kenya, Uganda, and Tanzania. *Small Business Economics, 51*(3), 687–708. https://doi.org/10.1007/s11187-017-9951-x
Jack, W., & Suri, T. (2014). Risk sharing and transactions costs: Evidence from Kenya's mobile money revolution. *American Economic Review, 104*(1), 183–223. https://doi.org/10.1257/aer.104.1.183

Koomson, I., Martey, E., & Etwire, P. M. (2022). Mobile money and entrepreneurship in East Africa: The mediating roles of digital savings and access to digital credit. *Information Technology & People*. Ahead of print. https://doi.org/10.1108/itp-11-2021-0906

Lorenz, E., & Pommet, S. (2021). Mobile money, inclusive finance and enterprise innovativeness: An analysis of east African nations. *Industry and Innovation, 28*(2), 136–159. https://doi.org/10.1080/13662716.2020.1774867

Mago, S., & Modiba, F. S. (2022). Does informal finance matter for micro and small businesses in Africa? *Small Business International Review, 6*(1), 10.26784/sbir.v6i1.415.

Molina-Azorín, J. F., López-Gamero, M. D., Pereira-Moliner, J., & Pertusa-Ortega, E. M. (2012). Mixed methods studies in entrepreneurship research: Applications and contributions. *Entrepreneurship & Regional Development, 24*(5–6), 425–456. https://doi.org/10.1080/08985626.2011.603363

Njoroge, P., & Murinde, V. (Eds.). (2021). *50 years of central banking in Kenya: Regional and global perspectives*. Oxford University Press.

Okello, G. C. B., & Munene, J. C. (2021). Analyzing the relationship between mobile money adoption and usage and financial inclusion of MSMEs in developing countries: Mediating role of cultural norms in Uganda. *Journal of African Business, 22*(1), 1–20. https://doi.org/10.1080/15228916.2019.1695189

Onyango, R. A., Eijdenberg, E. L., Masurel, E., & Obange, N. (2022). Business-financing options' effects on micro-enterprise performance in the tropics: The case of Kisumu County, Kenya. In J. Wood, T. Chaiechi, & K. Thirumaran (Eds.), *Routledge advances in business, industry and trade in the tropics. Business, industry and trade in the tropics* (pp. 1–19). Routledge. https://doi.org/10.4324/9781003153580-1

Prashaant, A., & Sharma, N. (2015). Vodafone's M-Pesa-A mobile wallet revolution. *FIIB Business Review, 4*(2), 26–29. https://doi.org/10.1177/2455265820150204

Prijadi, R., Wulandari, P., Desiana, P. M., Pinagara, F. A., & Novita, M. (2020). Financing needs of micro-enterprises along their evolution. *International Journal of Ethics and Systems, 36*(2), 263–284. https://doi.org/10.1108/IJOES-05-2018-0071

Ramayah, T., Lian, L. S., Rahman, S. A., & Taghizadeh, S. K. (2017). Modelling mobile money adoption: A Malaysian perspective. *International Journal of Mobile Communications, 15*(5), 491–513. https://doi.org/10.1504/IJMC.2017.086365

Rao, P., Kumar, S., Chavan, M., & Lim, W. M. (2021). A systematic literature review on SME financing: Trends and future directions. *Journal of Small Business Management, 1-31.* https://doi.org/10.1080/00472778.2021.1955123

Safaricom. (2022). *Fuliza*. https://www.safaricom.co.ke/personal/m-pesa/credit-and-savings/fuliza

Talom, F. S. G., & Tengeh, R. K. (2019). The impact of mobile money on the financial performance of the SMEs in Douala, Cameroon. *Sustainability, 12*(1), 183. https://doi.org/10.3390/su12010183

Tengeh, R. K., & Talom, F. G. S. (2020). Mobile money as a sustainable alternative for SMEs in less developed financial markets. *Journal of Open Innovation: Technology, Market, and Complexity, 6*(4), 163. https://doi.org/10.3390/joitmc6040163

World Bank. (2022a). *Overview:* Kenya.. https://www.worldbank.org/en/country/kenya/overview

World Bank. (2022b). *Population, total – Kenya | Data*. https://data.worldbank.org/indicator/SP.POP.TOTL?locations=KE

Chapter 24
Evaluating Financial Literacy Among Working Women in Pune: A Gender-Sensitive Approach

Vineeta Agrawal and Manisha Agarwal

Abstract Financial literacy among women in India has been a topic of concern for many years, given the gender gap in financial inclusion and the lack of access to financial services for women. In present study, authors have presented an association of financial knowledge, financial behaviour, financial attitude, need for financial training and demographic factors towards the financial literacy level among working women in Pune, India. The sample size of 105 working women has been incorporated for the research. A structured questionnaire designed on a 5-point Likert scale has been used based on convenience and snowball sampling. The result of the analysis revealed that even if the women are earning well, this does not translate into them being financial decision makers. It was also found that financial knowledge does not reflect into any improvement in their financial attitude.

Keywords Financial literacy · Financial knowledge · Financial attitude · Financial inclusion · Financial decision-making

24.1 Introduction

Women constitute around 49.58% of the world's population and around 48.04% of India's total population in 2020 (The World Bank Data, 2022). Though the women population in India contributes about 48% of the total population, their contribution to overall economic growth is not at par with the global average (Jha & Nagar, 2015). Gender inequality is the most prevalent in India. According to the United Nations Development Program (2022), India ranks 122 out of 191 countries on the

V. Agrawal (✉)
Lexicon Management Institute of Leadership and Excellence, Pune, India
e-mail: vineeta.agarwal@mile.education

M. Agarwal
School of Business, James Cook University, Singapore, Singapore
e-mail: manisha.agarwal@jcu.edu.au

E. L. Eijdenberg et al. (eds.), *Innovation-Driven Business and Sustainability in the Tropics*, https://doi.org/10.1007/978-981-99-2909-2_24

gender inequality index. Men dominate societal and family life in India. This has been the case in the past ages and continues to be practiced in most households. Though this mindset is changing with urbanization and education, there is still a long way to permanently change the scenario (GlobalData, 2022).

Since 2010, India has a good female literacy rate. In 2010, the female literacy rate was 80.35%. In 2021, the rate was 91.95%. This is above many developing nations and worldwide average of 83% (Statista, 2022). It is surprising that the high rate of literacy does not reflect in other indicators related to women development (India Briefing, 2022). India's female labor force participation rate (LFPR) is on a downward track. As per World Bank estimates, the female labor participation rate in India fell to 20.3 percent in 2019. This is much lower, when compared with the world average of 47% (International Labour Organization, 2022). Women are also more likely to work in informal employment and in vulnerable, low-paid or undervalued jobs. To make matters worse, the COVID-19 crisis caused unprecedented job losses, hitting women the hardest, further widening gender gaps. The participation of women in economic activity is very crucial for the inclusive growth of any developing country (Rawat, 2014; Chadda & Deb, 2013).

The existing gender gap and discrimination against women hit them financially. Women are not performing well in taking right financial decisions (Devi, 2016). Historically, low financial literacy has had a significantly greater impact on women than men (Lusardi & Mitchell, 2008). The OECD (2013) define "Financial literacy is a combination awareness, knowledge, skill, attitude and behaviour of individual that are required to make good financial decision and to achieve individual financial wellbeing." The lack of financial literacy impacts the ability of an individual to attain long-term objectives e.g., daily money management, pension, and financing (Ergün, 2018).

Women can be truly independent when they are financially independent (Srivastava, 2020). Having access over finance and financial matters helps in uplifting the status of women (Agarwal, 2021). Research shows that control over their own resources will translate into enhancing women's participation in decision making processes, developing self-worth and positively augmenting their status in the family, community and society (Klapper et al., 2016). Access to bank accounts, loans, insurance, and other financial services, result in direct improvements in outcomes of health, education, and employment. In turn, such progress helps achieve collective goals of eradicating poverty, promoting inclusive growth, and reducing inequality (Robino et al., 2018).

Financial inclusion and financial literacy are closely related concepts, as financial literacy is seen as a key driver of financial inclusion. Financial literacy is an effective means to close the gap between men and women's knowledge and confidence about managing finances (Goldsmith & Goldsmith, 2006). D'Silva et al. (2018) explore the current state of financial literacy and the factors that affecting their financial literacy levels though most of females do possess some sorts of investments, but they are still financially illiterate. Singh and Kumar (2017) in their study advanced the debate on women empowerment of women ghettoes through financial inclusion schemes of the government of India. The study identifies the substantial need for the development of formal financial system that may enhance the scale of financial inclusion.

There have been many studies in the past to measure the levels of financial literacy among women in India. It has been observed that there are minimum difference in financial involvement for urban and rural women. For urban women banking facilities are physically very near to them, but they are resistant to take part in these services and consider this as men's work. In case of rural women, it is also a constraint because rural areas lack the banking facility availability everywhere and sometimes women are not given freedom to manage their finances (Agarwalla et al., 2015; Baluja, 2016; Singh & Kumar, 2017).

Financial literacy is a complex construct that comprises several factors or components. A definition that properly covers this idea is proposed by the Organisation for Economic Co-Operation and Development (OECD, 2005) where financial literacy is regarded as a combination of awareness, knowledge, skill, attitude, and behavior needed to make sound financial decisions and ultimately achieve individual financial well-being (Delavande et al., 2008). Acquiring financial knowledge is a type of human capital that involves learning about managing income, expenses, and savings throughout one's lifetime (OECD, 2013). Financial behavior is the most important aspect of financial literacy, and positive financial behavior, such as planning expenses and building financial security and it can improve overall financial well-being. Conversely, negative behaviors such as overusing credit can harm financial well-being (Atkinson & Messy, 2012). A person's financial attitudes are shaped by their economic and non-economic beliefs, and they play a crucial role in personal decision-making. Past researchers concluded that there is a link between financial attitudes and financial literacy among youth (Grable & Lytton, 1998; Joo & Grable, 2004; Kasman et al., 2018). Financial satisfaction is related, both directly and indirectly, with diverse factors including financial behaviors, financial stress levels, income, financial knowledge, financial solvency, risk tolerance, and education. Findings support the continued and increased use of targeted education initiatives directed at improving the financial literacy and behavior of family and consumer economics constituencies (D'Silva et al., 2018).

The previous studies have indicated that occupation, income, educational qualification and marital status have a significant positive impact on the financial literacy level of unorganized sector working and youth population of India (Jana et al., 2019; Bharucha, 2019). Financial education programs can increase financial knowledge and improve financial behavior. Lusardi and Mitchell (2014) suggested that the effectiveness of financial education programs is influenced by the content and delivery of the program, as well as the individual's level of engagement and motivation. In a systematic review of financial education programs, Chen and Volpe (1998) found that financial education programs can be effective in improving financial knowledge, behavior, and attitudes. The authors also found that the effectiveness of financial education programs was influenced by the age and educational level of the participants, as well as the type of program and its delivery method.

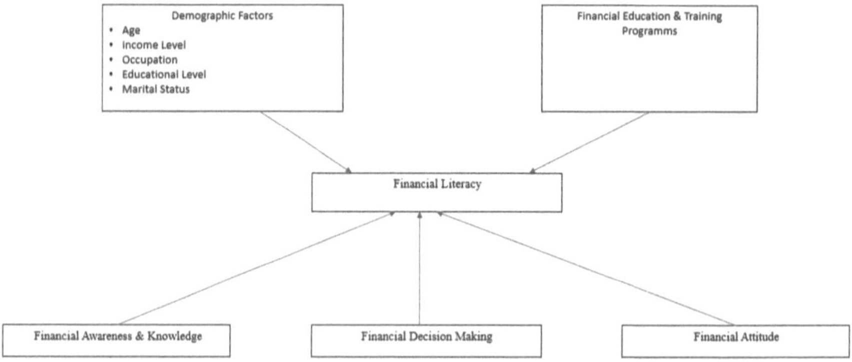

Source- Drawn by author

Fig. 24.1 Factors influencing financial literacy. (Source – Drawn by author)

In a similar context, two studies examined the effectiveness of a financial literacy training program (Kaiser & Menkhoff, 2020; Mandell & Klein, 2007). The studies found that the training program significantly increased financial literacy, as well as financial confidence and savings behaviour. The authors suggested that financial education programs should be integrated into the school curriculum to ensure that all students have access to financial education.

Overall, the research suggests that financial training programs and seminars can be effective in increasing financial literacy, improving financial decision-making, and promoting positive financial behavior. Based on the extensive literature review, the authors have proposed their own model for measuring the financial literacy of women (please see Fig. 24.1). This has been duly incorporated while framing the objectives and questionnaire for the study. The objectives of the study as presented in the next section.

24.1.1 Objectives

1. to examine the relationship among key financial variables such as overall financial awareness and knowledge, financial decision making and financial attitude among working women
2. to examine if the income level and overall financial awareness and knowledge affect the financial decision making among working women
3. to examine if the income level and overall financial awareness and knowledge affect the actual financial attitude (such as investment and budgeting) among working women.
4. to evaluate the requirement of decent information and training programs concentrating on the importance of personal finance.

24.2 Method

24.2.1 *Sample*

Working women in Pune, Maharashtra were requested to be a part of the survey. The convenience sampling combined with the snowball sampling technique was used to select a sample of 103 women in the service along with the women who are entrepreneurs from the population of working women from the different sectors in Pune (Maharashtra).

24.2.2 *Procedure*

The study first obtained ethical clearance from the academic department of Lexicon Management Institute of Leadership and Excellence. Primary data was the preeminent source of data collected through a structured questionnaire that was distributed among working women in Pune (Maharashtra, India). The questionnaire contained demographic, five-point Likert scale questions related to the objects of the study, incorporating various parameters that were framed to understand the financial literacy level of women in Pune.

24.2.3 *Data Analysis*

Data were analyzed with SPSS Version 27.0. For understanding and evaluating the significant factors impacting financial literacy and quality of life of working women, an appropriate statistical tool of mean, standard deviation, and Pearson correlation coefficient (r) and univariate analysis of variance was applied. A two-tailed $p < .05$ was considered statistically significant.

24.3 Results

For testing the internal consistency of the constructs, Cronbach's alpha was calculated. Cronbach's alpha for the study was 0.98. Cronbach's alpha above 0.6 is considered reliable and acceptable. Hence, the data collected from the study population is acceptable, highly reliable, and consistent as per the test conducted. Table 24.1 shows the socio-demographic profile of the respondents.

As per the results of the surveyed data, respondents are quite young and they might have joined the jobs as 72% of the respondents belong to the age-group of 20 years to 30 years. The same trend is reflected in the income levels as more than 50% of the respondents have shown low income levels. While 48% have an income level of more than Rs. 4,00,000. In terms of educational qualifications most of them have either a graduate or a Post graduate degree. Most of the working women are in service (66%). 19% are currently unemployed, which may be due to pandemic or family-related responsibilities. The next section presents the analysis of results by each objective of the study.

24.3.1 Objective 1: Relationship Among Key Financial Variables

The results obtained through data analysis indicate that financial awareness and knowledge has a significant and moderate level of positive correlation with financial decision making which is 0.595. Therefore, it can be interpreted that financial awareness of women is helping them to make financial decisions. As per the data the correlation values of financial awareness and knowledge and financial decision making with financial attitude has displayed a significant positive correlation i.e., .316 and .251 (see Table 24.1). The correlation though significant is rather low and this further indicates that even if the women if financially aware it does not translate into her showing financial attitude in the household matters (Table 24.2).

Table 24.1 Socio demographic profile of respondents

Socio – demographic profile		Frequency	Percentage
Age	20–30	74	72%
	30–40	23	22%
	40 years and above	6	6%
	Total	103	100%
Income level (Rs.)	Below Rs. 2,00,000	33	32%
	Rs. 2,00,000 to Rs. 4,00,000	19	18%
	Rs. 4,00,000 to Rs. 6,00,000	26	25%
	Above than Rs. 6,00,000	25	24%
	Total	103	100%
Educational Level	Senior Secondary	3	3%
	Graduation	49	48%
	Post – Graduation	50	49%
	Doctorate	1	1%
	Total	103	100%
Marital Status	Single	68	66%
	Married	35	34%
	Total	103	100%
Occupation	Not working	20	19%
	Self – Employed	9	9%
	Service	68	66%
	Business	6	6%
	Total	103	100%

Table 24.2 Correlations analysis of financial awareness and knowledge, financial decision making and financial attitude

Correlations				
		Financial awareness and knowledge	Financial decision making	Financial attitude
Financial awareness and knowledge	Pearson Correlation	–		
	N	92		
Financial decision making	Pearson Correlation	.595[a]	–	
	Sig. (2-tailed)	.000		
	N	86	94	
Financial attitude	Pearson Correlation	.316[a]	.251[b]	–
	Sig. (2-tailed)	.003	.017	
	N	86	90	99

[a]Correlation is significant at the 0.01 level (2-tailed)
[b]Correlation is significant at the 0.05 level (2-tailed)

Table 24.3 The univariate statistics for income level and overall financial knowledge and awareness affecting financial decision making and financial attitude

Univariate *F statistics*		
	Financial decision Making *F (df)*	Financial attitude *F (df)*
Income Level	0.054 (1,79) ns	61.67** (1,79)
Overall financial knowledge and awareness	28.37** (1, 79)	15.43** (1,79)

** p < .001, ns: non-significant

24.3.2 *Objective 2: Role of Income Level and Overall Financial Awareness and Knowledge in Affecting Financial Decision Making*

To achieve this objective, the income level of the respondents was coded into two categories of high (above 400,000) and low income (below 400,000). Overall financial awareness and knowledge variable was calculated after adding the data values in response to questions regarding financial awareness and financial knowledge. A median split method was applied to divide the groups in terms of their high or low financial literacy.

A univariate analysis of variance was conducted to find the differences. There was a significant effect of overall financial awareness and knowledge on financial decision-making $F\,(1, 79) = 28.37$, $p<.01$, partial eta squared = .26 indicating those women with higher financial awareness and knowledge had greater participation in financial decision making. However, there was no significant effect of income level on financial decision-making $p>.05$ (please see Table 24.3). This suggests that overall financial knowledge and awareness is more important to be involved in the financial decision making rather than actual income received.

24.3.3 Objective 3: The Role of Income Level and Financial Awareness and Knowledge in Affecting Actual Financial Attitudes (Such as Investment and Budgeting)

To fulfill this objective woman were divided into two group with high- or low-income level and with high or low financial awareness and knowledge as explained in previous section. The financial attitude was measured with five questions regarding their role in budgeting, financial consultation, investment, education, and retirement planning.

A univariate analysis of variance was conducted to find the differences. There was a significant effect of income level on financial attitude $F\ (1, 79) = 61.67, p<.01$, partial eta squared = .45 indicating those women with higher income level reported greater actual financial attitude. There was a significant effect of overall financial awareness and knowledge on financial attitude $F\ (1, 79) = 15.44, p<.01$, partial eta squared = .16 indicating those women with higher financial knowledge and awareness reported greater actual financial attitude (please see Table 24.3). The results further emphasize the role of financial awareness and knowledge in women independence.

24.3.4 Objective 4: The Requirement of Decent Information and Training Programs

Respondents were asked questions regarding the usefulness of seminar/training programs on financial literacy. In response to this, 27.5% women reported that they strongly agree to the usefulness of such kind of programs. 43% women reported that they agree to the usefulness of program. 17.6% women said that they are neutral and only 6% women reported that they do not agree to the usefulness of such programs. It is apparent from the data women have agreed that financial education and training is helpful. The response rate for women agree and strongly agreeing to this 70.6%, which is quite significant. It can possibly lead towards a higher level of financial literacy. There is a considerably high percentage of respondents who want more information on this subject to be available on the internet. Although several financial institutions, including Reserve Bank of India (central bank of the country), have provided basic information regarding finance and financial markets, further detailed information on the subject can be beneficial for the respondents in order for them to grow further financially and create wealth.

24.4 Discussion

This study aimed to understand the financial literacy and associated financial correlates such as financial awareness and knowledge, decision-making, and financial attitude of women. The aim of the study was achieved by testing four objectives.

Firstly, it was found that, financial awareness of women is important to make financial decisions. A significant correlation was found between financial knowledge, financial decision making and financial attitude. The low correlation values further indicate that even if the women if financially aware they might not be involved in making financial decisions and taking actions. The findings support similar studies to examine the relationship between financial education, financial literacy and positive financial outcomes (Fox et al., 2005; Lusardi, 2015). Grohmann et al. (2018) has suggested that good financial awareness and knowledge contributes to good financial decision making. However, the low correlation values also indicate the lesser involvement by women and the findings are similar to the study of Dutch adults where Van Rooij et al. (2007) found that those with low financial literacy are more likely than others to base their behavior on financial advice from friends and are less likely to invest in stocks. Agarwalla et al. (2013) found a significant positive association between financial knowledge and financial behaviour but negative relationship between financial behaviour and financial attitude and found no association between financial knowledge and financial attitude. There are also evidence to show that investment-related decisions are linked to the capacity to acquire knowledge and learn concepts (Lusardi, 2012).

The second objective of the study was to examine if income level and overall financial awareness and knowledge affect the financial decision making among working women. Findings indicated that those women with higher financial awareness had greater involvement in financial decision making. However, there was no significant effect of income level on financial decisions. This suggests that financial knowledge is more important to be involved in the financial decision making rather than actual income received. The findings indicate that creating avenues for financial awareness and enhancing financial knowledge of working women will increase their financial decision making and thereby contributing to further empowerment of working women. There are previous evidence in other contexts where seniors, who have significant wealth per capita, may have some difficulties since they sometimes struggle with digital literacy and communications disabilities, and may not be current with a changed market (Orton, 2007). Financial understanding is correlated with education and income levels, "highly educated consumers with high incomes can be just as ignorant about financial issues as less educated, lower income consumers" (OECD, 2005).

The third objective of the study was to examine if income level and financial awareness and knowledge affect the actual financial attitudes (such as investment and budgeting) among working women. The results showed that those women with higher financial awareness reported greater actual financial attitude. Financial knowledge and planning are closely related as women who display higher financial knowledge are more likely to plan and be successful planner. As per the results and findings, it can be concluded that both objective and subjective financial knowledge have significant influence on financial behavior (Robb & Woodyard, 2011).

The last objective of the study was to evaluate the requirement of decent information and training programs concentrating on the importance of personal finance. It is apparent from the data women have agreed that financial education and training is helpful. There is a considerably high percentage of respondents who want more information on this subject to be available on the internet. Although several financial institutions, including Reserve Bank of India (Central Bank of the country), have provided basic information regarding finance and financial markets, further detailed information on the subject can be beneficial for the respondents in order for them to grow further financially and create wealth.

The overall findings indicate that besides the basic information on personal finance and financial management, information can be provided regarding money management, wealth management, and investment. Women can be taught about portfolio management which will help reduce the risk and encourage investment. Workshops and seminars can be proven to be more effective for working women as these sessions are for a shorter period of time which they can attend without hindering their work. A similar observation has been shared by Huston (2010) that creation of financial education programs designed specifically to enhance financial literacy has been viewed as a solution to mitigating financial problems that individuals and families face. Financial education is a crucial foundation for raising financial literacy and informing the next generations of consumers, workers, and citizens (Lusardi, 2019). Given the lack of financial literacy among the population, it may be important to remedy it by adding financial literacy to the school curriculum (Lusardi, 2015).

Financial literacy can promote opportunity and innovation in financial markets with safeguards to prevent excesses, both the supply and demand side. It can help women who are the most vulnerable. Besides the basic information on personal finance and financial management, information can be provided regarding money management, wealth management, and investment. Women can be taught about portfolio management which will help reduce the risk and encourage investment. Workshops and seminars can be proven to be more effective for working women as these sessions are for a shorter period of time which they can attend without hindering their work.

The findings should be reviewed in the light of some limitations. One of the major limitations of the study is that the respondents volunteered for the study. Therefore, there are possibilities that the data produced from this study may not fully represent the general population of working women from Pune. The study is restricted to the region of Pune city. A nationwide study can be conducted to analyze the question at a larger level. There are chances that the respondents may have a biased view on the subject. These factors might have contributed to the disparity between accessibility to resources to learn the complex technicalities of financial matters and deploying the skills. These factors can be further assessed in future studies.

References

Agarwal, P. (2021). *Financial literacy and decision making among working women: an exploratory study of Punjab and Himachal Pradesh*. (Project Number: P2380) Indian Council of Social Science Research. Retrieved December 12, 2022, from https://icssr.org/financial-literacy-and-decision-making-among-working-women-exploratory-study-punjab-and-himachal

Agarwalla, S. K., Barua, S. K., Jacob, J., & Varma, J. R. (2013). *Effectiveness of financial literacy interventions in improving financial literacy among rural women in North India*. Retrieved from http://www.iimahd.ernet.in/fls/ReportLiteracy-Intervention-Web.pdf

Agarwalla, S. K., Barua, S. K., Jacob, J., & Varma, J. R. (2015). Financial literacy among working young in urban India. *World Development, 67*, 101–109.

Atkinson, A., & Messy, F. A. (2012). Measuring financial literacy: Results of the OECD/international network on financial education (INFE) pilot study. *OECD working papers on finance, insurance and private pensions*, 15, OECD Publishing, https://doi.org/10.1787/5k9csfs90fr4-en

Baluja, G. (2016). Financial literacy among women in India: A review. *Pacific Business Review International, 9*(4), 82–88.

Bharucha, J. P. (2019). Determinants of financial literacy among Indian youth. In *Dynamic perspectives on globalization and sustainable business in Asia* (pp. 154–167). IGI Global.

Chadda, R. K., & Deb, K. S. (2013). Indian family systems, collectivistic society and psychotherapy. *Indian Journal of Psychiatry, 55*(Suppl 2), S299.

Chen, H., & Volpe, R. P. (1998). An analysis of personal financial literacy among college students. *Financial Services Review, 7*(2), 107–128.

D'Silva, B., D'Silva, S., & Bhuptani, R. S. (2018). Assessing the financial literacy level among women in India: An empirical study. *Journal of Business and Management, 20*(5), 35–43.

Delavande, A., Rohwedder, S., & Willis, R. J. (2008). Preparation for retirement, financial literacy and cognitive resources. *Michigan retirement research center research paper*, (2008-190).

Devi, A. (2016). Financial literacy among women: A sample study in the Kamrup district of Assam. *EPRA International Journal of Economic and Business Review, 4*(2), 144–147.

Ergün, K. (2018). Financial literacy among university students: A study in eight European countries. *International Journal of Consumer Studies, 42*(1), 2–15.

Fox, J., Bartholomae, S., & Lee, J. (2005). Building the case for financial education. *Journal of Consumer Affairs, 39*(1), 195–214.

GlobalData, (2022, June). *Female Literacy Rate in India (2010–2021, %)*. (2022, June). www.globaldata.com. Retrieved February 18, 2023, from https://www.globaldata.com/data-insights/macroeconomic/female-literacy-rate-in-india/

Goldsmith, R., & Goldsmith, E. (2006). The effects of investment education on gender differences in financial knowledge. *Journal of Personal Finance, 5*(2), 55–89.

Grable, J. E., & Lytton, R. H. (1998). Investor risk tolerance: Testing the efficacy demographics as differentiating and classifying factors. *Financial Counseling and Planning, 9*(1), 61–73.

Grohmann, A., Klühs, T., & Menkhoff, L. (2018). Does financial literacy improve financial inclusion? Cross country evidence. *World Development, 111*, 84–96.

Huston, S. J. (2010). Measuring financial literacy. *Journal of Consumer Affairs, 44*, 296–316. https://doi.org/10.1111/j.1745-6606.2010.01170.x

India Briefing. (2022, April 18). *Women and Work in India: Trends and Analysis – India Briefing News*. India Briefing News. Retrieved January 15, 2023, from https://www.india-briefing.com/news/women-and-work-in-india-trends-and-analysis-24758.html/

International Labour Organization. (2022). *Gender and financial inclusion*. Retrieved February 10, 2023, from https://www.ilo.org/empent/areas/social-finance/WCMS_737729/lang%2D%2Den/index.htm

Jana, D., Sinha, A., & Gupta, A. (2019). Determinants of financial literacy and use of financial services: An empirical study amongst the unorganized sector workers in Indian scenario. *Iranian Journal of Management Studies, 12*(4), 657–675.

Jha, P., & Nagar, N. (2015). A study of gender inequality in India. *The International Journal of Indian Psychology, 2*(3), 46–53.

Joo, S. H., & Grable, J. E. (2004). An exploratory framework of the determinants of financial satisfaction. *Journal of Family and Economic Issues, 25*, 25–50.

Kaiser, T., & Menkhoff, L. (2020). Financial education in schools: A meta-analysis of experimental studies. *Economics of Education Review, 78*, 101930.

Kasman, M., Heuberger, B., & Hammond, R. A. (2018). Recommendations for improving youth financial literacy education. *The Brooking Institution.* Retrieved December 10, 2022, from https://www.brookings.edu/wp-content/uploads/2018/10/ES_20181001_FinancialLiteracy-Recommendations.pdf

Klapper, L., El-Zoghbi, M., & Hess, J. (2016). *Achieving the sustainable development goals: The role of financial inclusion*. CGAP.

Lusardi, A. (2012). Financial literacy and financial decision-making in older adults. *Generations, 36*(2), 25–32.

Lusardi, A. (2015). Financial literacy: Do people know the ABCs of finance? *Public Understanding of Science, 24*(3), 260–271. https://doi.org/10.1177/0963662514564516

Lusardi, A. (2019). Financial literacy and the need for financial education: Evidence and implications. *Swiss Journal of Economics and Statistics, 155*(1), 1–8.

Lusardi, A., & Mitchell, O. S. (2008). Planning and financial literacy: How do women fare? *The American Economic Review, 98*(2), 413–417.

Lusardi, A., & Mitchell, O. S. (2014). The economic importance of financial literacy: Theory and evidence. *American Economic Journal: Journal of Economic Literature, 52*(1), 5–44.

Mandell, L., & Klein, L. S. (2007). Motivation and financial literacy. *Financial Services Review, 16*(2), 105.

Organisation for Economic Co-operation and Development (OECD). (2005). *Improving financial literacy: Analysis of issues and policies*. OECD.

Organisation for Economic Co-Operation and Development (OECD). (2013). *Financial literacy and inclusion: Results of OECD/INFE survey across countries and by gender*. OECD Centre.

Orton, L. (2007). *Financial literacy: Lessons from international experience*. Canadian Policy Research Networks, Incorporated.

Rawat, P. S. (2014). Patriarchal beliefs, women's empowerment, and general well-being. *Vikalpa, 39*(2), 43–56.

Robb, C. A., & Woodyard, A. S. (2011). Financial knowledge and best practice behavior. *Journal of Financial Counseling and Planning, 22*(1), 60–70.

Robino, C., Trivelli, C., Villanueva, C., Sachetti, F. C., Walbey, H., Martinez, L., & Marincioni, M. (2018). Financial inclusion for women: A way forward. *G20 insights policy briefs: Inequality, human capital and well-being*. Retrieved November 15, 2022, from https://www.g20-insights.org/policy_briefs/financial-inclusion-for-women-a-way-forward/

Singh, C., & Kumar, R. (2017). Financial literacy among women: Indian scenario. *Universal Journal of Accounting and Finance, 5*(2), 46–53.

Srivastava, A. (2020). Role of financial independence in uplifting the status of women. *International Journal of Creative and Innovative Research in all Studies, 3*(7), 10–15.

Statista. (2022, November 23). *Global adult literacy rate by gender*. Retrieved from https://www.statista.com/statistics/1220131/global-adult-literacy-rate-by-gender/

The World Bank Data. (2022). *World Bank staff estimates based on age/sex distributions of United Nations Population Division's World Population Prospects: 2022 Revision*. https://data.worldbank.org/indicator/SP.POP.TOTL.FE.ZS?contextual=aggregateandlocations=IN

United Nations Development Programme. (2022). Human development report 2021–22: Uncertain times, Unsettled Lives*: Shaping our Future in a Transforming World*. New York.

Van Rooij, M., Lusardi, A., & Alessie, R. (2007). Financial literacy and stock market participation. *National Bureau of economic research*. Working Paper No. 13565. NEBR. Retrieved November 15, 2022 from https://www.nber.org/system/files/working_papers/w13565/w13565.pdf

Chapter 25
Kicking the Proverbial Can Down the Road, Across the Border: Sustainability at *Others'* Expense

Thomas Chong

Abstract We need to be sustainable – but at whose expense? Think about Bhopal, India where a 1984 industrial chemical accident exposed millions to toxic substances and affected Bhopal and its hinterland. Using case studies, we learned more about sustainability, economics, innovation, globalisation and psychology. Indeed, the world needs factories but no, it's "not-in-my-backyard" (NIMBY) but in the backyards of those hungry for investments. This NIMBY approach has resulted in nuclear plants, hydro-electric dams, lumber mills and other factories being located elsewhere. In 2022, activists around the Leech Lake reservation in Minnesota protested the environmental harm a lumber mill could cause, if approved. Nevertheless, there are a few success stories characterised by successful negotiation and application of sound psychological principles so NIMBY became "Yes, in my backyard". Thanks to economics (think: comparative advantage) and globalisation, customers world-wide could procure affordable timber products from outside their backyard. So how sustainable are we, really?

Keywords Sustainability · NIMBY · Economics · Globalisation · Ethics

25.1 Introduction

The paper is a case study of a few incidents that strongly suggests we still have a long way to go in demonstrating sustainability on a *global* scale. It warns of the detrimental effects of a "not-in-my-backyard" or NIMBY mindset..., and one that tends to 'export' environmental problems to another "backyard". The term, NIMBY which originated in the US, describes "the arguments of those opposing development in their vicinity while not necessarily against similar development *elsewhere*" (Hubbard, 2009). Indeed, the term, "NIMBY" has become a commonly-used term

T. Chong (✉)
Director Engagement, Newcastle Australia Institute of Higher Education, Singapore, Singapore
e-mail: tomchong4singapore@yahoo.com

E. L. Eijdenberg et al. (eds.), *Innovation-Driven Business and Sustainability in the Tropics*, https://doi.org/10.1007/978-981-99-2909-2_25

to describe one's (sometimes) loud opposition to locating something considered undesirable in one's neighbourhood. If one was to examine the NIMBY phenomenon, one might uncover a deeper issue which shall be briefly discussed later in this chapter.

According to Spiliakos (2018), "in business, sustainability refers to doing business *without* negatively impacting the environment, community, or society as a whole", addressing the effect business has on the environment and on society. Put in another way, to be sustainable is to ensure that our actions meet our needs *without* compromising the ability of others or future generations to meet their own needs.

Chouinard et al. (2011) suggested that sustainability would soon "simply be how business is done". This appears to be true given that "the number of companies filing corporate social responsibility (CSR) reports that use the Global Reporting Initiative standards – the most comprehensive ones available – has increased a hundredfold in the past two decades" (Pucker, 2021).

Hence, by these working definitions, we are not being sustainable if we are in effect 'exporting' our environmental malpractices to another community, out of our borders and as far away as possible. A few incidents that attest to such (mis)behaviour and misdemeanour are the Bhopal disaster, and for those in northern Minnesota, the Huber Mill. This chapter therefore seeks to examine and discuss what else is at play when we consider sustainability, and how we 'export' our less sustainable practices elsewhere whether or not we were exercising the NIMBY mindset.

25.2 Review of the Literature

The Bhopal gas tragedy of December 1984 at the city's Union Carbide India Limited (UCIL) pesticide plant exposed more than 500,000 people to methyl isocyanate gas or MIC (The Atlantic, 2018). It was, according to The Atlantic (2018), "the deadliest industrial disaster" in the world; after all, "40 tonnes of toxic gas spewed from the factory and scorched the throats, eyes and lives of thousands of people outside" those factory walls.

According to Varma and Varma (2005), MIC is a highly toxic substance that also made its way into and around the small towns located near the plant. Many around the world used the products of the Bhopal plant namely union carbide batteries but not many wish to have a similar factory in their own backyard. The Bhopal community benefitted from UCIL jobs but in the end, the trade-offs could turn out to be costly and catastrophic.

A study in Malaysia on the environmental impact of sawmilling industry suggested that several gases such as carbon dioxide, carbon monoxide, methane, nitrous oxide and sulphur dioxide were found discharged into the environment, impacting global warming, human toxicity and acidification (Ramasamy et al., 2015). There is no doubt that the sawmilling industry and its supporting industries created jobs. But how worthwhile is this? Aren't we able to create jobs without hurting the environment?

In Australia alone, Taylor and Warnken (2008) reported that "around 1,781,000 tonnes of wood waste was being generated in Australia per annum until 2007". Oftentimes, under-developed or developing countries do not have much of a choice if they are seriously yearning foreign direct investments which could create jobs for their people and provide almost instant cash for their land and raw materials beneath the land.

According to a report of the Foreign Policy or FP (2022, June), "the European Parliament voted to effectively outlaw the sale of new cars using gasoline or diesel by 2035". This can have serious ramifications or repercussions; after all, this would result in a very high and perhaps even sudden demand for batteries, quickening "the global transformation of the entire automotive industry to battery technology" (FP, 2022).

What is far more serious is probably what is not highlighted whether in the chambers of parliament the world over or in coffee shops: The world may not have enough supply of "minerals that go into batteries – lithium, nickel, cobalt, manganese, palladium, and others" and at the anticipated dizzying pace at which today's fuel-powered cars have to transition to electric cars.

In simple words, the anticipated demand for batteries will require faster extraction of raw materials (mostly) from under-developed countries "in a way that made developed countries unimaginably rich while leaving a trail of environmental degradation" in the mined countries (FP, 2022).

The NIMBY concept attempts to explain this phenomenon of low public acceptance to new development. Power plants and utilities are among the most affected, ranking fourth in a United States survey behind landfills, casinos, and quarries as the most unwanted project types in citizens' hometowns (Saint Consulting Group, 2011).

In a 2007 poll, 15% of Ontario residents said: "I support nuclear-produced electricity, but only if the plant is *not* located in my province" (Canadian Nuclear Association, 2007) – this is a clear example of the NIMBY mindset. Residents or locals in that particular backyard often form lobby groups to advance their agenda and together, resist and push back the locating and building of such amenities or plants in their backyards.

Closer to home (in Singapore), we have the following lobby groups or associations who advance their own agenda (not a comprehensive list): Climate Action SG Alliance (2023) is a non-profit organisation which "aims to harness the power of mass communication in strengthening the narrative for climate reformation so as to translate public awareness into action. Together, we will build a sustainable, resource-efficient and climate resilient Singapore" (n.p.).

Singapore Environment Council or SEC was established in 1995 as an independently managed, non-profit, non-governmental organisation (NGO). The SEC is the only recognised member of the Global Ecolabelling Network (GEN) in Singapore. The GEN is a non-profit association of leading eco labelling organisation worldwide. In 2018, SEC was granted United Nations Environment Programme (UNEP) accredited environmental NGO status. An approved Institution of Public Character with tax exemption status to donors, SEC influences thinking on sustainability issues and coordinates environmental efforts in Singapore and the region (SEC, 2023).

The Singapore Youth for Climate Action or S-Y-C-A (2023) was co-founded by Singapore youths ready "to take on responsibility of climate action, and being able to relate what we want for our shared future with decisions and negotiations happening at the global United Nations platform" (n.p.). Another not-for-profit and non-governmental organisation is Zero Waste SG which is dedicated to "help Singapore eliminate the concept of waste, and accelerate the shift towards zero waste and the circular economy. It started as a website in 2008 providing tips and resources on waste minimisation and recycling, and is officially registered as a non-governmental organisation in 2015" (Zero Waste SG, 2023).

25.3 Findings

The opposite of NIMBY is YIMBY i.e. "Yes, In My Back Yard". It takes persuasive engagement between the relevant authorities and constituents in order to arrive at win-win decisions, swinging from NIMBY to YIMBY. Opposition to the building of facilities like nuclear power plants, sawmills etc in any backyard is to be expected, especially from the local constituents. Indeed, even after securing YIMBY, it takes thoughtful planning and careful execution of plans to accommodate facilities like nuclear power plants, sawmills etc without suffering from hazards like what the community of Bhopal suffered.

From Table 25.1 below, it can be seen that with opposition, certain infrastructural projects had been cancelled or delayed as it comes under review. Hence, it appears that sustainability comes at another community's expense and the constituents of that community could oppose and fight against any decision or plans to locate a certain infrastructure in their backyard. We shall discuss each case in greater detail

Table 25.1 Energy-related development projects which have experienced local opposition. (Energy Education, 2013)

Energy type	Location	Details	Status
Wind power	Town of the Blue Mountains, Ontario	49.5 MW wind farm proposed by Brookfield Power (Brookfield Power, 2006).	Cancelled in 2006
Natural gas	Oakville, Ontario	A 900 MW natural gas-fired power plant to be built by TransCanada (Oakville, n.d.).	Cancelled in 2010
Nuclear power	Peace River, Alberta	Approval for a 4000 MW nuclear power plant sought by Bruce Power (CBC, 2011).	Cancelled in 2011
Hydroelectric power	Fort St. John, British Columbia	1100 MW hydroelectric dam proposed by BC Hydro (The Globe & Mail, 2013)	Under regulatory review.

and consider how NIMBY is so prevalent in each case and if other factors are also critical for successful negotiation.

25.4 Discussion

Wind power for the Town of the Blue Mountains, Ontario was cancelled in 2006 after much controversy (Brookfield Power, 2006). It was touted as "a major wind power development... and Brookfield Power is blaming the town" (National Wind Watch, 2006). As reported by the National Wind Watch (2006), its Mayor Ellen Anderson responded in bewilderment, wondering "how you could cancel something that never started" and she had asserted her "council never even received a proposal" and that they had "been engaging in a public process to develop an intensive renewable energy policy". After numerous claims and counter-claims made public through the town's mass media, it came down to allegations of 'she said, they said'. It reflected an atmosphere of poor communications and a lack of trust between parties and the people of the Town of the Blue Mountains never got to see even the plans for that 49.5 megawatt wind power project in their backyard.

This demonstrated that there is more to just NIMBY at play. Projects could be cancelled due to poor communications and a lack of trust and of course, an absence of rapport. In our efforts to advance our sustainability initiatives, it would be foolhardy to forget about respecting other parties in negotiations and striving for respectful communications and diplomacy to make our world a better one. This is why in advancing sustainability, economics, innovations amidst rapid globalisation, one should practise good principles of organisational psychology.

This is supported by research for example Triandis (1994), acknowledged by many as "the father of modern cross-cultural psychology" (University of Illinois, Urbana-Champaign, 2021) wrote of the need to consider the influence of culture on industrial and organizational processes amidst "increased cultural diversity" (read: globalisation) and urged the continued study of the effects on globalisation and organizational processes in today's age of innovation and sustainability efforts and attempts to resolve conflicts as we strive towards our respective goals.

The next case demonstrates the finesse of one of the parties to a failed negotiation. Despite cancellation of the project, TransCanada showed it could clearly state its noble intentions and willingness to be a good partner as well as stakeholder in the community:

> *We acknowledge the Government's decision that, in its words, a gas plant in Oakville is no longer needed and, as a result, the plant will not proceed. In order to comply with the Government's direction, TransCanada has been informed that the Ontario Power Authority (OPA) wishes to begin discussions where both sides mutually agree to terminate the contract and discuss reasonable payments TransCanada is entitled to. We appreciate the fact that the Ontario Government and TransCanada have had a positive working relationship and we look forward to discussing potential opportunities of working together in the future as the Government's Long Term Energy Plan is developed* (TC Energy, 2010).

Based on official postings and media releases from both parties namely the Ontario Government and TransCanada, no animosity was detected. Thus, even though the 900 MW natural gas-fired power plant project (to be built by TransCanada) was cancelled in 2010 (Oakville, n.d.), it appeared to have taken place with respect; moreover, relations are cordial enough for both parties to return to the negotiating table for future projects together. Such adept handling of the project (and its cancellation) is a good reflection of TransCanada's more than 50 years' experience and as "a leader in the responsible development and reliable operation of North American energy infrastructure including natural gas and oil pipelines, power generation and gas storage facilities" (TC Energy, 2010). This is a fine example to emulate.

The Bruce Power company had received approval for a 4000 MW nuclear power plant along the Peace River, in Alberta (CBC, 2011) but it ended on a sour note when there was significant pushback by the residents in towns close to the proposed site of the nuclear plant. Indeed, the hardworking and determined people of these concerned towns and their supporters had succeeded in lobbying for the cancellation of nuclear plant to be built by Bruce Power (Environmental Justice Atlas, 2022).

The Bruce Power company had made public their ambitious plan for a nuclear power plant in Alberta province, Canada, around Lac Cardinal which is about 30 kilometres west of Edmonton town. This was followed by much "heated debate and protests", according to The Globe and Mail (2009). When the company proposed another site about 30 kilometres north of Peace River, the locals there cried foul and the NIMBY cries shot out. The locals at the 2 proposed sites had expressed grave concerns about the proximity of the project to "freshwater sources that provides drinking water for the area" as well as environmental impacts on wildlife in the areas, besides "the risks of radioactive contamination of an aquifer that residents depend on for their water" (Reuters, 2008). Locals and activists had earlier written to the Canadian Environmental Assessment Agency, asking for an official review complete with public hearings which was acceded to. In fact, "the Alberta government appointed a panel of scientific, business, economic experts to study the pros and cons of nuclear power plant" (Reuters, 2008). Activists sought and secured an opportunity to be heard and to be actively "involved in any decision about a nuclear plant in their backyard" (CBC, 2008).

Indeed, the Globe and Mail (2009) reported that the locals did not want a nuclear plant in their own backyard and the NIMBY cries could grow longer and louder. After much controversy and protests, the Energy Minister declared that "Alberta won't fund nuclear power" (The Globe and Mail, 2009). Interestingly, in an official press release, Mr. Duncan Hawthorne, President and Chief Executive Officer of the Bruce Power company stated, "We've decided the new nuclear option in Alberta is not something our company will be progressing further" (Nuclear Monitor, 2011). That press release also paid "tribute to the hard work and intelligent criticism of the citizens of Alberta -- North, South, and Central -- that the project has been unceremoniously scrapped" (Nuclear Monitor, 2011).

Mr. Hawthorne also gentlemanly thanked "the dedicated citizens in various locations who worked tirelessly to educate their fellow citizens of the inherent dangers of nuclear power, as manifested most dramatically by the explosive self-destruction of 4 reactors in Japan earlier this (that) year" (Nuclear Monitor, 2011). This demonstrated how locals, when grouped together and galvanised, can be a force to be reckoned with and will be heard by the relevant authorities, leaving a project cancelled and abandoned.

A lot more is required to move NIMBY decisions to YIMBY. One significant group that is able to galvanise thousands upon thousands of activists is the World Wildlife Fund or WWF (2023a) who boasts "our community of over 11 million Activists worldwide have continued to give us hope as we make strides in protecting the diversity of life on earth" (n.p.).

It is important to note that the decision is not necessarily binary i.e. either NIMBY or YIMBY. After all, as suggested by Peace River Environmental Society: "I feel Alberta spoke up. We looked at this and said we really don't want this going on in our backyard. There's a lot of other options we need to exhaust before we consider nuclear" (Wilkinson, 2011). Film maker, Mr. Charles Wilkinson had retold the story of Peace River residents' resistance against the building of the proposed nuclear power plant in their backyard in the film entitled "Peace Out" (Wilkinson, 2011). Suffice it to state that the cost and benefits of each project must be carefully studied.

As reported by The Globe and Mail (2013), BC Hydro's proposed 1,100 MW hydroelectric dam at Fort St. John, British Columbia, Canada came under regulatory review after some resistance from locals then. However, today, Site C of the BC Hydro project, 7 kilometres southwest of Fort St John, BC down Peace River is being constructed at a cost of 16 billion Canadian dollars Salty Beaver Explores (2022). This shows that negotiation takes time and getting buy-in from the locals is an undertaking that takes patience, mutual respect, communication skills and of course a win-win mentality.

Today, according to Salty Beaver Explores (2022), the project is edging towards completion estimated to be in 2025. The project aims to provide a more reliable supply of water and cleaner energy to the people in the province. Moreover, according to Salty Beaver Explores (2022), the proposed dam project will also create "13 thousand person years of direct construction employment" and is expected to produce "enough energy to power (up) approximately 450,000 homes in British Columbia".

After all the debate and opposition (sometimes acrimonious and prolonged), one ought to consider if having such infrastructure in another backyard is sustainable, or not. After all, if we seriously consider the definition offered by Spiliakos (2018), sustainability is not achieved if what we do negatively impacts the "environment, community, or society as a whole".

However, if stakeholders and constituents synergise and work together in partnership then we would be in a better position to tackle issues like climate change, habitat protection, and pollution amidst the kaleidoscope of complex issues such as industrialization and its negative environmental impacts.

A chapter on sustainability issues would not be complete without a brief reference to and a discussion on the United Nations Framework Convention on Climate Change which is operationalized by the Kyoto Protocol by which industrialized countries and economies in transition commit "to limit and reduce greenhouse gases (GHG) emissions in accordance with agreed individual targets" (United Nations Climate Change, 2023).

According to the United Nations Climate Change (2023), this Convention only asks those countries to "adopt policies and measures on mitigation and to report periodically" (n.p.) The Kyoto Protocol sets "binding emission reduction targets for 37 industrialized countries and economies in transition and the European Union", and these targets add up to "an average 5 per cent emission reduction compared to 1990 levels over the 5 year period 2008–2012" (also known as the first commitment period).

On 8 December 2012, the Doha Amendment to the Kyoto Protocol was adopted, starting in 2013 and lasting until 2020 (also known as the second commitment period). The Kyoto Protocol establishes "a rigorous monitoring, review and verification system", complete with a compliance system to ensure transparency, requires the actual emissions of participating countries to be "monitored and precise records have to be kept of the trades carried out, ... tracks and records transactions by Parties" under its registry systems and mechanisms, keeps "an international transaction log to verify that transactions are consistent with the rules of the Protocol", and requires that reporting is done by Parties who would have to "submit annual emission inventories and national reports" regularly (United Nations Climate Change, 2023, n.p.).

Moreover, the Kyoto Protocol is developed to ensure via a compliance system that Parties are meeting their commitments, render Parties assistance so they may be able to meet their commitments if they have problems doing so, assist countries in "adapting to the adverse effects of climate change", and facilitate the "development and deployment of technologies that can help increase resilience to the impacts of climate change" (United Nations Climate Change, 2023, n.p.).

25.5 Recommendations and Learning Points

According to Harvard Law School (2015), NIMBY, if allowed to prevail, would be "counterproductive, costly and unnecessary". The Program on Negotiation staff at Harvard Law School (2015) recommended a tried-and-tested process to get from NIMBY to YIMBY, working through and/or settling disputes before they go out of control. Does this reflect a perpetuating practice in which people with more influence and means get their voices heard and their votes counted whereas those who (do not lobby) are not heard and whose views are often ignored or dismissed? Would the latter group therefore have to group together to get their voices heard. If so, this power differential or gaping inequity should be addressed.

It appears that in each of the aforesaid cases, the residents if and when they group together, they can succeed in being heard and getting projects contaminating their backyards cancelled. Indeed, if one was to examine the NIMBY phenomenon, one might uncover a deeper issue namely that there is a real power differential or gaping inequity whereby some people seem to get their voices heard and votes counted while others are left out of the conversation as well as the decision-making completely. This is a key learning point. Kritek (1994) alerts us to the pitfalls of conflict resolution especially "in situations where unacknowledged inequity influences disputes and their outcomes". Kritek (1994) went further by sharing insights on "how to recognize an uneven table -- as well as techniques that one might use to imagine alternatives to that unevenness".

Interestingly, there might be an occasion when a powerful state actually wishes to house a so-called undesirable plant in its own backyard – yes, not NIMBY but YIMBY. Let's take Texas for an example. When Elon Musk of Tesla fame was snubbed by Californian authorities and "local officials refused to let the car company reopen its factory during the coronavirus pandemic" (BBC, 2020), Elon Musk took his business to Texas who "welcomed" him (The New York Times, 2020).

Let's take another example – Shanghai, China, a powerful country that actually welcomes into its own backyard what others might not want in their backyard – yes, not NIMBY but YIMBY. This time, Shanghai China laid out the proverbial red carpet for Elon Musk and Tesla to purchase electric car batteries manufactured in Shanghai, China (Automotive News Europe, 2021). Why would China allow battery-producing factories in its own backyard? Didn't China officials remember what had happened to Bhopal? I see this China move to be shrewd – economically and politically. By being a large, if not the largest, producer of electric car batteries or *lithium iron phosphate (LFP) batteries*, China will create for itself more bargaining power. After all, according to Automotive News Europe (2021), "Tesla has been using LFP batteries in China supplied by Contemporary Amperex Technology Co. Limited (CATL), the world's largest battery maker" (n.p.).

A July report of the South China Morning Post (2020) suggested that "Tesla needs to succeed in China if it wants to dominate the world of electric cars, especially in a post-coronavirus world". Quick-witted entrepreneur, Elon Musk has already surged ahead to realise this by tapping on a certain man named Zeng Yuqun who is the same "battery engineer who once helped Apple extend the life of its MacBook laptops" (South China Morning Post, 2020). Indeed, Zeng Yuqun founded CATL and built it to become the largest global producer of rechargeable cells for the plug-in vehicles, making China the world's battery champion in less than 10 years. The products of this China-based company, CATL "are in almost every major global auto brand, and … they'll also power electric vehicles manufactured by Tesla at its new factory on the outskirts of Shanghai" (South China Morning Post, 2020).

Given that in Year 2019 alone, "Chinese consumers bought more than three electric vehicles for every one sold in the US", it makes economic sense to produce batteries in-country to save costs (South China Morning Post, 2020).

Interestingly, this can be one of China's ways to gain more leverage in negotiations, so that trade deals can become more equitable for the Chinese who for many years were under colonial masters. Isn't this a rather interesting and critical learning point?

Being sustainable helps us to live on planet Earth – this is true and commonsensical. It is also true that there is a lot of money to be made in producing environmentally-friendly electric cars except that the production of batteries for these cars are not that environmentally friendly so it is a case of NIMBY and YIMBY depending on how the costs and benefits stack up in one's favour.

Thus, it does not make sense for Elon Musk to insist on operating in a costly state or home country if his car factories in Texas are "losing billions (of dollars) amidst battery shortages, port issues" (The Globe and Mail, 2022). It would be a matter of time before he moves all of his operations elsewhere including China where the car batteries are produced and where demand for electric cars is 3 times as high as in the USA (South China Morning Post, 2020). So the discussion on sustainability is almost always to be discussed with topics like economics, innovation and globalisation.... which interestingly are the combined themes of the SEIGOP Conference 2023 being organised by the Centre for International Trade and Business in Asia (CITBA) of James Cook University. To get to a win-win-win situation for all parties, principles of organisational psychology could help and this requires participating stakeholders to exercise mutual respect, clear communication and a spirit of sincerely wanting to collaborate.

Indeed, by negotiating, compromises would be made so that all parties can find a solution that is more equitable and amenable. One such case can be illustrated by a survey reported by Karasmanaki and Tsantopoulos (2021): the local acceptance of a wind farm in Germany from the survey respondents was only 35% if a wind farm was located at a distance of 500 metres from their homes but as many as 66% were amenable to the idea of a wind farm to generate alternative and cleaner energy if the farm was located *offshore*. That study also uncovered critical factors in successful negotiation towards a win-win solution; these recommended factors include "trust in key actors and perceived fairness" as well as respectful communications even as stakeholders weighed the positive effects and benefits of wind farms (e.g. clean energy) against perceived risks and disadvantages (e.g. noise pollution). By working towards a win-win solution, none of the parties kicked the proverbial can into a neighbour's backyard.

Win-win solutions are possible as evidenced by the Vineyard Wind project off the coast of Massachusetts, which "would generate enough electricity to power 400,000 homes" (Davenport & Friedman, 2021).

Sadly, in the case of the Huber Mill in northern Minnesota, it was alleged that the relevant authorities did not clearly communicate their intent to build a sawmill near the Native American Reservation of Leech Lake and consult with its constituents regarding what is touted to be "the largest plywood or oriented strand board (OSB) plant in the country". *Economist and environmental activist* Winona LaDuke (n.d.) claimed the move to be "the latest bad idea: Huber Mill near Leech Lake Reservation" in an article in MinnPost; she also reported that "the Leech Lake Tribal government learned about the project from a press release". LaDuke (n.d.) further claimed that the 2019 Executive Order 19-24 was signed to affirm "government to government relationship between Minnesota and Minnesota tribal nations, providing for consultation, coordination and cooperation". It was further felt that the alleged lack of communications made matters worse because the executive order was intended "to establish mutually respectful and beneficial relationships between the state and Minnesota tribal nations" (Winona LaDuke, n.d.).

On the other hand, according to the Office of Governor Tim Walz and Lieutenant Governor Peggy Flanagan (2021), the Governor's Office had initiated the move to seek and secure from the Iron Range Resources & Rehabilitation Board a sum of "US$15 million in funding for the construction of the new Huber Engineered Woods LLC (HEW) OSB manufacturing facility in Cohasset, bringing 150 new jobs to the region". By any account, this is a laudable achievement, given that a lot had to be done to attract investments into the state of Minnesota including one from "one of the largest family-owned companies in the United States" namely HEW, a subsidiary of J.M. Huber Corporation.

While observers might remark that this is a case of "he says, she says", it nevertheless strongly suggests the parties involved have to lot more to work on in building mutual trust. Suffice it to state that respectful communications and timely consultation (both critical in organisational psychology) are also important in any negotiation – this is another key learning point.

One particular group that is leading the way in consulting with the American Indian people is the Office of the United States President. The White House (2022) has set aside resources in the form of New Consultation Trainings and Guidebooks, manifested in the following way: the Department of Commerce's Economic Development Administration will "launch a new staff training series on working with tribal communities. The training will ensure that EDA staff recognize and respect Tribal self-government and sovereignty, honor Tribal treaty and reserved rights, and strive to meet the federal government's trust responsibility toward Tribes". At the time of announcement, The White House (2022) had also assured that "in December 2022, the Department of Defense (DOD) will publish a Tribal Protocols Guidebook, which will serve as a resource guide for DOD components on how to build and enhance relationships with Tribal governments" (n.p.).

On the subject of plastic use, on a broader scale, the World Wildlife Fund or WWF (2023a), recommends that we urgently reduce our footprint or demand for the use of Earth's resources and opines that we currently would need to use about "1.5 Earths to produce all the renewable resources we use" (n.p.). In fact, WWF (2023b) urges that we "hold companies responsible for keeping plastic out of nature" (n.d.). We may do this by telling our Members of Parliament or elected officials that while we make recycling work, we should also coax and cajole companies to use environmentally-friendly products and even get rid of plastic straws. That should be the last straw so we keep unnecessary plastic out of nature. In this way, we save resources and money by removing from taxpayers and communities as much as possible the burden of recycling by incentivising the companies to urgently reduce their plastic footprint.

The dangers of plastic are all too familiar: marine wildlife including seabirds, fish, turtles and even whales are known to have mistaken plastic waste for prey, filling their stomachs with these pieces of plastic and subsequently suffering from "lacerations, infections, reduced ability to swim, and internal injuries" (IUCN, 2023). Besides, there are toxic chemical additives in plastic which pose serious health risks. According to the Geneva Environment Network (2023), these plastic additives include "endocrine disrupting chemicals which are linked to infertility, obesity, diabetes, prostate or breast cancer… and the health conditions linked to additives include reproductive, growth, and cognitive impairment and neurodevelopment disorders".

25.6 Conclusion

Suffice it to conclude that unless and until all parties trust one another and are able to negotiate on an even table, one may flex one's muscles and impose one's demands onto the other party who is weaker. It is about power differential, after all.

Hence, those with less negotiation power or holding the proverbial shorter stick would then end up housing the landfills, casinos, quarries and toxic-producing factories (including OSB manufacturing facility) in their backyard. Perhaps Congo stands out as a good example of an under-developed country exploited by one or more advanced countries who extracted raw materials from Congo to make electric cars and other products for themselves, leaving behind "a trail of environmental degradation, human rights violations, and semipermanent underdevelopment" in the former's backyard (FP, 2022). This is yet another sobering learning point.

How the locals had mitigated their 'small voice' is by joining other like-minded people to lobby the authorities or powers that be. There are many such lobby groups around the world besides the WWF, as discussed earlier in this chapter. Sometimes, it is difficult to win over large corporations to do more about the environment.

Tokenism sometimes takes place because of profits (it's business, after all). As reported in the Guardian (2015), one large drinks company who claims to have "a strong corporate responsibility program (with) savings in greenhouse gas emissions and water from efficiencies in its operations, its refrigeration equipment, its fleet and its supply chain… kept its greenhouse gas emissions constant from 2008 through 2012, while growing production volume in foods by 7% and beverages by 12%". The Guardian (2015) went further to report that "out of 50 companies that work with big environmental groups, only three – Mars, Starbucks and Google – publicly support the Clean Power Plan" (n.p.).

On the other hand, if all stakeholders respect and recognise one another as valuable partners then more can be achieved, together. When various parties come together with a win-win-win mindset, solutions may be produced for various problems whether these have to do with climate change, ozone layer depletion, loss of biodiversity, phosphorous and nitrogen cycles, water supply, ocean acidification, pollution or overfishing.

The case of the offshore wind farm off the coast of Germany is a case in point (Karasmanaki & Tsantopoulos, 2021). Another case is Site C of the BC Hydro project (Salty Beaver Explores, 2022). Indeed, this demonstrates that sustainability may be responsibly achieved resulting in a win-win-win situation, without negatively impacting the environment, community, or society as a whole, or in other words, without kicking the proverbial can down the road, across the border.

References

Automotive News Europe. (2021). *Tesla shifting to cheaper battery chemistry tried in China.* https://europe.autonews.com/automakers/tesla-shifting-cheaper-battery-chemistry-tried-china

BBC. (2020). *Tesla: Elon Musk moves to Texas in Silicon Valley snub.* https://www.bbc.com/news/technology-55246148

Brookfield Power. (2006). *Brookfield Power terminates Blue Highlands wind energy contract in the Town of the Blue Mountains.* http://brookfieldrenewable.com/content/2006/brookfield_power_terminates_blue_highlands_wind_en-30733.html

Canadian Nuclear Association. (2007, July). *Report: Canadian Views on Nuclear Energy – Ontario.* http://www.cna.ca/wp-content/uploads/Full_Report_July2007PPT.pdf

CBC. (2011). *Bruce Power dropping Alberta nuclear plant proposal.* http://www.cbc.ca/news/canada/edmonton/bruce-power-dropping-alberta-nuclear-plant-proposal-1.1046668

Chouinard, Y., Ellison, J., & Ridgeway, R. (2011). The sustainable economy. *Harvard Business Review.*. https://hbr.org/2011/10/the-sustainable-economy

Climate Action SG Alliance. (2023). *Welcome to the climate action SG Alliance.* https://www.climateactionsg.org/

Davenport, C., & Friedman, L. (2021). *Biden administration approves nation's first major offshore wind farm.* https://www.nytimes.com/2021/05/11/climate/climate-wind-farm.html.

Energy Education. (2013). *Not in my back yard syndrome.* https://energyeducation.ca/encyclopedia/Not_in_my_back_yard_syndrome

Environmental Justice Atlas. (2022). Bruce power nuclear power plant project abandoned in lac cardinal and peace river, Alberta. https://ejatlas.org/conflict/nuclear-power-plant-project-abandoned-in-alberta-canada

FP. (2022). *Green energy's dirty secret: Its hunger for African resources.* https://foreignpolicy.com/2022/06/30/africa-congo-drc-ev-electric-vehicles-batteries-green-energy-minerals-metals-mining-resources-colonialism-human-rights-development-china/

Geneva Environment Network. (2023, January). *Plastics and human health: Plastics and the environment series.* https://www.genevaenvironmentnetwork.org/resources/updates/plastics-and-health/

Harvard Law School. (2015). *Negotiation skills: Overcoming the Not-In-My-Backyard (NIMBY) Syndrome.* https://www.pon.harvard.edu/daily/negotiation-skills-daily/overcoming-the-not-in-my-backyard-nimby-syndrome/

Hubbard, P. (2009). *International encyclopedia of human geography.* https://www.sciencedirect.com/book/9780080449104/international-encyclopedia-of-human-geography

IUCN. (2023). *Marine plastic pollution.* https://www.iucn.org/

Karasmanaki, E. & Tsantopoulos, G. (2021). *Low carbon energy technologies for sustainable energy systems.* https://www.sciencedirect.com/book/9780128228975/low-carbon-energy-technologies-in-sustainable-energy-systems

Kritek, P. B. (1994). *Negotiating at an uneven table: A practical approach to working with difference and diversity.* Jossey Bass.

LaDuke, W. (n.d.). The latest bad idea: Huber mill near Leech Lake Reservation, *MinnPost.* https://www.minnpost.com/community-voices/2022/01/the-latest-bad-idea-huber-mill-near-leech-lake-reservation/

National Wind Watch. 2006). *Wind Farm blows away.* https://www.wind-watch.org/news/2006/09/26/wind-farm-blows-away/

Nuclear Monitor. (2011). *Bruce power will not proceed with nuclear option in Alberta.* https://www.wiseinternational.org/nuclear-monitor/739/bruce-power-will-not-proceed-nuclear-option-alberta

Oakville. (n.d.). *Proposed TransCanada power plant – Cancelled by the province.* http://www.oakville.ca/environment/proposed-transcanada-power-plant.html

Office of Governor Tim Walz and Lieutenant Governor Peggy Flanagan. (2021)**.** *Governor Walz announces Huber Engineered Woods LLC to bring 150 new jobs to Cohasset.* https://mn.gov/governor/news/?id=1055-486163

Pucker, K. P. (2021). Overselling sustainability reporting: We're confusing output with impact. *Harvard Business Review*. https://hbr.org/2021/05/overselling-sustainability-reporting

Ramasamy, G., Ratnasingam, J., Bakar, E. S., Halis, R., & Muttiah, N. (2015). Assessment of environmental emissions from sawmilling activity in Malaysia. *BioResources, 10*, 6643–6662.

Reuters. (2008). *Alberta names panel to study nuclear pros and cons.* https://www.reuters.com/article/canada-alberta-nuclear-idUSN2346067820080423

Saint Consulting Group. (2011). The Saint Index: United States 2011. http://saintindex.info/support-opposition

Salty Beaver Explores. (2022, May 26). *Site C hydroelectric dam at fort St John, BC* [Video]. YouTube. https://www.youtube.com/watch?v=GVfpbyHmNp0

Singapore Environment Council. (2023). *Why Sustainability Matters?* https://sec.org.sg/

Singapore Youth for Climate Action. (2023). *About Singapore Youth for Climate Action or SYCA.* https://www.facebook.com/sgyouthclimateaction/

South China Morning Post. (2020, July). *The battery billionaire who holds the key to Tesla's future in China and Elon Musk's global electric-car dominance.* https://www.scmp.com/business/companies/article/3092890/battery-billionaire-who-holds-key-teslas-future-china-and-elon

Spiliakos, A. (2018). *What does "sustainability" mean in business? Harvard Business School.* https://online.hbs.edu/blog/post/what-is-sustainability-in-business

Taylor, J., & Warnken, M. (2008). *Wood recovery and recycling: A source book for Australia.* Forest and Wood Products Research and Development Corporation.

TC Energy. (2010). *TransCanada Responds to Oakville Generating Station Decision.* https://www.tcenergy.com/announcements/2010/2010-10-07transcanada-responds-to-oakville-generating-station-decision/

The Atlantic. (2018). *The world's worst industrial disaster is still unfolding.* https://www.theatlantic.com/science/archive/2018/07/the-worlds-worst-industrial-disaster-is-still-unfolding/560726/

The Globe and Mail. (2009). *Alberta won't fund nuclear power, Energy Minister says.* https://www.theglobeandmail.com/news/national/alberta-wont-fund-nuclear-power-energy-minister-says/article4295604/

The Globe and Mail. (2013). *BC Hydro faces widespread community opposition over dam.* http://www.theglobeandmail.com/news/british-columbia/bc-hydro-faces-widespread-community-opposition-over-dam/article15816152/

The Globe and Mail. (2022). *Elon Musk says Tesla's new car factories 'losing billions' amid battery shortages, port issues.* https://www.theglobeandmail.com/business/international-business/article-musk-says-teslas-new-car-factories-losing-billions-of-dollars/

The Guardian. (2015). *In Washington, a handful of corporations lobby against climate change.* https://www.theguardian.com/sustainable-business/2015/apr/24/washington-climate-change-environmental-defense-fund-ceres-mars-google-starbucks-epa-clean-power-plan

The New York Times. (2020). *Welcome to Texas!': Musk's California Departure Stokes the States' Rivalry.* https://www.nytimes.com/2020/12/09/us/elon-musk-texas-california.html

The White House. (2022, November). *Fact sheet: Biden-Harris administration announces new actions to support Indian country and native communities ahead of the administration's second tribal nations summit.* https://www.whitehouse.gov/briefing-room/statements-releases/2022/11/30/fact-sheet-biden-harris-administration-announces-new-actions-to-support-indian-country-and-native-communities-ahead-of-the-administrations-second-tribal-nations-summit/

Triandis, H. C. (1994). Cross-cultural industrial and organizational psychology. In H. C. Triandis, M. D. Dunnette, & L. M. Hough (Eds.), *Handbook of industrial and organizational psychology* (pp. 103–172). Consulting Psychologists Press.

United Nations Climate Change. (2023). *What is the Kyoto Protocol?* https://unfccc.int/kyoto_protocol?gclid=EAIaIQobChMInP6mpNqg_QIVmX0rCh32DgFiEAAYASAAEgLu_fD_BwE

University of Illinois, Urbana-Champaign. (2021). *Celebrating the Life of Harry Triandis.* https://psychology.illinois.edu/news/2021-07-26/celebrating-life-harry-triandis

Varma, R., & Varma, D. R. (2005). The Bhopal Disaster of 1984. *Bulletin of Science, Technology & Society, 25*(1), 37–45. https://doi.org/10.1177/0270467604273822

Wilkinson, C. (Director). (2011). Peace out: Energy costs. *Film.* https://www.cinemapolitica.org/film/peace-out-energy-costs/

WWF. (2023a). *Tackling threats that impact the Earth.* https://www.worldwildlife.org/threats

WWF. (2023b). *Hold companies responsible for keeping plastic out of nature.* https://support.worldwildlife.org/site/Advocacy?cmd=display&page=UserAction&id=1090

Zero Waste SG. (2023). *Green groups in Singapore.* https://www.towardszerowaste.gov.sg/green-groups-in-singapore/

Chapter 26
Artificial Intelligence in Information Technology Infrastructure Management and Support in Singapore

Jireh H. I. Seow and Naveen K. Rajaharia

Abstract Artificial intelligence (AI) is gaining traction and acceptability across the information technology (IT) infrastructure management support services. High operational costs, reluctance to implement automation, and a dearth of a competent workforce in IT infrastructure management are among the factors driving the traction. This research also identifies potential barriers to using AI in IT infrastructure management support and operations as well as the potential advantages. Empirical data were collected qualitatively in a financial organization in Singapore; the research participants were in senior IT positions and the interviews probed their observations, experiences, and perspectives. Furthermore, the data was analyzed and interpreted using a phenomenological and narrative perspective. The participants' close ties to IT infrastructure management and operations inspired the study's adoption of a naturalist paradigm and epistemology. In addition, text-based open-ended interview questionnaires were also used to collect data as well as secondary data coming from electronic databases. They were then analyzed using a theme analysis framework to help see the bigger perspective. Finally, the paper discusses the findings and conclusion of the research, including the discovery of four overarching themes: hiring, opposition, benefits, and adoption. The conclusions drawn imply (1) workforce hiring considerations in IT infrastructure management; (2) barriers to adopting AI-based automation in IT infrastructure management; (3) advantages of AI for the organization and its employees; (4) prospective applications of AI. The practical implications for the industry include assessing the pros and cons of employing AI in IT infrastructure management and operations from the perspectives of both employers and employees, and recommendations on which aspects of managing IT infrastructure could most benefit from the incorporation of AI.

J. H. I. Seow (✉)
Innovation and Entrepreneurship Centre (i2e), Singapore, Singapore

S P Jain School of Global Management, Singapore, Singapore
e-mail: jireh.seowhi@spjain.org

N. K. Rajaharia
HCL Singapore Pte, Singapore, Singapore
e-mail: naveenrajaharia@hcl.com

E. L. Eijdenberg et al. (eds.), *Innovation-Driven Business and Sustainability in the Tropics*, https://doi.org/10.1007/978-981-99-2909-2_26

Keywords IT · Infrastructure management · Qualitative research · AI · Automation · Thematic analysis · Cost · Phenomenological · Hiring · Efficiency

26.1 Introduction

26.1.1 Business Issues

The infrastructure information technology (IT) operations in a banking and financial organization are one of the most critical functions of the organization's IT department. The IT infrastructure is the core technology component (Kuprenko, 2021), enabling the organization's business applications to generate revenue. For example, IT infrastructure elements include networking components, security appliances, and computing elements such as servers, databases, and storage. Continuous monitoring (24/7) and management of these elements must be done to keep the business running (Sumo Logic, 2021).

Traditionally, the IT infrastructure is managed by support personnel trained in specific technologies and works in a rotation shift structure (Hertvik, 2020). The legacy support method is manual in that the monitoring systems pick the alert from the infrastructure element such as network, security, and computation (Swanston, 2022). Then this alert will be sent to an infrastructure engineer or analyst for investigation. The support engineer picks the alert, logs in the device, and performs investigations based on particular standard instructions. Once the issue is isolated, the support engineer conducts remediation. They follow a manual approval process before initiating the commands or instructions in the device (Kark et al., 2019). After remediation of the issue, the incident is closed by the analyst.

Due to the manual nature of the IT infrastructure support model, there are issues faced by businesses. Following are the critical issues faced by financial organizations in IT infrastructure management:

- High operational cost for the company to deploy a workforce for 24/7 support considering the dependency on human skills instead of automated processes (Arundale, 2021). Manual execution of tasks is prone to human error, which results in penalties and low customer satisfaction.
- The cost of resources is high and so is the unavailability of technology skills in the market (Bughin et al., 2021). In addition, specialized knowledge is concentrated among specific staff.
- High-stress levels among employees working in the 24/7 environment leads to high staff turnover. There is also resistance to adopting automation using artificial intelligence (AI) (Donnelly, 2016).

26.1.2 Research Problems or Gaps and Research Objectives

By reviewing relevant literature, we realised that there are a number of factors influencing an organization's workforce or human resource (HR) hiring strategy. However, not much is known about such factors influencing a financial institution in Singapore, especially in relation to the workforce behind IT infrastructure and operations and in relation to AI. Moreover, little is known about resisting forces, especially from staff in senior IT positions, in the adoption of AI. In addition, relatively little is published about the possible solutions that AI can bring about in this area of that converges AI, HR, IT, and financial organizations.

Therefore, the key objectives of this research study are:

1. To discover the factors influencing a financial organization's workforce hiring strategy to support its IT infrastructure.
2. To discover the reasons for resistance in a financial organization to adopt AI in its IT infrastructure management and operations.
3. To discover the possible solutions from AI that can help a financial organization address workforce hiring and optimization.

26.1.3 Research Questions

Based on the research objectives above, the researchers developed the following research questions:

1. What are the factors influencing a financial organization's workforce hiring for its IT infrastructure management and support?
2. What are the main reasons preventing financial organizations from adopting AI in IT infrastructure operations?
3. How could IT infrastructure management and support of a financial organization benefit from using AI?
4. How could AI help address the workforce optimization for IT infrastructure management and support?

26.2 Literature Review

The IT infrastructure operations of any organization are fundamentally dependent on people, which means a large workforce is required to manage the network, compute, storage, and other technology systems so that the business can run properly. These resource costs keep increasing yearly due to resources getting seniority, cost of living increases, and inflation. This continuous flow of the revenue to resource costs leaves significantly less for the innovations and research on future technology products.

As per one study, there are benefits to adopting automation (Gupta, 2016). The cost control due to automation can be used to transform the verticals such as cloud, data, mobility, and internet of things (IoT). While this has benefits, the organizations are also cognizant of cutting jobs due to automation. As per the chief executive officer of Hexaware, automation will lead to shrinkage of the processes and, eventually, job cuts (Mandavia, 2017). The IT infrastructure operations are 24 × 7 function, which stresses employees working in shifts. As per (Donnelly, 2016), IT infrastructure operations employees' stress needs to be minimized. Along similar lines, Gartner's research suggests an AI for IT operations (AIOps) platform that can combine AI and data to replace the IT operations tasks, monitoring, IT service management, and processes in an enterprise (Preimesberger, 2019). Nevertheless, despite all these anticipated benefits, IT administrators are unwilling to adopt automation and AI technology. As per the results of one of the surveys, there is a reduction in the available talent related to automation, orchestration, and AI, resulting in this trend (Saran, 2017).

Cost for IT operations remains a significant concern for enterprises globally. In the US, a controller's report, 2011 mentions the potential of IT companies to reduce the cost of operations by 25% (Institute of Finance & Management, 2011) or more over 3 years. All this while the expenditure on IT spending is increasing exponentially. For example, in India, IT infrastructure spending increased by 1.5% from 2016 to reach USD 2.2 billion in 2017 (Sahoo, 2017). The IT operations landscape is changing rapidly, becoming more complex and data-heavy. As per a report (Masood & Hashmi, 2019), the IT operators are handling more alerts, events, and incidents while the vital performance measurements are getting more and more stringent, such as service-level agreements (SLAs), mean time to detect (MTTD), mean time to failure (MTTF), mean time between failures (MTBF), and mean time to repair (MTTR). Masood and Hashmi (2019) also point out that 41% of organizations have ten or more IT management tools, which is increasing with the adoption of multi-cloud, threat detection, and data analytics. This change is driving the growth of IT services in India, where automation is looked an alternative to the manual workforce (Vasudevan, 2022). The pandemic has deeply influenced all this. As per the report (Samik Chatterjee, 2020), the IT verticals will be driven by changes following the pandemic. This includes the (1) need for high bandwidth to support virtual working; (2) more adoption of public clouds to accommodate the surge in demand; (3) virtualization and abstraction of the hardware from software; (4) contactless banking transactions, payments, loans, and insurance; (5) 5G rollout and IoT. The use of AI is now needed more than ever. One of the reasons AI did not show its true potential is because the modern testbeds used for the analysis of critical infrastructure do not incorporate the real human operator in the experiment (Siaterlis et al., 2012). This caused AI to not have the data of real human decisions and hence not perceived as reliable. A survey was conducted to determine the uses of AI in operations management, which may be broadly divided into four areas (Kobbacy & Vadera, 2011). The outcomes demonstrate that there has been a remarkable growth in the usage of genetic algorithms since the year 2003, which means there is a widespread use of AI in the areas of planned maintenance, defect diagnosis, and quality assurance.

Talking about the current situation in the world, especially in the last 5 years, more and more companies are testing and trying to adopt AI and machine learning in their business operations. As per one report, AI has been used in Mazda North America operations for its global supply chain (Elias, 2018). Similarly, other companies are also investing in AI in their respective industries; some of them are:

- Ericsson has developed a managed services offering for communications service providers based on AI (Athena Information Solutions Pvt. Ltd., 2019).
- Hewlett Packard Enterprise (HPE) has brought the management of ProLiant, Synergy, and Apollo servers under its cloud-based AI management tool, driving down the operational cost (Athena Information Solutions Pvt. Ltd., 2018).
- IBM is transforming its Watson AI platform to diagnose and remediate IT infrastructure issues (Sayer, 2020). It will be built on the RedHat open-source software.
- AI will be going to be the next driver for semiconductor companies due to its rapid adoption of cloud and edge technologies (Hariharan, 2018).

While it is acknowledged that AI is revolutionizing operations and business, the road seems less mapped; Gray (2019) found that the foundation applications for AI to manage the critical infrastructure are not clearly mapped with the risk it contains. Schneider and Leyer (2019) did a test on 310 participants to study the impact of select complexity and cognitive discernments as to inclination to entrust a strategic judgement to an algorithm, resulting in a finding that workers with a low level of situational attentiveness are more likely to trust the task to a machine.

Another study by Balasubramanian et al. (2022) revealed that learning for human beings happens when distinct patterns developing in their minds by being engrossed in their environment and by employing substantive rationality. Machine learning can be a substitute for human decision-making. It is faster and does not have constraints as humans have, such as cognitive limitations and inflexibility. However, we need to understand that it is based on statistical analysis and not authentic sentient learning for decision-making. Furthermore, in another study by Tabesh (2021), it is found that humans monopolize the area of intuitive decision tasks compared to a machine. Managers in an organization have to make decisions quite often; it is essential that they can better use the technology to augment their decision-making and make it better. With the onset of the pandemic, the use of AI has created opportunities for enterprises where they can automate and reduce resources to save costs (Jarrett, 2021).

Considering the drivers for the future, AI will shape IT infrastructure operations. As per Korolov (2021), IT organizations are embracing the tools based on AI to predict interruptions and optimize and improve support. IT automation has reduced the technical services revenue so that the servers are easy to manage and cost-effective (Vizard, 2012). Another use case is to revamp the data centers, which includes the optimization to support emerging technologies, and installing self-cooling racks and smart power equipment (Cappuccio, 2021). Companies like NetEnrich invested in developing AI-driven solutions for their digital services (NetEnrich, 2019). In order to effectively use AI, data is the key. For example, Virtana focuses focussing on harnessing real-time analytics to build the AI-driven hybrid IT infrastructure management platform, helping customers and enterprises to manage complicated multi-cloud environments (Sliwa, 2019). Errors in IT operations are always challenging since they have a human dependency. One company named Mphasis has developed a DigiOps solution driven by AI to avoid human errors in IT operations (Athena Information Solutions Pvt. Ltd., 2016).

Another area of interest is the cybersecurity IT operations in the current scenario applicable for all organizations. Cybersecurity operations churn a vast amount of data that is not feasible for humans to read and take action. Instead, with the help of cognitive science and AI, it is feasible to augment the intelligence of humans with machine learning (Lyn Paul et al., 2019).

AI has the capability to automate the human decision-making practice; however, it has to be managed carefully (Alt et al., 2020). While the current machines have the power of learning, they are more like black boxes making humans extract valuable visualizations. Experiments show that human performance is improved with the help of algorithms (Bastani et al., 2022). As per a study by Henkel et al. (2020), advances in AI software are augmenting the front service employees to improve the interpersonal emotion regulation (IER) activities. There is an impetus for automated decision systems in the area of infrastructure and cybersecurity operations, where humans make decisions based on the analytics generated by AI and machine learning systems (Chamberlain et al., 2020).

The driving factors which are propelling the future of IT infrastructure are blockchain, machine learning, AI, and cloud computing (Mistry, 2018). The use of AI and automation has the potential to unlock the true value in IT infrastructure operations. As per Marx et al. (2021), the adoption of AI in operations can help an organization in:

- Operational resiliency, automated recovery, repairs, and maintenance.
- More frequent changes in products as per customer feedback, agile operations.
- Automating the low-value-added tasks to save cost.
- Securing the data and resilience.
- Make difficult decisions to achieve strategic goals.

As per the study by (Putra et al., 2020), IT infrastructure is critical for online media businesses such that it can handle surges in traffic. This calls for the capabilities of the cloud, which works on-demand basis. A company's decision to outsource the IT infrastructure benefits from cloud services resulting in a constructive stimulus on the organization. The associated benefits are improved strategy, capability, and cost-efficiency.

As per the report (Tien-tsin Huang, 2017), IT services are showing interest in investments in automation. However, the vendor capabilities are still at an early age.

The estimated global delivery centers increased by 177% in the last 4 years due to the high demand for digital services such as data analytics, IoT, cloud, etc. India and the Philippines have been observed to dominate the global delivery of BPO services with a share of 60% of the revenue, followed by countries like Europe, Latin America, and Canada. Tien-tsin Huang (2017) noted that hiring at the lower levels is affected due to automation with a 20–40% industry-wide shrinkage.

As per (NASDAQ OMX Corporate Solutions, Inc., 2019), the CAGR for remote infrastructure management is anticipated at a rate of 11%, which spans the services supporting networks, ERP systems, email systems, data centers, end-user devices, database administration, and technical support.

According to a study, IT infrastructure requirements trends have accelerated following the covid-19 outbreak; a few of them are (1) bandwidth requirements increased; (2) leverage more on the public cloud; (3) migrant physical computing to virtual; (4) adoption of contactless transaction (Samik Chatterjee, 2020).

There is always a worry among employees about organizations replacing them with AI. However, innovative companies are using AI to make an inclusive workforce and help to augment the human worker instead of replacing them (Moghaddam et al., 2020). There is a rapid change in the nature of work as companies become more digital, and the employees need to be empowered to support the innovations. The current in-demand skills and specialties that did not exist a decade ago will have a significant impact on the hiring of the workforce and how they apply these skills and make themselves ready to be competitive.

According to another study, the Labour Statistics Bureau expects the workforce demand for technology-related infrastructure to surge by 13.26% from the year 2014 to 2024 (Agrawal et al., 2017). In this survey, the growth estimation is 34.16% for human resources in the half-decade starting from 2016. The business value can be enhanced by fostering the business value of AI-based transformational ventures that influence the organization's performance. Wamba-Taguimdje et al. (2020) uses the sequential methodology in four steps (1) analyze the AI technologies; (2) consider various industry sectors to have a comprehensive exploration of the case studies; (3) collect data from AI-powered solution providers; (4) identify the impact on the organization's performance and the business value it adds up.

The revenue from selling IT infrastructure products such as switches, storage, and servers increased 34.4% year-on-year in the 2nd quarter of 2020 (IDC, 2021). This is in contrast to the fact that traditional IT infrastructure declined by 8.7% for the same period. Due to the pandemic, there are massive shifts in human interactions in terms of virtual events, shopping, collaborations, online meetings, telemedicine, entertainment, and the education field. The change in the increase in investments for the IT infrastructure is going to be consistent across all technology domains. Computing platforms will be the largest segment (50.9%) to benefit from this higher investment, along with the storage platforms, where the spending growth is observed at 21.2% (IDC, 2021).

Technology companies like TCS are investing significantly in intellectual property for their automation and AI or machine learning product offerings (TCS, 2021). ICT monitor reports highlight the commitment of TCS towards the enhancement of AIOps in the business by integrating cloud, agile, automation, and analytics. To keep up with the skill set needed, the company has adopted a talent transformation program in partnership with cloud service providers. The AIOps powered by AI and machine learning unlocks the vast potential that can be obtained by integrating the IT infrastructure component layer with the applications, and the corporate process level. The solution created is reusable, configurable, and prebuilt with previous experiences in managing customer operations. The solutions focus on (1) Agile infrastructure – autonomous management of the company's IT systems; (2) delivering agile, resilient, and scalable operations; (3) intelligent and intuitive workspaces for better user experiences; (4) cognitive virtual assistance acting as the proactive endpoint remediator.

26.3 Research Methodology

26.3.1 Qualitative Study

The qualitative method is used to obtain the answers from the experience, observation, perspective, and connotation from the standpoint of the participant (Hammarberg et al., 2016). This type of data usually doesn't acquiesce to the measurement quantitatively. The qualitative study techniques include group discussion to assess the normative behavior concerns, semi-structured interviews, text-based open-ended questionnaires to seek views on a specific topic of interest, and analysis of audio, text, videos, and documents.

The researchers selected a qualitative study method to reveal the potential issues and understanding of the IT infrastructure management of a financial organization supported by a renowned IT service company. Primary research data was collected from participants hold leadership positions at various levels. As per (*Your Guide to Qualitative Research in 2022*, 2022), there are five approaches to qualitative study, and two of them were employed:

1. **Narrative research**: It is the approach of examining the experiences and views of the participants explaining their choices and events.
2. **Phenomenological research**: This approach aims to derive an understanding of meanings through the interpretation of people's lived experiences.

The researchers employed a general qualitative inquiry that provided flexibility to phenomenology and narrative approaches. It also helped in the selection of a small number of participants with a greater flexibility for data collection methods such as text-based questionnaires, interviews, notes, and sample size.

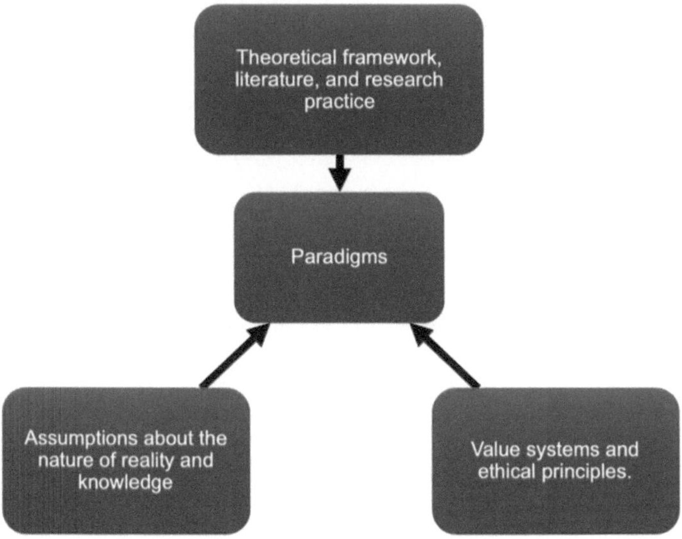

Fig. 26.1 Research paradigm. (Kawulich, 2012)

The other reason for the selection of narrative and phenomenological research approaches is that the participants, as well as the researchers, are bound by the non-disclosure agreements.

26.3.2 Research Paradigm

This research is constructed on the naturalist paradigm (Lincoln & Guba, 1985) for a qualitative study where the axiom is about the relationship of the knower to the known. In the scope of the study, the participants and their environment (IT infrastructure management and operations) are inseparable; they are also in a continuous interaction (Fig. 26.1).

26.3.3 Research Philosophy

Epistemology is associated with the conception of knowledge, aiming at by what means knowledge is gained and exploring the most acceptable approaches to reach the truth (Stainton, 2021). As per the aim and objectives of this research, the epistemological position is interpretivism (Hepler & Cloud, 2022) based on these assumptions:

- Employees or workforce are complex and intricate people.
- Some employees experience the working environment differently.

- The working environment factors drive human behavior.
- Scientific methods are not the most appropriate way to analyze employee perceptions.
- It is essential to interpret automation initiatives' motives, beliefs, and perceptions.

26.3.4 Data-Collection Methods

- Text-based qualitative open-ended questionnaires
- Unstructured interviews

26.3.5 Research Questionnaire

The following qualitative open-ended questionnaire was developed to be used offline or online to gather the responses from the selected participants.

Q1: Hello, what do you think factors influence your financial organization's workforce in IT infrastructure hiring?

Q2: Do you think the current workforce of your financial organization is adequate to support its IT infrastructure?

Q3: How could your financial organization's workforce be transformed to support its IT infrastructure fully?

Q4: What do you think about the hiring process for technical resources for IT infrastructure support?

Q5: Do you think the current workforce is appropriately skilled to support the organization's IT infrastructure?

Q6: What improvements do you suggest to optimize the workforce and offload the monotonous tasks to automated systems?

Q7: What do you think are the reasons preventing the organization from adopting automation in the IT infrastructure operations?

Q8: Do you think AI can augment the human workforce's capability to manage IT operations?

Q9: What initiatives do you think the organization shall take to avoid the resistance to adopting automation in IT infrastructure operations?

Q10: What IT infrastructure operations tasks can benefit from using machine learning and AI?

Q11: Do you think the manual human-assisted and repeatable tasks can be offloaded to AI?

Q12: What are the advantages or disadvantages of using AI-based operations in a financial organization's IT infrastructure?

Q13: How the AI can assist in hiring strategy for IT infrastructure support employees?

Q14: Do you think there is a resistance in the financial organizations to not let the AI handle the IT infrastructure for critical business systems?

Q15: Which area in the IT infrastructure support can be automated through machine learning?

Q16: How AI-based automation can drive the optimization inside the IT infrastructure support?

Q17: Do you see that AI is matured enough to take over manual business tasks from a human?

Q18: What benefits for the organization do you see when the manual work is transformed into automated?

26.3.6 Researchers' Biases

The subjective make-up of the qualitative study makes it obstruse to detach the researchers completely from the data, which at times leads to distortion of the objectivity and difficulty in avoiding bias (Shah, 2021). Due to this, qualitative research may often be perceived as lacking transparency and scientific rigor though it is flexible and allow creativity which results in additional insights that otherwise can't be collected in other research methods such as quantitative research (Johnson et al., 2020) (Fig. 26.2).

The researchers faced the following researchers' biases and the following mitigations were implemented.

1. ***Confirmation bias*** – is the most common type of bias where a researchers interprets the data in a way that supports his or her own hypotheses, at times ignoring the data that doesn't favor his or her claim (Nickerson, 1998).

   Mitigation: the researchers analyzed all the data collected with a transparent mindset. This needs continuous evaluation of the responses from participants and ensures that pre-existing assumptions are excluded.
2. ***Question order bias*** – this may have occurred; an interview or questionnaire question may influence the answers to subsequent questions (Thau et al., 2021). In some situations, participants judge the subsequent questions based on their response to previous questions, which leads to an inaccurate and biased response.

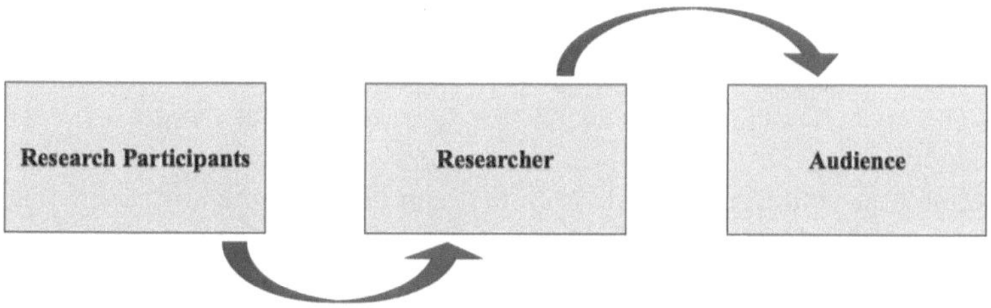

Fig. 26.2 Researchers role between participants and audience

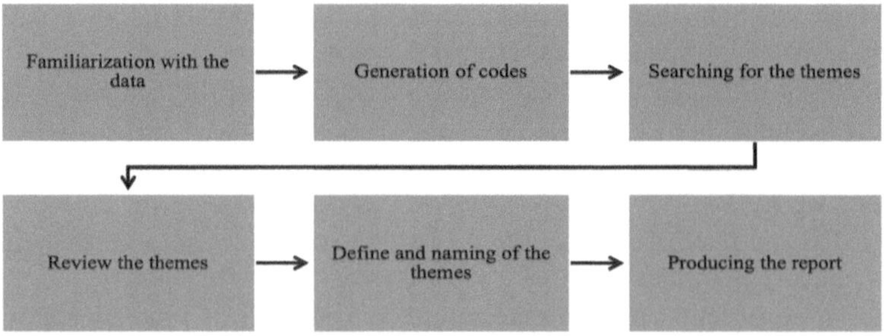

Fig. 26.3 Thematic analysis. (Braun & Clarke, 2006)

Mitigation: the researchers drafted the questionnaire in a way that asked general questions in the beginning and then moved over to the specific questions.

3. ***Leading question and wording bias*** – in several cases, the questions may influence the participants and prompt them in the direction of plausible outcomes that leads to a biased outcome (Schade, 2017).

   Mitigation: The researchers did not use any leading questions in the questionnaire and had kept all questions simple with a careful choice of words.

26.4 Analysis and Interpretation

26.4.1 Thematic Analysis

The method of thematic analysis is used in qualitative data analysis to explore the patterns in the data (Braun & Clarke, 2006). It is specifically helpful for the subjective information in the form of points of view, opinions, and experiences of the participants, the data collected through surveys, interviews, and conversations (Kiger & Varpio, 2020) (Fig. 26.3).

26.4.2 Reflexive Thematic Analysis

In this study, the researchers used the reflexive thematic approach suggested by Braun and Clarke (2006), and the reasons are:

- The study is having broad and narrow questions about people's perspectives and views.
- The method is theoretically flexible that can be used in a variety of fields and with a variety of approaches such as inductive, deductive, semantic, etc.
- It doesn't need to pretend to be a neutral stance from the researchers' perspective.

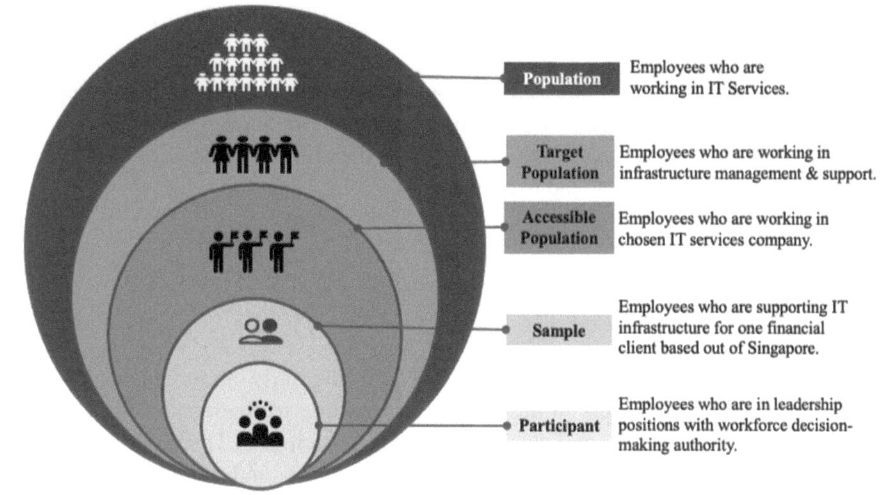

Fig. 26.4 Research population

- It doesn't make use of a codebook; instead gives freedom to the researchers to add, remove and change codes through the data.

26.4.3 Research Population

Population denotes the magnanimous compilation of individuals or objects which are the leading focus of the research (Hassan, 2023). In this research, the population is considered as all the employees who are working in the IT industry (Fig. 26.4).

The target group (population) consists of all of the employees working who are working in the IT infrastructure management and operations function. This set includes employees across all organizations. An accessible population is the segment of the target population to which the researchers has reasonable access (Themes, 2017). This category has all the employees working in an IT services company for IT infrastructure management functions. Using the method of purposive sampling, the sample from the accessible population is obtained. The sample selection criteria are that the employees are working in IT infrastructure management and operations in an IT services company supporting one of the Singapore-based financial clients. From this sample, we selected the participants who qualify all the previous criteria and are in the leadership and decision-making positions for workforce management.

26.4.4 Purposive Sampling

Purposive sampling is also known as the selective or purposeful sampling method where the researchers identify the participant as per preselected criteria. Each identified participant in this study is qualified against the criteria: occupation, company, function, client profile, role, and experience.

26.4.5 Number of Participants

A total number of 11 participants were selected for this study out of which eight are used. The selection is based on the purposive sampling technique considering the homogeneity, accessibility, and availability of the participants. Three of the participants responses are discarded as per data quality reviews, and the remaining eight are used for the purpose of the results of this study. Participants have been assigned a pseudonym (details in the appendix) to protect their identity.

26.4.6 Procedure

Data collection was carried out with each individual participant starting with an introduction and then obtaining the response in a text-based interview questionnaire both online and offline (Fig. 26.5)

1. ***Introduction*** – each participant is introduced to the study's objective and role in the research. The mode used in this study is phone conversations, face-to-face conversations, video conferencing, or text messages.
2. ***Consent*** – each participant has been informed to sign the consent form before answering the questionnaire.
3. ***Questionnaire*** – A total of 18 questions are included in the questionnaire sheet. The questions are purposefully kept subjective and open-ended. No leading questions were included to avoid any bias.

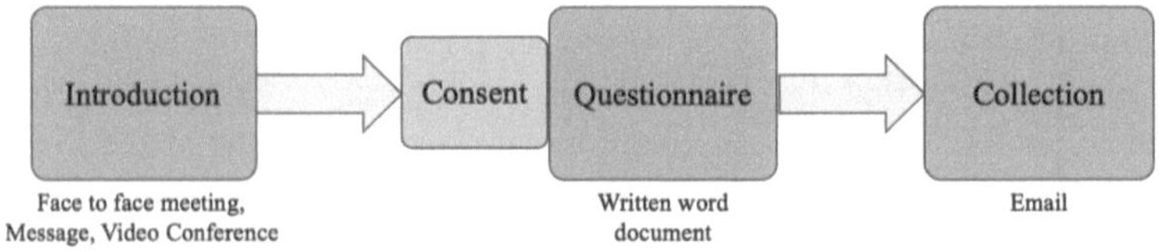

Fig. 26.5 Data collection process

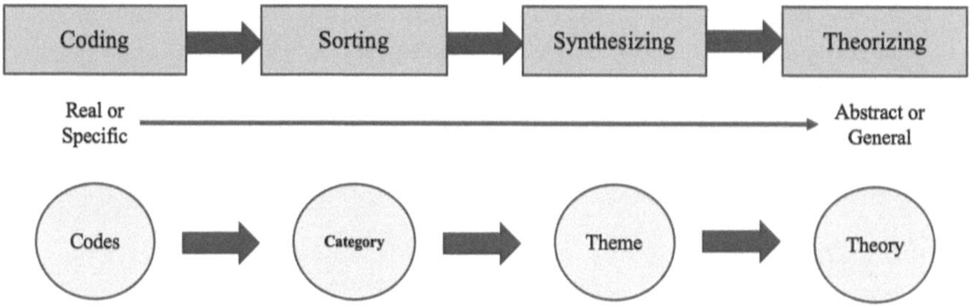

Fig. 26.6 Coding framework. (Saldana, 2015)

4. ***Data Collection*** – the responses are collected in text format in a MS Word document and sent over email to the researchers. The text data is then extracted to Microsoft Excel for further data analysis.
5. ***Timelines***

- Data collection time window: 2–3 weeks
- Questionnaire response time: 30–40 min per participant
- Data analysis time: 1–2 weeks

26.4.7 Analysis Methodology

The following framework is used to perform the coding process (Fig. 26.6):

Step 1: All the responses from each participant obtained in text format are read line by line, and codes (in vivo coding) are assigned as the comments to the answer or sentence of interest in Microsoft word. Inductive coding approach is used for generating the codes since it allows to use the code directly from the data.

Step 2: After creating the codes from each participant's response, the selected response text and codes are transported to excel along with page number, line number, and actual textual data.

Step 3: All the codes from all the participant responses are consolidated into one excel file arranged in columns.

Step 4: The codes are now reviewed again and sorted into various categories as per the pattern observed in the codes.

Step 5: Create Themes.

After further synthesis of the data in step 4, the following four high-level themes emerged and can be broadly classified as:

1. **Hiring** – related to the hiring strategy of the workforce in IT infrastructure management and operations.
2. **Resistance** – related to exploring reasons for resistance in adopting AI in IT infrastructure management and operations by financial organizations.

3. **Benefit** – aligned to the prospective use and benefits of AI in IT infrastructure management for a company as well as employees.
4. **Adoption** – related to the recommendation and implementation strategy for a company to adopt AI in IT infrastructure management and operations.

26.4.8 Inferences

26.4.8.1 Factors Influencing the Hiring of the Workforce in IT Infrastructure Management and Operations

Most participants shared similar observations on the influencing factors for hiring in IT operations. 50% of the participants said that attrition, attitude, and skillset are the primary influencing factors in hiring in IT infrastructure management. The participants shared that the organization is facing attrition primarily due to competitive pay in the market and the fast pace of technological advancement, which is challenging to catch. Other influencing factors are changes in business requirements, demand in the market, and enforcement of automation initiatives. Hiring decisions of individuals are based on cultural alignment, the experience of candidates, adaptivity of candidates in the continuously changing technology space, academic qualifications, and candidates' potential to add value to the organization. Organizations are facing challenges in retaining talent while the workforce is already lean in IT infrastructure operations. The long hiring process also adds to the impediments. Existing resource constraints experienced in organizations also includes staff reluctance to change their skillset, resulting in hiring externally, which increases cost. The thematic map below shows the connections of hiring in IT infrastructure management (Fig. 26.7).

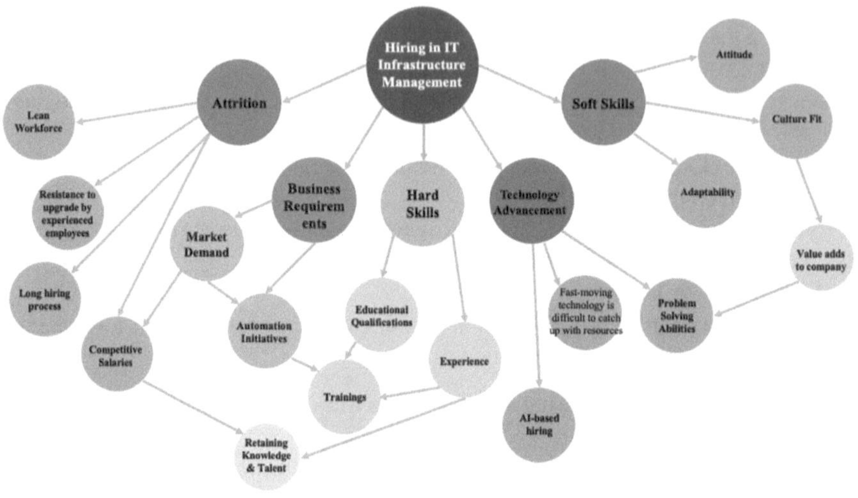

Fig. 26.7 Thematic map for hiring

The way forward to manage the hiring strategy for an organization is to develop in-house talent instead of being dependent on external hiring. 60% of the respondents comprehend that regular training, cross-technology training, and certifications can help to fill the talent gap. 25% think that the AI-assisted hiring process can help to find and map a candidate faster and without bias as human beings have prejudice. Organizations could hire staff with little experienced, even those in niche positions, and then train them after joining. This will ensure the cost of hiring be sustainable, and the newly-hired staff can be trained and prepared for their posts as needed by the organizations. The hiring process should be proactive instead of reactive, which means rather than waiting for to be hired after attrition, they proactively plan for rotation (role change or team change) for the workforce. Another strategy is to give incentives to existing employees for upskilling.

26.4.8.2 Resistance to the Adoption of Automation and AI

The employees and the organization have reasons to resist AI or automation in IT infrastructure management and operations.

Most participants (50%) comprehend that the organizations resist adopting AI IT infrastructure management due to cost (perceived low return on investment), non-availability of matured tools and infrastructure, and lack of availability of skillset and workforce to manage the automation. The other factors include the complexity of the AI configurations and logic, fear of the failure of the new technology, and ever-growing regulations. Financial organizations have a long culture of sensitivity and low-risk appetite regarding technology decisions.

The below thematic map shows the connections between resistance and the reasons stated by employees and organizations (Fig. 26.8).

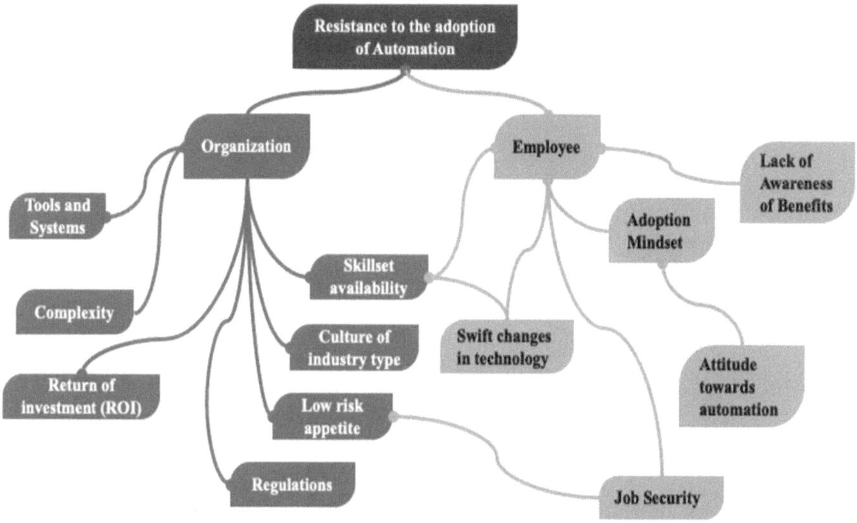

Fig. 26.8 Thematic map for resistance theme

As shared by most of the participants, the way forward for smooth adoption is to take up the challenge by leadership, knowing that the change is not easy for the employees. Respondents feel that resistance is unavoidable, and an influential leader can help to manage the difference in the organization when the work task moves to the automated AI-based machines. Regular training and awareness sessions also help overcome the resistance to adopting AI in the verticals of IT infrastructure support operations.

26.4.8.3 Benefits of Using AI in IT Infrastructure Support and Management

This study investigates the benefits based on the participants' responses categorized under advantages, disadvantages, and potential areas of use in IT Infrastructure Management.

Below thematic map demonstrates the connections between the benefits and the organization and employees (Fig. 26.9).

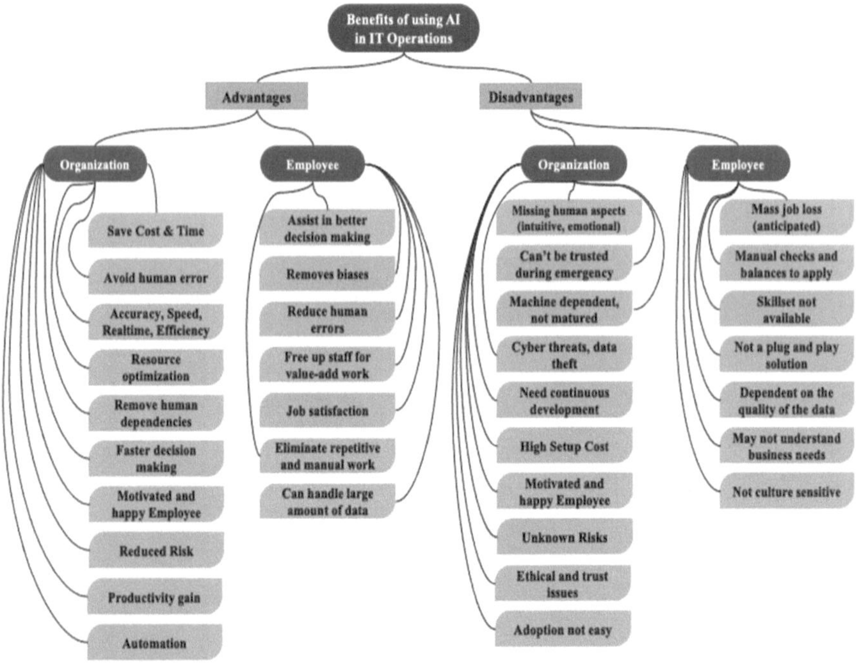

Fig. 26.9 Thematic map for benefits

Advantages

About 50% of the participants reflect that the key advantage of using AI is avoiding human errors in operations, automating repetitive tasks, and enhancing IT operations. Other benefits include accuracy, cost efficiency, speed in execution, and capability to handle extensive data. With the help of AI, human capability can be enhanced and assisted to be faster and better in decision-making. For an organization, automation saves time and cost for almost all the respondents. The participants feel that reduction in human error helps organizations save costs on the penalties, rework, and business impacts. Resource optimization is another area where organizations can take advantage of automation by eliminating resource dependencies, minimizing human intervention in the support task, and automating repeated tasks. Organizations can benefit from the productivity gain in IT infrastructure operations with reduced risk, resulting in contented employees and customers.

As the repetitive task will be automated, the employees will be unoccupied to do quality work, which will help to get job satisfaction. AI removes the biases and assists employees in faster decision-making with no manual errors.

Disadvantages

Most of the respondents (40%) feel that the primary disadvantage of AI is the risk and fear of mass job cuts. Twenty-five percent of participants think that AI can't replace human aspects such as intuitive, emotional, and culturally sensitive. They also mention that critical business tasks can't be off-loaded to machines, and this requires manual human control in emergency or disaster recovery situations. This also creates a dependency on machines, and manual checks and balances are always needed. AI technology is also not perceived as mature, leading to trust and ethical issues. A machine running based on data is limited to logically defined tasks, and it handles matters with no context. AI cannot match the out-of-box thinking of humans and it depends heavily on the quality of data.

Since AI is not a plug-and-play solution and it has to be customized for every customer organization, the solution setup incurs a high cost. It also needs continued development and management, and one solution may not simultaneously fit both large and small enterprises. Machine learning may not understand the business requirements, and change management is another obstacle to overcome in the organization. Other recent and more prevalent issues are related to cyber threats and data loss.

26.4.8.4 Potential Use

The participants had been equivocal regarding the probable areas where AI can play a key role in IT infrastructure management operations. 20% of respondents mark human error avoidance as the major area, while 30% feel that customer service can be improved significantly with automation. All the participants agree to a certain degree that AI can play a human helping role in the IT infrastructure management tasks, for examples, provisioning, monitoring, and correlating.

26.5 Conclusion

Inferences from the study revealed some of the eminent aspects and insights of IT infrastructure management in a financial organization. Furthermore, the analysis indicates some interesting relationships between hiring, workload, optimization, and advancement in technology. The data and thematic maps also give an understand and appreciation of the role of AI in the lifecycle of the IT infrastructure management in an organization. Furthermore, the researchers studied the challenges of hiring technical staff for the IT infrastructure operations as well as the plausible ways to improve the process with the help of AI. At the same time, the apprehensions and resistance of an organization as well as its employees in adopting AI in IT infrastructure operations are explored. Knowing various perspectives from the participants, the researchers constructed a theme centered around organizations and employees, thus showing the benefits of AI. In addition, the researchers produce a roadmap on an AI adoption strategy as well as recommendations for stakeholders to embrace AI and automation in IT infrastructure management and operations in a non-disruptive approach.

26.5.1 Recommendations

The automation-led initiatives driven by AI can be more beneficial in specific segments of the IT infrastructure management in the financial organization. As per the inference from this research, the following three areas could benefit from AI:

- *Human error avoidance*

As technology moves ahead and financial transactions get more and more complex they inevitably will be at risk if handled by humans. So, AI can be a good candidate to manage enormous volumes of data that otherwise may lead to errors by humans. Automation of repetitive tasks can lower the risk of errors and rework for the employees.

- *Customer experience*

Banking and financial companies heavily depend on customer service to retain existing customers and attract new customers. This essentially means the IT infrastructure needs to be available for the customer at all time and systems running without any glitch. Any small outage or issue impacting customers can seriously impact the customer satisfaction scores (CSAT) which is a success index for any company. Hence, using AI to proactively identify the IT infrastructure issues, performance issues, or predicting capacity issues can help to avoid the service outage and getting a better CSAT score.

- *IT infrastructure management tasks*
  - Provisioning of IT Infrastructure
  - Automation of business recovery IT functions
  - IT capacity and demand forecasting and planning
  - Automated system health checks at the start of the day
  - Event management and correlation
  - Detection of the faults and response
  - The downtime predictions, upgrades, and fault recovery
  - Elimination of time-consuming and repetitive manual tasks for the operators
  - Fraud detection and regulatory compliance

26.5.2 Limitations

This study is based on research from qualitative data. On one hand, qualitative data provides the opportunity to get the perspectives and feelings of participants unhindered while on other hand it is difficult to analyze. The analysis of qualitative data is done manually which becomes difficult as the data increases.

The data collection is done through open-ended questions that make it difficult for the researchers to verify the results objectively or mathematically. Hence the causality investigation is rather difficult (Radu, 2022).

The results of this qualitative research cannot be replicated over a large data set such as all the employees working in IT Infrastructure management to prove or reject any hypotheses. The reason behind this is that qualitative data contains the reactions, responses, and emotions of the participants which cannot be replicated (Naresh, 2021).

Other limitations which may had surfaced during the research are:

- Participants' responses might have been affected by the presence of the researchers and this is unavoidable.
- The presentation of the findings might result in complications due to issues of confidentiality and anonymity of participants.

26.5.3 Future Research

As mentioned, it may be a challenge to replicate the result of this research over a large data set. However, the researchers note this as a possible future research. A more likely scenario is to replicate this research in another or even a few more financial organizations in Singapore so as to affirm or overturn the results of this research.

If the researchers could have access to many staff in senior IT positions in many financial institutions in Singapore, then it is possible for a quantitative research to be carried out. Yet another potential future research is to investigate financial institutions beyond Singapore, starting with those in Southeast Asia.

References

Agrawal, V. K., Agrawal, V. K., & Taylor, A. R. (2017). Trends in IT human resources and end-users involved in IT applications. *Journal of International Technology and Information Management, 26*(4), 154–188. https://www.proquest.com/scholarly-journals/trends-human-resources-end-users-involved/docview/2051732262/se-2?accountid=162730

Alt, J.K., Klingensmith, K., & Faber, I. (2020). Growing an AI capability: Challenges and opportunities. In Proceedings of SPIE 11413, AI and machine learning for multi-domain operations applications II, 1141305 (22 April 2020); doi:https://doi.org/10.1117/12.2559126.

Arundale, A. (2021, October 19). *Using HR technology to reduce operating costs*. Advanced. https://www.oneadvanced.com/news-and-opinion/using-hr-technology-to-reduce-operating-costs/

Athena Information Solutions Pvt. Ltd. (2016). Mphasis launches AI-powered DigiOps to evade errors in IT infrastructure operations. *Trade Journal*, 1830826723. https://www.proquest.com/trade-journals/mphasis-launches-ai-powered-digiops-evade-errors/docview/1830826723/se-2?accountid=162730

Athena Information Solutions Pvt. Ltd. (2018). HPE delivers cloud-based AI-driven operations for HPE ProLiant, Apollo and synergy servers. *Trade Journal*, 2138512308. https://www.proquest.com/trade-journals/hpe-delivers-cloud-based-ai-driven-operations/docview/2138512308/se-2?accountid=162730

Athena Information Solutions Pvt. Ltd. (2019). Ericsson launches new AI-based operations engine to simplify network operations. *Trade Journal*, 2172562982. https://www.proquest.com/trade-journals/ericsson-launches-new-ai-based-operations-engine/docview/2172562982/se-2?accountid=162730

Bastani, H., Bastani, O., & Sinchaisri, P. (2022). Improving human decision-making with machine learning. *Academy of Management Proceedings, 2022*(1). https://doi.org/10.5465/ambpp.2022.17725abstract

Braun, V., & Clarke, V. (2006). Using thematic analysis in psychology. *Qualitative Research in Psychology, 3*(2), 77–101. https://doi.org/10.1191/1478088706qp063oa

Bughin, J., Hazan, E., Lund, S., Dahlström, P., Wiesinger, A., & Subramaniam, A. (2021, January 23). *Skill shift: Automation and the future of the workforce*. McKinsey & Company. https://www.mckinsey.com/featured-insights/future-of-work/skill-shift-automation-and-the-future-of-the-workforce

Cappuccio, D. (2021). Tips for revamping dated datacenters: IT infrastructure and operations leaders are increasingly focusing on new ideas and technologies alongside ways to deliver business value. Computer Weekly, 14–17.

Chamberlain, L. B., Davis, L. E., Stanley, M., & Gattoni, B. R. (2020). *Automated decision systems for cybersecurity and infrastructure security.* In *2020 IEEE Security and Privacy Workshops (SPW)* (pp. 196–201). doi: 10.1109/SPW50608.2020.00048.

Donnelly, C. (2016). IT infrastructure operations staff under stress, says HumanOps movement. *Computer Weekly*, 6–8.

Elias, M. (2018). Learning machines: How AI is already disrupting fixed operations. *Automotive News*, https://www.proquest.com/trade-journals/learning-machines/docview/2007154651/se-2?accountid=162730

Gray, J. (2019, November 25). Who's afraid of AI? *Utility Week*. https://utilityweek.co.uk/whos-afraid-ai/

Gupta, P. (2016). Automation could cut network costs and fund IT innovations. *Voice & Data, 23*(3), 18.

Hammarberg, K., Kirkman, M., & de Lacey, S. (2016, March). Qualitative research methods: When to use them and how to judge them. *Human Reproduction*, (31, 3), 498–501.

Hariharan, G. (2018). *AI and semiconductors: Exponential growth from AI adoption in the cloud and at the edge.* : JPMorgan Chase & Company. Retrieved from ProQuest one business https://www.proquest.com/reports/ai-semiconductors/docview/2001884971/se-2?accountid=162730

Hassan, M. A. (2023). Indian Ocean university | business administration – Academia.Edu. *Academia*. https://iouniversity.academia.edu/Departments/Business_Administration/Documents

Henkel, A. P., Bromuri, S., Iren, D., & Urovi, V. (2020). Half human, half machine – Augmenting service employees with AI for interpersonal emotion regulation. *Journal of Service Management, 31*(2), 247–265. https://doi.org/10.1108/JOSM-05-2019-0160

Hepler, R., & Cloud, D. (2022). Study.com | take online courses. Earn college credit. Research schools, Degrees & Careers. *Study*. https://study.com/learn/lesson/interpretivism-sociology-concept-origin.html

Hertvik, J. (2020). IT infrastructure management. BMC. https://www.bmc.com/blogs/it-infrastructure-management/

IDC. (2021). *Public Cloud IT Infrastructure Revenue Growth Remained Strong in Third Quarter of 2020, According to IDC.* https://www.idc.com/getdoc.jsp?containerId=prUS47279621

Institute of Finance & Management. (2011). IT costs: Strategies to cut IT infrastructure and operations costs. *Trade Journal, 2*, 08952787. https://www.proquest.com/trade-journals/costs-strategies-cut-infrastructure-operations/docview/853734029/se-2?accountid=162730

Jarrett, C. (2021). Don't try to beat AI, join it! Automation will give, as well as take, opportunities for human workers. *Quality*, 57–58.

Johnson, J. L., Adkins, D., & Chauvin, S. (2020). A Review of the quality indicators of rigor in qualitative research. *American Journal of Pharmaceutical Education, 84*(1), 7120. https://doi.org/10.5688/ajpe7120

Kark, K., Briggs, B., & Terzioglu, A. (2019). The future of work in technology. *Deloitte Insights*. https://www2.deloitte.com/us/en/insights/focus/technology-and-the-future-of-work/tech-leaders-reimagining-work-workforce-workplace.html

Kawulich, B. (2012). Selecting a research approach: Paradigm, methodology and methods. In *Doing social research: A global context* (pp. 51–61). McGraw Hill.

Kiger, M. E., & Varpio, L. (2020). Thematic analysis of qualitative data: AMEE guide no. 131. *Medical Teacher, 42*(8), 846–854. https://doi.org/10.1080/0142159x.2020.1755030

Kobbacy, K. A. H., & Vadera, S. (2011). A survey of AI in operations management from 2005 to 2009: IMS. *Journal of Manufacturing Technology Management, 22*(6), 706–733. https://doi.org/10.1108/17410381111149602

Korolov, M. (2021, December 13). How AI is reshaping IT operations. CIO. https://www.cio.com/article/221790/how-ai-is-reshaping-it-operations.html

Kuprenko, V. (2021). IT infrastructure explained: Definition, components, and types. *Stefanini*. https://stefanini.com/en/trends/articles/it-infrastructure-explained-definition-components-and-types

Lincoln, Y. S., & Guba, E. (1985). *Naturalistic inquiry* (1st ed.). SAGE Publications.

Lyn Paul, C., Blaha, L. M., Fallon, C. K., Gonzalez, C., & Gutzwiller, R. S. (2019). Opportunities and challenges for human-machine teaming in cybersecurity operations. *Proceedings of the Human Factors and Ergonomics Society Annual Meeting, 63*(1), 442–446. https://doi.org/10.1177/1071181319631079

Mandavia, M. (2017, July 13). In-house automation to cut more jobs: Hexaware CEO. *The Economic Times*. https://economictimes.indiatimes.com/tech/ites/in-house-automation-to-cut-more-jobs-hexaware-ceo/articleshow/59572878.cms

Marx, J., Martines, D., Quarta, L., & Desmartin, G. (2021). *How automation and AI can unlock value in IT operations.* : Boston Consulting Group. Retrieved from ProQuest one business https://www.proquest.com/reports/how-automation-ai-can-unlock-value-operations/docview/2584100274/se-2?accountid=162730

Masood, A., & Hashmi, A. (2019). AIOps: Predictive analytics & machine learning in operations. In: *Cognitive computing recipes*. Apress. doi:https://doi.org/10.1007/978-1-4842-4106-6_7.
Mistry, N. (2018). *What's driving the IT infrastructure of the future*? Enterprise innovation, N.PAG.
Moghaddam, Y., Yurko, H., Demirkan, H., Tymann, N., & Rayes, A. (2020). *The future of work: How artificial intelligence can augment human capabilities*. Business Expert Press.
Naresh, D. (2021, April 16). Strengths and Limitations of Qualitative Research. *Invoke*. https://invoke.com/blog/strengths-and-limitations-of-qualitative-research
NASDAQ OMX Corporate Solutions, Inc. (2019). Remote infrastructure management market is eyeing for an 11% CAGR to reach a USD 35 Billion valuation by 2023. *Wire Feed*, 2266744177. https://www.proquest.com/wire-feeds/remote-infrastructure-management-market-is-eyeing/docview/2266744177/se-2?accountid=162730
Balasubramanian, N., Ye, Y., & Xu, M. (2022). Substituting human decision-making with machine learning: Implications for organizational learning. *Academy of Management Review*. https://doi.org/10.5465/amr.2019.0470
NetEnrich, Inc. (2019, December 9). NetEnrich to launch AI-driven solutions for digital services integrity at the 2019 Gartner IT infrastructure, Operations & Cloud Strategies Conference. *GlobeNewswire News Room*. https://www.globenewswire.com/en/news-release/2019/12/09/1957921/0/en/NetEnrich-To-Launch-AI-Driven-Solutions-For-Digital-Services-Integrity-at-the-2019-Gartner-IT-Infrastructure-Operations-Cloud-Strategies-Conference.html
Nickerson, R. S. (1998). Confirmation bias: A ubiquitous phenomenon in many guises. *Review of General Psychology, 2*(2), 175–220. https://doi.org/10.1037/1089-2680.2.2.175
Preimesberger, C. (2019). How to prepare an enterprise for adding AI to IT operations. EWeek, N.PAG.
Putra, R. A., Putra, G. D., Arifin, N. F., Haryanto, B., Shihab, M. R., & Ranti, B. (2020). Benefit of using Cloud services in IT infrastructure in the capability, strategy and cost efficiency aspects: detikNetwork case study. IOP conference series. *Materials Science and Engineering, 879*(1). https://doi.org/10.1088/1757-899X/879/1/012045
Radu, V. (2022, January 31). *Qualitative research: Definition, methodology, limitation, examples – Omniconvert Blog*. Omniconvert Ecommerce Growth. https://www.omniconvert.com/blog/qualitative-research-definition-methodology-limitation-examples/
Sahoo, S. K. (2017). India's IT infrastructure spend to reach $2.2 billion in 2017: Report. *Voice & Data*, https://www.proquest.com/trade-journals/indias-infrastructure-spend-reach-2-billion-2017/docview/1895728143/se-2?accountid=162730
Saldana, J. (2015). *The coding manual for qualitative researchers* (3rd ed.). SAGE Publications Ltd..
Samik Chatterjee, C. (2020). Technology hardware: Near & long term implications of COVID-19 led IT infrastructure trends for IT hardware, networking, and semis. JPMorgan Chase & Company. Retrieved from ProQuest One Business https://www.proquest.com/reports/technology-hardware/docview/2385354391/se-2?accountid=162730
Saran, C. (2017). Automation and software-defined IT can help to bridge the server skills gap. Computer Weekly, 4–6.
Sayer, P. (2020). IBM retrains Watson AI for IT operations. CIO, https://www.proquest.com/trade-journals/ibm-retrains-watson-ai-operations/docview/2399574885/se-2?accountid=162730
Schade, A. (2017). *Avoid leading questions to get better insights from participants*. Nielsen Norman Group. https://www.nngroup.com/articles/leading-questions/
Schneider, S., & Leyer, M. (2019). Me or IT? Adoption of AI in the delegation of personal strategic decisions. *Managerial & Decision Economics, 40*(3), 223–231. https://doi-org.spjain.idm.oclc.org/10.1002/mde.2982
Shah, S. (2021, February 8). 7 biases to avoid in qualitative research. *Editage Insights*. https://www.editage.com/insights/7-biases-to-avoid-in-qualitative-research

Sliwa, C. (2019, October 22). Virtual Instruments becomes Virtana, adds cloud monitoring. *Storage*. https://www.techtarget.com/searchstorage/news/252472706/Virtual-Instrumentsbecomes-Virtana-adds-cloud-monitoring

Siaterlis, C., Genge, B., Hohenadel, M., & Del Pra, M. (2012). *Enabling the Exploration of Operating Procedures in Critical Infrastructures*. In J. Butts & S. Shenoi (Eds.), *Critical infrastructure protection VI. ICCIP 2012. IFIP advances in information and communication technology, vol 390*. Springer. https://doi.org/10.1007/978-3-642-35764-0_16

Stainton, H. (2021, August 30). Ontology and epistemology: A simple explanation. *Tourism Teacher*. https://tourismteacher.com/ontology-and-epistemology-simple/

Sumo Logic, Inc. (2021, October 14). Monitoring. *Sumo Logic*. https://www.sumologic.com/glossary/continuous-monitoring/

Swanston, M. (2022, July 7). IT monitoring | IT solutions | 24/7/365 IT support operations. *Bell Integration*. https://www.bell-integration.com/capabilities/run/it-monitoring/

Tabesh, P. (2021). Who's making the decisions? How managers can harness AI and remain in charge. *Journal of Business Strategy, 43*, 373–380. https://doi.org/10.1108/JBS-05-2021-0090

TCS. (2021). *TCS Named a Leader in Cognitive & Self-Healing IT Infrastructure Management Services by NelsonHall*. https://www.tcs.com/leader-cognitive-self-healing-it-infrastructure-management-services-nelsonhall

Thau, M., Mikkelsen, M. F., Hjortskov, M., & Pedersen, M. J. (2021). Question order bias revisited: A split-ballot experiment on satisfaction with public services among experienced and professional users. *Public Admin., 99*, 189–204. https://doi.org/10.1111/padm.12688

Themes, U. (2017, February 9). Examining populations and samples in research. *Nurse Key*. https://nursekey.com/examining-populations-and-samples-in-research/#s0230

Tien-tsin Huang, C. (2017). *IT services: The news flow: EY results, Euro Tech spending forecast, IT hiring improving, global sourcing data, and Harvey impact*. JPMorgan Chase & Company. Retrieved from ProQuest One Business https://www.proquest.com/reports/services-news-flow/docview/1937657912/se-2?accountid=162730

Vasudevan, S. (2022, May 23). How Automation is driving the next wave of growth for India's leading IT services companies. *Dataquest*. https://www.dqindia.com/how-automation-is-driving-the-next-wave-of-growth-for-indias-leading-it-services-companies/

Vizard, M. (2012). IT *automation reduces technical services revenue for the channel. Channel Insider, 1*.

Wamba-Taguimdje, S.-L., Samuel, F. W., Jean Robert, K. K., & Chris Emmanuel, T. W. (2020). Influence of AI (AI) on firm performance: The business value of AI-based transformation projects. *Business Process Management Journal, 26*(7), 1893–1924. https://doi.org/10.1108/BPMJ-10-2019-0411

Chapter 27
RFID Technology for Sustainable Fashion and Textile Manufacturing

Majo George, Rajkishore Nayak, Irfan UlHaq, Hiep Pham, Tarun Panwar, and Duc-Anh Nguyen

Abstract Radio frequency identification (RFID) technology is one of the greatest innovations that has been widely accepted in the supply chain and logistics for obtaining accurate and fast information. Utilizing RFID technology in a variety of industries, such as automotive, manufacturing, fashion, and textiles, can alter business dynamics and promote a sustainable future. RFID technology provides not only economic benefits in manufacturing and supply chain processes, but also numerous tangible business benefits, such as competitive advantage, improved customer relationships, resiliency, and increased profitability. Several brands of fast fashion have already adopted eco-friendly production techniques using RFID technology. Other brands should also begin focusing on sustainable practices to ensure their long-term success, which will benefit both the company and the environment. This paper investigates the sustainability benefits realized through the application of RFID technology in the fashion and textile supply chain focusing the manufacturing and retail operations in Vietnam. As Vietnam is one of the emerging economies that produces fashion and textiles for numerous international fashion brands, Vietnamese fashion and textile companies were selected for this study. The results revealed that numerous businesses, especially small and medium-sized enterprises (SMEs) were unaware of RFID technology and its benefits in the production and supply chain.

M. George · I. UlHaq · H. Pham
The Business School, RMIT University, Ho Chi Minh City, Vietnam
e-mail: majo.george@rmit.edu.vn; irfan.ulhaq@rmit.edu.vn; hiep.pham@rmit.edu.vn

R. Nayak (✉)
Centre of Communication and Design, RMIT University, Ho Chi Minh City, Vietnam
e-mail: rajkishore.nayak@rmit.edu.vn

T. Panwar
School of Fashion & Textiles, RMIT University, Melbourne, Australia
e-mail: tarun.panwar@rmit.edu.au

D.-A. Nguyen
Doctoral Student, Department of Economics and Finance, RMIT University, Ho Chi Minh City, Vietnam
e-mail: nguyenducanh@gmail.com

E. L. Eijdenberg et al. (eds.), *Innovation-Driven Business and Sustainability in the Tropics*, https://doi.org/10.1007/978-981-99-2909-2_27

There were several environmental, social and economic benefits, achieved through the implementation of new technologies such as RFID. Social benefits included customer satisfaction, reducing employee stress level and better labor management; the environmental benefits included saving energy, reducing wastage and pollution level; the economic benefits included saving resources, reducing cost and increasing profitability.

Keywords Sustainability · RFID technology · Fashion supply chain · Sustainable benefits · Emerging economies

27.1 Introduction

The current global warming, pollution, climate change, and resource scarcity have increased awareness of the need for sustainability in many manufacturing sectors, including the fashion and textiles industries (Caniato et al., 2012; Nayak, 2020). Sustainability has been pursued globally in supply chain activities as a strategic policy due to its growing importance in marketing and branding, as consumer awareness of environmental and social concerns is increasing (Bhardwaj & Fairhurst, 2010). Governments in several nations are also enforcing regulations requiring businesses to implement environmentally sustainable practices in their supply chains to reduce environmental degradation (Nayak et al., 2019a; Williams, 2015). The primary objective of sustainability in organizations is the development of long-term profitable business with minimal internal and external impacts on society and the environment (Fung et al., 2021). The future of manufacturing and supply chain activities can't be separated from the triple bottom line of sustainability (TBL), which relates to people, planet, and profit.

An organization would be able to achieve high and consistent profitability with low costs, while its members would receive fair compensation, supplementary benefits, improved working conditions, and safety (Nayak et al., 2020a). A company could achieve external sustainability, on the other hand, by increasing its competitiveness on the global market, providing more value to customers, increasing the number of jobs created, increasing transparency, increasing recycling, decreasing waste generation, consuming less energy, and reducing the release of hazardous chemicals into the environment (Mok et al., 2022; Guo et al., 2006). The fashion and textile industries are one of the most influential manufacturing industries in shaping the economies of many nations, particularly emerging economies (De Brito & Van Der Laan, 2009). This sector accounts for 2% of the world's Gross Domestic Product (GDP) and satisfies the second fundamental need for human civilization, namely clothing. Financially, this sector is worth more than 3 trillion US dollars, which is expanding, and employs over 33 million people, primarily women; this number has nearly doubled since 1990 (Collins, 2003). However, because sustainability practices are not strictly adhered to in this sector, it contributes significantly to environmental issues such as water and air pollution.

The concept of sustainability is gaining momentum in fashion sourcing, production, supply chain management, distribution and retail management, even though the adoption of sustainability in the fashion and textile industries is a difficult task due to the pressure of lower manufacturing costs and shorter lead time (Hsu et al., 2009; Desore & Narula, 2018; Goworek et al., 2020). Sustainable practices entail the incorporation of environmentally friendly processes into the production and supply chain process, including product design, sourcing of raw materials, yarn, fabric, and garment production, delivery of the final product to customers, and management of end-of-life (EOL) products (Nayak et al., 2020b). Many of the world's leading fashion brands are pioneers in integrating sustainable manufacturing and supply chain practices. The complex nature of the fashion and textile industries' supply chains and the trend of outsourcing from the global market have led to the decentralization of the supply chain, which creates difficulties in managing the industries' long-term risks.

Utilizing a variety of technologies in manufacturing and logistics processes can increase productivity, enhance efficiency, reduce waste, and reduce energy consumption, which are the pillars of sustainability. RFID or Radio Frequency Identification technology is one such technology that can contribute to environmental sustainability because it improves stock/inventory visibility and traceability during production and supply chain; automates inventory management; increases data accuracy; enhances status monitoring; and improves operational efficiency, waste reduction, and shrinkage reduction (Arkan & Van Landeghem, 2013; Choy et al., 2009; Dai & Tseng, 2012). RFID reduces the need for human intervention during storage, identification, logistics and transportation of inventory. RFID tags are entirely distinct from barcode tags in their design, capacity to store data, operational range, and method of data collection (Roberti, 2006). RFID technology has numerous applications in fashion production and distribution, including manufacturing, supply chain management, retail management, warehousing, theft prevention, stock identification, stock update, tracing and tracking of merchandise movement (Nayak et al., 2007; Nayak, 2019; Ni et al., 2011).

As the RFID technology can provide real-time information on the inventory, several fashion brands are adopting the technology to complement their sustainability practices (Weinstein, 2005; Zelbst et al., 2010). The use of RFID technology can help fashion brands in saving of materials, improved inventory turnover, waste reduction, and accurate stock keeping, which is related to environmental sustainability (Nayak et al., 2022; Denuwara et al., 2019). Furthermore, the use of RFID technology can help the brands to stay competitive in the fashion business as it can help to increase productivity and efficiency, and reduce the cost of manufacturing. Adoption of newer technologies such as RFID can help to reduce the cost of garments in the era of increasing material and labor prices. However, the number of research papers focusing on the use of RFID technology to achieve the concept of sustainability is very few. Therefore, the objective of this paper is to investigate the current status of RFID technology in the Vietnamese fashion and textile industries and how this technology is helping to achieve the concept of sustainability (Nayak et al., 2019b, Nayak 2021).

27.2 Literature Review

Sustainability was considered to be vital in recent times by numerous economic actors, including governments, organizations, and consumers. Sustainable development is not only concerned with environmental issues, but also with economic and social development as well as environmental protection (Macchion et al., 2018; Hiller Connell & Kozar, 2017). Furthermore, people and culture are the most important factors to consider when developing sustainable applications. Sustainability in fashion and textiles can be achieved through adopting new materials that are biodegradable, reducing carbon emissions during manufacturing, using renewable resources, recycling wastage, saving energy consumption and preserving resources (Aras-Beger et al., 2020). Further, taking care of society, employees, and animals has been a large challenge in the global fashion and textile manufacturing sector, especially in developing countries such as Vietnam, which is the third largest manufacturer of fashion (Thorisdottir & Johannsdottir, 2019). Hence, this research has selected Vietnamese fashion and textile industries for the research.

Radio Frequency Identification (RFID) is the technology that uses electromagnetic waves and radio waves to automatically identify objects, people, and animals at a considerable distance (Azevedo & Carvalho, 2012; Condea et al., 2012). RFID is one of the most promising modern technologies for automatically identifying, tracking, and tracing items. In several application areas, RFID technology can complement or completely replace traditional barcode technology. RFID is a method of automatic identification comprised of several components, including tags, tag readers, edge servers, middleware, and application software (Nayak & Padhye, 2017). Among these the most significant components are the RFID tag (also known as a transponder), RFID reader (also known as a transceiver or interrogator), and data processing software. RFID tags are small objects that can be attached to or implanted within a product, animal, or person. It consists of a tiny chip containing the data and an antenna for receiving and responding to radio-frequency queries from an RFID transceiver (Fig. 27.1). The tags contain Electronic Product Code (EPC) and product-related information, such as the manufacturer's name, batch and production

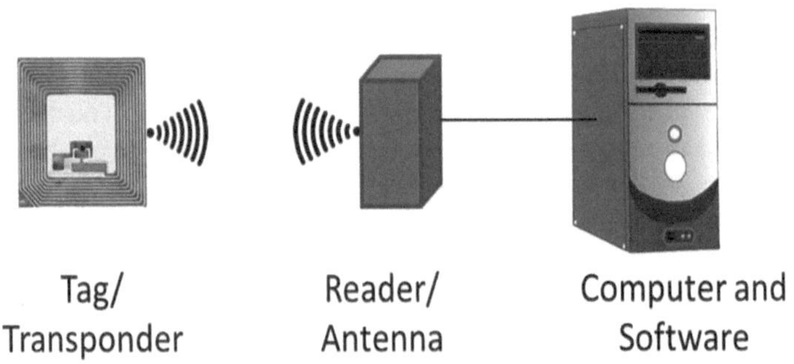

Fig. 27.1 A RFID tag with chip, software and antenna

year, price, etc. The RFID reader communicates with the tag within its read-range and decodes the data encoded in the tag. The RFID software is used to process data extracted by the reader from the RFID tags, which are related to product details.

As RFID systems can provide real-time inventory data, several fashion companies are adopting the technology to enhance their sustainability efforts. RFID technology can aid fashion brands in material conservation, increased inventory turnover, waste reduction, and accurate stock management, all of which contribute to environmental sustainability (Nayak et al., 2015). Furthermore, the use of RFID technology can help brands remain competitive in the fashion industry by increasing productivity and decreasing manufacturing costs. In an era of rising material and labour costs, the adoption of modern technologies such as RFID can help to reduce the cost of apparels. From the above discussions, it can be observed that RFID technology can provide several benefits relating to planet, people and profit. However, there are very few research papers that focus on the use of RFID technology to achieve sustainability. Consequently, the purpose of this paper is to examine the current state of RFID technology in the Vietnamese fashion and textile industries and how this technology contributes to the concept of sustainability. To achieve the research objectives, this study attempted to answer the following research questions (RQs).

- RQ1: How RFID technology is helping to achieve the benefits relating to sustainability?
- RQ2: How the implementation of RFID technology is helping the fashion supply chain in developing countries?

27.3 Methodology

To address the research questions, preliminary qualitative in-depth interviews with four Vietnamese fashion and textile manufacturing SME business owners were conducted. The selection of these businesses was based on two factors: (1) the belief that the interviewees are familiar with RFID technology and are implementing or have implemented it at their current or previous organization, and (2) the belief that the interviewees are familiar with RFID technology and its implications despite lacking practical experience. Inspired by the framework of TBL to measure sustainability marketing, a standard interview protocol was utilized to ensure interviewees' responses were comprehensive.

The interview questions focused on eliciting information regarding sustainability through the application of various technologies, such as RFID, and the obstacles encountered. It enabled us to compare diverse perspectives and gain valuable insights from the interviews. The interviews were recorded and then transcribed and coded using the NVivo software for qualitative data analysis. The interview questions were designed to capture the sustainability benefits using various technologies such as RFID. The study followed a four-step approach similar to Akbari (Akbari,

2018) and Farooque (Farooque et al., 2019) to investigate the sustainability benefits achieved by implementing RFID technology in Vietnamese fashion and textile supply chain.

The interviews were arranged with four apparel manufacturing units operating in Vietnam, who were using RFID technology. These industries have been operating at least for the last 3 years in Vietnam in fashion and textile supply chain. The participants were provided with the Participant Information and Consent Form (PICF) and explained about the interview process prior to the interview following RMIT's ethical guidelines. The interviews were organized both face-to-face and online, which lasted for about 60 minutes. The face-to-face interviews were conducted on the premises of the industries, whereas the online interviews were organized using Microsoft Teams platform, both conducted with two researchers and the interviewee. The following questions were asked to the interviewees to understand the benefits of using RFID technology relating to the TBL of sustainability.

- Environmental

How did the implementation of RFID technology help to achieve environmental benefits?

How did the implementation of RFID technology helping to reduce the process waste and materials waste?

- Social

How did the implementation of RFID technology help to achieve social benefits?

What benefits are you getting from RFID technology to manage labour productivity?

Do you think he implementation of RFID technology is helping to improve the transparency in the supply chain process? Describe in detail?

- Economic

How did the implementation of RFID technology help to achieve economic benefits?

What are the financial benefits are you getting from the RFID technology?

- Concluding questions

How does the implementation of RFID technology is helping to achieve sustainability in your fashion and textile business?

27.4 Results and Discussion

This study focused on the benefits of implementing RFID to achieve the TBL of sustainability. The implementation of RFID technology can contribute to the achievement of sustainability in the economic, environmental, and social spheres, as discussed in the following section.

27.4.1 Economic Benefits

In the fashion industry, economic sustainability ensures that the businesses sustainably uses resources while achieving their profit goals (i.e., the business is not creating environmental concerns or using excessive resources). To promote economic sustainability, businesses are increasingly considering their ties to the community and environment. A nation's economy is impacted directly or indirectly by the production of clothing and textiles for domestic as well as international consumption. RFID technology can be utilized by the fashion industry to manage the workplace and track inventory usage.

Implementing RFID technology improves manufacturing, supply chain, logistics, and warehouse management by facilitating more accurate inventory management. In addition, this enables businesses to comply with a variety of regulations, generate capital, and recycle obsolete assets efficiently and responsibly. The efficient management of assets improves the business's use of resources, provides greater clarity to distinguish between quality and defective products, and facilitates their identification. This can also aid in identifying the source of an error and taking the appropriate measures to correct it. This can also be used to recall any defective product that has reached retail stores. According to the first interviewee:

> **Extract 1** RFID technology is much more related to traceability and visibility as this kind of system is very helpful for quality control and aftermarket service when they have any quality feedback. We will be very accurate and precise to find out the products with defective components and feedback to the backlog, the production log, or purchasing orders. All information is collected from the traceability system: if one functional failure happened, there will have people who evaluate and analyze what are the root causes of this failure and which components, link back to the production site to identify how many items and quantities are in different stages or different areas and call back the products.

RFID technology can help to reduce the overall cost of a product by facilitating the efficient management of resources, such as inventory. RFID technology can assist in maintaining accurate inventory records and preventing shrinkage in the manufacturing and supply chain. Utilizing RFID technology can also reduce labour costs, which are considered the second most significant factor for garment costs after material costs. For instance, the RFID system can reduce payroll errors, increase employee transparency and motivation, provide information quickly, and reduce the processing time required for data. To improve the purchasing experience, the data processing advantage can also inform customers about the origin of the clothing or the availability of a fashion item at different store locations. In addition to the social impacts of this implication on customers, this can make customers feel more comfortable purchasing the article of clothing, thereby increasing revenue from this benefit. RFID technology aids in gaining a competitive advantage, and saves time by being more efficient and automatic, thereby enhancing productivity and reducing lead time. This was described by the third interviewee:

> **Extract 2** Competitiveness in the marketplace is a major factor leading to the application of RFID technology to meet the needs of customers. It will help manufacturing enterprises a

lot in saving time and human resources. Applying automatic machinery, enterprises will save some costs but not absolute, machinery helps reduce labour resources in production. RFID technology will help to increase productivity so that the company can receive more orders and shorten the production process.

In addition to the cost-effectiveness of RFID technology, as the trend toward sustainability awareness among younger generations continues to rise, the application of advanced technologies will increase the customer proposition perspectives, thereby directly increasing the revenue of fashion brands over the long term. RFID technology can increase the valuation of a fashion company from the perspective of investors because it will improve the ESG (Environmental, Social, and Governance) factor, thereby increasing the capital earned for future growth. Consequently, by incorporating a sustainability factor, a fashion company can increase its capital not only through the revenue generated by the possible expansion of its customer base but also through the investment capital from sustainable investors. This can also be a competitive advantage for any fashion brand, especially fast-fashion brands that sought a different perspective on their notoriously unsustainable business models. Also contributing to the argument was interviewee three:

Extract 3 With the growing trend of diversified ways for a person to look at the product, the need to be sustainable in the eye of the customer is important. Though the value of a product still plays a crucial role, other characteristics can also contribute to the decision-making process of a customer. An enhanced value proposition can be established through sustainability technology applications like RFID for an example.

27.4.2 Environmental Benefits

The production of clothing and textiles, particularly when the fabric is wet processed, requires a substantial amount of energy, water, chemicals, and auxiliary materials. This process generates a substantial amount of wastewater or effluent, which is frequently discharged untreated into the ecosystem. This effluent contains numerous hazardous chemicals that can hurt the environment. Therefore, all the steps involved in fabric wet processing should be evaluated critically for their environmental impact, which will aid in reducing land, water, and air pollution.

RFID technology makes it possible to measure and evaluate environmental pollution. RFID technology can be used to identify stocks that are not sold promptly. Promotions and discounts are implemented by retail establishments to increase the sales of these items. This aids in reducing the amount of waste at the end of the season that would have been burned. RFID technology reduces energy consumption because it is more efficient than barcode technology, which also reduces energy usage. This was explained by interviewee number three:

Extract 4 I believe the RFID technology can help to reduce waste, because one of the problems we are facing is that when we have many stocks, and our business is slowing down because of Covid-19, that makes difficulties as we cannot sell many products at the same time, so we have excess stock. Fortunately, because we are selling rackets, which can be in

> the warehouse for a long time, but some products will decrease in value when they are in the warehouse for a long time [...]. With such stocks, we cannot sell them anymore, and we have to dispose of them by burning or burying them. That is a huge waste, so I believe with RFID, stock shrinkage will be reduced, and we can sell more products to reduce the waste. [...] what we have is we are doing barcode scanning one by one and it takes a lot of time because the scanners run on electricity. I think with RFID we can do that faster as it can scan many tags at the same time, and I believe it decreases our electricity usage.

Using RFID technology to measure environmental impact will expedite the collection of large amounts of data using software that collects data automatically. RFID systems enable the collection of accurate, real-time data on emission levels, waste generated, effluent, and environmental impacts. As this data contains the exact emission level and waste produced, it can be used to identify the process causing the issue and take the necessary steps to reduce or eliminate the impact. The use of RFID technology can assist consumers in determining the environmental impact of a product and whether it is ecofriendly. This was explained by interviewee number four:

> **Extract 5** Any products with the RFID tag have information inside a tag so the customer can track the information inside the tag to see the supply chain process of producing that product and whether it is environmentally friendly. Not only for the customer, but it is also helpful for the company to "track the information" for improvements and convenience to achieve sustainability.

27.4.3 Social Benefits

Fashion and textile production has been characterized as a labor-intensive process. Despite the availability of automation tools and equipment, these industries are reluctant to adopt automation to maintain low production costs through the use of cheap labour and to avoid the high cost of installing automation systems. To avoid customer dissatisfaction, inventory that is running low is quickly replenished. The stress level of employees is decreased, and their job satisfaction is increased through an accurate and efficient stock management system. RFID technology can aid in establishing a better rapport with external parties, such as customers. As explained by interviewee two:

> **Extract 6** Thanks to the traceability system of RFID. Customers' satisfaction can be enhanced since the stock level and the product quality is fully checked with 100% of device functions tested [...]. [...] it puts the employees' working process in a more organized and rewarding way for our employees to make them feel like they create values. For example, if they can finish checking the whole warehouse in 2 days, it would be a lot more rewarding than finishing the tasks in a week. [...] RFID can increase the trust and the corporations within our company. Whenever something is missing in the warehouse, at least we have the information to track it down and the employees can work with each other with more confidence and more teamwork.

RFID technology improves customer satisfaction because it maintains an accurate inventory record. The integrated software system alerts the store manager of products with high demand whenever the stock level is low. These inventories can be promptly ordered by the store manager, thereby avoiding the problem of missing stock. This enhances customer loyalty and generates social benefits for customers. According to interviewee one:

Extract 7 The RFID system helps to manage inventory in retail stores and distribution centers in addition to the quantity, design, colour, and size of the products. The RFID system helps to look up information about the ingredients, and materials that make up the product as well as the place of production and the process of product formation, which helps to make decisions with a fuller view of the product. This can also help to keep the sustainability index of the product, which can be disclosed to the consumers.

27.5 Conclusions

In today's cutthroat fashion and textile industry, manufacturers and retailers are focusing on increasing their profits and maintaining a positive brand image. They frequently disregard the negative environmental and social effects of various production methods and the supply chain. To preserve a sustainable environment for future generations, the global community is focusing on reducing its carbon footprint. The application of RFID technology can transform business dynamics and pave the way for a sustainable future in numerous industries, including the fashion industry. Several high-end fashion labels have already begun to implement eco-friendly manufacturing practices. Other brands should begin focusing on sustainability issues to secure the future and benefit their businesses as well as the environment. RFID technology not only provides environmentally friendly production and supply chain processes, but also offers numerous tangible business benefits, such as competitive advantage, improved customer relationships, resilience, and increased profitability.

This study demonstrated that the use of RFID technology assists Vietnamese fashion and textile businesses in gaining sustainability benefits in the three aspects, social, economic and environmental. In terms of economic benefits, the efficient management of assets improves the business's use of resources, provides greater resource management, transparency, and contributes to the business's profitability. Additionally, RFID technology can be used to save resources with greater precision and efficiency. RFID technology also reduces labour costs and maximizes resource utilization. RFID technology can reduce the amount of waste produced and the amount of electricity used throughout the entire supply chain of fashion and textiles. This information can be made immediately accessible to garment manufacturers or other authorities as needed. In terms of social implications, RFID technology can be used to increase customer satisfaction in addition to employee satisfaction.

27.6 Limitations

This study focused on the applications of RFID technology in the fashion industry, even though RFID has been implemented in a wide range of industries such as automotive and construction. From other perspectives, numerous sustainable technologies may also suggest sustainable growth for organizations by minimizing costs and generating a higher return, even though the primary focus of this study was on RFID technology. In addition, a few suggestions were provided on how fashion businesses can implement the technology most practically and cost-effectively, as integrating new technology into an existing supply chain system always poses challenges for executives. Practicality is essential in any provided suggestion; however, as the study focused solely on the literature and theoretical aspects of RFID, it does not provide suggestions on the most recent technological advancements in the sustainable fashion industry. It is essential to consider all viable options for achieving sustainable growth, and the repercussions will vary across organizations, industries, and nations. Due to the omission of other technological options, a particular subject can lead to bias. In addition, technical analysis of proper RFID technology adaptations was not provided, as the focus of the study was on the sustainability benefits of successful RFID implementation.

References

Akbari, M. (2018). Logistics outsourcing: A structured literature review. *Benchmarking: An International Journal, 25*(5), 1548–1580.

Aras-Beger, G., Sağlam, B.B., & Bekki, N. (2020). *Case studies on sustainability for various fashion brands*. In *Supply Chain Management and Logistics in the Global Fashion Sector* (pp. 242–260). Routledge.

Arkan, I., & Van Landeghem, H. (2013). Evaluating the performance of a discrete manufacturing process using RFID: A case study. *Robotics and Computer-Integrated Manufacturing, 29*(6), 502–512.

Azevedo, S. G., & Carvalho, H. (2012). Contribution of RFID technology to better management of fashion supply chains. *International Journal of Retail & Distribution Management*.

Bhardwaj, V., & Fairhurst, A. (2010). Fast fashion: Response to changes in the fashion industry. *The International Review of Retail, Distribution and Consumer Research, 20*(1), 165–173.

Caniato, F., et al. (2012). Environmental sustainability in fashion supply chains: An exploratory case based research. *International Journal of Production Economics, 135*(2), 659–670.

Choy, K. L., et al. (2009). A RFID-case-based sample management system for fashion product development. *Engineering Applications of Artificial Intelligence, 22*(6), 882–896.

Collins, J. L. (2003). *Threads: Gender, labor, and power in the global apparel industry*. University of Chicago Press.

Condea, C., Thiesse, F., & Fleisch, E. (2012). RFID-enabled shelf replenishment with backroom monitoring in retail stores. *Decision Support Systems, 52*(4), 839–849.

Dai, H., & Tseng, M. M. (2012). The impacts of RFID implementation on reducing inventory inaccuracy in a multi-stage supply chain. *International Journal of Production Economics, 139*(2), 634–641.

De Brito, M. P., & Van Der Laan, E. A. (2009). Inventory control with product returns: The impact of imperfect information. *European Journal of Operational Research, 194*(1), 85–101.

Denuwara, N., Maijala, J., & Hakovirta, M. (2019). Sustainability benefits of RFID technology in the apparel industry. *Sustainability, 11*(22), 6477.

Desore, A., & Narula, S. A. (2018). An overview on corporate response towards sustainability issues in textile industry. *Environment, Development and Sustainability, 20*(4), 1439–1459.

Farooque, M., et al. (2019). Circular supply chain management: A definition and structured literature review. *Journal of Cleaner Production, 228*, 882–900.

Fung, Y.-N., et al. (2021). Sustainable product development processes in fashion: Supply chains structures and classifications. *International Journal of Production Economics, 231*, 1–15.

Goworek, H., et al. (2020). Managing sustainability in the fashion business: Challenges in product development for clothing longevity in the UK. *Journal of Business Research, 117*, 629–641.

Guo, Z., et al. (2006). Mathematical model and genetic optimization for the job shop scheduling problem in a mixed-and multi-product assembly environment: A case study based on the apparel industry. *Computers & Industrial Engineering, 50*(3), 202–219.

Hiller Connell, K. Y., & Kozar, J. M. (2017). *Introduction to special issue on sustainability and the triple bottom line within the global clothing and textiles industry* (pp. 1–3). Springer.

Hsu, C.-I., Shih, H.-H., & Wang, W.-C. (2009). Applying RFID to reduce delay in import cargo customs clearance process. *Computers & Industrial Engineering, 57*(2), 506–519.

Macchion, L., et al. (2018). Strategic approaches to sustainability in fashion supply chain management. *Production Planning & Control, 29*(1), 9–28.

Mok, A., Yu, H., & Zihayat, M. (2022). The trends of sustainability in the luxury fashion industry: A triple bottom line analysis. *Journal of Global Fashion Marketing, 13*(4), 360–379.

Nayak, R. (2019). *Radio frequency identification (RFID) technology and application in fashion and textile supply chain: Technology and application in garment manufacturing and supply chain*. CRC press.

Nayak, R. (2020). *Supply chain management and logistics in the global fashion sector: The sustainability challenge*. Routledge.

Nayak, R., & Padhye, R. (2017). *Automation in garment manufacturing*. Woodhead Publishing.

Nayak, R., et al. (2007). RFID: Tagging the new era. *Man-Made Textiles in India, 50*(5), 174–177.

Nayak, R., et al. (2015). RFID in textile and clothing manufacturing: Technology and challenges. *Fashion and Textiles, 2*(1), 9.

Nayak, R., Akbari, M., & Far, S. M. (2019a). Recent sustainable trends in Vietnam's fashion supply chain. *Journal of Cleaner Production, 225*, 291–303.

Nayak, R., et al. (2019b). The challenges for sustainability marketing approach: An empirical study in Vietnamese fashion SMEs. *International Journal of Trade, Economics and Finance, 10*(4), 104–108.

Nayak, R., et al., (2020a). *Sustainable supply chain management: Challenges from a fashion perspective*. In *Supply chain management and logistics in the global fashion sector* (pp. 3–32).

Nayak, R., Panwar, T., & Nguyen, L.V.T. (2020b). *Sustainability in fashion and textiles: A survey from developing country*. In *Sustainable technologies for fashion and textiles* (pp. 1–30).

Nayak, R., et al. (2021). Sustainable developments and corporate social responsibility in Vietnamese fashion enterprises. *Journal of Fashion Marketing and Management: An International Journal, 26*, 307–327.

Nayak, R., et al. (2022). Sustainability benefits of RFID technology in Vietnamese fashion supply chain. *Cleaner Logistics and Supply Chain, 5*, 1–12.

Ni, L. M., Zhang, D., & Souryal, M. R. (2011). RFID-based localization and tracking technologies. *Wireless Communications, IEEE, 18*(2), 45–51.

Roberti, M. (2006). RFID is fit to track clothes. *Chain Store Age, 82*(5), 158.

Thorisdottir, T. S., & Johannsdottir, L. (2019). Sustainability within fashion business models: A systematic literature review. *Sustainability, 11*(8), 22–33.

Weinstein, R. (2005). RFID: A technical overview and its application to the enterprise. *IT professional, 7*(3), 27–33.

Williams, B. (2015). The local government accountants' perspective on sustainability. *Sustainability Accounting, Management and Policy Journal, 15*(2), 84–92.

Zelbst, P. J., Green, K. W., Jr., & Sower, V. E. (2010). Impact of RFID technology utilization on operational performance. *Management Research Review, 33*(10), 994–1004.

Printed in Singapore by Markono Print Media Pte Ltd